THE NEW SHOSTAKOVICH

THE NEW
SHOSTAKOVICH

Ian MacDonald

OXFORD UNIVERSITY PRESS
1991

Oxford University Press, Walton Street, Oxford OX2 6DP
Oxford New York Toronto
Delhi Bombay Calcutta Madras Karachi
Petaling Jaya Singapore Hong Kong Tokyo
Nairobi Dar es Salaam Cape Town
Melbourne Auckland
and associated companies in
Berlin Ibadan

Oxford is a trade mark of Oxford University Press

First published by Fourth Estate 1990
First issued as an Oxford University Press paperback 1991

British Library Cataloguing in Publication Data
Data available
ISBN 0–19–284026–6

Printed in Great Britain by
Biddles Ltd.
Guildford and King's Lynn

TO
MY PARENTS

Contents

ACKNOWLEDGEMENTS   ix

PRELUDE: Truth   1

1 Innocence 1906–1925   16
2 Experience 1926–1931   32
3 Uncertainty 1932–1934   79
4 Terror 1935–1938   98
5 Togetherness 1938–1946   139
6 Isolation 1946–1953   184
7 Assertion 1953–1975   210

POSTLUDE: Immortality   245

APPENDIX 1: Stalinism and *Nineteen Eighty-Four*   265
APPENDIX 2: Akhmatova, Shostakovich and the 'Seventh'   271
APPENDIX 3: Chronology   277

SOME RECOMMENDED RECORDINGS   316
SOURCE NOTES   317
SELECT BIBLIOGRAPHY   323
INDEX OF COMPOSITIONS   327
INDEX OF CHARACTERS   331

Acknowledgements

Thanks are due to the following for permission to quote from published material in copyright: Century, extract from *Leningrad Diary* by Vera Inber; Collins Harvill, extracts from *Hope Against Hope* and *Hope Abandoned* by Nadezhda Mandelstam; Collins Harvill, extracts from *A Captive of Time* by Olga Ivinskaya; André Deutsch, extracts from *To Build a Castle* by Vladimir Bukovsky; the estate of the late Sonia Brownell Orwell and Secker & Warburg, extracts from *Nineteen Eighty-Four* by George Orwell; Robert Hale, extracts from *Pages From the Life of Dmitri Shostakovich* by Dmitri and Ludmilla Sollertinsky; Hamish Hamilton, extracts from *Testimony* by Solomon Volkov; Lawrence & Wishart, extract from *Dmitri Shostakovich, Composer* by David Rabinovich; Macmillan, extract from *Let History Judge* by Roy Medvedev; Oxford University Press, extracts from *Anna Akhmatova, A Poetic Pilgrimage* by Amanda Haight; Peters, Fraser & Dunlop, extract from *The Russian Mind* by Ronald Hingley; Praeger Publishers, extracts from *Music Under the Soviets* by Andrei Olkhovsky; Secker & Warburg, extracts from *Poems by Anna Akhmatova* (tr. D.M. Thomas) and *The Captive Mind* by Czesław Milosz; Tantivy Press, extract from *The Music of Dmitri Shostakovich: The Symphonies* by Roy Blokker and Robert Dearling.

Special thanks are due to Richard McKane, Peter Norman, and Anatoli Naiman for their kind assistance with Appendix 2; to David King for drawing my attention to the portrait photography of Moisei Nappelbaum; to Pamela Winterton for her valued advice and encouragement; and to Ewen and Olwen MacCormick for their support, without which this book could not have been written.

I always carry one end of a banner in the processions. I always look cheerful and I never shirk anything. Always yell with the crowd, that's what I say. It's the only way to be safe.

GEORGE ORWELL, *Nineteen Eighty-Four*

Prelude: Truth

Do you not think that history is really a whore?
SHOSTAKOVICH (?), *Testimony*

FOLLOWING HIS DEATH on 9 August 1975 in a Moscow hospital reserved for high-ranking *apparatchiks*, the composer Dmitri Dmitryevich Shostakovich was hailed in an official obituary circulated to all Soviet newspapers as 'a faithful son of the Communist Party' who had devoted his life to 'the ideals of socialist humanism and internationalism'. Five days later, as befits a Union First Secretary and Deputy to the Supreme Soviet, he was given a state funeral in the capital's Novodevichy Cemetery, an event televised in all countries signatory to the Warsaw Pact. East European newscasters recited the dead man's long list of official titles and awards: Honoured Artist of the Russian Soviet Federal Socialist Republic, People's Artist of the USSR, three times recipient of the Order of Lenin, Hero of Socialist Labour . . .

Coverage in the West followed the Soviet lead, describing the composer as 'a convinced Marxist-Leninist and lifelong Communist', but including the fact, overlooked in the Soviet bulletins, that he had twice in his life been severely reprimanded by the state for deviating from the official line. No comment was attached to this anomaly. The ups and downs of life in the Soviet Union are notoriously opaque to outsiders and obituaries hardly the place for speculation. Western classical stations played Shostakovich's Soviet-approved masterpiece, the Fifth Symphony, and commiserated with the Russian people over their loss. Newscasters proceeded to the next report and Shostakovich passed into history.

Four years later, Shostakovich – or someone using his name and identity – stepped back out of history through the pages of *Testimony*, claimed by its publishers to be the composer's memoirs as dictated to his amanuensis, Solomon Volkov. Volkov had been a music journalist in the Soviet Union until 1976 when he had travelled to America on an exit visa and settled in New York. Based on a typescript signed, chapter by chapter, by Shostakovich, *Testimony* was his first work published in English and an immediate succès de scandale, drawing a picture of the composer shockingly at variance with the image of him promoted by the USSR.

The Shostakovich of *Testimony* was a bitter man who denied allegiance to the Communist Party and repudiated any assumption that he had been in sympathy with the Soviet system: 'I never tried to flatter the authorities with my music. And I never had an "affair" with them. I was never a favourite, though I know that some accuse me of it. They say that I stood too close to power. An optical illusion.'

Going on to savage every aspect of his country's life and culture, this 'new' Shostakovich poured particular scorn on the Soviet policy towards the arts, which he claimed was crude, cynical, and antipathetic to any genuine creativity:

> A man has no significance in a totalitarian state. The only thing that matters is the inexorable movement of the state mechanism. A mechanism needs only cogs. Stalin used to call all of us cogs. One cog does not differ from another, and cogs can easily replace one another. You can pick one out and say, 'From this day you will be a genius cog', and everyone else will consider it a genius. It doesn't matter at all whether it is or not. Anyone can become a genius on the orders of the leader.

Castigating Stalin and his successors, the 'new' Shostakovich finally rounded, too, on Lenin, the very father of the Revolution and a figure of God-like status in Russia:

> Don't believe humanists, citizens, don't believe prophets, don't believe luminaries – they'll fool you for a penny. Do your own work, don't hurt people, try to help them. Don't try to save humanity all at once, try saving one person first. It's a lot harder. To help one person without harming another is very difficult. It's unbelievably difficult. That's where the temptation to save all of humanity comes from. And then, inevitably, along the way you discover that all humanity's happiness hinges on the destruction of a few hundred million people, that's all. A trifle. – Nothing but nonsense in the world, Nikolai Vasilyevich Gogol once said. It's that nonsense that I try to depict.

Failing revelation of the composer as a CIA agent, the contrast between the 'faithful son of the Communist Party' portrayed in the Soviet media and the scathingly anti-Communist Shostakovich of *Testimony* could hardly have been harsher. Suspecting a forgery, Western experts scrutinised Volkov's book for factual errors. One or two were found, but none of them seriously compromising. On the contrary, much of the information contained in it was unavailable in other sources.

Those in the know were privately heard to admit that a great deal of the book rang true. For example, it was no secret that the satirist Gogol – droll, obsessive creator of *Dead Souls* and *Diary of a Madman* – had been one of Shostakovich's favourite authors. Moreover, a taste for the works of this subversive individualist had periodically been deemed suspicious under the Soviet dispensation. It was therefore at least plausible that the publicly orthodox Shostakovich might, in private, have been given to a certain amount of grumbling about Soviet life, perhaps even to the point of mild dissidence on some basic tenets of Marxism-Leninism. But that a former Deputy to the Supreme Soviet and holder of the

Order of the October Revolution could be capable of completely rejecting his country's political system seemed to many commentators out of the question.

After all, Shostakovich had written numerous pieces celebrating Soviet anniversaries, four symphonies about Russian revolutionary traditions, and a small library of articles for papers such as *Pravda* and *Izvestia* insisting that music be harnessed to the wagon of Communist ideology. In well-known speeches, he had emphasised the political content of his work and declared himself proud to be a servant of the Soviet people. To accept all this as deception – on the part of the composer or the Soviet authorities, or both – would not only stand the study of Shostakovich on its head but also imply that the West was fundamentally incapable of distinguishing truth from lies in anything emanating from behind the Iron Curtain.

Some Western pundits were sufficiently taken by this idea to accept *Testimony*, 'slips' and all, as factual and hence revelatory. Others drew a compromise between extremes: Volkov may have interviewed Shostakovich on the understanding that the resulting material would be used in a memoir but, following his subject's death, had simply sprinkled this authentic data into a goulash of his own anti-Soviet convictions. *Testimony* was partly genuine, partly a cunning fraud. Only time would tell which ingredients were organic and till then judgement on the book would have to be reserved.

A more robust third position emerged towards the end of 1979 with an article in Moscow's *Literary Gazette*, collectively signed by several dozen ex-colleagues of the composer and headlined: 'Pitiful forgery – concerning the so-called *Memoirs* of D.D. Shostakovich.' Here, *Testimony* was contemptuously dismissed as a sham cobbled together by the renegade Volkov in order to secure a position for himself in the West. To back this up, members of Shostakovich's family, notably his third wife, Irina, went on Soviet TV to insist that Volkov knew little about the composer, had hardly ever visited the Shostakovich household, and had certainly never spoken to him long enough to acquire enough quotes to fill a book.

For a while, the increasingly rancorous debate about *Testimony* continued on the basis of entrenched opinion, no further facts emerging to change the balance of its warring standpoints. In October 1980, however, a decisive blow for the sceptics was struck by the American scholar Laurel Fay in the New York quarterly *The Russian Review*. Under the headline 'Shostakovich vs Volkov: whose *Testimony*?', Fay reported that she and Simon Karlinsky, an expert on Russian literature, had found passages in Volkov's book taken verbatim from reminiscences by the composer in various old Soviet sources. That these passages had been copied by Volkov was clear not only from the texts themselves, but from the way they had been altered to make them seem to have been uttered thirty or forty years later. Worse still for the Volkovites, the plagiarised passages appeared on the first pages of seven of *Testimony*'s eight sections – the pages that bore Shostakovich's authenticating signature. The inference was that Volkov had shown the composer a collection of old articles, ostensibly intended for an anthology, and, having obtained his signature at the head of each of these, had used them as the first pages of new chapters that he wrote and that Shostakovich never saw.

Within academic circles, Fay's piece was deemed conclusive. Volkov, known to have been preparing a conventional biography of Shostakovich, had clearly gone for the big money by turning his material into a set of bogus 'memoirs'. The fact that he had failed to rebut Fay's charges spoke for itself. Accordingly, the affair was smoothed over, *Testimony* now being routinely described in articles and reviews as 'spurious' or 'largely fraudulent' and Shostakovich's image resuming its familiar Soviet sobriety. To complete Volkov's debunking, the official Moscow publisher Progress made available in English a collection of the composer's speeches and articles under the title *About Himself and His Times*. This was the old, pre-*Testimony* Shostakovich: earnest, prosaic, impeccably versed in Soviet officialese, and strangely ingenuous – yet, so far as Western opinion was aware, the real thing.

The final nail in Volkov's coffin seemed to be provided in ˙ ᴐ81 by the unexpected defection to the West of Shostakovich's son, the conductor Maxim. Defection suggested dissidence which, in one so close to the composer, promised a revival of the *Testimony* scandal. Had his family lied about the book under pressure from the Soviet authorities, Maxim Shostakovich was presumably now free to speak his mind. Such hopes were soon dashed. Maxim withheld his imprimatur, venturing only that the scatological expressions attributed to Shostakovich in *Testimony* did not accord with the man he had known. 'It is a book,' he told the *Sunday Times*, 'about my father, not by him.' This condemnation by non-approval marked the nadir of *Testimony's* credibility. With Volkov discredited, some Western writers now began to re-promote, with far greater emphasis than had previously been customary outside Russia, the Soviet picture of Shostakovich as a proudly orthodox Communist and indefatigable musical 'populist'.

There remained isolated figures prepared to stand up for Volkov, though little notice was taken of them. One – surprisingly enough – was Simon Karlinsky, the professor of Russian literature who, with Laurel Fay, had unearthed *Testimony*'s plagiarisms. Despite these, Karlinsky thought the core of the book convincing and considered it, on balance, more authentic than not. Another witness for the defence was Gerald Abraham, the leading Western authority on Russian music, who observed that the Shostakovich of *Testimony* was consistent with his own impression of the man and with what he had heard about him from musicians behind the Iron Curtain. Two of these, newly defected to the West, let it be known that they concurred with Abraham's impression. They were the conductors Kyrill Kondrashin and Rudolf Barshai, who between them had premièred four of Shostakovich's fifteen symphonies during their time in the USSR. All were formidable attestants but, without the corroboration of the composer's son, they were unable to nudge academic opinion back to an open-minded outlook on the 'new' Shostakovich of *Testimony*.

Post-*Testimony* feuding continued to smoulder in musical circles, much of it centring on the composer's Fifth Symphony, held by Soviet critics to be his masterpiece. Western opinion on the work had always been divided. The official Soviet line was that it was autobiographical, representing the composer's own progress (under the guidance of the Party) from the internal conflicts of pessimistic self-preoccupation to solidarity with the optimistic struggle of the People against bourgeois reaction and 'the blind elemental forces'. While no Western commentator dissented from this edifying interpretation, many felt the 'optimism' of the symphony's finale to be forced and the work consequently flawed.

The traditional terms of this debate embraced two opposing hypotheses: (1) that Shostakovich had sincerely meant to write an apotheosis but had muffed it, possibly out of sheer anxiety to please the authorities (the 'Honest Communist' theory); (2) that he had known perfectly well that an apotheosis was required but in the event was powerless to override his own pessimism and so failed to bring it off (the 'Hamlet' theory). The 'new' Shostakovich of *Testimony* had offered a startlingly original view of the matter: 'I think that it is clear to everyone what happens in the Fifth. The rejoicing is forced, created under threat, as in *Boris Godunov*. It's as if someone were beating you with a stick and saying, "Your business is rejoicing, your business is rejoicing", and you rise, shaky, and go marching off, muttering "Our business is rejoicing, our business is rejoicing". What kind of apotheosis is that? You have to be a complete oaf not to hear that.'

Prior to the Soviet attack on *Testimony* and Maxim Shostakovich's non-endorsement of it, passages like this had seemed to some to be rather enlightening. Now, with Volkov established as a fraud, any approving reference to such enlightenment drew immediate condemnation from those Western commentators who felt their allegiance to the Soviet line vindicated by the trend of events. In 1983, for example, Christopher Norris, editor of the symposium *Shostakovich: the man and his music*, mocked Western liberals for imagining themselves 'too shrewd to be hoodwinked by the official view' of the Fifth Symphony. According to Norris, the discovery of 'subtle ironies' and 'cryptic messages of doom and despair' in music which 'sounds, to the innocent ear, like straightforward Socialist Optimism' was evidence not of genuine response but of 'ideological reaction'. This attitude, he contended, owed much, if not all, to that 'thoroughly mischievous ideological primer', *Testimony*. In future, he implied, responsible critics should think twice before associating themselves with Volkov's 'Cold War interpretative tactics'.

Unfortunately for the 'innocent ear' and its staunch refusal to hear anything ambiguous in music as supposedly guileless as Shostakovich's, events conspired almost immediately to prove it self-deceived. The first blow was administered by a new record of the Fifth Symphony in which the reading stridently concurred with the sour view of the work taken in *Testimony*. The conductor was Mstislav Rostropovich, a close friend of Shostakovich for nearly a quarter of a century prior to being forced out of the Soviet Union for supporting the dissident writer Solzhenitsyn. Discussing the symphony in his sleeve-note, Rostropovich tartly remarked that 'anyone who thinks the finale is glorification is an idiot'.

Next came the publication of a new edition of Boris Schwarz's standard work, *Music and Musical Life in Soviet Russia*, containing an interview given to its author by Maxim Shostakovich in New York in 1981. Here, while maintaining his previous reservations about *Testimony*, Maxim blew two devastating holes in the assumption, until then watertight, that his father had been a sincere Communist. Volkov, he asserted, was right in presenting Shostakovich as a man whose apparent loyalty to the Soviet regime was a 'mask': 'My father was a patriot of his people, which is not the same as a Soviet *apparatchik*.' Furthermore, in Maxim's opinion, the official pronouncements credited to the composer and assumed by most Western authorities to have expressed his personal views had actually been written by functionaries and merely signed or read by him.

Suddenly, a new groundswell of support for Volkov was evident among Soviet émigrés. Rudolf Barshai, already on record as believing *Testimony* to be 'all true', described Shostakovich's practice of wordlessly indicating to friends and pupils significant 'ambiguities' in his scores. Interviewed by Norman Lebrecht for the *Sunday Times*, Rostropovich called the composer's symphonies 'a secret history of Russia' (that is, a dissident critique of Soviet society), while Rostislav Dubinsky, founder of the Borodin Quartet and another close associate of the composer in his later years, confirmed that Shostakovich, though wary of discussing his music, had tacitly approved of its interpretation as a memorial to 'the (Soviet) destruction of Russian culture'.

Vindication of the 'new' Shostakovich escalated with the appearance of the singer Galina Vishnevskaya's autobiography in 1984. Rostropovich's wife, Vishnevskaya had, like her husband, known and worked with the composer for many years and holds the distinction of having had more Shostakovich works dedicated to her than any other artist apart from David Oistrakh (three each). Her portrait of the man differed in emphasis from Volkov's, but her view of Shostakovich's beliefs was identical. 'If music can be anti-Communist,' she declared, 'I think Shostakovich's music should be called by that name.'

Pianist Vladimir Ashkenazy, whose biography appeared in the same year, concurred with Vishnevskaya. A friend had told him that when Shostakovich joined the Communist Party (under pressure, at the late age of fifty-three, in 1960), he had evidently felt the decision to be 'a humiliation'. Speaking for Ashkenazy the pianist's co-author, Jasper Parrott, added that 'despite his much-publicized submission to the official line, it is clear now that Shostakovich in his later symphonies simply continued with his own, highly personal critique of the (Soviet) system which he so profoundly despised'.

With the official Soviet image of Shostakovich crumbling fast, Maxim Shostakovich now provided the clinching confirmation long hoped of him. Harried and vilified by the Soviet authorities since his defection, he had by stages moved away from the outright condemnation of *Testimony* required of him while he was still living in Russia, first by refusing to elaborate on the topic to the Western press in 1981, then by subsequently withdrawing what he had said without qualification. In 1984, expanding on his observation to Boris Schwarz that his father had worn a 'mask of loyalty', he admitted that there had been two Shostakoviches – the official version and the real one, who had been quite different. Finally, on 27 September 1986, he appeared in a BBC television interview with the composer Michael Berkeley, quietly dropping the bombshell of explicit authentification of *Testimony*: 'It's true. It's accurate. Sometimes, for me, there is too much rumour in the book, but nothing major. The basis of the book is correct.'

Thus, within a decade of burial amid the graves of scores of eminent and (presumably) committed Marxist-Leninists, the composer eulogised by *Pravda* as 'a faithful son of the Communist Party' turned out to have been a secret dissident waging, from behind the many masks of his music, a campaign of protest against the very system which had paraded him as its laureate.

The 'new' Shostakovich portrayed in *Testimony* has been confirmed beyond doubt. But how does that square with the fact that *Testimony* itself is not what it seems? If Volkov's portrait of Shostakovich is authentic, why the editorial sleight of hand? And what of the wider implications? Does the advent of the 'new' Shostakovich mean that the old Shostakovich, the official Soviet version, never existed? Did the composer change horses at some identifiable point in his career, or had he always been utterly unlike the state portrait painted by his Communist masters?

It is pointless to expect Western musicologists to have an opinion on any of this. A small department of their subject has just been turned upside-down and the hum of academic dissertation that once filled it has given way to open-mouthed silence. Nor is it clear whether even Shostakovich's latterday contemporaries – Rostropovich, Vishnevskaya, Barshai, and Dubinsky – know the whole story, for this stretches back to the 1917 Revolution itself at which time none of them were alive. Other émigrés with an intriguing tale may, like Maxim Shostakovich until recently, be unable to tell it in case of reprisals against relatives still living in the USSR. (The conductor Kondrashin, who met the composer in 1937, was himself bound to silence in this way until his death in 1981.) As for the Soviet scholars who have studied the documentary record on Shostakovich in far greater detail than has so far been possible outside Russia, not a word of theirs can any longer be taken at face value.

What, though, of Volkov? Refusing to respond to his critics or clarify the mystery surrounding *Testimony*, he has none the less continued to defend the integrity of his picture of Shostakovich – a picture endorsed, directly or indirectly, by half a dozen key witnesses. Moreover, while Laurel Fay has cast doubts on his probity, Volkov remains unique among contemporary writers on Shostakovich in having known the composer and studied him in situ for more than a decade. Leaving aside, for the time being, further evaluation of *Testimony*'s reliability, it is clear that Volkov's claims are both consistent in themselves and based on firsthand data unavailable to his Western detractors. This makes it vital to consider his outlook thoroughly before moving to a judgement on his methods of purveying it.

The truth, as presented to us by Solomon Volkov, is complex. In his view, there was never anything to the official image of Shostakovich in terms of congruence with the character and beliefs of the man himself. Almost religiously superstitious of power, the composer was, from his youth, on the side of the persecuted and against those who oppressed them, whoever they might be. What work he was forced to do for the state, he did reluctantly and with an innate revulsion which, in later life, he scarcely bothered to conceal. On the other hand, Shostakovich had as a young man been groomed for the post of musical laureate of the USSR, a position which he refused not at once, but gradually and with (in Volkov's words) 'much vacillation and inconsistency' – sufficient of each, some might say, to account for the common Western misapprehension that he had accepted it. Nor is it honest to ignore the evidence suggesting that, in the 1920s, Shostakovich was genuinely enthused by the Revolution and the new society it was supposedly bringing about; or the common knowledge that he diligently fulfilled the duties attached to the civic positions he held at various periods during his career.

Volkov does not sidestep such difficulties, but his explanation for the apparent contradictions involved is, to Westerners at least, almost as enigmatic as the mystery it purports to solve. Mention has been made of the 'Honest Communist' and 'Hamlet' theories of Shostakovich – hypotheses which possess the pedigree of long standing in Shostakovich scholarship, Soviet and otherwise, as well as the provisionally convincing virtue of partially overlapping each other. Volkov proposes a third theory, quite different from anything submitted before and sufficiently novel for it to have met with, as yet, little more than sighs of amused bewilderment from those called upon to assess it. Shostakovich, says Volkov, 'could not and did not want to enter into open conflict with the authorities. Yet it was clear to him that total submission threatened to become a creative dead end. He chose another path; whether consciously or not, Shostakovich became the second (Mussorgsky was the first) great *yurodivy* composer.'

The *yurodivy*, or 'holy fool', is a venerable Russian tradition whereby anyone wishing to mock the mighty may do so with relative impunity provided they behave in all other respects as if unworthy of serious attention. The parallel with the English court jester is more or less exact and it is significant that the Fool in *King Lear* was, after Hamlet, Shostakovich's favourite Shakespearian creation. (Apropos his score for a 1940 production of the play, the composer wrote: 'King Lear's Fool is a complex character, full of paradox and contradictions. Everything he says or does is original, unexpected, and wise.') Did Shostakovich, 'whether consciously or not', become a *yurodivy* in order to solve his dilemma with the authorities? Volkov's escape-clause begs the question, for even the most God-intoxicated of holy fools would be unlikely to have become so without noticing it – and Shostakovich was a very sober atheist. Rather oddly, Volkov goes on to abandon this initial caution completely: 'Shostakovich not only considered himself a *yurodivy*, but he was perceived as such by the people close to him. The word "*yurodivy*" was often applied to him in Russian music circles.'

Assuming Volkov not to be exaggerating here (his only example of this allegedly common practice being a remark by the conductor Yevgeny Mravinsky), the contention is clear enough. What is not so clear is whether there are trustworthy limits to *yurodstvo* (the practice of the *yurodivy*) and, if so, how they are to be recognised. Volkov, for example, tells us that 'stepping onto the road of *yurodstvo*, Shostakovich relinquished all responsibility for anything he said: nothing meant what it seemed to, not the most exalted and beautiful words. The pronouncement of familiar truths turned out to be mockery; conversely, mockery often contained tragic truth. This also held for his musical works.' Unfortunately, it is not entirely frivolous to wonder how far it holds for *Testimony*, too. For, even supposing that most, if not all, of it consists of verbatim Shostakovich, how can we be sure that these, alone among the composer's utterances, were 'responsibly' imparted to posterity? In fact, common sense should tell us that *Testimony*, if nothing else in Shostakovich's output, is to be excepted from the *yurodstvo* rule, its mockery being mostly open and always rationally expressed.

But is any of this true in the first place? One of the more immediate reasons why Western commentators have declined to take up Volkov's *yurodivy* thesis is that accepting it would return Shostakovich studies, formerly thought well advanced, to square one. Not only every statement attributed to him outside *Testimony*, but everything he did and every note he wrote would become subject to wholesale revaluation. Unhappily for the musicologists, if fascinatingly for the general audience, Volkov still holds the initiative. Confirmed by the accounts of others who knew Shostakovich well (and no one close to the composer, including his wife, Irina, now disputes the gist of *Testimony*'s version of him), his thesis has the dual merit of closely fitting the composer's character while offering a plausible explanation for the radical differences between the 'new' Shostakovich and the old one. All that is presently lacking is a preliminary study of the facts of the composer's life to establish how far Volkov's view of him is justifiable.

This book is a shot at that preliminary study – nothing more. Such is the subtlety of the issue as a whole that a complete assessment of it can be accomplished only by a Russian with a keen ear, a good grasp of musicological method, and a great deal of time. In advance of this, however, one important thing can be demonstrated beyond dispute: the greater part of Shostakovich's art, like that of his fellow Soviet composers and writers, is simply unintelligible when taken out of socio-historical context and, as such, attempts to grasp it as 'pure music' are doomed before they begin. As to final judgements and a rounded assessment of Shostakovich's career, these can come later. All that matters here is to show that they cannot come at all if its fundamental conditions remain, as they are at present outside Russia, wilfully misunderstood.

Until Volkov comes clean over how much of *Testimony* is genuine Shostakovich and how much pastiche, every sentence in it must be taken with a pinch of salt. On the other hand, Maxim Shostakovich's endorsement alone makes it impossible to reject the book in all but a few minor details. This being so, it will be referred to wherever doing so is relevant. What, though, of the many articles and speeches attributed to Shostakovich in the USSR? Are they all bogus? Is there anything at all in them we can trust?

The first rule for anyone wishing to gauge statements emanating from a totalitarian society is to remember that almost nothing spontaneous happens under totalitarianism. Everything – from squads of flag-waving infants at airports to collectively signed expressions of righteous indignation in the national press – is *planned*. Shostakovich's announcements for Soviet consumption need to be understood as products of this obsessively overseen system. What is required from Soviet artists in the way of statements to the media is not so much free opinions on whatever pops into their heads as 'correct' rehearsal of the official line on whichever subject happens to be under review. Since the official line may alter from week to week – so that no artist can be relied on to know what, at a given time, is the 'correct' thing to say – controls on the public voicing of even the most narrowly aesthetic views will always be tight. In other words, anything attributed by Soviet sources to Shostakovich must be presumed to be in reality the work of an officially sponsored journalist who may or may not have gone to the trouble of interviewing him before concocting it.

The fact that Shostakovich's name was regularly requisitioned for propaganda purposes seems to have been widely known in Soviet music circles. Maxim Shostakovich has more than once confirmed this, while Galina Vishnevskaya records it as common knowledge that Shostakovich signed letters of protest without looking at them, read prepared statements to the press without a pretence of sincerity, and generally allowed his reputation to be used by the state in any way it liked. To take one example of this (accepted as such by Boris Schwarz in his standard history of Soviet music), a piece 'by' Shostakovich appeared in *Pravda* on 7 September 1960 attacking the avant-garde's interest in the twelve-tone music of Schoenberg and accusing Stravinsky, then living in California, of being completely divorced from 'the true demands of our time'. This, treated as a major policy statement by the Soviet press, was followed throughout the sixties by a stream of similar articles condemning, as Schwarz points out, 'not only . . . experimentation, but the *right* to experiment'. In fact, these dreary pieces were written not by Shostakovich but by a functionary[1] assigned to promote the opinions in them by attaching them to the composer's name. The real Shostakovich showed a keen interest in avant-garde works of all kinds, defending such enfants terribles as Andrei Volkonsky, Edison Denisov, and Boris Tishchenko, and assiduously complaining to the authorities whenever their compositions were refused performance. As for Stravinsky, Shostakovich loved his music and kept a photograph of him on his desk throughout his career.

To the average Western democrat, the composer's attitude in 'allowing' this misuse of his name and reputation may appear to be alarmingly cynical and cowardly but, like so much that seems enigmatic about him, the mystery owes less to Shostakovich than it does to Soviet Russia itself as seen, through a perpetual fog of disinformation, from outside. Indeed, Western failure to arrive at anything remotely approaching an understanding of Shostakovich's music has less to do with the Machiavellian deviousness of its composer than with the political naivety of Western music critics.

A subject in themselves, the peculiarities of intellectual life in Communist Russia and Eastern Europe have never been analysed more penetratingly than by the Polish poet Czesław Miłosz in his study *The Captive Mind*. On the question of the signing of articles and reading of speeches with which one privately disagrees, Miłosz speaks of '*Ketman*', a form of pretence resorted to by anyone who, while harbouring thoughts of his own, wishes nevertheless to remain alive and, relatively speaking, unimprisoned. According to the poet, *Ketman*, an Iranian word, stood for the practice of Sufi mystics under orthodox Islam of at once hiding their heresy and mocking the establishment by professing orthodoxy in the most pedantically elaborate detail (and, where it was safe to do so, carrying their show of solemn conformism to the point of absurdity). In Miłosz's view, Westerners, by ignoring the ever-present element of *Ketman* in Communist life, persistently stop at the latter's moribund appearance, missing its vital undercurrents:

> Whoever would take the measure of intellectual life in the countries of Central or Eastern Europe from the monotonous articles appearing in the press or the stereotyped speeches pronounced there, would be making a grave error. Just as theologians in periods of strict orthodoxy expressed their views in the rigorous language of the Church, so the writers of the people's democracies make use of an accepted special style, terminology, and linguistic ritual. What is important is not what someone said but what he wanted to say, disguising his thought by removing a

---

[1] Probably the First Secretary of the Union of Soviet Composers, Tikhon Khrennikov.

comma, inserting an 'and', establishing this rather than another sequence in the problems discussed.

As for *why* this game is necessary, that, says Milosz, is a long story – and one which its protagonists find somewhat exasperating to have to explain to a layman (particularly when, as is usually the case, the said layman has arrived on a high horse):

> Unless one has lived there one cannot know how many titanic battles are being fought, how the heroes of Ketman are falling, what this warfare is being waged over . . . A Pole, Czech or Hungarian practiced in the art of dissimulation smiles when he learns that someone in the emigration has called him a traitor (or a swine) at the very moment when this traitor (or swine) is engaged in a match of philosophical chess on whose outcome the fate of fifteen laboratories or twenty ateliers depends. They do not know how one pays – those abroad do not know. They do not know what one buys, and at what price.

As a senior cog in the Soviet musical machine, Shostakovich cannot have helped being constantly involved in games of the kind outlined by Czesław Milosz and seems often to have traded his autograph in return for dispensations to those in his care (witnesses to his concern for colleagues and pupils are plentiful in Soviet biographies). Passages of *Ketman* occur in *Testimony* and it is clear enough from his music that he was capable of simulating conformity with as much deadpan irony as the next citizen. But what is unusual about Shostakovich is that, especially in his later years, he mostly didn't bother – and it is precisely from this publicly expressed indifference that it becomes possible to understand why Solomon Volkov calls the composer a *yurodivy*.

As a private act, signing a letter of 'protest' (that is, condemnation) without reading it is a gesture of cynicism or despair. Doing the same thing in public – for *everyone* knew that this was what Shostakovich did – is, on the other hand, profoundly subversive, in that it not only implies contempt for the powers that be, but also satirises their totalitarian bureaucracy (by insinuating: 'This is what we do: sign away our consciences, our memories, our souls, to keep the machine running'). Though to a Westerner this analysis of the composer's motives may smack of special pleading, Russians, well-schooled in the subtleties of self-expression under authoritarian conditions, would instantly recognise the *yurodivy* technique of 'taking the blame' (mimicking the foolish or reprehensible behaviour of others) described, for example, by Solzhenitsyn as being part of the repertoire of the extraordinary convict Petya Kishkin.

The roots of Shostakovich's *yurodstvo*, if that is what it was, lay in both the extreme experiences to which he was frequently exposed and their routine misrepresentation in both Russia and the West. For example, twice in his life – in 1936 and 1948 – he was publicly pilloried and temporarily 'unpersoned' for alleged musical crimes against the People which only the credulous or half-witted in his country ever took seriously. At these times, foreign misunder-standing of what was going on merely compounded his isolation and the many bitter diatribes against Western opinion in *Testimony* (apart from scuttling charges that the book is anti-Soviet propaganda) owe much to the readiness of Western musicologists not only to accept Soviet accounts of these ugly débâcles, but also to go along with the official view that they had somehow done him good as a man and an artist. These ordeals, humiliating and frightening in a way entirely obscure to people used to the concept of being able to answer back, marked the composer for life. In Vishnevskaya's words, he 'reacted in an agonizing, physical way, as if his skin were searing from the brand that had been put on him'. During these episodes, Shostakovich experienced total ostracism, lost both face and livelihood, and confronted the real prospect of imprisonment or even execution. Not surprisingly, he came to the conclusion that, since he had no alternative but to live in Russia and no mission in life beyond that of addressing his fellow citizens through his music, his only course was to avoid direct conflict with the authorities, however much the resulting damage to his good name should hurt him.

That Shostakovich was genuinely terrified at certain times in his life is almost certainly true and, in any case, hardly a matter for shame or rebuke. At these times, almost the entire population of Russia was in the same condition. Exactly why this was so can only be demonstrated at length – and it will be one of the tasks of the present book to place such a demonstration before the reader in the belief that without it no adequate grasp of the significance of Shostakovich's art can be achieved. For now, those in need of an index of fear by which to judge that of the composer may care to muse on the story, from the year 1937, of the poet Pasternak's pregnant wife publicly crawling on the floor before her husband in an attempt to persuade him to sign an official letter to *Pravda* applauding the recent execution of Shostakovich's benefactor and protector, Marshal Tukhachevsky. Pasternak, who less than a year earlier had signed a similar letter demanding the death penalty for the 'enemies of the People' Kamenev and Zinoviev, chose on this occasion to stand on principle and, despite his wife's hysterical entreaties, refused to sign, a decision predicated more on innocence than bravery. (Knowing that such a refusal could lead only to the Lubyanka, the poet's friends forged his signature to the document and what might have turned into an even nastier affair ended merely with further public vilification of the Tukhachevsky family.)

The truth is that, at certain periods in Soviet history, not to have abandoned one's principles would have amounted to a request to be done away with by the secret police. In 1937, millions of Russians were being shot or packed off to concentration camps for offences which, set beside Pasternak's potential 'treason', amounted to little more than a slight hesitation to cheer when told to. Shostakovich's behaviour in the face of all this was no different from anyone else's. Even the bold Solzhenitsyn (who referred to the composer as 'that shackled genius . . . that pitiful wreck' and disapproved of his refusal to advertise his dissidence) was himself daunted enough to have kept his own head well down during the earlier part of the post-Stalin 'thaw'.

As did hundreds of others in positions comparable to his, Shostakovich allowed articles and speeches, the content of which he despised, to be dignified with his name in order to survive. Most of what appears in a collection of these writings such as *About Himself and His Times* is, therefore, at best unreliable and at worst flatly mendacious. Some isolated clues can be disentangled from this material (chiefly from those passages disfigured, from the Soviet point of view, by remnants of the composer's personal style), but as any kind of guide to the thoughts of Shostakovich or the meaning of his music, it is useless.

If this is shocking to those Western commentators who have based their interpretations of Shostakovich almost entirely on the false perspectives presented in such sources, then it is fair to say that the shock is overdue. The reader will have to look far and wide in Western writing on the composer to find any mention in discussions of the Fifth Symphony of the fact that it, too, is a child of 1937. 'Experts' who venture opinions at great length on the significance of such a work without apparent awareness that it was composed in the midst of the most intense programme of state terrorism the world has ever known, are inexcusably presumptuous and in need of an admonitory jolt.

How then can the truth and value of *Testimony* be gauged against that of the mounds of documentation purporting to confirm the Soviet line? Two bodies of evidence exist to which our conclusions may be cross-referred.

The first is the testimony of Shostakovich's contemporaries – that of his fellow artists and of the ordinary people of Russia. By no means all of this witness relates directly to Shostakovich but acquaintance with it, however cursory, will aid greatly in placing his life and work in the context of life and work generally in the Soviet Union since the Revolution. This necessitates following the progress not only of the composer, but also of some of Russia's great writers, especially those with whom, either personally or via their work, he came into close contact. One of these is Anna Akhmatova, whose life is widely recognised to be a symbol of the dignity and resilience of the Russian people under the burdens they have borne during this century, and whose poems have provided the short inscriptions at the beginning of each of the following chapters.

The second body of evidence is Shostakovich's music itself. This, thanks to his preference for pragmatic survival over principled martyrdom, is extensive and, to say the least, multifaceted. It is also, because of its persistent misrepresentation (in the East by deliberate policy, in the West by a combination of credulity and complacent self-deception) effectively unheard. This peculiar state of affairs inevitably calls to mind Sir Thomas Beecham's remark concerning the English that while they don't like music, they absolutely love the noise it makes, and in turn prompts memory of Gustav Mahler's observation, apparently forgotten by most contemporary critics, that 'the music is not in the notes, but beyond them'. All that the West (or at least the majority of musical opinion-leaders in the West) has heard of Shostakovich's music so far is the noise it makes. The music itself, being beyond the notes, can only be heard if the listener is in tune with the composer's *intentions* – for to attribute inappropriate meaning to a piece of music is to experience not the music itself, but a sort of self-hypnotic dream one is having about it.

How far such dreams have value in themselves and indeed, how far we are dreaming about *all* our experience, are questions for the psychologist or the mystic. What is inarguable is that radical misunderstanding of a work of art will radically affect our assessment of its worth. Shostakovich's music is, at present, rated fairly highly in the West for the wrong reasons. It is conceivable that, were the right reasons to be discerned, it might be rated *very* highly. There is also, of course, the risk that it would be valued the less for being too dependent on knowledge of 'historical specifics' to conform to current notions of a properly timeless and subjective universal art.

Likeliest of all, however, is that its evaluation, while different in emphasis, will stay roughly where it already is. This, in the opinion of the present writer, will be because it is simply not within the compass of the Western imagination to assimilate the extremes of experience latent in Shostakovich's music. We will no more prove capable of holding in our minds the true significance of works like the Fifth Symphony than we have in the past proved capable of grasping the implications of the memoirs and 'camp literature' compiled by disaffected Soviet Russians and smuggled to the West. The meaning of Shostakovich's music will, as Alexander Solzhenitsyn has so mordantly remarked of its literary equivalent, 'go in one ear and out the other'. Then why bother?

You yourself will answer this question in the act of turning this page.

Chapter One

INNOCENCE 1906–1925

Do not torment the heart with earthly consolation;
Do not cling to your wife or to your home;
Take the bread out of your child's mouth
And give it to the man you do not know.
And be the humblest servant of the man
Who was your desperate enemy,
And call the forest animal your brother
And do not ask God for anything.

LOOKING BACK at the age of sixty-six, according to Solomon Volkov, Shostakovich dismissed his Petrograd childhood as 'totally average' and not worth recording, even supposing that he could remember anything about it, which, at his age, he mostly couldn't. After all, nothing of earth-shaking importance had happened to him as a child. Tolstoy hadn't dandled him on his knee, Chekhov hadn't told him any stories. Even what his Soviet biographers like to call the major event of his boyhood – his view of Lenin's arrival at the Finland Station in April 1917 – had gone practically unnoticed by him.

According to the official version of this story, the future composer had been deeply stirred by 'the spectacle of a billowing sea of people, the elemental force of the events taking place, and the figure of Lenin – all this being imprinted forever on his memory, to pour out later in sweeping symphonic canvases'. What actually happened, Shostakovich in his seventh decade claimed to be barely able to recall. He and some classmates from the Shidlovskaya Commercial School seem to have tagged along with the crowds converging on the station through the shabby streets of the Vyborg Side, Petrograd's proletarian-industrial district – but, either because mass demonstrations were then daily events or because he was too small to see what was going on, the ten-year-old Dmitri ignominiously failed to grasp the historic significance of the occasion. 'If I had been told ahead of time just what a luminary was arriving, I would have paid more attention, but as it is, I don't remember much.'

If we accept Volkov's version (and Maxim Shostakovich's is that his father *did* remember the day at the Finland Station, if only because the crowds badly frightened him), we are left with an interesting second question. One of the recurring themes of *Testimony* being mockery of the institutionalised overstate-ment of Soviet officialese, it is a moot point as to whether Shostakovich was really unimpressed by his early glimpse of Lenin or just damned if he'd go along with the historically 'correct' version of his private memories. The latter is far from unthinkable. In countries where truth is ordained from above, rather than muddled out below by each according to his creed, memory inevitably becomes a battleground vied for by the state on the one hand and the individual on the other. Where the state wins, memory disappears and only official history remains. Where the individual wins, there is at least a chance that the state's crimes will one day be recognised and the artificial past behind which they shelter dismantled.

As a deliberate gesture in the defence of memory, *Testimony* is polemical and needs to be approached with caution, no matter what the true nature of its authorship. This is not to say that it is unreliable in general or even in the tone of its detail – neither are any longer in doubt – but rather to recognise that Shostakovich (or Volkov, as the case may be) had considerable latitude for subtly altering the slant of awkward truths without actually falsifying the facts. Even if the authorship controversy did not attach to it, *Testimony*, pitching the personal memory of an embattled individual against the official memory of an all-powerful state, would still be contentious to the last full-stop. Echoing the grim sarcasm of many other works of its kind now available in the West, the book is part of a larger struggle and, as such, is necessarily a sort of counter-propaganda.

Shostakovich's jibe at Lenin in the story of the arrival at the Finland Station is a case in point. It serves the dual purpose of deflating Soviet official history and of suggesting that the composer was never a devotee of the Lenin cult, impressions highly convenient to someone wishing to present himself as a lifelong political sceptic. Consequently, we need to weigh this seemingly harmless anecdote to decide whether it is what it seems to be (the passing expression of an old resentment) or something less spontaneous (a minor revision of an embarrassing area in the composer's past). In this connection, it is worth noting that whilst *Testimony*'s condemnation of Soviet society is as wholesale as anything of the kind by Solzhenitsyn or Alexander Zinoviev or Nadezhda Mandelstam, Shostakovich never in his book explicitly renounces his country's political system or expresses a preference for any other. Naturally, there might be irreproachable reasons for this, but we cannot afford to take the possibility on trust; it is equally possible that the composer had something to hide. For example, there is the chance that, whilst wishing to distance himself from the Soviet state, he had nevertheless once been sufficiently firm a supporter of Lenin and Communism that explicit denial of them, even at the end of his life, simply stuck in his throat.

Accepting Shostakovich as having been a secret dissident in his old age is not difficult. Little he wrote then is hard to reconcile with such a position and the majority of it actually becomes more obscure if the option of dissidence is ruled out. Further back in his career, though, there appear to be many more obstacles to the dissidence theory and, by the time we reach his twenties (the years 1927–36), the case for believing him to have been fully sympathetic to Communism seems a great deal easier to maintain than its opposite. Surely the young man who dedicated his Second Symphony 'to October' and called his Third *The First of May* could hardly have been anything other than an orthodox Communist? *Testimony*, however, has nothing to say on the subject.

If Shostakovich did once go through a period of political commitment, the questions of when and to what extent he emerged from it are vital. It is not simply a matter of being able to draw a line across the list of his works so that anything above it may be said to represent 'the Communist' and anything below 'the Dissident'. Aside from the likelihood that the truth is fuzzier, the crux is that the longer the composer's support for Lenin and Communism lasted (supposing it ever to have begun), the more seriously *Testimony* becomes compromised by its refusal to so much as mention it.

Time, here, is paramount. A year or two's youthful fling in his late teens or early twenties would be as excusable as Shostakovich's reluctance to admit to it. But five years, ten years? This would be less of a whim than a way of life (and a way of life, moreover, extending some distance into the Stalin era). Excusing this would be harder and explaining its lack of acknowledgement in *Testimony* next to impossible. As for fifteen years or more, this would take us beyond the watershed of 1937, after which simple faith in Communism on the part of the average Soviet citizen, let alone an intellectual with a privileged view of events, can be ascribed only to moral inadequacy, conformism, or sheer terror. If it were shown that the composer stayed loyal to the cause this long, his stance as an inveterate sceptic would be demolished and the credibility of *Testimony* and its various emigré supporters drastically impaired.

Some readers may still be puzzled at this point. Why is the question of how long (if ever) Shostakovich was a Communist so important? After all, he lived in a Communist country – what else was he supposed to be? And why should any of this affect our view of his music, surely a subject ruled chiefly by the apolitical criteria of aesthetics? There is no short answer to these questions – except to say that without some knowledge of the circumstances in Russia during this period, very little about its cultural products can be adequately understood; and that since Shostakovich was himself such a product, there is no substitute for a brief review of his early life, however insignificant he considered it from the vantage-point of old age.

Born on 25 September 1906 in St Petersburg, he was the second of three children produced by Dmitri Boleslavovich Shostakovich and his wife Sofia, the other two being his sisters Maria, three years older than him, and Zoya, two years younger. Politically, the family regarded themselves as *narodniki* (literally, People-ists), which at that time[1] meant they were radical democrats with the

---

[1] The Narodnik faith, relatively tame by 1905, had not always been so reasonable. Originating as a strange fusion of European positivism and anti-European nationalism in the 1850s, it had begun by despising constitutional politics and advocating the revolutionary overthrow of the Tsarist regime. Repressed in 1874, the movement continued as a terrorist group (the People's Will) whose campaign of violence climaxed

then common tendency of the urban intelligentsia to idealise the Russian peasantry, by whose supposed innate goodness they believed the country might be saved. In the case of the Shostakoviches, this idealism was at least based on some knowledge of conditions outside their own class, both sides of the family having recently moved to the capital from the tough frontier-country of central Siberia. There, Dmitri Boleslavovich, the son of an exiled radical, had lived close enough to peasants to have picked up their speech-patterns and boisterous directness of manner, whilst Sofia's parents, though bourgeois and well-off, had worked in the administration of the Lena gold fields, devoting their lives to improving the lot of the local miners.

Since the newest political trends of the time were initiated by city-based intellectuals with European educations, it might be assumed that a Siberian upbringing would be comparatively backward in this respect. However, owing to the Tsarist practice of populating newly colonised areas by sentencing political prisoners to internal exile, the frontier was an excellent place to obtain a radical education. Three of Shostakovich's ten uncles and aunts are known to have been active in underground circles prior to the 1905 revolution and a fourth, his maternal aunt Nadia, was one of the many Petersburg students to be radicalised by the wave of Tsarist repression which followed it.

Nadia, who in those days lodged with the Shostakovich family, became a fully-fledged Bolshevik and wrote agitation propaganda which her sister and brother-in-law allowed her to distribute to students and workers from their house on Podolskaya Street. In the aftermath of 1905 this was a dangerous game, thousands then being imprisoned and hundreds hanged. Indeed, had it not been for the unexpected scale of events, which initially overstretched the resources of the secret police, the Shostakoviches, with their many revolutionary friends and acquaintances, would probably have been placed under immediate surveillance and Nadia soon arrested. As it was, it took the Okhrana (the Tsarist version of the KGB) more than a year to get round to raiding Podolskaya Street, on which day luck saw to it that there was nothing incriminating in the house.

All this amounts to an ideal pedigree for a Communist composer laureate and Soviet biographies accordingly make much of it, but the fact is that membership of the St Petersburg intelligentsia during this period was a virtual guarantee of sympathy for the radical movement and any impression that the

---

in 1881 with the assassination of Tsar Alexander II. Having by this act alienated the very 'People' they claimed to represent, the Narodniks spent the next twenty years in the political wilderness. Refloated as the Socialist Revolutionary (SR) Party in 1900, they regained their popularity by espousing parliamentary democracy and, in the 1917 election to the Constituent Assembly (a secret ballot by universal suffrage and proportional representation), won 417 seats to the Bolsheviks' 175 – an overwhelming majority. This, however, was academic, since Lenin immediately dissolved the Assembly and arrested the SR leadership. They and their party were formally 'liquidated' in 1922, following the first of the Soviet 'show-trials'.

Shostakovich residence was a hotbed of revolution is, to say the least, misleading. Naturally, the city had its quota of bourgeois reactionaries – Shostakovich notes that the families of Stravinsky and Prokofiev fell into this category – but amongst the academic and technical classes (the latter known in Russia as 'engineers') it was almost inconceivable to lack friends in radical circles. Shostakovich's father was himself an engineer (trained as a histologist, he worked in the Chamber of Weights and Measures) and his family's radical connections were about par for the Petersburg course. As with most decent and conscientious people of the time, their revolutionary fervour was really nothing more or less than a faith in the possibility of a just society, organised on rational principles rather than at the erratic whim of the Romanov dynasty. Again, like most, they had no firsthand experience of revolution before 1905 and were naively optimistic about the chances of change without chaos, it being largely this naivety that persuaded Dmitri Boleslavovich to allow his wife's sister to carry on her revolutionary activities under his roof – an innocence shared by Nadia herself, who would never have dreamt of putting the family at risk. The visit from the Okhrana came as a shock and altered the atmosphere in the household for several years afterwards.

Not that this unpleasantly direct encounter with the blunt end of a police state in any way frightened the Shostakoviches out of their radicalism. They stood by their principles and when, in 1907, Vyacheslav Yanovitsky, fiancé of Sofia's sister Lyubochka, was imprisoned on a false charge of murdering a policeman, they rallied round and got him off, notwithstanding that he was an active SR (Socialist Revolutionary) and therefore dangerous to know. Nor did the general spirit and significance of 1905 ever cease to be central to them. Though not himself a revolutionary, Shostakovich's father was great friends with his brother-in-law Maxim Kostrykin, who was enough of a firebrand not only to have been exiled to Siberia but also to have broken his parole. Together they were among the crowd in Palace Square on Bloody Sunday (9 January 1905), witnessing the famous massacre which, in a single hour, snapped the country out of its three-hundred-year trance of obeisance to the Romanovs.

Such experiences were not to be forgotten, and as they grew up the Shostakovich children were well-drilled in 1905 tradition, being taught to hope for a future in which its dreams of justice and self-government would eventually be brought to fruition. Such idealism is potent stuff to a young mind and it is conceivable that the composer continued to subscribe to it for a large part of his adult life (his son Maxim, for example, being named in honour of his father's revolutionary brother-in-law). However, the mature Shostakovich was anything but an idealist and his attitudes to 1905, to judge from his Eleventh Symphony, were by then at best ambivalent. Nor, more importantly, is it safe to assume that anyone believing in 1905 would automatically support the revolution of October 1917, for events in the interim ensured that there were crucial differences between the two upheavals.

During this period, a feeling described by the Petersburg Symbolist poet

Alexander Blok as one 'of sickness, of alarm, of catastrophe, of disruption' spread through the country. As the mystique of Tsarism, badly dented by 1905, became more tarnished with each new débâcle of the Great War, a revolutionary millenarianism began to make itself felt and the atmosphere in Russia grew strained with anticipation of an approaching storm. In the heat of this creeping hysteria, attitudes hardened and a brusque impatience with everything traditional appeared, particularly among the young whose interest in questions of right and wrong began to be overtaken by an aggressive impatience to affirm, without any reservation, the new over the old. As a consequence of this unforgiving mood, and especially of its triumphant sweeping of the field during the October Revolution, former radicals, such as Shostakovich's Aunt Nadia and Uncle Yasha, suddenly found themselves to be comparative moderates, while members of non-Bolshevik revolutionary parties, such as Vyacheslav Yanovitsky, faced the choice of either changing their allegiances or being 'liquidated'.[1]

Nor was it simply a question of attitudes. The 1905 ideal had been one of decentralised democracy, the pride and symbol of that revolution being the autonomous local councils known as *soviets* which had sprung up in the power vacuum left by the temporary withdrawal of Tsarist rule. However, when Lenin promulgated the slogan 'All power to the *soviets*' twelve years later, he was merely making use of a popular idea, democracy being the very last thing on his mind. October 1917 was an openly totalitarian revolution and, as such, a complete disavowal of the 1905 tradition and a slap in the face to those who believed in it.

So striking are the differences between 1905 and 1917 that any support Shostakovich unequivocally gave to the latter would, if nothing else, represent a break with his political upbringing and hence (though this should not be exaggerated) with his family. Perhaps significantly, just such a rupture seems to have occurred during the years 1927–36: the very period in which he seems most likely to have been a Communist. But little about Shostakovich's life is straightforward and, before threading our way through this particular hall of mirrors, we need to know something of how things seemed to him in his teenage years, bearing in mind that, far from pondering political comparisons, he was too young to think about anything much beyond playing soldiers until at least the early 1920s.

Shostakovich's childhood took place in the interim between 1905 and 1917 and he was still only a boy when the Bolsheviks seized power. Seemingly unaffected by the tension of the years immediately following 1905, he grew up happily in the bosom of his family, enjoying long dreamy summers with his sisters on the Irinovka estate outside Petersburg, courtesy of his mother's friendship with the owner's wife. Apart from regular illnesses, the only blemish on an otherwise

---

[1] See note on pp.18-19.

perfect childhood appears to have been the death, in 1914, of his young and much-loved Aunt Lyubochka, though even this is unlikely to have seriously disturbed an active seven-year-old.

Musically, Shostakovich was a slow starter. His mother Sofia was a good enough pianist to play chamber works with various neighbours and there was never a shortage of classical music in and around the household, but young Dmitri showed no great interest except when his ebullient father gave forth with 'gipsy songs' to his own accompaniment on the Spanish guitar. Apart from this, the boy's earliest intellectual passion was for reading – Hans Andersen, Krylov's fables, Pushkin, and anything about the wild Caucasus (or gipsies). Nothing daunted, Sofia and Nadia took him to hear *Tsar Saltan* in 1914 and he was duly entranced, but it was not until he was nine, when his mother got him to sit down at the piano and try out a few scales, that music really began to impinge on his awareness. Thereafter – in the way that some cheerfully shrug off as the ineffable mystery of genius and others find simply eerie – he commenced to work out most of it for himself, learning to read music with remarkable speed and becoming sufficiently adept at the keyboard to graduate to Bach's Preludes and Fugues by the age of eleven. At around the same time, he started writing his own music, revealing an undistractible facility which amused his father and thrilled his mother.

Although they continued his conventional education, it was clear that their son was not destined to be an engineer. Unusually watchful, if in other respects a healthily normal boy, he seemed to become a different person at the piano, assuming a commanding air of concentration often likened by surprised witnesses to that of a man twice his age. Moreover his maths teacher, who had previously regarded him as a promising pupil, complained that Dmitri no longer seemed capable of focusing his mind on his work and, when reprimanded for daydreaming, had replied in some puzzlement that his head was 'full of sounds'. The conclusion was obvious. Shostakovich's father conceded to his wife's insistence that they had a phenomenon on their hands and at thirteen their son became by far the youngest student at the Petrograd Conservatoire, studying piano with Leonid Nikolayev and composition under Rimsky-Korsakov's son-in-law Maximilian Steinberg.

The young Shostakovich was a model student – disciplined, hard-working, anxious to achieve and to be well thought of. Accordingly, his training went without a hitch and he graduated with honours in both courses, taking his piano finals in 1923 and obtaining his degree in composition two years later at the age of nineteen. The Conservatoire's director Alexander Glazunov, who recognised in Shostakovich an echo of his own prodigious youth, carefully monitored his progress in Steinberg's class and, in awarding him his doctorate, recommended the young man for a higher degree course which, under normal circumstances, would have led to the security of a professorship. However, times were hard and Shostakovich's need to earn a living would soon drive him too far from the academic orbit for this to be an option. He took the (largely extramural) course and graduated from it three years later, but was out in the world and pursuing his career from 1925 onwards.

Shostakovich may have been a great success as a composer, but his adult life, on the whole, was a disaster. In this, of course, he was similar to millions of other Russians, happiness under the Stalin dictatorship being at most a fleeting experience to all but the naturally servile. What seems clear is that most of his warmer memories clustered round his Conservatoire days, which in some respects seem to have been an extension of his blandly idyllic boyhood. Not that all was continuous sweetness and light. Conditions were always extremely uncomfortable, particularly during the Civil War years (1918–21) when any spare fuel was requisitioned by the Red Army and Nikolayev's piano class regularly congregated in dark and freezing rooms, muffled in greatcoats and gloves as they practised their graduation pieces. Food, too, was desperately short and malnutrition sapped energies, promoting the spread of disease and ensuring that death, even amongst the young, became a daily occurrence. Nor was Shostakovich's personal life a bed of roses.[1] Yet there was a camaraderie and group purpose about life in the Conservatoire which he would afterwards find difficult to replicate and which surely must have helped him through moments hard to bear under lonelier circumstances. Relatively sparing with dedications in later years, he inscribed nearly all of his earliest works to friends and teachers at the Conservatoire. Evidently the period meant a lot to him.

What kind of person he was then is less clear, since *Testimony* is not, on the whole, forthcoming on the subject and contemporary descriptions of his character conflict, some finding him reserved, others lively and amusing. The obvious explanation for this is that he behaved differently with different people, the self-control that in adulthood allowed him to be all things to all men apparently there in him from an early age. On the other hand, some Western critics subscribe to the theory that he had a divided personality, this being a by-product of the official Soviet line that the young Shostakovich was alienated from the People and hence either pessimistically tragic or flippantly satirical, only achieving a 'humane' synthesis of these elements under the paternal guidance of the Party. This was not, of course, how Shostakovich saw it (or latterly claimed to have seen it), but the idea that his was a double-aspected tragic–satiric style is too useful to pass over – especially since it illuminates the two things about him as a young man which all informants happen to agree on: his biting wit and the peculiar power he projected as a composer-performer.

Shostakovich's reputation for po-faced repartee dates to his earliest teens. Inherited from his mother, this talent needed to be quickly sharpened during his years at the Shidlovskaya Commercial School, a progressive post-1905 establishment catering to the children of engineer families, where his artistic leanings must have seemed to many pretentious. Not a strong boy, he learned to defend himself verbally, sizing up the weaknesses of those around him so as

---

[1] See Appendix 3.

to be ever ready with a piercing barb, a practice which *Testimony* refers to as the beginning of his disillusionment, claiming that becoming aware of the mechanical nature of much human behaviour ('what moves what . . . what pushes what') made him 'rather sad'. This revelation of people as puppet-like seems to have been so significant a discovery for Shostakovich (figuring, for example, in his first and last symphonies) that it is tempting to see it as that very focus of sarcasm and sadness from which his tragic–satiric style derived. But while a precocious cynicism no doubt nourished the satirist in him and can't have harmed his boyish gift for mimicry (impersonation becoming one of his favourite musical devices), to claim discovery of his tragic roots in a passing mood of adolescent melancholy would be fatuous. That these roots ran unusually deep even in his early teens is obvious in the music he was then writing – in particular his first substantial composition, the Suite for Two Pianos, Opus 6, completed in March 1922.

Unplayed after the twenties and published only in 1984, Opus 6 is a kind of homage to Rachmaninov's similar two-piano suites of 1893 and 1901, particularly the first of these, an apprentice work written at a comparable age. Like this and other pieces by Rachmaninov, Shostakovich's suite is haunted by the pealing of church bells and infused with a very Russian sense of the impersonality of fate. It should also be said that it shares the young Rachmaninov's tendency to overestimate the charm of his material, but the score nevertheless reveals an instinctive grasp of large-scale form and, in the halting melody of its slow movement, even approaches the older composer's shimmering lyricism. What is most striking about the Opus 6 suite, however, is its tragic intensity, no easy thing to accept as the work of a fifteen-year-old; and, since it would be altogether baffling for a composition so anguished to have come about without an external cause, it is no surprise that it was written under the impact of the first major calamity in Shostakovich's life: the sudden and unexpected death of his father at the age of forty-nine.

Throughout the starvation years of the Civil War, Dmitri Boleslavovich had been the life and soul of the family, cheering them up with his jokes and songs whenever he wasn't out of the house foraging for food or fuel. Though as underfed as everyone else, he so conspicuously held on to his energy and humour that when, one night in February 1922, he came home complaining of a headache and went straight to bed, it must have been difficult to believe it could be anything serious. But he never got up again and a fortnight later, to the stricken incredulity of his wife and children, he died of a brain haemorrhage. The shock of this tragedy went beyond immediate grief for, without a provider, the family could not survive the winter. Some days afterwards, Nadia, now married and living fifteen hundred miles away in the Urals, got a telegram from the children asking for help. Setting out immediately, she arrived in Petrograd a week later to find the Shostakovich apartment on Nikolayevskaya Street almost physically darkened by the absence of her brother-in-law and Sofia literally prostrate with sorrow. As a temporary solution, Nadia and her husband,

Professor Shohat, moved in with the family to boost the food allowance with their 'academic rations', whilst Sofia, now forty-four, got a job as a cashier; but when young Dmitri offered to give up his studies and look for work, his mother wouldn't hear of it. Things continued to be very grim for several months until, thanks to friends of her husband, Sofia found secure employment at the Chamber of Weights and Measures. Even so, the family's troubles didn't end there and things were never to run smoothly for them again.

The natural conclusion to draw from all this would be that Shostakovich found his tragic voice through the death of his father, but in fact the same tone is present in some of his earliest works (for example the five preludes from Opus 2)[1] – untormented, yet already displaying that strangely adult forceful-ness and ironic darkness of manner. (The G major prelude even features an early version of Opus 6's tolling funeral bells.) Moreover, one of his novice pieces, later suppressed by him, was a funeral march in memory of a boy he had seen hacked down by a Cossack during demonstrations on the Nevsky Prospekt near his home, an incident which, he assures us, remained with him throughout his life, finding its way into several works of his maturity. Clearly then, the original piece was, if nothing else, very deeply felt – and this at the age of ten! It seems as though the tragedian in Shostakovich has no starting-point, but rather recedes away into his childhood, perhaps even prior to the death of his Aunt Lyubochka. There is nothing necessarily mysterious in this. Russia, in the years immediately following the Revolution, was a country in which random outbreaks of violence could be witnessed almost every day and Shostakovich grew up as routinely acquainted with lawlessness and sudden death as any child in modern Belfast or Beirut, his famous self-control doubtless being partially a response to this unstable environment. But there was more to his tragic sense than can be explained in terms of what was happening immediately around him.

Given the predilections of his Petrograd professors, it is no surprise that the composer's first surviving 'public' compositions – the Scherzo, Opus 1, and the Theme and Variations, Opus 3 – are lightweight homages to (respectively) Rimsky-Korsakov and Glazunov. All the more striking, then, that the private world of his early preludes should be ruled by the gloomy influences of Rachmaninov and Medtner, conservative artists with serious outlooks and a strong sense of continuity with their nineteenth-century forebears. Even allowing for the prejudices of the Conservatoire's syllabus, the young Shosta-kovich seems initially to have felt more drawn to tradition than to revolt, a fact which becomes significant in the light of his disposition, once out of his rebellious twenties, to identify less with his extroverted Western contemporar-

---

[1] Shostakovich contributed the eight Opus 2 preludes to a set of twenty-four composed jointly with two friends at the Conservatoire in 1920, later withdrawing three of them as 'immature' and publishing the rest as 5 Preludes sans Opus. They are often listed as a separate work.

ies than with tragic figures from earlier generations, such as Tchaikovsky, Mussorgsky, and Mahler.

This mingled feeling for the past and for the tragic, if not inborn, is likely to have been instilled in the young Shostakovich by the extraordinary city in which he spent the first half of his life. With its huge sky, white nights, swooping bridges, and gloomy canals, St Petersburg was always a special place and, as his music often shows, Shostakovich had an acute sensitivity to atmosphere. Behind intense sound-pictures like *Palace Square* from the Eleventh Symphony lie timeless childhood impressions of grey stone and twinkling snow, long streets receding theodolite-straight to a low horizon, and the icy River Neva broadening to a mile-wide mirror between the Winter Palace and the Fortress of Peter and Paul. A city to inspire fantasy, Petersburg clearly fed Shostakovich's imagination from an early age, stimulating a vein of escapist romance preserved in his First Piano Trio of 1923 and sadly lost in two substantial apprentice scores he destroyed upon graduating in 1925: an opera based on Pushkin's *The Gipsies* and *Rusalochka*, a ballet after Andersen's fairy-tale *The Little Mermaid*. But the city also had its dark side, coming steadily to the fore as the composer grew up and probably encouraging his boyish fascination with the ill-starred and grotesque. By his early teens, he was devouring Gogol and Dostoyevsky, and fully aware of St Petersburg's ambiguous symbolism in Russian history.

This 'stern, dark city of many waters', as one of its latterday inhabitants, the poetess Anna Akhmatova, described it, is unique among European capitals in not having evolved through time but instead appearing almost instantly at the start of the eighteenth century in answer to Peter the Great's dream of a Russian 'window on the West' situated at the eastern end of the Gulf of Finland. Raised by slave-labour on a bed of logs in the marshy Neva estuary, Peter's city was a monstrous act of hubris, foreshadowing the grandiose excesses of Stalinism and costing so many thousands of lives that, though beautiful, it was in effect born in a state of regal illegitimacy for which the rest of Russia could hardly wait to see it suitably humiliated. In the two centuries during which it displaced Moscow as capital, Petersburg, with its European culture and élite privilege, became so perfect a token of everything wrong with Russia under the Romanovs that, when it finally met nemesis in the form of the three revolutions its own pomp had precipitated, the population at large made no secret of its satisfaction. Making Moscow capital again in 1918 was no act of neutral pragmatism to the Bolshevik government – and neither were the regular purges of Leningrad subsequently decreed from the Kremlin by the Georgian peasant Stalin.

St Petersburg had been the cultural centre of Russia throughout the nineteenth century, scarcely an artist of stature failing to be either born or based there. At the time of Shostakovich's arrival in the world, Balakirev was still alive and Glazunov newly in charge of the Conservatoire, where the young Stravinsky and Prokofiev were studying under Rimsky-Korsakov. In the world of the stage, the director Vsevolod Meyerhold ruled the theatre, while the impresario Serge Diaghilev was about to launch the epochal Ballets Russes, in which an extraordinary generation of dancers (Nijinsky, Karsavina, Pavlova) would make their names. Finally, it was the so-called Silver Age of Russian literature, with up to twenty major poets active, notably including the Petersburgers Blok, Akhmatova, and Osip Mandelstam. This era of phantasmagorical glamour (later commemorated in Akhmatova's hallucinatory *Poem Without a Hero*) was already fading in Shostakovich's boyhood and, by the time he'd begun to write music, had all but vanished. Nevertheless, its aura touched him and even at the age of thirteen he was indelibly impressed when Akhmatova, famous for her detached calm and majestic bearing, dropped in on a recital he was giving at the house of the Petrograd surgeon Grekov. Already a legend at thirty (it was said that every middle-class home in the city possessed a copy of her book *Rosary*), the poetess was too adult a taste to have then appealed to Shostakovich, most of the effect she had on him presumably being due to the sheer incongruity of seeing so mysteriously chic a woman abroad in the threadbare days of 1919. Later, however, he came to revere her.

Like her friend Mandelstam, who saw St Petersburg turning into a city of the dead and apostrophised it in his poems as 'Petropolis', Akhmatova was intensely aware of the halo of doom which began to glimmer about the place towards the start of the Great War. Watching Petrograd[1] fill with the deserting soldiers Lenin would use to seize power in 1917, she observed that the civilised city she had once lived in had degenerated into 'a camp of savages'. By the time of the October Revolution itself, the decay was complete – wild flowers sprouting in the department stores, wooden sidewalks rotting, and the cemeteries in ruins. Akhmatova, with a poet's love of extremes, was morbidly fascinated by this desolation: 'All the old Petersburg signboards were still in place, but behind them there was nothing but dust, darkness, yawning voids, typhus, hunger, damp firewood, and people swollen beyond all recognition.' The city, she concluded, had not merely changed but turned into its opposite: a cultureless wasteland. Like Akhmatova, Shostakovich spent many hours wandering around Petrograd at this time and the experience must have stamped itself permanently on his imagination. Though he would see other ruined cities in his life, he would never again witness the end of an age so clearly embodied in the fall of a great metropolis. Within a handful of years, the administrative and financial hub of an empire was reduced to a barter economy and emptied of over half its population. Too young to have taken this in intellectually, Shostakovich is sure to have wallowed in its imagery, the hollow textures of his later music holding memories of this dreamlike city of façades, his skeletal lines allusions to the wan lucidity of its humbled prospects.

---

[1] St Petersburg was renamed Petrograd in 1914, its former name then being thought inappropriately Germanic. Since Lenin's death in 1924, it has been called Leningrad – though its citizens still refer to it as 'Peter'.

On a day-to-day basis, of course, he would have been less concerned with perspectives on civilisation than with keeping warm in thin clothes, avoiding the drunken soldiers and the taunting prostitutes who serviced them, and finding ways to rise above the squalor all around him – what the novelist Ilya Ehrenburg recalled as 'a horrible life of millet gruel and dried fish, burst sewage pipes, cold, and epidemics'. The privations of the Civil War brought everyone low, but none so painfully as the Russian bourgeoisie, many of whom lacked the necessary street-sense to make the best of their reduced circumstances. (Such was the helpless poverty of Marina Tsvetayeva, Akhmatova's only rival for the title of national poetess, that a burglar who clambered into her Moscow quarters and saw how she was living gave her some of his own money and left.) Notwithstanding the emergency measures taken by his family, the death of Shostakovich's father might well have been fatal for them had not conditions as a whole begun to ease during the temporary return to a free-market system known as the New Economic Policy (NEP). Throughout the middle twenties, Sofia Shostakovich worked herself to exhaustion, but her meagre earnings never kept pace with inflation and, even after her daughter Maria secured a post at the College of Choreography, ends refused to meet. Towards the close of 1923, it became clear that Dmitri would have to combine studying with some sort of part-time job.

On and off for over two years, Shostakovich worked as a piano-accompanist to silent films in various Petrograd cinemas, hating nearly every minute of it. Not that he didn't love films – he was a born cinéaste, admiring the early work of Eisenstein and Pudovkin and greatly enjoying the comedies of Chaplin and Keaton (so much so that he was sacked from one establishment for persistent lacunae in his pianism owing to his being regularly convulsed with laughter at the on-screen action). But it was his ambition to make a big splash as a symphonist and composing was virtually impossible while his evenings were occupied with exhausting hours of hack-work.

As early as spring 1923 he had started to sketch a symphony, but had been forced to stop when infected with tuberculosis, a disease which was to afflict him for the next ten years. After various diversions and false starts, he gathered himself and began the work again in October 1924, this time pursuing it doggedly through half a year's hard luck and grinding toil to a conclusion on 1 July 1925, three months short of his nineteenth birthday. Submitted to the Conservatoire examiners as his diploma composition, Shostakovich's Symphony No. 1 in F minor, Opus 10, was immediately recognised as the most remarkable work of its type ever written by a composer under 20 years of age. Glazunov undertook to introduce it to the world and on 12 March 1926 it was premièred by the Leningrad Philharmonic Orchestra under Nikolai Malko, causing almost as great a sensation in the audience as the sight afterwards of its student composer awkwardly taking his bow.

As if a premeditated introduction to his double-aspected style, Shostakovich's

First Symphony is almost schematically divided into two halves (each of two movements), the first of these being dominated by the satirical mode and the second by the tragic. In a similar way the music itself, throughout displaying the composer's characteristically fidgety unease, moves from an abruptly contemporary vein in the opening movements to a frankly anachronistic expressiveness in the lento and finale, the presiding spirits being, respectively, those of Stravinsky and Tchaikovsky.

Thanks to the traditionalist bias of the Conservatoire's curriculum, Shostakovich discovered Stravinsky only in his late teens, the effect on him being instant and radical. As such, the First Symphony is, from the musicological angle, an excited spin-off from Stravinsky's *Petrushka*, a score of mesmerising originality which has temporarily fixated several other composers (for example, Messiaen in *Turangalila* and Tippett in *The Midsummer Marriage*). Shostakovich, however, would have found an extra fascination in the ballet's plot which, concerning the doomed antics of an animated puppet, reflected his schoolboy observations on the mechanical aspects of human nature, thus appealing directly to the satirist in him. The idea that human beings were machines or marionettes, their free will restrained by the bonds of biology and behaviourism, was in any case much in vogue at this time, inspiring a whole series of fate-harried puppet-heroes of which the most obvious examples, apart from Petrushka, are Schoenberg's Pierrot Lunaire and Berg's Wozzeck – both creations Shostakovich is known to have admired. Even his fondness for Charlie Chaplin is likely to have fallen into this category, explaining why the often-remarked 'Chaplinesque' tone of the symphony's early music is simultaneously so ominous.

The *Petrushka* legacy is strongest in the first two movements. Here we find ourselves in a psychological circus-world of disconcerting gestures and unexpected fanfares whose significance is never revealed. A march, by turns insouciant and sinister, alternates with a wistful 'ballerina' waltz and sudden menacing climaxes that rear up over the action like exaggerated shadows, suggesting some highly programmatic ballet of which the plot has been mislaid (or withheld). Brilliantly characterful though the music is, the most striking thing about it is the young Shostakovich's ironic distance from his material, the confident assertiveness of which reacts with its blankly enigmatic context to produce a tension in the listener based chiefly on the suspense of having no idea what to expect next. If there is an undercurrent of autobiography in all this, the peremptory silencing of the scherzo by a succession of deus ex machina piano chords would seem to suggest, more than a mere chapter ending, the ringing down of a curtain on an entire era of experience. (In his commentary on the work, Roy Blokker points out that 'in concert performance the final *fff* piano note, a low A for the pianist's *right* hand, presents a graphic image: the player crosses over to the bass of his instrument with a gesture oddly similar to the final, definitive closing of the end cover of a large book'.)

The symphony now unveils its greatest surprise, moving without warning or transition from Petrushkan pathos into stricken Tchaikovskyian tragedy. Clarifying the work's subjects as Fate and Death, Shostakovich now pours all his adolescent experience of mortality into its slow movement, punctuating its disconsolate sorrow with an implacably skirling tattoo of indifference. The cinematically graphic quality of the earlier movements returns in the finale, the symphony's puppet-hero almost visibly scurrying hither and thither, attempting to evade his destiny. Finally, Death looms over him in ascending piano-trills, eliciting agonised Mahlerian protests from the strings, and in a very nineteenth-century coup de théâtre the tattoo from the preceding lento is inverted into a question posed three times on unaccompanied timpani. The answer – a tearful soliloquy from a cello – reveals the young composer with mask at last doffed, this moment of calculated poignance trumped only by the resolve of the work's tersely stoical coda.

Since 'literary' interpretations of this sort tend to be frowned on in modern music criticism, Shostakovich's First Symphony is usually judged primarily as a formal structure, ignoring its dramatic content. In this case, the misconceptions this leads to (for example, that the work is flawed by its second half's 'stylistic retreat' from the boldness of its beginning), though unfortunate in themselves, are less regrettable than the consequent failure to appreciate the work's singular emotional maturity. The tragedy of the slow movement, for instance, is quite devoid of self-pity, while the symphony's closing bars display an experience of suffering and acceptance of the same normally found, if at all, only in middle age. Missing this prejudices any chance of understanding the music Shostakovich was to turn to next, and it is no surprise that the vagaries of his career during the years 1927–36 are invariably put down to immaturity, ignoring such objective factors as fluctuations in the political climate and the composer's strategy in responding to them.

This is not to pretend that he remained uncorrupted by what was then going on. The late twenties saw Russia subordinated to what Nadezhda Mandelstam called 'the cult of force' and Shostakovich, like almost everyone else, was affected by the often sadistic iconoclasm this brought with it. In this period of what Communists euphemistically call 'intensification of class-struggle', old values like civility and kindness were dismissed as bourgeois and the slightest hint of individualism mercilessly hounded. Many artists suffered the effects of this, though none more conspicuously than Anna Akhmatova who, vilified in the national press as a living symbol of bourgeois self-centredness and artistic decadence, found herself, in company with Osip Mandelstam, classed as an 'internal emigré' and her poetry unpublishable. Shostakovich can hardly have escaped having an attitude to this and it was probably unsympathetic.

Chief among Akhmatova's public persecutors (in private, he read her avidly) was the revolutionary poet par excellence, Vladimir Mayakovsky, who condemned her 'indoor intimacy' as having 'no meaning for our harsh and steely age'. Towards the end of the twenties, Shostakovich shifted his style sharply away from the Akhmatovian individualism of his early work towards the sort of populist radicalism demanded by Mayakovsky. This raucously anti-bourgeois phase was brief and he soon began to gravitate back to the more personal, interior, and truthful values for which Akhmatova stood; but for a while he at least *appeared* to allow the satirist in him to all but overwhelm his tragic other self – and it is during this short period that evidence suggestive of his affiliation to Communism is most persuasive.

Chapter Two

EXPERIENCE 1926–1931

Westward the sun is dropping,
And the roofs of towns are shining in its light.
Already death is chalking doors with crosses
And calling the ravens and the ravens are in flight.

IN A BOOK about his experiences in Russia during the late twenties and early thirties, the American journalist Eugene Lyons, then a member of the foreign press-corps, recalls how, in his act of the time, the Soviet comedian Vladimir Khenkin never failed to raise pained laughter with the line: 'One night I heard a pounding at the door – so I took my little suitcase and went to answer it.' Khenkin's reference was to the common custom, during times of 'intensified class-struggle', of keeping some clothes packed against the chance of being called away by the gentlemen of the security organs. In due course, Stalin's dictatorship would create an entire folklore of such syndromes: private codes for use in the presence of the police; blades hidden in shoe-heels for slashing one's wrists if torture became unbearable; the overdeveloped hearing born from listening in the small hours for a car pulling up outside or footsteps mounting the stairs (a variety of insomnia known in Stalinist Hungary as 'doorbell-fever').

'They always come for you at night' was a universal truism and its associated half-world of sleepless waiting is evoked in many long minutes of Shostakovich's music. Indeed, his son Maxim has recalled that, during a specially tense period in 1948, the composer not only had a suitcase ready, but would sit all night by the lift outside his apartment, convinced that the KGB were coming for him and hoping to persuade them to take him without disturbing his family. In this perspective, the legendarily nervous chain-smoking Shostakovich of later years – the 'pitiful wreck' of Solzhenitsyn's description – becomes an understandable figure. Yet he was one of many, the same lifelong strain having worn down millions of his generation.

Thanks mainly to Russia's dissidents, the truth of Stalinist terror is part of common awareness beyond its borders. Westerners with no more than an average knowledge of recent history know that Stalin's USSR was an extremely unpleasant place, while any reader of *Nineteen Eighty-Four* has a fair idea of conditions there during the late forties (see Appendix 1). Vladimir Khenkin's 'little suitcase' was, in truth, no joke. What is less well known in the West is how early the aura of fear around Stalinism began to develop. Eugene Lyons reviewed Khenkin's act in 1930.

On 5 December 1931, another American journalist, Rose Lee of the *New*

York Times, knocked on the door of Shostakovich's apartment in Nikolayev-skaya Street. Then twenty-five years old and still living with his mother, the composer struck Miss Lee, as he would many who met him throughout his life, as somehow timelessly young. Prepared to be awed by the world-famous laureate of Soviet music, she instead found herself met by a 'pale, tremulous' figure gazing earnestly at her through his glasses 'like a bashful schoolboy'. Once into his stride, however, the young man lost his gaucheness. Quoting Lenin to the effect that music was a unifying force, he dismissed as 'reaction-ary' figures such as Wagner and Scriabin, singling out Beethoven as the only revolutionary composer of pre-Revolutionary times. Seemingly fluent in Marx-ist-Leninist musicology, he spoke of Beethoven's ability to motivate the masses, observing of the *Eroica* that 'it awakens one to the joy of struggle'. Political analysis of symphonies was, he admitted, difficult. Nevertheless, all music had an ideological basis and, in Soviet Russia, it was consequently looked upon primarily as 'a weapon in the struggle'. There was plenty more in the same vein.

Muscular 'Bolshevik' certainties like these had a masochistic appeal for many Western intellectuals, conscious as they were of the softness of their own liberal values in an age of totalitarian vigour. Shostakovich's statements had just the air of scandal Rose Lee's readers were looking for and she avidly transcribed them, underscoring the desired frisson by remarking 'something alarming in the assurance of this young man, disposing of the past with no more apparent effort than a twitch of the fingers and a curl of his short upper lip'. Shostakovich, she observed, typified the 'strangely articulate' young intellec-tuals of the new Soviet society with their dogmatic manners – 'as if they had found the key to all questions'.

Turning the conversation on to a more personal track, however, Miss Lee soon discovered limits to this daunting assurance. Seemingly reluctant to talk about himself, the composer became suddenly wary, reverting to the pale, tremulous character who had answered the door. From a series of increasingly monosyllabic responses, it emerged that, whilst he had been working on an opera, he was for some reason afraid he would never finish it, having for the previous three years written little more than incidental music. The uneasy tone of Shostakovich's replies puzzled the reporter. He appeared to be 'embar-rassed' – but by what, she could not guess.

If a trained journalist on the spot inside Stalin's Russia was unable to deduce what was troubling Shostakovich, a mass audience in a different part of the world could hardly be expected to know better, and consequently this aspect of the *New York Times* interview was passed over in the West. The rest, however, was clear enough. Shostakovich was a 'Red' composer and his music different from anything being produced outside the USSR. This was the sound of world revolution, no less. The impact was great and for the next fifty years the phrases used by Shostakovich in this interview were to be recycled in every Western book and article about him.

Here then, surely, is the composer's free confession of Communist faith? He believed in the system in 1931 and everything he wrote up to that point must, therefore, be taken as Communist music. All that remains is to discover how much longer he subscribed to these opinions.

Unfortunately, the truth, particularly in a totalitarian country, is rarely that simple, and understanding Shostakovich's position at the end of 1931 requires rather more information than has so far been assembled in Western writings about him.

To begin with, the impression of a young man freely discussing his beliefs with an unbiased representative of the free press is misleading. In those days, the *New York Times* was openly friendly to Moscow's point of view, positive in its coverage of the Soviet programme of 'superindustrialisation', and disposed to turn a blind eye to Stalin's show-trials and the rumours of genocide surrounding his campaign of agricultural collectivisation. Rose Lee's privilege in being granted an interview with the country's leading composer can hardly have been an accident and the Soviet authorities must have expected a favourable result – which is to say that Shostakovich would have been told exactly what was wanted from him. Though her article makes no mention of this, Ms Lee would have been accompanied to Nikolayevskaya Street by a translator, a press-attaché, and at least one representative of the then ruling body of Soviet music, RAPM (Russian Association of Proletarian Musicians). There would have been nothing casual about the conduct of such an encounter.

The significance of this deepens in the context of the period during which the interview took place.

The pressure on Shostakovich to present an exemplary face to the West was insistent throughout his career. The public reprimands he received in 1936 and 1948, often seen in the West as perplexingly unique events, are, in fact, standard Communist policy towards non-Party intellectuals, official strategy on such matters being to spank with one hand while with the other waving away the very idea that anything of the sort is happening. It goes without saying that this requires the co-operation of those being disciplined, who must not only admit their errors but acknowledge the Party's wisdom in bringing these to their attention. The 1936 and 1948 reprimands were affairs of this kind and on both occasions Shostakovich toed the line as instructed.

What has so far been overlooked in everything written about the composer is that there was a *third* period during which he was required to make public his conformism: 1931. For the *New York Times* interview, far from being a spontaneous happening, can only have been a high-level stratagem designed to scotch rumours of cultural disunity at a time when the more independent of Western commentators were reporting huge cracks in the very foundations of Soviet art.

Having occurred within living memory and, more crucially, in the age of television, the Chinese Cultural Revolution of 1966–76 is a fact of mass acquaintance. Books like Nien Cheng's *Life and Death in Shanghai* and Zhang

Xianling's *Half of Man is Woman* have provided windows on an upside-down world in which culture was replaced by mechanised sloganeering, teenagers were turned loose on their seniors to 'teach them respect', and intelligence itself became a term of abuse. Having taken place long before television arrived, the Russian Cultural Revolution of 1929–32 is largely unremembered in that country and virtually unknown in the West – yet in every respect (including casualty figures) it is comparable with the mass psychosis precipitated in China by Mao Tse-tung thirty years later.

In short, Shostakovich's fateful declarations of Communist orthodoxy in December 1931 were made at the height of a period of violently enforced conformism every bit as frightening as those he subsequently experienced in 1936 and 1948. To understand his state of mind and the music he was writing at this time requires some consideration of the political background which conditioned it.

During the late twenties, a conflict was taking place across Russia at every level of society. Part of what Marxists call the class struggle, this was the phase of Soviet development called 'proletarianisation'.

Proletarianisation entailed the assumption of control of all aspects of society by the urban working class, ending the outmoded dominance of the bourgeoisie against whom the Bolshevik Revolution had originally been made. This process had begun in 1917 with Lenin's exhortations to the Petrograd workers to engage in 'class war' against the bourgeois and escalated the following year in the wake of Fanny Kaplan's attempt on his life. Accelerating genocidally with the onset of the Civil War, the class struggle only slackened off when Lenin, realising that economic revival would require bourgeois entrepreneurial skills, instituted the neo-capitalist experiment known as the New Economic Policy (NEP) in 1921. To hardline Bolsheviks, NEP was a betrayal in that it resuscitated the very class the Revolution had been designed to destroy. To the Russian bourgeois it was a blessed relief from four years of lawless persecution and an opportunity to find a place for themselves in Lenin's new world.

The Russian bourgeois were something of a special case, only distantly resembling the class Marx held responsible for the capitalist civilisation of modern Europe. In Russia, bourgeois meant 'educated', most of the segment of the population so called having come into being as a consequence of reforms in the Tsarist teaching system at the beginning of the nineteenth century. Nevertheless, the natural drift of the educated into better jobs and a higher standard of living marked them, in the eyes of revolutionaries like Lenin's Bolsheviks, as accessories to the ruling class. In fact, to the average revolutionary, almost always a bourgeois by birth, this intermediate class, with its 'affectations' of good manners and social conscience, was often more immediately offensive than the land-owning faction upon which Tsarist rule actually depended.

Himself exemplifying this brand of intolerance, Lenin made no attempt to conceal his dislike of what he saw as the 'rotten intellectuals' of the Russian bourgeoisie. Privately acknowledging soon after the Revolution that what he wanted was a programme of 'social extermination', he urged that 'class hatred' be taught in schools and ordered his secret police, the Cheka, to pursue a policy of 'the most cruel revolutionary terror' against the bourgeoisie. An organisation based on the operating methods of the Tsarist Okhrana and somewhat overcomplemented in psychopaths, the Cheka accordingly set about persecuting the educated class with staggering ferocity, rapidly establishing itself as the most feared agency in the land. During this period, thousands of bourgeois were taken as 'hostages', tortured, or shot in reprisal for the assassination of Bolshevik officials. Indeed, so terrified were bourgeois families of the Cheka that criminals posing as Chekists were able to blackmail them merely by threatening to arrest them, their victims generally being too cowed to ask to see warrant-cards. Protesting that one's family, though bourgeois in origin, had proletarian affiliations (that is, it included individuals who had sympathised with or even belonged to radical groups before the Revolution) was no guarantee of exemption. It depended which groups were on offer. For example, the Socialist Revolutionaries (several of whom were members of Shostakovich's family) became, after 1918, classed as 'enemies of the People', it being as unwise to be associated with them under Bolshevism as it had been under the Tsar.

How far the Shostakoviches suffered from the effects of the class struggle in this period is unclear. Victor Seroff, who co-authored the first biography of the composer with Shostakovich's maternal aunt Nadia, states that the family's bourgeois origin *was* a handicap to them, and notes that Sofia Shostakovich's indiscretion in wearing furs at the trial of Vyacheslav Yanovitsky in 1907 was on her record under the Bolshevik dispensation.[1] Concrete examples of persecution or disfavour go unmentioned by Seroff/Galli-Shohat, though some of the resentment of the Narodniks at their treatment after 1917 can be detected in Sofia's attitude to the Revolution, initially cool and later positively sulky. When, for example, Dmitri fell ill with tuberculosis in 1923, she cursed Nadia for 'her' revolution and the misery it had brought. (Nadia had joined the Bolsheviks in the wake of 1905.) By the thirties, however, her patriotism had got the better of her good sense and she was a staunch defender of the new regime.

Shostakovich's own attitude to all this is unknown. Seroff's statement that, in 1924, the eighteen-year-old composer considered himself 'wholly a part of the Revolution' is, in view of the pressures not to be otherwise, valueless. Nor, crucially, can it be taken as evidence of faith in Communism since, at that time,

---

[1] The Cheka knew the value, during interrogations, of seeming to know everything about their victims' lives. Julia de Beausobre, arrested during the early thirties, was amazed when her examiner remarked on the fact that her parents had rented a box at the Imperial Theatre before the Great War (*The Woman Who Could Not Die*, p. 43).

'October', as an idealised symbol of freedom, was common stock across the political spectrum. Furthermore, Seroff's conclusion seems to be based solely on a letter written by Sofia to Nadia in the USA near the end of 1924, in which she responds to her sister's suggestion that Dmitri seek a teaching post in America by expressing the hope that her son be offered a professorship at the Leningrad Conservatoire, since his love of his country would never allow him to leave it. 'It is amazing,' she adds, 'how early in his youth he understood the aims of the Bolshevik Revolution and how deeply he considers himself a part of them.' Leaving aside Sofia's own ambivalence about the Revolution, this sentence must be set against the fact that all mail then addressed abroad was being read by the Cheka. Mother of a family near to starvation, she would have every reason to wish to ingratiate herself with authorities who regarded her as a class enemy. (As for the longevity of her son's alleged revolutionary fervour, the conductor Nikolai Malko notes that he was unable to answer a single question in the political section of his piano exam in 1923.)

All that can be said with certainty about the politics (if any) of Shostakovich's youth is that his family tradition would have programmed him to regard 1917 with serious reservations. Everything that followed – Red Terror, the repression of workers' protests, the instigation of class war, and the setting up of concentration camps for its prisoners – would have ensured that someone like him had very mixed feelings about it. In addition, he would have known of the taking of hostages from bourgeois families, the purges of radical students during his days at the Conservatoire, and the mass arrests of the Bolsheviks' former fellow revolutionaries. Most of all, he would have felt the disturbing reverberations of the Kronstadt Uprising[1] – a tremendous blow to Bolshevik prestige in Petrograd and, if *Testimony* is to be believed, a deep influence on him.

For the composer to move from these attitudes into a rapprochement with Communism would have required drastically severing his ties with his family, class, and Narodnik tradition. Yet forces capable of effecting just such a break did exist and were acting on him at this time.

While still at the Conservatoire, Shostakovich had been relatively insulated

---

[1] Discontent among the workers in Petrograd in early 1921 burgeoned into strikes and protest-marches against Bolshevik economic policy. When the government declared martial law and started mass arrests, 5,000 sailors at the nearby naval base at Kronstadt formed a provisional revolutionary committee, demanding free speech, new elections, the release of all imprisoned socialists, and a devolution of power to the *soviets*. These being the very men who had ensured the success of the Bolshevik coup in October 1917, the government was severely embarrassed. Branding the Kronstadt rebels as Tsarist stooges in the pay of French counter-intelligence, Lenin had Marshal Mikhail Tukhachevsky storm the base with 50,000 men. The sailors were imprisoned and their many supporters in Petrograd executed.

from the facts of life in the new Russia. In general, choices had been simpler in the early twenties, survival being the chief focus of most people's attention until NEP brought a rise in living standards. When in 1926 Shostakovich stepped into public life in the echo of his First Symphony, the Revolution was moving towards its tenth anniversary and NEP prosperity nearing its height. The scenery in Bolshevik Russia had altered greatly in a very short time and a new atmosphere of assertion and competitiveness had introduced a fresh range of moral dilemmas.

For the young, the pressure to be smart and hard in mid-twenties Russia was difficult to resist. Shostakovich's was the first generation of Soviet youth – the first to live by 'scientific' precepts, free of the 'prejudices' of bourgeois culture. As such, its watchword was dogmatic exaltation of the new at the expense of the old, its self-image that of ironic, undeceived realism. 'Our duty,' announced the poet Mayakovsky, in his capacity as figurehead of contemporary Russian youth-culture, 'is to blare like brass-throated horns in the fogs of bourgeois vulgarity.'

That the vulgarity here invoked attached to the bourgeois rather than Mayakovsky was a reversal typical of the age, whose young iconoclasts saw themselves as the agents of a revaluation of all values and delighted in upturning tradition in every way (the clangorous percussion 'nocturne' from Shostakovich's 'anti-opera' *The Nose* being a typical instance). Mayakovsky's voice, amplified by the state propaganda machine, roared continuously over the hubbub, leading the chorus with ideas blunt enough to be wielded as weapons. 'I, who have scrapped the soul,' he declared, 'shout about things necessary under socialism.' Deliberately chosen, this metaphor sank deep into the national subconscious for, if one factor can be said to link all the many forms youthful cynicism adopted in the mid-twenties, it was the Revolution's abolition of the soul.

Identifying the Church as more than anything else responsible for the pre-Revolutionary status quo, the Bolsheviks set about severing its grip on the Russian mind within weeks of achieving power. As a supplement to shooting priests and razing monasteries, propaganda was set in motion to discredit the idea that human beings possessed a spiritual aspect which survived death. Half a century later, the success of this campaign was confirmed by surveys showing the use of the word *dusha* (soul) to have declined by 50 per cent since the Revolution. The immediate effect, however, was to usher in a materialistic phase in which Russian culture became aggressively body-centred.

In everyday life, the new stress on physicality took the form of a drastic loosening of sexual restraints. In line with the demands of 'revolutionary-proletarian expediency', Alexandra Kollontai's influential writings on 'free love' mocked marriage as bourgeois and exhorted the young to regard the slaking of sexual desire as of as little consequence as drinking a glass of water. Young men, at least, found this theory highly congenial and hastened to put it into practice in the name of the Revolution as often as possible. Young women, on the other hand, found themselves in the invidious position of being cheap if they acceded to demand and bourgeois if they didn't. As a result, demystification of sex in the twenties went hand in hand with devaluation of women and a literary atmosphere described by critic Ronald Hingley as 'bordering on sadism and pornography'. (Elements of this, too, can be found in *The Nose*.)

In art, physicality manifested itself most readily in visual terms. Here, state-directives to promote fitness became translated into images glorifying athleticism or homo-erotic idealisations of the muscular New Man of the proletarian revolution. Eisenstein was a case in point, his 'cinema-fist' philosophy being a typical reflection of the power-worshipping brutalism inherent in much Soviet art. Likewise, the machine-mysticism of groups like the Futurists and Constructivists found itself easily elaborated into theories conceiving the body, and hence the human being, as a system of valves and pistons. The theatre director Vsevolod Meyerhold, for example, began staging plays choreographed according to his doctrine of 'biomechanics'[1] (which, again, impacted on Shostakovich, who had his own ideas concerning human machinery).

This wholesale shift from soul-culture to body-culture was an inevitable consequence of Bolshevik ideology and would have happened in time anyway. What accelerated and intensified it was the pressure of necessity during the first years after 1917, when hunger ensured that physical needs took precedence over those of the mind and conversation rarely transcended complaints about the scarcity of bread. It took little enough of this to begin the passive erosion of inner values which the cynicism of the mid-twenties would elevate into an active crusade.

At a theatre in Petrograd in 1918, the audience's reaction to Othello's murder of Desdemona was to guffaw. 'This concentration upon such a personal emotion as jealousy,' wrote a witness, 'seemed too ridiculous to them in the midst of their own struggle for existence.' Eight years later, proponents of the new materialism were so assiduously debunking 'fictions' like freedom, truth, honour, conscience, and the sanctity of life that the novelist Yuri Olesha was moved to describe their efforts as an attempt to refurbish the soul clean of its old 'conspiracy of feelings'. Indeed, anyone retaining belief in the outmoded values of the soul-culture automatically became identified with the past. Anna Akhmatova and Osip Mandelstam, for example, even though still in their thirties, were by 1926 thought of as 'old people' irrelevant to modern life.

Looking about him at this time, memoirist Ilya Ehrenburg saw 'a generation

---

[1] Seeking a 'scientific art' of theatre, Meyerhold developed this system in 1920, deriving its elements from a casual study of Pavlov's theory of conditioned reflexes and his own observation of animal movements. An acrobatic and highly stylised extension of conventional acting, it was intended to complement the planes of Constructivist theatre-sets with predetermined movements designed to eliminate 'disruptive spontaneity'. According to Soviet critics such as Boris Asafiev and Ivan Martynov, Shostakovich's music between 1926 and 1932 was dominated by this theory and hence lacked 'inner' (psychological or emotional) qualities.

that roars with laughter at the circus and is in terrible sorrow; a generation without tears, callous, a stranger to tender passion and to art, devoted to the exact sciences, to sport, to the cinema'. To many, it seemed that this creeping dry-rot would prove irreversible. Asked why she had stopped writing, Akhmatova shrugged, 'It must be something in the air.' Certainly it was no time for poetry.

In the event, amputating the soul proved to be an unexpectedly complex operation involving many relapses. Regardless of the new body-culture's attempts to flatten out reality like a giant agitprop poster, Olesha's conspiracy of feelings persisted in creasing and tearing it. Depths lingered on in people despite Mayakovsky's stentorian calls to brassy shallowness; a sense of tragedy and memory of love survived amid the regimented cheers and brittle laughter.

The acutest awareness of what was happening belonged to the artists. Bearing the brunt of pressure to reflect the new materialism, it was clear to them that what they were really being asked to do was depersonalise their own talent – to project an art of complete self-effacement in order to pave the way for a regime of total collectivism. The brightest among them read the signs and – quietly, for in this era of tubthumping unanimity there was no other way – revolted.

These were the 'individualists' and, if his contemporary friends and heroes are anything to go by, Shostakovich was one of them.

'As a youth,' admits the composer in *Testimony*, 'I was very harsh and intolerant.'

No doubt much of his unpleasantness at this time derived from the fashionable behaviour of the iconoclastic young. Particularly chic among those kicking against a bourgeois upbringing was a rough directness borrowed from the proletarians and flaunted in mockery of the hesitant, fussy, snobbish circumlocutions of their own class, whose manners often resembled an elaborate apology for physicality itself. (Shostakovich's debunking of the Symbolist poet Sologub in 1924, recalled in *Testimony* with a relish undiminished by the intervening fifty years, exemplifies this.) Iconoclasm aside, the composer was also more than a little bent out of shape by overwork and disillusionment. His job as an accompanist in the Bright Reel cinema not only gave him insomnia, but exposed him to the high-falutin hypocrisy of one Akim Volynsky, who managed the place and who, when asked by Shostakovich for his wages, demanded to know how a young man who loved 'immortal art' could be so vulgar as to want money for it. Volynsky also wrote ballet reviews and whenever Shostakovich read these afterwards he saw through their pretension, so sharpening his precocious cynicism.

Excessive distaste for pretence veers easily into inverted snobbery, and when the young composer's sudden fame rapidly expanded his circle of acquaintances, the glitter of these must have made his former friends seem plain by comparison. The steam from the élitism this set in train was frequently let off on his family, Shostakovich's sister Maria complaining in a letter to Aunt Nadia that 'frankly speaking, he has a very difficult character – he is rough with us, hardly speaks to us . . . Towards those close to him [he] is impossible.' Though fond of the composer, Nikolai Malko observed him often self-betrayed by a mother-centred childishness and 'a petty and silly vanity'.

From 1927, the apartment on Nikolayevskaya Street was regularly awash with poets, musicians, and artists of every shape and size, Shostakovich numbering some of the most illustrious names in Soviet literature among his drinking partners. These included Yuri Olesha, author of the year's prose sensation *Envy*, Yevgeny Zamyatin, who wrote the classic anti-Bolshevik fantasy *We*, and the well-known humorist Mikhail Zoshchenko. His reading habits developing fast, Shostakovich would have been, through the influence of his new friends, immersing himself in the droll burlesques of Ilf and Petrov, the low-life wit of Valentin Katayev and Boris Pilnyak, and the bleak ironies of Isaac Babel. A particular favourite was Mikhail Bulgakov, later famous for his allegorical fantasy *The Master and Margarita*, whose plays and stories Shostako-vich looted for conversational tags he would still be using in old age.

These writers had one thing in common: they were sceptical of the Bolshevik regime. Referred to by their enemies as 'satirists', not all of them used out-and-out satire to express their points of view, but they were to a man independent. Literary individualists in an era of growing conformism, they were conspicuous amid a dull multitude of writers bent on divesting themselves of any attention-attracting uniqueness. Shostakovich's association with them almost from the moment he left the Conservatoire is one of the strongest arguments against his ever having been a Communist. (Again, though, it is important to separate 'October', the widely approved ideal of a new world of freedom, from Bolshevism. It was perfectly possible to be, in a general way, 'for the Revolu-tion' yet against the theory and practice of the party which engineered it.)

Independence similarly characterised the composer's taste in music, though here the transition from teenager to young man involved the solution of some basic questions and a period of thoughtful silence. The praise awarded his First Symphony, repeated abroad when the work was given in Europe by Bruno Walter in 1928 and in America by Stokowski in 1929, was tempered in Russia by reservations made from two specialist quarters – the aforementioned Russian Association of Proletarian Musicians (RAPM) and its rival body, the Association of Contemporary Musicians (ACM). Both focused on the influence of Tchaikovsky in the symphony's second half, RAPM deriding Tchaikovsky as a bourgeois individualist and urging Shostakovich to compose for the working man, the ACM advising him to modernise his methods or risk stylistic obsolescence. Jolted, the composer soon found himself locked in a creative crisis which took him a year to escape.

Why should an artist as self-possessed and technically secure as Shostako-vich have been so affected by the opinions of RAPM and the ACM? Previous commentators have tried to analyse the 1926–7 crisis in purely musical terms, but in Soviet Russia pure music does not exist. There, every part of life has its political aspect and, in confronting the rival criticisms of his First Symphony, the young Shostakovich was for the first time facing up to this. The opposition between RAPM and the ACM was a microcosm of the wider struggle going on in Soviet society as a whole: class warfare and proletarianisation. In this case, RAPM supposedly represented the interests of the proletariat, the ACM those of the bourgeoisie. Like anything else, it was never that simple.

The ACM, formed in Moscow in 1923, was a loose circle of composers and critics united only in believing that music should be independent and international. Responsible for inviting most of the leading Western modernists to perform in Russia during NEP, the ACM was nevertheless no avant-garde clique and included several conservative composers who had joined solely out of a principled concern for freedom of expression. Chairman of the Moscow section was the country's senior composer, the symphonist Nikolai Myaskovsky, a conservative whose periodic forays into anguished expressionism were still capable of shocking audiences in the late twenties. Other members included a pair of his pupils – the conservative Vissarion Shebalin, a close friend of Shostakovich, and Dmitri Kabalevsky, who trimmed a circumspect course between the ACM and RAPM – and the two leading avant-gardeists of the day: Nikolai Roslavets, known as 'the Red Schoenberg', and Alexander Mosolov, whose short orchestral work *The Iron Foundry* (a kind of poor man's *Pacific 231*) achieved a brief world-fame around this time. Heading the Leningrad branch were two modernists: the country's leading critic, Boris Asafiev, and the composer Vladimir Shcherbachov, Myaskovsky's opposite number at the Leningrad Conservatoire. Likewise sympathetic to the avant-garde in Leningrad were Vladimir Deshevov, notorious for his Constructivist piano piece *The Rails*, and Shcherbachov's talented pupil Gavril Popov, for whom Shostakovich had a high regard.

RAPM, founded like the ACM in Moscow in 1923, was a musical reincarnation of the Revolution's earliest 'worker's art' movement, the Proletkult (Proletarian Cultural and Educational Organisation) which, under the leadership of ex-Bolshevik Alexander Bogdanov, had started its own Workers' University in Moscow in 1917. Proletkult policy had been to proletarianise the arts – that is, eradicate bourgeois culture, replacing it with a completely new kind of creativity catering solely to urban labourers and peasants. Lenin, bourgeois enough to enjoy Beethoven and in any case on sour terms with Bogdanov, abolished the Proletkult in 1920, but its extreme left-wing membership lay low and reappeared in the form of several new organisations soon after his death, the most active being RAPP (Russian Association of Proletarian Writers) and RAPM.

RAPM, formed around the figurehead of the elderly proletarian composer Alexander Kastalsky, was instigated by the propaganda section of the Central Committee of the Communist Party to counter the influence of the newly formed ACM. Most of its members being musically semi-literate song-writers from the Komsomol (Young Communist League), RAPM produced little beyond crude polemics and was in any case perceived as being too close to the Party for the liking of the more serious Proletkult composers. Accordingly, several of these – notably Alexander Davidenko, Boris Shekhter, Viktor Belyi, and Marian Koval – formed their own Production Collective of Student Composers (Prokoll) at the Moscow Conservatoire in 1925. (The shrewd Kabalevsky, who had already joined the ACM, hastened to demonstrate the breadth of his sympathies by signing up with Prokoll too.)

Notwithstanding much mutual suspicion, the young Proletkulters of RAPM and Prokoll were at one in their impatience to take up proletarianisation where it had been dropped at the beginning of NEP. Demanding the liquidation of everything composed before 1917, they further announced their intention of suppressing anything else written since which, in their view, fell into the category of 'rotten product of bourgeois society'. In practice, this meant the ACM and, in 1926, RAPM published a letter attacking Anatoly Lunacharsky, the Commissar for Enlightenment, for referring to ACM members such as Myaskovsky, Shebalin, and Alexander Krein as 'our composers'. Not so, insisted the Proletkulters. Myaskovsky and his kind represented only 'the ideology of the decadent bourgeoisie', whereas Russia's true musical inheritance lay in the mass-songs and military marches of RAPM. Though the cultured Lunacharsky defended the ACM, he knew that it was solely his eminence which allowed him to do so without personal risk. No ACM composer engaged lightly in controversy with the Proletkult unless he was willing to put up with barracking from the back of the hall during his next concert. Only Nikolai Roslavets – who, though the country's most advanced composer, was shielded by his membership of the Communist Party – openly grappled with RAPM on a regular basis. 'Of course I am not a "proletarian" composer,' he snarled, 'in the sense that I do not write banal music "for the masses". On the contrary, I am "bourgeois" enough to consider the proletariat the rightful heir of all previous culture and entitled to the best in music.'

So quaint are the terms of the RAPM–ACM rivalry that it is tempting to see it as comic – a provincial play in which the protagonists wildly overact whilst maintaining an air of pomposity that would see them laughed off the stage in a more sophisticated theatre. However, the issues at stake in the twenties were anything but trivial. Works could be banned without appeal, careers curtailed at a finger-snap, while behind the scenes an endless parade of minor victims trudged away to living death in the labour camps now springing up along the shores of the White Sea in the far north.

Even as Shostakovich was writing his First Symphony in 1925, the Central Committee had convened a meeting to solve 'the problem of the intelligentsia' at which Nikolai Bukharin had called for 'standardized intellectuals . . . as though from a factory' while a delegate of RAPP, the writers' version of RAPM, demanded a dictatorship of the Party in literature and the establishment of 'a literary Cheka'. A letter signed by thirty-seven prominent writers (including

Babel and Zoshchenko) responded to this by, in effect, begging the Party for protection from the Proletkult. Times were dangerous. Very soon, even Nikolai Roslavets' outspokenness would cease.

Pausing to take all this in after the criticisms of his First Symphony in 1926, Shostakovich destroyed a small library of juvenilia, amongst which, according to Soviet sources, was a *Revolutionary Symphony*.

Destroying a work does not prove dissatisfaction with its content. Shostakovich may simply have disliked the *style* of his suppressed symphony (and, since the crisis of 1926–7 was partly about style, it may well be that this was all that was wrong with it). There again, perhaps the *Revolutionary Symphony* was not quite the celebratory work Soviet writers assume it was. It might, for example, have been about 1905 – about the 'People's Revolution' rather than the Bolshevik coup of 1917. A folk-like theme, composed by Shostakovich around 1920 and used in his 5th Prelude, later reappeared in his *Ten Poems on Revolutionary Texts* and Eleventh Symphony, both of which concern 1905. Maybe it also had some connection with the *Revolutionary Symphony*?

Or could it have been that the suppressed piece was about 1917 and unflatteringly so? A precedent for this existed in the form of Nikolai Myaskovsky's Sixth Symphony, premièred to considerable controversy in early 1924. Known in Russia as the 'Revolutionary', this gloomy hour of storm and stress was admitted by its composer to have embodied his outlook on events in the country after 1917. In its finale, the symphony pointedly contrasts two French Revolutionary songs, the *Carmagnole* and *Ça ira*, with the *Dies irae* and an old Russian chant called *The Parting of Soul and Body*. Deducing the nature of Myaskovsky's feelings from these clues is not difficult.

Shostakovich knew Myaskovsky's Sixth and would have been aware of the influence of the poet Alexander Blok on the views expressed in it. Blok, who in 1918 had hailed the Revolution with his apocalyptic *The Twelve*, subsequently grew famously disillusioned with it and his death in 1920 was taken by many Russian intellectuals as a symbolic burial of their faith in the new order. Dominating the inner landscape of the period with their images of awe and storm, the poet's portentous sonorities set up many musical echoes during the twenties (see Appendix 3). In short, Shostakovich's self-suppressed *Revolutionary Symphony*, quite apart from being stylistically dated, could easily have been the sort of thing the resurgent Proletkult would have loved to hate.

As it happens, all the available signs point to this very conclusion. With the exception of the 'circus' Scherzo, Opus 7, everything he had composed since his father's death in 1922 had been fundamentally tragic. Nor was this gloom confined to his more obviously personal works for, where the Revolution figured in his world, Shostakovich's introspection seems to have focused not on the flags fluttering in the sky, but on the blood slithering in the gutter. His *Funeral March for the Victims of the Revolution*, also discarded around this time, had been prompted by the death of one small boy in a flash of meaningless violence. The theme of his 5th Prelude would later be woven into two works alluding to the massacre of innocents on 'Bloody Sunday' in 1905. The tone of the wailing, tumultuous Scherzo, Opus 11b – surely, like the 19th of Proko-fiev's *Visions Fugitives*, an impression of crowds swirling crazily through the streets? – can only be described as grim. And if there is any 'revolutionary content' to the First Symphony, its character is beyond doubt pessimistic.

Even after a year's break from composition following the First Symphony, Shostakovich's mood, if his music is any guide, remained sombre. Resuming creativity in autumn 1926, he produced the positively demonic Piano Sonata No. 1, Opus 12, a work whose violent virtuosity serves as a reminder that he was then also a concert pianist whose repertoire included Liszt's *Funérailles*, *Réminiscences de Don Juan*, and B minor sonata. Though it might be supposed that a virtuoso piano sonata would have stuck out like a chaise-longue in the Bauhaus at this period, the genre was actually very popular during the mid-twenties, Mosolov writing a whole cycle of them and the Moscow Modernist Leonid Polovinkin sending up the trend in his so-called *Last Sonata* of 1928. Nor was Shostakovich's abrasiveness anomalous in itself. Encouraged by Lunacharsky, Scriabin's comparably dissonant piano sonatas were all the rage and similar works by Prokofiev and Bartok had recently been imported by the ACM.

What is remarkable is that the First Piano Sonata was originally entitled *October Symphony*. Apart from a possible relationship with the lost *Revolutionary Symphony*, the point here is that not only is the mood of the piece one of conscienceless ferocity, but its idiom is aggressively esoteric – making it the very antithesis of popular expression and the least characteristic of Shostako-vich's experiments in style. A clue to this lies in the sonata's second subject, where furious virtuosity declines into a clumsy pounding imitative of hack musicianship at its crudest. Like that of his Conservatoire-trained colleagues, the composer's attitude to the bellicose amateurism of RAPM is known to have been contemptuous. Do these bars, perhaps, embody this sentiment? The supposition might carry less weight were it not for the fact that imitative clumsiness was to become a standard satirical device for both Shostakovich and Prokofiev – or that Myaskovsky was to employ it to similar ends in the finale of his Eleventh Symphony in 1931. Be this as it may, the hieratic impenetrability of the First Piano Sonata solved nothing for Shostakovich. Prokofiev, on his first visit to Russia after emigrating in 1918, heard the young composer première the piece in Moscow and approved, but the general reaction was dour and a return to the drawing-board indicated.

At this point, Malko introduced Shostakovich to the man who was to become his greatest influence and closest friend, the multilingual polymath Ivan Sollertinsky. Four years his senior, Sollertinsky was not only an outstanding musicologist, but seemed to know everything about everything and find it all highly amusing. Accordingly, Shostakovich found himself taken in hand and introduced to poker, pub-crawls, numerous writers and artists, and the symphonies of then unknown Gustav Mahler. Excited by each other's minds, the two carried on an endless competition to see who could make the wittiest remark. Much of the hilarity of this friendship can be detected in the suite of ten piano grotesques, entitled *Aphorisms*, which next issued from Shostakovich's pen, though the darkness of the previous few years still clings to these macabre miniatures in spite of their drollery. As with the *3 Fantastic Dances* of 1922, echoes of Erik Satie are present; Shostakovich's *Dance of Death*, for example, recalls the French enigma's *Embryons desséchès*, while Satie's *Gnossiennes* lurk behind the concluding *Lullaby* with its baroque trills and inscrutable solemnity.

Meeting Sollertinsky reawakened the joker in Shostakovich and unleashed a sudden flood of fresh ideas, chief among these being the ambition, sparked by hearing Berg's *Wozzeck* at the Maryinsky Theatre, to compose a satirical opera. Lacking a subject, Shostakovich forthwith began buttonholing his literary contacts in search of a libretto. History, however, claimed priority. In May 1927, from Muzsektor (the musical department of the Commissariat for Enlightenment), came a commission for a work to mark the Revolution's tenth anniversary. It was an offer he could not refuse.

Inscribed 'Proletarians of the World, Unite!', the Symphony No. 2 in B, Opus 14 (*To October*) was uncherished by Shostakovich in later years. In fact, according to Maxim Shostakovich, his father latterly disowned both this and its sequel, the Third Symphony, making him promise not to conduct them. There can be no doubt that the source of Shostakovich's embarrassment over these pieces was their political content. The question is, was he embarrassed because they reminded him of a time when he believed in the ideology they expressed or because they recalled a former self too indecisive, opportunistic, or cynically flexible for his liking, even fifty years later? *To October* remains among the most intriguing mysteries of his career. Without an explanation of his attitude in writing it, no worthwhile assessment of his relationship with Communism is possible.

During the twenties, as has been stressed before, 'October' did not refer to the literal events of October 1917, but rather to the *spirit* of the Revolution as it existed in the minds of Russians across the political spectrum from the centre to the far left. 'October' symbolised an ideal New World of freedom and fellowship to which the nearest political idea was the Trotskyite doctrine of 'permanent revolution'. As such, it signified the very opposite of Bolshevik regimentation (it being in this sense, and despite his membership of the Communist Party, that Vsevolod Meyerhold referred to his iconoclastic productions of the early twenties as 'October in the theatre'). Shostakovich used the 'October' tag four times in his career: for the First Piano Sonata, the Second Symphony, the *October 1917* overture to his wartime suite *Native Leningrad*, and in the symphonic poem *October*, commissioned for the fiftieth anniversary of the Revolution in 1967. The two later works deal with the historical event; the two written in the mid-twenties concern its symbolic equivalent.

In this light, the Second Symphony's dedication looks harmless enough. The October mysticism of the twenties may then have been well on the way to being requisitioned by the Communist Party, but its freer meaning was still current, and what other symbolic references were available? In 1927 every artist in Russia was producing an October this or that. Unfortunately, this line of reasoning runs into an unavoidable obstacle. During the symphony's last seven or so minutes, its orchestra is joined by a choir, and the choir sings a poem, and the poem turns out to be a standard Komsomol paean to Lenin and Communism: 'Oh Lenin! You hammered resolve out of our misery, forged strength into our work-worn hands. You taught us, Lenin, that our destiny has but a single name: *Struggle!*' This, in other words, is not generalised Octoberiana, but plain and simple Bolshevik propaganda.

It is highly improbable that Shostakovich was a Bolshevik. In *Testimony*, Volkov has him holding forth unequivocally on this: 'Our family had Narodnik leanings – and, naturally, liberal views. We had a definite understanding of right and wrong.' Of course, this might actually be Volkov speaking, but there are sufficient indications from other sources to show that it need not be. Besides, unless Shostakovich had wholly lost his moral bearings since setting out to make his way in the world, he is unlikely to have become converted overnight to a Party which had crushed the democratic aspirations of Kronstadt and arrested students by the hundreds as recently as 1925.

Perhaps, though, the conversion had not been sudden? Perhaps he had been drifting towards reconciling the abstract 'October' and the concrete Revolution for some years? He would not, after all, have been alone in this. The contemporary slide into a body-culture, with its devaluation of old values, had swept many off their moral moorings and, as we have seen, Shostakovich was, to some extent, one such. In addition, six years free of proletarianisation had engendered a lulling effect of their own, introducing what memoirist Nadezhda Mandelstam has described as 'a progressive loss of a sense of reality . . . a general drowsiness' in which it was difficult to be sure of what was really going on. No inquisition seemed to be looming and living standards in 1927 were higher than at any time since 1914. The perennial Russian fear of a relapse into chaos had brought a deep yearning for stability, a willingness to close one's eyes and believe in a system which never tired of representing itself as unimprovably perfect. Did Shostakovich succumb to this, ceasing to draw the distinctions that would have kept him from toppling into the arms of Communism? Bolshevik propaganda was hard at work in 1927 to fuse the historical Revolution and 'October' mystique together again, part of this campaign being a war scare fomented to rally the populace into unanimity under the Red flag. Perhaps, in this atmosphere, the honour of a centre-stage appearance at the tenth anniversary celebrations turned the twenty-year-old composer's head?

Certainly the pressure on him to conform was intense at this point. Just as

Boris Pasternak was then being groomed by the Commissariat for Enlightenment for the role of Soviet poet laureate, so hints had been dropped to Shostakovich that he was in line for the post of court composer. The advantages – guaranteed fame, success, and money – were obvious. Yet what would his friends have said? This may seem a trivial question, but decisions of the sort Shostakovich was facing in May 1927 are very often made on the approval of colleagues and relations. His closest confidants then being Sollertinsky and the individualists of the literary scene, any advice the composer received is likely to have resembled Nadezhda Mandelstam's to Pasternak around this time: 'Watch out, or they'll adopt you.'

Supposing this to have been the case, and it is straining credulity to think otherwise, only one mystery remains: how did Shostakovich manage to move, within the mere month it took him to write the symphony, from sceptical reserve to the ranting 'Red Romanticism' of the work's finale? Did he simply snatch up a text he had no belief in and fling some music around it in a spirit of cynical pragmatism? Something of the sort – but the truth is probably subtler, more human, and more interesting.

Not least among the many worries preying on Shostakovich when he sat down to fulfil the Muzsektor commission in June 1927 was money, his only regular income then being his grant as a postgraduate student. He was to receive 500 roubles for the work and, though the fee was hardly generous (around £500 in current purchasing power), he needed it badly. However, at that price and with time limited by his wish to return as quickly as possible to his opera, there was no question of composing anything very ambitious. The problem was that the world, including Muzsektor, was expecting a worthy successor to his full-length First Symphony, which aside from being written in a style he no longer believed in, had taken him nearly a year to compose. Not easy to dream up a serious, conventional symphony when what one really wants is to scribble a fast, raspberry-blowing, avant-garde chamber opera. Clearly, Shostakovich had to find an acceptable compromise – and luckily there was an excellent one to hand.

It so happened that the Commissariat for Enlightenment's propaganda department, Agitotdel, regularly commissioned one-movement works on topical subjects, often featuring revolutionary tunes and invariably employing sung texts designed to make the required meaning clear. Though Shostakovich had been commissioned by Muzsektor rather than Agitotdel, and so was being asked for a piece of absolute music rather than a glorified broadsheet, he must have been attracted to the fact that, tailored to the attention-span of non-musical audiences, works of the second sort rarely lasted longer than a quarter of an hour. Writing a short agitprop symphony solved all Shostakovich's problems at once. Entirely appropriate to the occasion, such a work would be impossible for Muzsektor to turn down and guaranteed a friendly press, if only in Russia. Stylistically, it side-stepped the problem of producing a sequel to the

First Symphony, whilst offering carte blanche to experiment with orchestral effects in an entirely new vein. Most important of all, it would take only a short time to write, allowing him to get back to his opera at the earliest opportunity.

All that was missing was an appropriate text – something of a problem since such things were usually the work of Komsomol activists whose musical colleagues adhered exclusively to the anti-symphonic Proletkult. To judge from his opinion of RAPM, Shostakovich's acquaintance with Party and proletarian art organisations is likely to have been slim. Necessary consultations with Muzsektor and his literary friends produced the unanimous verdict that he should get in touch with the Komsomol-run Leningrad Working Youth Theatre (TRAM) which, under its director Mikhail Sokolovsky, was then the talk of the city's drama scene. What happened at this meeting is not recorded, but can be deduced from its outcome. Shostakovich agreed to become TRAM's musical consultant and in return went away with a poem by the company's resident writer, Alexander Bezymensky. With this act he had, in effect, solved the dilemma of choosing between RAPM and the ACM. For the time being, like Kabalevsky in Moscow, he would steer a prudent course between the two and await further developments.

How sincere was Shostakovich's new interest in proletarian art? Employing the confrontational techniques of Brecht and Piscator, Sokolovsky's theatre was reputedly well above the level of the average agitprop revue and the composer seems to have been genuinely excited by what he saw. On the other hand, Komsomol texts were notoriously awful and the strenuous bombast of Bezymensky's verses was all too typical. According to Malko, 'Shostakovich did not like them and simply laughed at them – his musical setting did not take them seriously and showed no enthusiasm whatsoever'. Given the sharpness of his literary nose, this is perfectly credible and the extent of his real commitment to TRAM is best indicated by the fact that he wrote nothing for them until two years later, by which time urgent new developments were influencing his decisions.

Back at his desk, Shostakovich plunged into composition at a speed fairly evident in the finished article. More than a year had elapsed since RAPM and the ACM had criticised his First Symphony as old-fashioned and he was ready to prove himself an artist as contemporary as the harshest Futurist, the most brutal Constructivist. Inevitably, the world of the Second Symphony is that of the militant mid-twenties body-culture. From the neo-Romantic First Symphony, with its confessional pathos and inner programme, Shostakovich had moved to its opposite: a gestural, geometric 'music without emotional structure', designed to reflect an external reality of speech-rhythms and movements. Much of this change can be put down to his fascination with Meyerhold's theory of biomechanics, but some of it at least must have been caused by loss of confidence in the subjective idiom he had grown up with in the Conservatoire. In effect, his *Othello* had been laughed at and, for the moment, part of him was ready to believe that personal emotion per se, let alone its public expression, was obsolete in the era of the Collective. Shostakovich, however, was never simple. Another part of him thought exactly the opposite and in the Second Symphony these two sides, satirist and tragedian, are simultaneously engaged without any apparent contact, like two artists working oblivious of each other at opposite ends of the same mural.

There is no real thematic material in the Second Symphony. Primarily interested in texture, the composer works quickly, slapping on the sonorities and substituting for contrapuntal clarity the layering method of Abstract Expressionism. But this is only half the story. Behind the wild Jackson Pollock exterior lurks the faint outline of a narrative. For example, one famous passage, in which nineteen unrelated lines are heaped into a howling crescendo, seems likely to be a musical representation of the ideological chaos in Russia between February and October 1917. (Ilya Ehrenburg recalls this as a period in which everyone stood on street corners all day arguing about what should be done and threatening to denounce each other. Asking Count Alexei Tolstoy what was going on, he received a shrug and the gruff comment: 'They're all off their heads.')

Following this, the sun of Bolshevism rises in a Scriabinesque tutti which comes close (figure 55) to quoting that composer's grandiloquent *Poem of Ecstasy*. Notwithstanding official statements printed over his signature to the effect that Scriabin was one of his favourite composers, it is well known that Shostakovich thought him madly pretentious and this passage is certainly tongue-in-cheek. Seriousness, however, returns as the noise subsides into a threadbare string line, strikingly prophetic of the composer's monochromatic later style, which in turn leads to the equivalent of this mini-symphony's slow movement. Here, the breathless pause before the megalomanic peroration uncannily anticipates similar moments in the finales of the Fifth and Seventh Symphonies. It is almost as if Shostakovich's imagination was programmed to produce specific musical formulae in response to particular emotional experiences – a thought almost immediately reinforced by what happens next. Bearing the work's only semblance of a theme (figure 64), a solo clarinet droops poignantly in a lament which, thirty years later, would reappear as the main motif in the closing movement of the Twelfth Symphony, *The Year 1917*. (This, we may infer from the composer's remarks on the subject, is the tune of his *Funeral March for the Victims of the Revolution*.) A short episode, recalling the death of the boy on the Nevsky Prospekt, concludes this section with ascending death-trills similar to those in the finale of the First Symphony. Personal emotion having been given its cryptic due, the Collective crashes in with its brief choral setting of Bezymensky's Komsomol poem, before a peremptory coda cuts the symphony off with a thud.

Having found a suitable form, Shostakovich had filled it with about equal gusto and carelessness. Though much of the symphony consists of sound-effects rather than music, it has incontestable vitality and is notable for coining the basic elements of the language he would be using for the rest of his career.

The leap in style from the First Symphony is enormous, with only that work's satirical mode surviving the change. Sadly, little else about it represents any artistic advance whatever over its predecessor, it being, by comparison, an unconsidered throwaway virtually devoid of serious content. In the end, the most remarkable thing about the Second Symphony is its ambivalence: its shocking contrasts of sunlight and shadow, of universal and particular. Such musical clues as are scattered about in it point to an underlying outlook deeply at odds with its apparent message of revolutionary enthusiasm. The rest is febrile transience, all too typical of its period.

Shostakovich was pleased with the orchestral effects he'd produced and, in a letter to Sollertinsky describing rehearsals in Moscow, confided that 'it sounded great'. However, reactions to the Second Symphony were mixed. The critics were politely lukewarm and Muzsektor disappointed. (The composer received no more commissions until 1929.) The public, whose taste is reflected in the fact that the hit of 1927 was Glier's dismal ballet *The Red Poppy*, showed no interest whatever and the symphony soon slipped out of the repertoire. In terms of the response it evoked, Shostakovich's Second Symphony was outstanding only in its unique feat of pleasing both the ACM and RAPM, the former delighted with its 'modernist' orchestral section, the latter approving the work's 'proletarian' chorale. By its première in November 1927, Shostakovich was already well advanced with his opera which, partly in celebration of an underrated sense-organ but mainly after the Gogol story on which it was based, was entitled *The Nose*.

Solomon Volkov dates Shostakovich's alleged decision to become a *yurodivy* to 1927 and identifies *The Nose* as the first work he wrote under his new persona. If the composer's contemporary claim that the opera was not meant meant to be funny is anything to go by, Volkov has a point. Unfortunately, Shostakovich reiterates this in *Testimony*, adding that he had never meant *The Nose* to be a satirical opera and insisting that it is 'a horror-story, not a joke'. This, if nothing else, is an exaggeration. The 'frivolity' of the work, whether or not apparent to its creator, was from the outset a bone of contention to official opinion, and the audiences which so enjoyed its individualism during its brief run in Leningrad in 1930 are unlikely to have done so with straight faces.

Shostakovich, however, has some justification for playing down the satire in his opera in that neither the literary nor musical version of *The Nose* is consistently satirical, or indeed consistently anything other than individualistic. Gogol was a one-off – moralist, surrealist, right-wing anarchist – and it is this singularity which so appeals to his native audience. His refusal to be pinned down, as much instinct as ploy, is essentially Russian. More to the point, it is quintessentially Shostakovichian and, in this perspective, the opera's dismissal by one Soviet critic as 'the handbomb of an anarchist' calls to mind Ravel's response to a listener's exclamation that the composer of *Boléro* must be mad ('She has understood!').

As satire, Gogol's story aims mainly at social pretension and the insolence of office. 'Major' Kovalyov, newly elevated to the rank of Collegiate Assessor in the Tsarist civil service, wakes to find his nose missing and subsequently discovers it to have assumed his identity and uniform and set off around St Petersburg pretending to be someone of consequence. The ensuing pursuit cocks snooks in all directions until, finally, the nose resumes its appropriate place and the tale peters out. A stylistic clue to the story is the offhand tone Gogol adopts throughout, peevishly complaining to the reader that he simply cannot imagine what any of this nonsense is supposed to mean. *The Nose* is, in fact, a satire within a satire, the hidden level being a quiet jeer at state censorship for which Gogol adopts the technique of criticising by overstating his disinclination to criticise. Satire by overstatement (*vranyo*) is, again, a Russian tradition much plundered by Shostakovich, but particularly interesting is that the kind used in *The Nose* – in effect, pleading stupidity – specifically belongs to the *yurodivy*.

Coincidence or plan? Gogol's story is not, on the face of it, an obvious subject for an opera and it is possible that Shostakovich selected it precisely because of its element of *yurodstvo*. Against this, however, it must be said that the opera makes no use whatever of Gogol's narrative device, whilst the composer's choice of story seems to have been prompted chiefly by nostalgia for his teenage reading habits. Volkov's contention that Shostakovich began acting in general like a *yurodivy* while he was writing *The Nose* is ultimately unverifiable. What is certain, however, is that this was a period in which those who saw the Soviet regime as the enemy of individual freedom increasingly took to hiding in irrational and inconsequential disguises. The Leningrad Dadaist group Oberiu were one example; Shostakovich's friend, the writer Mikhail Zoshchenko, another. Volkov calls both *yurodivye*, while Ilya Ehrenburg uses the term with reference to the individualist author Boris Pilnyak.

Much of the intellectual agenda for 1927–8 was set by the novelist Yuri Olesha's elusive satire *Envy*, which veiled a struggle between its rebel hero Kavalerov and the deindividualised functionary Andrei Babichev behind a dazzling downpour of outlandish similes designed to mock the middlebrow clichés of Soviet officialese. Shostakovich's *The Nose*, disapprovingly described by one of his Soviet biographers as 'a sort of cascade of musical witticisms', fits snugly into this background without, however, being remotely as focused as the work then being produced by writers like Olesha, Bulgakov, and Zamyatin. The libretto, written by the composer in collaboration with two fellow Gogolians, Sasha Preis and Georgi Ionin,[1] is very much the work of young enthusiasts, cultishly devoted to a favourite author. As such, its aims are

---

[1] Shostakovich originally asked Zamyatin to collaborate with him, but age difference (twenty-two years) produced a breakdown in communications and Preis and Ionin were drafted in. In the end, Shostakovich wrote most of the first two acts himself (apart from Scene 3, which survives in Zamyatin's version), and his collaborators the inferior Act III.

confused by its fidelity to style and no convincing overall scheme emerges. Magnifying the inconsequentiality of the story wherever possible whilst otherwise following it in pedantic detail, the text degenerates into tedious farce saved only fitfully by its music.

A fifteen-number opera in three acts and an epilogue, *The Nose* is often said to have been influenced by Berg's *Wozzeck* and there are several parallels between the two works. Both use an angular idiom designed to reflect speech-rhythms (Shostakovich claiming that his music was intended to form an equal partnership with Gogol's words, 'musicalising' them); both possess a symphonic inner structure (Shostakovich called *The Nose* a 'musico-theatrical symphony'); both are fast, episodic dramas beginning with shaving scenes; and so on. Influences of this order are, however, superficial and Shostakovich himself scornfully dismissed them. A more relevant influence might have been Prokofiev's *Love for Three Oranges*, scintillatingly premièred in Leningrad in 1926 (though Shostakovich claims to have been unimpressed by this, too). In fact, *The Nose* is largely without precedent, springing out of thin air as a response to its composer's intoxicating encounter with a large audience in the same year. At this stage of his career, Shostakovich had a young man's ambition to amuse and confuse his listeners which, combined with a boyish love of piling it on, simply ran riot in the work he seems to have regarded as the true successor (and antidote) to his First Symphony.

The Nose has been called an anti-opera, satirising the conventions of bourgeois opera by turning them upside-down. There are elements of this, but on this outing Shostakovich was only sporadically methodical and, unless doing so milks laughs or produces a striking effect, no theme or idea in it is pursued for very long. Indeed, most of the opera is less concerned with poking fun at bourgeois conventions than it is with debunking the ancient Russian tradition of soulful self-dramatisation – and, in this respect, its individualism is somewhat distorted by the influence of the body-centred cynicism then permeating Soviet life.

Relentlessly harsh and abrasive, the piece is at bottom an exuberantly heartless satire on humanity itself. Presented as two-dimensional puppets, the people in it are uniformly vain, stupid, violent, and prone to prolonged bouts of mass hysteria. Its few moments of lyricism are associated with false piety or self-pity, and the tragic idiom of the First Symphony recurs solely as accompaniment to the ridiculous Kovalyov's anguish concerning his truant proboscis. Here again is the Othello effect – the young man wincing at memories of disowned emotion. Self-dramatisation, of course, had dominated recent Russian symphonism, particularly in the works of Tchaikovsky and Scriabin, and

---

Preis insisted that material not in the original story should, as far as possible, be drafted in from other works by Gogol. Thus, the libretto contains borrowings from *Sorochintsky Fair*, *The Marriage*, *May Night*, and *Taras Bulba*, plus one interpolation from Dostoyevsky – Smerdyakov's song from *The Brothers Karamazov*.

Shostakovich had much to kick against. Myaskovsky, too, would recoil from an early rhetorical tendency into near self-effacement in his later symphonies; but Shostakovich, far younger than Myaskovsky, was less self-forgiving and, consequently, less forgiving in general.

The rapid, restless style of the piece, usually ascribed to the influence of Meyerhold (denied, of course, by Shostakovich in *Testimony*) is, in fact, a standard device of Russian satirical theatre, having evolved as a form of camouflage-by-speed intended to confuse the state censor. One or two significant motifs are nevertheless visible amid the mayhem. The police, for example, feature heavily, Gogol's references to them being underlined with ever-increasing gusto by Shostakovich's librettists – so much so that in the final act the process gets completely out of hand, degenerating into Keystone Cops slapstick. Elsewhere, restraint produces greater effect. The silent apparition of a policeman behind the barber, Yakovlevich, as he is toying with breaking the law is an eerily succinct evocation of all-seeing totalitarianism which must have caused a few gasps in 1930. However, *The Nose* is nothing if not an exercise in excess and Shostakovich can't resist drawing out a scene portraying the bribery of a police inspector to Dostoyevskyian lengths.

The sexual connotation of nose-loss is similarly prominent. In Scene 2, Praskovya Osipovna's taunting allusion to her husband's impotence, whilst securely based on Gogol scholarship, isn't in the original story. Nor is a long scene in which ten policemen tease and manhandle a pretty bread-roll seller. This is another infection from the twenties – the voyeurism of young men exacerbated into a fixation on female sexuality and the compulsion to punish which this arouses – and more of the same is present in gratuitous references to the frustrated desires of both Madame Podtochina's daughter and Yakovlevich's wife, Praskovya Osipovna. (Shostakovich, incidentally, acknowledges this erotic undercurrent in *Testimony*.)

Loss of nose may be a sexual symbol, but it also signifies loss of olfactory sensitivity and, in a more general way, *The Nose* is a comment on the decline in contemporary ability to distinguish between the sweet and the foul. The opera's first words (not in Gogol) obliquely signal this in an exchange between Kovalyov and his barber:

> *Kovalyov:* Ivan Yakovlevich, your hands stink.
> *Yakovlevich:* What of?
> *Kovalyov:* I don't know, old chap, they just stink.

If this seems oblique to the point of invisibility, it should be borne in mind that Russian audiences, having lived with censorship since the dawn of time, are constitutionally tuned to the tiniest subversive resonances in the music and poetry they value so highly. By this standard, the scene in which Kovalyov's advertisement of a reward for the return of his nose is refused by a sceptical newspaper clerk ('People already complain that we print too many tall stories and bogus reports') would have come as a veritable thunderclap of sedition in 1930.

Even so, there is only one specifically anti-Bolshevik squib in the whole opera, and that readily deniable. The Nose, challenged by Kovalyov in Kazan Cathedral, informs the Major that they have nothing in common; he, Kovalyov, is wearing the uniform of an official from the Ministry of Justice, 'whereas, sir, *my* chosen field is science'. This, not in the original (and presumably added by Zamyatin), would seem to be a poke at the theory of Dialectical Materialism in its self-appointed capacity as 'the only scientific description of history'. To anyone acquainted with history in its Soviet phase, the juxtaposition of 'science' with justice would have been richly suggestive.

Started soon after the Second Symphony, *The Nose* was completed a year later in May 1928 and submitted to Samuel Samosud and Nikolai Smolich at the Leningrad Maly Opera. They accepted it and rehearsals began in the autumn. In the meantime, however, great events outside the musical world had been set in train by the resolution, after a five-year power struggle, of the issue of Lenin's succession. There was a new ruler of all the Russias and for millions, not least Shostakovich, the rise of Joseph Stalin meant that life would never be the same again.

Stalin's announcement of the policy of 'Socialism in One Country' ended at a stroke the trance-like suspension of time under NEP. Suddenly, all was furious activity. The country was going to 'superindustrialise' – catch up in a matter of years with what had taken the West a century. Needless to say, doing this would entail mobilising the entire Russian people.

Unlike earlier Bolshevik leaders, Stalin was a real proletarian. Unencumbered by intellectual baggage or inverted snobbery, he was a patient schemer, as willing to bow to indignities on his way to power as, once there, he was meticulous in avenging them. Peasant-shrewd, he disliked cleverness, fine manners, anything cultivated. Meeting these, his predilection was to humiliate and destroy, wherein lay his only claims to refinement.

Brooding over the blueprints for the First Five-Year Plan in 1928, Stalin concluded that Lenin's moratorium on persecuting the bourgeois must come to an end. Their brains were needed for the technical and communicative realisation of what amounted to a second Revolution – and no proletarian could have any illusions that class enemies would co-operate in their own disfranchisement. They would resist by inertia and the pretence of solidarity. They would skive and sabotage. In short, they needed the whip.

This brutal logic was grounded in reality, if a severely stunted view of it. The deferment of the class war in 1921 had left proletarians and bourgeois polarised in mutual suspicion. Most of the educated class had retained their positions, or returned to them under NEP, and the more militant among the workers naturally resented this. Hadn't the Revolution been made precisely to extinguish injustices of this kind? As for the *intelligenty* themselves, they knew very well that they were camped on the edge of an abyss. Despite the relative ease of NEP, few of them were doing more than the bare minimum required, this being their way of participating in the Revolution without actively committing themselves to the destruction of their own class. But these were complex times and to conclude (as Stalin did) that the Russian intelligentsia fundamentally opposed the Revolution was a wilful misapprehension. It was not the Revolution the bourgeois distrusted, but the violently coercive uniformity stamped on it by the Bolsheviks. Many intellectuals of Sofia Shostakovich's generation were understandably torn between their socialist ideals and private anxieties over what might happen to them once these were implemented. It was a poignant dilemma from an era of lace-draped delicacy marooned naked in an age of arc-lights and steam-hammers.

From 1928 onwards, the pressure of this predicament, common among decent educated people over thirty, began drastically to intensify. To scare the intelligentsia into obedience, Stalin reactivated the process of proletarianisation, sending spies and overseers from the working class into the bourgeois-dominated bureaucracies, technocracies, and universities. As further encouragement, he began to make an example of those *intelligenty* who, 'like Egyptian slaves set to work to build pyramids which will form their own graves' (in the phrase of novelist Panteleimon Romanov), supposedly spent their days in skiving and sabotage. Towards the end of 1927, the papers began to feature reports of 'wreckers' – reactionaries allegedly found creating mischief in various sectors of the Soviet economy. The social origin of these creatures was unspecified but, since government bulletins had been predicting a bourgeois counter-revolution, there appeared to many citizens to be a simple explanation to hand. Notices exhorted workers to be on the lookout for wreckers and, naturally, to turn them in wherever they were found. Then in May 1928, around the time Shostakovich was completing *The Nose*, a sensational announcement appeared in the press. Agents of the GPU (the new title of the Cheka) had uncovered a huge conspiracy to sabotage production in the Donbass coalmines involving no less than fifty-three 'engineers' (technical intelligentsia), all of whom were to be put on public trial together in Moscow. It seemed that the anticipated bourgeois counter-revolution had arrived.

The so-called Shakhty trial, the most talked-about event in the USSR since the Kronstadt Uprising, ran clamorously through the summer for seven weeks. The first of the 'show-trials' of the Stalin age, it fascinated the Russian people, who daily queued at newspaper kiosks to read the latest on it in *Pravda*. Here they found accounts of angry workers' discussions about the case, editorials vilifying the defendants in unprecedently violent language, and pages of letters from outraged proletarians demanding death for these 'enemies of the People'. More remarkable still, they could read transcripts of the trial in which the accused abased themselves before the court, confessing to whatever charges were put to them and pounding their breasts with disgust over their own unutterable loathsomeness. The overacting and general gaudiness of the production were positively Oriental, and many simpler minds, conditioned by Soviet cinema to view life in terms of crude melodrama, fell for it. To Russians with an ounce of common sense, the Shakhty case and the chain of virtually identical affairs which trailed after it during the next ten years became known as 'witch-trials', and nothing about them was believed.

Why the grotesque exaggeration? In large measure it was sheer bad taste, a judicial parallel to the 'Stalin Gothic' skyscrapers raised in Moscow during the late forties. In so far as these circuses were ring-mastered by Stalin, they also smacked heavily of the pedantic sadism of the avenging paranoiac, determined to bury his enemies so thoroughly that there would be no danger of them rising from their graves to haunt him later. But the main factor, from the point of view of propaganda, was a wish to stun the Soviet people into a state of open-mouthed passivity in which they would be ready to accept anything, however absurd. The show-trials were, in effect, Stalin holding up four fingers to Russia and menacingly informing her that she saw five.

In the view of the émigré historians Heller and Nekrich, this was all part of an ongoing programme 'to kill human sensibility' in order to make way for the creation of the collectively-orientated Soviet New Man, a policy recognised as such by many contemporary writers. (The Nobel Prize-winning author Ivan Bunin described it as early as 1919 and the idea subsequently recurs throughout the work of the literary individualists.) Whatever else may be said about this, one thing is certain: it is inconceivable that Shostakovich could have kept the company he then did and still have believed in the Shakhty trial. If he had not already formed a disenchanted view of the ruling regime, he can hardly have avoided doing so after the summer of 1928.

If this is true, is it safe to say that he could not possibly have been a Communist at this time? Tiresome as it may seem, the answer is no. Despite the deepening degradation of the real-life Revolution, the symbol of October still held many of the best Russian minds in thrall. Typifying a common strain of self-deception, Boris Pasternak passed the late twenties denying his natural lyricism in order to serve what he saw as a millennial cause by producing noisy epics of the sort patented by Mayakovsky. In this sorry pose, he stood for a generation who had spent their lives awaiting the Revolution and for whom weeding out deep-rooted dreams of its perfect realisation was simply too painful a task to face. Shostakovich may have been among them. Like so many in his mother's generation, he might have been 'torn'. He could even have been a Communist.

What he cannot have been, given his circumstances and cast of mind, is the kind of Communist who believed without question everything his leaders told him. Under Stalin's rule, this scepticism would have been more than enough to qualify him as an enemy of the people awaiting discovery and 'extermination'.

For the remainder of 1928, Shostakovich marked time with minor pieces, his creativity focused mainly on rehearsals for *The Nose*. In daily life, he had two major distractions. The first was his love for Nina Varzar, a physics student and daughter of upper middle-class parents, whom he had met at the Scholar's Resort in Detskoye Selo a year before. The second was the air of fear spreading through the country like the foreblast of a singularly icy winter.

Already ominous currents were in motion within Soviet culture. The First Five-Year Plan had been launched on a platform of insanely unrealistic targets which the Russian people were expected to sacrifice all to fulfil. Arrests were on the increase and a new crime, refusing to inform (ie., putting one's 'narrow, class-based morality' before spying for the GPU), was swelling the northward flow of political prisoners into a small torrent. In the year's most talked-about play, Erdman's *The Suicide*, the hero remarked, to deafening silence in the auditorium, that there were 200 million people in the Soviet Union and all of them were scared. By 1929, a hundred thousand of them were also serving long sentences in labour camps. Though a negligible proportion of the general populace by later standards, these were mostly bourgeois *intelligenty* from the technical sector, Shostakovich's own background. He would have had much food for thought.

The new era hit him personally towards the end of 1928 when rehearsals of *The Nose* met resistance from the performers, ostensibly because of the work's complexity but actually because of its modernity. Proletarianisation had penetrated the opera house and Komsomol–Proletkult overseers were letting it be known that anything too clever could lead to unfortunate consequences for those involved. Shostakovich's response – to seek a broader range of opinion by including a suite of excerpts in a concert of his latest music that November – elicited a mixed reaction and the Leningrad Maly management continued to drag its heels. Meanwhile, two useful commissions arrived: to write history's first orchestral film-score for Kozintsev and Trauberg's *New Babylon*, then being edited at the Leningrad Sovkino studio; and to compose incidental music to Meyerhold's production of *The Bedbug*. The latter was the theatrical début of the legendary Mayakovsky, whose notorious willingness to place his muse at the disposal of every whim of Soviet propaganda must have been, if nothing else, a phenomenon of pressing curiosity to Shostakovich.

As a boy, Shostakovich had, like most of his contemporaries, admired Mayakovsky's pre-Revolutionary verse, However, the poet's later role as a mouthpiece for the Central Committee had alienated much of his audience and none more than Shostakovich's literary friends, who no doubt let their feelings concerning the proposed collaboration be known to him. (Nor would their case have been difficult to make. Some of Mayakovsky's work of this period resembles recruiting notices for the GPU, and lines like 'Think / about the Komsomol . . . Are all of them / really / Komsomols? / Or are they / only / pretending to be?' were bringing vers libre into disrepute.) An additional source of potential tension lay in the fact that the composer, as rising star of

Soviet culture, was poised to inherit the poet's mantle as figurehead of Soviet youth culture. Under these circumstances, their meeting was bound to be chilly.

Mayakovsky, whose musical taste was rough and ready, appears to have treated Shostakovich as a jumped-up bourgeois poseur which, whether true or not at the time, was certainly an instance of bickering amongst soiled kitchen utensils. The dislike was mutual and the description of Mayakovsky given by the composer to *Literary Gazette* in 1956 as 'a very gentle, pleasant, attentive person' appears to be one of his deadpan jokes. (Eugene Lyons recalled Mayakovsky as 'a burly, bellowing fellow', whilst to Max Eastman he was 'a mighty and big-striding animal – physically more like a prize-fighter than a poet – and with a bold shout and dominating wit and nerves of leather . . . probably the loudest and least modulated thing and nearest to the banging in of a cyclone that poetry ever produced'.) The irony is that, professional jealousy aside, the two artists almost certainly had something important in common: disaffection with the ruling regime.

Western musicologists who have either never read *The Bedbug* or remain impervious to its sarcasm tend to accept the line, fed them by Soviet critics, that the play satirises the Nepmen or 'grabbers' of the mid-twenties private enterprise culture. This is untrue. Like Olesha, Katayev, and Ilf and Petrov, Mayakovsky was using apparent satire on NEP as a front for satirising the government.

The poet's idealised view of progress had foundered on first-hand acquaintance with it during a visit to the industrial heartland of America in 1925 and his disillusion with Communism set in thereafter. By 1929 his revulsion against the soulless banality of the Collective was bitter and – owing to his compensating interest in alcohol – incautiously frank. Though *The Bedbug* uses the *yurodivy* technique of voicing its criticisms through the mouth of a buffoon (in this case, the Mayakovsky-like drunkard Oleg Bard), they are open and become steadily more blatant as the play proceeds.

Shostakovich thought the piece 'fairly lousy' and few would disagree with him. A hasty, manic, and finally insufferable farce, *The Bedbug* was knocked out chiefly in the hope of earning its author enough foreign royalties to pay for a sports car. On the other hand, it is also, in parts, a funny and occasionally brilliant satire, at least some of which must have wrung a reluctant chuckle from the composer. (Serious, too: the scene where the 'Zones of the Federation' block-vote on whether to 'resurrect' the cryogenically preserved hero Prisypkin alludes to the Soviet regime's liberal recourse to capital punishment. 'We demand resurrection!' chorus the conformist Zones where, a few years before, they would just as confidently have demanded death.)

Doing *The Bedbug* partly for the money and partly to please Meyerhold, Shostakovich was himself too much the satirist not to have known exactly what Mayakovsky was saying and must therefore have still been sufficiently naive to imagine that there would be no repercussions against himself for having participated in the project. If this is true, he was soon cured of his illusions. Opening in Moscow in February 1929, *The Bedbug* was attacked by the Proletkult for its form and by the Komsomol for its content. Meyerhold's theatre was soon finding audiences hard to come by and left-wing activists marked Mayakovsky down for special treatment. His passport was confiscated and within a year they had hounded him to suicide. As for Shostakovich, he discovered that KIM (the Communist Youth International, or Komsomol division of Comintern) had denounced *New Babylon* as counter-revolutionary with the result that cinema orchestras were refusing to play his music for it, claiming it to be too complicated. That it was nothing of the kind is demonstrated by the fact that it was nevertheless, as a result of some oversight, given a short and successful run in one Moscow cinema. But the reality was plain: *New Babylon* was not wanted. The score was withdrawn and not played again for nearly fifty years.

As yet the Cultural Revolution was a semi-spontaneous side-effect of proletarianisation, uncoordinated from the centre and prosecuted chiefly by activists. This would soon be rectified, but in the meantime the composer's first commission since the Second Symphony came through, unvetoed, from the Directorate of Theatres: a ballet to a scenario of outstanding idiocy entitled *The Golden Age*. Gaining in worldly wisdom by the week, Shostakovich accepted it without hesitation.

On this occasion, his timing was good, for the long anticipated storm now began to break. Having established the necessary precedent with the Shakhty trial, Stalin announced that 'bourgeois wreckers' were at work in every branch of Soviet industry. Reports of executions (of saboteurs, spies, counter-revolutionary priests, kulaks, speculators, and assorted 'backsliders and renegades') suddenly increased tenfold. A Communist hegemony was declared in the arts and the proletarian groups RAPP and RAPM began openly baying for blood. Their first victim was Alexander Voronsky, chief defender of the literary Fellow Travellers, whose arrest for 'Trotskyism' was one of the earliest made under this charge. Their second was the ACM's magazine *Contemporary Music* which, founded in 1924, ceased publication in March 1929.

Perhaps most significant for Shostakovich was the banning of the plays of his hero Mikhail Bulgakov. Bulgakov's story *Heart of a Dog* was one of the earliest works to be proscribed under NEP, and *The Days of the Turbins*, based on his novel *The White Guard* about a bourgeois family in Kiev after the Revolution, had been a cause célèbre since opening at the Moscow Arts Theatre in 1926. The Komsomol had picketed it and Mayakovsky had used a debate on Soviet theatre to call for legal reprisals against its author's 'whining'. A new ending, more acceptable to the left, was thereupon tacked onto the play – Shostakovich, who saw the production in January 1928, was disappointed to encounter this – but the compromise was a temporary measure. In May 1929 *The Days of the*

Turbins was taken off and within a month Bulgakov's entire oeuvre was outlawed.[1]

Shostakovich soon had problems of his own. In June a public hearing of *The Nose* at the All-Russian Musical Conference in Leningrad resulted in scandalous scenes, with RAPM delegates angrily denouncing the composer for 'Formalism' and 'anti-Soviet escapism'. Attacking the work as 'irrelevant to students, metal- and textile-workers', the Proletkult composer Daniel Zhitomirsky brandished a warning fist in Shostakovich's direction: 'If he does not accept the falsity of his path, then his work will inevitably find itself at a dead end.' This was threatening stuff with a futuristic ring to it, but as yet RAPM and the ACM were fairly evenly matched and the composer had enough supporters among the Modernists to protect himself. Accordingly, the debate ended in a draw, with a resolution to take excerpts from *The Nose* into Leningrad's factories and try them on the workers. But enough was enough. Nerves frayed from his growing struggle with the Proletkult, Shostakovich used the money from his ballet commission to fund a working holiday by the Black Sea with Nina. It was time to make himself scarce.

Safe in the Georgian resort of Gudata in July 1929, Shostakovich took less than a month to dash off his Symphony No. 3 in E flat, Opus 20.

Like the Second Symphony, it was an Agitotdel-style one-movement work with a choral peroration on a proletarian text, this time using incantatory verses by the talented working-class poet Semyon Kirsanov. The work, named after the poem, was entitled *The First of May*.

Why, without a state commission, did Shostakovich write a state propaganda piece? And why May Day? Conceivably there is no mystery. Shostakovich had composed a symphony for one of the Soviet calendar's two great annual festivals; now he had written a sequel to celebrate the other. But this is to take simplicity to ridiculous lengths. Aside from an uncharacteristic lack of ideas, only two things could have motivated the Third Symphony: genuine Revolutionary feeling, or a wish to ingratiate. As for the first, it has been argued that the October ideal may still have been in the composer's blood and that he may have identified himself with the proletariat against his own bourgeois background at this time. But too many contrary influences were working on him, too much disillusionment had soaked into his complex, ironic personality for simple revolutionary enthusiasm to have been real to him in 1929. On the other hand, alternative motives were abundant and need no resuming.

Clearly then, the Third Symphony was, largely, if not wholly, a pretence of orthodoxy at a time when anything else would have risked courting the kind of persecution visited on Mayakovsky or the technical *intelligenty* of the Shakhty trial. Hence the quite unnecessary Agitotdel format – and the slapdash

---

[1] Despite RAPP's incessant attacks on Bulgakov, Stalin took a shine to the play – presumably a torturer's interest in the discomfort of his victims – and, during 1932, sat engrossed through no less than fifteen private performances of it.

execution of the piece, so transparent to its unenthusiastic audiences. 'One cannot help feeling,' wrote the sympathetic English critic Gerald Abraham, 'that the composer is playing a part . . . He tries to be Marxian, but fantastic Gogolian humour keeps breaking in.' But though calculated insincerity was obviously the basis of the Third Symphony, its composer seems at first to have been satisfied with it and must surely have seen more in it than that. Though thematically not much richer than its predecessor, it occupies ten more minutes and has an aura of ramshackle ambition in proportion to its grander length. 'Gogolian humour' is present, but can't account for the whole, long stretches of which are defiantly unsmiling and cloaked in deep shadow.

Though more elaborately polyphonic, the linear, episodic idiom of the Third is a recognisable progression from the Second, even to the extent of hinting at a hidden programme. Possessing little integral form of their own, its more chaotic passages sound like responses to events in another dimension, such as an unseen film (a parallel perhaps to the First, with its hint of an unstaged ballet). Evidently the symphony is something of an extension of the cinema music Shostakovich had recently been writing. However, the main musical precedent for the work, both in detail and in general, is that of Mussorgsky.

Shostakovich's deepest artistic influence, Mussorgsky was greatly interested in the tradition of *yurodstvo*, concluded his epic opera *Boris Godunov* with a sorrowful prediction of doom from a *yurodivy*, and generally behaved like one himself (being known to enemies and friends alike as the Idiot). His *Complete Works*, jointly prepared by Pavel Lamm and Boris Asafiev, had been inaugurated in 1928 with a limited edition of the composer's original full score for *Boris*, an event of real fascination for Russian musicians. Shostakovich would have been poring over this in every free moment and the Third Symphony appears to have been the first creative by-product of this study.

In *Testimony*, Shostakovich describes Mussorgsky as 'an entire academy for me – of human relations, politics, and art'. His fascination with the composer was lifelong and it is unrealistic to imagine that his opinions on him in 1929 were as considered as they were fifty years later. However, *Boris Godunov*, with its portrayal of political tyranny in a highly specific Russian setting, would have had such relevance in the late twenties that it is difficult to conceive of Shostakovich not taking it instantly to heart. *Testimony*, at least, is sure that he did:

I always felt that the ethical basis of *Boris* was my own. The author uncompromisingly decries the amorality of an anti-people government, which is inevitably criminal, even inexorably criminal. It is rotten from within and it is particularly revolting that it hides under the name of the people. I always hope that the average listener in the audience will be moved by Boris's words, 'Not I . . . it's the people . . . it's the will of the people'. What familiar phraseology! The style of justifying villainy in Russia never changes, the stench of evil lingers.

These influences on the Third Symphony show in several ways. The speech-rhythmic phrases used by both instruments and voices, for example, conform to Mussorgsky's insistence on 'a musical reproduction of human speech in all its nuances'. The work's choral envoi has a massive unanimity and a gloomy incandescence, redolent of torchlight, which hark back to the chorus in *Boris Godunov* and its composer's vision of the People as 'a great personality, animated by a single idea'. A similar source is suggested by the dramatic drum-rolls, guillotine thuds, orchestral shouts, and sombre brass recitatives of the symphony's penultimate section. But if this is so, what is Shostakovich saying?

Celebrated by labour movements all round the world, May Day symbolises fraternal solidarity and the apotheosis of the urban working class. As such, it is the proletarian festival par excellence. So much for symbolism. In the Russia of 1929 the apotheosis of the working class was a reality and took the form of proletarianisation, state terror, and a Five-Year Plan predicated on turning the country into a giant labour camp. With its frenetic restlessness, belittling jeers, and towering blasts of brute sound, the Third Symphony speaks for its age in a manner as critical (and as carapaced in apparently contrary intentions) as Mayakovsky's *Bedbug*.

The individualism of Shostakovich's chosen artistic milieu perhaps finds expression in an eerie interlude sandwiched, like a dilapidated church between skyscrapers, at the centre of the work's tumultuous first fifteen minutes. Here, just as in an almost identical moment in the first movement of the Fourth Symphony six years later, the contrast of near-silence with the bombastic racket preceding it provokes a Mahlerian cry of anguish (figure 45). The fact that these passages are similarly characterised by keening strings and a nocturnal hush again suggests that the composer was programmed to associate certain soundscapes with corresponding emotional states and experiences. But it is the closing moments of the Third that drive its mood and message home. Here, the critic Boris Asafiev's contemporary view of the work as 'an attempt to produce a symphony from the oratory of revolution, from the characters and intonations of the orators' is borne out in a sequence of unison shouts over a long drum-roll, vividly suggestive of a demagogue haranguing a crowd. With pontifications from the deep brass drawing assenting growls from the lower strings – and, in turn, slavishly imitative cries from the violins – the atmosphere becomes sombrely Kafkaesque. Indeed, so ominous is this passage that it is tempting to hear in it the first appearance in Shostakovich's music of Stalin himself, perhaps denouncing wreckers or setting out the targets of the First Five-Year Plan.

There is no 'Red Romanticism' in the Third Symphony. Swinging between exhausting bustle and browbeating rhetoric, it is a realistic, not an idealistic, work. That most of the time it runs too fast in censor-evading circles to retain coherence is undeniable, and forgiving its twenty-two-year-old composer for this won't turn it into better art. But though a failure, it none the less survives through having something true to say of its time. However thin the inspiration, however hedged the creative bets, it communicates the agitation, grandiosity, and driven fear of the Russia Shostakovich was growing up in. If we are to look for a suitable epigraph to the piece, none could be more apt than Ilya Ehrenburg's verdict on the post-war generation of the forties: 'They wanted to rest but life would not let them.' To rest in 1929, and for years afterwards, was impossible and forbidden – unless one's eiderdown was made of earth.

On returning to Leningrad in the middle of August, Shostakovich swiftly dashed off an incidental score for Mikhail Sokolovsky's Komsomol theatre company, TRAM.

The Shot, to a play by Alexander Bezymensky, author of the proletarian verses used in the Second Symphony, was Shostakovich's first original work for TRAM since becoming their music consultant in 1927. As evidence of revolutionary conviction this is, to say the least, unimpressive; and while his admiration for Sokolovsky may have been genuine, the composer can hardly have been inspired by Bezymensky's propaganda puff for the so-called shock-worker movement. Apart from doing a favour for Meyerhold, in whose theatre the production was mounted, the only intelligible motive on Shostakovich's part is self-preservation – a musical sacrifice offered up to cover himself against further attacks from the Proletkult. This time, however, pragmatism betrayed him. Too shoddy even for the Proletkult, Bezymensky's play was savaged by RAPP for its 'schematism', a scandal which died down only after Stalin himself had gone into print to declare *The Shot* 'a model of revolutionary art for the present'. Shostakovich, whose main concern can only have been the then ubiquitous one of not being caught out of step, must have suffered some tense moments over this. (His score was later mysteriously 'lost'.)

Next on his schedule was the full-length ballet *The Golden Age*, for the writing of which he could doubtless have done with some peace and quiet. Unfortunately, these commodities were out of stock in Russia that autumn, for as the Cultural Revolution finally reached gale force, all hell broke loose. The branch of the arts most shaken by this fresh blast of proletarianisation was that of letters. But though this book is primarily about music, so integrated is the life of the arts in Soviet Russia that understanding Shostakovich's position at this time is impossible without some grasp of the contemporary situation in literature.

By 1929 RAPP, the literary equivalent of RAPM, was being covertly used by the Party to repress all non-Communist writers. There was little difficulty in engineering this since, to the zealots of the Proletkult, individualism in literature was anathema and independent operators, like the outlawed Bulgakov, were mere 'petit-bourgeois grumblers' who deserved no better than a bullet in the neck. Committed to dragooning the country's writers into 'literary brigades', they dreamed of fulfilling 'the Five-Year Plan in poetry', of building 'the Magnitogorsk of art and literature'.[1] Naturally, literature could only stand in for breeze-blocks by first being crush-packed in ice, and there were many writers for whom this prospect held little appeal. Others, realising that the time for protest had passed and preferring servitude to the grave, made the necessary adjustments. 'Let's ponder and repair our nerves,' sighed the poet Ilya Selvinsky, 'and start up like any other factory.' The analogy was only too precise. With superindustrialisation and proletarianisation gathering pace, the dominant metaphor for society in Soviet culture had become that of a vast machine in which its citizens were mere cogs, replaceable at a moment's notice and possessing no significance in themselves. According to this vision, what was required from Soviet writers were ecstatic hymns to selflessness in the service of the social machine; epic accounts of its heroic construction; glorified manuals for its smooth operation. The Russian people were building Metropolis; they did not need their time wasted by 'dreamers' who made them think or 'clowns' who made them laugh.

The only positive way to respond to demands like these was through external representation – meaning, chiefly, the visual arts. Hence the artists who thrived on this phase of Soviet development (and made the most show of their loyalty to the prevailing orthodoxy) were film-makers like Eisenstein, Dovzhenko, and Pudovkin. Men and women of letters were, by comparison, in a paralysing dilemma. Unable to hide in exuberant abstraction, how were they to divest themselves of their individuality without descending to lying platitudes? Watching these developments in 1929, the critic Boris Eikhenbaum drily noted the growing 'need for bad writing'. But things were already worse than that. Only the previous year a character in Erdman's *The Suicide* had called Russian culture 'a red slave in the People's harem'; by 1929 the bondage-metaphor was official and the Marxist critic Kogan was exhorting the country's writers to join in fomenting a spirit of 'new slavery'. Masochism became the latest literary style. In the eyes of playwright Vladimir Kirshon, the Party was 'an iron chain that yokes us . . . The chain may pain my body, but I can't live without it.'

Under these circumstances, anyone lacking the necessary submissive disposition drew attention to themselves by virtue merely of declining to kneel. When it came to identifying the 'literary Shakhtyites', as happened in September 1929, pointing them out required no university degree. A newspaper boy could have done it. Luckily for Anna Akhmatova and Osip Mandelstam, the regime's quota for lyric poetry had been set at nil for some years and they were no longer part of the literary scene. Mandelstam was on the poverty line in Leningrad with his wife Nadezhda, scratching a living from journalism; their friend Akhmatova was living quietly with an art historian on the Fontanka, a few miles away. Classified, rather poetically, as 'internal émigrés', they were

---

[1] Magnitogorsk is an industrial city in the Urals, founded in 1929 as part of the First Five-Year Plan and mythologised in Valentin Katayev's 'Five-Year Plan novel' *Time, Forward!*

considered redundant and the thunder passed over their heads. Instead, lightning forked down on two of the country's leading prose writers: Yevgeny Zamyatin and Boris Pilnyak.

Though formally accused of specific literary crimes (collaborating with foreign publishers to have work banned in Russia printed abroad – of which neither was guilty), Zamyatin and Pilnyak were in reality targeted by RAPP for a very simple reason. They were the heads, in Leningrad and Moscow respectively, of the Authors' League, the literary equivalent of the ACM and therefore RAPP's direct rival. The affair was no sideshow. Pilnyak was one of the country's most popular writers and Zamyatin a figure of immense prestige whose *Complete Works* were in the process of being published in Moscow. The RAPP agitators needed official help to overthrow them – and they got it in abundance. The result, in Max Eastman's suitably overheated description, was 'a veritable pogrom, a literary lynching at the hands of a mob instigated and egged on by the state power, a hounding and baiting and branding and pounding and menacing on the platform and in the press from one end of Russia to the next'.

Pilnyak, marked for special attention by Stalin,[1] was harried for 'apolitical-ness' (not being a Communist). The national press castigated his alleged failure to put his shoulder to the wheel of the Five-Year Plan, while his trips aboard (he was an insatiable explorer) were smeared as fraternisation with the international bourgeoisie. Every day the pressure grew more intense, the rhetoric more unreal. On 9 September, *Literary Gazette* devoted itself almost entirely to denunciations of Pilnyak and 'Pilnyakism' (which, growled the editorial, was 'eating up like rust the will to socialist construction'). It was cloddish hamming, heavily imprinted with Stalin's downturned thumb.

Demoralised, the individualist literary community cracked open, lifelong loyalties crumbling overnight. According to Eugene Lyons, 'every writer with an active will to survive was obliged in self-defence to spit at Pilnyak'. Authors' League members flocked to join RAPP. Even Mayakovsky, who as a Futurist despised the conservatism of the Proletkult, reconsidered his position and applied to enrol. Called 'submitting to the social command', it was, in fact, intellectual hara-kiri under duress.

The human effects were terrible. Pilnyak, described a year earlier by Lyons as 'a big, blond, unwieldy fellow with a huge smile and a huge appetite for wine, women, and life', turned overnight into a twitching wreck on the brink of suicide. Accused of 'philistinism' (in other words, failing to condemn NEP as a moral abomination on a par with Sodom and Gomorrah), the 'mirthful satirist' Valentin Katayev underwent a complete personality change, emerging as a model of sober conformism. Forced to recant his 'politically incorrect' *Comrade*

---

[1] He had written a story, *Tale of the Unextinguished Moon*, which hinted (with justification) that Stalin had murdered War Commissar Frunze in 1925 in order to replace him with his crony, Voroshilov.

Kislyakov, Panteleimon Romanov confessed that his novel (a cool look at genuine issues, recognisable as such to anyone in Russia) 'violated the normal proportion of life and gave an objectively untrue picture of reality'. Only the intellectually self-reliant Zamyatin managed to hold on to his dignity, defending himself tersely against specific charges and otherwise remaining aloof from the debâcle around him.

For this Shostakovich must have been grateful, since Zamyatin's name figured prominently among the credits for *The Nose*. In every other respect, however, the events of September 1929 can only have frozen his blood for, in a matter of weeks, the literary individualists with whom he was so closely associated had, as a body, been wiped out. How long would it be before the Proletkult swivelled their sights in his direction? Whatever was about to happen he, like everyone else, had only one option: to look optimistic and carry on with what he was doing. He had, in other words, to wear a mask.

As usual, this tells us nothing definite about Shostakovich's politics. In conditions of extreme uncertainty and incessant pressure to conform, hiding under a bright smile and a purposeful manner was the only way to get by. Everyone was doing it – even those who went along with the Stalin hard line. The only people in Russia uninhibitedly displaying their feelings in 1929 were the young iconoclasts of the Proletkult, confident that their hour had come. To them, the cowering bourgeois were fair game. 'Masks' must be ripped away and the philistinism behind them subjected to 'exposure'.[1]

They had every right to feel assured. Just as Mao would let loose the Red Guards on the Chinese middle class in 1966, so Stalin now decided it was time officially to unleash the Proletkult on the Russian bourgeoisie. On 4 December, a Central Committee resolution was issued, hailing RAPP as literary custodians of the Party line. The impact was immediate. All remaining groups and magazines were instantly wound up, the Commissariat for Enlightenment was abolished, and its director, the relatively benign overseer of Soviet culture since 1918, Anatoly Lunacharsky, was sacked. Growing rather than diminishing, the shock-waves spread quickly into the musical sphere. The ACM ceased to function and even the independent proletarian group Prokoll made haste to join RAPM, whose *Proletarian Musician* now became the only music journal in Russia. The Proletkult, with their ideal of a 'democratic' music founded on folk-song and march-rhythm, set about ousting all other genres from classical to the 'Western jazz' that had flourished in clubs and dance-halls during NEP. Modernism was placed under a virtual curfew, its adherents warned to change their styles and write for the People.

The rout of the Modernists accelerated in December with the scandal surrounding a performance of Prokofiev's industrial ballet *Le Pas d'acier* at Moscow's Beethoven Hall. Incensed by the work's dissonance, RAPM dele-

---

[1] 'Tear off the masks!' the dreaded rallying-cry of the thirties, was originally an RAPP slogan, coined by Averbakh from one of Lenin's commentaries on Tolstoy.

gates accused its composer, present during his second return to Russia, of 'dilettantism'. He responded contemptuously and the rumpus ended with RAPM condemning the ballet as 'a counter-revolutionary composition bordering on Fascism', a characteristically lurid verdict which gave the Bolshoi's directors no choice but to turn it down. Furious, Prokofiev went back to Paris. Apart from reflecting on Modernism in general, the *Pas d'acier* affair allowed RAPM to link the music of the ACM with 'Western bourgeois decadence'. In the xenophobic atmosphere of the First Five-Year Plan, associating with foreigners was tantamount to treason and, rather than find themselves on trial for Pilnyakism, many formerly innovative composers followed their literary colleagues by abandoning craft and inspiration for the artless formulae of the Proletkult. Mosolov, Shcherbachov, Deshevov, and Zhivotov all went this way. Kabalevsky, who had long prepared for just such an eventuality, calmly produced a *Poem of Struggle* written 'in sympathy' with Proletkult ideals. Shostakovich's friend Shebalin, a sophisticated conservative, joined RAPM, pretending interest in the coarse banalities of its leading light Alexander Davidenko. Perhaps most tragic of all, the potentially brilliant Gavril Popov, whose Chamber Symphony of 1927 movingly evokes the inner crises of life in the late twenties, hid his light under a proletarian bushel and took to drink.

By the beginning of 1930, the Proletkult had brushed aside its artistic enemies and was set to invade the country's educational system. At the same time, Stalin launched the first stage of his plan for agricultural collectivisation under the slogan 'Liquidation of the Kulaks as a Class' (kulaks being so-called 'rich peasants'). Russia huddled under the whirlwind.

Shostakovich meanwhile was nervously shepherding *The Nose* towards its première at the Leningrad Maly Opera. Finally opening there in January 1930, the work was immediately attacked by RAPM as 'lacking roots in Soviet reality' – and just as promptly defended against this and other charges by Ivan Sollertinsky. The real defenders of *The Nose* were, however, its audiences. Appreciating its individualism all the more in the stifling atmosphere of 1930, they filed through the turnstiles in sufficient numbers to fill fourteen performances (almost a record). Neither Proletkult interference nor faked workers' denunciations in the press were able to thwart the work's popular success. Aware of this as he was writing *The Golden Age*, Shostakovich must have taken heart – though when the première of his Third Symphony evoked indifference from all quarters, his first move was to insure himself against fresh attacks by knocking out another score for TRAM (*Soil*, Opus 25).

While he was doing this, news broke of the suicide of Vladimir Mayakovsky. The poet, pursued by Komsomol–Proletkult hecklers after the staging of his satire *The Bathhouse*, had lapsed into a depression and played one game too many of Russian roulette. For many of Shostakovich's generation, the death of Mayakovsky had much the same symbolism as the death of Blok for their elders: the spirit of the Revolution had blown out, leaving them in a new darkness. Having seen Mayakovsky up close, Shostakovich is likelier to have pondered more on the link between the poet's vodka-loosened tongue and the extra hole in his head. As for the dark, his eyesight was as good as anyone else's.

That the satirist in him was alive and kicking, seemingly undeterred by the eradication of this strain in contemporary literature, is plain enough from *The Golden Age*. The old delight in burlesque and caricature bursts out of almost every bar with a headlong energy that even Stravinsky never equalled. Nor was there a shortage of targets for this veiled raillery in the society the composer saw developing around him. Stalin's 50th Birthday celebrations in December 1929 were, for example, of such oafish ostentation that it is impossible to imagine Shostakovich contemplating them without a snigger. Fawning articles filled the papers with tributes to the Leader's greatness and 'genius', hailing him as a major theorist in Marxism–Leninism and insisting that he had been 'Lenin's most trusted aide'. Enormous portraits of this giant among men were promenaded like icons all over the country. Most significant for the future, a volume of essays on him by his cronies, published at state expense, featured a trend-setting revision of recent history purporting to show that Stalin, rather than Trotsky, had masterminded Red strategy during the Civil War. What was later to become euphemistically referred to in Russia as 'the cult of personality' began here, and Shostakovich's Gogolian funnybone cannot fail to have been tickled by this, by far the biggest 'nose' of all time.

Just as ridiculous and appalling was the new breed of *apparatchik* Stalin was bringing in. Eugene Lyons reported the replacement of the 'argumentative intellectuals' of Lenin's generation by 'tough-skinned, ruthless drill-sergeants from the ranks of the proletariat' whose dour chauvinism would henceforth set the style for Soviet officialdom. Their shoulders broad enough to bear chips by the sackload, these men needed little encouragement to allow their resentment of educated privilege to degenerate into an outright hatred of cleverness itself. Indeed, Stalin's dislike of intellectuals was so much the fashion in his Politburo that Lyons was moved to describe them as representatives of a 'revolt against intelligence', an impression depressingly borne out by policies adopted during the proletarianisation of the country's educational system. Carrying the Cultural Revolution into every department from research laboratories to primary schools, the Proletkult soon progressed beyond erasing inequality of opportunity to erasing quality itself. Their reasoning was forthright. Nature having been unfair enough to make some heads more capacious than others, egalitarianism must outflank her by decreasing the demand for brains. Just as in Mao's China the 'stupids' were exalted and anyone in spectacles branded a lackey of the bourgeoisie, so in the Russia of 1930 'the crucifixion of the intelligentsia' was the hottest topic of (sotto voce) conversation, and the war-cry of the young militants the brutally frank 'Up with mediocrity!'.

Storming into universities, libraries, museums and galleries, Stalin's Red Guard set about removing every vestige of the old system. In the conservatoires, non-musician Party members took over, banning all pre-Revolutionary music but Beethoven and Mussorgsky as 'alien to the proletariat' and scrapping traditional courses in favour of 'practical workshops' for the quota-production of mass-songs for farm and factory workers. (In line with this, students were required to do two hundred hours a year as paid labourers.) To ensure that the roots of the old bourgeois culture were thoroughly pulled out, every aspect of life in the conservatoires was methodically turned upside-down. Soloists were abolished and preference given to 'mass musicians'. Individual grades and examinations, held to foster 'an unhealthy desire to compete', were replaced by collective assessment on a 'brigade' basis. (Moscow students were allowed to graduate from composition class on the strength of two or three mass-songs.) Even the word 'conservatoire', having a common root with 'conservatism', was condemned as counter-revolutionary and outlawed.

Under Proletkult domination, politics became the most important part of the curriculum and no musicians could hope to advance their careers unless their ideological outlook was 'correct'. Sometimes the results were merely silly. Shostakovich's friend Vissarion Shebalin, one of the Moscow professors, confided: 'My pupils bring me some clumsy tune in 3/4. Then they start discussing whether it reflects the experience of the proletariat during the Kronstadt Uprising!' Elsewhere, things were more serious. People were losing their careers, their rights, even their lives. According to Yuri Yelagin, a violinist who studied under Shostakovich's friend Dmitri Tsyganov during the thirties, the Moscow Conservatoire suffered a kind of musical inquisition: 'With the students, the new director took a line of ruthless class discrimination. Irrefutable proletarian antecedents became the sole basis for admission. All students who could be classified as class enemies, including those who were in their last year, were expelled.'

The results of this reformation were spectacularly chaotic. By spring 1931, Maximilian Steinberg, Shostakovich's former composition teacher, was complaining in his diary that the new conservatoire regime had degenerated into 'real bedlam, threatening the annihilation of professional art'. All formal teaching had disintegrated, students were wandering from class to class in an atmosphere of anarchy, and anyone daring to protest was almost literally drummed out of town. When, for example, Steinberg's colleague Vladimir Shcherbachov suggested that order be restored, he was so shaken by the force-with which he was evicted that he fled to Tbilisi, a thousand miles away. Nor was this sort of treatment reserved for non-Party professors; the same happened to the Bolshevik avant-gardeist Roslavets who, kicked out of Moscow, ended up in Tashkent.[1]

Shostakovich, his postgraduate course complete, did not suffer directly from

---

[1] Abandoning Modernism, both composers attempted to disappear into the study of folk music. Roslavets accomplished his dematerialisation successfully and was never heard of again (he is believed to have died in 1944). Shcherbachov tried to appease the regime with a symphony called *Izhorsk* concerning the building of a factory. This failed and he, too, vanished from the pages of history.

the purge in the conservatoires. Even so, he had to be careful. The third issue of RAPM's magazine *Proletarian Musician* contains a letter from him – or at any rate signed by him – deploring the vogue for 'petit-bourgeois gipsy foxtrot ensembles' and welcoming the new Proletkult campaign against 'vulgar' light music. In a footnote, Shostakovich acknowledged that 'letting' Nikolai Malko conduct *Tahiti Trot* (his orchestration of the foxtrot *Tea for Two*) in November 1928 had been 'a political mistake' – though, in view of the fact that, shortly afterwards, he included the piece in Act III of *The Golden Age*, his confession seems not to have been entirely sincere. RAPM's hatred of jazz, one of a sizeable catalogue of bugbears with which it was perpetually 'struggling', was, in fact, a source of constant trouble for the composer, who loved it and smuggled as much of it as he could into his incidental scores of the period. To the puritanical Proletkult, however, it was loathsome – 'the music of the fat bourgeoisie', in Maxim Gorky's much-parroted definition – and during the next twenty years they rarely let slip an opportunity of denouncing Shostakovich's taste for it.

Gorky himself would have been another focus for the composer's satirical bent. As much of an enigma in literature as Shostakovich in music, Gorky had been a reformist folk hero before 1917, being popularly known, after his own poem of 1901, as the Stormy Petrel of the Revolution (to which there are several mocking references in *Testimony*). Having criticised Lenin's 'Red Terror', he spent the twenties self-exiled in Sorrento, whence he was inveigled back to Russia by Stalin's agents in 1928 and fêted with gifts and honours. Unsurprisingly, his attitude to the Revolution softened and soon the Great Humanist, as he was invariably referred to in the Soviet press, was lending his imprimatur to Stalin's harshest policies and his name to various factories, an entire city (his home town, Nizhny Novgorod), and even a few labour camps. The evidence is that Gorky tried to play a double game, accepting the role of Revolutionary beautician partly because genuinely flattered, but also in order to mitigate Stalin's brutality against the intelligentsia. However, the situation was deadlier than he realized and the compromises he was forced to make destroyed his integrity. He may not have written some of his more notorious denunciations, so shocking to the *intelligenty* of the thirties, and it is even conceivable that he secretly held on to his former principles whilst signing articles which grotesquely contradicted them. The laws of *Ketman*, as Czesław Milosz has pointed out, are often opaque to outsiders. None the less, the damage done by the Great Humanist in legitimising Stalinism, both at home and abroad, was incalculable.

How much of Gorky Shostakovich saw in himself around 1929–31 we can only guess. Gorky's dilemma, however, was a source of endless speculation in educated circles and the composer would certainly have had an opinion on it.

Whilst some pains have been taken to show that nearly everything Shostakovich wrote at this time has dark undercurrents, it is equally true that his satirical side then markedly outweighed the tragedian in him and several reasons have been suggested as to why this should be so. An important reason so far not considered (and one which, by 1930, had come to dominate all others) was the theoretical impossibility of tragedy under Soviet rule.

Here, after all, was a society on the road to perfection, marching in ear-splitting unanimity towards 'the radiant dawn of Communism'. There being no possibility of failure to reach this goal, it followed that there could be nothing tragic in Soviet life, which was therefore, during the thirties, officially decreed to be daily becoming more 'joyful'. 'People under dictatorships,' wrote Eugene Lyons, who saw the effects of this at first hand, 'are condemned to a lifetime of enthusiasm. It is a wearing sentence. Gladly would they burrow into the heart of their misery and lick their wounds in private. But they dare not; sulking is next door to treason. Like soldiers weary unto death after a long march, they must line up smartly for parade.' Often this 'lining up' was quite literal, whole neighbourhoods being summoned from their beds before breakfast to rehearse a street-march or practise a spontaneous demonstration. On other occasions, the imperative to counterfeit enthusiasm could reach almost psychotic dimensions. In a famous anecdote, Solzhenitsyn describes how a meeting at a factory during the thirties ended with a round of applause for Stalin which threatened never to end, no one present wishing to be seen putting a limit on his personal fervour. Finally, after about ten minutes during which there was no sign of it reaching a natural conclusion, the factory manager stopped the madness by sitting down, only to be promptly arrested after the meeting and told: 'Don't ever be the first to stop applauding!' Confirming this story, Mikhail Heller has recorded that, in the interval between speeches by Stalin at a conference in the Kremlin during the forties, delegates were offered buckets of salt water to bathe their hands, swollen from hours of clapping. Not for nothing was the Stalinist creed of Socialist Realism dubbed 'the cult of optimism'.

Under these circumstances, it is less surprising that Shostakovich's music of 1926–32 was predominantly animated and externalistic than that his subsequent work should often have been so nakedly tragic.

There was no shortage of reasons to be sombre in 1930. The murderous first phase of collectivisation may have been familiar only to the six million peasants it swept away, but the cities soon had their own mass-arrests amongst the educated classes to contend with. Most of the 600,000 by now in the Gulag were technical intelligentsia, people of Shostakovich's own class. Ousted from their jobs by incoming proletarians, charged with wrecking, and packed off to forced labour in the camps or *sharashkas*,[1] these men and women were the intellectual cream of Russian society: engineers, agronomists, biologists, linguists, and university lecturers (particularly historians slow to revise their

---

[1] Prisons in which scientists were put to work on government research projects. (See Solzhenitsyn's *The First Circle*.)

memories in accordance with the Party line). Few had done any wrong, most being mere random casualties of the revolt against intelligence.

It is important to understand that these waves of arrests, tiny by comparison with what was soon to follow, bore scant relation to real crimes. 'Wrecking,' writes the Marxist historian Roy Medvedev, 'as a conscious policy, pursued by the entire stratum of bourgeois specialists, never existed.' What the phenomenon really represented was an excuse for the crushing of independent thought at a time when Stalin needed unanimity in order to push through the First Five-Year Plan. The result, however, was that in every academic field the genuinely talented and authoritative were replaced by charlatans and second-raters, so destroying the base of Soviet science and technology for an entire generation. If any 'wreckers' were abroad in 1930, they were Stalin and his Proletkult proxies.

None of this, however, served to delay the endless parade of 'witch-trials' now passing like some nightmare variety act before the dazzled eyes of the Russian people. Some of these involved framing potential troublemakers by inventing subversive organisations to which they were then charged with belonging, the 'discovery' of each new conspiracy setting a precedent for the next. (The trial of the non-existent Union for the Liberation of the Ukraine led to the trial of the non-existent Toiling Peasants Party, and so on.) Other victims were selected as scapegoats for disasters of government policy incurred during collectivisation. Thus, when peasants protesting against expropriation slaughtered and burned their livestock, the blame was put on the Famine Organisers (demonic agronomists accused of somehow fomenting the resulting meat-shortage) and the Veterinary Shakhtyites (crazed bacteriologists alleged to have infected horses with the plague). In Medvedev's judgement, the show-trials of the thirties were bogus from beginning to end: 'a monstrous theatrical presentation that had to be rehearsed many times before it could be shown to spectators'.

One of the most ambitious of these monstrosities was the trial, during November and December 1930, of the so-called Industrial Party, a group of technicians accused of sabotaging factories and plotting to overthrow Stalin. An extraordinary Punch-and-Judy farce surrounded this affair, with the leader temporarily vanishing through a trapdoor (Western newspapers were full of reports of his assassination) and Gorky exhorting the proletariat to act fast before foreign agents swooped out of the sky to rescue the defendants. As a 'result' of this, half a million workers marched in Moscow on 25 November demanding that the accused be immediately executed. Eugene Lyons reported the case and witnessed the events: 'Hour after hour as night engulfed the city, the gigantic parade rolled past and its shouts of "Death! death! death!" could be heard in the columned ballroom where the trial was under way.'

Perhaps some of the grimness of the Industrial Party trial crept into *The Bolt*, Shostakovich's 'industrial' ballet, which he was writing in Leningrad at precisely this time? This dark, biting score, currently known only through its eight-number concert suite, stands in urgent need of recording. *The Golden Age*, lighter in tone, shows its satirical cards in some of its subtitles – 'A Rare Case of Mass Hysteria', 'Touching Coalition of Classes, Slightly Fraudulent' and (funniest, according to taste) 'General Exposure'. It does, however, contain one moment of striking seriousness: a slow, searing, bitonal pas-de-deux, the agonised climax of which abandons the ballet, with its simple-minded football-ing plot, for something much deeper. Shostakovich's first symphonic slow movement since the First Symphony, this piece (better known as the Adagio from the ballet's concert suite) is by far the weightiest thing he wrote between it and the opera *Lady Macbeth of Mtsensk*. Hints of the style of Berg inhere in its opening minutes, but the last fifteen bars are pure Mahler, a simultaneous allusion to the codas of the first and fourth movements of that composer's tragic Ninth Symphony. Utterly unlike anything else in the ballet, this piece seems deliberately designed to give the lie to everything around it, as if hinting at Shostakovich's underlying seriousness of mind.

Premièred at Leningrad's Kirov Theatre in October 1930, *The Golden Age* pleased neither the Komsomol–Proletkult militants, who found its levity trivial, nor the audience, bored by its propagandism. If this wasn't bad enough after a year's work, the ballet's early closure sufficiently weakened Shostakovich's position to allow the zealots to kill two birds with one stone and get *The Nose* off too. There was now no one left to help him. The Cultural Revolution had reached its zenith and the Proletkult were at the height of their power, able to hold national conventions, publish their views without contradiction, dictate the ideological content of art in enormous detail, and destroy any dissenters foolish enough to stand in their way. Even the victors could feel the chill they were generating. 'We are living,' acknowledged the RAPP playwright Alex-ander Afinogenov coolly, 'in an epoch of great fear.'

The ACM, existing more or less nominally since 1929, finally collapsed in mid-1931 following the secession of Myaskovsky and Shebalin. Myaskovsky, whose symphonies of the twenties had been dangerously pessimistic, read the signs early and turned to apparently harmless[1] chamber pieces, such as his 'village concertos', Opus 32. Shebalin emulated his teacher with his own concertinos of 1930–32, but such self-imposed restrictions soon grew stifling. In mid-1931, Myaskovsky, Shebalin, Kabalevsky, and others tried to found a 'new creative association' to produce symphonic music implementing Marxist–Leninist methods. Rather too obviously a ploy to reinstate the orchestral repertoire, this initiative was quashed by RAPM, who saw to it that Shebalin's *Lenin*, an almost-listenable exception among Soviet propaganda symphonies, was 'buried' at its première later in the year. Myaskovsky's solution was to produce two symphonies at the same time: the Twelfth, or *Collective Farm*

---

[1] The Lyric Concertino, Opus 32, No. 3, contains in its agonised 'Andantino monotono' a remarkably explicit musical protest against Proletkult uniformity and the attack on individualism in the late twenties.

Symphony, in naively euphonious style; and its extraordinary predecessor, the Eleventh, described by his Soviet biographer as an 'outlet to more subjective moods' and, in fact, a furiously direct response to the destruction of Russian musical culture over the preceding three years. Both works, needless to say, were rejected out of hand by the Proletkult.

Shostakovich, meanwhile, lay low. He had an opera inside him and this time no Dadaist facetiousness: the full-blown, four-act real thing. However, if this era was inauspicious for symphonies, it was no time at all for composing grand opera. Under attack throughout 1930, *The Nose* had been killed off so thoroughly that it would not be resuscitated for another forty years. Lev Knipper, a Moscow Modernist and composer of *The North Wind*, an opera targeted with *The Nose* in this campaign, had been frightened into a spectacular somersault, emerging as the acme of faceless banality. If opera was viable at all, it would have to be ideologically spotless and structured like a suite of choral folk-songs. Nothing else would do.

Approached by the Bolshoi to produce just such an ear-sore based on Eisenstein's film *Battleship Potemkin*, Shostakovich declined. Instead, and in spite of pressures to the contrary, he began to plan *Lady Macbeth of Mtsensk*, a 'tragi-satiric opera' (his own description) based on a story by the nineteenth-century writer Nikolai Leskov. The risks were obvious. Apolitical, Leskov was unacceptable to the Proletkult and his story perilously devoid of a pious moral. In the menacing crowd-mentality of 1931, Shostakovich could only continue with *Lady Macbeth* if he covered himself by taking on the sort of projects RAPM approved (which, as incessant innuendo in the press made clear, boiled down to his incidental scores for TRAM). Thus, as soon as he had finished *The Bolt* and his music for the film *Alone* in January 1931, he scribbled his third and last incidental score for TRAM, *Rule Britannia!*, and – his personal low of lows – the 'circus revue' *Allegedly Murdered*. However, the strain of pasting together these hack jobs whilst planning the opera was too much and in July he took his fate in his hands by writing to the RAPP periodical *The Worker and the Theatre* to explain that he was pulling out of no less than four contracts for incidental music. Pleading exhaustion, he argued that the endless demand for this instant art was 'depersonalising' Soviet music and, in a transparent attempt to disarm his enemies in advance, promised to start work immediately on 'a large symphony dedicated to the fifteenth anniversary of the October Revolution' (in 1932). Far from mollifying the Proletkult, the news of this piece, edifyingly entitled *From Karl Marx to Our Own Days*, merely prompted fresh swipes at him for 'ideological wavering'.

The extent of Shostakovich's commitment to the new symphony, to be composed on a libretto of political texts and contemporary poetry, is best illustrated by the fact that immediately after announcing it he went on holiday to the Black Sea and began writing *Lady Macbeth*. This time there was more than usual to keep him away from Leningrad. Among the 'loose ends' he had left was one of the four projects cancelled before coming away: an incidental score for Nikolai Akimov's production of *Hamlet* at Moscow's Vakhtangov Theatre to the contract for which the management had decided to hold him. Unsurprisingly, the holiday grew longer, stretching through September into October and taking in a full-scale tour of the Caucasus.

Finishing Act I of *Lady Macbeth* in Tbilisi in early November, Shostakovich could no longer postpone the evil day and returned to Leningrad. Here he had the pleasant shock of discovering that the film *Alone* (like *New Babylon*, directed by Kozintsev and Trauberg) was doing healthy business largely on the strength of his score. Planned as a silent and completed as such in May 1930, *Alone* had been held back for a year until Shostakovich could join the production team in Kiev. Working there in early 1931 with Kozintsev and Lev Arnshtam, a friend from his days at the Leningrad Conservatoire, he had created a deftly illustrative soundtrack scored for an ensemble of wind instruments, double basses, and percussion. The novelty of this greatly intrigued Russian filmgoers, but it was the heroine's song, *How Beautiful Life Will Be*, which they came out humming and which assured the success of *Alone* both at home and abroad.

Without question, Shostakovich needed this. His break with theatre music had gone down badly with RAPM and the watchdogs of the Cultural Revolution were waiting for him to make a fatal mistake. 'Alone' was, in fact, an exact description of his predicament. His musical colleagues were either gagged or meekly churning out the folk-nationalist fodder RAPM required of them, leaving Shostakovich as the only composer in Russia writing music with the sound of his own voice. His literary friends were likewise muted or altered out of all recognition. For the average writer, the imperative to embrace the 'new slavery' was irresistible, those already broken being paraded in the press to cow any remaining impulse to dissent. Yuri Olesha, recently one of Shostakovich's friends, had become an abject conformist who, within four years, would betray him to save his own skin. Boris Pilnyak, once a jovial bear of a man, seemed to Max Eastman to have physically shrunk:

> He has become Russia's leading expert in recantation, abjection, self-repudiation, sighs of repentance and prayers of apology for the sin of having had thoughts, impulses, fancies, emotions, reactions, reflexes, tropisms or any perceptible knee-jerks or eye-winks that he could call his own. The literary journals are soggy with his unctuous promises and tears of contrition. He begs for Marxian instruction. He asks to have special censors appointed to watch over his novels and dissect out in advance any malignant matter foreign to the policies of the party . . .

The Orwellian extremity of Pilnyak's humiliation was common, indeed usual.[1] Isaac Babel's famous adoption of what he called 'the genre of silence' could not have been sustained without his international reputation, his contacts

---

[1] To be fair to him, Pilnyak was almost certainly playing the *yurodivy* in at least some of his confessions.

in the security organs, and the protection of Gorky, who regarded him as Russia's greatest living prose writer. Otherwise, 'self-criticism' was de rigueur and boot-licking the rule.

Creative style was now rigidly prescribed. At the Congress on Proletarian Art held in Kharkov in November 1930, Leopold Averbakh, leader of RAPP, had dictated a set of formulations to be adhered to without question. Art, now defined as a 'class weapon', was to be collectivised and organised on a military model, all remnants of individualism and other 'petty-bourgeois attitudes' being replaced by 'discipline'. In this new art-army, the primary duty was political study: 'The method of creative art is the method of Dialectical Materialism. Every proletarian artist must be a dialectical materialist.' Far from being a fanatic's day dream, Averbakh's formulations were seriously meant and immediately implemented. Soon, artists who had not studied their 'Diamat' were being made to stand in the corner like naughty children. Under 'the careful and yet firm guidance of the Communist Party', grown men and women were catechised and drilled into submission to the 'correct' world view, no deviation into personal opinion being tolerated. When RAPP promulgated the slogan 'Liquidate Backwardness!', everyone understood that 'backwardness' meant anything failing to exalt the shock-worker movement. In these bleakly restrictive conditions, art became somewhat less glamorous than a weapon. It was, rather, a setsquare, a level, a plumbline.

The prevailing ethos of mechanical conformism depended on minute critical surveillance. Mayakovsky's *The Bedbug* includes a satire on this lowbrow literal-mindedness in the form of the Usher at the wedding, programmed to look for subversion in key words and so constantly prone to comical blunders in his anxiety to bowdlerise. A boggling example of this is recorded by Nadezhda Mandelstam who, having reflected in one of her lectures that 'the young English gerund is ousting the old infinitive', found herself charged by the Komsomol with 'hostility to youth'. The Sentinels of the Revolution even kept an eye on each other. In 1931 the Komsomol attacked RAPP for their slogan 'Overtake and Surpass the Classics' on the grounds that proletarian writers were already *far in advance* of 'bourgeois and landlord literature', a squabble which rapidly mutated into a major scandal. 'Every day,' wrote Osip Mandelstam, 'I find it harder to breathe.' He spoke for millions.

This, then, was the chokingly oppressive background to Shostakovich's interview with Rose Lee of the *New York Times* on Nikolayevskaya Street that December.

'I consider that every artist who isolates himself from the world is doomed. I find it incredible that an artist should want to shut himself away from the people, who, in the end, form his audience. I think an artist should serve the greatest possible number of people. I always try to make myself as widely understood as possible and, if I don't succeed, I consider it my own fault.'

In the light of events sketched in this chapter, these words from the *New York*

Times interview sound a little less nobly unforced than they otherwise might. Indeed, considering that Shostakovich was now, understandably, a reclusive introvert whose only confidant was Ivan Sollertinsky, his repudiation of privacy seems rather ironic. As for his political statements, so striking to Western ears that the composer was thereafter rarely mentioned outside Soviet Russia without a tag from the *New York Times* interview in tow, these appear to be nothing more than straight quotes from Averbakh's notorious formulations of 1930. 'No music without ideology', 'music is a weapon in the struggle' and so on – these slogans, though always implicit in Marxist–Leninist aesthetics, became part of the coinage of Soviet culture only after the Kharkov Congress. Shostakovich need not have pondered them deeply, let alone believed them. They were the sort of things one was expected to say in 1931. He said them.

If the content of the *New York Times* interview was orthodox enough to keep the Proletkult–Komsomol zealots off his back, the respite was brief. As 1932 dawned, questions began to be raised in the proletarian papers concerning the 'large symphony' *From Karl Marx to Our Own Days*, which he had promised them six months earlier. Though still in the middle of Act II of *Lady Macbeth*, he took the implied threat seriously enough to break off and knock out the first of the symphony's five projected sections, using a text by the poet Nikolai Aseyev. Aseyev, like Semyon Kirsanov – librettist of the Third Symphony – had been a friend of Mayakovsky and may have been among those artists Shostakovich met while working on *The Bedbug* at the Meyerhold Theatre in 1929. He also resembled Mayakovsky and Kirsanov (and, come to that, Meyerhold) in having started as a revolutionary leftist before becoming disenchanted with the Soviet system and going his own way.[1] There is a consistency here that might, at a stretch, indicate something of Shostakovich's own position, though it must be said that he differed fundamentally from these artists in possessing an innate tragic sense, based on an inability to ignore the sufferings of others, which almost certainly constituted an insurmountable obstacle to simple political commitment. What is certain is that he had small interest in *Karl Marx*. Having sketched the first section of it, he went straight back to *Lady Macbeth*.

Then came the bombshell which changed everything in Soviet culture overnight and brought to an abrupt conclusion this hectic second period in the composer's life.

---

[1] Pasternak, who knew Aseyev during this period, describes him as 'a gifted and intelligent man who retained his inward freedom and refused to blind himself to anything.' (*Essay in Autobiography*, 4; tr. Manya Harari.)

Chapter Three

UNCERTAINTY 1932–1934

Now mirrors learn
Not to expect smiles

O UT OF THE BLUE on 23 April 1932, the Central Committee of the Soviet Communist Party published a resolution abolishing all existing 'creative associations' and announcing the unionisation of the arts forthwith. Overnight, the dreaded arbiters of Soviet culture, RAPP and RAPM, simply ceased to exist. Worse still for them, they immediately found themselves on the receiving end of exactly the kind of persecution they had been handing out to their political enemies for the previous three years. Their leaders were arrested and removed from the positions they had usurped in the universities, galleries, museums and conservatoires, the former administrators of which were instructed to resume their positions and curricula pending a national review by Party officials. A total ban was placed on any resumption of proletarian artistic activity. Finally, to emphasize that an era was over and a new one in force, *Pravda* printed a swingeing attack on the Proletkult, characterising its recent rule as a period of 'cliqueism, left vulgarisation, and time-serving'. The Russian Cultural Revolution had ended.

The resolution of 23 April came as a complete surprise to most Russian artists. Few understood that it was merely the cultural by-product of a political gear-change ordained by Stalin for purposes which had nothing to do with art and everything to do with social engineering. Just as Mao would foment the Chinese Cultural Revolution for motives of political expediency, so Stalin had elevated RAPP and RAPM not for ideological reasons but in order to drill and browbeat the country's intellectuals while the First Five-Year Plan was going through. Drawing no distinction between artists and workers, he and his Politburo had assumed that, once 'disciplined' by the Proletkult, the country's creative minds could easily be made to produce whatever was politically appropriate at a given time. The zealots of the Proletkult, however, hardly saw themselves as cultural NCOs carrying out a mechanical task on behalf of officers of superior initiative, but rather as major strategists in their own right. Imagining that Stalin had chosen them for the purity of their faith in Marxism– Leninism rather than for their loud voices and ready fists, they had gone all out to bludgeon the *intelligenty* into a proletarian revolutionary conformity which even selfless fanatics would have found bracing. Their inspiration departed with their comfort and privacy, Russia's artists were, by 1932, uselessly mute and miserable.

This would have mattered less had the First Five-Year Plan been an obvious success, but to the ordinary citizen at the beginning of 1932 it had every appearance of being a disaster. To finance the import of heavy industrial machinery, Stalin had, for the previous five years, steadily exported most of Russia's productivity in basic foodstuffs and materials. Despite famine in 1930, wheat had been sold abroad in millions of tons causing bread-queues in every city throughout the following year, while meat had become a fabulous rarity owing to the ruination of stock-breeding during collectivisation. By 1932, the Russian people were slaving to build socialism in a drab world of constant shortages, ersatz substitutes, and raging inflation, the strain of which was only too apparent in their mood of rebellious resentment. Clearly something had to be done.

Stalin's solution was to create an illusion of relaxation – something that could be talked about as a relative improvement – by easing his stranglehold on the bourgeois. Instead of throttling them, he would chain them together by their necks.

His first step was to curtail the persecution of the technical intelligentsia and order that the country's scientific brains be pooled in a new institutional system. (A trial of 'wreckers' in the porcelain industry had been under way, all the defendants denouncing each other and confessing in the customary unison, when the news of Stalin's announcement came through. Immediately, they began, in louder unison, to protest their innocence.) The resolution on restructuring the arts was, in effect, simply a cultural analogue of Stalin's declaration on the sciences.

The thinking behind these decrees was cunningly practical. Clearly intellectual life in the Soviet Union had to be controlled, but it had also to be productive and this could plainly not be best effected by state terrorism. What was needed, Stalin decided, was a self-policing intelligentsia trapped in a centrally regulable system of rewards and punishments. Thus unions, banned by Lenin in 1919 for being hotbeds of independent thought, were resurrected in 1932 as an ideal machinery for intellectual coercion. At the same time, Stalin announced the abandonment of Leninist 'egalitarianism' in favour of a new system of pay-differentials and allied privileges, such as special rations and 'closed' stores for the use of those in particular favour. Designed to create an 'interested' class (that is, interested in preserving the status quo), Stalin's drive against egalitarianism was a carrot to the stick of unionized conformity. After years of grim scarcity, this invitation to partake of the Soviet good life in exchange for one's independence of mind was, for most Russian *intelligenty*, not a dilemma to be agonised over at length.

Shostakovich himself was too relieved to have RAPM off his back to notice that the new Composers' Union which everyone was hurrying to join was innately more repressive than anything seen during the Cultural Revolution.

Testimony confirms other sources in suggesting that the crisis of 1931 had driven him to the brink of a mental breakdown ('I was in terrible shape. Everything was collapsing and crumbling. I was eaten up inside'). The downfall of the Proletkult allowed him to cancel the *Karl Marx* symphony and finish Act II of his opera *Lady Macbeth of Mtsensk*, while the economic security promised by membership of the Composers' Union at last made it possible for him to marry Nina Varzar. Most of all, the end of the Cultural Revolution meant that, for the time being, he and his musical colleagues could mix socially and artistically without the dread of political interference. *Testimony* vouchsafes no secrets in describing this and the following two years as the happiest of his life.

As a measure of the relative licence Shostakovich was to enjoy under the new dispensation, nothing could be more convincing than his immunity from the scandal surrounding his part in the Vakhtangov Theatre's internationally notorious 'materialist' production of *Hamlet*, staged in Moscow during the summer of 1932.

Having spent 1931 trying to evade being typecast as a composer of incidental music, Shostakovich was naturally reluctant to get involved in more theatre work. However, since he had already spent the Vakhtangov's advance on a Black Sea holiday, he had no choice but to come up with the goods and duly did, albeit not in the best of tempers. His resentment only partly defused by the calculating charm of the play's director Nikolai Akimov, he turned in a score which, while no masterpiece, possesses in certain passages a definite baleful power. It was, however, the snook-cocking cynicism of other sections, tailored to the production's iconoclasm, which ensured that Shostakovich became embroiled in the resulting furore.

It was Akimov's idea to present Hamlet as a revolutionary struggling against the old order as embodied by his adulterous uncle and mother. In this scheme, Elsinore stood for the rotten bourgeois state, its denizens becoming emblems of capitalistic futility (Polonius an ageing conman, Ophelia a tipsy nymphomaniac, and so on). So far, so unexceptionable. Where the production got too clever for its own good, thereby invoking the wrath of the Party, was in endowing its unlikely prince-revolutionary with feet of clay, presenting him as a dissolute bully faking his father's ghost to gain popular support and wistfully addressing 'To be or not to be' to his uncle's crown. This, to Stalin's suspicious watchdogs, rang a distinctly subversive bell.

Shostakovich's bearing during rehearsals, observed by violinist Yuri Yelagin from his seat in the Vakhtangov orchestra, was characterised by an enigmatic blend of blankness and subterranean intensity:

> He was very modest and refrained from criticizing or complimenting anyone at the rehearsals . . . One evening some member of the company gave a supper in his honour. He had a lot to drink, but the drinks made him even more distant, silent and polite. His pale face became whiter

than usual. Our girls vied with one another in an effort to entertain him, but he paid little attention to them. Toward the end of the evening one of our actresses sang some gipsy songs to the accompaniment of a guitar. She had a fine voice and Shostakovich sat next to her and listened intently. As he was leaving, he thanked her and kissed her hand.

The composer's iron control, inborn but stoutly reinforced by recent experience, struck many who knew him but slightly as distinctly un-Russian in its apparent coolness. In fact, his determination not to give himself away only made him stand out in the usual demonstrative Slavic crowd and more than one witness has compared his aloofness to that of a man from Mars. Behind the mask, however, the Martian seethed with sarcastic bitterness. Yelagin records that in one of his numbers for *Hamlet*, Shostakovich mocked the Proletkult by making the Prince appear to fart through a flute while, in the orchestra pit, a piccolo squeaked out a parody of Davidenko's famous mass-song *They Wanted to Beat Us*. Cracked six months earlier, this joke[1] would have invoked instant retribution from RAPM. By June 1932 it was merely rather risqué.

The Vakhtangov *Hamlet* caused a tremendous kerfuffle during its short run and was packed out at every performance. Indeed, such was the interest in the production that government-inspired protests were insufficient to stop it and it was only pulled off 'in response to public opinion' after Karl Radek, megaphone of the Central Committee, had officially attacked it in *Pravda*. For Akimov, the affair was useful publicity to boost a scandalous career; he lasted till 1940 before the authorities eliminated him. To Shostakovich it was, at most, another blot in his official copybook, for the unruly state of which he would soon be taken to task. In the summer of 1932, however, he was apparently free to be as *terrible* an *enfant* as he wished.

Although happily married, Shostakovich continued to experience difficulties in his domestic life. Having tried in vain to find another room in a crowded

---

[1] The idea was stolen from Yuri Olesha's much-discussed play *A List of Assets*, produced a year earlier at the Meyerhold Theatre. In this largely conformist work, Olesha had attempted to square himself with the regime while clinging to the last vestiges of his self-respect, a feat Shostakovich would have found instructive, if nothing else. Part of the play's action involves a debate on the Socialist significance of *Hamlet* in which a Proletkult spokesman attacks the tragedy as 'slobbering soul-searching' inappropriate to 'the breathtaking whirl of national development'. To this, Olesha's actress-heroine Goncharova replies by quoting Hamlet's remark (III: 2) to the effect that he is not a pipe for others to play on, adding: 'Esteemed comrades, I submit that in this breathtaking, swirling era, an artist must keep thinking slowly.' Listening in the audience, the twenty-four-year-old Shostakovich must have been impressed. 'Thinking slowly, writing fast' became his creative motto, while Hamlet's declaration of independence was still haunting him fifty years later in *Testimony*: 'A marvellous passage. It's easy for him, he's a prince, after all. If he weren't, they'd play him so hard he wouldn't know what hit him.'

Leningrad, he was forced to bring Nina into the Nikolayevskaya apartment (displacing his mother Sofia to a couch in the sitting-room) and it would be eighteen months before the Composers' Union was sufficiently organised to get the couple a place of their own on the Kirovsky Prospekt. Nor, though Nina's family had money, were they able to live it up very much prior to the worldwide success of *Lady Macbeth* two years later. Nevertheless, compared with the raucous hell of the Cultural Revolution, their married life was bliss.

During August and September, they holidayed at Gaspra in the Crimea where Shostakovich wrote Act III of the new opera and met the violinist Dmitri Tsyganov, founder of the Beethoven Quartet which subsequently premièred most of the composer's string quartets. Returning to Leningrad in the autumn, he worked fast to finish *Lady Macbeth*, scribbling the final bars on 17 December and dedicating it to his wife. He had started the work in October 1930 and to bring it to a conclusion must have been considerably more than a matter of professional satisfaction. He and his opera had survived the storm.

A further welcome boost to his confidence arrived with the success of his score for the film *Counterplan*, made for the fifteenth anniversary of the Revolution and premièred in Leningrad that November. The hit of *Counterplan* was *Song of the Meeting*, which he subsequently milked for instant appeal whenever he needed it.[1] Originally to words by the poet Boris Kornilov (who, like Mayakovsky, drank too loudly and consequently 'disappeared' in 1939), the song became internationally famous during the forties, being reworded by Harold Rome as the *Hymn of the United Nations*.

Emboldened by this, Shostakovich invited Nikolai Aseyev, author/collator of the text for *Karl Marx*, to collaborate with him on a comic opera, *Big Lightning*. Sadly, this ran out of electricity after a few pages[2] and, while negotiations for *Lady Macbeth* dragged on through the winter, the composer turned from the clamour of the theatre to the solitary world of the piano, producing a set of 24 Preludes written, seemingly as daily exercises, between the end of December and the beginning of the following March. None of these pieces lasts much longer than a minute and almost all are casually satirical in tone, veering off at unexpected angles in a sub-Prokofievian mood of perfunctory sarcasm. According to Ivan Martynov, one of his Soviet biographers, Shostakovich thought of the Opus 34 preludes as a series of psychological sketches. If this is so, which there is no reason to doubt, he must have been in an especially caustic frame of mind that winter. Uniformly barbed, bitter, and disenchanted, the Preludes delight in their own cantankerous unpredictability, as if acting out all the individualism their composer would have otherwise expressed had there not been a gun of conformism at his head. Obviously coasting after the effort of

---

[1] As the finale of *Poem of the Motherland*, in the film *Michurin*, and (twice) in the operetta *Moscow, Cheryomushki*.

[2] The remnants of this project were found, assembled and performed in Leningrad by Gennadi Rozhdestvensky in 1981.

completing *Lady Macbeth*, he does not seem to have taken these pieces very seriously and their cumulative effect is dry and rather tiresome. The Sixth Prelude, a vaingloriously simple-minded march, may have been another swipe at the Proletkult, but detailed decoding of its companions is hardly encouraged by the quality of their music which, while never less than clever, is also stubbornly unmemorable. Only the abruptly anguished Fourteenth, later re-used by the composer in his score for the war film *Zoya*, strikes a deeper note.

As if emerging from a private inner world by carefully decompressive stages, Shostakovich moved, within a week of finishing the 24 Preludes, to his next piece, the Concerto for Piano, Trumpet, and String Orchestra in C minor, Opus 35 (better known as the First Piano Concerto). Here, the orchestra provided a public context for his more personal feelings as represented from the keyboard – or, at any rate, appeared to do so. Less vengefully weighted to the satirical end of his personality than the Preludes, the First Piano Concerto is a darkly glittering conundrum whose heart, but for some declamatory bars in its slow movement, is wholly hidden from public view. What it means, if anything, has never been guessed at in print. Admitting from the hindsight of his sixties that the Concerto was not one of his best works, the composer told his Soviet interviewer that it was 'written under the influence of American folk music', though whether this was meant to mitigate or mystify is unclear. While bulging with quotations from other composers, the piece contains no observable American folk music whatever. Probably what Shostakovich actually said was 'American show music', since there is a strong whiff of Broadway in some of the Concerto's brasher moments (for example the piano two-step at figure 76, which subsequently accelerates into the closing peroration from Tchaikovsky's Fourth Symphony). Unfortunately, this fails to clarify further the work's intentions, other than to draw attention to its obsessive imperative to debunk.

In certain respects, Shostakovich's Opus 35 follows the example of Prokofiev's First Piano Concerto which, written in 1911, is a quietly droll send-up of the Romantic fervour of composers like Tchaikovsky and Rachmaninov. When, in his opening movement, Shostakovich sets up the conventional string cue for a swooning Rachmaninovian second subject only to leap into a suspender-flashing can-can, he seems on the face of it to be doing the same sort of thing. But while the issue of Romantic inflation was very much alive when Prokofiev penned his subtle satire, it was dead and buried by 1920, let alone 1933. Were Shostakovich's First Piano Concerto simply an entertainment, its debunking allusions to the music of the past might be no more significant than, say, Poulenc's in his Double Concerto. However, the work's slow movement is so obviously serious that, ignoring outmoded notions of the composer as fundamentally schizoid, we can only conclude that the surrounding facetiousness is actually serious too. (This is not as perverse a judgement as it may seem. In interviews of the period, Shostakovich voiced resentment of critics who held that he had 'at last' managed to express 'depth and humanity' in his opera *Lady Macbeth*, having, in their view, previously frittered away his gifts in the unseemly pursuit of frivolity. His comic stuff – such as *The Nose*, the First Piano Concerto, and the Polka from *The Golden Age* – was, he insisted, just as deep and humane in its way.)

What, then, is the serious subtext of the apparently offhand Opus 35? The most likely answer would seem to be the relationship of private to public, of the individual to the crowd. As a leading motif in Shostakovich's recently completed *Lady Macbeth of Mtsensk*, it would from now on be returned to frequently in his opus list.

The 24 Preludes, classically sequenced in fifths after the example of Chopin, seem to have represented for Shostakovich a symbolic return to pure music after the aggressive illiteracy of the Cultural Revolution. Having got this off his chest (and aware that too much of this 'élitism' could still attract unwelcome attention), he responded to the call of civic responsibility by producing a Piano Concerto complete with its own instrumental commissar in the shape of a solo trumpet. As such, the Concerto's substance seems to have grown out of the recent concerns of Shostakovich's intellectual life, being a kind of dialogue between the frenetic world of Soviet materialism and the spiritual calm of the classical composers he had been revisiting during the winter of 1932–3 (among those quoted in his score being Bach, Haydn, Beethoven, and Weber). Thus, opening with a 'serious' theme which promises to develop along relatively conventional lines, the Concerto suddenly cartwheels away into a circus-world of comic turns and raspberries ringmastered by the trumpet. Here, the past is made to caper in a red nose for easy laughs, every attempt on its part to regain dignity or defend itself being swept away on a tide of raucous double entendres.

The implication – that great art has no place in a culture shrunken by cynicism – is pursued further in the fractured beauty of the central lento. Curbing the relentless activity of his outer movements, Shostakovich evokes an aching nostalgia suggestive of a genuine longing for grace, albeit a basically angry one. (When the piano strays into self-pity at figure 37, its pose is subverted by comically tiptoeing cellos and basses.) Despite his lurking scepticism, the composer talks straight for most of this movement, alluding (five bars after figure 33) to Mahler's patent vein of wistful world-weariness without apparent irony. Only when his search for classical consolation has found nothing but empty style, irrelevant to a world aeons away from its vision of sublime order, does he turn wry again, bringing the movement to an end on a conspicuously sour note.

The short third movement, a baroque recitative of chilly Brittenesque luminosity, rises briefly above the poignant dilemmas of this world before relapsing, to the accompaniment of braying donkey noises, into the dance-mad finale. Driven by the trumpet's incessant horse-race fanfare, its slapstick is piled on so remorselessly that, by the time the Concerto finally squeals to a halt, the joke has worn sufficiently thin to have entirely vanished. The alienation–

effect is unsettling – though not enough to have deterred the public who, taking the First Piano Concerto at face value, have made it one of Shostakovich's popular successes.

Critics, both Soviet and Western, have taken the composer to task for his failure to write anything sincerely affirmative during this period, hearing his then typical blend of tormented lyricism and acrid satire as evidence either of anti-social wilfulness or a basic flaw in his character (Soviet critics would draw no distinction here). The question of why Shostakovich was unwilling or unable to compose the sort of music they would have preferred him to is spun out through page after page of the books on him, often resulting in theoretical convolutions of grotesque complexity. Seen in the context of contemporary Soviet history, however, the mystery evaporates.

Whilst relaxed by normal standards, life in the cities in 1933 was disturbed enough by currents from the recent past to manifest a mildly hysterical undertow of live-now-for-tomorrow-we-die. The First Piano Concerto is, to some extent, a product of this. Similarly, while the Shostakovich of *Testimony* will have nothing to do with cynicism, 1933 was more thoroughly saturated with this attitude than any year since the Revolution, and it is unlikely that he remained immune to it. The megalomanic inflation of production targets during the First Five-Year Plan had become a kind of mass psychosis which reached a deafening zenith in 1931. The years 1932 and 1933 were lived in the echo of a huge door of disbelief slammed on this insanity and in that respect the tone of Shostakovich's Concerto and Preludes is very much of its period.[1]

In any case, he could not afford to relax too much even now for, while he was finishing the Concerto, his ballet *The Golden Age* came under attack in the Moscow press for its 'oversimplifications'. The coded message was that Shostakovich was not taking Communism seriously enough and, with the fate of Boris Pilnyak fresh in his mind, he cannot have shrugged off the insinuation lightly. Indeed, he would shortly be obliged to sign an article confessing that both *The Golden Age* and *The Bolt* had been 'gross failures' and admitting that 'the depiction of Socialist reality in ballet is an extremely serious matter which cannot be approached superficially'.

As usual, this fresh menace was only one element in a grand plan being directed from the Kremlin. The new cultural bureaucracy was hurrying to establish its pecking-orders and Shostakovich was again being considered for the Soviet musical laureateship, a post of solemn responsibility for which he was clearly expected to sober up. His nomination and due election to the minor post of deputy to the Oktyabrsky District of Leningrad in November 1933 seems to have been part of the plot and almost certainly out of his hands. Though he performed the minimal duties the position entailed, it would be

---

[1] It was during 1933 that Stalin stopped Afinogenov's play *The Lie*, then in rehearsal at three hundred theatres, and personally rewrote it, having taken exception to the heroine's condemnation of the falsehood now dominating Soviet life.

improbable that he did so in a spirit of profound political conviction. Yuri Yelagin, who had observed the composer at the Vakhtangov in 1932, saw him again while he was working there on Balzac's *The Human Comedy* a month or two after his civic elevation: 'At the rehearsals, Shostakovich was usually silent, calm and outwardly indifferent to the way in which his composition was played. He always seemed relaxed, though he seldom smiled. He did everything casually as if he were toying with an idea and his entire manner seemed to imply that whatever was taking place around him was totally devoid of any serious meaning.' Whatever else this represents, it is hardly a picture of a committed Communist toiling to create a musico-theatrical art worthy of the People.[1]

In January 1934 occurred the most prestigious event in Soviet music since the première of Shostakovich's First Symphony in 1926. Opening simultaneously in Leningrad and Moscow, his opera *Lady Macbeth of Mtsensk* was a runaway success. Hailed by Soviet critics as the greatest Russian opera since Tchaikovsky's *Queen of Spades*, it went on to receive nearly a hundred performances at the capital's Nemirovich-Danchenko Theatre and was still playing there and in Leningrad two years later.

Lady Macbeth derives from a novella published in 1865 by Nicolai Leskov, a story-writer and satirist famous in Russia for his use of the vernacular and criminal slang. A humanitarian sympathetic to the Russian underclass but without any formal political programme, he was a foreign figure in the regimented air of thirties Russia and, like Dostoyevsky, was soon to be posthumously unpersoned and banned.

Bridging the divide between Gogol and satirists like Zamyatin, Pilnyak, and Zoshchenko, Leskov was a natural choice for Shostakovich's sequel to *The Nose*, though the story itself was lurid and, by Soviet standards, appallingly amoral. In the composer's ironic précis, *Lady Macbeth* is 'the truthful and tragic portrayal of the destiny of a talented, smart, and outstanding woman, "dying in the nightmarish conditions of pre-revolutionary Russia", as they say'. In fact, the heroine, Katerina Ismailova, the 'Lady Macbeth' of the title, is a bold triple-murderess who, having done away with her husband, walls up his corpse in the cellar and proceeds to make riotous love to his manservant. For Shostakovich, however, her actions are understandable – indeed, justifiable. 'A turn of events is possible,' observes the narrator of *Testimony*, 'in which murder is not a crime.' In this case, the turn of events is that Katerina is the victim of vicious circumstances: a woman trapped into marrying the foolish son of a

---

[1] Nor is such a figure very audible in the Suite No. 1 for Dance Band, composed at the same time. Sometimes called a suite for 'jazz band', these pieces have less to do with jazz than with the Berlin cabaret of Weill and Eisler. Defying warning-noises from on high, the final Foxtrot, a concoction of sleazily decadent hauteur, is straight out of the world of *The Golden Age* and is, in fact, used in the Bolshoi's contemporary production of the ballet.

brute and condemned to drag out her days in tedious rural isolation among mindless bumpkins. Longing for life-validating love, in which subject Shostakovich rates her 'a genius', she can realize this dream only by slaughtering her male chauvinist oppressors.

Lady Macbeth is, in fact, an overtly feminist opera and was planned as the first of a tetralogy ('a Soviet *Ring*') dealing with the progressive liberation of Russia's women. The second of these was to centre on Sofia Perovskaya, the People's Will revolutionary who led the gang responsible for blowing up Tsar Alexander II; the third concerned the struggle for emancipation of an unnamed woman of the early twentieth century; and the fourth featured an unlikely Soviet Amazon combining the qualities of glamorous Bolshevik Larissa Reisner with those of Zhenya Romanko, a record-breaking shock-worker on the Dnieper Dam.[1] How consistent Shostakovich's feminism was, only the women in his life can say. Certainly he was not as devoted to it as Borodin, who sacrificed his composing career to fight for women's rights. In fact, the theme was a standard constituent of Narodnik intellectual baggage which figured in the work of most of the great nineteenth-century writers and was, officially at least, a central plank of the Bolshevik platform. Quite possibly what feminism really meant to Shostakovich was a safe metaphor for liberation from Communism which he hoped to develop as the cycle evolved. What is more certain is that Katerina, a woman (as he describes her) 'on a much higher level than those around her . . . surrounded by monsters', was for him, during the period of the opera's composition, a projection of himself and her embattled situation an exterior embodiment of his own.

The extent to which Shostakovich sympathised with Katerina is clear in his various commentaries on the opera – indeed, sympathy with her was for him the moral cornerstone of the work. That he went further and actively identified with her can only be inferred, but it is both obvious and understandable. In effect, Katerina acts out what Shostakovich was unable to do: she destroys her tormentors and lives by the law of her heart. She is, in her own terms, honest, brave, and true – and yet, not unlike the composer, she is betrayed by everyone around her. A key element in this, the brief aria 'Seryozha, my love' from Act IV, in which Katerina begs her faithless lover not to leave her, recurs twenty-five years later at the climax of the autobiographical Eighth Quartet. The cellist Mstislav Rostropovich has recalled that 'during a rehearsal I played that particular phrase in such a manner that Shostakovich couldn't help himself and cried . . . I put the same amount of soul into it as he did when he composed it.'

Betrayal is, in fact, a major motif in *Lady Macbeth*. The growing activity of informers and provocateurs in Soviet society, the mutual recriminations of the

---

[1] How far Shostakovich got with this massive project is unclear. On 28 December 1934, he announced that his librettist, Sasha Preis, was working on the second opera in the cycle, using material from Saltykov-Shchedrin and Chekhov. In *Testimony* (p. 206), he says that Preis completed a libretto on 'the life of women who want to be

accused in the show-trials, the recantations of his artistic colleagues during the Cultural Revolution – all of these are likely to have been seething in Shostakovich's mind as he wrote the opera. Particularly symbolic for him may have been the case of Pavlik Morozov, a twelve-year-old boy declared a national hero in September 1932 for denouncing his father.[1] (*Testimony* speaks witheringly of the Ismailov family as a microcosm of Stalinist society: 'A quiet Russian family who beat and poison one another . . . just a modest picture drawn from nature.') Yet the brunt of his anger is directed not at the sneaks and bullies of the Ismailov household, but at Sergei, the smooth-talking gigolo who pretends love for Katerina only to throw her over as soon as trouble arrives ('a petty scoundrel, a clerk who has picked up a little "culture", read a few books, and speaks in an affected way – his sufferings are all pretence'). By betraying a heroine so close to Shostakovich, Sergei seems to have become the composer's private symbol of perfidy, imposture, and disillusionment. The tone of *Testimony*'s musings on *Lady Macbeth* is, accordingly, highly personal – indeed, almost primal. It is, says Volkov's Shostakovich, about 'how love could have been if the world weren't full of vile things . . . the laws and properties and financial worries, and the police state'. In effect, Sergei stands for the betrayal of the composer's childhood innocence and idealism by an outside world predicated on force, deceit, and self-interest. Katerina's despairing plea to him is as much to Shostakovich's shattered dreams of happiness as to her own lost love.

At the time *Lady Macbeth* was being written, the Proletkult was attempting to impose a collectivist aesthetic in which the individual was not only obsolete, but fundamentally counter-revolutionary, a theme incorporated into the doctrine of Socialist Realism soon after the Cultural Revolution had finished. In focusing on individual psychology in *Lady Macbeth*, therefore, Shostakovich was going out on a dangerous limb. Nor was his treatment of the Collective (the chorus is almost always presented in a menacing light) any the less unorthodox. In strictly commercial terms, this could be considered rather shrewd for, music aside, it was the opera's emphatic individualism that attracted the crowds, a syndrome with which the composer would have been familiar from working on *The Nose*. Certainly *Lady Macbeth* plays to the gallery throughout much of its length (a fact disdainfully noted by some American critics when it was premièred in New York in 1935). In so often resorting to sheer volume it lays

---

emancipated', which sounds like the third opera. It is unknown whether these texts survive or were ever worked on by Shostakovich, who abandoned several other operatic projects around this time (including an operetta on Ilf and Petrov's *The Twelve Chairs* which, drafted in mid-1937, was scrapped the following year).

[1] As an example to Soviet youth, Morozov became famous – which is to say, infamous – throughout Russia. Maxim Gorky, presumably paying off some debt to Stalin, campaigned for a national monument to him, while Eisenstein spent three years making a film about the boy called *Bezhin Meadow* which he had to abandon when attacked by *Pravda* in 1937.

itself open to accusations of catering to the lowest common denominator, its main musical flaw deriving from its twenty-five-year-old composer's inability to gauge how much rampaging fortissimo the ear can stand. Its blatancy, too, tends to the over-exuberant, a fact Shostakovich acknowledged when he toned the score down during the sixties, taking the riper language out of the libretto and removing the sexually explicit trombones from Scene 3. All of which goes to prove that *Lady Macbeth* knew how to please the crowd, even if she disapproved of it. How far, though, was Shostakovich's individualism a conscious stance rather than one of the colours in his creative palette?

In answering this politically loaded question, it has to be said that Shostakovich in old age was somewhat more restrained than he was in his twenties and that *Testimony*, whatever its ultimate standing, is unlikely to be an exhaustive account of his motives in composing *Lady Macbeth*. (His revised version of the opera, *Katerina Ismailova*, is palpably staider than the original and not, one feels, solely because it had to be to qualify for filming in 1965.) *Lady Macbeth* is about many things: boredom, for instance, and cruelty. But if it is about one thing above all, it is about sex – and that makes it dangerously easy to misinterpret. For one thing, Leskov's novella is, for its period, audaciously carnal; that an opera based on it should be so is no surprise. For another, *Testimony* claims that whilst eroticism dominates the opera it conceals a serious point, derived from conversations with Ivan Sollertinsky during 1931 about the then imminent 'abolition of love'. According to this idea (common currency at the time in intellectual circles), the sexual licence of the twenties had so trivialised relationships that love was in danger of being diverted wholesale into Stalin-worship and the cult of the Party. Were this to continue unchallenged, future generations might, as in *Nineteen Eighty-Four*, come to know love solely as an impersonal devotion to Big Brother. Hence (to paraphrase the composer's exposition), *Lady Macbeth* was conceived as a kind of happening, Katerina's passion being a bomb of authentic feeling set to explode nightly in the souls of its sexually deracinated audience.

This is a persuasive argument, corresponding to the reality of Soviet sexual politics in 1931–2 and offering a depth of rationale to the opera which conforms impressively with Shostakovich's depth of feeling in composing it. If true, however, it would be the first categorical proof of his antagonism to Communism – an antagonism which, even if only in artistic terms, could justly be called counter-revolutionary. This being so, it is necessary to see whether the work itself, as written in the early thirties, is reconcilable with the composer's view of it forty years later.

Shostakovich worked out the libretto of *Lady Macbeth* with his friend Sasha Preis, who had collaborated on *The Nose* four years earlier; and as with *The Nose*, their text is scrupulously faithful to its source, condensing Katerina's steamy affair with Sergei but otherwise following Leskov's outline with only one deviation. This is the opera's third act, which (again, like *The Nose*) introduces new material concerning the police and is musically and dramatically less convincing than the other acts. (*Lady Macbeth* departs from this odd pattern of parallels by improving in its Act IV.)

Among several further parallels with *The Nose*, *Lady Macbeth* includes an apparently gratuitous and unnecessarily protracted scene in which a woman (the serving-girl Aksinya) is teased and humiliated by a crowd of baying men. Shostakovich's claim concerning the opera's subtext has to be self-consistent and it must be said that the lack of dramatic justification for the equivalent scene in *The Nose* tends, on the face of it, to vitiate claims to serious intention in the portrayal of Aksinya's teasing in *Lady Macbeth*, particularly since the latter grotesquely inflates Leskov's original. *The Nose* vents a strain of gang-minded male cruelty common in the literature of the sexually liberated twenties and, with so many of its schemes echoed in *Lady Macbeth*, it seems reasonable to wonder whether the same thing is going on there, too. Against this, the Shostakovich of *Testimony* dissociates himself very specifically from any sympathy with sadism and dilates at length on his fear and hatred of mob mentality. Further, the flogging of Sergei in Scene 4 is as fantastically exaggerated as the tormenting of Aksinya, and for obvious alienative reasons. On balance, then, the Aksinya scene has to be accepted as a functional satire on the insensitivity of Russian men to Russian women.[1]

Apart from this, the opera contains no downright obstacles to Shostakovich's retrospective account of its inner message. Certainly the portrayal of physical sex in Scene 3 is very vulgar and it could be argued that this contradicts his alleged aim of restoring dignity to the idea of love. This, though, can easily be defended either as one of the opera's many shocking ironies or by pointing out that a lofty distinction between sex and love was never part of its agenda. In the final analysis, the scene is simply ambiguous, which is why Shostakovich later de-vulgarised it, erasing the graphically detumescent trombones as 'irrelevant and distracting from the main idea'.

In the absence of solid proof, such as a letter from Shostakovich to Sollertinsky spelling out his intentions, the deeper design of *Lady Macbeth* has to remain to some extent conjectural. This does not, however, mean that common sense cannot deduce the truth, for the concealed message alleged in *Testimony* is not only historically plausible (and uncontradicted by the music), but also finds support in other aspects of the work. Shostakovich called *Lady Macbeth* a 'tragic-satiric opera' and, whether accepted or not, his hidden rationale certainly illuminates its satirical side. To be specific, it allows the blatancies of the work to be understood as parodies instead of unrestrained expressions of the composer's own vulgar streak, as *impersonations* rather than

---

[1] Wife-beating was so thoroughly institutionalised in pre-Revolutionary Russia that a husband who refrained from it was thought abnormal. An old manual of etiquette published in Moscow included instructions to husbands on how to whip their wives 'courteously, lovingly' so as not to blind or deafen them (Hingley, *The Russian Mind*, p. 154).

inflated descriptions. For example, the strident interlude between Scenes 2 and 3, which might otherwise be taken as embodying Katerina's resentful excitement over her first joust with Sergei, now looks more like a spoof on peasant ribaldry in which a rudely winking procession to the marriage chamber becomes a terse comment on contemporary Soviet sexual attitudes. In this and other similar passages, seeing *Lady Macbeth* from the point of view of the Shostakovich of *Testimony* upgrades it as art, bringing it into line with the subtlety on display in the best of the rest of his work.

If this revaluation of *Lady Macbeth* is to be accepted, what of the corollary – that conceiving and performing it in that spirit amounted to a counter-revolutionary antagonism to Communism?

Shostakovich was no fool. He knew that anything with tragic undertones could, were the authorities so inclined, be interpreted as contrary to the Soviet principles of doctrinaire optimism. Olesha's discussion of *Hamlet* in *A List of Assets* had examined this in detail and he had evidently absorbed the lesson. Yet despite his misgivings, expressed at the time to the *New York Times*'s Rose Lee, he went ahead. Clearly, he *had* to write *Lady Macbeth* – it was an emotional necessity which, if repressed, might have led to a breakdown (or, as with so many stifled Soviet artists, suicide by alcoholism). He had to express individuality and all those associated feelings denied to the Collective: love, boredom, loneliness, doubt, fear. Some of these were dangerous to mention, let alone express (boredom, for instance, though a traditional Russian concern, was not supposed to exist under Communism). Yet he let it all out, knowing the risks he ran in so doing.

Feelings, though, are one thing, thoughts another. If the intellectual subtext of *Lady Macbeth* is as he says in *Testimony*, then the opera is a great deal more than a glorified emotional safety-valve.

The most overt signs in the opera that Shostakovich was at odds with Communism in his mind as well as his heart occur in Acts III and IV. In the former, the scene at the police station, not in Leskov, was instantly accepted by its Russian audiences as a satire on the security organs, and when Stalin saw the Bolshoi production in 1936 it was this that infuriated him most (it seems he thought the Police Chief was meant to be a parody of him). And though by 1934 there were enough prisoners slaving in Russia's labour camps to have populated a respectable country,[1] such things were never talked about, the very existence of the Gulag being officially denied. That Shostakovich had set his finale in convict Siberia was, to his thirties audiences, his most daring stroke. It hardly mattered that this was Tsarist rather than Stalinist *katorga* (penal servitude). *Katorga* was *katorga*. The convict songs that weave through this music (played to Shostakovich as a child by his mother who had heard them

---

[1] Galina von Meck, imprisoned during the first wave of arrests among the intelligentsia in 1930, saw the official figures for deportation to the camps in secret files at Borovlianka in 1933: 17½ million (*As I Remember Them*, p. 412).

while passing through Siberia in 1898) were, in a real sense, still contemporary. Before the Revolution, convicts had been called *neschastnenkie*, or 'poor little wretches', and it was considered a duty to look kindly on them if ever a column of such unfortunates trudged by. Under Communism, the fear of *katorga* was too universal to be sentimentalised and the custom perished. 'I wanted,' insists Volkov's Shostakovich, 'to remind the audience that prisoners are wretched people and that you shouldn't hit a man when he's down. Today you're in prison, tomorrow it might be me.' If Katerina's love was a bomb set to explode in his audience's hearts, her imprisonment was a candle left to burn in their minds.

The attitude behind all this was, of course, not peculiar to Shostakovich. It was the liberal outlook of the non-Party intelligentsia, of the composers of the Association of Contemporary Musicians, and of the individualist writers he knew personally or by repute: Bulgakov, Zoshchenko, Akhmatova, Pasternak, Mandelstam, and company. That during the years 1934–5 he alone was able to get away with voicing it depended on a fragile coincidence of factors. Firstly, Stalin and most of those close to him were musically illiterate and so uninterested in monitoring events on the compositional front. Secondly, with Nazism ascendant in Europe, Russia needed to cultivate her allies and *Lady Macbeth* was a prize exhibit among her musical exports to the West. And, thirdly, the post-1932 state-takeover of the arts, masterminded as it was by Gorky, proceeded faster in literature than it did in music, leaving Shostakovich with a field temporarily free of meddling functionaries. (By the time they had sorted themselves out, *Lady Macbeth* was being hailed as a masterpiece in Europe and its composer was world property.)

On balance then – and unless critically bowdlerised beyond recognition – *Lady Macbeth of Mtsensk* can reasonably be interpreted as a deliberate, if necessarily disguised, expression of antagonism to Communism. As yet only reactive, it cannot be called positively anti-Communist (although it may well have been conceived of in just such a spirit and is obviously moving strongly in that direction). Nor, more importantly, is it likely to have leapt from nowhere into the composer's head in 1931 – in fact, given his interests and contacts, it is difficult to see how it could not have been gestating there for several years.

All told, there is in *Lady Macbeth* sufficiently strong evidence of Shostakovich's disenchantment with the Soviet regime to provide a base from which to trace the trend back through a line of works otherwise classifiable only as *probable* products of such an outlook. In the light of previous analyses, there seems to be no compelling reason why we should not follow this strain of scepticism all the way to his student days.

The sustained tragedy of the finale of *Lady Macbeth* was something unique in Soviet culture of the early thirties. Elsewhere in music and in all the other arts the new official aesthetic, Socialist Realism, served to confine creative expression rigidly to narratives of heroic struggle and hectoring optimism. This was the age of the 'Five-Year Plan novel', typically a multi-volume blockbuster depicting the construction of a giant power plant. Later, as the list of industrial projects to be glorified lengthened dispiritingly into the future, writers ran out of rhetoric and turned to a dogged, gritty substitute referred to – unofficially – as 'grey realism'. In this period, however, the strenuous purple of Red Romanticism was mandatory. Literary behemoths such as Marietta Shaginyan's *Hydrocentral*, Leonid Leonov's *Sot*, and Mikhail Sholokhov's *Virgin Soil Upturned* were saluted as flagships of Communist art and anything reflective, downbeat, or short taken as a guarantee of dissent. Those who could manage the expansive manner abandoned their hard-won concision for the New Grandiosity (the satirist Valentin Katayev, for example, secured his survival by turning out the model behemoth *Time, Forward!*). Those who gagged at the thought – ironists like Isaac Babel and Andrei Platonov, lyricists like Akhmatova and Mandelstam – found themselves unpublishable and were forced to hack for their living in journalism and translation.

Meanwhile, Stalin's public insistence that, despite appearances, life was becoming 'more joyful' was translated by his cultural *apparatchiks* into a demand on artists for an unalloyed diet of ecstastic selflessness. Once again, the pressure to be positive quickly became suffocating. During the First Congress of the Writers' Union in August 1934, at which delegates from every branch of Soviet industry lobbied writers to produce novels about the workers they represented, Shostakovich's ex-friend Yuri Olesha, now a script-writer, addressed his colleagues fervently in the Red Romantic high style: 'All doubts, all sufferings are past. I have become young . . . A whole life lies before me.' Afterwards he admitted privately to Ilya Ehrenburg that he was hopelessly blocked. 'If I write "the weather was bad", they'll tell me it was good for the cotton crop.'

While the most advanced form of state control was exerted on the writers, Soviet composers were being almost as mercilessly dragooned into churning out musical behemoths of their own. For now, choral symphonies were in vogue, the leader in the field being former Modernist Lev Knipper, whose Fourth Symphony, *Poem of the Fighting Komsomol*, was something of a contemporary hit and lingers in the regular Soviet repertoire today. Works like this invariably came in three parts: an heroically struggling first movement, stern and resolute in character; a song-like adagio or funeral march (or, better still, a combination of the two); and, finally, a conclusion of rumbustiously banal triumphalism. No musical argument was pursued for more than a few bars and the writing, particularly of the choral sections (distributed at regular intervals throughout so as not to bore the audience with too much instrumental music), was of elementary simplicity.

The main selling-point of such pieces was the so-called 'mass-song', a crudely monophonic setting of facile verses apostrophising Stalin, Party, and Motherland, designed so as to be easily reproducible by local farm and factory choirs. (Knipper's Fourth, for example, owes its success solely to the hummability of its mass-song, *Little Field*, familiar to older Western listeners from the Red Army concerts of the sixties.) A twenties invention of the Proletkult, the mass-song was adopted by the new regime as an ideal propaganda medium, and by 1934 was being injected into any musical idiom that would take it. 'Song-symphonies', such as Knipper's, were soon succeeded by 'song-operas', stage-works bearing a closer resemblance to vaudeville than Verdi or Wagner. By the end of the decade, the mass-song could claim to be the main distinguishing characteristic of the species *Soviet music* and its dominance has never diminished since. 'In the Soviet Union,' wrote the emigré musicologist Andrei Olkhovsky in 1955, 'the mass-song resounds from early morning until late at night. Soviet citizens work and rest – in so far as it is possible to rest at all – with its insistent melody in their ears.'[1]

Shostakovich was as contemptuous of the new song-symphonies as Babel and others were of the Five-Year Plan novels. Unlike Babel, who could express his distaste only by refusing to write anything (a gesture which later cost him his life), the composer was able to use the success of *Lady Macbeth* as a shield from behind which to campaign for improved music criticism and even to attack song-symphonism at a Composers' Union conference in February 1935. However, whilst doubtless satisfying in itself, resistance was useless and would shortly afterwards become suicidal. By the summer of 1935, Shostakovich had joined Babel in the eloquent solidarity of silence.

The success of *Lady Macbeth* considerably alleviated its composer's financial worries and during the winter of 1933–4 he and Nina frequently appeared at parties and restaurants. Soon afterwards, though, they began to be seen together in public less often and Shostakovich resumed drinking with his éminence grise Sollertinsky. Little is known of events in his married life at this time, except that Nina seemed to be ill and away on rest-cures rather a lot. Obviously the strain of overcrowding at the Nikolayevskaya Street apartment had something to do with it. By the spring of 1935, things had degenerated sufficiently for Shostakovich to be filing for divorce when an apartment at the Home of Soviet Composers fell vacant, allowing him and his wife to get out from under mother's feet. The divorce was thereupon dropped and by the autumn Nina was pregnant.

On 1 August 1934, following an explosive row which had resulted in Nina catching the train for Leningrad, Shostakovich found himself left to his own devices in Prokofiev's rooms in Moscow. (The older composer had vacated the premises in June and gone to spend the summer in Paris with his family.) Leaving aside the orchestrally textured octet movements of Opus 11, Shostakovich had composed nothing small-scale since the Three Pieces for Cello and Piano, Opus 9 during the winter of 1923–4. Ten years later, and disregarding

---

[1] The genre has, unfortunately, proved to be translatable. The citizens of China and North Korea suffer it too.

the fact that no chamber music had been either written or requested in Russia since the Cultural Revolution, he dashed off the first movement of his Cello Sonata in D minor, Opus 40, in a mere two days. If true (our source is Solomon Volkov), this ranks as one of the composer's more remarkable feats, since the opening allegro of the Cello Sonata is a subtle structure built on two unusually attractive themes. In reality, he had probably been mulling these ideas over for some time and merely used the pressure of emotion as a circumstantial device to get them down on paper. (Indeed, the fact that the piece had been commissioned by the cellist Viktor Kubatsky, its subsequent dedicatee, suggests that this was so.)

The Cello Sonata is a deceptive piece. The Soviet critic Dmitri Rabinovich, who claims to have been a close friend of the composer, describes it as 'a sudden ray of sunshine'. Others, in Russia and the West, have referred to it as 'mainly lyrical' and pointed to the 'peasant joy' of the second and fourth movements as indicative of its essentially genial character. In fact, comments like these are typical of the distortions caused by accepting the anodyne Shostakovich so assiduously peddled by Soviet propagandists and it does not require especially attentive ears to discern that the work is actually strained, sardonic, and distinctly bitter.

Opening with a melody which casts a yearning glance at Late Romanticism (had Prokofiev perhaps imported Fauré's sonatas from Paris?) Shostakovich establishes a mood of delicate, even genteel, nostalgia. In 1935, a pro-Communist critic for a Prague newspaper acidly described this as 'a model of bourgeois music', an opinion subsequently used against the composer in 1936. He was more perceptive than he realised. This is pre-Revolutionary music, presented without irony as an evocation of a gentler way of life. Carried sweetly by the cello, it is soon, however, in trouble and tussling with a refractory triplet phrase on the piano until, with a murmur of reassurance, the radiantly lyrical second subject enters, every bit as charmingly old-world as the first. Swelling to an intense crescendo, there is something maternal about this theme and the cello shows a childlike reluctance to relinquish it, yielding a wan cry as a drumming figure on the bass-notes of the piano supervenes. A fretful development of the first subject follows in which the protesting cello hoists it high above the dark swirl of the piano as if trying to prevent disaster. Again, the maternal second subject appears, dispensing calm and comfort, but this time the cello parts with it unrefreshed and the drumming figure begins to dominate. Upset by more agitated development, the unhappy cello is sighing tiredly in its lower register by the time the mother-motif comes to its rescue for the third and final time. Cut short by an ominously pacing piano, their communion is fruitless and the movement closes darkly on the drumming figure.

Having completed the first movement, an insomniac Shostakovich decamped to the Crimea (the first time for five years that he had holidayed without Nina) and finished the sonata within a month. The second movement, described by Rabinovich as 'sincere merriment, inoffensive humour, and not caricature or grotesquerie', is in fact a brutal folk-dance, full of clumsy stamping, which anticipates the pounding peasant scherzo of the Piano Quintet of 1940. The 'country' allusion is hard to interpret (how much Shostakovich then knew of collectivisation is unknown); in all probability, he is satirising the 'revolt against intelligence' mounted by Stalin's provincial recruits after 1928. The third movement, a gloomily vehement monologue which winds to a rasping climax before dwindling back into silence, gives way to a finale of vitriolic sarcasm. Here, a one-finger rondo melody, idiotically pleased with itself, 'wrong notes' and all, parades up and down between interludes of deranged academic exercises, sagely quoting the initial theme of the first movement as if to show that it *knows all that*. The last of these interludes, with piano scales cascading around a cello part of cheerful imbecility, suggests the inspirational presence of the Proletkult.

Shostakovich and Kubatsky toured the Cello Sonata extensively during 1935. Despite its sourness it was liked and, under happier circumstances, things could only have got better for all concerned. However, three weeks before they premièred the piece in Leningrad, one of those historically pivotal events took place after which everything changes and the past becomes forbidden territory, impossible to visit again.

On 1 December 1934, a young man called Leonid Nikolayev walked into the Smolny in Leningrad, pulled out a revolver and, from point-blank range, fired a single bullet through the head of Sergei Kirov, the most important Communist in Russia after Joseph Stalin. And the Great Terror began.

Chapter Four

TERROR 1935–1938

How the Russian earth
Loves the taste of blood

IN THE IMMEDIATE aftermath of the Kirov assassination, forty thousand Leningraders were deported to the labour camps for collusion in the crime, a further four hundred committing suicide before the NKVD got to them. As the months rolled by, the Kirov investigation spread out all over Russia and the list of arrested conspirators expanded in proportion so that, by 1936, those implicated in the murder were numbered in millions. The most remarkable thing about the Kirov conspiracy, however, was that it never existed – or rather that it did, but was actually mounted by a few secret agents working for Kirov's colleague and friend, the Beloved Father himself, Joseph Stalin. Leonid Nikolayev, a man with a grudge, had been merely an expendable pawn in their game.

Stalin had several reasons for killing Kirov, the least important being personal jealousy. In recent years, Kirov had attained a level of adulation within the Party modestly comparable with his own and was even being referred to in some quarters as the Stalin of the North. The leader tolerated no rivals. His backwoods hatred of cosmopolitan Leningrad also played its part, the post-Kirov purge allowing him to make a clean sweep of the remnants of the old Petersburg nobility and arrest as many intellectuals as he pleased. (Anna Akhmatova's husband and son were pulled in soon after the assassination in order to keep her quiet while the NKVD went about its work.)

But there were greater issues at stake. Stalin's collectivisation of agriculture, commenced in 1930 and more or less complete by 1934, had been largely concealed from the nation's city-dwellers, who felt its effects mainly in the form of food shortages. Among the intelligentsia, however, rumours were rife that the campaign had been a major catastrophe, destroying Russia's rural productivity and costing thousands of peasant lives. Osip Mandelstam, for example, thrown out of Leningrad in 1931, had wandered off the beaten track before arriving in Moscow and discovered the truth. Though his *Poem About Stalin*, which addressed the dictator as 'murderer and peasant-slayer', was never written down and only recited privately to friends, its mere existence was dynamite. Meeting Pasternak on the Tver Boulevard in March 1934, Mandelstam held him by the arm and whispered the poem into his ear. 'I didn't hear this,' responded a grim Pasternak, 'and you didn't tell it to me.' Shortly afterwards, the NKVD were informed about the poem and Mandelstam was arrested. Possibly due to the pleas of Pasternak, who petitioned Bukharin, and Akhmatova, who went straight to the Kremlin, Mandelstam and his wife Nadezhda were sentenced only to three years' internal exile in the Urals. Amazingly, Pasternak was then allowed to visit the Ukraine, ostensibly to gather material for an heroic ode on collectivisation, but really to see whether Mandelstam had been telling the truth. What he saw shocked him so badly he was unable to sleep for a year afterwards.

By 1934 the Ukraine, once a lush prairie supporting over forty million people, had become, in the words of historian Robert Conquest, 'one vast Belsen'. Nearly fifteen million peasants had died. Starving hordes were wandering the country in search of something to eat. Russia's agriculture had been rationalised to death.

If the genocide in the Ukraine had gone all but unnoticed in the cities, it was the talk of the Party. Many *apparatchiks* had gone mad from the horrors they had been forced to inflict and there had been some embarrassingly prominent suicides (the most conspicuous being Stalin's second wife, Nadezhda Alliluyeva). Stalin managed to keep the lid on by purging a million members between 1931 and 1933, but he had no excuse for removing the many senior Bolsheviks who had known him since pre-Revolutionary days and were immune to the hyperbole of his personality cult. When his glorification reached surreal dimensions at the 17th Party Congress in 1934, the revulsion of his old comrades was obvious. To forestall exposure of the truth about collectivisation or perhaps even a coup, Stalin had to liquidate the Party and replace it with a new one. He began by killing Kirov. Then he blamed Zinoviev for the murder and killed *him*. And so on.

Shostakovich's reaction to the Kirov affair goes unmentioned in *Testimony*, but he can only have been as anxious as everyone else. Anyone who had known Kirov was suspect and the composer had probably met him at least twice (during the 1930 run of *The Nose*, which Kirov eventually banned, and while working on the film *Counterplan*, which Kirov supervised in 1932). With widespread arrests among the Leningrad intelligentsia, Shostakovich must have known many of the 'disappeared' and would certainly have felt the shuddering impact on the city's cultural life of Kirov's replacement, Andrei Zhdanov, a brutal man later famous for his persecution of Russia's intellectuals in the forties.

In the tense periods following his public reprimands in 1936 and 1948, the composer kept his head down by devoting his time to film scores and suites of previously published material. Significantly, he did the same during the winter of 1934–5, writing two soundtracks (for the films *Maxim's Youth* and *Girlfriends*) and cobbling together the conformist ballet *The Limpid Stream*, which he padded out with unadapted material from *The Golden Age* and *The Bolt*. A potboiler to a Socialist Realist scenario about collective farmworkers in the Kuban grain region of the North Caucasus, *The Limpid Stream* featured some of his least inspired music (preserved in the Ballet Suites Nos 1–3) and it was probably toiling on this piece of drudgery that prompted him to complain about aspects of Socialist Realism at the Composers' Union in 1935.

When Shostakovich made his critique of Soviet music criticism and the phenomenon of song-symphonism at this debate, he was protected by the international success of *Lady Macbeth* and emboldened by the warm reception awarded, the week before, to *Maxim's Youth*. He needed to be. Though Socialist Realism had been in existence for a mere two years, its canons had already acquired an aura of infallibility which very few at the conference would have been rash enough to violate. In addition, the doctrine had the self-seeking support of the many ex-Proletkulters now jockeying for position in the Union's hierarchy, and the elusively irreverent Shostakovich was almost as much of a hate-figure to these leftists as the dandified Prokofiev.

'Socialist Realism' was a term originally coined in an anonymous *Literary Gazette* editorial of 29 May 1932, later ascribed to Stalin. That it was designed to fill the ideological vacuum left by the Proletkult was clear from a circular from the Orgburo of the Writers' Union issued that December, informing members that Averbakh's Kharkhov Resolution of 1930 had been cancelled. From now on, Soviet artists were to cease being Dialectical Materialists and start being Socialist Realists. Doubtless a relief to those Soviet artists who had never had any idea what Dialectical Materialism was, this announcement unfortunately left the nature of its replacement almost as obscure.

Fully expounded in an essay by Maxim Gorky in 1933, it emerged that Socialist Realism was nothing less than the aesthetic face of 'Marxist truth'. To Marxists, the truth is that history is heading inevitably for a climax of static perfection called Communism (Socialism being merely the final stage of the approach-phase). Communism being a utilitarian faith, the only useful task art can do for it is that of hastening the arrival of this millennium by helping to instil the values needed to bring it about. Socialist Realism, said Gorky, would do this by portraying reality 'in its revolutionary development' as though looking at the present from the future Golden Age.

Socialist Realism, in other words, was to be a kind of political science fiction, based on a theory about a hypothetical future, by means of which lying about the present could be made to seem both necessary and noble.

Looking at the present as though from the future being confusing even for a Socialist Realist, the theoretical side of the doctrine tended to be stressed less than the practical methods of carrying it out. Since this was an aesthetic of heroic fulfilment, it had to be optimistic. No tragic heroes, no unhappy endings. Because 'the radiant future' (as it was customarily referred to) would be collective, individuals could only be treated as symbols of qualities or tendencies. Idealisation was to be encouraged and 'naturalism' (dwelling on the sordid side of things) strongly to be avoided. An essentially public art, Socialist Realism had no place for nuance, introspection, or reflection. All was unflagging action in its externalised world, loud with the megaphone language of Red

Romanticism (defined, in appropriately delirious style, as 'the artist's justified emotion in the face of the real mass heroism of the struggle for Socialism').

Of its many internal contradictions, eventually the most destructive to Socialist Realism was one which appeared, at first, to be purely theoretical. It was that if reality is to be considered literally as in perpetual 'revolutionary development', no artist can ever hope to fix it in his work. Any art produced according to such a theory will be obsolete before it is started, let alone finished – especially if it happens to coincide with one of those moments when history's steady progress towards the radiant future mysteriously moves sideways or even goes into reverse.

This syndrome, inadequately grasped by observers outside the Communist bloc, has long been familiar in Russia, where attentions forced on artists in the name of Socialist Realism have invariably been seen not as stages in the consistent pursuit of an aesthetic ideal, but rather as side-effects of arbitrary changes in the official political line. A famous example is the case of the post-war novel *The Young Guard* which, as a major contribution to Socialist Realism, was awarded a Stalin Prize in 1947. A year later, Stalin saw Gerasimov's film of the book and flew into a rage over the 'insufficient emphasis on the role of the Party' in the lives of its heroes and heroines. The author, Alexander Fadeyev, no less a personage than the General Secretary of the Writers' Union, was ordered to rewrite the novel from top to bottom in accordance with the principles of Socialist Realism. Several years later, he completed this revision and submitted it for assessment – only to be told that things had changed yet again and another complete rewrite was due. Not long after this, Fadeyev shot himself. Asked what Socialist Realism was by some Czech writers at a conference in 1958, the Nobel laureate Mikhail Sholokhov quoted the deceased General Secretary's answer to the same question confided to him a few weeks before he died: 'The Devil alone knows.'

That Socialist Realism was really nothing more than what was useful to Stalin at any given moment had to be tactfully concealed and, since the best way of diverting attention has always been to let the dog see the rabbit, emphasis was laid less upon what Socialist Realism was than on what it was *not* – that is, identifying its mortal enemy. This was Formalism, originally the name of a twenties art-for-art's-sake literary group but adopted by Stalinist theorists in the thirties to play the role of scapegoat and whipping-boy to the state's new aesthetic doctrine. Formalism, defined in *The Soviet Political Dictionary* as 'putting to the forefront the outer side of a question, the detachment of form from content', was a charge used initially against abstract art. However, since the 'content' alluded to in the *Dictionary* really meant '*political* content', the scope of Formalism was, like that of the Kirov investigation, constantly broadening.

It has been said that the basic flaw in Socialist Realism is Communism's inability to legislate for an individualistic pursuit like artistic creativity. While true enough in itself, this overlooks the fact that, rather than waste time formulating a consistent theory of art, Communism's priority has always been to assimilate art as quickly as possible into its general propaganda effort. In this perspective, Socialist Realism is simply art useful for building Socialism, Formalism art useless for it. But even this is to glamorise the truth for, since 'building Socialism' in the Communist bloc means whatever those in power wish it to mean, Socialist Realism for practical purposes merely signifies art the authorities happen to like and Formalism art they don't.

Shostakovich's unusual forthrightness in criticising these concepts at the February 1935 Composers' Union conference may have been partly the product of looking not at the sinister overall pattern, but instead at its incongruous details. Had he fully grasped the political motives behind Socialist Realism, he might have seen that making a fuss about its façade was not only dangerous but pointless. In the event, his winter of toil on the sloganeering banalities of *The Limpid Stream* seems to have provoked a bout of uncharacteristic candour amounting to an open invitation to be assaulted from all sides. Socialist Realist criticism, he declared, contained 'too much discussion about whether the music adequately conveys that the collective farm has fulfilled its plan by one hundred per cent'. As for song-symphonies, the criteria for success in this idiom were childishly naive: 'Add a verse, that's "content"; no verse, that's "Formalism".' These things were quite so, but to say as much was extraordinarily undiplomatic.

Seizing their chance (or perhaps put up to it by the powers behind the Composers' Union), Shostakovich's Proletkult enemies began publicly attacking *Lady Macbeth* as a piece of individualistic/pessimistic/naturalistic Formalism. Shostakovich fought back through the pages of *Izvestia*: 'I have never been a Formalist and never shall be. To malign a work as Formalist on the grounds that its form and meaning is not instantly apparent is to be inexcusably superficial.' Referring to this in her autobiography, Galina Vishnevskaya comments: 'In those days, that took a great deal of courage.' (This is particularly true in view of the fact that Raya Vasilyeva, screenwriter of *Girlfriends*, for which Shostakovich wrote the music, had just been arrested for participation in the Kirov conspiracy – any connection with the 'disappeared' being perilous in the extreme.)

If, as it appears, the liquidation of the Proletkult in 1932 had let out the fighter in Shostakovich, then the spring of 1935 seems to have marked the climax of his battling mood. There again, he would have been unable to contribute to *Izvestia* had his prestige not been appropriately high – and if this was apparent to others, it must have been clear to him too. *Lady Macbeth* had made him Russia's leading composer. For the moment, that gave him confidence and a certain amount of clout, which he used.

Reality, however, was rushing onward in its customary revolutionary development and in June the première in Leningrad of *The Limpid Stream* drew distinctly unfriendly notices from the critics. Articles had appeared over Shostakovich's signature promising that this work would rectify the 'mistakes' of *The Golden Age* and *The Bolt* and confessing that in his earlier pieces he had sought to entertain to the detriment of serious revolutionary art. (This was the standard Proletkult view of him and the line which would be taken against him in 1936.) *The Limpid Stream*, however, showed no sign whatever of any serious intention – almost as though the composer was deliberately subverting his previous 'public statements' (a gesture smacking strongly of *yurodstvo*). Further controversy was forestalled when the ballet's audiences, grateful for its light-hearted choreography, turned it into an unexpected success.

At the Composers' Union conference in February, Ivan Sollertinsky had expressed warm anticipation for his friend's Fourth Symphony, having, he said, reason to believe that it would be 'at a far remove' from the previous three, being more ambitious and heroic. (As with *Lady Macbeth*, he and the composer had discussed the work's design in some detail.) Notwithstanding this, the only composing Shostakovich did during the first half of 1935 took place on a single day (26 April) and consisted of five allusive Fragments for small wind group and strings. Of these, the first two are 'impersonations' in a subdued version of his usual satirical style, perhaps drawn from nature at the Composers' Union conference. The third, the most striking, is a chill pianissimo nocturne, suggesting isolation and insomnia, a mood which seeps through into the wan polytonal line-drawing of the fourth. The concluding Fragment sets a waltzing violin against the quiet, regulatory rasp of a snare drum, a theme which recurs in the finale of the Fourth Symphony. The last things Shostakovich wrote before embarking on that ill-fated colossus, the Opus 42 Fragments are among the most understated works in his opus list. The stillness at the heart of the cyclone, they belie their thunderous epoch with the lucidity of a congenital outsider – of a man from Mars.

In September 1935, Shostakovich was one of a Russian musical delegation sent on a concert tour of Turkey as part of a drive to improve relations between the two countries. The tour was diligently played up in the Soviet press and, upon his return, he was offered a number of guest appearances 'at very flattering terms'. All seemed well and he set about fulfilling these engagements in relaxed mood. Having begun his Fourth Symphony on the Turkish tour, he continued with it while travelling between dates in Russia so that by 28 January 1936 it was already well advanced. That morning, he was waiting at the station in Arkhangelsk when he happened to see the early edition of *Pravda*. On page three was an article, headlined 'Muddle Instead of Music', attacking his opera *Lady Macbeth* as a cacophonous and pornographic insult to the Soviet People and threatening that unless the composer of this degenerate work changed his ways things 'could end very badly'. Though unsigned, the article was obviously by Stalin himself.

To be publicly condemned by Stalin was tantamount to a death sentence. In a single day, Shostakovich went from being a cosseted piece of Soviet property to an anathematised outcast – and this at a time when outcasts were being packed off to Siberia in scores of thousands every month. When, a week later, *Pravda* published a second article, 'Balletic Falsity', attacking *The Limpid Stream* in similar terms, it seemed a foregone conclusion that Shostakovich was about to 'disappear'. All at once, friends and colleagues were out to his calls. 'Everyone,' recalls the narrator of *Testimony*, 'knew for sure that I would be destroyed. And the anticipation of that noteworthy event – at least for me – has never left me.' Unable to do anything about it, he went home to his wife and waited.

A few days later, he was summoned before a special conference of the Composers' Union in Moscow. Here, in contrast to the year before, he had to sit quietly and take the most abusive criticism without protest. *Lady Macbeth*, banned after the first *Pravda* attack, bore the brunt of the hostility, being vilified for its sympathetic treatment of a murderess, for insulting Soviet womanhood with its 'untypical' heroine, and for the 'vulgar naturalism' of its libretto. *The Limpid Stream*, too, was condemned both for cynical banality and for failing to use the Cossack folk songs of the region in which it was set. All this, however, was merely a prelude. As in the case of the campaign against Zamyatin and Pilnyak in 1929, what had been launched as special criticism of individual offences rapidly expanded its scope to the dimensions of a general purge.

The watchword was Formalism – the first time the Soviet public had heard a term which had, until then, been bandied about solely within the confines of the various artistic unions. That Shostakovich was the leading musical purveyor of this trend was supposedly demonstrated by the sackloads of letters which poured into the Composers' Union during the conference, denouncing him as a 'bourgeois aesthete and Formalist' and demanding 'music for the millions'. No more authentic than the usual fusillade of communications from 'incensed workers' accompanying every ritual of public humiliation in Stalin's Russia, this 'tide of popular protest' was nevertheless welcomed by a national press keen to get the idea of Formalism across to its readers in plain terms. Adapting to the simplest outlooks and shortest tempers, *Pravda* and *Izvestia* presented Formalism as incomprehensible music written by bourgeois counter-revolutionaries, quite possibly in code and definitely in flagrant contradiction to the interests of the international proletariat. For the ordinary Russian this, while puzzling, was at least as plausible as any of the other new crimes which the papers were forever 'unmasking'. If there could be 'wreckers' in the porcelain industry, then why not in the composing industry too? What turned tepid distaste into outrage was the accompanying insinuation that these Formalists were playing them for fools. Portrayed as 'anti-People music', a game of the intelligentsia at the expense of the workers, Formalism touched on natural resentments and was soon evoking genuine anger.

At the Composers' Union, new victims were needed to feed the growing furore and the choice fell inevitably upon the cosmopolitan Prokofiev and his reserved and studious colleague Nikolai Myaskovsky. Absent in Paris, Prokofiev was charged with Formalism by a young proletarian composer called

Tikhon Khrennikov, keen to make a name for himself. Myaskovsky, upbraided for his tragic Sixth Symphony of 1923, was forced to repudiate it as 'a weak-willed, neurasthenic, and sacrificial concept', and warned not to try anything like it again. Anyone connected with Shostakovich was similarly reprimanded – Samuel Samosud for conducting *Lady Macbeth*, Dmitri Rabinovich for giving the opera a good review, and Ivan Sollertinsky for being a bourgeois aesthete and all-round bad influence. Initially attempting to defend Shostakovich, Sollertinsky quickly saw that doing so would only get both of them into deeper trouble and so changed tack, repenting his Formalism and disavowing his former approval of works like *Aphorisms* and *The Nose*. *Pravda*, reporting the proceedings, exulted with characteristically prefabricated frenzy:

> The editorials of *Pravda* have caught off guard the masked defenders of decayed bourgeois music. This is the reason for the bewilderment and anger of these men. The idolator of this trend which disfigured Shostakovich's music, the untiring troubadour of Leftist distortion, Sollertinsky, correctly appraised the situation when he declared at the session of Leningrad music critics that there is nothing more for him to do in Soviet musical art and that he will terminate his 'activities'. The mask is torn off! Sollertinsky speaks his own language.

Shostakovich himself said nothing during the conference, rising only at the end to apologise for his Formalism. (*Testimony*: 'Like the sergeant's widow, I had to declare to the whole world that I had whipped myself. I was completely destroyed. It was a blow that wiped out my past. And my future.') Some of those present, apparently touched by his plight, back-pedalled on total condemnation. Lev Knipper, whose work Shostakovich had lambasted only twelve months before, generously urged against 'driving nails into his coffin'; the composer's colleagues, he suggested, ought instead to 'help him straighten himself out'. Concurring, the critic Boris Asafiev, who had earlier denounced *The Limpid Stream* as 'Lumpenmusik', warned that it would be wrong to relegate Shostakovich from the front rank of Soviet composers. However, these remarks had no effect on the mood of the conference as a whole, which adjourned with a unanimous condemnation of Shostakovich and musical Formalism in general.

The composer's fall was resounding. Now mentioned in the press only amongst lists of enemies of the People, he was persona non grata to society at large – 'unpersoned', as the jargon had it. To know him was dangerous, to associate with him suicidal. (People literally crossed the street to avoid passing too close to him.) With Nina five months pregnant and no money coming in, he was in a desperate situation. Like millions of others, he took to keeping a suitcase packed with two changes of warm underwear and some stout shoes. Like millions of others, he now lay awake every night, listening for the sound of a car drawing up outside, of boots thudding on the stairs, of a sharp rap at the door.

After a few weeks, understandably unable to work in this state, he went to Moscow to see a powerful friend, Marshal Mikhail Tukhachevsky, the most prestigious senior officer in the Red Army. The two had first met in 1925, when Shostakovich, then eighteen, had told Tukhachevsky, then thirty-two, that he was writing a symphony. An amateur musician, the young military genius recognised a fellow wunderkind and took Shostakovich under his wing, conferring with him regularly during the late twenties to advise him on his career and help him with money. Greeting his distraught protégé in February 1936, Tukhachevsky talked quietly with him for some time, solemnly promising to intercede on his behalf with Stalin should that ever become necessary, and counselling him to put his mind at rest and go back to his work. According to a witness, Shostakovich was a new man after leaving Tukhachevsky's study, going straight to a piano and improvising with his usual incongruous power.

Setting about the Fourth Symphony, he finished it in short-score by mid-April. He then took a further month to orchestrate its finale, confiding in a letter to his composer friend Vissarion Shebalin that he was 'very bitter', did not know what to do next, and was deliberately dragging his heels. The cause of this bitterness was the composer's betrayal at the hands of so many he had believed to be his friends. Indeed, according to *Testimony*, the loneliness was such that he lived for some while on the verge of suicide: 'The danger horrified me and I saw no other way out . . . I desperately wanted to vanish, it was the only way out. I thought of the possibility with relish.' Gradually, however, and with the aid of advice from his writer friend Zoshchenko, he pulled back from the brink. 'The hostile forces didn't seem so omnipotent any more and even the shameful treachery of friends and acquaintances didn't cause me as much pain as before. The mass treachery did not concern me personally. I managed to separate myself from other people, and in that period it was my salvation.'

Considering Shostakovich's perilous personal situation, the fact that the Fourth Symphony was accepted for rehearsal by the Leningrad Philharmonic shortly after being finished is something of a puzzle. The composer was popular among the city's musicians and strings may have been pulled, but his works had otherwise been withdrawn from performance and publication and, under such conditions, string-pulling would have had small effect on its own. The greater mystery is the question of why, having so publicly condemned-Shostakovich, Stalin had done nothing further to him at a time when he was daily signing death-warrants by the hundred. In his introduction to *Testimony*, Solomon Volkov suggests that Stalin had made 'a private decision concerning Shostakovich that would never be rescinded'. This was that the composer, despite his links with known and condemned enemies of the People, was not to be arrested but instead taken aside and whipped like a jester out of favour with the king: 'In the framework of Russian culture, the extraordinary relationship between Stalin and Shostakovich was profoundly traditional: the ambivalent "dialogue" between tsar and *yurodivy*, and between tsar and poet playing the role of *yurodivy* in order to survive, takes on a tragic incandescence.'

Volkov's theory is compelling. Stalin's relationships with certain artists undoubtedly exuded an almost medieval air of court ritual. 'He thinks poets are shamans who'll put a spell on him,' Osip Mandelstam told his wife Nadezhda, shortly before his arrest in 1934 – and the fact that, for a gross poetical insult to the leader, Mandelstam received only three years' internal exile strongly bears this out. Stalin had a peasant superstition of the oracular kind of artist. Workaday, journalistic types did not impress him and, when he chose to, he destroyed these in quantity.[1] He was, however, fascinated by those around whom the charisma of inspiration wove a tangible magnetism, treating them with a gruff deference appropriate to holy fools or those likewise in thrall to the unseen. A fascinating passage in *Testimony* discusses this vis-à-vis the dictator's relationship with the otherworldly piano virtuoso Maria Yudina, and it seems likely that Stalin had similar feelings concerning Akhmatova and Pasternak, whom he spared in situations which would have been fatal to individuals less obviously possessed by their art. Though Volkov's Shostakovich presents himself as a 'proletarian' artist (in that he did not sit around waiting for inspiration to strike, but treated his work as far as possible like a job), his enormous nervous energy made him intensely charismatic to others, and the strange impression of a boy in a man's body is recorded by many who committed their memories of him to writing. He conformed, in other words, to Stalin's idea of a 'real artist': not a smart operator, but someone who simply couldn't help bursting into verse or song – a sort of higher village idiot.

Caution, however, is necessary on this subject. That Stalin and Shostakovich had the sort of tsar–*yurodivy* relationship suggested by Solomon Volkov is likely to have been true at a later stage, but not, perhaps, as early as 1936. In fact, prior to his *Pravda* editorial on *Lady Macbeth*, Stalin had probably been completely unaware of Shostakovich's career as a serious musician, his own taste inclining more to folk songs and military marches. He was, on the other hand, a lifelong film buff and, with his shrewd nose for propaganda effects, he can hardly have overlooked Shostakovich's pre-eminence in Soviet cinema music – indeed, it was likelier to have been this that initially protected Shostakovich in 1936 rather than his international reputation as a symphonist and opera composer, which would have meant little to Stalin. That the leader quickly got interested in who and what Shostakovich was, though, is more than possible. He liked to sit up at night in the Kremlin, studying the files of his victims and sometimes phoning them to let them know that his all-seeing eye was upon them.[2] Conceivably, the 1936 campaign against Formalism, which

---

[1] Of the seven hundred writers at the First Congress of the Writers' Union in 1934, Ilya Ehrenburg estimates that 'possibly fifty' were still alive in 1960 (*Eve of War*, p. 41).

[2] Naturally, news of these famous calls spread rapidly through the intellectual community, serving as effective ways of maintaining the dictator's terrifying mystique. Bulgakov and Pasternak were recipients of much-discussed midnight telephone conversations and *Testimony* (p. 148) describes how Shostakovich got one in 1949.

he would have overseen if not personally directed, led him to investigate Shostakovich and, as Volkov suspects, issue a special order on him. And it is possible that the rehearsals for the Fourth Symphony were allowed to go ahead on Stalin's nod, to see what Shostakovich would do next.

The problem for Shostakovich was that, whether or not in 1936 he considered emulating Myaskovsky and Shebalin[1] in turning out compromised work to please the authorities, the Fourth Symphony had been conceived and largely completed before the *Pravda* attacks and had nothing placatory about it at all. If Stalin was waiting to hear what he'd do next, that work would need at least to *appear* to toe the line – and yet the Fourth was the most extreme thing he had written, or would ever write. As the rehearsals began under the conductor Fritz Stiedry, Shostakovich must have been in an agony of indecision. The descent of Damocles' sword had been postponed and the possibility of survival seemed good, provided he made the right move. A week after he had finished the symphony, his wife Nina had given birth to their daughter, Galya. With thoughts of suicide put firmly behind him, he had everything to live for.

For a while, he tinkered with the score and hovered nervously at the rehearsals, where Stiedry, terrified at having to conduct anything by an enemy of the People, was making an appalling mess of it and showing no sign of improving. Finally, after ten increasingly tense orchestra calls, he made the only possible decision. In December 1936 he announced that, as it stood, his Fourth Symphony was a failure and would be withdrawn from preparation pending further work on its finale.

Placed in a drawer, the manuscript was lost during the war and Shostakovich had to rewrite it in a two-piano arrangement from his initial sketches in 1946. Periodically questioned about it in the Soviet press, he repeated his line about the symphony's finale and alluded vaguely to its 'grandiosomania', giving the impression that it was beyond repair. Later, using the instrumental parts made for the rehearsals with the Leningrad Philharmonic in 1936, the entire symphony was reconstructed as it had stood at the moment when Shostakovich originally withdrew it – and when, during the Khrushchev period, he was invited to work it into some kind of performable shape, he merely handed this reconstruction to the conductor, Kyrill Kondrashin, saying 'Let them eat it'.[2]

On 20 December 1961, twenty-five years after it had been withdrawn as a failure, the Symphony No. 4 in C minor, Opus 43, was premièred by the Moscow Philharmonic Orchestra note for note as Shostakovich had written it

---

[1] Shebalin had composed a song-symphony, *The Heroes of Perekop*, in 1935, and Myaskovsky's Socialist Realist Sixteenth Symphony, *The Aviators*, elicited an enthusiastic response at its première in Moscow on 24 October 1936.

[2] Kondrashin had suggested cuts, which the composer refused. Later, he tinkered with some of its dynamics and tempi to produce a 'definitive version', authenticated by Boris Tishchenko and published posthumously in 1984.

between 13 September 1935 and 20 May 1936. Clearly he had meant what he said when he had first said it. What, though, had he meant?

While a great deal of ink has been spilled over the worth and significance of Shostakovich's Fourth Symphony, it has so far been done exclusively in technical, rather than historical, terms. No one has attempted to suggest what the Fourth *means* – apart from Shostakovich himself in the more contentious pages of *Testimony*. 'The pre-war years,' he is alleged to have told Volkov in 1973, 'that is what all my symphonies, beginning with the Fourth, are about.'

In the present case, this is almost certainly true. A realist writes about what he sees around him and the fact that the Fourth, conceived between 1934 and 1935 and composed in 1935 and 1936, should concern those years is hardly a surprise. But in what way does it concern those years? Some have guessed that the symphony portrays an emotional crisis in its composer's personal life. Others hear it as a grandiose panorama of Soviet society in the making, its mountainous crescendi as heroic and triumphant. Agreement exists only on the manner in which it achieves its effects: that it is, for one reason or another, a piece that drives its point-making to a pitch of intensity and volume so extreme that this becomes a point in itself. The symphony, wrote the late Hugh Ottaway, is 'on any normal reckoning greatly overscored – but there is no doubt that the effect of physical assault is deliberate'. In other words, this is to some extent a work *about* 'grandiosomania', rather than one merely displaying it. Shostakovich's Fourth, on one level, concerns overstatement and its gigantic orchestra is in itself partly a comment on giganticism.

'Gigantomania' is, in fact, the word used by the thirties economist Nicholas de Basily to describe the mood of public life in Russia during the First and Second Five-Year Plans. From a sense of inferiority to the industrialised West had emerged a tub-thumping boastfulness which quickly departed from any basis in fact or reason, claiming production quotas as 'overfulfilled' by ten times or more and inflating already ambitious estimates into, in de Basily's phrase, 'astronomical figures and projections on a planetary scale'. This was the era of collective farms so huge that labourers spent more time travelling to work on them than driving their tractors; of Pharaonic follies like the vast White Sea Canal, excavated in record time at the cost of 100,000 lives and thereafter hardly used; of an art of titanic impersonality and a public language predicated on relentless exaggeration.

Inevitably, this outer inflation produced reciprocal inner distortions. As the Russian taste for 'scenes' and self-display found new expression in the stentorian melodrama of the show-trials, so the national love of the fantastic lie (*vranyo*) became institutionalised in government statistics and officialese, blending indistinguishably with the downright lie (*lozh*) of conventional political propaganda. Prior to Socialist Realism, literary purveyors of *vranyo* had been merely tall-story tellers, charming their readers with the poignant transparency of their yarns. Ronald Hingley, in his study *The Russian Mind*, has shown how *vranyo* is endemic to Russian life and amusedly tolerated so long as it does not degenerate into compulsion and its practitioners become more tragic than comic. 'How much more painful,' he observes,

> must be the predicament of an internally protesting Soviet *vranyo*-monger who is humiliated by the obligation to produce officially sponsored fantasies. Perhaps he wishes to protest and dissociate himself from the performance, yet he is not prepared to face the penalties for failing to produce *vranyo* at all – or, worse still, for substituting the truth in its place. There is, however, one kind of protest which he can make with relative safety. By subtly overdoing his performance, he can deride the whole process, separating himself mentally from his humiliating position, and thus preserve a measure of self-respect. He is safe in so doing, for who can be certain that the exaggeration is deliberate? Moreover, though interfering 'activists' can easily embarrass someone who shows insufficient zeal, they are less favourably placed when confronted by one who shows an approved brand of zeal, however synthetic, in excess.

As an example of this satire by overstatement, Professor Hingley adduces the straightfaced absurdities of Leonid Leonov's Five-Year Plan novel *Skutarevsky*, which mocks the Stalinist *lozh* by spinning out its optimism to ridiculous lengths. Since *Testimony* makes a similar claim for the finale of Shostakovich's Fifth Symphony, it seems legitimate to wonder whether his Fourth is not cut from the same cloth.

The composer's three previous symphonies open quietly, even slyly, pacing themselves in preparation for later developments. The Fourth, following three brazen Oriental skirls on everything but the bass instruments, crashes straight into a barbaric fortissimo stamping which maintains the same level of snarling ferocity for twenty-seven bars. The shock is considerable. Pasternak had written of 'our unprecedented, impossible state' and there is a towering brutality about this music that speaks of similar things – though Shostakovich, never a merely illustrative composer, is at least as concerned with the psychology of exaggeration as its outer manifestations. The dislocating upward twist in the theme's third bar is, for example, both arbitrary and exasperated, suggesting a destructive rage fundamentally infantile in nature. Likewise intrinsic – to the point of ubiquity – are snappish two-note phrases, expressive of crass irritability (and, as such, prefigured in the satirically crude and stupid policemen's music from *Lady Macbeth*). The very personification of tyranny and egomania, these measures are almost certainly a musical mirror to the excesses of the Stalin personality-cult.

Fanfared by a famously hagiographic article by Radek, the dictator's deification had intensified dramatically at the so-called 'Congress of the Victors' in 1934, where frenzied delegates had hailed him as a superman who could do no wrong. The atmosphere of hysteria at such rallies conceded nothing to the mass-psychosis of Hitler's appearances at Nuremberg. Though not a charismatic psychopath of the Führer's calibre, Stalin as *Vozhd* (leader) employed propaganda and presentation to magnify his image in exactly the same way, a fact clear from *Pravda*'s account of the 7th Congress of the Soviets in January 1935:

> At 6.15, Comrade Stalin appears. All the delegates rise as one man and greet him with a stormy and prolonged ovation. From all parts of the hall come the shouts of 'Long live the Great Stalin', 'Long live our Vozhd.' A new outburst of applause and greetings. Comrade Kalinin declares the congress open, and reminds the audience that it is Comrade Stalin who is the 'instigator, inspirer, and organizer' of the whole gigantic work of the Soviet Union. A new storm of applause passing into an endless ovation. The entire assembly rises and greets Stalin. Cries of 'Long live Stalin! Hurrah!' Comrade Filatov proposes to elect a Praesidium of twenty-six members. The first elected on the Praesidium is Iosef Vissarionovich Stalin. Again cries of 'Hurrah' fill the hall, and the roar of applause is heard for a long time . . .

At the same rally, the writer Avdeyenko epitomized the masochism of the Vozhd's worshippers in a speech that quickly became a touchstone of absurdity in intellectual circles:

> I must sing, shout, cry out aloud my delight and happiness. All is thanks to thee, O great teacher Stalin. Our love, our devotion, our strength, our hearts, our heroism, our life – all are thine. Take them, great Stalin – all is thine, O leader of this great country. People of all times and all nations will give thy name to everything that is fine and strong, to all that is wise and beautiful. When the woman I love gives me a child the first word I will teach it shall be 'Stalin' . . .

That an assiduous *Pravda*-reader like Shostakovich could have been unaware of all this is frankly unbelievable. Indeed, at the time of the planning and writing of his Fourth Symphony, Russia was so much in the grip of a political cult-madness modelled on Fascism that absence of reference to this in so major a work by so tenacious a realist would be, to put it mildly, difficult to explain. As it turns out, the symphony is obviously saturated in the megalomanic spirit of its time and to approach it under any other assumption would be to misunderstand it completely.

Following its aggressive initial outburst, the music subsides into a quieter second group, the strings drifting in what appear to be inchoate reminiscences of classical form and phrasing, somewhat like disintegrated equivalents of the 'old world' themes in the first movement of the Cello Sonata. Psychologically the most penetrating of modern Russian memoirists, Nadezhda Mandelstam has written in detail on the inner impact of outer upheavals under Stalinism and is particularly illuminating on the emotional consequences of being terrorised into artificial enthusiasm: 'An existence like this leaves its mark. We all became slightly unbalanced mentally – not exactly ill, but not normal either: suspicious, mendacious, confused and inhibited in our speech, at the same time putting on a show of adolescent optimism.' Coincidentally or not, the strings of Shostakovich's second subject ramble very much as if in feverish semi-consciousness, until barking trumpets summon them back to the deafening rally of the symphony's opening.

Re-establishing itself, the stamping rhythm builds massively around a glimpse of the first subject (like the view, over the heads of a crowd, of an enormous portrait being carried by in procession) until, energy spent, it finally throbs away into the distance along another street. There is a moment's silence and then the individual responds to what has gone before – not articulately, as in conscious repose, but expressionistically, as in a waking dream. A crescendo rises rapidly from the lower strings into a hysterical, hair-tearing scream of raging Mahlerian anguish (marked *fffff*): a cathartic musical release of the self-repression vital under totalitarianism (recalled by Mme Mandelstam as 'an inner pain greater than the worst of heart attacks')[1]. Stifling itself abruptly (as if terrified to be overheard by the neighbours), the music sinks into the unquiet nocturnal mode of the third of the Opus 42 Fragments or the tensely expectant third scene of *Lady Macbeth*. Here, the distracted strings of the movement's second subject toss restlessly around a tired, vigil-keeping idea introduced on solo bassoon and punctuated softly by the harp-chimes of a faraway clock. The image of a man pacing his apartment at four a.m., brooding and chain-smoking, is irresistible. As with the night-scene in *Lady Macbeth*, suspense and concentration are heightened by pointilliste effects, both passages employing the eerie tolling of a celesta to evoke an atmosphere of nerve-racked hypersensitivity. Again, Nadezhda Mandelstam provides the key: 'If you live in a state of constant terror, always listening for the sound of cars drawing up outside and the doorbell ringing, you begin to have a special awareness of each minute, of each second. Time drags on, acquiring weight and pressing down on the breast like lead. This is not so much a state of mind as a physical sensation which becomes particularly oppressive at night.'

Taken to a choked crescendo by the strings, the vigil theme is resumed by bass clarinet until, as a quiet horn greets the dawn, a bird stirs on E flat clarinet, its drooping two-note motto uncomfortably suggesting that of a cuckoo-clock. (This motif, first heard inconspicuously on bassoon as part of the second subject at figure 7, is destined for a dominant role in the symphony.) The music's skeletal textures now begin to fill rapidly, tension rises, and the dreaded thing finally happens: the secret police arrive, audibly climbing the stairs (figures 46–7) and bursting in through the door on a triumphant crescendo. In a brilliant alienative stroke, Shostakovich switches the two-note motto around

---

[1] In Shostakovich's 1941 *King Lear*, a nearly identical crescendo accompanies the blinding of Gloucester.

in the upper orchestra like torch-beams while the NKVD move grimly through the darkened apartment in the guise of the vigil theme, growled out on tubas and bass clarinet – an uncanny parallel to Orwell's similar use of the nursery rhyme 'Oranges and Lemons' in the arrest scene in *Nineteen Eighty-Four*.

A cinematic jump-cut reveals the first subject capering nonchalantly on piccolo and E flat clarinet (in Roy Blokker's words, 'as if happy to be back and innocently unaware of what has been taking place'). Nonchalance, however, soon turns to mockery, the music accelerating and fuguing with itself, dancing with the shadow of its own dangerousness like a gang of tearaways strutting down an alley. With the apparent implication that such street-bully bravado is the seed of all herd-violence, this swaggering banter suddenly erupts into a *real* fugue – a stampeding presto on the strings which sucks the rest of the orchestra in, section by section, like some sonic tornado. A galloping juggernaut climax of vengefully overstated fury now turns into a reprise of the stamping rhythm before segueing absentmindedly into an inconsequential waltz. Taking Shostakovich at his realist word, the simplest interpretation is that this represents exhausted distraction – an interlude of thankful ease in which the vodka passes and there is time to forget that anything unpleasant has happened. (Memory is a major theme for memoirists of the Stalinist period and this is the first appearance of a motif Shostakovich would return to often, notably in the Tenth Symphony.) The horror, though, won't let go. Six shuddering crescendi rear up, as if trying to haul something back to mind (the last, perhaps significantly, using the *fffff* marking again). Evoked like a demon, the stamping first subject reappears in 6/8. However, it has nothing new to say and the music's impetus is clearly running down. After a dejected reprise of the vigil theme on cor anglais and strings, a reminiscence of the two-note bird-call figure leads into a fatalistic soliloquy on solo violin, the prototype for many 'post-catastrophe' meditations in later Shostakovich works. Though the enormous movement is over, it seems reluctant to make an end of it, continuing to toss restlessly in its sleep as a final, quietly menacing recapitulation of its opening material ticktocks sombrely down to silence.

Some commentators have claimed to see conventional sonata form beneath this wayward design. Something like it is certainly present, but in the form of wreckage, like a bombed building reconstructed in the mind's eye from the pattern made by its collapsed remains. Shostakovich lends shape to his chain of episodes by cross-references and derivations, many of which have not been referred to in the preceding account (the tornado fugue, for example, being an impacted abbreviation of the stamping first subject). Essentially, though, this is concertedly untraditional symphonism, relying more on the innate force of its ideas than on the acquired force of their structural relationship.

As if to satisfy his audience's need for reassuring form, Shostakovich presents his interludial second movement in a simple A-B-A-B-A layout, the A section led by a four-note motto in Beethovenian mould, the B section being a dissonantly angular lament. Conceivably relevant to this is a well-known announcement of the Central Committee in 1932 to the effect that, during its heyday, RAPM had spent too much time discussing the works of Marx and Engels and not enough studying the works of 'Comrade Beethoven'. While it would not do to take this over-literally, it is interesting to note how the thoughtful initiatives of the strings, with their attempts at classical variation and fugue, are repeatedly frustrated by the vulgar mimicry of the woodwind and mutinous crescendi in the brass. Important, too, are the peremptory interruptions of the timpani, reintroducing the ugly two-note motif from the first movement and showing it to have been implicit in the music's steady 3/8 metre from the outset.

The second movement's pattering, interlaced percussion coda – rattling bones, tremolo violins like dead souls hurrying home to the graveyard before sunrise – sets the stage for a finale as expansive as the first movement and even less traditionally symphonic in design. Mahler's is the presiding spirit, the first of the movement's four sections being a funeral march similar in effect to that of his Fifth Symphony. Soft pizzicato basses introduce the rhythm (once again the drooping two-note phrase) and a bassoon announces the theme – a lugubrious, somnambulistic thing dominated by a three-note figure most prominent on solo oboe as an upward-leaping fanfare falling just short of an octave. As in Mahler, there is about all this an objective edge of mockery, a deliberate hollowness, which keeps the listener's ears alert to tell-tale nuances of expression, such as the theatrical sighing of muted violins at figure 157. However, as the cortège gets nearer, rising in pitch and weight, Shostakovich scales new grim heights of visionary satire: inverting the three-note fanfare in a blaze of trumpets, the plodding automaton sorrow throws back its hood to reveal a grin of insane triumph. What, the audience is forced to ask, is being buried here?

Hushing into a wistful violin epitaph for the lost past, the march resumes its plodding tread, passing slowly out of ear-shot in the manner of the processional music at the beginning of the first movement. Rippling Mahlerian woodwind mark a scene-changing pause until the familiar two-note motto leaps from the basses to land in the second section, an agitated 3/4 allegro apparently hell-bent on jumping out of its own skin. As if to underline the two-note motto's symbolism of brutal stupidity, Shostakovich now strips the texture away to leave it mechanically interlocked with a shadow of itself (and then of a third version upside-down). This starkly Constructivist passage proceeds in its own isolation for no less than ninety bars, getting nowhere, before the rest of the orchestra overrules it and begins to build up a head of steam over a motor-rhythm bass. At the crest of a runaway crescendo, the whole orchestra erupts in thunderous unison on a version of the vigil theme from the first movement. Things are happening too fast for reflection, however, and the music begins to break up under its own weight, trombones throwing two-note figures all over the stave as the noise slackens away on a falling three-note motif (♪♪ ♩) screamed out on the violins and echoed emphatically on the timpani.

This, an allusion to Sergei and Sonietka's smugly perfidious duet from Act IV of *Lady Macbeth*, is one of Shostakovich's most complex musical codes, versions of it occurring throughout his work. Sometimes sly, often menacing and occasionally even spiteful, it has many faces and one of its meanings would appear to be 'mask'. Prominent in the first movement of the First Symphony, it also features in The Fool's music for the 1970 *King Lear*, implying clowning with serious intent; the Fourteenth Symphony uses it similarly, in its sixth movement, to suggest mirthless laughter. More frequently, as in *Lady Macbeth*, it denotes a kind of derisive duplicity – a trickster figure bringing disillusionment – and as an archetypal experience seemingly formative in the composer's life it can best be summarised as signifying 'betrayal' (of trust or, originally, of innocence). So it does at this point in the Fourth Symphony where, as the horns sustain the first of the movement's prolonged pedal-points, the scenery changes yet again to usher in its third section: a beguiling ballet divertissement on the subject of treachery.

Referring to the bitter, suicidal feelings induced by his 'show-whipping' before the Composers' Union in February 1936, the Shostakovich of *Testimony* plausibly observes: 'Some of these thoughts you can find, if you wish, in my Fourth Symphony. In the last pages, it's all set out rather precisely.' In the light of this, it seems probable that the appearance of the betrayal motif marks the point at which he resumed work on the Fourth after his public reprimand. This divertissement, foreshadowed by the inconsequential waltz at figure 81 in the first movement, develops, during its ten or twelve minutes, into one of the most complex and allusive passages in all of Shostakovich. So intricate is its interplay between the crude two-note figure and the betrayal motif, and so virtuosic the mingling of the music's rhythmic and stylistic elements that it would require several pages of orthodox analysis to do it justice. All that will be done here is to characterise the whole and mark out its main subdivisions.

In all probability this movement-within-a-movement is a musical dramatisation of Shostakovich's humiliation at the Composers' Union conference. With his talent for mimicry and interest in characterisation by 'intonation', he was ideally suited to pen a sequence of instrumental character sketches drawn from those he observed during the course of this charade. A sensitive performance (such as, on record, Kondrashin's or, with reservations, Rozhdestvensky's) makes almost visible the cavalcade of Gogolian grotesques by whom the composer was traduced and condemned in February 1936.

A little strutting promenade for bassoons and giggling piccolo leads us into the hall where thrumming harps call the conference to order. A wan waltz (the composer?) enters and sits dejectedly while flute and piccolo trill the opening remarks in a mood of schoolboy hilarity soon dispelled by three table-thumping chords across the full orchestra. The dismal subject of the two-note figure is now raised by a horn and seconded by the violas, over another brooding pedal-point. For a moment, the music freezes, as though lost in thought – then perks up and resumes waltzing in sentimental mood (short, by a hair's breadth, of actual Mahlerian string glissandi). Impatient with this, the rest of the orchestra hastens into a brisk *galop*, leaving the waltz behind. An opinionated bassoon now takes the floor, cheered on by skittering Rossinian violins and eagerly agreed with by an excitedly gesticulating xylophone. The blustering of a trombone momentarily attracts the attention of a pair of sycophantic piccolos, but when the bassoon insists on repeating itself word for word, the rest of the orchestra switches smartly back into waltz-time. A half-hearted attempt by some clarinets to smooth things over is sternly rebuked by the imperturbable bassoon and the 'betrayal' motif, insinuated on piccolo and trombone, quickly becomes a topic of heated debate among the woodwind, some of whom, in their anxiety to see the question from all sides, consider it standing on their heads. Meanwhile, the trombone, sounding a little the worse for wear and in any case ill-equipped to keep up with the intricate rhythmic discussions proceeding in the strings, relapses gratefully onto the two-note figure before finally running out of puff. Another pedal-point is reached, an adjournment is wearily requested by clarinet and oboe, and, after grave consideration, the lower strings consent. Flute and piccolo make the closing remarks and the violins file out in spirited conversation.

The aforegoing resembles nothing so much as a musicalisation of the trial of the Knave of Hearts in *Alice in Wonderland*, and it is a strange coincidence that the only other music like it, Stravinsky's *Jeu de Cartes*, was being composed at exactly the same time in Paris. However, Shostakovich's deceptive frivolity has a serious intent and, as the longed-for peace of a pedal-point beckons once again, he snaps a carefully prepared trap. Looming up on a rolling timpani tidal-wave, a dissonant four-chord sequence (*fffff* for the third time) sweeps us without warning back into the gigantomanic world of the symphony's opening bars. Much debated during the divertissement, the fanfare from the funeral march reappears in the midst of this terrifying din and soon the march itself is climbing up through an obliterating landslide of sound, as if determined to achieve a crazed apotheosis. The final explosion, quite possibly the loudest music ever written, subsides onto a vast 129-bar pedal-point over which the funeral fanfare rises in desolate resignation. Fusing the personal and the universal, Shostakovich has reached the end of his world and the end of the world at large. Lit fitfully by the cold radiance of the celesta's valediction, the symphony pulses gradually away into lifeless darkness.

Frequently dismissed, in the absence of any grasp of its context or motives, as an undisciplined and bombastic failure, the Fourth Symphony, properly comprehended, emerges as a triumph of intellectual control, energetic drive, and auditory imagination. At twenty-nine, Shostakovich had created a milestone in symphonism that, under any other circumstances, would have gone on to alter the course of Western music. Born, however, in an age of unprecedented tyranny and under a regime fundamentally hostile to the human spirit, it almost vanished forever and found its audience only after a quarter of a century of imposed silence. A further thirty years on, neither this amazing work nor the terrible circumstances which shaped it are any closer to being generally understood.

Western writers have often confessed themselves mystified by the *Pravda* attack on *Lady Macbeth* and Shostakovich's withdrawal of the Fourth Symphony during the difficult time which followed it. Some, unable to accept the affair as simply a matter of Stalin's incoherent wrath, have examined the statutes of Socialist Realism for a sensible solution expressible in purely cultural terms. Others, accepting the involvement of political purposes, have tried to understand it as a necessary symbolic expression of national intellectual solidarity at a time when the rise of Fascism was threatening peace in Europe. Obviously, the common factor behind such explanations is a wish, for whatever reason, to avoid imputing sordid or irrational motives to the Soviet system as a whole. In the light of *glasnost*, however, it is easier to accept that events like the 'disciplining' of Shostakovich in 1936 might have been side-effects of something altogether more sinister and less excusable than its first observers suspected.

The complete truth of what happened in 1936 is still not clear. Galina Vishnevskaya contends that it was a plot on the part of Shostakovich's Proletkult enemies, whereby Stalin and Molotov were inveigled into visiting the Bolshoi's new production of *Lady Macbeth* by disaffected singers who wanted the opera taken off. Stalin's adverse reaction was, in their view, guaranteed by his recent enjoyment of Ivan Dzerzhinsky's simple-minded 'song-opera' *Quiet Flows the Don* which suggested that a real modern opera would confuse and annoy him. The scheme worked as expected and, in due course, *Pravda* conveyed Stalin's approval of *Quiet Flows the Don*, hinting that the work was henceforth to be taken as a model of Socialist Realist music by all Soviet composers.[1]

Though this rings true enough, it fails to explain why the attack on musical Formalism was followed immediately by a wave of similar assaults on architecture, painting, drama, literature, and the cinema (see Appendix 3). Some commentators see the Formalism campaign as a temporary fad of the security forces during the steady build-up of the Terror, a fixation triggered by Stalin's disgust over *Lady Macbeth* which soon metamorphosed into a full-scale purge. Again, there is probably some truth in this – indeed, the well-informed Isaac Babel thought so at the time, telling Ilya Ehrenburg: 'In six months they'll leave the Formalists in peace and start some other campaign.' There again, his guess

---

[1] The irony of this is that, had it not been for Shostakovich (to whom it is dedicated), *Quiet Flows the Don* would never have been staged. Dzerzhinsky showed his effort to his hero, Shostakovich, in 1932, who saw how bad it was and offered to help him with it. Premièred in 1934, the opera flopped. After the 1936 affair, it was awarded a Stalin Prize and stayed in the repertoire for thirty years. While, during Shostakovich's ordeal before the Composers' Union, Dzerzhinsky joined Knipper in urging that he be 'helped', at the 1948 inquiry he changed sides, violently denouncing his former idol.

on this occasion was wrong. The drive against Formalism continued through the Terror and was still going when he himself was arrested in 1939.

The likeliest explanation of all is that the cultural purge of the late thirties was a premeditated stage in the progressive mechanisation of Soviet intellectual life, a process which had been initiated by the Cultural Revolution and was to be taken up again after the war during the late forties. According to this view, the attack on Shostakovich was a piece of opportunism by Stalin, who had long been pondering an artistic extension of the post-Kirov Terror and simply seized the opportunity presented to him by *Lady Macbeth*. The advantages of this thesis are that it accounts for the speed at which the campaign against Formalism developed and explains why Shostakovich, though publicly unpersoned for eighteen months, was unofficially let off the hook towards the end of 1936. Stalin, in other words, though genuinely displeased by *Lady Macbeth*, was by no means as infuriated as he made out. (As for the view, frequently expressed in Western writing on Shostakovich, that the 1936 affair did him good both personally and artistically and was therefore justified whatever its original motives may have been, this will be examined towards the end of the present book, touching as it does on issues beyond the scope of the present narrative.)

In as much as he did not, officially, exist after the February reprimand (the only references to him in the press being reprints of unsympathetic reviews from abroad), Shostakovich understandably kept his head down during the summer of 1936, confining himself to revising his 1931 film score *Golden Mountains*. The Terror was intensifying in the approach to the first of the three late thirties show-trials, and the Formalism campaign was now resulting in the the harassment of many writers who were friends or ex-friends of his.[1] A ray of hope broke through in October when Leningrad's Pushkin Drama Theatre commissioned three numbers from him for their production of *Salute to Spain!* by the former RAPP playwright Alexander Afinogenov. This, however, faded away in November when Afinogenov was criticised and the play pulled off.[2] (It was in the wake of this fiasco that Shostakovich withdrew the Fourth Symphony.)

---

[1] Among those criticised in 1936 were Pasternak, Babel, Zabolotsky, Leonov, Katayev, Fedin, and Vsevolod Ivanov. Boris Pilnyak and the Communist writer Galina Serebryakova were tried together for treason and sent to the camps. Yuri Olesha (who, during the *Lady Macbeth* affair, had testified that the opera personally insulted him) was arrested for his screenplay *Stern Youth*, which so fervently hymned the image of the young Soviet Superman that he was accused of importing Nazi ideals of Aryan purity and jailed as a Fascist.

[2] Another score quashed at this time was his miniature comic opera *The Tale of a Priest and His Servant Balda*, after a story by Pushkin and set to animated pictures by Mikhail Tsekhanovsky. About to be released, the film was suddenly withdrawn and later destroyed during the bombing of Leningrad in 1941. Shostakovich rescued part of the opera as a suite of six numbers, and his Soviet biographer, Sofia Khentova, has since reconstructed it from other fragments.

During the winter of 1936–7, he received three further commissions: Four Songs on Verses by Pushkin for bass and piano (on the occasion of the centenary of the poet's death) and two film scores, *Maxim's Return* and *Volochayevsk Days*. These he had finished by the end of January, at which point the anti-Formalism drive hit the cinema and, fearing to be swept up in a second wave of persecution, he again stopped working. Named as 'saboteurs' of the Soviet film industry were Russia's leading directors, Eisenstein and Dovzhenko, neither of whom were anything but models of political orthodoxy. The shock of this reverberated through the intellectual community: if such men were not safe, no one was. At a three-day conference in February which pedantically re-enacted the scenes in the Composers' Union a year before, the internationally famous Eisenstein was accused of 'overweening conceit and aloofness from Soviet reality' and forced to acknowledge the 'individualist illusion' of his film *Bezhin Meadow*.

One can only speculate on Shostakovich's attitude to these events. Probably he felt some grim satisfaction in not being alone in suffering persecution and perhaps an element of hysterical relief that it was now happening to someone else instead of him. On the other hand, unable to foresee the future, he must have despaired that the nightmare would never end or that the secret police might yet come stamping up his stairs. Most of all, he would have been gripped by the fear now stitched tightly and from top to toe into the fabric of Soviet society. This, however, whilst paralysing an individual's power of expression, was not in itself a wholly static condition. As with solitary confinement, an immobilising fear could eventually serve to stiffen the resolve and discipline the will. 'Better scared than spared,' writes Nadezhda Mandelstam. 'Akhmatova and I once confessed to each other that the most powerful sensation we had ever known – stronger than love, jealousy, or any other human feeling – was terror and what goes with it: the horrible and shameful awareness of utter helplessness, of being tied hand and foot. There are different kinds of fear. As long as it is accompanied by a sense of shame, one is still a human being, not an abject slave. It is the sense of shame that gives fear its healing power and offers hope of regaining inner freedom.' Very possibly, shame was healing Shostakovich that winter. At any rate, *something* must have happened to him – or subsequent developments become impossible to understand.

Along with greater determination and control, anyone surviving the kind of experience referred to by Nadezhda Mandelstam would have been bound to feel another powerful, and powerfully motivating, sensation: anger. Disciplined anger is, for instance, the driving force behind the enormous, obsessive, painstakingly vengeful works of the leading literary chronicler of Stalinism, Alexander Solzhenitsyn. To a large extent, the same is true of Shostakovich's output after 1936. Certainly it would explain how and why, having been reduced to disowning a work of monumental antagonism to Stalinism in December 1936, he should, only three months later, decide to embark on a sequel expressing precisely the same sentiments in only slightly less obvious form.

In his monograph on Shostakovich, Norman Kay is alone among Western writers in acknowledging the courage the composer displayed in writing his Fifth Symphony, in that it wholly ignored the rigid prohibitions on tragedy and abstraction in force in 1937. The work, he guesses, must have involved 'a gargantuan effort of will'. This is true, but not precisely for the reasons Kay gives. To even begin to understand the incredible single-minded bravery of the Fifth requires first having some idea of its historical background – the terrifying life of 'black marias at night and demonstrations by day' described in the books of Shostakovich's literary brother-in-arms Solzhenitsyn and the many other memoirists of this extraordinary period.

Under Article 58, Section 12 of the Soviet Criminal Code (1926), failure to denounce anyone guilty of crimes listed in other sections of the Code was punishable by death or imprisonment for an unlimited period. As a corollary of this, the 'duty to inform' was endlessly played upon by the government and security organs. 'The authorities,' recalls Nadezhda Mandelstam, 'did everything to encourage "fearless unmaskers" who, "without respect for persons", showed up "survivals of the old psychology" in their colleagues.' Under such conditions, the practice of denouncing neighbours and even relations out of sheer malice was common, while 'unmasking' one's workmates rapidly became an accepted way of gaining promotion. Once Stalin had control, however, the duty to inform was institutionalised by simply bringing people in off the street and scaring them into spying for the police.[1] The idea behind this was not so much that of creating a centralised network of informers as of binding those involved irrevocably to the system. 'The more people who could be implicated and compromised,' observes Mme Mandelstam, 'the more traitors, informants, and police spies there were, the greater would be the number of people supporting the regime and longing for it to last thousands of years.'

By comparison with the piecemeal strategy of recruiting informers, the Terror was a blitzkrieg, a full-scale invasion. Denunciation being too slow a process to keep up with the demands of so vastly expanded an operation, the NKVD were directed to detain people at random, torturing the names of 'accomplices' from them so as to ensure that arrests would proliferate at the required rate of thousands per week. As the madness intensified in late 1936, orders were sent out from NKVD headquarters for indiscriminate arrests by quota – 10,000 enemies of the People from this town, 15,000 from another. (Stalin had fixed the number of 'unreliables' in the population at five per cent, and this was the only way to make up the figures.) The quota system was soon

---

[1] This happened to the concert pianist Vladimir Ashkenazy as a young man in Leningrad and he found it extremely difficult to extricate himself from his predicament (Parrott, pp. 77–84).

so prevalent that the police gave up all pretence. Robert Conquest records the case of a Tatar woman who, arrested as a Trotskyite, was reallocated by her interrogators as a bourgeois nationalist on the grounds that they had enough Trotskyites but were 'short on nationalists', even though they'd arrested all the Tatar writers they could think of. Dreaming up plausible crimes to fill out these quotas rapidly became a joke and the entries on charge-sheets correspondingly absurd. Conquest writes of a Jewish engineer accused of designing a scientific institute in the form of half a swastika, of a Kiev professor arrested for mentioning the depth of the Dnieper River in a textbook, of a woman arraigned for saying the disgraced Marshal Tukhachevsky was handsome (she got ten years). Nadezhda Mandelstam recalls that the wife of the poet Sergei Spasski was accused in 1937 of having wanted to blow up a monument to her uncle, even though no such monument existed. 'The police interrogators – with higher permission, needless to say – amused themselves with gruesome jokes of this kind, particularly in Leningrad.'

Such random instability swiftly shook Soviet society to its foundations, cracking social relations apart like rotten floorboards. Returning to Moscow from assignment in Spain, Ilya Ehrenburg found the city in a state of paranoid catatonia with every other friend or acquaintance he asked after 'taken'. In the offices of *Izvestia*, even the boards displaying the names of department chiefs had gone. A secretary told him that it wasn't worth having new ones made: 'Here today, gone tomorrow.' A writer he met sighed, 'What terrible times! You're at a loss to know whom to butter up and whom to run down.' After nearly three years of incessant stress, social cohesion had completely collapsed. People no longer trusted each other and love was a rare and improbable bloom hanging on here and there in a landscape of sterile grey. The unshockable Isaac Babel told Ehrenburg: 'Today a man talks frankly only with his wife – at night, with the blanket pulled over his head.' In fact, it was then common for couples not to talk at all in case one of them should turn out to be an informer.[1]

Why had things reached this state? What sensible reason could there be for smashing a society to pieces like this? These questions were much whispered about within the intellectual community and it is a tribute to the success of Stalin's self-deification that, despite all this tense speculation, the Terror was rarely laid at his door – indeed, most thought it was entirely the work of Nikolai Yezhov, then head of the NKVD (after whom the events of 1935-8 came to be known as the Yezhovshchina, or Yezhov's Time). Stalin was looked up to as a mythical being far above day-to-day affairs. Rumour (almost certainly started on his orders) had it that he knew nothing of the mass disappearances; 'they' were concealing them from him. 'If only,' cried Pasternak to Ehrenburg one

---

[1] Mikoyan, referring to a confidential memorandum from Yezhov in 1938, mentions by name several who denounced brothers, husbands, and fathers, declaring proudly: 'Such facts are impossible in a bourgeois country, but here numerous examples can be cited' (Basily, p. 141).

night on Lavrushensky Lane, 'someone would tell Stalin about it!' Babel, who knew Yezhov's wife and occasionally visited their house in order to study the psychology of the new barbarism at close quarters, was unusual in holding a different view. Passing Ehrenburg at the Metropol Hotel in 1936, he murmured, 'Yezhov is only the instrument'.

The questions so urgent in 1937 remain so today. At the apex of the Terror, half a million were shot and seven million dispatched to the camps in a period of just over a year. Cautious estimates of the population of the Gulag by 1938 range between nine and fifteen million.[1] One in ten adults were behind the wire. Why did Stalin do it?

Beyond doubt, the first purpose of the Terror was to freeze independent thought in order to allow Stalin to hold on to power. As Nadezhda Mandelstam explains:

> The principles and aims of mass terror have nothing in common with ordinary police work or with security. The only purpose of terror is intimidation. To plunge the whole country into a state of chronic fear, the number of victims must be raised to astronomical levels, and on every floor of every building there must always be several apartments from which the tenants have suddenly been taken away. The remaining inhabitants will be model citizens for the rest of their lives.

A second important motive was the creation of a huge slave labour force with which to exploit the virgin territories of Siberia – to work in the mines and forests, to build roads, railways, dams, factories, new cities, and more concentration camps. Such a labour force was cheap to run because, having no rights, it was unable to demand adequate food and shelter. This, though, meant a high death-rate[2] and a consequent need to ensure that slave caravans streamed steadily out of the cities of the west and into the taiga and deserts of the east. In 1937 Akhmatova secretly wrote a poem describing the once-beautiful city of Leningrad as a needless appendage of its prisons, through which hundreds of thousands of its citizens were being processed into the Gulag. She was not exaggerating. By 1941 slave labour would account for more than one-fifth of Russia's total work force.

The third reason for the Terror is, however, perhaps the most terrifying of

---

[1] The lower figure is Robert Conquest's (*The Great Terror*, pp. 333ff.), the higher an average of official NKVD estimates. Galina von Meck (see above, p. 92n) reckoned the total nearer twenty-five million. The most recent figures released in the USSR support the higher estimates.

[2] The death-rate on the White Sea Canal was seven hundred per day (Conquest, *The Great Terror*, p. 364). Conquest estimates that most camps lost half their prisoners every two to three years. Two million died in the Gulag between January 1937 and December 1938.

all. Ultimately planned as one phase of a sustained programme of internal repression which commenced at Stalin's takeover in 1928 and was still in progress when he died in 1953, it was deliberately taken far beyond all reasonable bounds in order to smash conventional social relations forever, so making way for the creation of Homo Sovieticus, the New Man of Communism. 'The word "conscience",' writes Nadezhda Mandelstam of the early thirties, 'had gone out of ordinary use since its function had been taken over first by "class feeling" and later by "the good of the state".' This, however, was only a prelude. Using Pavlovian methods, those behind the Terror took things a stage further, working to disintegrate relationships in such a way that everyone in Russia was in effect placed in solitary confinement. The next stage, in which those isolated by fear were, by propagandist brainwashing, to have their individual feelings replaced by communal ones, was interrupted by the Second World War. As soon as the war was over, though, the process was resumed, reaching its chilly zenith around 1950. The Terror, in other words, was part of a social experiment into the adaptability of human nature with the ultimate goal of producing a nation of human robots programmed to love only the state.[1]

Apart from the obvious fact that it could never be publicly declared, let alone advertised to the rest of the world, the secrecy in which the Terror proceeded was a functional part of its Pavlovian method. With public life full of non-stop optimism and the metallic braying of loudspeakers, the individual entered a condition akin to schizophrenia: nocturnally isolated, diurnally overwhelmed by bogus communality ('black marias at night, demonstrations by day'). The technique was designed gradually to artificialise all feelings (especially those which might produce independent thoughts), an effect reinforced by broadcasting incessant falsehoods through the propaganda media. (To admit that you did not believe what you read in the papers was in itself a crime.) Preparing the way for the final abolition of privacy, this splitting of public and private produced a society of masks behind which real faces were maintained only to the extent that their owners realised what was happening and could summon the inner strength to resist. The stress of this was terrible. 'We were capable,' recalls Nadezhda Mandelstam, 'of coming to work with a smile on our face after a night in which our home had been searched or a member of the family arrested. It was essential to smile – if you didn't, it meant you were afraid or discontented. This nobody could afford to admit – if you were afraid, then you must have a bad conscience. The mask was taken off only at home, and then not always – even from your children you had to conceal how horror-struck you were; otherwise, God save you, they might let something slip in school.'

It was this society of masks which filed smiling into the Philharmonic Hall in Leningrad on 21 November 1937 to hear the world première of Shostakovich's Symphony No. 5 in D minor, Opus 47. It was this society of masks that broke

---

[1] A thoughtful analysis of this is made in Mikhail Heller's *Cogs in the Soviet Wheel* (1988). See also Chapter 6 and Appendix 1 of this volume.

down and wept during the symphony's slow movement and, at the work's close, erupted into passionate applause that raged longer than the music itself.

Inasmuch as the concert might have ended with his arrest, the Shostakovich of *Testimony* understandably remembered the occasion well: 'The atmosphere was highly charged, the hall was filled – as they say, all the best people were there, and all the worst too. It was definitely a critical situation, and not only for me. Which way would the wind blow? That's what was worrying members of the select audience – people in literature, culture, and physical culture. That's what had them in a feverish state.'

By the end of the evening the issue was beyond doubt. Shostakovich had regained his supremacy in Soviet music at a stroke and guaranteed his own rehabilitation to the world of the officially existent. As for the deeper significance of what had happened, that was difficult to gauge, and it became more so forty years later when *Testimony* cast serious doubts over the symphony's meaning. Was it, as Soviet critics held, a confessional work in which its composer rehearsed his own redemption by the grace of the Communist Party? Or was it, as certain revisionists now insisted, a musical memorial for the millions of Russians who had disappeared or died at the time it was being written?

Most Western writers stuck to the Soviet line, shaking their heads at those who fell for the 'Cold War interpretative tactics' they saw in their opponents' views. Emigrés who had known Shostakovich took the revisionist line, arguing that the Fifth Symphony was a dissident work cloaked in a disguise deceptive only to the uninformed. The most eloquent revisionist was Solomon Volkov: 'In the thirties, at the time of the great purges, music was the only real force that could speak to the people – and could say "Look, that's what happened to us. Hear closely, I am speaking for you. You are all silent because there is a tremendous fear and purges and deportations going on. But I will speak for you." – That's what the Fifth Symphony is all about.'

An important plank in the revisionist platform was that Russian audiences had seen the inner meaning of the Fifth from the very beginning. Volkov's Shostakovich is unequivocal on this: 'Of course they understood, they understood what was happening around them and they understood what the Fifth was about.' But did they? In another part of *Testimony*, the composer is recorded as admitting to his astonishment that 'the man who considers himself its greatest interpreter does not understand my music. He says that I wanted to write exultant finales for my Fifth and Seventh symphonies but I couldn't manage it.' The man in question was Yevgeny Mravinsky, conductor of the Leningrad Philharmonic Orchestra from 1937 to 1985. Mravinsky premièred Shostakovich's Fifth, Sixth, Eighth, Ninth, and Tenth Symphonies and was for years the composer's most trusted interpreter. (Maxim Shostakovich affirmed in 1983 that, notwithstanding the remarks on Mravinsky in *Testimony*, his performances remained 'closest to my father's thoughts'.) That so close a colleague was capable of mistaking Shostakovich's basic intentions in the Fifth Symphony argues that the margin for error in understanding the work was wider than the composer and his apologists make out.

Yuri Yelagin, who was at the Leningrad concert, reports a general euphoria afterwards, but says nothing about the music's meaning, let alone whether he or anyone else had grasped it: 'Everyone rose and the auditorium shook with applause. Shostakovich came out and took dozens of bows. When thirty minutes later my friend and I left the auditorium the ovation was still under way and Shostakovich was still acknowledging the applause. Shaken by the emotional experience we wandered for a long time along the shores of the Neva. We could not bear the thought of returning to the hotel and going to sleep.' Yelagin's is a description of intense feeling, rather than of an experience absorbed and understood – nor is such a thing to be found in any contemporary impression of the Fifth Symphony. In fact, the commonest reaction the Fifth seems to have called from contemporary Russian listeners was simple relief at hearing tragic emotion expressed during a time when genuine feeling was being systematically destroyed by the Terror. Galina von Meck, in a passage on the effect of hearing music in the labour camps, describes a radio broadcast of the Fifth in just such generalised terms. The music's emotion was, to her as to others, evidently authentic – and, in an era of enforced artificiality, that in itself was almost unbearably moving.

On the face of it, this weakens the revisionist case for the Fifth Symphony in that the mere presence of tragic feeling in a work cannot be taken as a guarantee of any specific underlying attitude, even in a society where tragedy is banned. Indeed, the tragic side of the Fifth was recognised immediately by Soviet critics and used as the basis for a theory of its meaning diametrically opposed to that of the revisionists. Nor does it discredit the Soviet critics to point out that they had either to find a way of assimilating this tragic aspect or condemn a work which had sparked a reaction unprecedented in modern musical history.[1] Probable motives are one thing, facts another. Even the overwhelming evidence of background and association documented in this book would be insufficient to counter Soviet claims about the Fifth Symphony if the work itself did not demonstrably do the same.

The Soviet theory of the Fifth, developed to accommodate it within the framework of Socialist Realism, is that it expresses the progress of an intellectual from a state of 'individualist illusion' to triumphant self-transcendence in solidarity with the people and recognition of the inevitable apotheosis of Communism. According to the thinking behind this view, the condition of individualism,

---

[1] According to Mstislav Rostropovich, 'The government would have been delighted to execute (Shostakovich), the same thing they did to Meyerhold at the same time. But it so happened that the ovations after the Fifth Symphony lasted more than 40 minutes. They had never seen such an audience success. And of course the government knew that, so they put a face on it, saying, "We've taught him and now he's writing acceptable music" ' (Rothstein, pp. 50–2).

because isolated, is tragic – but it is also superficial (as all tragic feelings are) in that it ignores the redeeming profundities of 'Marxist truth'. Since the staging of Olesha's *A List of Assets*, the commonest symbol of individualism in Soviet culture had been Shakespeare's Hamlet, a man locked in the torture chamber of his own limited ideas. Incorporating this ready-made concept into their analyses of the Fifth, Soviet critics were soon talking about its individualism as 'Hamletesque' and referring to the work itself as the 'Hamlet Symphony'. From here, it was a short step to identifying its beleaguered hero as Shostakovich himself and discussing all his music in terms of its composer's so-called 'Hamlet aspect'.

The Hamlet theory of Shostakovich and his Fifth Symphony was not born without a struggle, the debate first focusing on whether the work was 'subjective' (autobiographical) or 'objective' (about society). The latter view, a conventional Socialist Realist answer, was rejected for failing to explain why the music had so much tragedy in it, but the final choice could not help being some sort of compromise between the two and, in the end, it turned out to be a highly effective one. With the Hamlet theory, the Soviet authorities invented a myth about the composer which could be used to account for all deviations from optimism on his part and as a simple explanation for any punishment they deemed it necessary to wreak on him as a result. This official Soviet view of Shostakovich as a Hamlet figure was received with great interest in the West.

It must be said that Shostakovich himself contributed to all this in no small measure. Interviewed about the symphony at the time, he let himself be quoted to the effect that it concerned 'the making of a man' and signed (perhaps even draft-wrote) articles similarly helpful to the authorities – notably including one on 'the possibility of Soviet tragedy' which smoothed the work's assimilation into the mainstream of Socialist Realism. Most dutiful of all was the Fifth Symphony's famous subtitle: 'A Soviet Artist's Practical Creative Reply to Just Criticism.' With such apparent eagerness to please, it is hardly surprising that the piece was for so long accepted as officially described.

In *Testimony*, Shostakovich fiercely renounces all this, in particular denying that the Fifth's finale was ever meant as the exultant thing critics took it for: 'What exultation could there be? I think it is clear to everyone what happens in the Fifth. The rejoicing is forced, created under threat, as in *Boris Godunov*. It's as if someone were beating you with a stick and saying, "Your business is rejoicing, your business is rejoicing", and you rise, shaky, and go marching off, muttering, "Our business is rejoicing, our business is rejoicing". What kind of apotheosis is that? You have to be a complete oaf not to hear that.'

There is about this passage a vehemence that stands out sharply from the sardonic dryness of *Testimony*'s prevailing style. Questions about the Fifth Symphony seem to have been a sore point for its composer – indeed, sore enough for him to feel no remorse in implying that the supremely sensitive conductor Yevgeny Mravinsky was an oaf. Suddenly we find ourselves back at square one, wondering if he had something to hide, whether the Fifth was truly the sacrificial offering it was originally thought to be and Shostakovich's latterday anger about it actually rooted in shame. There were, after all, many illustrious precedents. Both Osip Mandelstam and Pasternak had humiliated themselves in verses praising Stalin during the Terror and Prokofiev had done likewise in his *Cantata for the 20th Anniversary of October*. No matter what the evidence of his previous career (or of the indisputably dissident Fourth Symphony), there remains a possibility that Shostakovich gave in to fear in the finale of his Fifth Symphony and compromised himself in a way he later found hard to face.

If the Shostakovich of 1973 is to be believed over the Shostakovich of 1937, the Fifth Symphony must speak for itself – with reference to its background, but without *depending* on it.

The absolute minimum which Shostakovich can be assumed to have deduced from his reprimand in the Composers' Union is that his music was too complex, technically and emotionally, for the requirements of Socialist Realism. *Pravda* had described *Lady Macbeth* as 'a farrago of chaotic, nonsensical sounds'. Knipper, Asafiev, and Dzerzhinsky had said that its composer should be helped to 'straighten himself out'. Shostakovich knew that he was being told to simplify his music. More than that, he knew that this meant submitting to the deadening one-dimensional naiveties of Socialist Realism, itself a kind of revenge of the Proletkult, whose work he had openly derided. Yet, unpersoned in an era of unprecedented state terrorism, he appeared to have no choice but to comply.

Faced with this situation in April 1937, he must have looked for a way out. All eyes were upon him – or would be when he submitted the finished article. If he were to do anything but yield, it had to be subtle. His old vein of satire had been denounced and would not be tolerated so blatantly again. On the other hand, to fall back on giving cautious vent to his tragic side, whilst otherwise thumping the tub like everyone else, would have amounted to self-betrayal. A man of such strong feelings cannot have contemplated abandoning his inner principles with anything but nausea. To be obliged to speak like a fool was bad enough in the realm of words; to have to do it in his own first language of music would have been an admission not merely of cowardice but of technical inadequacy. Somehow he had to turn simplicity into a virtue, mocking it by the unanswerable device of making great art of it.

One work had pulled off this paradox thirty-seven years before: Mahler's Fourth Symphony. Commencing in a mode of childish simplicity which had its audiences scoffing, it went on to develop this material so bewilderingly that even the dullest listeners would realize they had been fooled. Shostakovich could not afford to enlighten the dullards in his audience, but he could let the intelligent know what he was up to by adapting Mahler's opening trick: repeating a single note over and over again. (Mahler's Fourth starts with twenty-four quaver F sharps tapped along with by infant-school sleighbells.)

The first four bars of Shostakovich's Fifth Symphony consist of an austere vaulting theme in canon on the strings, descending via a motto rhythm to three repeated A's on the violins. (The resemblance of the vaulting theme to the opening of Stravinsky's *Apollon Musagètes* of 1928 is striking, but probably coincidental.) A large part of the first movement is based on these initial bars and they are packed with the same meaningfully truncated phrases that characterise the Fourth Symphony. The vaulting theme, for example, is a succession of two-note figures reminiscent of the Fourth's dominating two-note motif; the descending motto rhythm in bar 3 is that of a military side drum; and the reiterated A's are the seed of Shostakovich's Mahler strategy – his blackly ironic attempt to 'straighten himself out' and comply with the simplifications required of him by *Pravda* and the Composers' Union. There is little Mahlerian gentleness here, though. At the end of the symphony, these A's, deprived of even their initial minimal rhythmic interest, will be screamed out by the entire orchestra 252 times in a regular quaver row (as Vishnevskaya puts it, 'like nails being pounded into one's brain').[1]

As a core component of the symphony, the motif of repeated notes recurs throughout the exposition, rising, for example, to eleven high A's at figure 8 before dissolving into a thrumming accompaniment for the pensive second subject, a derivation of the vaulting theme. Descending through the strings to a cluster of glumly repeated chords on low woodwind, a rhythmically softened incarnation of the 'side drum' motto is taken up on solo flute in a mood suggesting pastoral peace before a storm, an item of musical scenery which would, henceforth, be rolled on frequently at similar moments in Shostakovich's works. A gusting crescendo releases the repeated notes again, yearning skywards (in groups of three) as though to escape their own monotony, before a clarinet returns them to the subservience of the thrumming accompaniment. So far, the atmosphere has been chastely severe, the vaulting theme feminine in its longing for a fugitive ideal beyond its frugal means. Indeed, were it not for its unvocal quality, one might guess an origin in the composer's abandoned opera *Sofia Perovskaya*. Be that as it may, this fragility is now shattered by a rough masculine directness.

Lassooing the accompaniment figure for a mount, a menacing new theme on horns whips up the pace and a classic Shostakovichian allegro develops, drawing the orchestra in section by section like a rumour running wild in a frightened community. Not long into this occurs a key passage easily missed because so understated. Just before figure 22, piano and strings toll out another line of repeated notes, at which trumpets chime in with strutting two-note figures, the reiteration pattern passing to horns and high woodwind. Immedi-

---

[1] Rows of repeated notes are, of course, a Shostakovich trademark to be found in his scores from the First Symphony onwards, nearly always as accompaniments (the Fourth being particularly rich in these). It is, however, with the Fifth that the idea is elevated to a motto-thematic role, as if discarding the picture in order to admire the frame.

ately afterwards, violins imitate the trumpet line before resolving onto yet another sequence of repeated notes. Clearly these ideas are related by more than simplicity, their exchanges suggesting a relationship of master (two-note) to servant (one-note) which, in the light of the dominant role played by the two-note figure in the Fourth Symphony, implies significance. Two-note figures in *Lady Macbeth* stand for crudity or brute authority – especially that of the police, in which context Stalin supposedly recognised himself. Are these configurations musical ways of saying 'Stalin'?

If they aren't, something coming soon almost certainly is. With the thrumming accompaniment tossed from trumpets to high strings and back again, the 'menace' theme drives to an agitated climax – whereupon a startling cinematic cut sends us tumbling out of the world of abstraction and into representation of the most coarsely literal kind. We are at a political rally, the leader making his entrance through the audience like a boxer flanked by a phalanx of thugs. This passage (the menace theme dissonantly harmonised on grotesquely smirking low brass to the two-note goosestep of timpani and basses) is a shocking intrusion of cartoon satire. Given the time and place in which it was written, the target can only be Stalin – an amazingly bold stroke.

The appearance of the Vozhd evokes an extraordinary musical image of obeisance, the orchestra thrumming the one-note motto in excited unison before bowing down to the symphony's keynote D (figures 29–31). Suddenly, the vaulting theme from the movement's beginning is there amidst the mob, desperately trying to find a way out through the grinning brass. At the peak of a wildly struggling crescendo, its basic two-note component abruptly, and with vertiginous ambiguity, turns into a flourish of colossal might on drums and brass, punctuating a frenzied unison declamation of the motto rhythm. Here, the Fifth connects with the oratorical world of the Third. There can be absolutely no doubt that introspection plays no part in this, that it is objective description – Shostakovichian, as opposed to Socialist, realism.

As this declamatory passage ends, the brass and drums decrescendo in triumph on the three-note pattern from bar 4, as if grimly satisfied with their brutalisation of the rest of the orchestra and of the symphony's earnestly questing opening bars, all elements of which have been deformed during this convulsion. Over the thrumming rhythm, flute and horn now converse in a major-key transposition of the second subject: two dazed delegates agreeing that the rally had been splendid and the Leader marvellous. (A typical stroke of black comedy here has the horn doggedly copying everything the flute says, to the point of reaching for a B clearly too high for it.) A wry conversation for departing woodwind merges into evening in a curfewed city, the menace theme inverted on flute, the second subject on solo violin, and a nine-note valediction on celesta (another reference to the Fourth Symphony) bringing the movement to rest.

The scherzo, a cross between the confident 'full sail' bravado of the scherzo from Mahler's First and the uneasy sidestepping irregularity of that of his

Sixth, is only five bars gone before the lower strings are snagged on a fusion of the two-note and reiteration pattern ideas which, in due course, will obsess the symphony's finale. For now, the 'Stalin' motif is everywhere, the strings are repeating notes in their high register (figure 52), and all is as normal in this smilingly hollow world. Glissando toasts in the high strings help the tasteless merriment on its way, the trio portraying a grown-up violin teaching an infant flute its political catechism to fondly sentimental sighs from the harp. Amused approval booms in the strings and the beer-festival spirit resumes, disclosing as many caricatures per page as the divertissement in the Fourth Symphony. Finally called to order by the two-note pounding of the timpani, the orchestra drowns out a wearily unconvinced oboe with its last stamping tutti.

So far, the Fifth has been a quietly dazzling exhibition of structural control, mood and character portraiture, and discreetly applied sarcasm. Shostakovich's new masked method, a step or two back from his pre-1936 posture and far less explicit, has worked brilliantly. But it has all been rather dry – he hasn't yet moved us.

The fruit of a three-day burst of creativity towards the middle of the symphony's gestation period (1 April to 20 July 1937), the Fifth Symphony's largo is the first real slow movement in a Shostakovich symphony since that of the First in 1925. That its intensity of feeling is more nakedly direct than anything the composer had written before is especially remarkable in view of the new obliqueness prevalent in the rest of the work. Here is Shostakovich the tragedian, author of the First Symphony, the adagio from *The Golden Age*, and Act IV of *Lady Macbeth*: no disguises, no ironies. It was during this movement that the Leningrad audience began to cry, and no wonder. Understanding music like this is simple – particularly if half your family have been arrested and you are alone and terrified and trying to smile.

Between 1939 and 1940, Anna Akhmatova composed her poem-sequence *Requiem*, confiding it to her friend Lydia Chukovskaya in her squalid apartment, whispering the verses in fear of hidden microphones. *Requiem*, in many ways the poetical sister of Shostakovich's Fifth, concerns the seventeen months she passed, following her son's arrest in 1938, waiting for news of him in queues of the similarly bereaved outside various Leningrad prisons. In the poem's preface, she writes: 'One day somebody "identified" me. In the queue beside me, there was a woman with blue lips. She had, naturally, never heard of me; but she suddenly came out of the trance we were all in and whispered in my ear (everyone whispered in those days): "Can you describe this?" I said: "Yes, I can." And then something like the shadow of a smile passed over what once had been her face.' There can be little doubt that the slow movement of the Fifth describes 'this' too, speaking for the Russian people in their hour of darkness in a way which must have been overwhelming to audiences of the period. But its intensity may also have owed something to a personal tragedy in Shostakovich's life at the time. On 27 May, Marshal Tukhachevsky was arrested in Moscow on a charge of conspiring with Hitler to overthrow Stalin. Two weeks later, on 13

June, the newspapers announced that Tukhachevsky and his fellow conspirators had been shot.[1] 'It was a terrible blow for me,' recalls Shostakovich in *Testimony*. 'When I read about it in the papers, I blacked out. I felt they were killing me.'

If the funereal character of the Fifth Symphony's slow movement suggests that, on one level, it represents a requiem for the composer's friend and patron Mikhail Tukhachevsky, this in no way detracts from its broader significance as a meditation on the tragic situation in Russia as a whole. In fact, so transparent is its intention that close description is unnecessary. The music is a moonlit nocturne, at one point (figure 87) disturbed by the clock-chimes of a glockenspiel. Arching in two helplessly grieving crescendi, it has as its centrepiece a soft exchange concerning the three repeated notes from the first movement (first introduced on high violins at figure 78). Here, a grim Beethovenian recitative on the lower strings is mollified by the oboe before an ugly woodwind progression ignites the second main crescendo, its repeated notes ringing indignantly over a long death-trill similar to those in the First and Second Symphonies.

Despite its sadness, the largo is, due to the absence of the brutal brass and percussion, a sanctuary of quiet at the symphony's heart. This quiet is, however, full of tension and the finale shows why, blasting off with a snarling crescendo on a trill aimed sarcastically at the whispering tremolando sensitivity of what has preceded it. Its leading theme, an outburst of uncouth laughter on low brass accompanied by 'Stalin' two-note timpani figures and based on the opening of the Fourth Symphony, releases crowd upon crowd of mechanically jabbering repeated notes over which scraps of melody rage and posture. The music's gravitational pull towards unity is immediately felt in the thicket of high A's at figure 100 – in fact, this entire passage is based on the familiar repeated note pattern, the score at figure 109 already resembling a parade-ground of identical quavers. Propelling all this is the two-note motif which finally brings the whole thing to a hammering crescendo of repeated notes obvious enough for even the sleepiest ear to grasp. A horn now smoothly suggests the dawning of a bright new day, but the violins will have none of it, wailing miserably at having to hold their one note (figure 113) before giving up the struggle and sinking into a doleful 'ripple' pattern around distant echoes of the movement's main theme.

The 'ripple' is a quotation from the composer's four recent settings of Pushkin, being an accompaniment (in the first song, *Rebirth*) to the following

---

[1] The plot against Tukhachevsky, a sordid collaboration between the NKVD and the Gestapo, was one of the first indications that Stalin's paranoia was degenerating into madness. Fearing a military coup, he faked the evidence for one and then executed most of Russia's senior army officers for being involved in it. Because of this, the Red Army lacked experienced leaders when Hitler invaded in 1941 and was consequently routed with massive loss of life.

words: 'And the waverings pass away / From my tormented soul / As a new and brighter day / Brings visions of pure gold' (tr. George Hanna). This quotation,[1] the cornerstone of the Hamlet theory of the symphony, is supposed to signify a musical confession of its composer's surrender to 'Marxist truth' and the Party line. The irony of it is, however, painfully obvious to anyone listening to the music rather than to a set of tired preconceptions about it. This interlude, based on the finale of Mahler's First, is followed not by triumph but by something horrible. Over growling horns and the ominous pulsing of the two-note timpani figure, seedy woodwinds reintroduce the movement's crude initial theme. The oboes, now obediently in step with the clarinets, weave a counter-melody – a counter-melody full of repeated notes. If this is to be a new and brighter day, it is evidently going to be a conformist one. On cue, the strings take up the repetition pattern and the music ponderously ascends to a grandiloquent D major peroration constructed almost entirely of reiterated high A's and the two-note swagger of the timpani, cloddishly reinforced in the closing bars by the bass drum. Pushkin's vision of pure gold has been dashed by the Soviet vision of brass. 'What kind of apotheosis is that?' demands the Shostakovich of *Testimony* furiously, and it is difficult to disagree with him.

The music is over, but several important questions still require answers. Why, for instance, does Shostakovich quote the Pushkin setting if all he wanted to do was suggest a false reconciliation? Surely this could have been done, without sowing confusion, by using elements from the symphony itself? The answer to this is simple: the quotation was *meant* to confuse because it was part of what Churchill once called a 'bodyguard of lies' behind which Shostakovich hid his real intentions in order to preserve his life. The Fifth Symphony was expected to be an expression of apologetic conformism on the part of an artist living in public disgrace. Envisaged by the *apparatchiks* as a kind of musical version of the confessions customary at the show-trials, it was scheduled as the centrepiece of Leningrad's celebration of the twentieth anniversary of the Revolution. Clearly, a new work by a composer whose existence was not officially acknowledged could not be scheduled without some explanation – and Shostakovich had his explanation well prepared. In order to live and compose more music, he conveyed to Party watchdogs and journalists a *false programme* for the Fifth which presented it as the harmless tale of 'the making of a man'. By now aware of the need to cover himself, he hid a clue in the symphony to support this alibi: the Pushkin quotation. Found by official musicologists, it would look like evidence in his favour. As for future generations, they would be able to deduce the ambiguity from its musical and historical contexts. The symphony's subtitle, 'A Soviet Artist's Practical Creative Reply to Just Criticism', was likewise part of the lie – although this time it

---

[1] Some modern commentators appear to believe it to be a new discovery, but in fact it was recognised from the beginning and is, for example, discussed in Rabinovich's resumé of the orthodox line on the symphony, published in 1959.

was not Shostakovich's idea, but one forced on him by the authorities in return for letting the work be performed. *Vechernyaya Moskva* for 25 January 1938 (four days before the work's Moscow première) reports that the symphony's subtitle was 'suggested' to Shostakovich by an 'unknown journalist' and accepted by the composer 'with gratitude'. Naturally.

If these convolutions strike some readers as unlikely, it has to be said that no Russian would see them as such.[1] Many instances of similarly elaborate deceptions can be found in Soviet cultural life – the shenanigans surrounding the première of Shostakovich's Thirteenth Symphony being a notable example. After all, 'disinformation', a term coined by Soviet propagandists, has long been employed to discredit Soviet citizens whose views fail to coincide with those of the Party (Solzhenitsyn, for example, being with official approval, slandered as a spy and Gestapo collaborator). Individuals seeking to survive in a society which routinely falsifies their every word and gesture can scarcely be blamed for fighting fire with fire.

The truth, of the matter is, in any case, clear both in the life of the composer and the notes of his symphony which, stripped of its protective shell of nonsense, is so outspoken an attack on Stalinist tyranny and the sinister inanities of Socialist Realism that one can only marvel at its composer's courage and self-belief in seeing it through, bodyguard of lies and all. As a work of art, it is, perhaps, limited by its own specificity, but no more so than any other in the genre. In so far as it speaks not merely for Russia in 1937 but for hundreds of millions of others in the twentieth century who have suffered under political oppression, it is actually more universal than, say, Tchaikovsky's Sixth which, while generally loved, speaks primarily for Tchaikovsky.

Musically the symphony represents a radical slimming down of Shostakovich's previous superabundance of means: a refinement of his pithiness and a deepening of his already considerable resources in ambiguity. Since the Fourth, a lot of colour has gone from his palette, but the music's discourse is clearer for it and the only serious loss incurred in its exchange of exuberance for austerity is that of its predecessor's awesome visionary sweep. The Fifth, in short, embodies what Czesław Miłosz, referring to similar background conditions in his native Poland, calls 'the elimination of emotional luxuries'. Gauntly disciplined music born from necessity, it is ready for the guerilla war its composer would wage against his country's jailers for the rest of his life.

This, however, is only half the story of the creative *perestroika* to which Shostakovich was forced to subject himself during the three months of the

---

[1] Vishnevskaya has no doubt that Shostakovich's 1937 description of the Fifth Symphony was a lie to throw the Leningrad Party *aktiv* off the scent and that the alternative was certain annihilation. She points to the ambiguous phrases in one of the composer's statements of submission: 'Our Party has so closely followed the growth of all musical life in our country. I have been aware of that close attention throughout my creative life' (*Galina*, pp. 212–13).

symphony's composition. Without understanding something of the substance and method of this music, it is impossible to gauge the refinement of tone its composer arrived at in realising it. Specifically: unless listeners see how sarcastic much of its straightforwardness is – how crucial to separate the pared from the satirically puerile in its 'simplifications' – they will miss the anger and ambition of a piece they may have listened to with pleasure many times without ever really hearing.

For several years after its première, the Fifth Symphony completely dominated Soviet concert programmes, being paraded as the greatest triumph to date of Socialist Realism. To a large extent, this was good for its composer in that it both sheltered him from attack, in the way *Lady Macbeth* had during 1934–5, and led to commissions which boosted the family income.[1] On the other hand, it exposed him again to the glare of publicity at a time when both the Terror and the anti-Formalism campaign were still in full swing and any false move on his part could have resulted in disaster. Mandelstam, Babel, and Meyerhold were all to fall in the succeeding months and the drive to conformism in the arts would not ease until the beginning of 1939. It was an uncomfortable position to be in and Shostakovich could not afford to relax. (According to *Testimony*, he did not properly 'come back to life' until the outbreak of the war three years later.)

The most important event in Russia during the spring of 1938 was the last of the show-trials, that of the so-called 'Right-Trotskyite Centre', the chief accused being the most eminent surviving Bolshevik of Lenin's generation, Nikolai Bukharin. As an apparently conscientious Communist and an open patron of independence in the arts (at various times he had helped Pasternak, Akhmatova, Mandelstam, Bulgakov, and Meyerhold), Bukharin was something of a beacon of integrity in the eyes of contemporary Russian *intelligenty* and they followed his trial with horrified fascination.[2] His famous confession at the trial (to a ludicrous catalogue of crimes that included an attempt on Lenin's life in 1918) was the climax of Stalin's wilful assault on common sense, the most brazen instance of 'two and two makes five' the Russian people were ever required to swallow. The atmosphere in the country immediately after it was breathless with fear.

---

[1] His financial problems had already been partially alleviated by an invitation from the Leningrad Conservatoire in the spring of 1937 to give tutorials in composition and orchestration.

[2] Currently elevated to sainthood in left-wing mythology, Bukharin was not always the tolerant sage of later legend. In, for example, the programme of the Bolshevik Party at the beginning of 1917, he theorised, in characteristically ruthless Leninist fashion, that 'proletarian violence in all its forms, beginning with shooting . . . leads to the transformation of the human material [sic] of the Capitalistic age into Communist citizens' (Basily, p. 142).

At this point, Shostakovich let it be known that he was about to start on a song-symphony – a massive choral-orchestral work 'inspired by' Mayakovsky's poem *Vladimir Ilyich Lenin* and dedicated to the Father of the Revolution himself. With the possible exception of Bukharin's confession, a more perfect avowal of conformism would have been difficult to conceive. The authorities were suitably gratified and bulletins on the progress of the Lenin symphony were regularly solicited from Shostakovich during the next three years. Always this great work was 'going well' or 'nearly finished', its composer 'hard at work' on it. Yet Stalin's sixtieth birthday came and went in 1939: no sign of the Lenin symphony. The year 1940 arrived and the seventieth anniversary of Lenin's birth went by: still no sign. Puzzled journalists came to him in December 1940 and asked how the masterpiece was coming along. 'Nearly finished,' Shostakovich told them. 'It should be ready next year.' That Shostakovich was having problems with the Lenin symphony was obvious from the fact that he kept producing pieces of music which had nothing to do with it: a string quartet, a second Suite for Dance Band, numerous film scores, another symphony (his Sixth), a piano quintet, and a complete re-orchestration of Mussorgsky's massive opera *Boris Godunov*. Word had it that he kept getting stuck and having to go and write something else. Finally, when the war arrived, the Lenin symphony had to be shelved; and, when eventual victory brought forward other pressing projects, the composer regretfully admitted that the legendary magnum opus had, perforce, been abandoned.

The official version of this chapter of accidents now dates Shostakovich's laying aside of the hoped-for Bolshevik chef d'oeuvre to early April 1939 – two years before he last told journalists it was 'nearly ready' and just after completing the apparently far more urgent business of writing a comic operetta entitled *The Silly Little Mouse*. In fact, he had stopped work on the Lenin symphony even earlier than that – at the end of May 1938, six weeks after first announcing it. The incident puzzles Soviet commentators. Shostakovich had supplied a detailed outline of his plan, claiming that he was immersed in a 'profound study' of 'the poetry and literature, folklore, legends, and songs about Lenin'. In the end, he produced absolutely nothing. Was it all some kind of joke?

Anyone familiar with the composer's character and tastes would have smelt a rat from the start. The idea of Shostakovich writing a song-symphony after savaging the genre in 1935 and practically discrediting it with his own Fifth in 1937 is, to put it mildly, somewhat quaint. That he should, after *The Limpid Stream*, be prepared to go along with the folk-nationalist demands of Socialist Realism by including some settings of Kazakh poetry by Dzhambul Dzhabayev is very strange indeed (if true). That he should select a hackneyed ode by Mayakovsky, whose person and post-Revolutionary verse he frankly disliked, is even stranger – particularly since his friend Shebalin had already used the poem in his own song-symphony, *Lenin*, of 1931. Furthermore, Shostakovich had assured reporters that the idea for a symphony about Lenin had first come to him in 1924, a project that had filled him with excitement and burned in his mind ever since. If this was, in fact, the case, why had he taken so long to get around to it?[1]

In the light of *From Karl Marx to Our Own Days*, the non-existent choral symphony of 1931 behind which Shostakovich hid from the Proletkult his work on *Lady Macbeth*, it becomes virtually certain that the Lenin symphony was a similar hostage to fortune sent out in the hope of persuading the Soviet authorities to leave him alone for a year or two. Like *Karl Marx*, forgotten as soon as the Proletkult had gone, the Lenin symphony found its final excuse for non-existence in the Nazi invasion. All the verisimilitude Shostakovich had fed to the reporters was exactly that and no more. A song-symphony with a dash of folk-nationalism was something they would understand – all the other composers were churning them out. A piece about Lenin was about as safe as it was possible to be – no one could attack you for that. A choral setting of Mayakovsky was smart because Stalin had just made him the national poet, decreeing indifference to his verse to be a crime. (Shebalin need not worry, since the thing would never be written.) Even the Revolutionary songs Shostakovich claimed to be studying as source-material for the symphony were really to do with something else – his current crop of film score commissions: *Volochayevsk Days*, *Friends*, and *The Great Citizen*.

In the uncertain aftermath of the Bukharin affair, and having already put one over on the *apparatchiks* with his tale about the Fifth Symphony, Shostakovich seems to have decided to take out some extra insurance. As to whether it was a joke, it has to be said that the ploy did have its facetious side. For years, Shostakovich was 'having problems with the Lenin symphony' and seeing no result. In a sense, it could be said that the rest of the country was experiencing the same trouble.

The work Shostakovich turned to six weeks after announcing the Lenin symphony in April 1938 was the exact opposite of it: mild, intimate, determinedly unambitious. The String Quartet No. 1 in C, Opus 49, was the composer's first essay in this form. No student quartets are mentioned in any of the sources on him[2] and he told journalists at the time that it was written 'as an exercise', as though he were trying the medium on to see if it suited him. As

---

[1] Shostakovich's supposed reverence for Lenin is somewhat deflated by Nikolai Malko's story (*A Certain Art*, p. 190) that, during the twenties, he was given to baffling admirers by telling them 'I love the music of Ilyich'. 'Ilyich' being the name by which Lenin is popularly known in Russia, the composer's victims would naturally express puzzlement – whereupon, affecting surprise, he would explain 'I am talking about the music of Petr Ilyich Tchaikovsky'.

[2] In 1985 two quartet pieces from 1931 were found in Moscow – arrangements of Katerina's aria from Scene 3 of *Lady Macbeth* and the popular Polka from *The Golden Age*. The Prelude and Scherzo, Op. 11, is scored for double quartet.

for its significance, this was, he assured them, minimal, explaining that he had considered and rejected the idea of calling it *Spring*.

Audibly a reaction to the enormous strain of the preceding two years, the scale and dynamic range of the First Quartet are small. Scarcely fifteen minutes long, it rarely rises into forte and is curiously passionless, giving the impression of having been visualised at a distance, as through the lens of memory. The childlike title which Shostakovich rejected may have been another blind (there is nothing especially seasonal about the work), but more probably it was meant to carry the suggestion of youth, this being, like the Cello Sonata, a flirtation with nostalgia for the composer's pre-Revolutionary boyhood. Just as Prokofiev in his autobiography *Childhood* and Myaskovsky in his Violin Concerto were then turning inwards under the pressure of external events, so Shostakovich in the First Quartet seems briefly to slip away from Stalin's Russia to take refuge in some fleeting (and crucially, *private*) memories of happier times.

Being Shostakovich, it is, of course, not entirely that simple. Recollections of his mother's domestic chamber concerts may lie behind the bustling finale; a game of 'horsey' on the Irinovka estate seems to be the idea behind the tiny scherzo. These relatively unguarded moments evince a naive charm that won the quartet the kind of popularity in Russia which Britten's *Simple Symphony* achieved in England in 1934. Elsewhere, though, there is a watchful calm about the music, derived partly from its use of classical devices but more fundamentally from a deliberate withholding of feeling on the part of its composer. For example, the second movement, a miniature funeral march on a deceptively tricky nineteen-bar passacaglia theme, is twice halted by distressed outbursts as though one of the pall-bearers has collapsed in uncontrollable grief. The marionette scale of the drama will not, however, sustain this for long and the proffered emotion is quickly withdrawn, as if it had never happened.

Here, the First Quartet transcends the state of being merely drained by traumatic experience to imply a condition in which one is *not allowed to feel anything*. This could be related to the sort of voluntary desensitisation expressed by Akhmatova in two telling lines from her poem *The souls of those I love are on high stars*: 'How good that there is no one left to lose / And one can weep' (tr. D. M. Thomas). Shostakovich must have been as familiar with this syndrome as anyone in Russia in 1938 – indeed, his Sixth Symphony can be read, in part, as a musical exploration of it. The obverse of this coin, however, was Stalin's intention, by terror, to scour from the individual soul all personal feelings preparatory to the imposition of collective ones. Shostakovich had circled around this subject in the last two movements of the Fifth Symphony, and it is significant that the First Quartet's first movement muses much on three crotchet C's, alluding to the three-note motif in the symphony. The quartet is, in fact, full of long, clucking rows of repeated notes, though these have more of the accompanying function usual in Shostakovich's music and, unlike the Fifth Symphony, rarely become a subject in themselves. Both works, however, share a common 'interest' in extremely simple formulae (Norman

Kay describes the quartet's material as 'almost derisively uncomplicated') and, given the composer's Mahlerian habit of cross-referring his compositions, a continuity of meaning between them is highly probable. Among other such cross-references, for example, are a sad whisper of the two-note idea (figure 13) – which returns in more emphatic form in the finale – and intrusions of the 'betrayal' motif both in the second subject of the opening movement and during the scherzo. The reiteration of the three C's in the work's last bars likewise suggest a serious subtext.

Another possible explanation for the studied simplicity of the First Quartet is that three weeks before Shostakovich began it, Nina gave birth to their son, Maxim, so that their apartment would have been ringing to a baby's cries as he sat down to compose. Shostakovich, however, was able to seal himself off from his surroundings and write under the most trying circumstances. More importantly, as this chapter may have demonstrated, he rarely let personal concerns obscure his view of the outside world or come between him and his vocation, as a realist, to characterise and criticise it.

Chapter Five

TOGETHERNESS 1938–1946

I have woven for them a great shroud
Out of the poor words I overheard them speak

BY THE END of 1938, the Terror had reached overload. One in ten of Russia's adult population had 'disappeared' and, with arrests now proliferating among the security forces themselves, the system was beginning to collapse under its own weight. Eugenia Ginzburg, detained in Moscow's Butyrki prison between 1937 and 1939, recalls this period in her memoir *Into the Whirlwind*: 'All the agencies were inhumanly overworked. People were run off their feet; transport was insufficient; cells were overcrowded to bursting; courts sat twenty-four hours a day!' Clearly, this could not continue forever – indeed, had the arrested gone on 'naming accomplices' at the same rate, it has been estimated that by 1941 the whole country would have been in jail. With one eye on the rise of European Fascism, Stalin resolved to call a halt, confining his henchman Yezhov (with the pretence of having suddenly discovered what was going on) and replacing him with the barely human Lavrenti Beria. Ordering the mass arrests to be stopped, the dictator blamed the Terror on Trotskyite saboteurs and had Yezhov shot for plotting to assassinate him. By mid-1939, things had subsided to the usual level of informer arrests and denunciations.

The Terror's final phase claimed many famous names in Soviet culture. Boris Pilnyak was shot as a Japanese spy. The playwright Sergei Tretyakov was executed for sabotage. Boris Kornilov, author of the words to Shostakovich's *Song of the Meeting*, disappeared – as, finally, did Isaac Babel, who had sailed too close to the wind for too long.[1] Osip Mandelstam, arrested for counterrevolutionary activity, was sentenced to five years' hard labour. As had happened to Shostakovich in 1936, his wife Nadezhda's friends (with the exception of Pasternak and Akhmatova) avoided her through fear of association. In December 1938, maddened by starvation and abuse, the poet died alone in a camp compound at Magadan near Vladivostok.

Most celebrated of all artists to fall in this period was the great theatre director, Vsevolod Meyerhold. Stalin's dislike of Meyerhold dated from the latter's production of Mayakovsky's dissident drama *The Bathhouse* in 1930. In

---

[1] His official death-date is March 1941, but documents recently discovered in the archives of the KGB show that he was, in fact, tortured and shot in 1939.

139

1935, following the Kirov affair, Party meetings began to revolve around public confessionals on prescribed themes, one of which, under Stalin's direction, was remorse for 'former infatuation with the theatre of Meyerhold'. During 1936 'Meyerholdism' became a popular alternative to Formalism as a term of cultural invective, and when the anti-Formalist campaign reached the theatre in 1937, Meyerhold was subjected to blistering attacks in the Soviet press, letters from 'ordinary workers' demanding 'simple and accessible' productions and denouncing his as 'unrealistic and anti-People'. Regarding himself as a pure Communist and the Revolution as betrayed, Meyerhold was sufficiently 'unrealistic' to be outraged by this and, called to account at a public meeting, defended himself with a vigour no less courageous for being fundamentally naive. Obsessed with one particularly debased journalistic attack on him, he kept an underlined copy of it in his pocket, buttonholing colleagues and reading it to them with indignant exclamations.

While Eisenstein, pilloried with Meyerhold in 1937, fell on his feet with *Alexander Nevsky*, a Party-supervised anti-Nazi epic which gained him the Order of Lenin, Meyerhold refused to conform. In December 1937 *Pravda* attacked him as a crypto-Trotskyite 'introducer of alien elements' and 'father of theatrical Formalism'. A month later, his theatre in Moscow was closed. Despite this, he stuck to his guns and respect for him among the intelligentsia, while somewhat wry, was none the less profound. Emboldened by the applause that greeted him at the Actors' House on 13 June 1939 (an occasion compared by Yuri Yelagin to Shostakovich's Fifth in that the director was expected to confess his sins), Meyerhold dropped his notes and launched into a suicidally principled attack on the root of all evil in contemporary Russian culture: Socialist Realism.

> What [he demanded of the stunned Party officials on the platform with him] is your definition of Formalism? I also would like to ask the question in reverse: what is anti-Formalism? What is Socialist Realism? Apparently Socialist Realism is orthodox anti-Formalism. I would like to consider this question in practical rather than theoretical terms. How would you describe the present trend in the Soviet theatre? Here I have to be frank: if what has happened in the Soviet theatre recently is anti-Formalism, if what is happening today on the stages of the best Moscow theatres is an achievement of the Soviet drama, I prefer to be considered a Formalist. I, for one, find the work in our theatres at present pitiful and terrifying. Where men of art once searched, made mistakes, experimented and found new ways to create productions some of which were bad and others magnificent, now there is nothing but a depressing, well-meaning, shockingly mediocre and devastating lack of talent. Was this your aim? If so you have committed a horrible deed. In your effort to eradicate Formalism, you have destroyed art!

Apart from Pasternak, who questioned Socialist Realism and the Mayakovsky cult at the Writers' Union in 1936 (surviving by simultaneously addressing two odes of praise to Stalin), Meyerhold was the only figure in Russia to publicly criticise official policy during the Terror. It was an extraordinarily brave thing to do and he paid horribly for it. A week later, the NKVD hauled him away to jail where, over a period of six months, they tortured him to death. Shortly after his arrest, his wife, the actress Zinaida Raikh, was murdered in their apartment, dying of seventeen stab-wounds, two of them through her eyes. Meyerhold had stood up to Stalin and the gangster retribution visited upon him was an expression of the dictator's special fury.

Meyerhold's fall stilled all remaining dissent in the intellectual community, and for some months the silence in the arts was deafening. The valedictory character of the first movement of Shostakovich's Sixth Symphony, written at this time, may to some extent represent a reflection on the fate of Meyerhold and other cultural figures of the age. He and the great director had met during the previous year to discuss a collaboration on Lermontov's *A Hero of Our Time*, but a political embargo had been placed on the project and Shostakovich accordingly saw out 1938 by concentrating on film-scores, issuing occasional 'progress reports' on the Lenin symphony, and toying with various stage-projects. Among the latter were two further Lermontov ideas: a ballet about him for the Kirov and an opera based on the poet's play *Masquerade*, which the composer promised an interviewer he would start as soon as he had finished the Lenin symphony. (At that moment, he was actually re-orchestrating Strauss's operetta *Vienna Blood*, a piece of escapism which secured two performances at the Kirov in 1941.)

Shostakovich's interest in light music at this time may not have been wholly an allergic reaction to the Lenin symphony. On orders from the Politburo, the Soviet cultural authorities had decreed a new musical policy designed to boost morale in the face of Fascism and provide a soundtrack for the 'new happy life' the nation was supposedly enjoying under Stalin's munificent rule. Contradicting all previous announcements, this new policy demanded, amongst other things, a steady supply of light music. More significantly, it de-emphasised the heroic values of Socialist Realism, allowing composers the freedom, within reason, to compose from inner rather than outer necessity.

If, after the recent anti-Formalist campaign, this detour seems peculiar, closer examination reveals it to have been absolutely consistent with Stalin's usual warped pragmatism. Survival had motivated the dictator's decision to enforce the Terror and it was survival that prompted his reassessment of the role of music in 1938. To resist Hitler (with whom he was hastily negotiating a non-aggression pact), Stalin needed to strengthen Russia's ties with potential allies by rebuilding cultural links, for which work the usefulness of pieces like Shostakovich's Fifth Symphony had not been lost on him. If the USSR was to gain friends abroad, it had to normalise its image, and music was undeniably effective in raising international prestige. The catch was that the bourgeois Western nations had no interest in Socialist Realist music, which not only had a (to them) disagreeably totalitarian sound, but more crucially did nothing to dispel the impression abroad that Russia was little more than a glorified prison. The only way to do *that* was to present Soviet music in a guise normal by Western standards – hence, the institution of limited free expression. Stalin wished to grow a swift crop of bourgeois symphonies, ballets and operas for war-export.

As a result, Soviet musicians experienced a sudden change in their fortunes. Hitherto underpaid and badly housed, they now found themselves second only to Russia's film-makers in the country's cultural pecking order, enjoying the kind of privileges – 'closed shops', dachas, and chauffeured cars – normally allowed only to the Party favourites, the *nomenklatura*. The new freedom, which Yuri Yelagin recalls as 'a musical NEP', was, however, strictly relative. Supervision, censorship and coercion may not have intensified, but neither did they cease. Any composer straying from the straight and narrow could still find himself the target of official censure, as Shostakovich and Prokofiev soon discovered. The main difference was that sinners would not automatically be unpersoned, imprisoned, or shot – which, compared with the preceding decade, was very heaven.

Shostakovich's first response to the neo-NEP mood was his Suite No. 2 for Dance Band, premièred in November 1938. Nevertheless, the general atmosphere was still icy, and the Terror, while decelerating, continued to be ferociously violent during 1938–9, up to a thousand per day being shot in Moscow alone. It was difficult to be jolly under such conditions, though Shostakovich, like everyone else, put a brave face on it, trying as far as possible to carry on as normal. During these years, he never missed a chance to indulge his love of soccer, attending matches and keeping the results of all Soviet league games in a notebook. (A lifelong supporter of Leningrad Dynamo, he not only knew his football statistics, on which he enjoyed challenging friends to test him, but appreciated team strategy and harboured dreams of qualifying as a referee.)

The frosty ambivalence of this period ensured that, far from healing over, the split between public/diurnal and private/nocturnal life only pulled wider apart. Though the Terror (officially referred to as 'the recent purge') was over, millions had vanished and only a token handful ever returned from the Gulag. Adding to the psychotic tone of late thirties 'Soviet reality' was the signing on 27 August 1939 of the pact between Communist Russia and its erstwhile arch-enemy Nazi Germany. Abruptly, after years of anti-Fascist catechising in all walks of Soviet life, Hitler was the Great Friend of Socialism, the word 'Fascism' disappeared from Soviet newspapers, and saying anything against Germany became a deportable crime.

On the day that the Soviet–Nazi pact was signed, Shostakovich finished the second of the three movements that constitute one of his most enigmatic creations: the Sixth Symphony. A puzzle to every commentator on its composer's output, the Sixth was particularly opaque to those Soviet critics at its

1939 première who, perplexed by its lack of a sonata-allegro first movement, dubbed it a 'symphony without a head'. To them, its long opening largo bore no discernible relation to the pair of short, fast movements which followed it, the work's two halves existing in schizoid isolation, apparently oblivious of and irreconcilable with each other. Why this should be so, the Soviet critics – stepping out of the concert hall and back into the psychotically fractured world of Stalinist society – simply could not imagine.

Shostakovich began his Symphony No. 6 in B minor, Opus 54, on 15 April 1939 and finished it, six months later, in mid-October. Apart from the First, written in snatched moments over nine months, and the Fourth, which took as long but was similarly protracted by external circumstances, the Sixth was the longest in gestation of all Shostakovich's symphonies.[1] He wrote nothing else that year except for the operetta *The Silly Little Mouse*, completed in March, and a re-orchestration of Mussorgsky's *Boris Godunov*, commenced in late November and pursued at leisure into the summer of 1940. Compared with the restlessness of 1938, his career between 1939 and 1940 was as quiet and static as the Sixth Symphony's first fifteen minutes.

Much of this seems to have been to do with the strangeness of the time itself: meaningless activity cloaking an underlying bleakness. As recorded by Volkov in *Testimony*, Shostakovich recalled the period as 'difficult and mean, unbelievably mean and hard . . . Every day brought more bad news, and I felt so much pain, I was so lonely and afraid . . .' In this state of mind, his election to deputy of the Leningrad city council in March 1939 (again a matter outside his hands and presumably a side-effect of the new musical policy) can hardly have delighted him. The only good news for him that year was his confirmation as a professor of composition at the Leningrad Conservatoire. Here, cloistered with a select circle of students (including Georgi Sviridov, Kara Karayev, and Veniamin Fleishman), Shostakovich could retreat into the ostensibly neutral world of musical analysis for a few hours each week, an atmosphere he had not enjoyed since finishing his postgraduate course in 1928.

Soviet critics have seen the influence of Bach in the first movement of the Sixth Symphony and guessed that this derives from a study, in the composer's Conservatoire class, of the *St Matthew Passion* or the 48 Preludes and Fugues. All that is known of Shostakovich's tutorials is that they were demonstrative and dynamic rather than pedantically explicatory. Perhaps conditioned by

---

[1] The Seventh took five months, but would have required half that time had it not been for interruptions caused by the Wehrmacht and Shostakovich's evacuation to Kuibyshev. Apart from the Second and Third, dashed off in little more than a month each, the composer wrote most of his symphonies in three-month bursts. The Fifteenth arrived slightly faster (two months) and the Ninth, including an unusual false start, took a little less. Like, for example, Mozart and Mendelssohn, Shostakovich did the bulk of his composing in his head before sitting down to, in effect, write it out.

caution, he liked to teach by playing things rather than talking about them, a favourite exercise being the reduction of a full orchestral score to a four-hand piano arrangement. Two of the scores he himself reduced around the time of composing the first movement of the Sixth were the adagio of Mahler's Tenth and Stravinsky's *Symphony of Psalms*.

Another important element identified by some Soviet critics is the similarity between the Sixth's opening largo and the *Palace Square* movement of the Eleventh Symphony of 1957. Both are static pieces, bleached of colour and tense with tremolando strings. More significantly, both feature material related to the popular music of 1905, the Eleventh quoting these sources literally, the Sixth hinting more vaguely at the characteristic contours of workers' and revolutionary songs of the period. The Soviet writer Lukyanova, for example, hears in this music a memorial gathering, punctuated by a series of brief funeral orations: 'the rustle of footsteps, the flutter of lowered flags, subdued voices, bitter exclamations, and mournful silence'. Certainly Shostakovich had studied such revolutionary material in 1938. However, to go further and deduce, as some have done, that the first movement of the Sixth belongs to the abandoned Lenin symphony is overstepping the mark. Admittedly, had Shostakovich worked at any length on the latter, he would probably have concentrated at first on the motif of burial and valediction, using grief for the death of Lenin as a front for grief for the death of Russia under Leninism. But there is no internal evidence to suggest that the largo of the Sixth has anything to do with a song-symphony about 1917 or 1924.

According to *Testimony*, the 'first part' of the Sixth Symphony, like the Fourth, concerns Shostakovich's state of mind during the traumatic months of 1936. If this is to be reconciled with the music itself, we must assume that he is referring not to the betrayal and humiliation of the Composers' Union debate, probably dealt with in the divertissement section of the Fourth's finale, but to the intense isolation he felt subsequently. Isolation and vigil, themes in both the Fourth and Fifth, feature strongly in the largo of the Sixth and, if Shostakovich's allusion is to an emotional condition, the parallels between all three works are easy to see. However, as Lukyanova suggests, the movement also carries a specific train of thought. Of its three melodic cells, two are introduced in the opening measures, the third emerging on cor anglais after the first of two searing crescendos. This four-note figure, accompanied by soft slow-march thuds on the basses, has a rhythm in common with the funeral march at the beginning of the Fourth Symphony's last movement (indeed, the first of the three aforementioned melodic cells is also in march rhythm). If this funerary parallel between the two works is part of what Shostakovich was drawing our attention to, the train of thought in both symphonies seems likeliest to be mourning for the death of democratic revolutionary idealism – for the non-Communist Narodnik ideals of the composer's own background.

The most striking thing about the Sixth's largo is its plainness. Teetering on long tremolando pedal-points, it hardly moves, employing only pallid colours and restricting its discourse to a brooding game of patience with its germinal cells. Sharing the austerity (suggestive of selfless revolutionary idealism) of the Fifth's opening bars, it lacks the energy or will to put its material through its predecessor's ambiguous transformations, instead drifting in a mood of drained and distracted meditation. Compared with the Fifth, it seems only half-alive – a bloodless, tremulous, whispering thing.

In the energetic context of Socialist Realism, this frozen passivity was an anomaly which much exercised the symphony's first Soviet critics. A theory grew up, undiscouraged by the composer, that (in the words of Rabinovich) the largo represented the Hamlet hero of the Fifth taking a last look back on 'the drama that has been played out in his mind' before joining 'real life . . . its sparkle and joy' in the form of the concluding movements. To suggest anything else – for example, that this music concerned the suspension of inner life in late thirties Russia, when to have any feelings at all was to invite mental breakdown – was obviously impossible, even if writers like Rabinovich and Martynov suspected it. This, however, is almost certainly the emotional subtext of the largo which, beneath its funereal outer garments, is yet another vigil-keeping nocturne after the style of those in the Fourth and Fifth Symphonies. In the central section, a passage for two flutes which alludes to the 'grosse Appell' in the finale of Mahler's *Resurrection*, the usual celesta clock-chimes can be heard (two bars before figure 28) while immediately afterwards, as in the Fourth, horns herald the dawn. This is indeed a reverie – but not on personal problems.

The symphony's second and third movements burst on the rapt stillness of their predecessor much as the finale of the Fifth explodes into the silence of its own slow movement. Jeering woodwinds lead the first allegro, plunging us into the heartless bustle of the morning street. This is not so much 'real life . . . its sparkle and joy' as a Groszian caricature of it, focusing on the surge of crowds (cascading octave semiquavers) and the brash jollity of street bands. In the midst of this, menacing low brass begin a tune related to the melodic cells in the largo, following which a sudden hysteria calls up rows of conformist repeated notes and a brutal climax on four fortissimo chords across the whole orchestra. Repeated notes similarly dominate the melodic lines of the third movement, which sets off at an even faster pace and in the same grotesque Groszian manner. The scene now is circus-like, but again crude forces invade the relentless merriment, driving it to another stampeding climax. The coda – high-kicking vulgarity imported about equally from Broadway and the Folies Bergères – is Mahlerian in its enthusiastic embrace of traditionally unsymphonic material. The Soviet authorities had demanded light music and they were getting it: light music with a vengeance. Shostakovich's use of alienation is nowhere more disquieting. Trying to hold in mind the Sixth's beginning while listening to its ending induces a kind of aesthetic vertigo.

In refusing to reconcile the antagonistic elements in his Sixth Symphony, Shostakovich put meaning so far before conventional ideas of formal balance that some commentators have expressed difficulty in recognising the work as a symphony at all. That he did so deliberately and not out of creative exhaustion is obvious from the music itself, which, in its later stages, is so packed with rampant energy that the last two movements, while together lasting five minutes less than the first, take up more than four-fifths of the score. Shostakovich rarely wrote faster music than this in a symphony: it flashes by at such a rate that few following it can turn its pages quickly enough not to fall behind, let alone grasp the details of what is going on. Nor is the invention cheap – indeed some of the symphony's orchestration (for instance, the coda to the second movement) is special even by Shostakovich's standards.

This said, the Sixth Symphony remains a piece whose lop-sidedness, whilst deliberate, vitiates its value as a work of art once divorced from its historical context. Both the Fourth and the Fifth stand as musico-dramatic designs in their own right, independent of their background. That knowledge of this background charges these works with heightened meaning, altering perspectives on their designs in the most radical way, is purely contingent. Ultimately, they do not beg to be explained. The Sixth, its provocative originality notwithstanding, does.

Shostakovich was conspicuously absent from the list of composers making musical offerings to Stalin on the occasion of his sixtieth birthday on 21 December 1939. Myaskovsky dutifully knocked out a *Salutation Overture*; Prokofiev produced an appropriately meretricious cantata called *Hail to Stalin*. Shostakovich, meanwhile, sat quietly at home, re-orchestrating *Boris Godunov* on a commission from Samuel Samosud at the Bolshoi Opera.

Testimony has much to say on this subject: 'Doing the instrumentation of *Boris* was like a poultice for a wound . . . I wanted to distract myself somehow, to spend some time with a musically like-minded man, tête-à-tête. The Sixth Symphony was finished and I knew for sure what the next one would be about, so I sat down with the complete composer's piano reduction of *Boris* . . . I put it on the desk and there it lay, for I didn't disturb it too often. After all, I do know the music rather well, in fact, quite well.'

Immersing himself in the opera during the winter of 1939, the Shostakovich of *Testimony* claims more than ever to have seen its message as contemporary for his country:

Mussorgsky's concept is profoundly democratic. The people are the base of everything. The people are here and the rulers are there. The rule forced on the people is immoral and fundamentally anti-people. The best intentions of individuals don't count. That's Mussorgsky's position and I dare hope that it is also mine. I was also caught up in Mussorgsky's certainty that the contradictions between the rulers and the oppressed people were insoluble, which meant that the people had to suffer cruelly without end, and become ever more embittered. The government, in its attempt to establish itself, was decaying, putrefying. Chaos and state collapse lay ahead, as prophesied by the last two scenes of the opera. I expected it to happen in 1939 . . . I remember that I was very bothered by one other thought at the time. It was clear to everyone that war was coming, sooner or later it was coming. And I thought that it would follow the plot of *Boris Godunov* . . . The time of troubles was ahead. 'Dark darkness, impenetrable!' And 'Sorrow, sorrow for Russia, weep, oh, weep, Russian people! Hungry people!' cries the *Yurodivy*. In those days it sounded like news from the papers – not the official brazen lies that paraded on the front pages, but the news that we read between the lines.

The re-orchestration of *Boris Godunov* was finished in June 1940 but, owing to the replacement of Samuel Samosud as principal conductor at the Bolshoi, did not receive its first performance until twenty years later. With the ink still wet on the score, Shostakovich turned to his next work, the Piano Quintet in G minor, Opus 57, a request from the Beethoven Quartet who, after giving the Moscow première of the First Quartet, had asked the composer for 'something we can play together'. According to Shostakovich, the Quintet was written 'almost simultaneously' with the work on *Boris Godunov*, by which he presumably meant that the Quintet was coalescing in his mind during his long 'tête-à-tête' with Mussorgsky. In other words, we should expect the Quintet to be permeated with the thoughts and presentiments quoted in the above extract.

Beyond doubt, it is. The oracular Bachian prelude which opens the work is unmistakably the jeremiad of a modern Mussorgskyian *yurodivy*, foretelling weeping and the gnashing of teeth. Similarly, the slow fugue which follows it is a graphic evocation of the grief of a people destined to suffer 'cruelly without end' like the chorus in *Boris*. Between these passages, however, is something which does not fit so neatly: a carelessly waltzing entr'acte which treats the solemn gestures of the Quintet's opening measures like so many fashion accessories. This, a satirical imitation of complacency on the model of the waltz in the first movement of the Fourth Symphony, strikes a tone of banality in sharp contrast to the biblical loftiness of the greater part of the Quintet's first two movements. Having left his tragic and satirical aspects on opposite sides of the street in the Sixth Symphony, Shostakovich here brings them back together, creating an unstable mixture the more subversive for bubbling quietly.

The classical grandeur and clarity of many passages in the Piano Quintet, combined with the memorability of its thematic material, brought it instant popularity and, in 1941, a Stalin Prize. Seizing on it gratefully, Western groups made it the most recorded of Shostakovich's chamber works apart from the Cello Sonata and Eighth Quartet (around twenty versions available at the last count). However, the haste with which the work was taken up in the West led to a performing tradition in which important aspects of the music's elusive character became smoothed over in the pursuit of incongruous felicities of phrasing. Interpreting Shostakovich's classical movement titles (prelude, fugue, scherzo, intermezzo, finale) at face value, Western performers have tended to play the Piano Quintet as 'pure music', overlooking the fact that, like everything else its composer wrote, it is a volatile hybrid of the abstract and the representational.

An outstanding example of this is the Quintet's scherzo, habitually tossed off by Western groups as a display piece devoid of irony. The fact is that ignoring the movement's allegretto marking obscures both its many caustic nuances and, worse still, the satirical continuity of the work as a whole.[1] Far from being harmlessly high-spirited, the scherzo is a clumsy rustic dance with brutal undertones directly related to the second and fourth movements of the Cello Sonata and the scherzo of the Fifth Symphony. Its hammering of tell-tale repeated notes is loutish, not mischievous, and the 'wrong notes' in the piano part are as sarcastic as those in the second movement of Prokofiev's contemporary Sixth Piano Sonata. This, in other words, is another allusion to the 'revolt against intelligence' – Stalin's generation of cultureless country bullies. In the same way, the return of the keening lamentation of the first two movements in the intermezzo should move the heart – but not to the extent that the mind overlooks the menacing stalk of the piano's staccato bass-line. Had he wished to achieve a pure, one-dimensional effect here, Shostakovich would simply have written this part legato. As a 'tragic-satiric' artist, however, he worked by striking disturbing sparks from irreconcilable elements, and this passage is an uncomfortable case in point.

Nowhere is the Quintet's tragic–satiric ambivalence more obvious (and, to a 'pure music' interpretation, more perplexing) than in its finale. To the Jewish-Gipsy anguish of the intermezzo's closing bars, the finale responds in the manner of a kindly *babushka* murmuring 'never mind, never mind' – the sound of credulous self-deception (and a version of the 'betrayal' motif, itself to be found on violin in the previous movement). The second subject, announced with naive grandeur by the piano, inverts the fanfare traditionally played to signal the coming of the clowns at Russian circuses, quickly drumming up such excited throngs of repeated notes that it loses track of its own chords. On cue, the *babushka* returns, drowsily reiterating 'never mind' in the bass-register of the piano like a cooing woodpigeon, before a puzzled recollection of the Quintet's intermezzo momentarily stills the music's placid motion. But the finale is too foetally asleep to be troubled by the composer's forebodings and its blandness resumes, linking arms with the 'clowns' theme and wandering dreamily off into the wings.

In its way, the end of the Piano Quintet is as disjunctive as that of the Sixth

---

[1] The fact that in his 1955 version with the Beethoven Quartet Shostakovich persistently hurries the music appears to contradict this. The trait was, however, typical. Remarking on it, Nikolai Malko, for example, notes (*A Certain Art*, p. 161) that the composer's tempi in playing a piano reduction of the First Symphony were 'constantly too fast' (such that a complete performance would have lasted a mere twenty minutes!).

Symphony. In both works, serious questions are answered with middlebrow platitudes, uproarious in the Sixth, dozily mild in the Quintet. With the latter, Shostakovich, as Mussorgsky's *yurodivy*, stands in storm-light at the edge of a great darkness, crying like Cassandra of coming catastrophe. Hearing him, Russia stirs vaguely in her dreams before rolling over and going back to sleep – a vision at once comic and terrible which could have come from no other composer. *Echt*-Shostakovich, the Quintet is the very essence of his artistic uniqueness and, in its five-part design, he had shaped a creative template he would return to many times in later works.

Shostakovich's individualism having made him a focus of expectation for the intellectual community, anticipation among the audience at the Quintet's première in Moscow on 23 November was intense. Arriving at the Composers' Union plenum in Kiev the previous year, he had found, to his embarrassment, the entire assembly standing to applaud him – an event which drew the attention of the NKVD, who assumed it to have been contrived by agitators. Six months later, and despite a cool official reception, the Sixth Symphony had impressed its audiences simply by sounding real in an otherwise cardboard world of Socialist Realist bombast. Thus when Shostakovich and the Beethoven Quartet took the stage in Moscow to play the Piano Quintet, the atmosphere was not unlike that attending the première of the Fifth Symphony three years before – and this time tension was heightened by an additional issue. Chamber music, held to be a bourgeois idiom, had been firmly discouraged under both the Proletkult and the reign of Socialist Realism. Could Shostakovich, the audience wondered, set a precedent and break this philistine taboo? Much hung on the outcome of the evening for the many composers (notably Myaskovsky, Shebalin, and Prokofiev) who longed to be allowed to write in a more personal style. So clamorous was the applause at the end of the performance, however, that questions about the future of Soviet chamber music dwindled before what, in the view of Andrei Olkhovsky who witnessed it, rapidly assumed the proportions of a political demonstration.

As at the Kiev conference, Shostakovich can only have been embarrassed by this. The sole individual in the USSR allowed standing ovations was the Caligula of the Kremlin himself, and had Stalin not needed Shostakovich for propaganda purposes the composer might there and then have followed in the footsteps of Mandelstam, Meyerhold, Babel, and Tukhachevsky. That he did not probably depended more on his cinema work than on the quality of his serious music. In May he had been given the Order of the Red Banner of Labour for his services to the Soviet film industry, and in 1941 two film cycles for which he had composed soundtracks, the *Maxim* trilogy and the bipartite *The Great Citizen*,[1] would be awarded Stalin Prizes. Stalin was clearly pleased enough with Shostakovich to let the faux pas of his popularity for the moment

---

[1] A propaganda biography of Kirov ordered and supervised by Stalin in order to 'explain' the Moscow show-trials.

go unpunished. As for the Quintet's subversive meaning, this, whether or not guessed at by the authorities, had little practical importance, the audience for chamber music being small. In fact, oblique as it is, the work's significance is unlikely to have been widely grasped, its impact, as with the Fifth Symphony, deriving mainly from the shock of hearing real feeling and an independent voice in an era of conformist mediocrity.

'The withering away of illusions,' observes Volkov's Shostakovich in words which might describe the Piano Quintet, 'is a long and dreary process, like toothache. But you can pull out a tooth. Illusions, dead, continue to rot within us.' In fact, he is referring to the work he turned to after finishing the Quintet: the incidental music for Grigori Kozintsev's production of *King Lear*. Shostakovich seems to have had other things on his mind at this time,[1] and his contributions, falling short of Kozintsev's requirements, had to be supplemented with numbers from the 1932 *Hamlet*. None the less, his love of Shakespeare spurred him to one of his finest theatre scores, drenched in the Mahler of the *Des Knaben Wunderhorn* march songs: *Revelge, Der Tambourg'sell*, and *Wo die schönen Trompeten blasen*. (A curiosity of the piece is the sequence *Ten Songs of the Fool*, a set of lugubrious vocal variations on the tune known in Britain as *Jingle Bells*.) *King Lear*, finished in the early winter of 1939–40, was followed by a film score (the comedy *The Adventures of Korzinkina*) and three pieces for solo violin, subsequently lost during the war. Thereupon, Shostakovich fell silent for six months, seemingly deprived, by fear of surveillance and the general desolation of the times, of the will to compose.

If the Piano Quintet had cried in the wilderness of illusion that was 'Soviet reality' in 1940, the grandest illusion of 1941 was that woven around the mind of the great deceiver Stalin himself. Time and again, messages from London, Washington, and Paris had warned him of Hitler's plans to invade Russia. Stalin either ignored them or dithered, hesitating to commit himself to preparations for war. On the evening of 21 June, he replied to Defence Commissar Semen Timoshenko's anxious assertions that Hitler was about to invade with an impatient snort: 'We are starting a panic over nothing.' Six hours later, under a Luftwaffe strike which destroyed most of the Soviet airforce on the ground, three and a half million Axis troops poured over the border.

A staple misconception about Shostakovich in the West is that his output is largely concerned with grief over Russia's twenty million war dead. To put it bluntly, this is absurd. The Great Patriotic War, as it is referred to in Russia, was catastrophic and the suffering of those enslaved by the cold Nazi racists atrocious. It was, however, a relatively short interlude during twenty-five years of comparably atrocious suffering under Stalin, whose repressions took the

---

[1] In late 1940, Anatoli Maryengov provided Shostakovich with a libretto for *Katyusha Maslova*, an opera based on Tolstoy's *Resurrection*. Several sheets of a draft of this were discovered by the composer's biographer, Sofia Khentova, in 1979.

lives of at least three times as many Russians as died through Hitler's invasion.[1]
The war's deprivations were terrible, but its virtue so far as ordinary people
were concerned was that, while it lasted, terror ceased, the isolation of the late
thirties melting in the warmth of a sudden sense of togetherness. At last people
could talk to each other, trust and love each other, co-operate in a cause they
knew to be right. While the war raged, Stalin and the Politburo lay low, the
loathed political indoctrination meetings were cancelled, and the security
forces concentrated on processing prisoners of war. Far from being a time of
special sorrow to most Russians, the war was a time of heightened awareness,
of feeling more alive than they had since the distant days of their youth.

Part of this release came from being able to grieve openly for the first time –
that is, for losses sustained during the Terror, rather than, as later, from enemy
action. 'We could talk about it,' recalls Shostakovich, in one of the more flowery
passages of *Testimony*. 'We could cry openly, cry for our lost ones. People
stopped fearing tears . . . Spiritual life, which had been almost completely
squelched before the war, became saturated and tense, everything took on
acuity, took on meaning.' Ehrenburg, Pasternak, Nadezhda Mandelstam, and
other Russian memoirists attest to this. Indeed, Anatoli Kuznetsov, in his
documentary novel *Babi Yar*, records that the early war-mood in Russia was
one of welcome to the Nazi invasion as a chance to get rid of Communism
forever.

Shostakovich had no illusion that the Nazis were potential liberators – let
alone (as desperate Soviet propaganda claimed) 'fraternal workers' who would
lay down their arms rather than turn them on their Russian brothers and
sisters. Within days of the invasion, he had sent his family out of Leningrad in
case the city should be bombed. His ambition to enlist in the Red Army
thwarted by his bad eyesight, he immediately joined his pupil and friend
Veniamin Fleishman in applying for the Civil Guard. Fleishman was accepted
(and killed early in the siege). Shostakovich's eyes let him down again and he
was eventually enrolled as a fireman in his local Civil Defence brigade. When
evacuations from Leningrad began in July and the composer was offered a
chance to ship out with the Conservatoire to Tashkent, he declined, turning
instead to the rapid production of twenty-seven arrangements for front-line
concerts (of works by Beethoven, Bizet, Dargomyzhsky, and Mussorgsky) and
a pair of choral songs (*Vow of the People's Commissar* and *The Fearless Regiments*

---

[1] The figure of twenty million, much brandished by later Soviet leaders, is almost
certainly inflated. In 1947 Stalin gave the number of Russian military dead in the
Patriotic War as seven million. In 1959 Khrushchev revised total Soviet losses to the
higher estimate. It is now widely believed that the latter figure was boosted by between
five and seven million of those killed in the Terror, in the course of Stalin's wartime
deportations from the Crimea and Caucasus, and during the return of Russian POWs
from allied-occupied Europe after 1945. (The lastest Soviet estimates of deaths due to
internal repression under Stalin are more than high enough to warrant taking this
hypothesis seriously.)

Are on the Move). Ignoring further exhortations to leave, he then began composing the Seventh Symphony. Working with a new fluency, he completed the twenty-five-minute opening movement in just over a month.

At this stage, Shostakovich had no plans to extend the work any further and, having envisaged a one-movement symphony, began to arrange his schedule on the assumption that it was nearly finished. Two weeks before completing the movement, however, he had a last meeting with Ivan Sollertinsky, who visited him on his way to being evacuated with the Leningrad Philharmonic. Playing his friend what he had written, Shostakovich realised that it was merely the start of something much bigger and that he must decide whether to continue it straight away or leave the city and face what might be a long interruption. After Sollertinsky had gone, Nina pointedly remarked that, for her, the most important thing was the children's safety. Shostakovich brooded on this and, next day, notified the authorities that he and his family would leave the city with Kozintsev and the staff of the Lenfilm Studios. It was too late. In the final week of August, German advance troops cut the rail-link and the siege of Leningrad had begun.

On 4 September, the day the initial bombardment began, Shostakovich started the symphony's second movement. Working at high intensity, broken by regular sprints to the neighbourhood bomb-shelter, he finished it within a fortnight, accepting a request to broadcast to the city within hours of scribbling the final bars. Akhmatova, now fifty-two and working as an air-raid warden, did the same. Temporarily removed from official disgrace, she was put in front of a microphone at Radio Leningrad and curtly directed to address the city's women. In the event, the effect of her voice calling gravely through the now-incessant storm of bombs and shells was so electrifying that the authorities, knowing good propaganda when they heard it, overruled her wish to remain in the city and flew her out to Moscow at the end of the month. For his own broadcast, Shostakovich adopted a matter-of-fact tone, assuring his fellow Leningraders that for him it was business as usual – he was in the middle of a new symphony. Such sangfroid counted for much. Missing the broadcast but finding a reference to it in the local paper, the poetess Vera Inber confided to her diary: 'I am moved by the thought that while the bombs rain down on this besieged city Shostakovich is writing a symphony. *Leningrad Pravda*'s report on it is tucked away between communiqués of the southern front and reports of petrol bombs. And so, in all this horror, art is still alive. It shines and warms the heart.'

That evening, Shostakovich played a piano reduction of the Seventh as it then stood to a small audience of Leningrad musicians. Though a pause had to be made at the end of the first movement for a visit to the shelter during an air-raid, the party reconvened as soon as the all-clear sounded and their host performed his brand-new second movement. So enthusiastic was their reaction that he started that night on the third – a large-scale adagio.

Owing to bomb-damage and requisitioning, the city was now without electricity, and Shostakovich often had to work by candlelight. Rationing was in force since the Germans had blown up the food depots and when he celebrated his thirty-fifth birthday on 25 September, it was with a meagre feast of black bread, potatoes, and vodka. In the streets, hunger was beginning to bite. The municipal horses had been slaughtered and soon people would be reduced to eating their pets. Vera Inber noted that Leningrad's skeletal citizens had green and lumpy faces and were walking slowly to conserve energy. It was the beginning of the starvation which, during the seventeen months of the siege, would kill almost a million of them.

Shostakovich finished the Seventh Symphony's adagio four days after his birthday and would have gone on had not City Defence Headquarters ordered that he and his family be flown out while it was still possible. With no time to pack anything but suitcases and no room for anyone apart from himself, Nina, and the children, he grabbed the scores of the Seventh and his beloved *Lady Macbeth* and left for the airstrip, remembering on the way that he had forgotten to bring his friend Fleishman's unfinished opera *Rothschild's Violin*. This, and the fact that he had been forced to leave his mother behind with his sister Maria and her husband, preyed on his mind all the way to Moscow.

After a tense fortnight in an overcrowded city where it was impossible to do any work, he and his family were collected and put on a train going east to the war capital of Kuibyshev. Chaos ruled the rail system and the journey was agonisingly slow, their carriage halting in sidings for days at a time while hospital trains overtook them or long columns of supply trucks passed in the opposite direction. Galya and Maxim were bored and restless, and Shostakovich was grateful for the company of his Moscow friends, the composer Shebalin and the pianist Lev Oborin. Finally, on 22 October, having taken over a week to cover six hundred miles, their train crossed the Volga and arrived in Kuibyshev.

A major gateway to Siberia, Kuibyshev was jammed with refugees and the Shostakoviches were lucky to be given a two-room apartment, albeit an unfurnished one. The local music school found the composer a battered upright piano and, while Nina hastened to turn their rooms into a home, he sat down after nearly a month's interruption to begin the Seventh Symphony's finale. Finishing the work at last on 27 December, he inscribed it: 'To the City of Leningrad'. As the *Leningrad* Symphony, it was, during the next two years, to become the most talked-about musical composition in the world.

Naturally, Shostakovich wanted Mravinsky and the Leningrad Philharmonic to première it, but since they had been evacuated to Novosibirsk, fifteen hundred miles further east in the very heart of Siberia, this was impracticable. Fortunately, Samuel Samosud and the Bolshoi Theatre Orchestra were billeted in Kuibyshev and rehearsals on the symphony started in February 1942. On 5 March, the Seventh was premièred in the city to a tremendous reaction. Moving swiftly, the authorities sent the score to Moscow where, on 29 March, Grigori Stolyarov conducted its second performance in an epoch-making global radio transmission which even an air-raid in the middle failed to halt. Western interest was intense, the phoenix symbolism of a symphony born from the flames of Leningrad catching the popular imagination. Conductors vied with each other to mount its Western première and the Soviets exploited their propaganda coup by microfilming the score and spiriting it out, Mata Hari style, via Teheran and an American naval ship, to the USA. Toscanini's US première, broadcast from New York's Radio City on 19 July, was heard by millions across the country and sixty-two performances of the work followed in America alone during 1942. Played all over the world, the Seventh Symphony made Shostakovich more famous than any other modern composer, photographs of him appearing in newspapers from Stockholm to Rio and *Time* devoting its cover to a celebrated picture of him in his Civil Defence fireman's helmet.

Amid the hullabaloo, the most important première of all went virtually unnoticed. In Leningrad, only the Radio Orchestra had failed to be evacuated and the Soviets knew that morale would be greatly improved if they could manage to perform the Seventh in the city of its inspiration while it was still under siege. The snag was that most of the performers were dead, having enlisted in the Civil Guard and disappeared into some of the fiercest fighting seen in the war outside Stalingrad. By mid-1942, of over a hundred musicians a mere fifteen were still playing. To mount the Seventh Symphony, a work lasting seventy minutes and employing an orchestra surpassed in size only by that of the Fourth, seemed out of the question. Disregarding this, the Soviets flew the score in on a medical transport and put up posters all over the city ordering every available musician to report to the Philharmonic Bolshoi Hall. Surveying his ragged band, the conductor Karl Elias saw that more were needed. Messages were accordingly sent to the front-line units requesting the release of anyone who could play an instrument. Gathering in a hall partly open to the sky from bomb-damage, an emaciated, dysentery-ridden orchestra of tramps began, shakily, to rehearse 'their' symphony. A week later, on 9 August, Leningrad's commander-in-chief General Govorov ordered the city's batteries to knock out as many German guns as possible to prevent them from drowning the broadcast ('Operation Squall'). As the bombardment faded, Elias signalled the downbeat on what must surely have been the most emotional concert ever given.

Such is the legend of the *Leningrad* Symphony, the 'war symphony' which brought Russia's epic struggle with Nazism onto the radios and into the homes of hundreds of millions of foreigners to whom it might otherwise have meant nothing. For years the legend hung round the symphony like a dust-cloud that refused to settle, rendering it at best only partially audible. Sold as a work of urgent topicality, the Seventh's currency was brief, and by 1944 it had vanished from concert programmes everywhere but in Russia. Hearing in it only the sound and fury of heroic propaganda, Western critics dismissed the symphony as a string of bombastic platitudes beneath serious consideration.

And so matters remained until 1979 and the appearance of *Testimony*.

'Actually, I have nothing against calling the Seventh the *Leningrad* Symphony, but it's not about Leningrad under siege, it's about the Leningrad that Stalin destroyed and that Hitler merely finished off.' Among those subscribing to the orthodox line on Shostakovich, passages from *Testimony* such as this caused especial outrage.

Their anger was understandable. As with the Fifth, Shostakovich had gone into print at the time of the Seventh's early performances (either as author or authenticator of ghost-written copy), supplying a programme note to it and attaching descriptive titles to each of its four movements: 'War', 'Memories', 'Our Country's Wide Vistas', and 'Victory'. According to this scheme, the first movement begins with Leningrad happily at peace. War arrives in the work's next and most notorious passage, a forty-page crescendo representing the Nazi invasion, following which, in a pensive epilogue, 'the ordinary people honour the memory of their heroes'. And so on.

Though the composer later withdrew these titles, he never renounced the programme and, since his music seemed broadly to fit it, there seemed no reason to believe that he had not meant what he had originally said. What infuriated Volkov's critics more than this, however, was the insinuation that under the guise of a patriotic epic Shostakovich had actually been satirising Communism and attacking Stalin, the alleged architect of Russia's victorious war strategy. That Volkov should suggest as much of any honourable Russian, let alone the composer of the *Leningrad* Symphony, appeared to them to be beyond the bounds of civilised discourse.

Ironically, *Testimony* is far from definite about the meaning of the Seventh. On the one hand, Shostakovich insists that it had nothing to do with the war:

> The Seventh Symphony had been planned before the war and conse-
> quently it simply cannot be seen as a reaction to Hitler's attack. The
> 'invasion theme' has nothing to do with the attack. I was thinking of other
> enemies of humanity when I composed the theme. Naturally, fascism is
> repugnant to me, but not only German fascism, any form of it is
> repugnant. Nowadays people like to recall the prewar period as an idyllic
> time, saying that everything was fine until Hitler bothered us. Hitler is a
> criminal, that's clear, but so is Stalin. I feel eternal pain for those who
> were killed by Hitler, but I feel no less pain for those killed on Stalin's
> orders . . . There were millions of them in our country before the war
> with Hitler began.

While this is categorical enough, the composer mysteriously contradicts himself in another passage, opposite this:

> I couldn't not write it. War was all around. I had to be with the people, I
> wanted to create the image of our country at war, capture it in music . . . I

wanted to write about our time, about my contemporaries who spared neither strength nor life in the name of Victory Over the Enemy.

The reason for this discrepancy is that the second excerpt comes from one of *Testimony*'s plagiarised 'autograph' pages, while the former is (allegedly) from the composer's conversations with Volkov in 1973. Strange to say, this does not necessarily invalidate Volkov's text. The 'autograph' passage, after all, originates in a Soviet wartime propaganda puff, while the 'Volkov' has, in effect, been authenticated by the composer's son. Since this leaves the debate about Shostakovich's Seventh at an impasse, our only resort is to test the rival theories against the score. If the music will not speak for itself, neither it nor any amount of talk about it can ultimately be worth very much.

The Symphony No. 7 in C, Opus 60, has, in fact, had a rather more controversial career than is often supposed. As early as 1943, Soviet critics were claiming that the 'exultation' of the finale was unconvincing and pointing out that what was then seen as the work's most effective music (the march in the first movement) represented not the glorious Red Army, but the Nazi invader. They were not, of course, suggesting that Shostakovich was a closet Fascist, but that his pessimism, his Hamlet complex, had frustrated what might otherwise have been a masterpiece of the calibre of Tchaikovsky's *1812*. These grumbles, born from impatience with the tragic mood of his Eighth Symphony of 1943, soon developed into a whispering campaign encouraged by the many mediocre Soviet composers who resented Shostakovich's fame and wished to see him humiliated.

The Seventh was not, however, merely the innocent victim of professional jealousy. Its contemporaries were aware of a darkness in it, an ambivalence that betrayed the apparent straightforwardness of its C major tonality. Shostakovich's Soviet biographer Dmitri Rabinovich, for example, refers to the first movement, notwithstanding its composer's programme, as 'a tremendous requiem'. Akhmatova, too, heard this in the symphony and, on cue, *Testimony* echoes her: 'Akhmatova wrote her *Requiem* and the Seventh and Eighth are my requiem.'[1] Even some Western writers, relying on their ears rather than on tradition, have heard the symphony in a way very different from that presented

---

[1] In his memoirs, Ilya Ehrenburg makes what may be a telling 'deliberate mistake', claiming that in November 1943 Shostakovich invited him to a performance of the Seventh: 'I came away from the concert deeply stirred: voices of the ancient choruses of Greek tragedy had suddenly resounded. Music has one great advantage: without saying anything it can express everything.' In fact, the concert in Moscow on 4 November 1943 was the première of the far more obviously tragic Eighth Symphony and the temptation is to assume that Ehrenburg has made a simple error. Solomon Volkov does so in *Testimony* (p. xxxiv), quoting the passage as though it refers to the Eighth. It is, however, hardly credible that, of all pieces of modern music, Ehrenburg should not have heard the Seventh and been aware that on that night in Moscow he was listening to something else. In fact, on musical evidence alone, it is the Seventh, rather than the Eighth, which

by orthodox commentators. For example, Roy Blokker and Robert Dearling, in a study written prior to the publication of *Testimony*, reject the official programme's description of the work's opening as expressive of a 'peaceful, happy life', instead calling it 'melodically . . . earthbound and frustrated', its scoring 'serious and almost heavy-hearted', and the second subject 'subdued and doubtful'. Even an apparently idyllic and sunny expanse of G major is, in their view, not what it seems: 'The ambivalent mood continues . . . the bass line making subdued ominous threats, and a muted violin closing the exposition with a pathetic question.'

Blokker and Dearling's intuitions are, in some respects, amply borne out by the score. There is an inbuilt ambiguity about much of the Seventh's music caused by a slow-rocking tonal scheme in which keys swing mesmerically to and fro between their relative major/minor – an effect bound to unsettle an attentive listener. Ambiguity, though, is unremarkable in itself. While 'ominousness' is clearly there, lurking in cloudy modulations on an otherwise bright blue horizon, the most striking things about the symphony's opening are its strangely glassy smile and the banality of the things it says. Compared with the sensitive hesitance of the Fifth and the troubled cogitation of the Sixth, the Seventh opens in a businesslike mood of almost stupid confidence – and, given the deadpan intelligence displayed in the rest of the composer's music (let alone in *Testimony*), it seems only fair to credit Shostakovich with being stupid on purpose. This, surely, is the studied simplicity of totalitarian poster-art – of the big, square-jawed smiths and lathe-workers, the ruddy-faced milkmaids and harvest-girls of Socialist Realism's 'radiant future'. That Shostakovich is up to something along the lines of the Fourth's mock-grandiosity and the Fifth's false naivety is confirmed (coincidentally?) in bars 4 and 5 where, beneath unison strings, a 'Stalin' two-note[1] motif strikes up on trumpets and

---

resounds with 'voices of the ancient choruses of Greek tragedy' (in its long slow movement). Ehrenburg, in other words, may have been making a subversive point whilst simultaneously covering himself in case of official comeback (Ehrenburg, *The War, 1941–45*, p. 123).

[1] Why two notes? At its simplest because, in the 'conformist' passages of unison octaves in the Fifth and Sixth Symphonies, that is one note more than anyone else. Likewise, two notes (tonic and dominant) are the simplest reduction of a given key. Again, philosophically, two notes indicate the simplest, most reductionist outlook: either/or, black/white, good/ungood. (For the parallels between Socialist Realism and Orwellian Newspeak, see Appendix 1.) From the psychological point of view, two notes signify compulsive symmetry. Cultural purges in Russia have, from Zamyatin and Pilnyak to Daniel and Sinyavsky, invariably been conducted in symbolic pairs, reflecting Stalin's paranoiac view that he was surrounded by conspiracy (a pastime requiring a minimum of two participants). His list of great Russian artists, announced in a speech promoting patriotism in November 1941 (Pushkin and Tolstoy, Gorky and Chekhov, Repin and Surikov, etc.), provokes an aside from Shostakovich: 'You know, two of every living creature' (*Testimony*, p. 67).

timpani, as if beating time for the rest of the orchestra. As at the start of the Ninth Symphony (where a trombone incessantly repeats the two leading notes of the second subject), the equivalent motif in the exposition of the Seventh disregards the unison line above it, eventually pulling it rudely down to six repeated G's. Seven bars later, conditioned to obey, the orchestra fervently reiterates the dominant G seven times of its own accord. Using the simplest symbolism, Shostakovich has established the continuity of the Seventh with the code language of preceding works. Which is to say that the ambivalence of this music resides less in its 'ominousness' than in the fact that, beneath its apparently simple optimism, its intentions are *satirical*. The 'peaceful, happy life' of the *Leningrad*'s opening is that of Socialist Realist fiction and its music a poker-faced send-up of Socialist Realist symphonism.

Immediately after the seven repeated G's, high woodwind tootle a phrase built on a pair of clucking tonic C's – a blithe foreshadowing of the 'Nazi' march. (Not for the first time Orwell's 'duckspeak' comes to mind, Shostakovich's flutes, oboes, and clarinets here indulging in some classic 'doubleplusgood quacking'.) A repeat of the movement's first bars, complete with its Stalin motif, subsides onto the second subject: a dreamily expansive string cantilena evoking the perfect poster image of the wheat prairies of the Ukraine. As in the first subject, the pull to G deforms the melody, creating uncouth cadences and three-note clusters of tell-tale repeated G's in an oboe's rustic lullaby (figures 8–9). Sedated by a slow cradle rocking between G and B major, the symphony, already complacent, is beginning to fall asleep. Clouds (in B flat) darken the hot summer sky. With a lark rising overhead, the music relaxes in the comfort of B major, oblivious of the bird's allusion to the jagged falling intervals of its composer's *Funeral March for the Victims of the Revolution* (figure 18). The semitonal flattening of a few bars earlier turns out to have been a premonition. As stasis is reached, a side drum sounds on the horizon, tonality wavers back out of the heat-haze in the traditional key of triumph, E flat major, and the notorious *Leningrad* march begins.

Readers will have noticed that, unlike previous descriptions in this book, this one has begun to involve reference to key-relationships. The subject of tonality has been avoided so far because most listeners experience its effects by feeling rather than analysis, making dissection of Shostakovich's key-schemes less productive than 'literary' characterisation. In the case of the Seventh, however, the tonal design, in common with the rest of its composer's technical apparatus, is both unusually simple and a clue to the work's inner meaning. Criticised by detractors for its stationary key-centres (so noticeable that it has been described as little more than a series of doodles on pedal-points), the work presents itself in this way precisely because, as a sustained satirical impersonation of a Socialist Realist symphony, its disguise is ingenuousness. The advantage in this for the ordinary listener is that grasping the gist of the piece from its tricks with tonality becomes relatively easy. As Shostakovich said in 1941, the Seventh Symphony was written for the people – 'my contemporaries who spared neither strength nor life in the name of Victory Over the Enemy'. The difference between the approach of Shostakovich and that of an orthodox Socialist Realist lies in the fact that Shostakovich, unlike his putative colleague, refuses to underestimate his audience's intelligence. The Seventh Symphony waits for its listeners to come to it. Its meaning is lying there for all to see, but the work itself almost never points it out.

The famous march is a prime example of this. Western critics of the forties, missing the irony, took the tune's grating fatuity at face value and (like Mahler's detractors in the case of the first movement of his Third Symphony) complained that it was unworthy of a serious composer. This was, of course, true; but then that was the point. It was, on the other hand, only natural that Western listeners should accept the notion that Shostakovich's march represented the advancing German army. In the first place, he said so in his own programme. In the second place, the Seventh was a symphony written in time of war and displayed every sign of being *about* war. In the third place, no precedent (apart from the brief march in the Fifth Symphony) existed for such an episode in anything the composer had written before. Since the most overwhelming fact of life in Soviet Russia in 1941 was the German invasion, the idea that the march in the first movement of the *Leningrad* symphony concerned anything else was never even considered.[1] Yet, in Russia, the march was by no means generally accepted as advertised, the conductor Yevgeny Mravinsky, for example, describing it as 'a universalized image of stupidity and crass tastelessness'. He, though, like his fellow Soviet intellectuals (but unlike Western critics), had lived under the tyranny of Socialist Realism and could understand why creating such an image might be of concern to Shostakovich. More importantly he, like the rest of Shostakovich's Russian audience, knew the composer's language and proclivities, and instinctively peered beneath the surface to see what was going on underneath. Still, the contradictions remain. Even a conformist critic like Rabinovich accepts the march as 'a generalized image of evil' while at the same time pointing to its 'German colouring'.

The simplest explanation is that, like the rest of the symphony, the *Leningrad* march is two things at once: superficially an image of the Nazi invasion; more fundamentally a satirical picture of Stalinist society in the thirties. That is to say: the 'war symphony' legend, along with the composer's programme and movement titles, was, like the Fifth's similar accoutrements, a bodyguard of lies for his deeper intentions.

In the case of the march, its apparently crass simplicity hides a sophisticated process of secretion. Rabinovich is right about the 'German colouring', for example. This comes partly from an overt likeness to a tune from *The Merry Widow*, Hitler's favourite operetta, and more subtly from the fact that a

---

[1] Later, this changed – and, what is more, before *Testimony* appeared; see, for example, Hugh Ottaway, 'Shostakovich's "Fascist" theme', *Musical Times*, 111 (March 1970), p. 274.

prominent sequence of six descending notes in the seventh of its twenty-two bars bears a passing resemblance to the third bar of *Deutschland Über Alles*. There again, Solomon Volkov claims that a version of the tune already existed Russia, set to the words 'I'll go and see Maxim' and jokingly sung in the Shostakovich household to the composer's son. Shostakovich, in other words, allegedly fashioned a tune that would sound German and Russian at the same time.

In fact, he went considerably further than that. Seven bars after figure 49, at the height of a tremendous racket and following a scarifying six-bar trill across most of the woodwind section, the march modulates grimly into C sharp minor to quote the first theme of Tchaikovsky's Fifth Symphony – or rather six descending notes from it: those (appropriately transposed) referred to above in connection with *Deutschland Über Alles*. The virtuosity of this coup is comparable with Strauss's delayed revelation of the use of a fragment from the *Eroica* in his *Metamorphosen*. Shostakovich, though, goes one better by managing to quote the Tchaikovsky motif not in its fateful initial tonality but in the key of its hectic triumph in the symphony's finale. The effect of this is to identify the march, at the very peak of its hysteria, as Russian rather than German (and, incidentally, to prove that Shostakovich has been in control of this ambiguity from the outset). Here is one of the composer's most open clues – yet it has never been identified in any previous commentary on the work.

The reason for the march being arranged in twelve variations is, on the other hand, obscure. That there is a hidden symbolism is fairly certain – variation VIII, for example, is virtually identical to variation VII and evidently inserted so as to make up the required number; but why is unclear. (Twelve years from 1905 to 1917?) As for variation IV, this is *yurodivy* lunacy at its most impenetrable, a frankly asinine affair in which a bassoon traipses around two bars behind an oboe, doggedly reiterating everything it says. Aside from the Tchaikovsky quotation during the succeeding fortissimo surge, the most significant bar in the march comes eight bars after figure 52, where B flat grinds against B natural (in allusion to the swing from sleepy B major to aggressive E flat major at its outset). This clash, which will become pivotal in the rest of the symphony, is a musical way of showing a fork in the road – one leading home, the other to disaster.

Shostakovich's huge crescendo now declines over a G flat pedal-point (a dazed semitone below the home key) to reveal a bassoon hobbling dolefully through a broken memory of the moment's idyllic second subject. Searching for the shelter of C major, this melody wanders again into the perilous region of C sharp minor before eventually finding its long-lost dominant G waiting for it in the horns. Soothing strings essay the first subject over a rocking alternation between C and C sharp, but this leads only to the 'duckspeaking' premonition of the march and the music rears back in fright, the horns again sounding their admonitory G's. Now high strings float the sleepy closing measures of the second subject, faintly sour with the clash of B against B flat (and the consequent danger of C sharp). No good will come of this either and, for the third time, the solemn G's of the horns call a halt. Finally, side drum and trumpet quietly recall the march and, reaching no resolution, the movement ends, as it began, in C.

The use of horns as harbingers and warnings goes back, via Wagner and Mahler, to the rustic scherzo of Beethoven's *Pastoral*, Shostakovich's employment of the device in the Seventh being the first of several such instances (of which the third movement of his Tenth Symphony is the most famous). Here though, his horns are ambivalent, rejecting all of the movement's Socialist Realist thematic material, yet doing so on the very dominant G that brought its exposition so often to earth. Presumably, the opening movement of the *Leningrad* is to be understood as a world of its own, beyond salvation and oscillating perpetually between false optimism, somnolence, and violent mass hysteria. The first movement of Nielsen's Fifth Symphony, with which it shares several features, possesses much the same irredeemable quality but, in view of what follows, the more apposite comparison is with the *Todtenfeier* of Mahler's *Resurrection*. Conceived, like the first movement of the *Leningrad*, independently of the chain of movements which follow it, Mahler's *Todtenfeier* is left as an insoluble problem, its composer turning instead to what initially seems to be a harmlessly unrelated allegretto. Shostakovich may have had this design in mind at the same point in his Seventh. Certainly the apparent harmlessness of his own second movement is every bit as deceptive as Mahler's.

The key feature of its first subject – skipping in semiquavers like a serious and solitary child – is the recurrence, in bar 8, of spooky quaver duplets clearly related to the 'Stalin' two-note idea. As the theme is elaborated, these duplets proliferate, their musical implication (cf. figure 113 in the finale of the Fifth) being that of enforced restriction to something irksomely simple. The same is true of the oboe-led second subject, whose every attempt to slip away from the prevailing B minor is frustrated by its nursing strings. A cor anglais manages a brief outing into the fresher air of C minor/E flat, but the first subject is soon back, pizzicato, in its original key. This time, however, the semitonal flattening of its eighth bar (G/G flat) is speculatively raised a tone, pushing the music into C sharp minor, the 'danger' key of the first movement. If what has gone before has been pure Mahler, the childishly triumphant cavalcade which follows finds Shostakovich at his most Brittenish (though the accelerando most conductors impose on the score at this point usually disguises this). Waking from its nightmare with a xylophone shriek, the music plunges abruptly back into its original B minor, running nervously through its exposition like a frightened little boy muttering a nursery rhyme to calm himself. In its final repeat, having prudently dropped its eerie eighth bar, the first subject sighs gratefully to sleep.

Described in the official programme as 'a lyrical scherzo recalling times and events that were happy . . . tinged with melancholy', this movement's graphic evocation of childhood fears (with Stalin as bogyman?) clearly has little to do with the symphony's advertised meaning. Rather, it seems to hark back to the

Petersburg of its composer's early years, lending weight to his retrospective account of the work in *Testimony* as about 'the Leningrad that Stalin destroyed and Hitler merely finished off'.

If the second movement's original title ('Memories') serves both its official programme and the interpretation placed upon it here, that of the third ('Our Country's Wide Vistas') seems more arbitrary, suggesting that these inscriptions were, like the subtitle of the Fifth Symphony, chosen for the composer by Party *apparatchiks*. Given the focus of the work as a whole, it seems natural to see this great adagio, one of Shostakovich's finest symphonic slow movements, not as a broad picture of Russia but rather as a meditation on the Leningrad of his adult years – a logical progression from the St Petersburg childhood evoked in the preceding movement. As if to confirm this, the music's idiom time-travels forward a generation, for while the second movement is imaginatively related to the hobgoblin scherzo of Mahler's Seventh, its successor opens with harshly hieratic Stravinskyian wind-chords straight from the neoclassical world of the *Symphony of Psalms* and *Oedipus Rex*. Here, the *Leningrad* mines the oracular vein of the Piano Quintet (whose 'Intermezzo', uncoincidentally, bears a likeness to the slow movement of Stravinsky's neoclassical Piano Concerto).

Here, again, is the voice of the prophet–*yurodivy*, and *Testimony* has some apposite – and convincingly unexpected – things to say on this aspect of the Seventh: 'I began writing it having been deeply moved by the Psalms of David; the symphony deals with more than that, but the Psalms were the impetus . . . David has some marvellous words on blood, that God takes revenge for blood, he doesn't forget the cries of the victims, and so on. When I think of the Psalms, I become agitated. And if the Psalms were read before every performance of the Seventh, there might be fewer stupid things written about it.'[1] If indeed the symphony's third movement is a kind of Old Testament lamentation for the victims of Stalin's Leningrad purges, it may be that Shostakovich himself chose its misleading title so as to avoid further provoking the persecutor's wrath. Writing a symphony about a city Stalin particularly loathed was risky enough in itself. To have laboured the point at a time when he and the Party required something to inspire the entire nation would have been imprudent, to say the least.

The adagio's first section consists of a declamatory line for violins (the voice of the prophet?) framed by solemn chordal tuttis from the woodwind. Featured prominently in the violins' second paragraph is the symbolic grinding of B natural against B flat, familiar from the symphony's earlier movements, following which the music sinks sorrowfully into the depths before modulating into an optimistic E major. To a bass pattern derived from the first movement's rustic second subject, a flute announces a graceful new theme, inspiring the cellos to brave the air of C sharp before returning safely to D major with an allusion to the love-softened adagietto of Mahler's Fifth. It is time, however, to

---

[1] Shostakovich seems to have had Psalm 9 especially in mind.

face the ugly truth, and an obsessive two-note motif (♪♩., the B/B flat clash reversed and raised a fifth) pushes the movement suddenly into G sharp. Marked moderato risoluto (and not, as many conductors play it, allegro agitato), the resulting crescendo climaxes on a descending bass-progression again reminiscent of the *Funeral March for the Victims of the Revolution*. Ignited by a stark Tchaikovskyan cymbal clash, the movement's opening chordal theme now blazes out defiantly against the relentless repetition of the two-note motif – the spirit of Leningrad versus the void of Stalinism, perhaps. Crisis over, the tension eases into a soulful reiteration of the gentle second subject and when the two-note motif is reached again, the violas quietly sidestep it into a final reprise of the first subject. All pretence at a patriotic panorama of the Motherland now dissolves in the face of the movement's uncompromisingly funerary mood.

By contrast, the *Leningrad*'s finale opens with what sounds like straightforward war music. A snare drum rattles and the wind fanfares at figure 151 are so obviously military that Britten borrowed them virtually intact for his *War Requiem*. Yet other things in this tumultuous passage refer less to images of battle than to motifs from Shostakovich's recent symphonies: a tendency to relapse into hosts of jabbering repeated notes; a pull towards huge unison octaves; the fact that most of the thematic material is based on two-note cells. Especially incongruous is a passage of peremptory pizzicato slaps set against a version of the 'betrayal' figure quoted in the finale of the Fourth Symphony. A clue to this comes in what follows: an imperious Beethovenian statement built from pairs of 'Stalin' crotchets complete with a snarling horn trill (figure 182). With hints like these in evidence, it is reasonable to assume that here, as elsewhere, the *Leningrad* symphony conceals the usual hidden agenda.

In *Testimony*, Shostakovich pairs the *Leningrad* with the Fifth as works whose perorations are only superficially exultant. Suffice it to say that the music offers abundant confirmation of this. Settling on to the ♪♩. figure from the climax of the adagio, the finale ascends to a huge fortissimo C major coda bursting with subversive similarities to the Fifth: disreputably gurgling low woodwind (figure 197); hammering unison repetitions (of the dominant G); cloddishly pounding timpani duplets. The *Leningrad*, in other words, maintains its Janus face to the end.

What the work fails to maintain, however, is an even quality. Rising in its third movement to genuinely elevated heights, it relapses in its finale to the level of inspired efficiency. The movement 'comes off', but it fails to cap what has gone before – indeed ignores key elements of the wider musical argument (such as the recurring clash between B and B flat, left unresolved at the end of the adagio). Though far deeper and more disciplined than its reputation has it, Shostakovich's Seventh Symphony is fatally distorted by the strain of seeming other than it is: a war story rather than a civic requiem. Nor can the month between finishing the adagio in Leningrad and starting the finale in Kuibyshev have helped, there being signs that this delay induced in him a wish to escape the work and its burden of public responsibility as soon as he could. On the other hand, to deny the *Leningrad* its greatness as an expression of the human spirit would be grossly unfair. No other modern composer has possessed the energy or attitude required to create anything like it – particularly under the demanding circumstances out of which it arose – and certainly no composer since Mahler has been capable of thinking on the monumental, yet paradoxically concentrated, scale of its slow movement.

The true dimensions of its ambition unsuspected, the *Leningrad* stands as a derided work whose significance for modern music remains to be realised. Nor will this realisation come until the symphony is recognised as subtler and more intelligent than most of the contemporary pieces now commonly assumed to be superior to it.

Shostakovich's weariness with the *Leningrad* is witnessed by the fact that, finishing it on 27 December 1941, he turned, *the following day*, to his third opera, *The Gamblers*, an escapist work which absorbed his interest (and utility so far as the authorities were concerned) for most of 1942. A striking instance of the self-regulating nature of the creative drive, this abrupt switch from high epic to low comic convinced more than one of his Soviet biographers that the 'infantile disorders' he supposedly outgrew in the Fifth Symphony were actually still at work. While his colleagues were able to apply their shoulders to the wheel of the war effort without requiring regular vacations in which to indulge their private whims, Shostakovich, it seemed, could not remain serious for more than a few months together without having to divert himself with what the musicologist Rabinovich bemusedly reported as 'a paradoxical story about card-sharpers'.

Shostakovich's Soviet critics had a point. Ruled by his tragic-satiric temperament, he was incapable of submerging his personality in the collective shallows for long without needing either to gulp the fresh air of irony or dive into worlds of feeling which, by virtue of their very depth, were inimical to a society founded on militant superficiality. Having picked up Gogol's satirical play *The Gamblers* in Moscow and re-read it on the train journey to Kuibyshev, he had evidently decided that turning it into an opera was just the thing to see him through the winter. The Hamlet theory of the composer's psychology – according to which this decision was a clear symptom of an immature compulsion to subvert – surely underestimates his practical acquaintance with his own creative inner rhythms.

Unfortunately, Shostakovich failed to allow for the success of the *Leningrad* symphony which, demanding his presence at rehearsals in February 1942, shattered the congenial Gogolian spell which he had carefully woven around himself since finishing it. Moreover, when his mother and sister Maria arrived in Kuibyshev in March, he was further distracted by earnest discussion of the fates of friends and relatives. Reluctantly returning from small-town nineteenth-century Imperial Russia to the wartime USSR, he put *The*

Gamblers aside and began the song-cycle *Six Romances on Verses by English Poets*, dedicating each setting to someone from whom the war had separated him. However, as spring turned to summer and world interest in the Seventh Symphony grew, he found even the song-cycle too much to cope with. Finishing it at last in October, he returned briefly to *The Gamblers* before thinking again and abandoning it for good. *Testimony* explains why:

> The important thing was, who would put on this opera? The subject wasn't heroic or patriotic. Gogol was a classic, and they didn't perform his works anyway. And me, I was just dirt to them. They would say that Shostakovich was making fun, mocking art. How could you have an opera about playing cards? And then, *The Gamblers* had no moral, except perhaps to show how unenlightened people used to be – all they did was play cards and try to cheat one another. They wouldn't understand that humour was a great thing in itself and that it didn't need additional morals . . .

The surviving fifty minutes of *The Gamblers* show Shostakovich returning to the caricatural style of the divertissement from the Fourth Symphony. The action is rapid, the mood ironic, and in the last and largest of the opera's eight scenes, Stravinskyian neoclassicism asserts itself in mock-portentous baroque recitatives interspersed with passages tartly reminiscent of *Pulcinella*. The impression of lightness may, however, be misleading for the scoring exists only in sketch-form ('I intended to use a full orchestra, as in *Katerina Ismailova*'). Projecting the scale of the work, Shostakovich had realised that he had let himself in for a running-time of around four hours – a labour at odds both with the offhandedness of the subject and his own reserves of energy.

By contrast, the *Six Romances on Verses by English Poets*, Opus 62, are pithily condensed and (especially in the composer's 1971 orchestration) constitute some of his most appealing work. With their wryly skeletal fake folk-style, they possess a vigorous directness which relates them to the *Songs of the Fool* from the 1940 *King Lear*. Indeed, the most substantial of the sequence is a setting of Pasternak's translation of Shakespeare's Sonnet 66, which sourly stresses the Russian equivalents of the lines 'And art made tongue-tied by authority, / And folly (doctor-like) controlling skill'.[1] This is the *yurodivy* as jester – and, by Soviet standards, a remarkably outspoken one.

Bored with the provincial music scene in Kuibyshev, Shostakovich can hardly have enjoyed being roped into writing incidental music for *Native Leningrad*, a 'spectacle' mounted by no less a band of wandering thespians than

---

[1] It was, of course, for the sake of these lines that Pasternak chose in 1940 to translate this poem which, in his version, became famous in Russia during the forties. At a recital at the Moscow Polytechnic Museum in 1948, the poet turned an evening scheduled as a celebration of Stalin's 'struggle for peace' into what amounted to an anti-Stalinist demonstration by refusing to read conformist verses from the platform, instead

the Song and Dance Ensemble of the NKVD. Obliged to attend their rehearsals during October, he tempered his revulsion with a conscientious patriotism and managed to come up with one popular success (the *Lantern Song*). This, however, was the last straw and he was planning to join Sollertinsky in Novosibirsk when Vissarion Shebalin, newly appointed Director of the Moscow Conservatoire, offered him a post there as Professor of Composition. Wasting no time in accepting the offer, Shostakovich was in the middle of making the necessary arrangements when he went down with gastric typhoid and found himself confined to bed for a month. Forced in on himself, he discovered a piano sonata taking shape in his mind and, impatient to begin writing it out, summoned his friend the pianist Lev Oborin to help him with any technical problems this might entail. Still under treatment, wincing with pain, and in dogged disregard of his doctor's advice, he left his bed in January 1943 and within a week had got as far as the second movement. The strain, however, proved too much for him and he ended up having to finish the piece two months later in a sanatorium at Arkhangelskoye, near Moscow.

Awarded the opus number (61) which he had hopefully reserved for *The Gamblers*, the Piano Sonata No. 2 in B minor was premièred by him, along with the *Six Romances on Verses by English Poets*, in Moscow during June. An interior piece whose emotional remoteness and intellectual rigour place it beyond the reach of the general audience, it bears the signs of having been influenced by the Modernist idiom of Prokofiev's recent Sixth Piano Sonata, with which it shares a hothouse lyricism, a flavour of acrid dissonance, and a vein of rather tactless anti-militarist satire. Harmonically recherché, the slow movement in particular recalls its composer's 1926–7 period, though this may be less a product of stylistic nostalgia than of a clinically fevered imagination. Hearing in this livid, glittering nocturne 'a sort of unpleasant and at the same time cold sorrow', Shostakovich's biographer Rabinovich spoke for officialdom in dismissing it as 'simply an unfortunate piece of music'. A different kind of remoteness informs his finale, a set of variations on a passacaglia theme whose lofty and enigmatic abstraction recalls the Arietta of Beethoven's Opus 111 and forecasts Shostakovich's own Preludes and Fugues of 1950–1.

Conceived in the isolation of illness, the Second Piano Sonata has a special depth of its own but, for obvious reasons, suffers from an absence of its composer's usual vitality. A premonition of the withdrawn, whispering style of his convalescent late period, it stands like a tarn of contemplative stillness at the heart of one of its composer's most mountainously ambitious periods. Only a searching performance can reveal the strength of feeling its sparse and dispassionate lines conceal.

---

descending into the hall to chant his own poetry. Wildly excited, the audience demanded 'the Sixty-sixth' which, to thunderous applause, he thereupon recited. As always superstitious of poets, Stalin did not punish Pasternak directly for this, instead striking at him by sending his lover, Olga Ivinskaya, to the Gulag.

Still weak from his illness, Shostakovich was granted a Moscow apartment in April and, gratefully quitting the sanatorium, moved into it with Nina. Believing it wise for the time being to leave their children in the care of the composer's mother in Kuibyshev, the couple set about making a home for themselves, and by July Shostakovich felt sufficiently restored to begin a new symphony: his Eighth. Working at the new Composers' Retreat at Ivanovo, he finished the score, one of his longest in the genre, in a little over two months.[1] The conductor Yevgeny Mravinsky, who visited him during the late stages of the work, was excited by what he saw and had it in rehearsal with the USSR Symphony Orchestra as soon as it was finished.

Premièred in Moscow in November, the Symphony No. 8 in C minor, Opus 65, was immediately controversial. Seemingly the second instalment of a symphonic war trilogy, the most obvious thing about it was its blatant and virtually unalleviated tone of black tragedy. Even by the relatively relaxed standards of the early forties, tragedy was anathema to Socialist Realism – particularly at a time when the People were officially deemed to require nothing but uplift or light entertainment. With the *Leningrad* still thundering around the world, the Soviet authorities had been expecting another major propaganda piece: a Victory symphony which would blazon the exploits of Stalinism and the Soviet nation to the ends of the earth. First performed in the echo of the Germans' massive defeat at Kursk and the Red Army's recapture of Kiev and Smolensk, Shostakovich's Eighth, with its brooding catastrophism and depressive sense of doubt, rang a very dissonant – not to say dissident – note.

Behind the scenes, Stalin's cultural *apparatchiks* were doubtless furious – yet they could do nothing. Temporarily the world's most famous artist, Shostakovich was beyond their reach and would continue to be so until Western radio stations tired of scheduling his Seventh Symphony. Putting a brave face on it, they floated the idea that Shostakovich's Eighth was a musical memorial to the dead of Stalingrad – and, though never adopted outside Russia, the 'Stalingrad symphony' tag is still current there fifty years later, notwithstanding the composer's disinclination to approve it.

As for Shostakovich's musical colleagues, they were free to speak their minds and did so with undisguised relish. Reviews of the Eighth ranged from the dubious to the openly derogatory, the main complaint being the elementary observation that it was an offence against the institutionalised optimism of Socialist Realism ('the tragedy remains without solution, the problems are not overcome, no conclusions are drawn', etc.). On cue, Shostakovich's old Proletkult enemies, now led by Tikhon Khrennikov, seized the opportunity to

---

[1] This included interruptions to compose his entry for Stalin's National Anthem competition and to collaborate with Khachaturian on the *Song of the Red Army*. An amusing account of these episodes and Shostakovich's subsequent audience with Stalin is offered in *Testimony* (pp. 256–64).

step up their whispering campaign against him. Only the novelist Leonid Leonov made a point of defending the Eighth Symphony, praising its composer in the pages of *Literary Gazette* for at least having the courage of his convictions. Tepidly promoted in Russia while hostilities lasted, Shostakovich's Eighth was further criticised after the war and then dropped from the repertoire for some fifteen years. Nor did it fare any better on the international scene. Premièred in Britain and America during the summer of 1944, it was coolly received and vanished from concert halls as soon as the war was over. In fact, the Eighth's stock did not revive until the sixties – since when it has gained a high reputation, especially in the West where nowadays it is generally regarded as one of its composer's greatest symphonies.

So wildly have the fortunes of Shostakovich's Eighth Symphony fluctuated since it was written that it would be rash to take anything about it for granted, let alone its stature as a work of art. Indeed, in the post-*Testimony* era, a new look at the work has long been called for and it is curious that, alone of the symphonies whose meaning Shostakovich 'revises' in his autobiography, the Eighth has been tacitly agreed by Western pundits to be above question – as if the very idea of re-evaluating it is somehow in bad taste. It is interesting to examine why this should be so.

Until recently, more or less the only thing the average educated Westerner knew about the USSR was that it had lost a huge number of its citizens during the war. Thus, before the publication of *Testimony*, the 'dark side' of Shostakovich's music was almost exclusively ascribed to his supposed feelings of anguish concerning this. To the extent that they thought about it at all, Western liberals were able to assuage any guilt they harboured about admiring the work of someone they assumed to be an orthodox totalitarian by concentrating their praise upon the musical manifestations of what they saw as his copious grief for the victims of Nazism. Moreover, during the sixties and seventies, it became chic to ascribe the defeat of Nazism, irrespective of the efforts of the Western Allies, to the long-suffering Russian people alone (and in particular to the victors of Stalingrad). According to this theory, Germany's defeat was effectively due to Stalin and 'his' people, and the West should (a) be suitably grateful and (b) desist from waging the Cold War, which was clearly its own fault. The status of Shostakovich's 'wartime' Eighth Symphony grew at the same rate as this specious oversimplification, and to a large extent the work's present critical inviolability continues to depend on it. It is not unfair to guess that most Western liberals admire Shostakovich's Eighth not for what it is, but for what they believe it represents: gigantic suffering, righteous anger, superhuman Socialist resolve to resist the depredations of Fascism, and so on. Since *Testimony*, however, an alternative interpretation of the work has been available: the composer's alleged insistence that it is not about the Great Patriotic War at all, but about Stalin's persecution of his own people during the Terror of the thirties. If this is so, the apparatus of liberal guilt and intellectual myth surrounding Shostakovich's Eighth Symphony crumbles and it becomes imperative to listen to the work again – not as a set of virtuous preconceptions, but as a piece of music which, belonging to a sequence of similar works, probably deals in the same clues and attitudes as they do.

In its capacity as 'one of Shostakovich's greatest symphonies', the Eighth is inevitably assumed to contain some of his finest symphonic music. It is, for example, axiomatic in Western musicology that, next to the first movement of the Tenth Symphony, its opening adagio is the best thing of its kind he ever wrote. Here, though, myth and preconception have combined to produce an extraordinary mass delusion for, by the standards of the composer's previous four symphonies, the Eighth's opening movement is a bloated and unfocused mess. For once, Shostakovich deploys used wares: the inaugural gesture lamely rehearsing that of the Fifth; his second subject following the pattern of second subjects in both the Fifth (I) and Seventh (III); the general harmonic and dramatic scheme familiar, again, from the Fifth and Seventh. That this is due less to a concern for continuity than to a basic lack of inspiration is confirmed both by the essential vagueness of the material and its peculiarly pallid orchestration. Indeed, the charges of redundant longevity and repetition usually levelled at the Seventh Symphony are far more aptly laid against the first movement of the Eighth, with its over-exploited second subject and interminable 'post-disaster' cor anglais solo.

However, the most convincing evidence of degeneration comes with the movement's central crescendo. Similar in tone to the screaming climax of the adagio of Mahler's Tenth, this ambitious gesture is for once inflated and chaotic to the point of incoherence. It could, of course, be argued that this is intentional. Soviet critics had bickered over whether the Seventh Symphony was as good as *1812*, and it is possible to see the collapse of the Eighth's adagio under its own emotional weight as a derisive riposte to this academic elevation of art over life. Certainly its massive crescendo is at least partly aimed at bourgeois standards of acceptable behaviour, its howls of demented noise deliberately calculated to put truth so far beyond beauty that not even the deafest ears in the concert hall could miss the point.

That Shostakovich *meant* his crescendo to be not merely brutal and ugly but also confused and drunkenly formless is conceivable – but, if true, argues a peculiar abandonment of his usual astuteness. Such a strategy, while defensible in its own terms, cannot be productive in the long run if only because audiences, rarely pleased to be shrieked at, will either cover their ears or cease paying to listen to you. A composer as aware of his listeners as Shostakovich is unlikely to have made so simple a mistake. It is, on the other hand, perfectly possible that he simply lost grip on his material under the weight of its emotional burden, producing a chaos more inadvertent than intentional. Taking into account the staleness of the movement as a whole, it seems reasonable to conclude that its central climax is badly botched. Why should this be?

The question begs the more basic one of what the music is about. *Testimony*, at least, is clear on the subject: 'Akhmatova wrote her *Requiem* and the Seventh and Eighth symphonies are my requiem . . . The terrible pre-war years. That is what all my symphonies, beginning with the Fourth, are about, including the Seventh and Eighth.' As with the Seventh, anything symphonic Shostakovich wished to say about the thirties during the early forties would have had to be disguised in martial dress and the Eighth's more obviously military movements (such as its third) do not necessarily discredit *Testimony*'s claims to an alternative meaning. What is odd, though, is that, having dealt with aspects of Stalin's Terror in his music since 1935, Shostakovich should still have felt sufficiently strongly about it in 1943 for this to have blown his structure apart and plunged him into raging inarticulacy. Surely the volcanic passion of the Eighth's first movement can only have been the result of fresh emotional input – a new influx of outrage post-dating his own experience of the thirties? And surely the obvious source of this was, contrary to the composer's later assertions, the horror of Nazi atrocities, then being described in the Soviet press in relentless and appalling detail?

There is, however, another possible source for the fresh outrage evident in the Eighth Symphony's opening movement. The Fourth, Fifth, Sixth, and Seventh Symphonies were composed in Leningrad, a city traditionally aloof from the rest of the country and, because of censorship, largely deprived of communication with it. Until 1942 Shostakovich may, like many of his fellow 'Peterites', have been under the impression that the brunt of Stalin's Terror had fallen on his home city. (In fact, the feeling in Leningrad that the city was being treated as a convenient scapegoat for disaffection in the rest of the country did, at times, reflect the truth.) Making new acquaintances in Kuibyshev and Moscow, however, Shostakovich would have discovered that the scale of arrests and executions in the thirties, far from bearing down especially on Russia's second capital, had been so gigantic as to exceed the capacity of all but the most delirious imagination. (As Solzhenitsyn wearily admits in *The Gulag Archipelago*, 'Even the most broad-minded of us can embrace only that part of the truth into which our own snout has blundered.') This revelation of Stalin's incredible genocide would have been more than enough to provoke the explosion of the Eighth – indeed, is more likely to have done so than horror stories of the occupation, which were hard to distinguish from propaganda.

If this fails to explain the full extent of the first movement's uncharacteristic loss of control, the equation can be balanced by a probable additional factor. There is about the Eighth a certain earthbound quality – an absence of the *vital electricity* which above all distinguishes Shostakovich's music from that of most other composers. Apart from its featherlight coda, the ungainliness of the symphony's march-like second movement seems to owe as much to its composer's tiredness as to any intention of mocking totalitarian pomposity, while a more direct musical image of terminal exhaustion than the fourth movement's dirge-like passacaglia would be hard to imagine. It is not so much that the ideas behind the symphony's three central movements are weak (on the contrary, they are as incisive as ever); rather that they lack the necessary imaginative charge to bring them to life. Not to beat about the bush, the likelihood is that, in ignoring medical advice and going on with the Second Piano Sonata when he should have been in bed, Shostakovich blew a fuse somewhere – a fuse which had not properly mended when, three months later, he started the Eighth Symphony. The speed at which he wrote it is immaterial; the fact that he could work steadily through an attack of gastric typhoid is proof enough that his willpower was, even if only in bursts, stronger than his body. Indeed, both sonata and symphony bear the signs of having been pushed through by intellectual force alone and, in the case of the latter, the impression of a man trying too hard is frequently all too vivid. In the final analysis, what is wrong with the first four movements of Shostakovich's Eighth is that they are one-dimensional in the way that the works of composers like Penderecki and Schnittke are one-dimensional. The tragic earnestness is laid on too thickly and too monotonously; there is little sense of perspective and no ironic contrast, characterisation, or humour. To be precise, the fuse that Shostakovich blew during his illness seems to have been the one governing his function as a satirist. In much of the Second Piano Sonata and Eighth Symphony we hear only one side of his normal, electrically interactive stereo signal: the tragedian. Of the jester there is no sign. A crucial dimension is missing.

Unmistakable confirmation of this comes with the symphony's fifth and final movement. Whether Shostakovich had planned his finale from the beginning or, as it were, backed into it, is unknown. Mravinsky had visited Ivanovo just before he wrote it and his enthusiasm for the first four movements meant enough to the composer for him to make the unusual gesture of dedicating the finished score to him. Conceivably, Shostakovich had been uncertain of how to go on with it – perhaps even doubtful of the worth of what he'd done. Whatever the truth, the difference of approach after Mravinsky left is very marked. From the ruins of the moribund passacaglia buds new life – but hardly the edifying cliché of rebirth dear to the Socialist Realist. Here, at last, the jester awakes and a familiar irony arrives to rescue the situation with one of the composer's most searingly satirical inventions.

Turning away from the pulverised wasteland of the previous movement, Shostakovich reveals a caucus of Pooterish bassoons small-talking their way through a smug little tune reminiscent of the 'never mind' theme of the finale of the Piano Quintet. Reproducing the Quintet's five-movement design, the composer borrows its main idea as well: that of bland refusal to face the truth and of the consequent death of memory. Thus, when the strings, taking up the bassoons' tune, stray into emotion too effusive to be tolerated in respectable society, they gently pooh-pooh themselves (nine bars before A in the Breitkopf edition) before relapsing into conformist self-effacement. A sportive flute celebrates the fact, drawing yawns of approval from a horn and, with a sighing hint of the pooh-poohing phrase from the violins, the movement reaches its second subject: a dignified, lyrical cello cantilena. Pedantically paced by the bassoons, the cellos swoop deep and dark – too deep and dark for the oboes, who indignantly pooh-pooh them (figure C) and return, with comic officiousness, to the blandness of the first subject.

Exposition over, the chastened lower strings attempt to rehabilitate themselves by accompanying the violins' elaboration of the pooh-poohing phrase with a chain of repeated notes. Forty bars after figure C comes another clue: a quotation of the 'Sergei' or 'betrayal' motif from the finale of the Fourth Symphony. (Indeed, the movement's first subject is nothing more than a variation on this three-note cell, as the violins disclose only a few bars later.) What the composer seems to be suggesting here is that, after the war (movements three and four?), rather than reward them for their efforts, Stalin will betray the people by reviving the Terror which Hitler had forced him to abandon. Since the thought was a common one at the time – being, for example, the subject of the letter for which Solzhenitsyn was arrested in 1945 – this interpretation is well worth considering. (If accepted, the climactic point of the Eighth's finale becomes, as *Testimony* maintains, a traumatic reacquaintance with 'the terrible pre-war years'.)

Sounding remarkably like the sourly satirical finale of Nielsen's Sixth Symphony, Shostakovich's closing movement heads steadily for its rendezvous with reality – yet even here tiredness shows through, with a debilitated fugue on the first subject standing in for genuine development, and the climax, a collapse into the screaming crescendo of the opening movement, emerging in strangely laborious style. With the recapitulation, Shostakovich returns us, via the 'betrayal' motif on bass clarinet, to the movement's platitudinous beginning. Drained of any will to protest, the violins drift to sleep on a pedal C, the first subject limping home in heavy pizzicato basses. Far from being the poignant dying fall it is usually said to be, the symphony's coda is bleakly ironic.

To an extent, the finale of the Eighth Symphony humanises the rest of the work, almost turning it into a retrospective success. However, this late revival is illusory. Compared to the acute sureness of touch of the Fourth, Fifth, and Seventh Symphonies, the Eighth swings a sandbag against the listener's skull, its emphases and alienative contrasts displaying the strained excesses of a depleted imagination. Tremendous in conception and often overwhelming in execution, it is none the less more admirable for its intentions than its deeds.

Three months after the première of the Eighth Symphony, the composer suffered one of the worst losses of his life. Visiting Moscow to stay with him during November, Ivan Sollertinsky had secured a professorship in music history at the city's Conservatoire and a delighted Shostakovich had seen his friend off, expecting him back as soon as he had settled his affairs in Novosibirsk. On 11 February 1944, however, a telegram brought the news of Sollertinsky's death, at forty-two, from a heart attack. Probably the only intellectual equal Shostakovich was ever able to talk to without having to compromise or disguise his meaning, Sollertinsky had been a lifeline to him for seventeen years. At times he had lived for conversations with him and, without that unique closeness, he must have felt suddenly very alone.

Within days of hearing of Sollertinsky's death, Shostakovich began his Piano Trio No. 2 in E minor, Opus 67, in whose opening bars the cello, muted in its highest register, weeps like an abandoned little boy. In fact, so dolorous is the blow the composer has suffered that the whole first movement appears to be yet another flight into his untroubled childhood along the lines of the Cello Sonata (I), First Quartet (*passim*), and Seventh Symphony (II). Here again are the memories of summer games on the Irinovka estate, of his first faltering music lessons, and of boyish night terrors (figure 18).[1] Parallels with earlier works proliferate in the second movement, a clumsy peasant dance after the pattern of the scherzi in the Cello Sonata and Piano Quintet. Just as most Western groups wantonly distort the Quintet's scherzo, so they routinely ignore the composer's insistent markings at the head of this movement – allegro non troppo, marcatissimo, pesante (not too fast, heavily stressed, ponderous) – in order to toss it off as a flashy display piece. To judge from its prominent two-note patterns, the likelihood is that the movement is another swipe at Stalinist anti-intellectualism (although the central trio-section, with its exuberant waltz and hint of Spanish gipsy music, argues a link with Shostakovich's home life during his Conservatoire days). Again, the third movement calls on established personal practice, being a funerary passacaglia on an eight-bar theme distantly related to the finale of Mahler's Ninth (a kinship revealed in the last of the six variants). Like nearly all of the work's material, it is extremely simple, and in this respect the Second Trio, with its one-finger lines and 'untutored' discords, harks back to the Fifth Symphony and (especially) to the First Quartet. Here, though, simplicity is treated as both vice and virtue: on the one hand, a talisman against falsity; on the other, the easy victim of deceit. As with Britten, innocence abroad in the twentieth century is an abiding theme for Shostakovich – and its musical characterisation in the Second Trio once more suggests that, some time during 1943–4, he studied Carl Nielsen's Sixth Symphony (*Sinfonia semplice*).

The simplicity of the people is formally invoked in the folk-like material of the Trio's finale. Written rapidly in late July and early August, it is the first of Shostakovich's 'Jewish' pieces, in this case provoked by reports in the Soviet press of the Red Army's liberation of the Nazi death camps at Belzec, Sobibor, Majdanek, and Treblinka. Horrified by stories that SS guards had made their victims dance beside their own graves, Shostakovich created a directly programmatic image of it. This harshly realistic movement is meant to shock and,

---

[1] There may even be a quotation from one of his destroyed teenage works. Two bars before figure 9 is a theme briefly held up to the light, like a dusty page discovered among long-lost treasures in an attic. Though it plays no further part in the Trio, Shostakovich was sufficiently taken with it to use it later in the year as the main theme of the finale of his Second Quartet.

at its height, the impression of someone stumbling about in exhaustion is painfully vivid. Soon after this, death mercifully supervenes in pealing baroque arpeggios, leaving the ghost of the main theme dancing sepulchrally in the bass, like the murdered Petrushka at the end of Stravinsky's ballet. With a final memory of the passacaglia, the Trio twitches to a stop: a broken puppet.

Although begun in grief and concluded in anger, the Second Piano Trio did not come easily to Shostakovich, taking him a full six months to compose. Interrupted by his tutorials at the Conservatoire, work on the score of the film *Zoya*, and the noisy arrival of Galya and Maxim from Kuibyshev in April, it shows signs of an artist running on the spot and, in the finale, straining to say something beyond the top of his voice. Compared to the Eighth Symphony, however, it has an energy and humanity which preserve it and which probably stem from a spiritual link with its dedicatee, the composer's much-mourned soulmate Ivan Sollertinsky.

Further delaying the Second Trio was the fact that Shostakovich had been simultaneously pondering two other works: the Second Quartet and Ninth Symphony. Written in a remarkable nineteen days at Ivanovo in September, the Quartet No. 2 in A major, Opus 68, must have been long premeditated. A huge leap from the modest scale of the First Quartet, it runs for nearly forty minutes and is in effect a chamber symphony, having a grandeur of conception more suited to the concert hall than the recital room. Like the Piano Quintet, it uses classical titles and techniques, but its driving contrapuntal power is thoroughly modern and again, particularly in the opening movement, suggests familiarity with the music of Nielsen. Entitled 'Overture', this strident double-exposition sonata is the most energetic opening to anything Shostakovich had written since the Seventh Symphony and, with its simple major tonality, immediately establishes the Second Quartet as a public work of comparable directness.

As in the case of the *Leningrad*, the obvious question is: why the aggressive confidence? Unlike the opening of the Seventh Symphony, that of the Second Quartet bears no sign of being a parody of Socialist Realist optimism. Its style is combative and, at first glance, devoid of irony. Like the opening movement of the Fifth Quartet of 1952, it speaks of resistance and overcoming, a mood very much in the air when it was being written. With the surrender of Finland and Marshal Zhukov's drive into Poland, the Great Patriotic War was clearly won and few Russians, no matter how critical of their government, could fail to be elated. The adoption of the People's victory by Stalin and the Party was, however, a common topic of conversation[1] and, since Shostakovich had

---

[1] Little was seen or heard of Stalin by the Russian public during the war, which was fought on the basis of nationalism rather than a defence of Communism. The Nazis were defeated by a combination of Red Army generalship and a huge effort by every Russian man, woman, and child – not by Stalin and the Party who, claiming the credit after hostilities were over, had tried to buy Hitler off with territorial concessions when things were going badly. If any single figure was popularly credited with winning the war, it was Zhukov.

incorporated this into the finale of his Eighth Symphony, it would be surprising if the Second Quartet had nothing to say on the subject. In fact, closer examination shows that it does, disclosing an intriguing pattern of codes and ambiguities which the composer would from now on develop through a whole sequence of interrelated works.

Underpinning the Overture's exposition are a succession of strange, squeezed crescendi on single notes, usually in the lower register. Present during the first subject, they become particularly active during the second subject which, constructed chiefly from the ♪♩. 'Stalin' motif of the Seventh Symphony (III–IV) and pitched in that work's dark key of C sharp minor, seems likely to be another of Shostakovich's characterisations of the dictator himself. That this is so is confirmed by the presence, four bars before figure 5 (and twice more during the ensuing passage), of a four-note motto later employed in the scherzo of the Tenth Symphony (described by the composer in *Testimony* as 'a musical portrait of Stalin, roughly speaking'). It would seem, therefore, that the squeezed one-note crescendi (which also appear in the peasant scherzi of both the Piano Quintet and Second Piano Trio) are Shostakovich's way of representing some mannerism of Stalin's personality or style of speech.

The scheme of the quartet's opening material can thus be represented as follows: the first subject corresponds to the various nuances of the Russian people's victorious mood in summer 1944; the second subject corresponds to Stalin and the Party, readying themselves to resume control once the war is over. The development section of the movement, too intricate to be disentangled here, pitches these ideas at each other, climaxing in a passionate protest from the first violin against an accompaniment of stabbing duplets (figure 18), before swerving into a telescoped recapitulation that drops the second subject altogether.

Extending its parallels with the *Leningrad*, the quartet reproduces in its second movement, 'Recitative and Romance', that symphony's static pedal-point tonalities: a solo violin freely exclaiming over a series of sustained chords from the other instruments. Here, Shostakovich universalises the predicament of persecuted Jewry, mingling the voice of the cantor with that of the Bachian Evangelist – though, in concluding, the violin descends to its lower register to shake its head sombrely over the ♪♩. 'Stalin' motif. The pensive mood continues in the third movement, 'Waltz', which abandons its shadowy reflections only briefly for an agitated memory of the finale of the Fourth Symphony.

Concluding his quartet, Shostakovich produces the theme 'discovered' in the first movement of the Second Trio, to which he prefixes a solemn, admonitory fanfare and adds a set of fifteen variations. Very folk-Russian, the theme is at first treated with deliberation, passacaglia-style. In the seventh variation, however, the dense part-writing of the first movement reappears, igniting an excitement which, by the twelfth variation, is bordering on hysteria. At this point, the admonitory fanfare sounds and the music calms down, as if remembering itself. The thirteenth variation, airy and liberated, is followed by a second calming transitional passage and the final pair of variations unravel poignantly into a vista of elusive freedom. Finally, the fanfare returns and, in chorale harmony, the theme rises to a defiantly prophetic assertion. Little doubt remains as to what this closing message is: the People will overcome, will be avenged.

Dedicating this magnificent work to his colleague Vissarion Shebalin (then rated the leading Soviet quartet-composer), Shostakovich let the Beethoven Quartet première it in Moscow in November, playing the piano part in the first performance of his Second Trio on the same programme. Fluent, organic, and unaccountably underrated in the West, the Second Quartet was a considerable breakthrough for its composer. Having effectively avoided the quartet genre for more than half of his life, he would henceforward write an average of one every thirty months until he died.

Shostakovich saw out 1944 with a cluster of minor pieces: the *Children's Notebook* (a piano primer for his daughter Galya) and two patriotic 'spectacles', *Russian River* and *Victorious Spring*, none of which took him more than a day or two to finish. His duty done, he then paused to ponder one of the most difficult and dangerous decisions of his entire career: what to make of his Ninth Symphony.

According to the Shostakovich of *Testimony* – and there is no good reason to doubt him on this point – the problem was one of number and occasion:

> They wanted a fanfare from me, an ode, they wanted me to write a majestic Ninth Symphony . . . And they demanded that Shostakovich use quadruple winds, choir, and soloists to hail the leader. All the more because Stalin found the number nine auspicious: the Ninth Symphony. Stalin always listened to experts and specialists carefully. The experts told him that I knew my work and therefore Stalin assumed that the symphony in his honour would be a quality piece of music. He would be able to say, There it is, our national Ninth.

Not since the Fifth Symphony had Shostakovich been so inescapably trapped in the spotlight. Were he to fail his masters at this critical juncture, punishment could be postponed only by his international fame, which would soon fade along with memories of the war. Perhaps envisaging a smokescreen strategy along the lines of *Karl Marx* or the Lenin symphony, he told the Soviet press he was writing a 'Victory Symphony' complete with 'apotheosis' – but this time he had miscalculated for there was no deus ex machina to save him from coming up with the goods. This might have mattered less had his revulsion over a project hailing Stalin as victor been milder than he foresaw, but when he started composing he found himself unable to overcome it ('I couldn't write an apotheosis to Stalin, I simply couldn't'). Finishing the exposition during the summer of 1944, he tried it out on some friends – then stopped. Thereafter avoiding the subject, he returned to it only when he absolutely had to: in the summer of 1945, three months after the fall of Berlin. Knowing then that if the Ninth was to be ready for the twenty-eighth anniversary of the Revolution in November he could prevaricate no longer, he set to work in August and poured out the entire score in under a month.

Following Soviet custom, the Symphony No. 9 in E flat major, Opus 70, was pre-premièred in September at the Moscow Composers' Union in a two-piano reduction played by Shostakovich and Sviatoslav Richter. Controversy duly ensued. Having anticipated the triumphant third panel of a war triptych scored for large orchestra and choir and lasting at least an hour, Shostakovich's peers were baffled to be confronted with a strange, manic-depressive neoclassical piece for standard forces which stopped suddenly after a mere twenty-five minutes. Handed a weapon on a plate, the composer's Proletkult enemies hastened to display their outrage. The world, however, was watching and the Soviet authorities had no option: cancelling the Ninth, which had been scheduled as the centrepiece of the November festivities, would be more embarrassing than letting it go ahead. As with the Eighth Symphony, the only choice was to maintain an air of unified decorum and deal appropriately with the situation at a later date. Thus, to a reception of politely lukewarm puzzlement, Shostakovich's Ninth was premièred in Leningrad under Mravinsky's baton on 3 November.

Officialdom maintained its straight face. *Culture and Life*, the Central Committee's new arts periodical, expressed measured disappointment with the Ninth, but closed ranks against the anticipated mirth of foreign observers by summarising Shostakovich as 'a composer of immense talent, of whom our Soviet country is justly proud'. Feeling obliged to defend the symphony, Mravinsky offered the opinion that it was 'a work directed against philistinism . . . which ridicules complacency and bombast, the desire to "rest on one's laurels" '. The Ninth's apparent triviality, he insisted, was satirical impersonation, its 'deliberate and laboured gaiety' expressive not of the composer's feelings but of those of 'the self-satisfied, short-sighted philistine who is essentially indifferent to everything'. Though twenty years obsolete, this reference to the archetypal bourgois Nepman was perpetually current in Soviet mythology. ('Philistinism', like Formalism, was a flexible term of abuse which meant whatever those in power wished it to mean.) By using Stalinist jargon, Mravinsky was attempting to place Shostakovich safely within the laager of conformism, thereby rendering his friend's act of subversion, paradoxically, plus royaliste que le roi. It was a brave, if wasted, effort. The disjunction between the demands of the time and the tone of Shostakovich's offering was, for once, too blatant to be ignored. Only a dunce could have failed to realise that the composer was up to something in this score,[1] and the fact that it was not entirely obvious what this was merely exacerbated the wrath of the authorities.

Puzzlement over Shostakovich's Ninth still persists, Western critics in particular displaying an apparently bottomless capacity for missing the point of it. Passively accepting the Soviet view of the work as a typically schizoid miscalculation on its composer's part (dimly proffering light entertainment at a time when what was required was solemn grandiosity), some have remained content to see it as a piece gaily innocent of depth – a sort of P. G. Wodehouse 'silly fool' symphony. Hugh Ottaway, for example, refuses to hear any ambiguities in it at all: 'Only the cynical will misinterpret as cynicism the brashness and asperity of some of this music.' Others, sensing its subversive undercurrent, are more cautious if no less mystified. Thus, expressing the British left-wing analysis of the work, Robert Stradling describes it as an 'unhelpful . . . regression to satirical characteristics'. (Note the standard implication of infantility.) The idea that Shostakovich could have mistaken what was wanted from him in 1945 is, however, palpably ridiculous. All the evidence points to the conclusion that he knew exactly what he was doing in the Ninth and – whether through bravery or a weary inability to do otherwise – compromised his intentions by not so much as a semiquaver.

No one familiar with the code language developed in Shostakovich's music after *Lady Macbeth* and the Fourth Symphony will find difficulty in interpreting the Ninth Symphony. Subverting its own billing as a paean to Stalin Victorious, it is a frankly satirical work, mocking the Wagnerian pretension of the dictator's cult by restating it as Rossinian opera buffa. 'When the war against Hitler was won,' recalls the composer in *Testimony*, 'Stalin went off the deep end. He was like the frog puffing himself up to the size of the ox . . .' Effectively confirming this, nothing by Shostakovich is more ruthlessly targeted on Stalin than his Ninth, almost all of its material being constructed from two-note cells and other 'Stalin' patterns. Likewise, its various Wagnerisms – the most prominent being the allusion to Wotan's motif in the fourth movement – are probably expressions of Shostakovich's view, outlined in *Testimony*, of Stalin and Hitler as 'spiritual relatives'. (Indeed, the farce of Eisenstein's 1940 production of *The Valkyrie*, described in the same passage, may also have been in Shostakovich's mind while writing the Ninth.)

Emulating the Second Quartet, the Ninth begins with a double-exposition sonata movement whose second subject (a crude quick-march led by a two-

---

[1] Alone among his otherwise obtuse accounts of Shostakovich's symphonies, the composer's Soviet biographer Rabinovich offers an unusually perceptive analysis of the Ninth (*Dmitri Shostakovich*, pp. 100–4), seeing it as a symphonic twin of the Second Piano Trio: 'a symphony of warning, a political pamphlet embodied in music'. This argues that, in Russian musicological circles at least, the aims of Shostakovich's Ninth Symphony were transparent enough to be broadly understood.

note tonic-dominant trombone) is clearly symbolic of the Vozhd. Instead of the quartet's striving, heroic first subject, however, the Ninth's opening bars mimic the ordinary citizen's carefree relief at the victorious conclusion of the war, an atmosphere of foolish horseplay conveyed in clownish, cartoon-like language. In the development section, though, the mood changes, larger crowds spilling onto the street and the brutally grinning heavy brass of the Fifth and Sixth Symphonies elbowing the rest of the orchestra aside. Fights break out and, when the strings attempt to restore the first subject, brass and drums attack them, roaring two-note war-cries. For a hectic moment the music continues in two keys at once until the trombone wrests control in favour of the second subject. Learning fast, the strings join in and, while the brass step down for a breather, the woodwind sneak a repeat of the first subject. Spotting the bullies coming back (seven bars after I in the Breitkopf edition), two flutes whistle up the second subject and the recapitulation ends on sneering trills, the quick-march in control.

In the second movement, Shostakovich's clownish tone takes a different tack. Both the clarinet's wan 'sad-face' first theme, with its tell-tale two-note pendant, and the heel-dragging second theme, a chain of two-note cells, subtly mock conventional grief. When real feeling briefly breaks through, the horns warn it off and soon the 'happy-face' clowns reappear with a cheery scherzo. Taking its rhythm and effects from the pell-mell second movement of the Sixth Symphony, this is yet another street-party that goes violently wrong. (Note the squeezed crescendi at figure B, bars 3–16, and the menacing proliferation of two-note figures in the wind and brass ten bars after C.) Over in a few hectic minutes, it plunges abruptly into the stillness of a bassoon recitative over sustained string chords, again recalling the Second Quartet. By now it is impossible to tell whether Shostakovich's solemnity is serious or just another mask, and when the bassoon, too, turns out to have been fooling us, we are at least relieved of the tension of uncertainty. The strings, though, are not so sure. Setting off into another clownishly tiptoeing two-note tune (a sort of burlesque of the Fourth Symphony's stamping first theme), the soloist only gradually tempts them to join in. At last, they 'get' it, take up the tune on their own account, and the finale is under way. Again it is the horns that apply the pressure and, as suspense finally erupts into action, they chortle in two-note triumph (four bars before G). A dark whirlwind now seizes the movement, driving it to a climax of teetering expectation – but all that emerges is the clownish main theme, hammered out on the entire orchestra in a peroration of towering bathos. Shostakovich's contempt is scalding. Here are your leaders, jeers the music: circus clowns. Point made, the Ninth Symphony summons a helterskelter coda and slams itself shut.

'I knew what I was in for when I wrote the Ninth,' admits the narrator of *Testimony*. 'Stalin was incensed. He was deeply offended because there was no chorus, no soloists. And no apotheosis. There wasn't even a paltry dedication. It was just music, which Stalin didn't understand very well and which was of dubious content.' The understatement is extraordinary. Given its context, the Ninth Symphony was an open gesture of dissent and it is hardly surprising that its exit from Soviet concert life was virtually instantaneous. Unrecorded in Russia until 1956, it was so thoroughly condemned in the press that, having written a symphony every two years since 1935, Shostakovich prudently waited a full seven years before returning to the genre.

The wartime mood of togetherness in Russia was not immediately dispersed by the return of normality after Germany's surrender in May 1945. A mood of escapism persisted till the end of the year, floated on the hope that, in the absence of the Nazi threat, the domestic regime might soften. The hope was, as Shostakovich and other intellectuals had foreseen, a forlorn one. Having identified the USA as his new 'external enemy', Stalin was already plotting another internal clamp-down to go with it. From this moment, the Cold War, semi-officially declared in early 1946, became inevitable. Soviet fear of the West swiftly mutated into a campaign against 'kowtowing to foreigners' under the auspices of which anyone who had ever spoken to a non-Russian or said a word in favour of the Allies risked deportation to the Gulag. In a drive to forestall contamination from beyond the USSR's borders, Russians who had been held prisoner in Europe during the war were bartered back from their countries of sanctuary and liquidated en masse. Altogether two and a quarter million were forcibly repatriated, of whom less than a fifth escaped summary execution or imprisonment once back in Russia. (Many of those who evaded the net were tracked down and killed abroad by Beria's NKVD.)

In the Soviet musical community caution and pessimism prevailed. Until the drift of events was clear, few composers were prepared to risk doing anything as explicit as setting a text in case their choice should later turn out to be counter-revolutionary. Instrumental works were the rule and, with Socialist Realism by default still in abeyance, these could, with a fair degree of safety, act as repositories for the darker feelings then common among Russian intellectuals. It was now that Prokofiev finished his First Violin Sonata, commenced in the grim days of 1938, and started his tragic, dissident Sixth Symphony. Myaskovsky and Khachaturian each wrote a troubled, introspective cello concerto. For his part, Shostakovich turned once more to the string quartet, his third in the genre.

All the wariness of the time seems to be distilled in the pinched, flinching central section of its second movement, the first of the five to be written. Composed in Moscow during late January 1946, it would later receive the temporary title 'Rumblings of unrest and anticipation'. However, work on the quartet lapsed almost as soon as it had begun, Shostakovich's next three months being taken up with teaching and the marking of exam papers at the Conservatoire. It was not until May that he went back to it and it took him three more months to finish the piece.

The only thing Shostakovich wrote in 1946, the Quartet No. 3 in F major,

Opus 73, gathers all the strands of code and design which he had developed during the war years. Here, again, is the five-movement layout with its variant of an underlying fourfold scheme: innocent, folk-simple prelude; brutal, disruptive scherzo; static, grieving passacaglia; ambivalent finale with climactic quotation from an earlier movement.

The first movement, the third double-exposition sonata the composer had written in three years, plays the now-familiar 'Mahler Four' trick of beginning with simple ingredients before transforming these in a complex development (in this case, a knotty fugue). Similarly, the relationship of first to second subject appears to echo that of the Second Quartet and Ninth Symphony: the People first; Stalin second. In this case, the People are symbolised by the number three, as against Stalin's usual two. The cellular grouping of three repeated notes or of three notes of equal value, begun in the Fifth Symphony and First Quartet, had also been used in the fugue of the Piano Quintet and the later stages of the Second Quartet, but it is here that Shostakovich finally establishes it as a major symbol. From now on, it would play a key role in almost everything he wrote.

In the Third Quartet, the terms of debate are laid out in the opening bars, the cello prodding gruffly at F, second violin and viola tapping out a three-note motto, and first violin playing a naively open melody based, again, on three-note cells. Of these, the most important is the cello. Apart from its repeated low F,[1] its first contribution is to copy an ostentatious semiquaver run by the first violin; then, when the violin does something too clever for it, it drops out for three bars, returning only when it hears a two-note phrase it can cope with; in bar 29 it squeezes out a single-note crescendo; and so on. During the development section, the cello's part consists almost entirely of two-note figures, squeezed crescendi, copycat phrases, and bars tacit to ponder its next remarks. Typically lagging two beats behind the other instruments, it is a classic 'Stalin' cypher.

The usual codes continue to prevail. Drooping to a dismal C major/minor for its second subject, the music clucks out a rustic two-note pattern before losing patience with the paucity of this and breaking briefly into two bars of sprightly triple-time. Later, at the climax of the fugue, having doggedly reiterated the first phrase of the first subject three times, the cello throws out, double-forte and double-stopped, an angry expansion of it reminiscent of the totalitarian scherzo of the Eighth Symphony (seventeen bars after C) and predictive of the 'Stalin' scherzo of the Tenth. Finally, following a recapitula-

---

[1] An insight into the significance Shostakovich invested in such details is provided by Valentin Berlinsky, cellist of the Borodin Quartet. Rehearsing the movement, they decided this note sounded better pizzicato. When they played their version to Shostakovich, however, he stopped them immediately, insisting that the note be played arco. Objecting that pizzicato sounded better, Berlinsky was gently informed: 'Of course pizzicato is better, but please play it arco.' The crude effect is, in other words, deliberate (interview with Michael Oliver, BBC Radio 3, 1983).

tion in which the first subject is allowed additional triplets, the triple-time bars from the second subject rush nervously through a scurrying codetta.

With its ponderous three-note bass-line and Jewish violin theme, the second movement recalls the 'dance of death' finale of the Second Trio. However, droning hurdygurdy bitonality, two-note cells, and one-note crescendi soon reveal a familiar presence and the music hunches into a grotesque tiptoe, as if trying not to be noticed. In a sourly sinister rustic coda, the cello sings 'cuckoo' on its inevitable two notes (a device perhaps appropriated from the end of the allegretto from Nielsen's Fourth Symphony). The struggle between two and three continues in the scherzo's jagged alternating bar-pattern of 2/4 and 3/4.[1] Again prefiguring the 'Stalin' scherzo of his Tenth Symphony, Shostakovich drops in and out of a duple gopak-rhythm without breaking the overall alternation (though the effect is of a growing dominance of two over three and, by the scherzo's final page, 3/4 has, in fact, disappeared).

Visiting Leningrad in July, Shostakovich took his half-finished quartet with him and the austere elegy of the quartet's adagio, composed while staying with his mother, may owe something to his feelings upon viewing the ruination of his home city. (A recent visitor, Ilya Ehrenburg, had been gravely impressed: 'Each house bore a scar. There were still notices on walls here and there, warning against the danger of walking on this or that side of the street. Many houses had scaffolding up; most of the workers were women . . . ') This short and very intense movement, a kind of recitative-passacaglia based on bar 7 of the finale of the Second Quartet, resolves sombrely on the work's three-note motif: a memorial to the People's dead.

The wry, spectral 6/8 melody which starts the finale, reminiscent of the second of the *Six Romances on Verses by English Poets*, is another death-dance, though this time a dance *of* the dead: of Stalin's victims returning to haunt him (and bringing with them the memorial passacaglia of the preceding movement). Oblivious to this, the cello sets off in complacent 2/4, but soon the first violin is sounding insistent triplets and the metre shimmers ominously back into 6/8. Like the ghost of Banquo at the feast, the passacaglia rises up in a chilly aura of hair-raising double-stopped violins, wailing the three-note motif of the People. Dumbstruck, the cello chokes and falls silent. Fading like mist at the movement's end, the spectral 6/8 melody leaves the People's motif strummed, jester-style, in three broken pizzicato chords over a numbed F major.

Composed without an overt programme, the Third Quartet had acquired one by the time its dedicatees, the Beethoven Quartet, premièred it in Moscow in December 1946. Presented as a 'war quartet', the work's five movements had been given explanatory subtitles by its composer: 'Calm unawareness of the future cataclysm', 'Rumblings of unrest and anticipation', 'The forces of war unleashed', 'Homage to the dead', and 'The eternal question: Why? And for what?' Aside from a hint in the last subtitle that war was not exactly what

---

[1] See also the Second Piano Trio at figures 79–81.

Shostakovich had in mind, the strongest evidence that this programme was a bodyguard of lies after the fashion of those surrounding the Fifth and Seventh Symphonies is the fact that he later dropped it. While no more obviously subversive than anything else he had written in recent years, the Third Quartet was his first venture following the outrageous Ninth Symphony and he may reasonably have felt it needed some extra protection. If, on the other hand, its programme was a last-minute precaution, this might be more simply explained as a response to a major change in the political weather – for on 14 August 1946, less than a fortnight after he had finished the quartet, Russia learned to fear a new name: Zhdanov.

Chapter Six

ISOLATION 1946–1953

They cursed me so all the world could hear
And gave me slander for my drink
And gave me poison for my food.
They took me out to the very brink
And for some reason left me there -
I will roam the silent squares,
As if I were the town's mad fool.

THERE can be few countries in which poetry means more than it does in Russia. In that semi-European, semi-Asiatic hybrid, verse has not long outgrown shamanic chant and poets are still expected to behave as if possessed of and by The Truth. Bringing volatility and a touch of the unpredictable to an otherwise regimented way of life, the poet is a kind of precarious safety-valve, and the verse recital a spiritually tense event prone to spontaneous outbursts of collective anger or grief.

Soviet Russia has seen many such occasions: Marina Tsvetayeva's 1922 recital of her counter-revolutionary White Russian verses; Mayakovsky's noisy appearance at the House of Komsomol in 1930; Mandelstam's 1933 recital in Leningrad – at which, asked by a provocateur for his opinion of contemporary Soviet verse, he replied coldly and to cheers from the audience that he was 'Akhmatova's contemporary'. But the most famous of all was a recital given by Akhmatova herself in the Moscow Polytechnic Museum in May 1944. By then unofficially recognised as one of the country's two greatest living poets (Pasternak being the other), she had become a living symbol of fortitude in the face of suffering. So charged was this feeling that when she made her entrance the audience stood and applauded her for, in effect, merely existing. 'No good will come of this,' murmured the reluctant focus of attention; and she was right. Informed of Akhmatova's standing ovation, a jealous Stalin demanded to know who had 'organised' it. From this moment, his revenge on her was guaranteed.

As soon as the war was over, the dictator and his colleagues began planning the resumption of their campaign to create a Soviet New Man. As in the late thirties, the key to this was the mechanisation of intellectual life through coercion, selective purges, and the strict enforcement of Socialist Realist dogma. Independent thought being at its most obvious in the printed word, Stalin chose literature as his first target and Andrei Zhdanov, the Party boss of Leningrad and a rampant philistine, as his Witchfinder General. A shrewd politician with the manner of a street bully, Zhdanov craftily catered to his leader's prejudices by concentrating on the Leningrad literary scene, singling out its two most eminent representatives: Shostakovich's friend the popular humorist Mikhail Zoshchenko, and Stalin's special bête noire Anna Akhmatova. Thus, on 14 August 1946, the Central Committee issued a ban on two Leningrad literary magazines for the 'anti-patriotic' crime of purveying 'the reactionary cult of the old St Petersburg' in the form of the writings of the 'extreme individualists' Akhmatova and Zoshchenko. A stunning shock to the Russian intelligentsia, this was the first salvo in a relentless barrage of intimidation against them which, during the late forties, became known among the population at large as the 'Zhdanovshchina' (Zhdanov's Time).

Zhdanov's method when attacking a given group of intellectuals was to assemble it in a public hall, pick out its two or three most prominent representatives, and personally insult them in the most brutal terms. As a result, their colleagues could be relied upon either to relapse into dazed conformity or, should they wish to ingratiate themselves with the authorities, join in the vilification from the floor. Thus summoned before the Writers' Union, the fifty-five-year-old Akhmatova had to sit quietly while Zhdanov lashed her as 'a demented gentlewoman dashing to and fro between her boudoir and her confessional – half-nun, half-harlot, mingling prayer with fornication'.[1] Zoshchenko, in his turn, was derided as 'a conscienceless literary hooligan' guilty of mocking the Soviet order and Soviet people – 'all this mockery being seasoned with empty wit and rubbishy humour'. Having been thoroughly spat on, both writers were banned from publication and stripped of their union membership and ration cards. Akhmatova, immunised by experience, left the hall in silence, her head high. A sobbing Zoshchenko, for whom this treatment was horribly new, tried to buttonhole friends, but they walked round him in a wide circle, terrified of being associated with an enemy of the people.

Like Akhmatova, Shostakovich would have seen it all before and *Testimony* plausibly represents his view of the literary purge as hard-bitten: 'People shied away from Zoshchenko on the street, just the way they had from me. They crossed the street, so that they wouldn't have to say hello. And they smeared him even more at hurriedly arranged meetings, and it was his former friends who did it the most, the ones who yesterday had praised him the loudest. Zoshchenko seemed surprised by it all, but I wasn't. I had gone through it at a younger age and the subsequent storms and bad weather had hardened me.' Under such circumstances, though, stoicism was not enough. The new 'anti-

---

[1] This epithet, which Volkov reports Shostakovich as finding typically meaningless (*Testimony*, p. 56) was, like most of Zhdanov's invective, supplied to him by his minions from established sources – in this case from the critic Boris Eikhenbaum's seminal character-assassination of 1923. Despite Alexandra Kollontai's sisterly defence, Akhmatova was from then on routinely dismissed in Soviet criticism as a neurasthenic 'boudoir' poetess with a martyr-complex. Ironically, considering Zhdanov's uncredited use of his insult, Eikhenbaum was a self-proclaimed Formalist.

patriotic' strand in official vituperation may well have been what prompted Shostakovich to take the precaution of disguising his Third Quartet as a piece about the war.

If so, it was a prudent move, for, in the afterblast of the Akhmatova–Zoshchenko affair, the Soviet cultural scene rapidly froze over. Restructured, the Writers' Union became openly repressive, with branch secretaries ordered to maintain 'vigilance' against any deviations from the tenets of Socialist Realism. Instructions were passed down to all writers to add generous measures of patriotic xenophobia to whatever they were currently working on and, to ensure that the point had been taken, further attacks on 'reactionary individualism' followed in the spring of 1947, with Pasternak as the main target. Meanwhile, hard on the heels of his swoop on the writers, Zhdanov tore into the film industry, among the many works he banned or scrapped outright as 'un-Soviet, anti-patriotic, and anti-People' being Kozintsev and Trauberg's *Simple Folk* (with a score by Shostakovich), Pudovkin's *Admiral Nakhimov*, and Eisenstein's *Ivan the Terrible Part II*. Soviet cinema now faced a decade of virtual standstill, while Eisenstein, who had trusted himself safe from further persecution, cracked up and, within two years, was dead.

Luckily for Shostakovich, duty now called sufficiently often to provide an excuse for writing nothing ambitious enough to be controversial. Elected Chairman of the Leningrad Composers' Union, he was called upon to make frequent time-consuming trips to the city. Similarly appointed a deputy to the Supreme Soviet of the RSFSR (an establishment whose main function is to rubber-stamp directives from the Central Committee), he found himself obliged to deal with a continual stream of queries from his constituents. Apart from scoring the film *Pirogov*, the only composing he did for most of the year took the form of the patriotic cantata *Poem of the Motherland*, knocked together from popular songs for the thirtieth anniversary of the Revolution in November. Finally, towards the end of 1947, he returned to serious composition with two works written almost simultaneously: Three Pieces for Orchestra and the First Violin Concerto. The former has never been published and has no opus number.[1] The latter, started in October 1947 and finished six months later, took a further eight years to see the light of day, receiving its première in 1955.

Written for David Oistrakh, with whom the composer gave many recitals during this period, the Violin Concerto No. 1 in A minor, Opus 77, was too hot a potato for its time – though exactly how hot its composer could hardly have realised when he began it. The first of a group of works written, as the Russians say, 'for the drawer', it shares with its companions (the song-cycle *From Jewish Folk Poetry*, the Fourth Quartet, and the Prelude in F sharp minor, Opus 87, No. 8) a fascination with Jewish folk music which, in the Russia of the late forties, was actively dangerous. To what extent Shostakovich intended the

---

[1] This work is possibly identical with the Ballet Suite No. 4, published in 1953.

concerto as a specifically 'Jewish' work is, however, unclear. As in the case of the Eighth Symphony and the war, Western commentators have been quicker to link the First Violin Concerto with the Holocaust than the score itself may warrant – for, even supposing that its 'Jewishness' is paramount, this aspect of the work is less likely to have been inspired by the crimes of the Nazis than by the potential for their replication in Russia after the war.

Though Russian anti-Semitism reached its nadir with the era of the great pogroms between 1870 and 1920, it continued to flourish under Soviet rule, often within the ranks of the Party itself. Stalin signed a statement condemning anti-Semitism in 1931 but, by the late thirties, had apparently changed his mind, liquidating most of the Jewish Communists during the Terror and closing all Yiddish schools and cultural associations in the interlude of Russo–German 'friendship'. Later, undiscouraged by the authorities, anti-Semitism infected Red Army recruiting policy and, after hostilities ceased, Stalin's own prejudice became increasingly blatant. Under his direction, the late forties saw an officially sponsored wave of anti-Semitism in Soviet life which, in the guise of the campaign against 'rootless cosmopolitans', persisted until his death in 1953.

According to *Testimony*, Shostakovich was aware of the initial stirrings of the anti-Jewish movement in late forties Russia as he was beginning the First Violin Concerto: 'All I heard people saying was, "The kikes went to Tashkent to fight". And if they saw a Jew with military decorations, they called after him, "Kike, where did you buy the medals?" That's when I wrote the Violin Concerto, the Jewish cycle, and the Fourth Quartet.' However, Stalinist anti-Semitism (as distinct from its populist equivalent) did not properly emerge until 1948; nor is it certain that, even in a work like the song-cycle *From Jewish Folk Poetry*, Shostakovich meant to address purely Jewish suffering.

Originally drawn into sympathy with the Jewish predicament by the revelation of the Nazi death camps in 1944–5, the composer both felt for the Jews as individuals and identified with them collectively as victims of systematic persecution ('Jews became a symbol for me. All of man's defencelessness was concentrated in them'). It is therefore probable that, when expressed via the abstract medium of music, Shostakovich's partly metaphorical sentiments would assume forms more general than specific – particularly since, musically, his identification with Jewishness went to the heart of his own creativity. 'Jewish folk music,' he acknowledges in *Testimony*, 'has made a most powerful impression on me . . . It's multifaceted, it can appear to be happy while it is tragic. It's almost always laughter through tears. This quality of Jewish folk music is close to my ideas of what music should be. There should always be two layers in music. Jews were tormented for so long that they learned to hide their despair. They express despair in dance music.' Indeed, so similar are Jewish ambiguity and Shostakovich's tragic–satiric temperament that, on his own admission, their relationship emerges in pieces not usually thought to belong to his 'Jewish' canon ('Many of my works reflect my impressions of Jewish music.'). Because of this, it seems sensible to seek in the First Violin Concerto not a particular Jewish theme – let alone a concrete historical event – but rather a feeling and method close to those of Jewish music conceived as a folk expression of the experience of the persecuted outsider.

The fact is that, though the predicament of Soviet Jewry became a major issue in Russian moral life after 1948, there were forces of a different sort at work in late 1947. Severe food shortages had brought malnutrition to Russia's cities for the first time since the war and the emotional tenor of everyday life was correspondingly depressed. Those who blamed the Communist system for this and had hoped to see its hold on Russia broken by the war (among whom we can presumably count Shostakovich) were faced with the dispiriting fact of a Stalinist hegemony in Eastern Europe and recent Communist takeovers of Poland and Hungary. Show-trials in the satellite countries were swelling the flow of recruits to the Gulag, as was the increasingly oppressive campaign at home against foreigners and anyone 'associated' with them.[1] In the camps themselves, an already strict regime was hardening and consequent riots, albeit unreported in the national press, were being suppressed with extraordinary ferocity.[2] But it was in the world of thought that the growing freeze was most insidious for, having dealt with literature and film, Zhdanov's programme of ideological purification was now exercising its frigid energies on a drive to establish the 'primacy' of Soviet science. Some of the results of this were merely ridiculous. Claims that supposedly Western inventions – of radio, internal combustion, penicillin, and the aeroplane – had actually been made by obscure Russians, led to popular cracks about the USSR being 'the home of the elephants' (though an announcement that Russia had discovered Antarctica seemed apt enough). Few jokes, however, were made about Zhdanov's continuing intellectual purges; indeed those economists, lawyers, linguists, and historians old enough to remember the Cultural Revolution recognised, in the humiliation of professors by their students during and after 1947, hideous parallels with the débâcle of 1929–32.

The return, after an absence of seven years, of full-scale Stalinist repression destroyed the togetherness of the war overnight. Recalling a period of mass paranoia in which people took to mounding cushions over their telephones because of a rumour that they contained listening devices, Nadezhda Mandelstam noted the grim similarities with 1937: 'Nobody trusted anyone else, and

---

[1] Prokofiev's Spanish wife, Lina, was one such victim. Sentenced to eight years in the camps for communicating with the American embassy in Moscow (an attempt to get some money to her mother in Paris), she never saw her husband again.

[2] In order to prevent the truth of the Gulag from reaching everyday society, those who had survived ten-year sentences handed down during the late thirties were, without trial, given the same again when their original terms expired. One of these 'repeaters' was Eugenia Ginzburg, author of a classic *samizdat* account of life in the camps (*Into the Whirlwind*), whose first sentence expired in 1947, but who was then rearrested and held for another six years.

every acquaintance was a suspected police informer. It sometimes seemed as though the whole country was suffering from persecution mania, and we haven't recovered from it.' This was the background to Shostakovich's First Violin Concerto which, in occasionally adopting Jewish mannerisms, did so less to point to the racial isolation of the Jew, than to speak, with a suggestive Jewish accent, of the political isolation of the Russian – not least of a Russian called Shostakovich. Around the time he began the concerto in October 1947, he had been told that *Poem of the Motherland*, his perfunctory offering for the thirtieth anniversary of the Revolution, had been rejected as politically inadequate. Hardly surprising, then, that the concerto's first movement should be informed with a very personal sense of foreboding.

Here, for the first time since the late thirties, Shostakovich composes a vigil-keeping nocturne along the lines of those to be found in his 'Terror symphonies': the Fourth, Fifth, and Sixth. No ominous dawn birds appear, yet the First Violin Concerto's slow opening movement paints its austerely silver-grey picture of haunted insomnia every bit as painstakingly as its predecessors. While a division into first and second subject is discernible, the abiding effect is of a seamlessly unfolding soliloquy, its contours bowed with sorrow and chained with heavy two-note phrases. Only in the central episode – where, to soft celesta chimes, the music gives way under its own weight and the violin plummets through a dreamscape of moonlit clouds – is there any glimpse of lightness or freedom. As if provoked by this, the questing second subject struggles to rise into a clearer atmosphere, but a dissonant crescendo drags it back to earth and, in tones of broken fatalism, the movement fades into a pale and comfortless dawn.

This drained and static mood is shattered by a crowded scherzo whose Jewish idiom suggests the experience of stigmatisation. Solomon Volkov speaks of 'an autobiographical motif: the lone individual against the raging, stupid mob' – and the identity of the individual concerned is spelled out in the movement's second section: D-Eb-C-B (in German notation, D-S-C-H, or D. Schostakowitsch). As in the Fourth Symphony's finale, the subject is the composer, beset by fools and knaves, scorned by his inferiors, and forced to demean himself with fatuous articles and speeches. (The notes of the main theme, later to reappear in the Tenth Symphony, are a sort of garbled version of his own motto.) The predominant style is of Mahlerian caricature – a kind of modernisation of songs like *Des Antonius von Padua Fischpredigt* and *Lob des hohen Verstandes*. Indeed, during a grotesque high-kicking folk dance that harks back to the Second Trio, the soloist – all pedantically slashing discords and squeezed crescendi – seems to be apeing a specific style of speech. Could this be an impersonation of Zhdanov? Shostakovich had yet to face him in anger, but is certain to have heard his radio addresses and may have met him during his work at the Composers' Union. As prime mover of the post-war cultural freeze – not to mention the merciless persecutor of a friend (Zoshchenko) and a living liberal legend (Akhmatova) – Zhdanov would have been much on the composer's mind at this time. That the two fast movements of the First Violin Concerto are, partly, satirical pictures of the Zhdanovshchina would make both historical and musical sense.

The sardonic anger of the scherzo spills over into the third movement, a searing passacaglia with fanfare accompaniment which at once mourns the dead of the Patriotic War and scourges the leaders who rewarded their sacrifice with a return to repression. Ending on the fanfare, the violin continues to toy with this in its cadenza until memories of the scherzo's crudity goad it to a withering virtuoso outburst that accelerates into the finale. Entitled 'Burlesque', this movement has all the complex ambiguity of Shostakovich at his most allusive, the soloist's interaction with its two-note material running the gamut from mock-conformism to open contempt. Varying the 'revenant' theme of the finale of his Third Quartet, the composer reintroduces the passacaglia – shrilling along in the sky above the racing presto below it – before switching into a kicking 'Stalin' gopak and closing on a final fist-shaking assertion of the third movement. Again, the inference is that the People will triumph in the end.

An extension of the Second and Third Quartets, the spirited defiance of the First Violin Concerto is, given its time, remarkable. Even more so is the fact that, somewhere between composing the passacaglia and the finale, Shostakovich was summoned to face the second of his public reprimands at the Composers' Union – an event for which he was doubtless prepared but which, astounding the foreign press-corps, echoed in headlines all around the world.

The 1948 campaign against Formalism in music repeated the pattern of the 1936 campaign fairly precisely. Prepared by the authorities in cahoots with Tikhon Khrennikov and the ex-Proletkult group, it had probably been ready for some time (perhaps since 1946) and, when finally activated, needed to be given the illusion of spontaneity by attaching it to a current issue. In the case of 1936, this had been Stalin's anger over Shostakovich's opera *Lady Macbeth*. In 1948, it was Stalin's anger over the Georgian composer Vano Muradeli's opera *The Great Friendship*. Arguably, both scandals were fakes.

Convened in Moscow in January 1948, the First Congress of the Union of Soviet Composers was chaired by Andrei Zhdanov, who, fresh from purging science, was raring to lay down the law in classical music and dominated the conference with boorish gusto. As with the writers, film-makers, philosophers, lawyers, and historians, his bullying vulgarity hit the sheltered community of composers like a thunderbolt, swiftly reducing grown men to frightened infants. A Western observer, the journalist Alexander Werth, recorded with distaste that 'many at the conference behaved like schoolboys laughing at teacher's jokes' – teacher, in this case, being the overbearing Zhdanov.

Called to account for the Formalism of his opera, Muradeli hastened to confess his guilt but, with an inconsequentiality which can only have been pre-arranged, blamed it on the 'Big Four' of Soviet music – Shostakovich, Prokofiev, Myaskovsky, and Khachaturian – who he claimed were able, through their eminence in the Composers' Union, to impose their Formalist perversions on everyone else. Zhdanov, delighted to have unearthed a conspiracy so soon in the proceedings, allowed the subject of Muradeli's opera to be dropped forthwith in favour of the more interesting game of hounding the Formalists, a theme taken up with enthusiasm by the Proletkult composer Vladimir Zakharov. All classical music, declared Zakharov, was worthless. The only arbiters were the people and what the people wanted were mass-songs. Likewise, the ongoing debate over Shostakovich's Eighth Symphony was pointless since Shostakovich's Eighth was, by definition, 'not a musical work at all' and anyone who denied this was in league with the West ('the reactionaries against whom we fight – the bandits and imperialists'). Rising in the stupefied silence after Zakharov's speech, Tikhon Khrennikov, who had first made his mark on Soviet music by attacking Prokofiev in the wake of the general denunciation of Shostakovich in 1936, broadened the scope of affairs by drawing attention to the Formalism of Prokofiev's Sixth Symphony and Myaskovsky's Cello Concerto. No doubt voicing his own jealous resentment of the Big Four, he blamed their success on the connivance of corrupt critics, a charge eagerly seconded by Ivan Dzerzhinsky,[1] to whom Soviet critics were mere 'flunkeys in the service of the big composers'. These accusations, which drew gasps in the hall, were too outrageous not to have been carefully worked out beforehand.[2] Called upon by Zhdanov to wind up the first day's discussion, Shostakovich delicately turned the anti-critical theme into a plea for freedom of speech, agreeing that what was needed was a truly honest exchange of opinion ('We lack a creative atmosphere; composers write their works in a cell – as it were'). Following a few inconsequential summarising remarks, he concluded with a shrug of resignation: 'Now, I take it, instructions will be given.'

The second day saw some brief signs of resistance, brave speeches by Khachaturian and Shebalin encouraging several speakers to take issue with Zakharov's wholesale rubbishing of their profession. The Proletkult, however, rallied with an attack by Viktor Belyi on Shostakovich's 'repulsive, ultra-individualist' Eighth and the old jibe about the Leningrad's best tune belonging to the Germans. On the third day, finally tiring of setting his captive audience at each other's throats, Zhdanov delivered his verdict. In a speech notable for its equally casual menace and ignorance, he announced that Soviet music was threatened by an invidious 'Formalist school' whose methods were 'radically wrong'. To cheers, he remarked that the modern music this school composed

---

[1] The same Dzerzhinsky whom Shostakovich had unselfishly helped in 1934–6.

[2] Designed to further isolate the leading composers, the Khrennikov/Dzerzhinsky line possessed the additional advantage, so far as Stalin was concerned, of mobilising anti-Semitism. (Most Soviet music critics happened to be Jewish. Prominent among the pro-Shostakovich critics disciplined in 1949 were Dmitri Rabinovich and Israel Nestyev.)

reminded him of nothing so much as 'a dentist's drill or a musical gas-wagon, the sort the Gestapo used'. A cumbersome attack on the principal 'Formalists' – Shostakovich, Prokofiev, Myaskovsky, Khachaturian, and Shebalin – drew further appreciative laughter. The embarrassing fact that these composers had between them won half the Stalin Prizes awarded during the previous decade was dismissed by Zhdanov without missing a beat: 'We did not consider, when we awarded you these prizes, that your works were faultless, but we were patient and waited for you to take the right road. Now, obviously, the Party has had to step in.'

In the aftermath of the ovation which greeted Zhdanov's harangue, delegates vied with each other to claim themselves 'deeply moved', even 'shattered', by its sweeping profundity. Again required to close the meeting, Shostakovich seems to have played the *yurodivy*, returning, as if oblivious of its irrelevance, to Muradeli's opening contention that he had written a bad opera because the Formalists had made him do it. Muradeli, he submitted, had written a bad opera because he was incapable of writing a good one. Furthermore, Soviet music was not (as Zhdanov had just spent half an hour insisting) in a terrible state but, on the contrary, 'advancing along a wide front'. To a tense silence, he concluded by re-adopting his usual ambiguity: 'I think that our three days' discussion will be tremendously valuable, especially if we think carefully about Comrade Zhdanov's speech. I, and I'm sure others here, would very much like to examine the text of it. A close study of this remarkable document ought to be of great help to us in our work.'

This sort of veiled insolence was not going to be tolerated. Sacked from the directorate of the Composers' Union, Shostakovich, Prokofiev, Khachaturian, Myaskovsky, and Shebalin were replaced by their talentless Proletkult foes: Zakharov, Chulaki, Belyi, and Koval. For his services as unofficial Congress co-ordinator, Tikhon Khrennikov was made Secretary-General, a post he thereafter continued to hold for forty years.[1] On 10 February, Zhdanov issued a Central Committee resolution condemning Muradeli's opera and the 'anti-People Formalism' associated with it. A further conference in April saw a complete revision of the history of Soviet music, establishing the Proletkult/ Socialist Realist tradition as the official mainstream. Dismissing Shostakovich's symphonies en masse as 'frantically gloomy and neurotic', Khrennikov declared almost everything by him and the other major composers 'alien to the Soviet People' and unfit for performance. All records and tapes by them and their fellow Formalists were ordered to be destroyed and their scores recycled to save paper.

---

[1] Universally hated (Viktor Seroff and Andrei Olkhovsky both refer to him as 'the evil genius of Soviet music'), Khrennikov made Prokofiev's last years a misery and never missed an opportunity of needling Shostakovich. Called to account under *glasnost* in 1988, he defended himself against his furious victims by pleading that he had only been obeying orders and that his family would have suffered had he not done so.

In the West, media speculation over the 'sharps and flats purge' (as *Newsweek* called it) was busy and, as usual, bewildered. How, pundits wondered, could famous and comparatively audience-friendly composers like Prokofiev, Shostakovich, and Khachaturian be considered too modern for the world's most 'progressive' society? Why were workers all over the USSR up in arms about Formalism and besieging the Soviet press with complaints about it? And, most perplexing of all, why were the composers in question confessing their sins and grovelling in thanks to the Communist Party for showing them the error of their ways? Only the more sophisticated commentators (mostly émigré Russians) grasped that the whole thing was centrally orchestrated and part of a very much grander design. The average left–liberal opinion was that Stalin and Zhdanov were perfectly within their rights to demand a non-élitist art consistent with 'Socialist' aims. To this constituency, warnings like George Orwell's – 'If we find ourselves in ten years' time cringing before somebody like Zhdanov, it will probably be because that is what we have deserved' – seemed little more than reactionary gloom and distortion.

Even in Russia itself it was possible to misunderstand what was really going on. Olga Ivinskaya records that, ignoring her opinion that Shostakovich would recant the following day, Pasternak sent the composer a letter of support – and was duly dismayed when his mistress turned out to be right: 'Oh Lord, if only they knew how to keep silent at least! Even that would be an act of courage!'[1] Myaskovsky, in fact, did just this and got away with it. He, though, was an old man who habitually shunned the public eye. Neither Prokofiev nor Shostakovich, well known figures with young families to consider, could afford to follow his example. Pleading illness, a terrified Prokofiev made his confession by letter. For his part, Shostakovich had to face a week of self-criticism meetings at which the only card he could play was the *yurodivy* joker – as with Boris Pilnyak during the early thirties – of blaming himself a little too readily for a little too much. (In the free conditions of *perestroika*, the theatre director Yuri Lyubimov has spoken – laughingly – of Shostakovich's willingness in 1948 to 'restructure' himself by confessing to absolutely anything.)

Nor, this time, was there to be any respite after the initial frenzy. Zhdanov had harnessed the entire Soviet propaganda machine to the anti-Formalism campaign and for months the country was convulsed with debates and demonstrations about it. At school, children were drilled to despise the 'mercenary Formalists' who had been caught trying to wreck the Soviet music industry and 'Formalist' became part of the common repertoire of insults, despite the fact that few had any idea what it meant. The consequences were inevitable. Windows were broken in the Shostakovich household and, during one especially nasty period, young Maxim defended his father by sitting in a

---

[1] Only a year later, Pasternak, who had evidently forgotten writing a pair of obsequious odes to Stalin in 1936, found himself once again poetically on his knees to the dictator over Ivinskaya's arrest.

tree outside the house with a catapult, shooting at anyone who stopped to yell an insult or throw something. The cellist Mstislav Rostropovich, then twenty-one, saw the effects of all this at first-hand: 'Shostakovich was like a lunatic. He didn't sleep. He drank a great deal, I am sure. Terrible. That was the first time I felt the problems of the Soviet system.'

Despite appearances, however, Shostakovich was still in control. While Prokofiev, Khachaturian, and Shebalin fell seriously ill after the January–February purge, he worked on with the energy of a man possessed, finishing the First Violin Concerto before turning to an extraordinary new work: *Portrait Gallery (Rayok)*, a cantata satirizing the events in the Composers' Union and of the Zhdanovshchina in general. Explicit where the Fourth Symphony's finale had been oblique, the piece was written not so much 'for the drawer' as for the sake of its composer's sanity – an act of vital, if private, catharsis. Hidden in the Shostakovich family archive for forty years, its existence was revealed in one of Solomon Volkov's footnotes to *Testimony* (p. 147), but it was not till 1989 that the composer's third wife, Irina, deemed it safe to exhibit the manuscript.[1]

Like his late *Preface to the Complete Edition of My Works*, the text of *Portrait Gallery* (by Shostakovich himself) is a parody of vacuous officialese. Headed, in the style of a bureaucratic circular, 'To assist students', the title page consists of the following announcements: 'The struggle between the Realist tendency in music and the Formalist tendency in music. Text and music by unknown authors. The Section of Musical Security has informed us that the authors are being sought. The Section assures us that the authors will be found.' Next comes a bogus introduction 'from the publisher' explaining how the score was discovered, buried in excrement, by 'the candidate for the Fine Sciences, P. I. Opostylov' – a swipe at Pavel Ivanovich Apostolov, senior Party *apparatchik* in the Moscow branch of the Composers' Union. (Shostakovich's version of his name is a pun on a Russian root meaning 'tiresome' or 'detestable'.) Opostylov's 'report' on 'this outstanding work' mercilessly debunks the clanging clichés, fatuous tautologies, and pretensions to 'scientific' status of Soviet critical style – a sarcasm which continues in the libretto itself, the first 'aria' of which runs as follows:

> Comrades! Whereas Realist music is written by those we call composers
> of the People, Formalist music is for some reason written by composers
> who are against the People. Comrades, one must ask why it is that Realist
> music is written by those we call composers of the People, whereas
> Formalist music is always written by composers who are against the

---

[1] According to André Lischke's sleeve-note to the Erato recording (ECD 75571), issued in autumn 1989, Mstislav Rostropovich believes *Portrait Gallery* to have been composed, not in 1948, but around ten years later. The composer's third wife, Irina, contests this in an interview given to *Soviet Culture* (20 January 1989), maintaining that Shostakovich's close friend Isaak Glikman saw the work, complete with the exception of Troikin's last speech, during summer 1948.

People? Those composers who we call composers of the People write Realist music, comrades, because, being by nature Realists, they simply cannot help but write Realist music, whereas those composers who we call anti-People composers, being by nature unrepenting Formalists, simply cannot help but write Formalist music. It follows, then, that we should create conditions in which our People's composers will be able to develop melodies of a Realistic nature, whereas those composers who are against the People should at once abandon their highly questionable and dubious experiments in Formalist music.

Sung to the Georgian melody *Suliko*, Stalin's favourite song, this is a send-up of the Leader's lumbering radio speeches, notorious for their elephantine progressions from A to B by way of self-answering rhetorical questions. A parody of Zhdanov's equally heavy-handed jocularity follows this and the work ends with a Red-Army-style rendition of the popular song *Kalinka* to the words 'Sonatas, cantatas, quartets, and motets!'.

Deliberately banal, the musical aspect of *Portrait Gallery* is negligible. None of the usual codes feature in it and, without knowing who the composer was, it would be hard to identify it as by Shostakovich. But while its blistering satire is too topical to be of more than documentary interest, this interest is so great as to qualify it as a major discovery. Bearing out Solomon Volkov's claims to have obtained information from Shostakovich of unprecedented intimacy, *Portrait Gallery* also confirms the lacerating wit of *Testimony* and its subject's controversial use of scatological expressions. Indeed, Dvoikin's rhapsodic encomium to 'a legitimate *lezghinka*' corresponds precisely to a vitriolic passage in *Testimony* (pp. 143–5) concerning Muradeli's part in the 1948 fiasco.

What is most convincing about *Portrait Gallery*, however, is its amplification of Shostakovich's creative creed. Two-thirds of its acid is flung not at the political but at the cultural attitudes of the Soviet establishment – specifically at its middlebrow elevation of 'beauty and elegance' over truth and directness. The subject of further satire in the finale of his Thirteenth Symphony, this vital and neglected element in Shostakovich's outlook will be examined more fully in the final chapter of this book.

Now more or less deprived of income from serious music and unable to support his family on his teaching salaries, Shostakovich was forced to find work in the film industry. Had it been Stalin's intention to destroy him, no openings would have been found, but the monarch–jester relationship was intact and the composer's luck had not entirely deserted him. Gerasimov's epic *The Young Guard* had been in production at the Gorky Studio since 1947 and, though Stalin ordered script changes when he saw a rough cut in 1948, Shostakovich's score met with his gruff approval. Because of this, no objections were raised to him working on two more films that year: Dovzhenko's *Michurin* and Alexandrov's *Meeting on the Elbe*. It is a measure of Stalin's estimation of Shostakovich as a cinema composer that these were virtually the only films made in Russia in 1948 and, as such, were under the dictator's personal supervision. Aware of the delicacy of his situation, Shostakovich took pains to please, re-using his famous *Song of the Meeting* (from *Counterplan* in 1932) in *Michurin*,[1] and writing two more hits, *Homesickness* and *Song of Peace* for *Meeting on the Elbe*. It was, however, his fate to be always at the centre of controversy in Soviet life and so it turned out with the film *Michurin*. A 'biopic' about the Russian horticulturist Ivan Michurin, it had been planned to accompany the latest stage in Zhdanov's campaign of intellectual mechanisation: the establishment of the 'primacy' of Soviet biology. Events, however, assumed an unpredictable pattern and the film had to be held up for alterations stemming from late developments at the Congress of the Soviet Academy of Agricultural Sciences in Moscow that August.

Falling ill while finalising the campaign, Zhdanov died soon after the conference he had intended to chair,[2] but his place was taken by Trofim Lysenko, Stalin's favourite biologist, who dominated the Congress every bit as effectively as his mentor had dominated the arts and sciences conferences of the previous two years. Lysenko's theory, based on Michurin's, was that acquired characteristics were inheritable (that is, changes experienced by an organism in its lifetime would be transmitted to its offspring). That this contradicted every known law of genetics daunted Lysenko not one whit. Claiming that the idea that heredity had anything to do with genes and chromosomes was 'imperialist' and that those promulgating it were ipso facto 'lackeys of American imperialism', he bullied and humiliated the leading figures in the Soviet life sciences until they 'repented'. Just as, six months earlier, Russia's best composers had been made to forswear Formalism for Socialist Realism, so the finest Soviet biologists and agronomists were forced to abandon genetics for 'Michurinism', an outcome that set research in Russia back a decade and made her the laughing-stock of the international scientific community. How much of this Shostakovich understood is unknown. At the very least, he would have been reassured that Stalinism was capable of asserting anything about anyone as long as it served its purpose.[3]

September brought a further blow: Shostakovich was sacked from his teaching posts for 'professional incompetence', so cutting off his only guaran-

---

[1] He had already re-used it once in the previous year, as the final number of *Poem of the Motherland*.

[2] Some, of course, say he was poisoned by Stalin (or Malenkov).

[3] There was, in fact, a serious issue at stake in the Lysenko affair. Stalin's aim of engineering the Soviet New Man depended on two strands of theory: Pavlovian conditioning and Michurinist biology. From Pavlov came the idea of draining individual identity by isolation and fear before filling it again with thoughts and reflexes approved by the authorities (as diagnosed by Orwell in *Nineteen Eighty-Four*). This achieved, Michurinist biology would, it was hoped, breed out the old characteristics within a generation (see, for example, Heller, pp. 80–1).

teed source of income. Again, a kind of compensation was the fact that he was not alone, all the other 'Formalists' receiving the same treatment (the most spectacular instance being Shebalin's removal from the directorship of the Moscow Conservatoire). Designed to exclude their enemies from contact with the new generation of composers, this putsch was the work of Khrennikov and his Proletkult allies who, as in 1931 and 1936, were going all out for a final solution on the vexing issue of genius. Indeed, judging from the viciousness of the attacks they made on him during this period, there is no doubt that, had these jealous mediocrities taken over the Politburo instead of the Composers' Union, Shostakovich would have been shot in 1948 and his case closed for good.

Stalin, however, had plans for him. While evidently approving of the life of penury to which the composer had been reduced – the image of a slave living on crumbs flicked from his master's table must have occurred to both of them – he also wished to confuse foreign opinion on the subject of the Zhdanovshchina, it being important not to give the unequivocal impression abroad that Soviet domestic policy had put Russia beyond the pale of civilisation. Thus, soon after Zhdanov's death in August, *Pravda* carried a note mildly approving the 'realism' of Shostakovich's score for *The Young Guard* and, some weeks later, announced that he had been made a People's Artist of the RSFSR. (Prokofiev had received the same honour a year earlier, shortly before being criticised for his Sixth Symphony and attacked by Zhdanov at the Composers' Union.)

Something of the hopeless spartan regime he and his family were reduced to between 1948 and 1953 can be felt in the work Shostakovich turned to next: *From Jewish Folk Poetry*, Opus 79. Written for soprano, contralto, tenor, and piano, the starkness of this cycle is unsettling even in the orchestrated version its composer made of it in 1963. It is as if, with these songs of poverty and starvation, Shostakovich wished to make a point about 'realism' – *real* realism rather than the bogus 'Socialist' variety. Music whose bones show through its withered skin, *From Jewish Folk Poetry* is one of the most devastating expressions of twentieth-century protest art and anyone who can sit through it without squirming is well advised to check that they still have a pulse.

The official launch of Stalinist anti-Semitism had come in September 1948 with the arrest of the Jewish Anti-Fascist Committee. Soon afterwards, all Jewish institutions and newspapers were closed and the leading Jewish writers rounded up, many of them later to be shot as 'Zionist agents of American imperialism'. As the months went by, the persecution grew increasingly rabid, 'rootless cosmopolitans' being targeted in every walk of life and scarcely a day passing without *Pravda* reporting fresh discoveries of 'nests' of 'these passport-less beggars'. Sickened by this, Shostakovich searched for a text which would suit the directness of his feelings. While the book of artless Jewish folk poems he settled on may not immediately have reminded him of Mahler's use of *Des Knaben Wunderhorn*, the parallel is clear. Like Mahler's pioneeringly low-ironic song-cycle (so influential on Brecht and Weill), the eleven settings of *From*

Jewish Folk Poetry employ a stylised naivety to cut through their audience's protective shell of refinement. Too raw to evade and too sophisticated to dismiss, these songs take the listener out of the comfort of the concert hall and into the bleak squalor of village and ghetto. This alienative effect is carefully prepared, the cycle gradually shifting from ironic resignation into anguished satire. *Warning* quotes the finale of the Second Trio, while a harrowing poem in which a woman lying with her sick baby in a cold cottage weeps to see winter coming is followed by *Song of Plenty*, a shepherd's hymn of joy ('My country is beautiful!') set in a parody of Socialist Realist concord.

From *Jewish Folk Poetry* was obviously too contentious for 1948 and Shosta-kovich bitterly consigned it to his drawer, along with *Portrait Gallery* and the First Violin Concerto. ('Not one of these works could be performed then. They were heard only after Stalin's death. I still can't get used to it.') Worse, however, was to come. In order to repair the damage done to Russia's international image by his recent purges, Stalin decreed a 'struggle for peace'. Every available intellectual was conscripted into this effort and the peace crusade filled the newspapers, vying for space with the ongoing campaign against rootless cosmopolitans. No use to Stalin in hiding, Shostakovich was hauled out of seclusion and sent with a Soviet delegation to the Cultural and Scientific Congress for World Peace, convened at New York's Waldorf-Astoria Hotel in March 1949. 'People sometimes say that it must have been an interesting trip,' grits the narrator of *Testimony*. 'Look at the way I'm smiling in the photographs. That was the smile of a condemned man. I answered all the idiotic questions in a daze, and thought, When I get back it's over for me.' The émigré composer Nikolai Nabokov, no fan of Shostakovich's music, attended the Congress and found himself sitting opposite him, close enough for their knees to touch.

> Throughout the conference [Nabokov recalls], I watched his hands twist the cardboard tips of his cigarettes, his face twitch and his whole posture express intense unease. While his Soviet colleagues on the right and left looked calm and as self-contented as mantelpiece Buddhas, his sensitive face looked disturbed, hurt and terribly shy. I felt, as I lit his cigarette or passed a record to him from an American admirer, that he wanted to have it over with as quickly as possible, that he was out of place in this crowded room full of rough, angry people, that he was not made for public appearances, for meetings, for 'peace missions'. To me he seemed like a trapped man, whose only wish was to be left alone, to the peace of his own art and to the tragic destiny to which he, like most of his countrymen, had been forced to resign himself.

At a press conference two days later, the composer (in 'a nervous and shaky voice') read a xenophobic speech, dripping with vitriolic references to Prokof-iev and Stravinsky, which Nabokov, familiar with the traits of Soviet official style, knew immediately had been written by someone else: 'I sat in my seat petrified by this spectacle of human misery and degradation. It was crystal clear to me that what I had suspected from the day I heard Shostakovich was going to be among the delegates representing the Soviet Government was true: This speech of his, this whole peace-making mission was part of a punishment, part of a ritual redemption he had to go through before he could be pardoned again.' The torture reached heights of exquisite Oriental refinement when the composer was required to perform a piano version of the scherzo from his Fifth Symphony in front of thirty thousand people at Madison Square Garden. ('I thought, This is it, this is the last time I'll ever play before an audience this size.')

Back in the USSR, Shostakovich discovered to his surprise that his guilt had been sufficiently expiated for pictures of him to have begun appearing in the papers again. Furthermore, though the ban on his earlier works remained, it seemed that he was free to submit new material provided it was written in a 'democratic' (that is, depersonalised) style. Interest in both Russia and the West concerning what Shostakovich would come up with in 'answer' to 1948 was intense. Another Fifth, perhaps? The long-lost Lenin Symphony? In fact, informed that he might redeem himself by composing something to glorify Stalin's reafforestation plan,[1] he had small choice. Cutting his losses, he produced the oratorio *The Song of the Forests*, Opus 81, the monumental blandness of which had Western pundits sadly writing him off as a burnt-out case. Only in the work's penultimate number, with its echoes of the finale of the Eighth Symphony, were there any signs of life. Otherwise, the 'Fifth of 1949' was received with disappointment as the nearest thing to a musical vacuum Shostakovich had ever created. To Khrennikov, however, *The Song of the Forests* was exactly what the Soviet People wanted, being, he claimed, far superior to its composer's dreary symphonies. Clicking smoothly into action, the Soviet propaganda machine confirmed this with a Stalin Prize, First Grade. Though vital so far as the money went (10,000 roubles – equivalent to around £1,000 at today's rate), this, to Shostakovich, must have seemed the lowest point of his career. For the sake of self-respect, he had to compose something he could be proud of, even if that meant locking it in a drawer as soon as he had finished it.

His solution, the String Quartet No. 4 in D, Opus 83, was the last of his 'Jewish' works and, like the others, it was withheld by its composer, receiving its première only after Stalin died in 1953. Commencing in 'democratic' style with folk violins skirling up and down the scale of D major over a sixty-four-bar hurdygurdy pedal-point, the piece presents the very image of collectivist unison. However, as its textures mass like a crowd rising in applause, it grinds

---

[1] 'The Great Stalinist Plan for Remaking Nature', begun in October 1948, was a fifteen-year tree-planting project designed to protect southern Central Asia from drought. Thomas Whitney, then attached to the American embassy in Moscow, saw it as 'Stalin's King Canute complex': 'Even the hot drought wind from Central Asia – the feared *suhkovei* – would submit to the will of Stalin!' (*Russia in My Life*, p. 171). Comparable to Mao's campaign to wipe out sparrows, this madly impractical grand design struggled on while Stalin was alive, but was dropped immediately after he died.

into dissonance with the violins striving shrilly to escape into E flat. At the height of the pandemonium, three high A's suggest the Fifth Symphony, an allusion confirmed when no less than fourteen high A's shriek out consecutively at figure 5 (bars 4–7). As dominant as it was in in the Fifth, the initial key exerts so tight a hold over the first movement that no modulation can last long enough to establish a second subject and, exhausted by its explosive opening, it declines onto another pedal-point D and stops. (Without antithesis, there can be no development. Shostakovich may have had in mind the then-famous 'no conflict' theory, according to which, having attained perfect unanimity, Stalinist society had outgrown the era of dialectic.)

The second movement, a wanly beautiful 'ballerina' waltz to a persistent two-note accompaniment, expands the range of allusion to include the Third Quartet, citing its symbolic alternation of 3/4 and 2/4. Swooning gratefully from F minor to the 'escape' key of E flat, the music is dismayed to find itself sliding into D minor and, in trying to regain E flat, writhes in a fraught crescendo. A sombre chorale introduces an allusion to the fanfare figure from the cadenza of the First Violin Concerto (figure 29), before fading quietly into an F major twilight.[1] The trotting, dreamlike third movement – seemingly another of the composer's reveries of boyhood – dwindles sinisterly into a sequence of seesawing semitones, the minimal expression of which music is capable beyond the repetition of a single note. The chill greyness of this motif is haunting. Many of Shostakovich's harmonic schemes are based on the clash of adjacent notes and keys, but the swing of these bare descending minor seconds, like a rocking-horse nodding imperceptibly in an empty room long after its child rider has forgotten it, would gradually come to dominate his music, especially that of his late period.

Other 'late' mannerisms – skeletal pizzicati and pinched, tapping high notes – occur in the finale, which, extending the sepulchral mood of the third movement, takes the form of a grotesque Jewish dance paced by octave D's in the bass. Now pitching D flat against the home key, a tremendous dissonant crescendo peaks in D major unison before subsiding into a wistful recollection of the chorale from the second movement. A clue to what this means follows with a second reference to the fanfare figure from the First Violin Concerto (figure 98). Hounded beyond endurance in that Orwellian age of 'the struggle for peace', Shostakovich may perhaps have been brooding on the ultimate peace: death. As in the Second Trio and Third Quartet, the quartet's final crescendo hints at the idea of the return of the dead, but this time the composer seems not so much to be evoking ghosts as identifying with them. In this respect, the premonitions of his death-fixated late style may be more than coincidental.

---

[1] Further references to the First Violin Concerto (first movement) occur in the quartet's spectral third movement (cello at figure 38, violin at figure 49), while there is a veiled allusion to the Second Quartet's finale at figure 42.

If, however, the Fourth Quartet is partly the work of one exhausted by the world and longing to be out of it, its exuberant invention and rich system of allusion belie this. Tired and frightened as he may have been in his conscious mind, Shostakovich was clearly intact and thriving on the deeper creative levels.

During the years 1949–52, Russia froze rigidly in the icy grip of Stalinist terror. Conformism in all walks of life became obligatory, and cultural life went into hibernation, little of note appearing in any of the arts. Living, like Akhmatova and Zoshchenko, largely on loans from friends, Shostakovich supplemented his income with film-work and 'democratic' vocal pieces, the latter usually in collaboration with the conformist poet Yevgeny Dolmatovsky.[1] His major source of earnings came in the form of Stalin Prizes awarded to a stream of Socialist Realist pieces written, as Vishnevskaya observes, 'as a last resort – to get a crust of bread'. (These were the films *Pirogov*, *The Young Guard*, *Michurin*, *Meeting on the Elbe*, and *The Fall of Berlin*, and the vocal works *The Song of the Forests* and *Ten Choral Poems by Revolutionary Poets*.) In addition, Shostakovich's friend and colleague Lev Atoumyan, who regularly worked for him as an arranger of the suites from his film scores, created three Ballet Suites between 1949 and 1952 by taking extracts from *The Golden Age*, *The Bolt*, and *The Limpid Stream*, and some numbers from the film *Michurin* and the incidental score for *The Human Comedy*. (These, in turn, were eked out even further by the composer as his *Dances of the Dolls* for piano in 1951.)

Shostakovich's only substantial serious work during this stagnant period was a set of 24 Preludes and Fugues for piano, Opus 87, composed between October 1950 and February 1951. Inspired by a reacquaintance with Bach's *Well-Tempered Klavier*, which he heard at a festival in Leipzig, this was his longest work under a single title apart from *Lady Macbeth*. Some great music is contained in it – in particular Nos 12 and 24 – but the set was written to be performed under existing political conditions and is, with some outrageous exceptions, conservatively styled. Composed in numerical order, the work was probably as therapeutic for Shostakovich as his earlier Preludes, Opus 34,

---

[1] Shostakovich's Dolmatovsky settings began in 1942, with two items in *Native Leningrad*, and concluded in 1970, with the eight choruses *Loyalty*, Opus 136. Dolmatovsky also wrote the words for *Patriotic Song* (Shostakovich's entry for the National Anthem competition in 1943); one song in *Victorious Spring*, Opus 72 (1945); two songs in the film *Meeting on the Elbe*, Opus 80 (1948); *The Song of the Forests*, Opus 81 (1949); the hit song *A Beautiful Day* from the film *The Fall of Berlin*, Opus 82 (1949); *Four Songs*, Opus 86 (1951); *The Sun Shines over Our Motherland*, Opus 90 (1952); and *Songs of Our Days*, Opus 98 (1955). Their most popular collaboration, *The Homeland Hears* from *Four Songs*, Opus 86, was sung by Yuri Gagarin while in orbit around the earth on 12 April 1961 – the first song to be sung in space.

though this time satire was necessarily rationed (Nos 2 and 15) and the tone of some of the fugues (for example Nos 4 and 6) introverted to the point of depression. (A clue to his state of mind upon starting the cycle occurs in the fugue of No. 1 in C major, which, in the *'beklemmt'* style of the Cavatina in Beethoven's Opus 130, almost breaks down as though choked with inexpressible feeling.) Premièred, after a delay of nearly two years, in December 1952, the work was cautiously received as a possible case of Formalism.

By this time, the USSR had been in Stalin's deep-freeze for nearly five years. Living in a state uncomfortably close to the conditions portrayed by Orwell in *Nineteen Eighty-Four* (see Appendix 1), most Russians were paralysed by a mixture of fear and propaganda-drilled Stalin-worship. Yet the dissidents of Stalinism – Nadezhda Mandelstam calls them 'the secret intelligentsia' – remained, like the Winstons and Julias of Orwell's novel, resentfully obstinate and unbroken. A typically grim Russian joke of this period conveys the tone of contemporary dissident life: a man comes to a kiosk to buy *Pravda*, scans its front page, and then hurls the paper away. He does the same the next day and the day after that. Finally, the intrigued kiosk-owner asks him why he throws the paper away without reading the rest of it. 'I only need the front page,' the man replies. 'I'm waiting for an obituary.' 'But they don't print obituaries on the front page.' 'Take it from me, friend, the obituary I'm waiting for will be on the front page.' Rumours about Stalin's declining health were rife among the secret intelligentsia in 1952 and, during the latter half of the year, Shostakovich may have got wind that the dictator's days were numbered – either that, or he simply had an intuition that the hell Russia was in was about to end. Some explanation, at least, is needed to account for the extraordinary final work of his enforced period of self-censorship: the titanic, battling Fifth Quartet.

Like several of the composer's wartime pieces, the Quartet No. 5 in B flat major, Opus 92, begins with a double-exposition sonata movement. In its virile Beethovenian energy, however, it resembles one previous work in particular: the Second Quartet. Many other parallels exist in the Fifth – indeed, most of its tonal and metrical symbolism is derived from the Fourth Quartet – but the sense of militant resistance in its magnificent opening movement had not appeared in Shostakovich's music since the Second Quartet nearly a decade earlier and, in fact, the spiritual kinship of the two works is made explicit by an important quotation in the Fifth's finale.

The tremendous struggle of the Fifth Quartet's opening allegro is implicit in its seemingly harmless opening bars. An ascending three-note phrase is hastily corrected to a stable eight by the viola, whose A flat tonality pays no attention whatever to the violins' B flat. Holding truculently to its motif (much like the trombone in the first movement of the Ninth Symphony), the viola canvasses support from the cello, which, rudely compromising between keys, introduces a bellicose A major sculpted in terse two-note blocks. As in the Fourth Quartet, a grating dissonance results, the violins screaming out E flat (the Fourth's 'escape' key) until the forces of aggression subside, allowing the appearance of a gracefully waltzing second subject in G. Before long, though, a stabbing 2/4 counter-theme (written as 2 against 3) begins to dominate and, slumping dejectedly into E flat minor, the exposition returns to its starting-point. The rhythm of the 'betrayal' motif from *Lady Macbeth* now ushers in the vast development section – a passage which, for scale and ingenuity, foreshadows the first movement of the Tenth Symphony, written a year later. A war for control of key and metre, it mounts towards a rending climax in which, through the brutal offices of A major, the key of A flat (and a numbed, limping unison) is forcibly imposed on the waltzing second subject. A final, sorrowful visit to E flat minor heralds the restoration of the home key but, as at the end of the Seventh Symphony's first movement exposition, what sounds idyllic is actually sinister – another angle on the deceptive smile of Socialist Realism.

Segueing to its central slow movement, the quartet relapses into an icily muted B minor. Desolately akin to the fourth movement of the Eighth Symphony, this three-note threnody for crushed aspirations and deformed lives also recalls the 'ghost music' of the Third Quartet. Haunted by its musical ancestors, the Fifth now begins to echo increasingly with recollections. At figure 64, a pleading 'vocal' melody, reminiscent of Katerina's despairing aria 'Seryozha, my love' (*Lady Macbeth*, Act IV), leads to a chorale similar to that in the Fourth Quartet's second movement – while, back at B flat major in the third and last movement, a complacent waltz fulfils the same ironic role as the finales of the Piano Quintet and Eighth Symphony. Here, the quotations fall thick and fast: the rhythm of the 'betrayal' motif (two bars before figure 86); the 'pooh-poohing' phrase from the Eighth's finale (for example, figure 89); the ominous C sharp minor of the Seventh Symphony (figure 90). As the inevitable crescendo builds, two-note figures on first violin (marked *feroce*) evoke the four-note motto first mooted in the Second Quartet's opening movement (and later used as the basis of the 'Stalin' scherzo of the Tenth Symphony). The triumph of brutality now assured, the cello brings the music to a breathless halt, alternating the four-note motto with flurrying semiquavers that suggest a hand furiously trying to erase the score. In a tense pause, the first violin salutes the slow movement with three high F sharps, a gesture seconded by a three-note pizzicato flourish, quoting the execution scene from *The Young Guard* (figures 117–19). Indifferent to this, the waltz resumes its careless course, but, unlike the Eighth Symphony, the Fifth Quartet will not compromise, concluding in a mood of resolute valediction over a glacial pedal-point.

With Stalin still alive, Shostakovich could hardly summon a joyously victorious finale – yet the striving spirit of resistance of the epic Fifth Quartet was not far short of it. Nor would he have long to wait for the real thing.

In his final years, Stalin's paranoia set in with a vengeance. Seeing conspiracies everywhere, he accused even his oldest cronies of spying for the West and took to living in an isolated woodland dacha surrounded by mines and booby-traps. To forestall any plot against himself, he planned purges of the Politburo, the

Party, and the security organs (now known as the MGB and under the control of Viktor Abakumov). Most serious of all, he was contemplating another Terror to match that of 1935–9. In January 1953, two ominous themes appeared in the Soviet press: a campaign for greater 'vigilance' (accompanied by slogans contending that there was no nobler act than denouncing your best friend); and what amounted to a call for a national pogrom against the Jews. The key element in the latter was the so-called 'Doctors' Plot', announced by an article in *Pravda* by Stalin himself. According to this, the Jews were literally poisoning Soviet society: Jewish doctors by injecting their patients with carcinogens or syphilis, Jewish pharmacists by serving their customers with pills made of dried fleas. Lest anyone take this for insane fantasy, a group of Jewish doctors, suitably prepared in the interrogation chambers of the MGB, were on hand to confess that the all-wise Stalin was right again and had brilliantly caught them red-handed in their abominable machinations.

During February, the atmosphere in Russia blended dread of a new Terror with a punch-drunk inability to admit so appalling a prospect. Prayers made an understandable comeback in these eschatological weeks and, at the last minute, they were answered by Stalin's death on 5 March. Merciful to the nation, the dictator's passing was considerably less than merciful to him. Choking slowly to death from a stroke over an agonising twelve hours, he seems (according to his daughter Svetlana) to have had a last-breath death-bed vision, pointing with an awful expression at something he saw through the ceiling.

The passing of Stalin – and, with him, the cruellest dictatorship the world has so far seen – released a spasm of violent emotion throughout the country. Brainwashed by twenty-five years of propaganda, many took to the streets in tearful hysterics over the death of The Greatest Genius of All Times and of All Peoples. On the final day of his lying in state in Moscow, hundreds were crushed to death by MGB tanks defending his coffin against a panic-stricken rush to see the departing demigod for the last time.

Within weeks of Stalin's funeral, his supporters were bewildered to read of a Ministry of Internal Affairs report that the Doctors' Plot had been a 'provocation' got up by criminal elements within the security forces. As a stunned lassitude settled over Russia and the Politburo busied itself with a leadership struggle, Shostakovich retired to Komarovo outside Leningrad and, from July to October, composed a major new work: his Symphony No. 10 in E minor, Opus 93. Premièred in Leningrad by Yevgeny Mravinsky on 17 December, it drew a mixed response from the critics who were, as yet, uncertain which way the wind was blowing. Shostakovich's Proletkult enemies could afford to be less cautious; Khrennikov, Koval, and Dzerzhinsky all launched vituperative attacks on the Tenth and controversy duly flared in the Composers' Union. Describing the work as 'the tragedy of the profoundly isolated individual, helpless in the face of the forces of evil', the critic Boris Yarustovsky added, menacingly: 'Such a conception of the world is very far from that which is experienced by the majority of Soviet people.' As for the composer, he kept his thoughts to himself, except to issue a statement offering spoof 'self-criticism' for any mistakes he may have made in estimating the proper length of his symphony. Some, for example, might have said that the first movement was too long; the second, on the other hand, was possibly too short. 'As for the third movement, I think that my calculations worked out pretty well, except that it is a bit long. Here and there, though, there are places that are a bit short. It would be very valuable to have the comrades' opinion on this.' Asked what the symphony was about, he replied: 'Let them work it out for themselves.' In spite of *Testimony* ('It's about Stalin and the Stalin years'), the question still stands.

In terms of neutral formal analysis, few of Shostakovich's symphonies have had more written about them than his Tenth; nor has any single movement he wrote been more thoroughly described, from the external point of view, than its opening moderato. The movement's unusual structure, in which three themes weave in and out of each other with effortless ingenuity, inevitably attracts the musicologist and, as a result, enough detailed exegesis exists to obviate the necessity of any more here.[1] Little headway, however, has so far been made in attempting to characterize the music – to say what its form expresses. Yet long before *Testimony* it was obvious that, written when it was and given its composer's outlook, the Tenth Symphony can hardly have been unrelated to the most important event in post-war Soviet history: the death of Stalin. As a realist, Shostakovich saw his art (and, in particular, his more public art) as inextricably bound up with real life. What happened around him – from trends to actual events – was intrinsic to the dynamism of his music, down to its smallest nuances. This being so, to treat the Tenth as an emotionally affective formal design without objective meaning has never been likely to prove very illuminating. On the other hand, neither *Testimony* nor historical probability are sufficient to establish anything by themselves. If there is objective meaning in the music, it must be audible.

With the menacing presence of Stalin out of the way, it is unsurprising that the Tenth should be, generally speaking, more relaxed and direct than anything Shostakovich had written for many years. What, though, given the stylistic codes developed in earlier works, should the Tenth be expected to display in the way of specific details? Stalin (two) has gone; the People (three), though enslaved and abused, survive. We should therefore expect three to dominate, though not necessarily in any easily triumphant manner.

The opening movement of the symphony is, in effect, a vast slow waltz, of which almost all the material is constructed from three-note cells. The first theme, announced on cellos and basses, consists of two three-note cells which, raised by a tone, are then repeated, the notes in the second cell being doubled in length to emphasise the all-important triplicity. The grouping into six, inherited from the finale of the Fifth Quartet, seems to signify the People

---

[1] E.g., David Fanning's *The Breath of the Symphonist: Shostakovich's Tenth* (Royal Musical Association, 1988).

ascendant,[1] and, though heavy with thoughtful (or cautious) pauses, the mood is very much that of a slow stirring to life. On the other hand, the atmosphere is also clouded with dark memories, and when the lower strings shift to the movement's second theme, they do so by dropping the first crotchet of the opening six-note phrase, creating a bar of two notes: a bad omen. The folk-like second theme, introduced on clarinet, again consists of six-note phrases, but trails off in a pair of two-note bars and, in the unhappy crescendo that ensues, it is the rare two-note phrases that provoke most passion. As this climax recedes with the second idea now on the strings, it is again the pair of two-note bars that provoke a troubled pause, the brass gravely reiterating the phrase in which they occur. With the third theme, brought in on flute, the infection of two-ness (duplicity?) is growing. Though notated in six-quaver bars and played legato, its melody is phrased in three groups of two – and concludes on the same pair of two-note bars as the second theme. All in all, it is as if the 'revenant' motif of the Third, Fourth, and Fifth Quartets has been reversed: there, the ghost of the people haunted Stalin; here the ghost of Stalin haunts the people.

In the enormous crescendo that forms the movement's central span, the insidious two-ness asserts itself with greater force and frequency. Following a run of demi-semiquavers which blazes like a fuse to a tell-tale high A, the trumpets seize the third theme and, in a bar of 2/4 all to themselves, strip it of its legato phrasing, so that, following a fortissimo tutti, it emerges as *written*, as well as played, as three groups of two instead of one of six. (Note, how, in the aftershock of this transformation, dissonant high woodwind mock the movement's unhappy second theme.) As the crescendo builds higher, Shostakovich, with very little actual metrical change, manages to suggest a conflict of 2/4 with 3/4 – and, at its height (figure 43), the two-note fanfare from the third movement of the Seventh Symphony can be heard screaming at the top of the orchestra, disguised in triple-time. Though three is, with painful deliberation, reasserted in the end (figure 64), the purely rhythmical message of the Tenth Symphony's first movement is that two is contained within three and can exert a malign influence even without overtly displaying itself.

In the raging scherzo, the crash of two-note figures clearly denotes the presence of Stalin, portrayed as a kind of malevolent tornado. Written in the 2/4 of the Georgian gopak, the music is constructed almost entirely from a four-note motif which, as we have seen, has already appeared in both the Second (I) and Fifth (III) Quartets. As might be expected, the basic 'Stalin' double-quaver signature is here writ very large indeed – and on 'his' instruments: brass and drums.

No matter what the point of view of the commentator, the allegretto third movement of the Tenth Symphony has, in the end, always been shrugged off as an insoluble enigma. Inarguably, it has a 'programme' – the layout of the music

---

[1] Soviet analysts have traced much of the work's thematic material to sources in Russian folk song.

and the portentousness of its gestures leave no room for doubt – but what that programme is has so far remained unsolved. In fact, the music abounds in suggestions that irony, if not frank satire, is its central characteristic. Its opening theme quotes from the First Violin Concerto's satirical scherzo, while the mood and language of the movement as a whole resembles the finale of the Fifth Quartet which, in turn, is closely related to the finale of the Eighth Symphony – again, both of them satirical pieces. Apart from this, the main components of the movement are the composer's D-S-C-H motto and a Mahlerian horn-call which occurs ten times. The simplest explanation for this constellation of clues is that, having dealt with collective experience in the Tenth's first two movements, Shostakovich now wished to turn to his own individual experience, treating it as specifically as he had in the finale of the Fourth Symphony and the scherzo of the First Violin Concerto. However, the assumption that the composer is here stepping out for the first time as himself may be misleading, for the fact that the allegretto's first theme is built on a 'misspelling' of his D-S-C-H signature suggests that it concerns not the real Shostakovich but the false one created by Soviet propaganda.

To judge from its embedded clues, for example, the chief characteristic of this passage is *deception*. What erupted with brusque intolerance in the First Violin Concerto is now presented with a honeyed sweetness which fails to conceal its dishonest intentions: the squeezed crescendo at figure 101; the 'conformist' canon which follows it; and – most significantly – a rat-a-tat rhythm, which features inauspiciously in the finale of the Fifth Quartet, bulks large in the Tenth's 'Stalin' scherzo, and can even be traced back to Shostakovich's oldest cypher: the 'betrayal' motif. The simplest interpretation of this would seem to be that, in the absence of Stalin, Communist disinformation will become subtler, if identical in its basic aims.

As though to illustrate this, the second subject is in garish contrast, tart winds trilling a staccato combination of D-S-C-H and the rat-a-tat rhythm accompanied by two-note timpani. The rat-a-tat figure seems, in fact, to be part of the travesty: the People's three notes appropriated by the authorities to legitimise their rule. This becomes clearer when, as the music's cockiness turns positively bumptious (figure 113), a warning horn sounds and the *real* People emerge sadly from the shadows in the guise of the symphony's initial slow, six-note theme. As if waking from some dim dream, the movement modulates with a sigh into a clear, peaceful D major – but the forces of evil are not to be thwarted. Abetted by the soft strokes of a sinister gong, the strings slip quietly into a pizzicato two-note accompaniment to the horn's fanfare, blurring the issue so subtly that soon the cor anglais is wheedling at the first subject again. (Here – figure 125 – the rat-a-tat motto assumes the characteristic falling intervals of the 'betrayal' motif.) Its initiative regained, the bumptious mood returns with a jubilantly strutting restatement of the second subject. Accelerating back into the first subject, its squeezed crescendi now vulgarly obvious, the sound expands to a battering climax, punctuated by urgently protesting cries of D-S-C-H from the strings. Again, the horn call halts the madness and the movement slowly dissolves, its travesty D-S-C-H squeaking away to the bitter end.

In the finale, it is D-S-C-H which assumes the warning role. Now understandably hesitant to commit itself, the music moves through a sequence of doubtfully conferring woodwind solos, before shifting into E major and a precipitous allegro. The tone is vulgar, the time-signature is 2/4, and there are a lot of two-note phrases around, but there is no sign of anything threatening and, in any case, it is time for rejoicing. As the excitement mounts, however, it becomes clear that, as in the scherzi of the Sixth and Ninth Symphonies, a brutal element is taking over. Breaking into a gopak, the movement stampedes rapidly towards a violent recapitulation of the symphony's 'Stalin' scherzo – but, just as things are getting out of hand, D-S-C-H slams down the lid. Returning to the tonality and triple-time of the introduction, Shostakovich impresses his signature on the music three more times. Inoculated with irony, it is now free to rejoice without risking an infection of mass hysteria. A breathlessly absurd bassoon plays the main tune of the allegro in huffing 'Stalin' two-note style; and suddenly the atmosphere lifts. Eschewing the violence of the gopak for a hilarious can-can, the finale whirls into an exultant coda, driven home by the all-conquering D-S-C-H.

The release of psychic energy in the Tenth's finale is so tempestuous that it can seem unequal to the weight of the symphony's earlier movements; indeed, this is the usual criticism of the work offered by Western critics. Western critics, however, are notoriously unimpressed with Shostakovich's symphonic finales as a whole – a fact not unconnected with their wholesale ignorance of the composer's intentions in writing them. If there is a provisional quality to the finale of the Tenth Symphony, it is there because Shostakovich, being no fool, saw nothing to be conclusive about. And if its uproar is nevertheless indecorously eruptive, he and his audience had earned the right to it a hundred times over. A symphony of pauses – cautious, fearful, sombre, shrewd – the Tenth ends in (by Shostakovich's own definition) truly *proletarian* jubilation: unsnobbish and unbuttoned, yet level-headed. Nevertheless the work's heart is in its great opening moderato and in the tidal wave of grieving emotion poured out in it. 'How good that there is no one left to lose / And one can weep,' wrote Anna Akhmatova. Thus wrote Shostakovich also, in his memorial Tenth Symphony – a musical monument to the fifty million victims of Stalin's madness and the supreme thing of its kind composed in the last half-century.

Chapter Seven

ASSERTION 1953–1975

I, like a river,
Have been turned aside by this harsh age.
I am a substitute. My life has flowed
Into another channel
And I do not recognize my shores.

WITH STALIN'S cold breath stilled, the Russian air grew gradually warmer and the ice of his final tyranny, dirty with sordid murders and squalid defamations, began to crack. Ehrenburg's novel *The Thaw*, published in 1954, fixed the metaphor in the public mind. It was spring, a new age – or so it initially appeared. In fact, the political situation, relatively volatile for the first time in decades, was now also dangerously unpredictable.

In theory ruled by a triumvirate of Malenkov, Molotov, and Stalin's executioner Beria, Russia lacked commanding leadership, and control over its intellectual life started to slacken. The first sign of liberalisation in the arts came with an anonymous *Pravda* article in November 1953 calling for 'a broad-minded approach' to Socialist Realism. Taking this up in the magazine *Novy Mir* (*New World*), Vladimir Pomerantsev suggested that truth should be measured by ordinary, rather than 'ideal', standards (code for 'Socialist Realism is institutionalised lying; let's get rid of it'). Under the editorship of Alexander Tvardovsky, *Novy Mir* now became a modest rallying-point for the literary liberals. In music, the lead was taken by the ever-optimistic Khachaturian, whose plea for greater freedom of expression for composers, published in *Soviet Music*, anticipated Pomerantsev's article by a month. Shostakovich, though, had been here before. Waiting until Beria was out of the way (deposed in July, he was shot in December), he set his name to a cautious piece in *Soviet Music* in January 1954, entitled 'The Pleasure of Finding New Ways'. Hedging his bets with the blatantly spurious claim that the goal of the liberal artist was identical to that of the conformist, he argued that creative freedom was no danger to Soviet power – indeed, could only fortify it, depleted as it was by 'superficiality, dullness, clichés [and] the wrong-headed "no-conflict" theory'. His caution proved prescient. With Beria replaced by Khrushchev, the Soviet leadership realised that too rapid a liberalisation would entail taking the lid off Stalin's crimes and dealing with the fact that around five million of his victims were still languishing in the Gulag. Accordingly, Tvardovsky was sacked from the editorship of *Novy Mir* for publishing Pomerantsev's polemic, the primacy of Socialist Realism was reaffirmed and, by the end of 1954, the 'thaw' was over.

Any lightness of heart Shostakovich may have felt in the aftermath of Stalin's passing soon evaporated in the heat of daily living. Though his new work was being performed, everything of his banned by the 1948 resolution remained unpublished and unplayable, while he himself continued to be officially unpersoned and therefore, on any permanent basis, unemployable. Earning money from what incidental scores and film projects he could secure, he was on the poverty-line till, during the 1954 thaw, the Bolshoi took him on as a music consultant. An apparently spontaneous gesture of quasi-rehabilitation, this appears, in fact, to have been a trade-off in exchange for which Shostakovich was expected to co-operate in the post-Stalin refurbishment of Russia's image abroad. As in 1931, the deal seems mainly to have depended on him giving an interview to the ever-amenable *New York Times*, this time conducted by the writer Harrison Salisbury. Taken to meet Shostakovich in a luxurious five-roomed apartment on Mozhaisky Boulevard, Salisbury found the composer in possession of four pianos and a Pobeda car and, to all appearances, thoroughly at ease with life. Insisting that everything was fine with Soviet music and that, contrary to misleading reports in the foreign press, Soviet composers were freer than those in the West, Shostakovich explained that, with the exception of a few proscribed compositions, the government continued to support his work – 'and generously too'. Impressed by the 'honesty and sincerity' of these, on the face of it, surrealistic remarks, Salisbury duly conveyed them to the free world.

Thirty years on, Eric Roseberry, in one of the better accounts of Shostako-vich's life, accepted the *New York Times* piece at face value: 'What with Ministry of Culture fees, sales of music and performance royalties, Stalin Prizes, etc., the composer was earning a very good living.' However, according to Maxim Shostakovich and Galina Vishnevskaya, the exact opposite was the case. Indeed, Vishnevskaya, who met Shostakovich within weeks of the Salisbury interview, found him so poor as to be unable to entertain except very primitively, and – oddly – living not on Mozhaisky Boulevard but round the corner on Kutuzovsky Prospekt. Contrary to Roseberry's happy picture, Vishnevskaya claims that Ministry of Culture fees for the composer's new works were few and far between, none of his music was on sale, and all foreign royalties were seized by the authorities. As for Stalin Prizes, his last one – second grade, awarded in 1952 – had provided him with approximately enough folding cash to purchase three standard blue serge suits. Far from earning vast sums of money, Shostakovich was for the first time since the twenties having to play the piano in public in order to make ends meet.

Unless the composer's nearest and dearest are lying through their teeth, it can only be concluded that Harrison Salisbury was misled. How, though, could this have been done? In truth, the trick was not difficult and has been played on visiting Westerners by Soviet propagandists time and time again: a recently condemned public figure is produced to the foreign press, well fed and full of emollient assurances that the 'fraternal' criticism to which he or she has recently been subjected was both kindly meant and entirely justified; suitably impressed, the journalists report to their Western readers that there was nothing to previous stories of censure and reprimand, which were merely items of Cold War propaganda. Tiresomely familiar to Soviet dissidents, the most famous instance of this practice involved Akhmatova and Zoshchenko who, only three months before Salisbury's Shostakovich interview, were produced from impoverished obscurity in Leningrad to answer questions about their downfall in 1946 from visiting Western students. Knowing that she spoke freely at her peril, Akhmatova told her interrogators that Zhdanov had been right to criticise her and the Central Committee correct to deprive her of her union card. Not so worldly-wise, Zoshchenko misread the situation as an opportunity to register a few mild complaints about his treatment. For the benefit of their fellow writers, the consequences were brutally simple: Akhmatova was awarded a *dacha*, while Zoshchenko was returned to poverty and neglect. All that the Western delegation saw, however, was what their interviewees did and said at the meeting.

The probability is that Salisbury's Shostakovich interview was conducted on a basis similar to that of the Akhmatova–Zoshchenko charade and, while it would be interesting to know who really owned the luxury apartment on Mozhaisky Boulevard, little else about the *New York Times* piece would appear to warrant serious attention – apart from the fact, noted by Boris Schwarz, that 'as if by prearrangement' the claims made by Shostakovich to Harrison Salisbury were also made, in virtually identical language, by Khachaturian in the April 1954 edition of *Soviet Music*. As Czeslaw Milosz had written a year before in *The Captive Mind*, 'They do not know how one pays – those abroad do not know. They do not know what one buys, and at what price.'

Another element in Shostakovich's instalment plan for 1954 seems to have been the democratically styled *Festival Overture*, Opus 96, written for the thirty-seventh anniversary of the Revolution. Like the Concertino for Two Pianos, Opus 94, composed a year earlier, the *Festival Overture* is alive with an unforced laughter that can only reflect its composer's relief over not having Stalin to worry about any more. Unfortunately, his joy was short-lived for, in early December, he received news that his wife Nina, then working with radioactive materials at a high-security physics institute in Armenia, had suddenly fallen terminally ill. Catching the next plane to Yerevan, he arrived at the hospital in time to be reunited with her shortly before she died. Now withdrawn and preoccupied, Shostakovich left the upbringing of Galya and Maxim to his maid, Marya, apparently unwilling to interfere in their lives in case his own woes should somehow rub off on them. Vishnevskaya notes that the family apartment was in chaos and the teenage sister and brother were growing up spoiled and undisciplined: 'Shostakovich loved them with a kind of abnormal, morbid love, and lived in constant fear that some misfortune would befall them.' Temporarily unable to face his afflictions, the composer took to drowning his sorrows in vodka every evening and going to bed early.

The last thing Shostakovich needed now was to be seen in public, let alone to be back at the centre of controversy, but this is exactly what happened when, on 15 January 1955 in Leningrad, he played the piano in the première of his 1948 song-cycle *From Jewish Folk Poetry*. Though anti-Semitism in Russia had ceased to be as overt as it had been under Stalin, it was still rife and there was much behind-the-scenes opposition to the concert. Nevertheless, it was a great success and the public interest might have jolted him out of his depression had not his mother been taken ill during rehearsals. Tending her throughout the summer, he composed little apart from his score for the film *The Gadfly*, and even the belated success of his First Violin Concerto, premièred by Mravinsky and David Oistrakh in Leningrad in October, failed to raise his spirits. His mother's death in November seems to have left him unable to orientate himself and his decision soon afterwards to remarry turned out to be impulsive and ill-considered. Seeing Margarita Kainova, a teacher and Komsomol leader, at a conference early in 1956, he proposed to her on the spot (solely, Vishnevskaya thinks, because of her physical resemblance to Nina). A simple girl who had no idea who Shostakovich was, Margarita failed to set his household in order and was never accepted by his children. The composer's disastrous second marriage ensured him a further four years of misery at a time when he was long overdue for some ordinary happiness.

On 25 February 1956, the currents of unrest set in motion by Stalin's death were unexpectedly canalised by Nikita Khrushchev's dramatic power-play at the 20th Party Congress. At last breaking with the dictator, Khrushchev charged him with the deaths of the leading Communists of his time and for failing to take adequate defence measures before the war. Leaked to the West, this 'secret speech' set the tone for the next year in the Soviet bloc and anti-Stalinist protest spread rapidly in Russia and Eastern Europe.

Though unmentioned in Khrushchev's speech, the occupants of the Gulag were major beneficiaries of the liberalisation which followed it. Several million political prisoners were released in 1956 and a stream of newly freed friends of the Shostakovich family passed through the composer's apartment during the next two years. ('Our home,' recalls his son Maxim, 'was sometimes like a small hotel for people who came back.') In the midst of this, Shostakovich produced his first serious composition since the Tenth Symphony: the Quartet No. 6 in G major, Opus 101. The shortest and lightest of its kind since the First Quartet of 1938, it is also one of his more deceptive and personal creations.

Like the Third Quartet (the second subject of whose first movement it quotes at figures 3 and 7), the Sixth begins in the mock-simple style of Mahler's Fourth Symphony. Two-note motifs abound, but their cuckooing falling thirds are harmless and the general mood is rather insipid, a marked contrast with the energetic muscularity of the Fourth and Fifth quartets. One reason for this is that the cello, so often associated with Stalin in Shostakovich's early quartets, has relatively little to say – indeed, for bars at a time says nothing at all. But, then, this is not a work pitched angrily at Stalin and his era.

'Refusing to dwell on the past', the Sixth's bland expression speaks more of the situation in Russia when it was written than of earlier tragic history.

In the Soviet bloc 1956 was, above all else, about censorship. In Russia, particularly, it was a second thaw – another bout of creative struggle against the bowdlerising restraints of Socialist Realism (or, as Solzhenitsyn more pithily puts it, of 'shying the first pebbles at Goliath's stupid brow'). Pre-eminent among contemporary writers was Vladimir Dudintsev, whose novel *Not by Bread Alone* went to the heart of things by attacking the corrupt, repressive materialism of the Stalinist 'new class'. Though Stalin was gone, his technique of implicating others in his crimes by a strategy of rewards and menaces had created a new social stratum: the Soviet bourgeoisie. These people had profited from Stalinism and were prepared to surrender neither their privileges nor the system which perpetuated them, since doing so would expose them to retaliation from those they had betrayed during the years of Terror and freeze. To the liberal intelligentsia, the situation was equally clear: the moribund weight of this mass of venal mediocrity was smothering the national spirit and, unless heaved off, would stifle Russia to death. Only by dismantling the Socialist Realist aesthetic, which censored the truth about Soviet society, could the country's artists attack the new class and, ultimately, the anti-democratic Communism upon which it depended.

Mimicking the smugness of the Stalinist bourgeois, Shostakovich's Sixth Quartet quietly satirises the palliative pseudo-art with which their leaders disinfected the Russian air of 'dangerous' ideas. Every movement ending on a sleepy perfect cadence, the work encounters crisis only briefly in its outer movements when a falling minor second disrupts its diatonic daydream to produce a characteristic tussle between adjacent keys. In the second movement, Shostakovich's ambivalent feelings towards the People take the form of a placid rustic dance around the usual three-note motif – though, when it recurs in the gently sorrowful third movement, the symbol is treated with respect for the suffering which the sounds around it seek to forget. Stalin's name (two bars before figure 60), evokes a grave pause before this folk-like threnody continues, but the seriousness is skin-deep and it takes only a word from the cello to transform sad B flat minor into a smiling major cadence at the movement's end. Beginning on a folksy drone, the finale is a satire on complacency in the mode of the last movement of the Eighth Symphony, its rhythm being that of the familiar 'betrayal' motif. The underlying conflict of the first movement is slyly hinted at (figure 64, bars 7–9) and later calls up memories of the slow movement, leading to a typical agitated attempt to escape into E flat. However, the cello is on hand to pick up the pieces, reintroducing the quartet's banal opening measures and guiding it to a suitably soporific conclusion.

More relaxed and discreet than Shostakovich's previous four quartets, the Sixth is a cunning piece that occasionally trespasses a little too close to Socialist Realist insincerity for its own good. It is, however, fascinating both in itself and as a link in an ongoing chain of codes and cross-references – particularly in its allusion (figure 33) to the second subject of the Seventh Symphony's first movement, characterised above (pp. 157–8) as a satirical image of the Socialist Realist heaven on earth.

Less rewarding was the composer's next work, the Piano Concerto No. 2 in F, Opus 102. Written for Maxim's nineteenth birthday in May 1957, it is a jeu d'esprit, full of private jokes (such as the scale-exercises in its finale) and, aside from a beguiling Tchaikovskyian andante, little else. Shostakovich must have composed the work with at least one eye on sweetening the Soviet authorities, for the upkeep of his extended family[1] was by now becoming too great to be borne without state sponsorship. Needing to compose for his supper, he had to write for the broadest audience and so turned to projects with direct appeal.[2] The most obvious example of this was *Moscow, Cheryomushki*, a comic operetta about one of Khrushchev's new housing projects, reinforced not only with his ever-popular *Song of the Meeting*, but also with Vasili Soloviev-Sedoi's worldwide hit *Moscow Nights* (known in the West as *Midnight in Moscow*). Another was an editing job on Mussorgsky's *Khovanshchina* for Vera Stroeva's film version of 1958. Only too pleased to be involved with his favourite composer again, Shostakovich worked long hours and ended up not only re-orchestrating the entire opera, but writing part of the screenplay. However, his chief effort towards relocating himself in the mainstream was the work he turned to soon after finishing the Second Piano Concerto early in 1957: his Eleventh Symphony. Conceived from the start as a popular piece, the Eleventh was an instant success in Russia (his greatest since the *Leningrad* fifteen years earlier). At a stroke re-establishing him at the centre of Soviet music, it was the turning point of his post-Stalin career, and from then on his financial situation steadily improved – ironic considering that, far from being the Communist Revolutionary epic it was taken for in both Russia and the West, the symphony, a work of despairing darkness, was in reality one of the many subversive products of the anti-Communist 'Year of Protest', 1956.

His largest symphonic score apart from the Fourth and Seventh, Shostakovich's Symphony No. 11 in G minor, Opus 103, subtitled *The Year 1905*, was for years dismissed outside the USSR as 'film music' – a tawdry agitprop broadsheet with neither discipline nor depth. However, under the influence of left-inclined pop culture during the seventies, the Eleventh Symphony gradually acquired the same kind of virtuous posthumous reputation as the Eighth. Since it was about 'the people', it had to be simple and direct – what was wrong with that? Entering into what they took to be the Red Romantic spirit of

---

[1] For the composer's many commitments, see Vishnevskaya, *Galina*, p. 231.

[2] Party pressure was also involved. Around this time, Minister of Culture Nikolai Mikhailov ordered a group of leading composers (including Shostakovich) to write more popular music, indignantly demanding to know how long the USSR would take to produce its own Yves Montand. One of the assembled was heard to murmur, 'Two Five-Year Plans'. (Gunther, *Inside Russia Today*, p. 162.)

the thing, sleeve-note writers focused less on the music than on its avowed historical background: the protest march of 9 January 1905 which, ending in the 'Bloody Sunday' massacre in St Petersburg's Palace Square, sparked Russia's first revolution. Those who regarded the Eleventh as a humanist monument beyond the purview of ordinary criticism were naturally outraged by *Testimony*'s contention that it was actually a double-edged work dealing as much with Soviet Russia as with the imperial past. Apart from anything else, Shostakovich's image as an Honest Communist depended on taking the symphony's meaning at face-value; to doubt this would be to admit the possibility of a different Shostakovich altogether.

Just such a Shostakovich, the alleged author of *Testimony*, spoke of the Eleventh Symphony as his most 'Mussorgskyian' composition – Mussorgsky for him symbolising two key ideas: 'the people' and 'recurrence'. According to this scheme the people, destined to be forever at the mercy of indifferent autocrats, would periodically protest in the name of humanity only to be betrayed or punished, this archetypal situation recurring throughout Russian history no matter who happened to be in control. 'I wanted,' the composer purportedly told Volkov, 'to show this recurrence in the Eleventh Symphony. I wrote it in 1957 and it deals with contemporary themes even though it's called "1905". It's about the people, who have stopped believing because the cup of evil has run over.' Critics of this passage found its analogy far-fetched: what relevance had the Hungarian Uprising, a revolt against progressive Communism, to the Narodnik revolution of 1905, a rebellion against reactionary Tsarism? Surely this talk of 'recurrence' was an intellectual fancy imposed on Shostakovich to bolster Volkov's misrepresentation of his beliefs?

In fact, the concept of recurrence was central among Soviet artists and writers in the wake of the Hungarian Uprising, an event which held tremendous significance for the community of *intelligenty* of which Shostakovich was a member. No country outside Russia had suffered so cruel a Stalinist Terror as that of Matyas Rákosi's Hungary. Under Rákosi, during the late forties and early fifties, denunciations, public confessions, and purges had been as much part of life as under Stalin himself. Millions passed through the country's prisons and torture-chambers (about one in ten of the population) and, while Rákosi had gone by 1956, the popular wish to be rid of Communism was by then ungovernable and its effects were watched anxiously by liberals throughout the rest of the Soviet bloc – not least in Russia itself. There, in spite of propaganda to the effect that the Hungarian troubles were caused by reactionary agitation, it was known that what was really going on was a broad-based revolution in the mould of 1905 and February 1917. An acting-out of their own urge towards freedom, Hungary's struggle was, for Russian intellectuals, the very heart of the Year of Protest – and when, on 25 October 1956, the Hungarian secret police machine-gunned a peacefully demonstrating crowd in Budapest's Parliament Square, killing six hundred, the analogy with the twelve hundred dead of Palace Square in 1905 was flatly unavoidable.

The Red Army's suppression of the resulting uprising shook Russia to the core. A rallying-point for Soviet youth, it was, as Vladimir Bukovsky recalls, the catalyst for the creation of modern Soviet dissidence:

After all the exposures, denunciations, and posthumous rehabilitations [of the 1956 thaw], after all the assurances about the impossibility of repeating the past, we were now presented with corpses, tanks, brute force and lies all over again. Just one more convincing proof that nothing had changed at all. Boys just like us, fifteen or sixteen years old, were perishing on the streets of Budapest, rifles in hand, in defence of freedom . . . On the one side there was *our side* – the Russians, who were cold-bloodedly sent in to kill. And on the other there was also *our side*, for I would have done exactly the same thing if I had been in the place of those young Hungarians . . . After those red-starred tanks, the pride and joy of our childhood, had crushed our peers on the streets of Budapest, a bloody fog blinded our eyes. The whole world had betrayed us, and we believed in nobody.

The obvious parallel today is with the mood in China after the 1989 massacre in Tiananmen Square. With an equivalent feeling abroad in Russia in 1956–7, it is inconceivable that a piece of sound-painting as naturalistic as the massacre in the second movement of Shostakovich's Eleventh Symphony should have struck its early audiences as mere coincidence.

The composer had first considered a symphony on 1905 in 1955, the revolution's fiftieth anniversary. That he did not begin writing it until nearly two years later is more than adequately accounted for by factors in his personal life – his mother's illness; his upsetting remarriage; the arrival of many newly freed friends from the Gulag. Yet there remains the possibility that, prior to the Parliament Square massacre, Shostakovich had no adequate psychological peg from which to hang such a work. True, this had not stopped him exploring the theme in his *Ten Choral Poems on Revolutionary Texts* of 1951 but, in the absence of further stimulus, having painted the scene already is unlikely to have been anything but a disincentive to doing it again. In fact, judging from the low-profile Sixth Quartet, he lacked the energy to tackle anything as ambitious as *The Year 1905* until 1957 – after the Hungarian Uprising. To someone like Shostakovich, the events of October and November 1956 would have been more than enough to stir him out of his inertia. Stalinism was abroad again and needed to be resisted.

That the squashing of the Hungarian Uprising was an extension of Stalinist censorship was clear from two developments in early 1957: the end of the second 'thaw' (symbolised by Khrushchev's public reprimand of Vladimir Dudintsev); and the dissolution of the Hungarian Writers' Association on a charge of 'assaulting the Soviet system'. Much of the intellectual impetus for events in Hungary had come from writers like Tibor Dery, Gyula Hay, and Georg Lukacs. Unable to admit that the Uprising had possessed a genuinely popular base, the Kremlin could only tighten the leash on its own intelligentsia in order to prevent the same thing happening in Russia. Absent from the frontline of dissidence in the Year of Protest, Shostakovich made his own protest in 1957: the Eleventh Symphony. In this respect, the work's populism can be understood as an attempt, in the face of government propaganda to the contrary, to establish the integral link between the aspirations of the liberal intelligentsia and those of the people at large. Naturally, the composer was at the same time seeking, from motives of simple survival, to restore his standing in the Soviet cultural sponsorship system – yet there is no hint of compromise in the piece. His style is not surrendered to 'democratic' facelessness and entirely lacks the one self-defining attribute of Socialist Realist falsehood: optimism. On the contrary, the Eleventh is a grim, grey, obsessional thing whose essentially despairing tone is made palatable to a wide audience solely by its pictorial immediacy and adroit use of revolutionary songs.

The work's relationship to Shostakovich's main sequence of closet 'protest' pieces is clear from the outset. Conforming to its composer's established code system, this symphony 'about the people' is built almost entirely on the number three, beginning with the timpani motto at the start of its first movement. Derived from the triplet rhythm of the revolutionary song *Listen*, announced by two flutes at figure 8, this motto, in one guise or another, saturates the symphony from beginning to end – indeed, there are more triplets in the Eleventh Symphony than most composers write in their entire careers. Likewise ubiquitous are the Sixth Quartet's ambiguously clashing major and minor thirds. Two-note figures, though relatively rare, are always consistent with their symbolism in the 'Stalin' works of 1935–53. Ominous in the first movement's distant Mahlerian fanfares[1] (for example five bars before figure 3), they erupt in full savagery with the attack of the Tsar's Cossacks in the second movement and completely dominate the raging bluster of the finale. The Eleventh, however, has been formally described many times. Far more pressing a necessity is the question of what it means.

The failure of the 1905 Revolution, a popular uprising in Shostakovich's own Narodnik tradition, guaranteed a further more organised and ruthless revolution in the future. Had Tsar Nicholas II liberalised in 1905, extremism would not have returned twelve years later to destroy him. This chain of consequences is explicit in the plot of the Eleventh Symphony, its first half linked by the repetition of the song *Listen*, its second half by the dourly determined *Bare Your Heads* (one of two themes borrowed from the *Ten Choral Poems* and originally from the Fifth Prelude of 1920).[2] Failing to listen, the

---

[1] Shostakovich's use of the same muted tremolando strings and trumpet calls in the 'Dresden in Ruins' sequence from his film score *Five Days, Five Nights* (1960) suggests a common provenance in the introduction to Mahler's First Symphony.

[2] Contrary to a common misapprehension, this is not a folk song but a folk-like theme of the composer's own (see: Brown 'An Interview with Shostakovich', p. 88).

Tsar reaps the whirlwind of the symphony's finale; but this is by no means an occasion for carefree rejoicing. In Shostakovich's scheme, denial of the People merely incites violence and a further cycle of recurrence – specifically, a Bolshevik cycle (hence the last movement's brutal two-note swagger and the hint of a 'Stalin' gopak five bars after figure 130). Summoned by an evilly gurgling bass clarinet, the symphony's coda, in which recurrence is embodied by a recapitulation of the People's swirling, agitated music from the second movement, is a positively sinister prediction of 1917.

Sealing the finale's inauspicious message is its title *Nabat* (*The Alarm-Bell*). *Nabat* was a nineteenth-century review edited by the fanatical first-generation Narodnik Petr Tkachev, notorious for maintaining that nothing, however immoral, was forbidden the true revolutionary. Anticipating Lenin (upon whom he was a formative influence), Tkachev advocated that revolution, far from being the province of the People, should be carried out by a small, motivated Party unafraid of using whatever violence it thought necessary. Similarly important to early Bolshevik theory was Tkachev's friend the Nihilist Sergei Nechayev, whose milieu was fictionalised by Dostoyevsky in his monumental satire on political extremism *The Devils* – long banned in the USSR and, according to Shostakovich's daughter Galina, the composer's favourite novel. Taking all this into account, his Eleventh Symphony, premièred as a work of orthodox triumphalism at the fortieth anniversary of the October Revolution, can be seen as, in reality, a covert attack on the very festivities of which it was nominally the prize exhibit.

So much for politics. What of the music as music? Despite its abidingly depressive mood, the symphony is charged with an energy and quasi-Tchaikovskyian passion absent from the composer's work for some years. With its subtle integration of revolutionary songs, the piece has a cinematic immediacy that can make a powerful first impression on sympathetic listeners. By the standards of earlier works, however, the Eleventh is disappointing. In terms of musical invention one of his most monotonous scores, it too often spins out thin material to minimal effect (the finale's cor anglais solo, for example, vying for tedium with that of the Eighth Symphony). Lacking his usual precision, the music blurs into impressionistic smudges in the first movement, hyperinflating bombastically in the second and fourth. Only in the concentrated third movement does Shostakovich strike gold, producing a funeral march of overwhelming emotional force. The rest of the symphony – often described as a huge symphonic poem, but actually more like a wordless one-act opera – is prolix in the extreme and it is hard to imagine it surviving in the non-Soviet repertoire as anything more than a curiosity.

Returned to favour by the Eleventh's popular success, Shostakovich was awarded the Lenin Prize for it in April 1958, his rehabilitation being further confirmed when the authorities asked him to chair the first Tchaikovsky Piano Competition in Moscow that year. A month later, a Central Committee resolution 'correcting the errors' of the 1948 decree absolved all Zhdanov's

victims of guilt, restoring them to official favour and blaming their treatment on
'J. V. Stalin's subjective attitude to certain works of art and the very adverse
influence exercised on Stalin in these matters by Molotov, Malenkov, and
Beria'. His ten years of disgrace and penury erased at a stroke, Shostakovich
was once more the state's blue-eyed boy. Galina Vishnevskaya, with him when
the news arrived, recalls his bitter laughter. An Historical Decree had abro-
gated an Historical Decree. 'It's simple,' he kept muttering, between tumblers
of vodka. 'So very simple.'

If the strenuous rhetoric of the Eleventh Symphony had suggested a loosening
of the composer's grip on his own essentially clipped and concentrated style,
his next major work showed that the aberration was temporary. The First Cello
Concerto, written during the summer of 1959 and premièred in Leningrad in
October by its dedicatee Mstislav Rostropovich, incisively summarises the best
points of Shostakovich's anti-Stalinist series in language which, at once plain
and electrically alive, wastes not a note.

On past form, it would seem that some current event had affected the
composer, impelling him to a fresh creative initiative – and in this case the
probable cause is easy to find. Towards the end of 1958 Russia had been
obsessed to the exclusion of almost everything else with one thing: the
'Pasternak affair'. Pasternak's novel *Doctor Zhivago* had been published abroad
in November 1957, where its truthful picture of the Stalin years had made it the
international literary event of the year, much to the fury of Khrushchev's
cultural *apparatchiks*. Opinion on Pasternak's unprecedented strategy of foreign
publication divided the Soviet artistic community. (According to Vishnevskaya,
Shostakovich tutted, saying: 'When in Rome, do as the Romans do.') The
award to Pasternak of the 1958 Nobel Prize inflamed the situation still further,
and taking sides for or against him soon became an unavoidable moral issue.
Shostakovich, who respected Pasternak as, alongside Akhmatova, the greatest
living Russian poet, can have had no trouble making up his mind – especially
when the government launched a hate-campaign against 'this literary weed'
which rapidly took on the crazed intensity of the Zamyatin/Pilnyak affair of
1929. Despite the fact that no one in Russia had read a word of *Doctor Zhivago*,
anti-Pasternak letters swamped the press, while 'spontaneous' demonstrations
demanded that the author be deprived of his citizenship ('Throw the Judas out
of the USSR!'). In October, the Writers' Union convened a special session to
revile Pasternak for 'spitting in the face of the People'. Berating him for
reactionary individualism, the critic Viktor Pertsov jeeringly described the
poet's exquisite style as 'eighty thousand miles round his own navel'. Alexander Bezymensky – Proletkult librettist of Shostakovich's Second Symphony
– fondly reminisced about having persecuted Pasternak during the thirties
before calling for his deportation ('Weeds should be uprooted!'). Compelled to
decline the Nobel Prize, Pasternak addressed a confessional letter to *Pravda*,
Shostakovichian in its seemingly artless ambiguities: 'It does indeed appear as

if I maintain the following erroneous propositions [in *Doctor Zhivago*]. I seem to be saying that every revolution is a historically illegitimate occurrence, of which the October Revolution is an example, and that it has brought misfortunes on Russia, and led to the demise of the traditional Russian intelligentsia.' In fact, the Russian intelligentsia, though badly frightened by Pasternak's public pillorying, had not ceased to exist, and, at his funeral two years later, hundreds turned out to mourn him.

If not present in body on this occasion, Shostakovich must have been in spirit. He owed his acquaintance with Shakespeare to Pasternak's translations and was aware that, like him, the poet had been treated by Stalin as a shaman-cum-jester who, though punishable, was none the less for superstitious reasons to be preserved. (On one occasion presented with documents giving grounds for Pasternak's arrest, Stalin had pushed them away saying 'Do not touch this cloud-dweller.') Far more than the 'recurrence' of October 1956, Pasternak's persecution would have touched Shostakovich personally. Once again a sensitive, defenceless individual had been set upon by a mob whipped up by cynical demagogues. It must have seemed as if Zhdanov had returned from the grave.

No coincidence, then, that the Cello Concerto No. 1 in E flat, Opus 107, is a kind of update of the composer's First Violin Concerto, written at the height of the Zhdanovshchina in 1947–8. Except for the earlier work's slow introductory nocturne, the First Cello Concerto follows its layout closely, the biting mood of its quick opening and closing movements in particular echoing that of the First Violin Concerto's scherzo and finale. Here, again, the soloist, confined to variations on a four-note motto similar to the composer's own D-S-C-H, is nagged by mocking woodwind and forced by an intolerant orchestra to sign its cocksure statements. Pasternak's poem *The Nobel Prize* inevitably comes to mind: 'I am caught like a beast at bay. / Somewhere are people, freedom, light. / But all I hear is the baying of the pack. / There is no way out for me' (tr. Max Hayward).

Though the usual metrical codes obtain – the cello's pleading triplets at figure 54; its three notes against the timpani's two at figure 77 – the number five, too, is prominent, both in five-note phrases and bars of 5/4. Dating from the late Forties, Shostakovich's use of five is hard to read. For instance, a five-note phrase accompanies the repeated word *khokhochu* ('laugh') in the sixth movement of the Fourteenth Symphony, while the same quintuple cackling occurs in the opening allegretto of the Fifteenth Symphony. In other passages, though, the number five has a mournful or menacing association. The simplest solution would seem to be: two-plus-three or 'Stalin-plus-the-People' – in other words, the populace manipulated by the state for the kind of persecution inflicted on Pasternak. In the present case, though, the composer may have had even more specific developments in mind. Under Khrushchev, the use of civilians to police civilians attained a new sophistication, notably in the form of the *druzhiny* or People's Guards, authorised by the Supreme Soviet in 1959 to rid the streets of 'parasites' and harass anyone generally failing to conform. By exhorting neighbours to spy on each other, sanctioning 'comrades' courts', and encouraging the Komsomol in their traditional role as moral vigilantes, the Soviet authorities mobilised 'the wrath of the People' against the people themselves. Conceivably this, too, was in Shostakovich's mind while writing the First Cello Concerto.

Between 1957 and 1961, Soviet intellectuals faced a return to the isolation they had experienced during 1929–31, 1935–39, and 1946–53. Severely tested by the Pasternak affair, some retreated into silence while others abandoned their principles altogether to join in the concerted abuse. With younger artists unafraid to protest in Mayakovsky Square, conscience became a central issue for the older intelligentsia, most of whom had suffered under Stalin and, given the option, would have preferred to avoid enduring more of the same in their fifties and sixties. Seemingly embodying this in his concerto, Shostakovich has a horn follow the cellist around, half-conscience, half-confessor. While mostly commenting on the action at a distance, the horn acts as a shadow soloist and at figure 31 the two principals have a brief confabulation all to themselves.

If the First Cello Concerto reflects a depressing reality, it is anything but depressing in its effect, being one of its composer's most spirited works. Even when the soloist is turning cartwheels for the amusement of tittering wood- wind, his teeth are gritted in a rictus grin of resistance. Though tears fall in the solitude of its slow movement, this deeply ironic work never bends its knees and its final treble-stopped vows of conformism are slashed out with an incon- gruous power that utterly denies their apparent capitulation.

Shostakovich's return to economy and control was confirmed with his next work, the Quartet No. 7 in F sharp, Opus 108. Dedicated 'In Memoriam' to Nina, it is a diamond-hard design of three linked movements whose twelve- minute duration makes it its composer's shortest masterpiece. Apart from the violent canonic allegro at the beginning of the third movement, most of the music has a triple structure or feel to it – though the central section of the middle movement introduces one of the variants of the First Cello Concerto's four-note motto. As to what lies behind the work, it is tempting to see it as programmatic: the bustling first movement a portrait of its dedicatee (with perhaps, a 'vocal' impersonation hidden in the bridge between first and second subject); the nocturnal second, with its unhappy memories or premonitions, a picture of husband and wife separated; and, in the third, the composer flying fretfully to the hospital – the whole concluded by further recollections of Nina's personality. On the other hand, the first theme of the middle movement bears a distant resemblance to the march from the Fifth Symphony, while the finale's allegro seems rather too violent to fit the suggested scheme. Conceivably the secret of the Seventh Quartet is known to the Shostakovich family and will one day be made public. For now, its crystalline precision and intimate eloquence are sufficient in themselves.

By contrast, the Quartet No. 8 in C minor, Opus 110, written three months later, was for years as much obscured by its own legend as were the Seventh,

Eighth, and Eleventh Symphonies. Known in the USSR as the 'Dresden' quartet, the Eighth was composed in three days during the composer's visit to the ruined city of Dresden in July 1960. Sent there to provide a score for the East German war film *Five Days, Five Nights*, Shostakovich had supposedly been so shocked by the devastation he saw that he poured out his feelings in music, inscribing the work 'To the Memory of the Victims of Fascism'. This went down well with the Soviet authorities, who assured the quartet a global publicity similar to that awarded to the *Leningrad* and *The Year 1905*. Yet, from the beginning, there was a clear disjunction between the Eighth Quartet's programme and its music, which, far from aiming for impersonal universality, consisted of the densest mass of self-quotation Shostakovich ever committed to paper. Were the work's programme and dedication, then, like those of many of his earlier works, no more than a bodyguard of lies? According to Vishnevskaya, the composer told friends that, far from concerning the dead of Dresden – victims not of Fascism but of Western democracy working to Soviet military request – the quartet was actually a musical autobiography; hence the self-quotations. *Testimony*, is, of course, unequivocal on the matter: 'Everything in the quartet is as clear as a primer. I quote *Lady Macbeth*, the First and Fifth symphonies. What does fascism have to do with these? The Eighth is an autobiographical quartet, it quotes a song known to all Russians: "Exhausted by the hardship of prison".'

More often translated as 'Tormented by lack of freedom', this nineteenth-century convict song occurs in the work's fourth movement, following a wizened citation of D-S-C-H. The message seems explicit enough: 'Shostakovich is tormented by lack of freedom.' In fact, taken as a whole, the quartet is probably the most explicit thing in the composer's output. In the first movement, a mournful D-S-C-H introduces the ambiguous opening theme of his First Symphony. The violent second movement brings slashing two-note figures and an incipient gopak rhythm, with the 'dance of death' theme from the Second Piano Trio turning up over very deliberate triplets. The motto from the First Cello Concerto follows in a satirical fast waltz and the finale links D-S-C-H with the unifying motif from the 'Siberian' Act IV of *Lady Macbeth*, reinforcing the message that Shostakovich is, in effect, 'in prison'. The funeral oration of the fourth movement quotes the hammering figure from the execution scene in *The Young Guard* and, after a quotation from the third movement of the Eleventh Symphony, the cello sings part of the aria 'Seryozha, my love', again from Act IV of *Lady Macbeth*.

Other quotations, variations, and recurrent motifs are to be found in the Eighth Quartet – it is, for example, particularly rich in five-note cells – but its meaning is clear enough already. The question is: why did such a work burst out so forcefully in Dresden? While the music he later wrote about the place in *Five Days, Five Nights* is of low voltage, dutifully invoking the shades of Beethoven and Richard Strauss with no hint of personal involvement, it is probable that the ruin of so proud a cultural symbol would have held an immediate significance for him in terms of his own life. How else, after all, would a razed ex-Fascist city have provoked such a concentrated study not merely in autobiography, but also in self-justification? Previously content to signal his own position in hints, he had never before felt the need to spell it out so clearly. Was the sight of Dresden, then, merely a catalyst for the composition of something he had been planning for some time? Once again, an examination of context suggests the answer.

Following the successful première of the Eleventh Symphony in Moscow in October 1957, the Soviet authorities had set about incorporating Shostakovich into their cultural propaganda operation. The chairmanship of the Tchaikovsky Competition, the Lenin Prize, the removal of the Formalist stigma applied to him by Zhdanov – these were gestures calculated to demonstrate to the West that Shostakovich was restored to state approval. All that remained was to show that the composer, in his turn, approved of the state. Thus, on 8 February 1958, at a Kremlin reception for the Soviet intelligentsia, Shostakovich rather than Khrennikov was called upon to reply on behalf of the assembled composers to Khrushchev's address. In so doing, he was required to toast 'the Communist Party and its Leninist Committee, the Soviet Government, and the Soviet People'. The resolution rescinding the verdict of 1948 followed, as effect follows cause, some three months later. Shortly afterwards, Shostakovich's name appeared under a piece in *Pravda* (13 June) offering fulsome appreciation of the recent decree and claiming that he had been 'deeply moved by the manifestations of the Communist Party's care and attention for Soviet music and Soviet composers'. In his standard history of Soviet music, Boris Schwarz admits that he finds the tone of the composer's article 'somewhat curious . . . as if he had never been personally involved'.

The scheme to purvey Shostakovich as an obedient conformist continued in 1959 when he was sent to America with a delegation of Soviet composers headed by his arch-enemy Khrennikov. Described in *Musical America* as 'highly nervous, a chain-smoker with darting eyes and fidgeting hands, ill at ease most of the time', he was asked by reporters if he still believed that the USA was a nation of 'war-mongers'. In no position to deny the spurious Waldorf-Astoria speech of 1949 in which this sentiment had been expressed, Shostakovich embarrassedly explained that he had always been friendly to the USA and that his remarks ought not to be taken to refer to the American people as a whole. 'Cautious and non-committal', he later declined to answer questions about the *Lady Macbeth* affair on the grounds that he was 'too tired'. Though some witnesses were struck by the strangely mechanical unanimity of the six Soviet composers on show, the damage had been done: in the eyes of the outside world Shostakovich was confirmed as an orthodox Communist. The logical next step was to make this an incontrovertible fact.

On returning to Russia, Shostakovich was informed that the government wished to reappoint him First Secretary of the RSFSR Composers' Union – but that this would require him joining the Communist Party. Unable to decline this suggestion, Shostakovich put a brave face on it though, according to both Volkov and Ashkenazy, he felt the charade to be a humiliation. On 7 September 1960, a week before the ratification of his candidate membership, the composer 'contributed' another article to *Pravda* welcoming Party ideologist Mikhail Suslov's minimal redefinition of Socialist Realism and attacking the 'individualism' inherent in Schoenberg's twelve-tone system: 'We do not conceal that we reject the right to fruitless formal experimentation, to the advocacy in our art of pessimism, scepticism, and man-hating ideas, all of which are products of the individualism on the rampage in the contemporary bourgeois world.' The first of a series of similarly philistine articles 'by' him in *Pravda* over the next decade, this was received in Russia as a major policy statement, setting the seal on Shostakovich's new orthodox image both at home and abroad. This time the damage was serious, even those sympathetic to his predicament finding his total acquiescence to the demands of the regime mystifying. Commenting on the *Pravda* piece, Boris Schwarz wrote, disapprovingly: 'Shostakovich, whose usual prose style is angular and artless, may not have written this pretentious drivel, but he signed it and thus identified himself with its propaganda content.' Yet, as usual in such situations, it is hard to see what else the composer could have done. Refusal to co-operate would have driven him back into the wilderness and rebounded on his family and friends. Committed to producing an art of honesty in a culture of lies, he had long ago made the decision that what people thought of him was less important than ensuring they had the chance of being emotionally confronted by his music. Part of the bargain for signing on the Party's dotted line was the unbanning, after fifteen years, of the Eighth Symphony, while soon the Fourth, too, would be finally allowed to see the light of day. Furthermore, he could easily debunk the fake Shostakovich who regularly sounded off on the Party's behalf in *Pravda* by continuing to write music equally as dissident.

Thus, a fortnight after the announcement of his candidate membership of the Party, the Eighth Quartet was premièred in Leningrad, disguised as a piece about Fascism, but in fact reassuring those with ears to hear that, far from acting out of his own free will, Shostakovich was, as usual, being pushed about by the authorities.

A similar declaration of independence was on show in the composer's song-cycle *Pictures of the Past*, Opus 109, premièred by him and Vishnevskaya in February 1961. Setting pre-Revolutionary verses by the ironist Sasha Cherny so as to point up their contemporary relevance, *Pictures of the Past* drew roars of approval and demands for two complete encores from its first-night audience, who evidently had no difficulty in understanding that the Communist Shostakovich was a fiction created by the Kremlin. Vishnevskaya, the cycle's dedicatee, was particularly delighted with it, noting that it 'scoffed' like the boldly iconoclastic work of its composer's youth. Clearly Shostakovich was in assertive mood. The state had a fight on its hands.

The next round was, however, a rough one. Due to be confirmed as a full member of the Party in October 1961, he was commissioned to write a new symphony for its 22nd Congress, scheduled for the same month. To make matters worse, the symphony was to be a sequel to the Eleventh, celebrating not the Narodnik revolution of 1905 but Lenin's coup of October 1917. In effect, the commission placed Shostakovich in the same quandary he had faced when asked for something to mark the tenth anniversary of October in 1927. 1917 was holy ground. A repetition of the minor gloom of the Eleventh Symphony was out of the question; anything about October had to be upbeat and painted in the brightest 'democratic' colours.[1] Nor could he afford to disappoint his sponsors – for, if annoyed, they might renege on their promise to allow the long-lost Fourth Symphony to be performed, or even withdraw their favour completely.

As with the Ninth Symphony, Shostakovich was at first unable to come up with a solution to the problem and the Twelfth consequently went through several drafts. His first plan, given out in a broadcast on Radio Moscow in October 1960, consisted of four movements: 1. 'Lenin's arrival in Petrograd'; 2. 'The heroic events of November 2nd'; 3. 'The civil war'; 4. 'The victory of the October Socialist Revolution'. However, he soon abandoned this in favour of concentrating on Lenin himself and, during the first half of 1961, the work assumed the working title of the 'Lenin Symphony'.

A sacred figure in the USSR, Lenin was (and still is) worshipped as a kind of latterday Christ, his cult imitating that of Jesus in its claim to omnipresent immortality.[2] Hardly a topic close to Shostakovich's atheistic heart, the demigod had been the subject of one of his several stillborn works of the late thirties (see pp. 135–6) and the Twelfth Symphony may contain some themes he had prepared for it. Certainly it features at least one tune resurrected from an earlier period: the *Funeral March for the Victims of the Revolution*, first deployed in his other 'October' symphony, the Second.

Apparently as uninspiring to the composer as he had been in the late thirties, Lenin was soon deposed from the leadership of the new symphony, Shostakovich returning to his broader original scheme in which the Revolution itself was hero. His final score consists of four linked movements: 1. 'Revolutionary Petrograd'; 2. 'Razliv' (named after Lenin's hideout following the unsuccessful July coup); 3. 'Aurora' (the cruiser which signalled the start of the October Revolution by shelling the Winter Palace); and 4. 'The Dawn of Humanity'. Surviving in the slow movement, Shostakovich's sketch of Lenin was quietly critical, though tentative by comparison with his portrait of Stalin in the Tenth

---

[1] That Shostakovich had darker thoughts about 1917 is clear from his grim symphonic poem *October*, Opus 131, of 1967.

[2] See Tumarkin, *Lenin Lives!* Lenin's saintly image has, of course, been successfully exported to the West. In reality a self-proclaimed autocrat, his approval of dictatorship and terror was, in essence, no different from Stalin's.

Symphony. In *Testimony* he is reported as admitting as much: 'I understand that my Twelfth Symphony isn't a complete success in that sense. I began with one creative goal and ended with a completely different scheme. I wasn't able to realise my ideas, the material put up resistance.'[1] Notwithstanding these reservations, he managed to hide many clues to his real intentions in this subtly ambiguous score.

The Symphony No. 12 in D minor, Opus 112, *The Year 1917*, opens with a ponderously self-assured melody in the low strings which, in its 10th–12th bars, adopts an oddly crab-like motion suggestive of the main motif of Liszt's *Faust Symphony*. Sternly resolute, despite continually circling back upon itself, it speaks of indomitable endeavour and, for identification's sake, will be referred to here as the 'struggle' theme. Accelerating to a fast two-note mutation of itself, the 'struggle' theme works up to a tremendous climax before declining quickly down to a dry, pedantic enunciation of the People's three-note call. Beginning again in the low strings, a hymnal melody takes over, ascending to a second climax over two-note thuds in the drums and basses. Very much the theme of a quasi-Christ 'luminary' figure, this is almost certainly a suitably idealised portrait of Lenin (with the same Faustian sting in its tail as the 'struggle' theme). First and second subject deployed, Shostakovich now proceeds to his development section – an energetic and, it has to be said, extremely exciting 'battle' sequence, dominated by curt two-note figures, which rages to an explosive climax on the 'struggle' theme. So tense and active is this passage that the recapitulation can only be a sustained decrescendo – but interesting things are happening here, too. For example, at figure 51, the violins allude to the binding motif from Act IV of *Lady Macbeth* (quoted in the last movement of the Eighth Quartet), while the horn, playing the 'Lenin' theme, closes on a pair of fateful two-note semitonal oscillations – perhaps foreseeing the transformation of Tsarist Siberia into Stalinist Gulag?[2]

The rocking semitones recur in the slow movement, as does the tolling three-note motif of the People. This interlude, portraying Lenin in meditative retreat on the eve of October, is subtly tongue-in-cheek, evoking the religious overtones of the dictator's cult in a sanctimonious chorale if anything more self-righteous than the 'Lenin' theme itself (which alternates with it). At first, darkness prevails; Lenin cannot find inspiration. Then seraphic light streams into the monk's cell in E flat major and the People's motif rings out. Grateful for this heaven-sent grace, a clarinet contemplates it in the rhythm of the

---

[1] The main reason for supposing that the Twelfth borrows from unused earlier material is that it employs melodies rather than motifs – an essentially non-symphonic strategy that caused Tchaikovsky, for example, endless problems. That the Twelfth is Shostakovich's most Tchaikovskyian symphony is, perhaps, made clearer by comparing its rushing passage-work to that of the Overture to *The Gadfly*, where the Tchaikovsky inheritance is more obvious.

[2] In the *Collected Works* (Vol. 6) these bars (four before figure 52) are given a variant form: that of the *Lady Macbeth* figure.

'Lenin' theme while pious violins raise their eyes skywards in a saccharine glissando (three bars after figure 70). From satire to tragedy: a sinister gong chills the atmosphere and the clarinet wanders, via a pair of seesawing semitones, into the first four notes of the *Funeral March for the Victims of the Revolution* (figure 73). Tremolando strings shiver, a trombone soliloquises prophetically on the People's motif, and the movement ends with a quiet pizzicato allusion to the memorial third movement of the Eleventh Symphony. Thus, with infinite finesse, Shostakovich lays at Lenin's door the ultimate guilt for the fifty million victims of his Glorious Revolution.

Setting two against three as in so many of the composer's scherzos, the symphony's third movement is rhythmically one of his most original inventions. Dramatic, too: arriving to a cold, high woodwind chord of C sharp, the 'Lenin' theme is growled out by low brass over ominous divided strings and distant thunder-effects. Exhilarated by this, the two-versus-three fight boils up over expectant triplets and, in two-note triumph, the finale looms suddenly into view, massed horns calling out the *Funeral March for the Victims of the Revolution*. Full of five-note phrases, an optimistic second subject alters the mood, but the sky clouds over when it meets the 'struggle' theme. Ambitious, the finale now goes for a synthesis, fusing its second subject, 'Lenin', and the *Funeral March* – but the rhythm of the 'betrayal' motif brings memories of the Eleventh Symphony's finale (figure 104) and the 'struggle' theme reappears. Two more climaxes are cut off by fortissimo three-note statements; facile jubilation, it seems, will come only when the People are given their due. Accordingly, the strings return to the depths for a resumption of the 'struggle' theme in its original tragic colours before, swinging into a blinding D major, the symphony at last reaches its peroration. High A's as usual screaming monotonously at the top of the orchestra, the coda mercilessly exceeds even the preposterous climax of the Fifth Symphony.

Taking all this seriously, the Communist audience on the opening day of their 22nd Congress applauded heartily. Equally earnest, critics at the symphony's Western première at the Edinburgh Festival in 1962 were appalled. Neither were right. Once it is grasped that there was never room in the Twelfth Symphony for Shostakovich to say anything serious – or even overtly funny – it becomes easier to see the work for what it is: a dazzlingly resourceful *impersonation* of the very symphony its early audiences thought they were hearing. It may not be very profound, but nor is it by any means as trivial as it may seem and, on the grounds of sustained ingenuity alone, it deserves a considerably higher reputation than it has been allowed so far.

The Soviet success of Shostakovich's Twelfth was completely overshadowed by the main event of the 22nd Congress: Khrushchev's second denunciation of Stalin. The high-water mark of de-Stalinisation before the Gorbachev era, this speech and the subsequent removal of the dictator's remains from the mausoleum in Red Square sanctioned a new 'thaw' – the third since his death in 1953. In fact, a current of independent thought had been coursing through Russian intellectual life ever since the Pasternak affair of 1958, notably in the form of *samizdat* ('self-published') literature circulated from hand to hand in carbon copies. Just prior to the Twelfth Symphony, *samizdat* magazines had begun to publish both new writing and works banned under Stalin's rule, and 1961 saw the first semi-official manifestation of this: *Tarusa Pages*, a symposium published in Kaluga under the editorship of the well-known memoirist Konstantin Paustovsky. Containing poems by Tsvetayeva and Zabolotsky and articles in praise of Meyerhold and Bunin, *Tarusa Pages* was a direct challenge to Socialist Realism and readers all over Russia looked to it as a manifesto of liberal 'revisionism'.

The most outstanding literary event of the year, however, was the appearance of *Babi Yar* by the twenty-eight-year-old Yevgeny Yevtushenko, then considered to be the standard-bearer of liberal youth culture. A poem about the Nazi massacre of seventy thousand Jews in a ravine outside Kiev in September 1941, *Babi Yar* was at the same time a bold and highly controversial indictment of contemporary Soviet anti-Semitism.[1] Having just finished the Twelfth, Shostakovich bought *Literary Gazette* to read the poem and was electrified by its identification with the Jew as victim (this, of course, being precisely the way he felt himself). Seizing on *Babi Yar* as embodying the opposite of what his Twelfth would inevitably appear to represent, he quickly sketched a setting before, almost as an afterthought, phoning Yevtushenko to ask his permission. Delighted to be set by Shostakovich, the poet promptly suggested extending the collaboration and the project accordingly grew, acquiring three more existing poems and a new one, *Fears*, written specially for what had by then become the composer's Thirteenth Symphony. With interruptions for the premières of the Twelfth and Fourth Symphonies and the fulfilment of a promise to Vishnevskaya to orchestrate Mussorgsky's *Songs and Dances of Death*, Shostakovich was unable to continue with the work until the summer of 1962 – but he then moved fast, finishing it shortly before leaving Russia to attend the Edinburgh Festival.

The Thirteenth Symphony was very deliberately allotted the opus number 113, next after the Twelfth. Though *Songs and Dances of Death* came between the two symphonies, unlike his re-orchestrations of *Boris Godunov* and *Khovanshchina*, Shostakovich never gave it an opus number. Clearly he wished to juxtapose the seemingly conformist Twelfth Symphony with something overtly dissident – much as he had juxtaposed his apparent submission to the Communist Party with the Eighth Quartet. His intention, however, was apprehended by the authorities and, in the approach to the Thirteenth's première in Moscow on 18 December 1962, a backstage struggle developed,

---

[1] After Stalin's death, anti-Semitism continued in a lower key. There was no recognition of any 'Jewish problem' and no restoration of Jewish institutions. Between 1956 and 1965, nine out of every ten synagogues in Russia were closed.

with a caucus of Stalinist *apparatchiks* trying, through threats and blackmail, to get the concert called off.

The situation was finely balanced. Khrushchev – who, in Vishnevskaya's words 'had not yet dismounted the soapbox' of the recent 22nd Party Congress – was committed to de-Stalinisation and the new thaw. Moreover, even if the Stalinists had had a free hand, Shostakovich's profile in the West was too high after the Edinburgh Festival to permit an outright ban on him.[1] Yevtushenko, too, was well known outside the USSR and his reputation increased when in October *Pravda* published his poem *The Heirs of Stalin*. But the surest protection Shostakovich and Yevtushenko enjoyed during the Thirteenth's rehearsal period was afforded by the appearance in *Novy Mir* of Alexander Solzhenitsyn's taboo-smashing account of Stalin's Gulag, *One Day in the Life of Ivan Denisovich*. Having bided his time through the first two thaws, Solzhenitsyn had taken Khrushchev's second anathematisation of Stalin as a sign and submitted his novella to Alexander Tvardovsky (reinstated as *Novy Mir*'s editor since 1958). By-passing the bureaucracy, Tvardovsky had sent a copy to Khrushchev who, recognising ammunition for his war with the Stalinists, ordered *Ivan Denisovich* to be published immediately. The resulting scandal convulsed the Soviet cultural scene, diverting attention from the equally explosive event brewing up at the Moscow Conservatory Bolshoi Hall.

Despite these factors, getting the Thirteenth Symphony played turned out to be a complex game for which those organising it – Shostakovich, Yevtushenko, Khachaturian, Rostropovich, Vishnevskaya, the conductor Kyrill Kondrashin, and the composer Moisei Vaynberg – needed all their wits about them. Before rehearsals began, the *apparatchiks* had informed them that the poem *Babi Yar* was ideologically unsound in that it made no mention of the native Russians who had died in the war against Fascism. The Party, it was said, wanted the text changed or the performance cancelled. Reading this as a bluff, Shostakovich's group took no notice and, when their soloist was strong-armed into withdrawing, they merely recruited another one (Viktor Nechipaylo) and carried on. Their enemies however, had another card to play.

On 1 December disaster had struck the Russian liberals. Invited to an exhibition of Russian abstract art, Khrushchev had flown off the handle, calling the painters pederasts and storming out shouting 'Gentlemen, we are declaring war on you!' In effect, the third thaw had ended there and then – a fortnight before the Thirteenth Symphony was due to go. Hastening to draw Khrushchev's attention to the 'unpatriotic' words of *Babi Yar*, the Stalinist faction duly

---

[1] In August, Shostakovich sweetened the authorities by arranging two popular Proletkult choruses by Alexander Davidenko, having noted their existence during an ironic lament for their 'unfortunately half-forgotten' composer in 1959. Originally from a collectively composed Prokoll 'oratorio', *The Road of October* (described by Olkhovsky as 'in reality only a suite of mass-songs'), they are of the utmost banality and cannot seriously have appealed to him.

enlisted his displeasure and, the day before the concert, Yevtushenko found himself the target of the Soviet premier's crude baiting at a hastily convened arts conference. Non-committal on Khrushchev's pointed observation that anti-Semitism no longer existed in the USSR, the poet took cautious issue with him over the banned abstract artists, venturing that the 'Formalistic trends' in their work would soon be straightened out. Blustering, Khrushchev responded with a rustic proverb: 'The grave straightens out the humpbacked.' To the astonishment of his fellow artists, Yevtushenko refused to be browbeaten: 'Nikita Sergeyich, we have come a long way since the time when only the grave straightened out humpbacks. Really, there are other ways.'

That evening, having expended their arsenal of threats on Viktor Nechipaylo without result, the plotters managed to eliminate him by arranging his last-minute secondment to the Bolshoi's production of *Don Carlos*. Luckily, Shostakovich's group had been coaching yet another bass, Vitaly Gromadsky, who was able to step in at the eleventh hour, giving their enemies no time to react. Official sabotage, however, persisted throughout the day of the concert. The TV cameras originally set up to cover the event were noisily dismantled and at one point the entire choir tried to resign, only a desperate speech by Yevtushenko shaming them into staying. Finally, with a packed house of excited liberals and only the government box empty, the symphony went ahead to a tremendous ovation. Two days later, the Shostakovich group managed to mount a second performance of the work before the authorities cut their losses and banned it.

Shostakovich's last major clash with the Soviet state, the Symphony No. 13 in B flat minor, Opus 113, is – by the standards of its time and place – an astonishingly outspoken piece. Its music pared and simplified to lend maximum impact to the text, the work is a high-art Russian equivalent of the 'protest' songs then current in America, Yevtushenko's ramshackle apocalyptic irony being very much that of a Soviet Bob Dylan. In fact, it was his words more than Shostakovich's settings which thrilled the work's first-night audience and it was inevitable that, in taking their revenge, the authorities came down harder on the poet than the composer. Heavily 'persuaded' during the days after the concert, Yevtushenko eventually sanctioned a censored version of *Babi Yar* in *Literary Gazette*[1] – a surrender which marked the beginning of his fall from grace with the Soviet public and a long phase in his career deformed by efforts to please the state while retaining a modicum of self-respect and independence. (Many

---

[1] 'I feel myself a Jew. / Here I tread across old Egypt. / Here I die, nailed to the Cross. / And even now I bear the scars of it.' [Changed to: 'Here I stand as if at the fountainhead / That gives me faith in brotherhood. / Here Russians lie, and Ukrainians / Together with Jews in the same ground]'; 'I become a gigantic scream / Above the thousands buried here. / I am every old man shot dead here. / I am every child shot dead here.' [Changed to: 'I think of Russia's heroic deed / In blocking the way to Fascism. / To the smallest dew-drop, she is close to me / In her very being and her fate'.]

of his fellow liberals despised Yevtushenko for his behaviour, but his predicament was a difficult one and Shostakovich, who knew it well, declines to condemn the poet in *Testimony*.)

Earthily vernacular, the work's five poems cover every aspect of Soviet life. *Babi Yar* slams Russite anti-Semitism; *Humour* invokes Mullah Nasruddin in a paean to tyrant-deflating laughter; *In the Store* uses the hardship of Soviet women to point to the failure of materialistic Communism to deliver anything on the material level; *Fears* is a coruscating attack on state represssion; and *A Career* sends up cynical self-interest and robotic unanimity. A wholesale rejection of 'Soviet reality', the Thirteenth Symphony was forbidden in Russia for ten years and has rarely been played there since.

Musically, the work employs Shostakovich's standard shorthand, hateful or lifeless things (for example, the central orchestral fortissimo in the first movement) etched in two-note rhythms, decency and folk-simplicity appearing always in triple forms. Starting with a burlesque impersonation of the arrogance of power, *Humour* uses the tune of *MacPherson Before His Execution*[1] (introduced on low strings at figure 45) to colour Yevtushenko's image of the endlessly murdered and endlessly resurrected spirit of mockery. At the pregnant line 'His appearance displayed obedience', the orchestra voices the composer's exasperation by blasting out its tutti in two keys at once. *Fears* is remarkable for its orchestral effects, the tuba, for example, harking back to the 'midnight arrest' section of the Fourth Symphony's first movement. Passing, via the ponderous tick of an ancient clock,[2] into the oleaginous flute theme of the finale, these pages contain, for sheer sound, some of Shostakovich's most adventurous measures since his Modernist period. *A Career* follows in the footsteps of earlier satirical finales, such as that of the Eighth Symphony – but particularly those of the Fourth Quartet (from which it plunders bars 5–6 after figure 92) and the Sixth Quartet (quoting the cello at figure 70, etc.). In fact, the tone of this movement is as deceptive as that of the Sixth Quartet, the irony in its glutinous main theme only becoming inescapable in its final appearance on solo violin and viola. (*Testimony*: 'They'll talk about beauty, grace, and other high qualities. But you won't catch me with that bait. I'm like Sobakevich in *Dead Souls*: you can sugarcoat a frog, and I still won't put it in my mouth.')

Returning to plainness in its coda, the Thirteenth Symphony ends with the celesta tapping out the People's three notes to the steady chime of a high bell.

---

[1] The third of the composer's *Six Romances on Verses by English Poets*, Opus 62, of 1942. An echo of it also occurs in the eighth movement of the Fourteenth Symphony (*The Zaporozhian Cossacks' Answer to the Sultan of Constantinople*).

[2] Regular notes behind the beat (that is, across the bar-line) – an effect used also in the fourth movement of the Eighth Symphony (ten bars before figure C, *et seq*., in the Breitkopf edition) and the slow movement of the Second Violin Concerto (figure 61, bars 6–8).

Not as dominant as in recent symphonies, this motif nevertheless plays an important part in the Thirteenth, permeating its second movement (where it is punched out in triumph at figure 42); swirling up in memories of the Eleventh at figure 103; and speaking, all but inaudibly, of love in *Babi Yar* (figures 17–18). Five-note figures, too, feature throughout the work (see above, p. 220).

In terms of artistic achievement, the Thirteenth is a fascinating piece, intensely sensitive to its text and yet writhing with an independent musical life of its own. If, occasionally, its fortissimo passages seem gesticulatory rather than precisely articulated, compensation is provided by expressive detail in the lighter scoring of a kind not heard in the composer's work since the Fourth Symphony. This seems to have been a product of his reacquaintance with the Fourth during the Thirteenth's planning stage (though it is equally possible that, liberated in the Thirteenth, Shostakovich regained contact with areas of creativity closed to him since the comparably full-throttle days before 1936). The presiding colour of the Thirteenth Symphony is, however, like that of the Eleventh, grey – a word sadly stressed at figure 23 – and it is the wavering semitones of *In the Store*, the work's most monochrome and eventless movement, that point the way forward to the gradually deepening despair of its composer's late style.

Chief among the characteristics of this late style is a stark sparseness of line, harmony, rhythm, and colour which has been plausibly ascribed to the increasingly sick Shostakovich's disinclination to tire himself out with scribbling too many notes. He had begun to feel pain in his right hand just before starting the First Cello Concerto in 1958 – a complaint which afflicted him for the rest of his life, frequently obliging him to stop writing and rest. This must, of course, have conditioned his general working schedules, but to assume that it altered the way he composed is to place too much importance on mechanical necessity. After all, there are many very full pages in the scores of his Fourteenth and Fifteenth Symphonies, his Twelfth Quartet and Violin Sonata, and the symphonic poem *October* – not to mention *Katerina Ismailova*, his revision of *Lady Macbeth*, completed in 1962. Clearly, before any lesser consideration, Shostakovich wrote more simply not because he had a progressive neural disorder but because simplicity was what he was aiming for as an artist.

In this respect, the closing pages of the Thirteenth are arguably seminal for his late style which, though usually dated from 1966, can be seen emerging from the symphony's shadow in the form of works like his music for Kozintsev's film of *Hamlet* and the cantata *The Execution of Stepan Razin*, Opus 119, in 1963–4. Linked by a motto-rhythm used first in the film's *Duel and Death of Hamlet* number, these scores share a militant simplicity, almost puritanical in its distrust of anything colourful or soft-edged, which seems to stem from the Thirteenth's closing juxtaposition of the three notes of the People against a smarmily harmonised, fluttering melody indicative of preciousness and pretension.[1] The symphony's quasi-religious bells further suggest the presence of Mussorgsky's People-mysticism – and *Stepan Razin* is nothing if not religiously devoted to the idea that the People will, ultimately, smell corruption and see through evil. Similarly inherited from the Thirteenth is an edge of irascible Old Testament violence, crashing down in vengeful blows from an enlarged percussion section (instrumentation which, again, may derive from renewed acquaintance with the Fourth Symphony). Both *Stepan Razin* and *Hamlet* feature these flagellating chords, cracked out with the help of the whip and wood-block introduced in the Thirteenth's third movement. The Eleventh Symphony, too, looms behind these works (particularly *Hamlet*). However, the most significant common factor is their ascetic severity – a quality likewise to the fore in the composer's frugal song-cycle *From Jewish Folk Poetry*, which he chose to orchestrate soon after the Thirteenth during summer 1963.

That Shostakovich had a need for sackcloth and ashes after the Twelfth Symphony is possible – but it squares neither with his usually forceful creativity nor his, by now, extreme toughness of mind. More probable is that after the failure of the third thaw (and more particularly, the banning of one of his most personal and outspoken works) he was simply furious with the Soviet mediocracy and the morally rotten art it brandished as exemplary. While concerts were filled with flaccid confections by the like of Khrennikov, Kabalevsky, and Shchedrin, the score of his Thirteenth Symphony had to be smuggled out of the country and the Soviet première of *Katerina Ismailova* was cheapened by cloak-and-dagger farce.[2] A similar situation prevailed in literature, and Solzhenitsyn's description of the Writers' Union as 'a rabble of hucksters and moneychangers' voices the same vituperative disgust as Shostakovich's *Hamlet* and *Stepan Razin*. It is this disgust and avenging plainness that shaped the composer's late style, more than any wish to give his fingers less work to do.

Though now happily married to his third wife Irina and allowed to travel abroad to attend foreign productions of *Katerina Ismailova*, Shostakovich refused to moderate the new puritanical fury of his art. Composed during a very busy summer in 1964, his Ninth and Tenth Quartets displayed his 'late' proclivities for squealing glissandi, biting sforzandi, and listlessly oscillating semitones. In the midst of a period of frenetic activity, they also anticipate the late period's preoccupation with silence and very slow music, featuring more

---

[1] A similarly fey configuration occurs, without apparent irony, in the cycle on poems by Tsvetayeva twelve years later (No. 2: *Whence Such Tenderness?*). The feminine delicacy of the latter was, however, untypical of the plain-spoken Shostakovich, and the tone of this song, which has nothing else in common with *A Career*, is unique in his output.

[2] The revised opera was given on 26 December 1962 with no publicity and no press coverage. Posters claimed that *The Barber of Seville* would be played, although everyone in Moscow art circles knew that it would be replaced at the last minute by *Katerina Ismailova*. (Those in the know joked on the night of the concert, 'See you at the barber!').

minims and semibreves than anything the composer had written before.[1] Apart from this, the works are typical two-versus-three struggles, featuring the rhythm of the 'betrayal' motif and forlornly deformed derivations of D-S-C-H (the Ninth at figure 67; the Tenth at figures 12 and 82). The Quartet No. 9 in E flat, Opus 117, possesses a structure unique in its composer's output: five movements 'cross-fading' each other, the last being itself cast in five meshed sections. Starting with an ambiguous smile (and the 'betrayal' motif as early as the eighth bar), it shows signs that Shostakovich's recent re-involvement with the Jewish problem had included a review of his Fourth Quartet. Central, both metaphorically and actually, is an evocation of Stalinist dreariness which stirs the first violin to an agonised three-note protest. In the finale, three and two join battle, at one stage passing through a wild Central Asian folk dance probably influenced by the composer's visit to Tashkent shortly before beginning the work. The Quartet No. 10 in A flat, Opus 118, recycles a familiar format, savaging an uneasily provisional introduction with a ferocious scherzo (à la Tenth Symphony) and recapitulating its desolate passacaglia at the climax of a capricious finale capped with a three-note sign-off. Though strong pieces (especially the Ninth), neither quartet has the depth or breadth of their finest predecessors and one can be forgiven for thinking that we have been over this ground once too often.

In October 1964, having drummed Soviet artists into line by sanctioning the imprisonment of the poet Josef Brodsky for 'parasitism',[2] Khrushchev was ousted by the old-style Stalinist Leonid Brezhnev. While the new regime was finding its feet, a fourth 'thaw' developed and Shostakovich, in lighter mood, wrote a little group of settings using texts from the state's tame satirical magazine, *Crocodile*. Soon, however, trouble erupted, with writers and students protesting against the government's surreptitious attempts to rehabilitate Stalin (by blaming the Terror on a Trotskyite plot to liquidate the old Bolsheviks which only he had seen through). The customary clamp-down followed, and by 1966 this last gasp of liberalism was stilled. With the imprisonment of the writers Yuly Daniel and Andrei Sinyavsky, Brezhnev's

---

[1] Partly a product of Shostakovich's habit of writing in large note-values, the trend in these works is, none the less, essentially one of thought rather than technical contingency.

[2] According to the poet Anatoli Naiman's autobiography (Russian edition, p. 137), Akhmatova asked Shostakovich, in his capacity as deputy to the Supreme Soviet for the Leningrad district in which Brodsky lived, to intercede for him. At a meeting with Akhmatova in the writer Viktor Ardov's Moscow house during December 1963, Shostakovich expressed his 'deep and sincere respect' for her, but was pessimistic about the chances of helping Brodsky, who had been specifically targeted as a leading figure in *samizdat*. His gloom was prophetic. Though he did what he could, the composer was unable to prevent Brodsky from being sentenced to five years' internal exile. (This, incidentally, was not the meeting with Akhmatova described on page 274 of *Testimony*, which seems to have taken place at her *dacha* in Komarovo during 1958.)

gerontocracy of 'grey men' inaugurated a neo-Stalinist freeze which paralysed Russian culture for the next twenty years. Shostakovich would die long before his unhappy country glimpsed the sun again.

Despite perpetual illness and the tedious necessity of having to supply the state with regular tokens of obeisance,[1] the composer's last decade was consistently productive. From 1966 to his death in 1975, he wrote two symphonies, two concertos, five quartets, two string sonatas, and three major song-cycles – more than many manage in a career.

These creations of Shostakovich's increasingly convalescent sixties form a group of their own, separate from the main body of his work (if, as argued above, implicit in it). Here, turning away from confrontation with the state and dogged by the possibility of sudden death following his first heart attack in 1966, he focused with growing austerity on eternal and universal subjects: time, love, betrayal, truth, morality, and mortality. Withdrawn and cryptic, these compositions are often compared with Beethoven's own late period – a parallel of which Shostakovich was aware and which he acknowledged, with varying degrees of directness, in the finales of the Twelfth Quartet, Violin Sonata, and Viola Sonata. Inasmuch as it is essentially subjective, the scope offered by this late work for precise critical characterisation is smaller than with the composer's pre-1966 output. On the other hand, the code language developed in his earlier period survives intact into his late period, allowing even a brief overview to throw objective light into areas of it which might otherwise seem tenebrously personal.

If Shostakovich's late period is to his main sequence as the outer planets are to those revolving closer to the sun – cold, remote, obscure, solitary, and relatively simple in constitution – then the asteroid belt via which the listener voyages into their dark and archetypal sphere can be said to consist of three sparsely minimal works dating from 1966: the Eleventh Quartet, the Second Cello Concerto, and the song-cycle *Seven Romances on Poems of Alexander Blok*, Opus 127. Together, these pieces contain the basic elements of almost everything evolved in the compositions which follow them. Here, simplicity is elevated to an article of faith – a kind of all-purpose prophylactic against a world steeped irredeemably in imposture and deceit.

The first of the group, the Quartet No. 11 in F minor, Opus 122, adopts a style of artless naivety, somewhere between that of child and clown (in other words, that of the *yurodivy*). An extreme solution which seems to preclude any

---

[1] These were *A Year as Long as a Lifetime*, a film score to a biographical script about Karl Marx by the Stalinist hack Galina Serebryakova; the *Funeral-Triumphal Prelude*, Opus 130 ('In memory of the heroes of Stalingrad'), and the violent and gloomy symphonic poem *October*, Opus 131, both commissioned for the fiftieth anniversary of the Revolution in 1967; the eight choruses entitled *Loyalty*, Opus 136, for the centenary of Lenin's birth in 1970; and the *March of the Soviet Police*, Opus 139, a commission dedicated, ironically, to his friend Mikhail Zoshchenko (see *Testimony*, p. 179).

sophistication at all, this recurs in its purest form in very late works like the Thirteenth Quartet, the finale of the *Suite on Verses by Michelangelo*, the *Four Verses of Captain Lebyadkin*, and the first movement of the Viola Sonata. A more hard-bitten, adult version – a knowing parsimony capable of complex development – appears, fused or contrasted with the purer *yurodstvo*, in the Cello Concerto No. 2 in G, Opus 126 and, on its own, in the cosmically oracular Blok cycle. Through this triple aspect – child/clown, disillusioned adult, and prophet/soothsayer – simplicity rules Shostakovich's late music with a rod of iron, assuming, at its severest, a quasi-religious tone first heard in the Piano Quintet of 1940. It is as if the composer has seen too much evil, suffered too much duplicity. Like Britten, he ponders in old age a kind of Noh theatre of moral parable, chiselling away the superfluous to expose the essential human beneath, bereft of its camouflage of vanity and pretence. The further into the late period this theme is pursued, the more extreme it becomes. Lashing 'infamy and crime', 'those who jabber lies', and 'the malevolent crowd' in his Michelangelo suite, Shostakovich prowls the verge of misanthropy like some latterday Ecclesiastes, the whipcrack chords of *Hamlet* and *Stepan Razin* raining down in its eighth movement as though the scars of calumny were as livid to him in 1974 as they had been in 1936, 1948, and 1962.

Such outbursts of fury, though frequent in the late period, none the less emerge from a deeper background of detached inaction and silence. As Shostakovich gradually retires into himself, the axis of tension shifts away from the earthly war of good and evil towards a dialogue between himself and death. So central to the works of the forties and fifties, the opposition of two and three is absent from the transitional pieces of 1966 and only rarely manifests itself thereafter (for example, on the last page of the Twelfth Quartet). Similarly, though aggressive two-note phrases still occur – notably in the violently virtuoso second movement of the Violin Sonata, written during the Soviet invasion of Czechoslovakia in 1968 – they are more commonly present as drily impotent gestures (as in the first movement of the Twelfth Quartet) or short-winded grumbling (throughout the Viola Sonata). In fact, by far the commonest form of two-ness in Shostakovich's late music consists of monotonous oscillatory figures, usually semitonal, which distil what once stood for Stalin into a general, life-denying dreariness. In parts of the quartets (for example, the Eleventh's fifth movement and the Fifteenth's 'Epilogue'), such oscillations seem to embody life at a flickering minimum: its ultimate mechanical reduction to heart-beat, brain-wave, or breath.

Just as the number two becomes generalised after 1966, so three – the number of the People, of the victimised, of love – dissipates in frequency and strength during the late period, although something of a rally occurs in the last three quartets. In the Thirteenth, the three-note motto from *The Young Guard* pounds out yet again; the Fifteenth's first movement is a slow three-note lament in folk idiom; and, in the Fourteenth, triplets break out at what would otherwise be inexplicable places (figures 24, 31, and 66 – the last with an incongruous Philip Glass effect). Most significant of all is the finale of the composer's last work, the Viola Sonata, Opus 147, based on the adagio of Beethoven's *Moonlight* sonata – or, rather, on the first three notes of both the theme and its arpeggio accompaniment. Actually funereal in character, this movement had nothing to do with moonlight, the title having been coined by the poet Heinrich Rellstab and imposed on Beethoven by his publisher, a process so familiar to Shostakovich that this, as much as the three repeated notes of the adagio's melody, is probably why he chose it. His last finale, it seems to be the composer's departing hint that his music has been misrepresented and is often not what it seems. (As for whether he knew it was his swansong, there is evidence of this, too, on the score's final page, where a quotation from his youthful Suite for Two Pianos acts as a theatrical last glance back across his career to its very beginning.)

In marked contrast to the decline of two and three, the late period sees an increasing focus on the 'betrayal' motif, which appears, for example, in its characteristic intervals before the final allegretto of the Twelfth Quartet (figure 64), in *The Fool* and *Dinner at Goneril's* from the score to Kozintsev's film of *King Lear*, and in *The Zaporozhian Cossacks' Answer to the Sultan of Constantinople* (punctuating the line 'horrid nightmare that cannot be told'). In the form of its rhythmic outline, it is everywhere from the march in the Second Cello Concerto to the Serenade in the Fifteenth Quartet – indeed, certain works, such as the Second Violin Concerto, Violin Sonata, and Fourteenth Quartet are positively obsessed with it. Shostakovich's withdrawal from the world in his late works seems at least partly to have been founded on a growing distrust of humanity per se, and one reason for the scarcity of the classic three-note pattern is that the 'betrayal' motif, being itself in three notes, gradually usurps its position. In the sixth movement of the Fourteenth Symphony a lady, having mislaid her heart, dismisses it as 'just a trifle' (evoked by a blasé three-note figure on xylophone) before laughing 'at the love which is cut off by death' in the almost identical rhythm of the 'betrayal' motif. The misanthropic insinuation that to be human is to be shallow and undependable is implicit in such other encounters of the three-note figure and the 'betrayal' motif as the song *We Were Together* from the Blok cycle and the finale of the Fourteenth Quartet. (Indeed, figures 69–73 of the latter display an apparent indifference even to the distinction between two and three which would seem downright cynical were it not for the warm restoration of the three-note figure in its radiant Janáčekian conclusion.)

From those who knew him, it seems that Shostakovich's philosophy, at its simplest, was to value the individual and fear the crowd. If, beyond the late period's bouts of angry misanthropy, there is an abiding feeling, it is for those he loved – the love in them that made them individual, differentiating them from the heartless Collective. The ultimate treachery of the 'betrayal' motif can thus be seen as the abandonment of love for cynical self-interest – in a word, faithlessness. Speaking of this in one of the most convincing passages of

Testimony, he told Volkov: 'I think the greatest danger for a composer is loss of faith. Music, and art in general, cannot be cynical. Music can be bitter and despairing, but not cynical . . . When a man is in despair, it means that he still believes in something. It's the smug little music that is often cynical. Quiet and calm it is, for the composer doesn't give a damn about anything. It's just drivel and not art. And it's all around us.' Aside from the fury directed at his country's political leadership in pieces like *Poet and Tsar* from *Six Romances on Poems by Marina Tsvetayeva*, Opus 143, and *The Zaporozhian Cossacks' Answer* in the Fourteenth Symphony, most of the anger of Shostakovich's old age is expended on those 'working to make our era cynical'. Explicit in the *Suite on Verses by Michelangelo*, Opus 145, this subject is no less determinedly addressed in non-vocal works such as the Second Violin Concerto.

Written at the beginning of the Brezhnev freeze, the Second Violin Concerto is the first major work following the meditative transitional group of 1966. Earthy and direct, it is arguable whether it really belongs among its composer's 'outer planets' for in almost everything but orchestration (which is sparse, in typical late style) it shares the aims of his anti-Stalinist main sequence, owing its character to conflicts in the public rather than the private sphere. The sixties had witnessed the coining of the word 'dissident', meaning one committed to public expression of his disagreement with government policy. Confronting the authorities on basic issues of legality and human rights, men like Petr Yakir, Yuly Kim, General Petr Grigorenko, and Andrei Sakharov had brought honesty back to Soviet public life for the first time since Lenin had banned Gorky's *Untimely Thoughts* in 1918. Though pleased by this, Shostakovich had seen enough false dawns not to offer himself as a sacrifice in the flagrant style of the dissidents. Instead – and in a typically guarded way – he became what was known, in another new coinage, as a 'signer': one of a reservoir of leading Soviet intellectuals willing to lend their names to open letters on issues of natural justice and violations of the country's legal code. Thus, early in 1966, he joined the physicist Petr Kapitsa and the writers Kornei Chukovsky, Konstantin Paustovsky, and Sergei Smirnov in drawing the Central Committee's attention to the poverty then the lot of Alexander Solzhenitsyn, while in spring of 1967, following the arrests of many prominent intellectuals, he stood with Sakharov and other academicians in a letter deploring the new laws against anti-Soviet statements and demonstrations. Soon afterwards, however, open dissidence became a ticket to a psychiatric hospital and Shostakovich stepped quietly out of the firing-line, henceforth expressing his views either obliquely or not at all. When, in May of the same year, Solzhenitsyn sent a famous letter to the Writers' Union demanding an end to censorship, Shostakovich invited him to his *dacha* in Zhukovka where, in a cordial spirit which did not last,[1] he called the writer a 'truth-seeker' (meaning one who, in an era of

---

[1] They fell out in 1969, the Christian Solzhenitsyn offended by Shostakovich's grimly atheistic Fourteenth Symphony.

ostrich conformism, refused to have his memory recreated for him by the Communist Party). By recent standards, this was tame stuff, but the composer had other ways of expressing himself and, within days of meeting Solzhenitsyn, was putting his suppressed feelings into his Second Violin Concerto.

Composed exactly twenty years after the First Violin Concerto and in analogous circumstances, the Concerto No. 2 in C sharp minor, Opus 129, contains several references to its older cousin and commences in a comparably twilit hush. Soon, though, the violin's sorrowful theme, based on the rhythm of the 'betrayal' motif, is overruled by a two-note interval derived from its accompaniment, a restraint on its freedom with provokes an outburst of indignantly double-stopped octave E flats. With mocking cuckoo-calls, a jocular five-note second subject now brings the 'betrayal' motif into the open and a sinister circus mood develops, the soloist jumping through hoops to the imperious military beat of a tom-tom. The analogy here is with the First Cello Concerto (a link spelt out at figure 31 and hinted at further in the first of the work's three cadenzas). The slow movement, in sombre triple-time, resumes the midnight meditation of the First Violin Concerto's nocturne, rising at one point to a bat-squeak fourth G above middle C in its quest for release from the darkness surrounding it. Having already alluded to the nocturne in its first movement (figure 1, bars 6–8, etc.), the Second recalls it again, in tandem with a reference to the First's passacaglia, at figure 56. Ending abruptly on a two-note oscillation, the short, furious second cadenza leads to a recapitulation in which the soloist dwells tearfully on the People's three-note motif.

If the apotheosis of the two-note figure is the third movement of the Eighth Symphony, that of the 'betrayal' motif occurs in the Second Violin Concerto's extraordinary finale. Present in rhythmic form throughout, it is paired with a vulgarly grinning two-note counter-theme against which the violin's introspective melody from the first movement is no match. When a complex two-versus-three contest breaks out (figure 83), the rhythm of the 'betrayal' motif springs up all over the orchestra and the ensuing chaos is halted by an angry two-note shout from the wind section. Two-note figures in slashed double and quad-ruple-stopped dissonance make the final cadenza one of the most vitriolic passages anywhere in Shostakovich's work and, as triplet fanfares in its concluding bars sound a last-ditch challenge, the concerto explodes into an astonishing display based almost entirely on the 'betrayal' rhythm.

A summary of the string concerto as he used it (a drama of the individual against the mob), the Second Violin Concerto may be exhilarating in its anger, but to hear its conclusion as positive is to miss its satiric thrust. The same goes, in a different way, for the Second Cello Concerto (whose central march is quoted in the Second Violin Concerto's third cadenza: bars 73–82). As with so much of Shostakovich's music, the tone of the Second Cello Concerto's haunting finale is deceptive, and what at first seems (in Malcolm MacDonald's words) a 'warm, heart-easing' mood becomes, on closer inspection, more like deadly parody. Yet another satirical analysis of the culture of moral expedience, this movement quotes the motto-theme and mechanistic percussion of the Fourth Symphony's second movement to underline its parable of puppetry and dehumanisation.

But the traps, tricks, and intricate cross-references in Shostakovich's last period deserve a book in themselves and, regretfully, there is space here for little further consideration. Until their general language and atmosphere is adequately understood, it will be as hard to guess how many of his late works are masterpieces as it is to gauge the stature of, say, Samuel Beckett's novels. So simple are many of their pages that one can stare at them in puzzled disappointment for long periods before realising with a sinking feeling that one's preconceptions are blocking one's apprehension of something very unusual and very great. Nowhere in his output is Shostakovich's ironic elusiveness more disconcerting or his recourse to impersonation more subtly unannounced. Often, what can seem like mere enervation may only disclose its inner life once the phenomenal energy of adjoining passages has been assimilated.

Like the late music of Beethoven, Liszt, and Fauré, Shostakovich's last works ignore convention in pursuit of integrity of vision. Like Lear's Fool, they say things of such unsocialised directness that cultivated ears may fail to recognise them as sane, let alone consequential. They are not, however, an anarchic law unto themselves and comparing their signs and traits with those of the main body of the composer's output reveals much of their hidden logic. As with nearly everything Shostakovich wrote, however, they will remain opaque to the extent that the attitude of the mind behind them is misconceived or disregarded as conjectural – and this is nowhere more true than in the last of the composer's works we shall look at in any detail: the Fifteenth Symphony of 1971.

In terms of ambiguity, it is generally agreed that Shostakovich surpassed himself with his last symphony – so much so that, though the work has attracted more speculation on its meaning than any three of his other pieces, no conclusion about it has yet been arrived at. Written in a couple of months during summer 1971, it has four movements, features solos for nearly every instrument in its orchestra, and is full of gnomic quotations (of which more seem to be unearthed with every passing year).

The basic problem with the Symphony No. 15 in A major, Opus 141, is that of identifying its tone of voice. Clearly, it is a very dark piece, yet much of its music seems upbeat in mood and trivial in inspiration. Indeed, the composer's pupil Boris Tishchenko claims that Shostakovich told him he had meant the symphony's first movement to be 'cheerful' – a puzzling statement considering the music itself and its probable deeper motivations. Brezhnev's USSR was a country paralysed by conformist mediocrity, rampant corruption, and alcoholism. Had Shostakovich remained true to his disgust of 1962–4, he would have found it hard to be anything but contemptuous of what was going on in 1971;

and, in fact, the Fifteenth Symphony turns out to be just so, the lash of righteousness returning from *Stepan Razin* to flail savagely in the tutti of its slow movement. It is, perhaps, significant that the nearest symphonic thing to the Fifteenth is the satirical Ninth of 1945; and also that, despite being written quickly, both works gave their composer trouble at the planning stage. Did Shostakovich mean to write a cheerful first movement and find himself as incapable of doing it as, twenty-five years earlier, he had been unable to stomach glorifying Stalin? It seems unlikely. All that is certain is that anyone feeling cheerful after the opening allegretto of the Fifteenth Symphony will find the rest of the work rather bemusing.

The movement's 2/4 metre and the two tinkling chimes which start it signal that what follows will primarily concern the negative forces in Soviet life. Very little three-note action is observable and apart from a struggle between 2/4 and 3/4 in the development section, the number two has its own way. Metrically the most significant passages are those in which (harking back to the constructivist episode in the finale of the Fourth Symphony) crotchet triplets, and then quintuplets, play against pairs of quavers – apparently confirming the additive link between the three groupings suggested above (p. 220). In tone, the music recalls the shallow carelessness of the first movement of the Ninth Symphony and just as the trombone there can only play two notes in the dominant, so in the Fifteenth the brass can only manage Rossini's *William Tell* overture in E major. There, however, the parallels end, for while the Ninth is a 'public' work whose action takes place in the full light of day, the Fifteenth, in common with many other of Shostakovich's late works, is nocturnal and interior, its pages beset with a sense of the macabre not far removed from the hallucinatory grand guignol of *The Suicide* from the Fourteenth Symphony. Clearly there is a contradiction at work here.

A clue to the mystery lies in a statement about the Fifteenth which Shostakovich made shortly after the work's première in 1972: 'The first movement describes childhood – just a toy-shop, with a cloudless sky above.' It is fair to say that no Western critic has ever been able to reconcile this with the music itself, which veers from the uneasy to the nightmarish. Nor is the 'toy-shop' tag a matter of doubt for foreigners alone. When Maxim Shostakovich was asked about it by Boris Schwarz in 1981, he laughed dismissively – and in view of the fact that he conducted the première under his father's supervision it might seem safe to conclude that the composer was not wholly serious on this point. There again, the movement does confirm his description in several ways, echoing the mood of the 'childhood' scherzo of the *Leningrad* and (at figure 32) quoting a fanfare from the first movement of Mahler's children's symphony, the Fourth.[1] The *William Tell* overture, too, was one of Shostakovich's earliest musical memories, imprinting his vocabulary much as barrel-organs,

---

[1] Significantly, the one which Mahler later used as the leading motif of his initially dark and tormented Fifth.

bird-song, and military bands imprinted the young Mahler's. Yet another childhood reference comes with an allusion (flute at figure 1, bars 6–8) to the *Funeral March for the Victims of the Revolution*.[1] Indeed, with its rattling clockwork percussion and burlesque march episodes, the Fifteenth's opening movement conjures up most vividly the classic infant fantasy in which toys jerk into life and parade across the nursery floor. In effect, the only thing conspicuously missing from the composer's description is the 'cloudless sky above'. How, though, can these incongruous elements – maturity of diction, infantility of content – be reconciled?

United by a sense of hollow menace, the movement's two aspects imply an analogy between the grotesqueries of infancy and adulthood. Like Prokofiev, Shostakovich was fascinated by automata and the pseudo-life of machinery and, if *Testimony* is to be believed, he had progressed from an interest in wind-up dolls to a study of wind-up people quite early in his teens. The present study has identified such thoughts as the basis of his irony and suggested that they underlie most of his satirical passages. It hardly needs saying that the Fifteenth Symphony's first movement is probably another case of this. The composer is said to have remarked apropos of it, 'We are all marionettes' – and, in fact, the human-as-puppet motif seems to be the presiding idea of the work as a whole.[2]

Taking Shostakovich at his word (*Testimony*, pp. 175–7), we must accept that despair rather than cynicism is the shaping force behind such music. In his old age, much like Nadezhda Mandelstam, he seems to have lost faith in people of both his own and younger generations. Under Brezhnev, concern for memory, truth, and justice dwindled in the face of the imperative merely to survive, creating a trivial, time-serving society without hope for the future or interest in the past. In 1971, it must have seemed to the composer as though the victims of Stalin, among them hundreds of his friends and colleagues, had perished for nothing and would soon be forgotten.

Accordingly, the Fifteenth's opening movement seems best understood as portraying a society in which people, their control over their own lives little greater than that of puppets or mechanical toys, do not act so much as *behave*. Shostakovich dramatises this in childhood terms, setting his action in an allegorical nursery, just as in the first half of his First Symphony he evokes an allegorical circus. The method is similar to that of Lewis Carroll's *Alice* books, and the grandfatherly double bass that creaks out an admonitory three-note phrase at figure 35 is straight from the pages of children's fiction. Shostakovich's subject is, however, more serious and his atmosphere correspondingly knowing and sinister. For example, the rhythm of *William Tell*, often used in his

---

[1] The outline of the *Funeral March* can also be discerned in the *De Profundis* movement of the Fourteenth Symphony.

[2] Shared configurations suggest that the same can be said of the Fourth Symphony (II) and Second Cello Concerto (III).

music, is, more significantly, also the rhythm of the 'betrayal' motif[1] (itself introduced by solo bassoon two bars before figure 6). The betrayal here is of the broadest kind: of decency, of the past, of self. There is, too, the suggestion that as puppets (or relative children) human beings are prone to playing dangerous games with life, games which can get out of control – an idea taken up again in the symphony's finale.

After the mad shadows and youthful energy of the first movement, the almost stationary bareness of the adagio comes as a shock. Here, again, is the composer in his study late at night, sunk in contemplation of his own and his country's terrible past. Attended by heavy-hearted brass, a solo cello weeps for a sadness so profound that listening to it brings an embarrassing sensation of unwarranted intrusion. Commenting on the Soviet society of her time in 1971, Nadezhda Mandelstam wrote: 'The only approved way [to talk about the past] is to show that, however bad things may have been for you, you nevertheless remain faithful to the idea of Communism, always able to distinguish the truly important – our ultimate objective – from minor factors – such as your own ruined life.' Audible in the atonality of his cello line and a pair of sarcastic perfect cadences reminiscent of the Sixth Quartet, Shostakovich's alienation from the ideology which ruined his life finally erupts in a cataclysmically furious outburst in funeral rhythm.[2] The symphony's bitter heart, this moment is also in effect the climax of his entire late period. Aside from Vaughan Williams's apoplectic Fourth Symphony, it is difficult to think of music in which anger has been more devastatingly expelled.

While the symphony's caustic third movement has been plausibly compared to the *Humoreske* from Nielsen's Sixth, a more precise parallel might be with the critics' music from Strauss's *Ein Heldenleben*. Here, with asthmatically squeezed crescendi and the percussive rattle of dry bones, the number three is travestied and the number two desiccatedly affirmed, the whole accompanied by much ponderous play on the 'betrayal' rhythm. Just before figure 92, the brass yawn a bleary misrepresentation of D-S-C-H.

Announcing the burial of Russian culture by means of appropriate quotations from Wagner, the finale progresses via three-note pizzicati from the Eleventh Symphony's third movement to a hesitantly graceful melody based on Glinka's song *Do Not Tempt Me Needlessly*. Exactly what temptation Shostakovich had in mind here is unclear. Possibly it was the 'smug little music' of easy gratification for which the post-Stalin Soviet government would certainly have rewarded him very amply. On the other hand, the movement's confluence of

---

[1] The link is spelt out at figure 44 in the Ninth Quartet – a work which, curiously enough, Shostakovich described to *Pravda* (21 October 1964) as 'a "children's" quartet, about toys and playing'.

[2] The same rhythm features in symphonies Eleven (III), Thirteen (I), and Fourteen (VII); in quartets Eleven (VI), Twelve (II), and Fifteen (V); and in the *Suite on Verses by Michelangelo* (X).

allusions suggests rather that the lure in question is the broader enticement of millennial Communism with its hubristic promise of a state-planned heaven on earth. (In *Testimony*, Shostakovich describes the Fifteenth as sharing ideas with his projected opera on Chekhov's *The Black Monk*, a story about a man who disastrously surrenders himself to delusions of grandeur.) Haunted by 'revenant' triplets, a banal passacaglia (deconstructed from the *Leningrad* march so as to emphasise its two-note element) winds to a climax of clumsily bathetic anguish before sagging back in exhaustion on the Glinka theme. The very image of a hollow culture unable any longer to say anything real, Shostakovich's last symphonic movement tapers gradually away to the spasmic twitch of puppet-strings, the dispiriting click and whirr of clockwork.

And thus, with a whimper, ends the twentieth century's greatest symphony cycle.

Was it written by the sterling orthodox Communist buried in Novodevichy Cemetery on 14 August 1975? It was not. That figure, a ghost created by Soviet propaganda, certainly did not exist after 1931 and in all probability was as much of a mirage beforehand.

Was it, then, written by the embittered secret dissident introduced to the world in 1979 via Solomon Volkov's *Testimony*? It was.

Is the new Shostakovich the real Shostakovich?

Of course.

POSTLUDE: Immortality

And it's quiet, Lord, so quiet,
Time has become audible
And one day the age will rise
Like a corpse in a spring river

How much of a fake is *Testimony*? The detective work of Laurel Fay and Simon Karlinsky has established beyond doubt that the book is a dishonest presentation. Represented as 'The Memoirs of Dmitri Shostakovich as related to and edited by Solomon Volkov', *Testimony* in fact consists partly of 'memoirs' related to (and edited by) earlier Soviet journalists. Moreover, the motive for this is clearly that of deceiving Western opinion into accepting Volkov's material as authenticated by the composer, which, in the sense of his having read and signed the manuscript, it evidently was not.

On the other hand, the frontispiece of the book presents a photograph showing, smiling conspiratorially together on a sofa in Shostakovich's Moscow apartment, the composer, his third wife Irina, his favourite pupil Boris Tishchenko, and his alleged amanuensis Solomon Volkov. Underneath, in shaky handwriting, is scrawled 'To dear Solomon Moiseyevich Volkov in fond remembrance. D. Shostakovich. 13 XI 1974. A reminder of our conversations about Glazunov, Zoshchenko, Meyerhold. D.S.' This is hard to dismiss, and even Volkov's firmest opponents admit that the parts of *Testimony* concerning the three artists mentioned in the inscription are probably genuine. How much of the rest of the book can be regarded in a similar light is impossible to say; nor, were the whole to be accepted as emanating from the horse's mouth, would it be any simpler to assess its more general authenticity as fair opinion. Even if every word in the book is pure Shostakovich, he could still, in theory, have been spinning a line to Volkov for any number of disreputable reasons.

Actually, if accepted as verbatim Shostakovich, the sour wit and wry disenchantment of *Testimony*'s passages on Glazunov, Zoshchenko, and Meyerhold would be quite sufficient to justify the tone of the rest of the book – a fact of which Volkov's critics seem comfortably oblivious. Not that they need worry, since *Testimony*'s fraudulent elements logically place this material out of court too, it being clear that an editor prepared to fake chapter-beginnings is unlikely to think twice about misrepresenting whatever authentic material he may hold.

Leaving aside a small number of insignificant disputed facts, the point at issue in *Testimony* is that of the attitude of mind displayed in it. Did Shostakovich feel like this, think like this, talk like this? And, if he did, had he always done so? Such questions can be answered only in terms of probability. For example, few would deny that the tone of the composer's late period music matches that of *Testimony* rather precisely. From the Thirteenth Symphony of 1962 onwards, Shostakovich's music is clearly dissident in the sense of rejecting his country's political environment root and branch. Even his careful refusal to make an explicit denial of Communism in *Testimony* perversely redounds to the book's credit, since it would have been as easy for Volkov to put such words in his mouth as to take out those which persistently attack the West for its glib vulgarity. (*Testimony* is by no means the simple Cold War fodder its critics maintain.) But how far back can this attitude be legitimately traced? Is the crucial pre-1962 narrative in *Testimony* authentic in the sense of reflecting how the composer felt about the characters and events in it *at the time?*

The present study has gone to some lengths to show that, for many compelling reasons, the outlook expressed in *Testimony* has a very high probability of having been present in Shostakovich's mind since his mid-twenties. It is possible that there may have been a short period (his 'misty youth', roughly corresponding to the era of the New Economic Policy)[1] in which he felt at one with his country's political system, though enough contrary factors suggest that this was not so. Shostakovich may have been something of a cynical opportunist at this time – between 1927 and 1931 he was regarded as a sort of national musical clown – but in this he was no different from other iconoclasts of his age. Furthermore, his return to tragedy in the opera *Lady Macbeth*, six years after his First Symphony, was clearly the most important creative decision he ever took in the absence of outside pressure – a decision which, in context, can only have been made in conscious disregard of political orthodoxy. If he had ever concluded a compact with Communism, Shostakovich broke it in 1931. How long it took for this impulse towards freedom to mature into consistent dissidence is, again, a question answerable only in terms of probability. There seems, however, to be little room for it to have been later than 1935 and the Fourth Symphony – unless, of course, convincing alternative interpretations of this and other works of the following years can be advanced, which, on the evidence adduced in these pages, seems unlikely.

The match between the tone and content of the composer's 1931–62 output and that of corresponding passages in *Testimony* is, therefore, arguably as exact as that of the later material. In fact, *Testimony* can be said to be a very fair reflection of the mind behind Shostakovich's music all told – which is presumably why his son Maxim describes the book as 'true, accurate'; why Rudolf Barshai calls it 'all true'; and why a dozen other key witnesses have assented to its view of the man they knew and worked with.

Testimony is a realistic picture of Dmitri Shostakovich. It just isn't a *genuine* one.

How many of the words in *Testimony* can we trust as Shostakovich's own? Sadly,

---

[1] See *Testimony*, p. 123.

none of them (not even the passages stolen from earlier Soviet sources, since these are even likelier to have been paraphrased, altered, or censored). This is a disappointing conclusion to have to draw for, were *Testimony* trustworthy word for word, it would certainly be one of the wittiest and most perceptive books by a composer, out-sparkled only by Berlioz's memoirs or Constant Lambert's *Music Ho!* and surpassing both in psychological depth. If Solomon Volkov wrote it, he deserves credit for his skills as a pasticheur and an aphorist – indeed, if not one word of his book is genuine Shostakovich, it must stand as one of the most stylish fakes of all time.

It is, in fact, the very debunking cleverness of *Testimony* which most upsets supporters of the 'Honest Communist' and 'Hamlet' theories of the composer, both of which depend on seeing him as, to some degree, bewildered or naive. Inevitably, such views have severely limited the capacity of many critics to expand their appreciation of what Shostakovich may have been attempting. Starting from the assumption that they are brighter than their supposedly muddled subject, Western academics like Christopher Norris and Robert Stradling seal their ears to anything which might otherwise come as an illuminating surprise to them. The consequences of this superiority complex range from the merely constipated (Norris's vision of Shostakovich as 'forced back upon the stoical limits of repetitive auto-suggestion') to the frankly insulting (Stradling's remark that the Tenth Symphony is 'mainly compounded of that mixture of self-congratulation and guilt which marked all the "survivors" of Stalin's indiscriminate bloodletting').

To a great extent the concept of the stupid Shostakovich inferred by so many Western pundits owes its origin to the often inane articles he signed, a collection of which was published in 1981 by the Moscow house Progress in order to discredit the clever Shostakovich advanced in *Testimony*. As has been explained, these pieces are largely worthless and the book they appear in virtually pure propaganda. (Progress are also the publishers of Tomas Rezac's hatchet-job *The Spiral of Solzhenitsyn's Betrayal*.) Yet, crucial though this rubbish has been in misrepresenting Shostakovich's intellect, at least as effective in achieving the same thing has been the ingrained twentieth-century habit of approaching music as abstract form devoid of intrinsic meaning.

An example of this is contained in the way Shostakovich and Prokofiev have so far been assessed outside the USSR. Admiring Prokofiev's relatively guileless eloquence and bemused by apparent crudities in Shostakovich which their aestheticism prevented them from identifying as sardonic mimicry, Western critics have invariably treated Prokofiev as essentially more intelligent than Shostakovich. Compounding the irony, they have deduced from this that Prokofiev is the more self-aware of the two, stereotyping Shostakovich as self-indulgently subjective (the 'Hamlet' theory). Thus Alexander Werth, discussing the two composers in his *Russia: The Post-war Years*, accepts the politically illiterate Prokofiev's suave facility as intellectually superior to the infinitely more pointed, if far less ingratiating, work of the most resourceful political satirist music has ever seen. Shostakovich, claims Werth, is 'too introspective, too concerned with himself and his own depths and chasms, even though sometimes he did feel passionately about the sufferings of his own country, during the war and since'.

This line was standard in the West for so long that it found little difficulty in surviving even *Testimony*, a recent example being David Pownall's play *Master Class*, in which a war-haunted Shostakovich sobs uncontrollably before Stalin and Zhdanov, while a quietly assured Prokofiev urges him to pull himself together. Featuring a similarly imaginary Stalin likewise prone to bursting into tears, *Master Class* perpetuates all the silliest Western misconceptions about the characters it purports to present. Portrayed as though in some rough and ready way genuinely concerned with the future of Soviet art, Stalin and Zhdanov are drawn from propagandist images at least thirty years out of date. Prokofiev, too, though he wrote his quota of secretly dissident music,[1] is misrepresented as self-possessed and on top of the situation instead of as the cowed and unhappy victim of Socialist Realist bullying he had become by 1948.

Like his hero Mahler, Shostakovich has suffered badly from the musicologist's perennial insensitivity to humour in music. Anyone, for example, deaf to the spoof-academicism of the finale of Mahler's Seventh is bound to miss the tongue-in-cheek ponderousness of the much-debated tone-row in Shostakovich's Twelfth Quartet. In the same way, the poker-faced sarcasm of those few of his Soviet pronouncements that are identifiably genuine has nearly always been misconstrued outside the USSR. The number of Western writers content to describe as 'bewildered' the composer's nervously double-edged remarks before Zhdanov in 1948 beggars belief. Similarly, it has taken thirty-five years for a Western critic (David Fanning) to spot that Shostakovich's commentary on his Tenth Symphony for the Composers' Union in 1954 is a series of bitter jokes – 'a calculated insult to the audience to which it is addressed, with an attendant sense of unease (the insult must be calculated so as not to be too obvious)'.

More damaging than their imperviousness to wit has been the tendency of Western critics to stigmatise as subjective almost anything in music lacking in formal neatness. Just as Mahler's philosophical adventures in sonata form are commonly assumed to be the autobiographical ramblings of a man incapable of abiding by the rules, so Shostakovich's unannounced impersonations and alienative leaps from the abstract to the concrete have often been mistaken for the nervous twitches of an artist trapped in his own compulsions. His alleged psychological instability is a favourite theme in Russia too, albeit with special national variations. Thus, even the shrewdest Soviet musicologist to have been

---

[1] The First Violin Sonata (1938/46), the so-called 'War sonatas' (conceived in 1939 and more appropriately entitled 'Terror sonatas'), the Sixth Symphony (1947), the closing pages of the Fifth Symphony (1944), the finale of the Second Quartet (1942), and so on.

published in English, Andrei Olkhovsky, describes Shostakovich's music as driven by a morbid fear of death and 'a desire to be among the People . . . to lose one's own ego and to be merged in the mass'. While it would be hard to think of an artist less suited to submersion in the mass than the self-conscious and crowd-phobic Shostakovich, the oddest thing about this judgement is its assumption that the creator of works so carefully designed could none the less be little more than a passive reflector of subjective impressions. Again, like Mahler, Shostakovich is assumed to be not in control of his effects, to be a sort of human Aeolian harp playing whatever the wind of emotion happens to blow – to be, in a nutshell, intellectually inferior to the musicologist commenting upon him.

It must be said that the portrait of the composer painted in her autobiography by Galina Vishnevskaya is not far short of the Hamlet stereotype described above. Here is a troubled, superstitious, and self-contradictory introvert, given to dwelling obsessively on pregnant phrases. Abrupt and spasmodic of speech, Vishnevskaya's Shostakovich sits uneasily with the fluently ironic raconteur presented by Volkov (whom she pointedly never mentions). On the other hand, a recurrent theme in first-hand impressions of Shostakovich is that of his peculiar ability to adjust his personality to the needs of whoever he happened to be with. ('I could not read his mind,' confesses a witness quoted by Lukyanova. 'I always wondered whether he was excited or calm.') Speaking of this chameleon talent, the composer's friend Dmitri Frederiks observes that many who imagined that they knew the real Shostakovich were, in reality, acquainted only with a blankly compliant reflection of themselves. While partly a form of kindness – he was known only to criticise performers of his work if he thought them capable of grasping his remarks, otherwise smilingly assuring them that they were doing fine – it is worth observing that this 'mirror' tactic is also a classic *yurodivy* device. Vishnevskaya, an emotional lady with a typically Slavic love of gush, may chiefly have seen the sort of Shostakovich – the tormented artist – she wished to see.

Others recall a very different character: tight-lipped, controlled, sardonic, self-contained. His pupil Boris Tishchenko, for example, paints a formidable picture of a man who seems to have treated him as an intellectual equal: 'He disliked half-heartedness and indecisiveness in anything – in opinions, tastes, even minor matters. What he said was concrete and specific: every thought was expressed in a strict yet ample literary form – sometimes it was even a short story. Shostakovich was hostile to diffuse, abstract discussions and platitudes. There was no magniloquence, no pathos, everything was specific and well-rounded.' This is the Shostakovich presented by Volkov in *Testimony* and the same persona can be found in other reminiscences of the composer collected by the Leningrad musicologists Dmitri and Ludmilla Sollertinsky in their book *Pages from the Life of Dmitri Shostakovich*.

Far from being the rambling, preoccupied Hamlet of myth, Shostakovich was a man of intense energy and concentration, able to work under the most distracting conditions and ferociously attentive at rehearsals, even in old age. The writer Chingiz Aitmatov recalls his 'tense aquiline posture' during work with the Beethoven Quartet on his Fourteenth Quartet in 1973, while Royal Brown, who interviewed Shostakovich for *High Fidelity Magazine* in the same year, found himself magnetized by the sixty-seven-year-old composer's 'obviously enormous inner strength': 'When he speaks, it is in a high, somewhat sibilant voice that comes out in fast, almost youthfully enthusiastic bursts that are highly accentuated, even for the Russian language. And it is the latent energy of the speech as well as the intense concentration one can observe and feel in the presence of this composer that left not only me but many others who had the chance to be with him with a strong feeling of both warmth and admiration.'

To do her justice, Vishnevskaya was similarly impressed by Shostakovich's 'extraordinary restraint and discipline', adding the shrewd feminine observation that behind the façade he was physically somewhat aloof and, though devoted to his children, found it hard to be natural with them. Again, however, this slight stiffness, if true,[1] has to be seen as but one part of a multifaceted personality – an aspect which manifested itself in more positive form as an incorruptible conscience and undeflectable sense of duty. Stories of the composer's generosity are legion and, like Rachmaninov, he never turned down a deserving request for a public appearance if his health allowed it. Nor was this kindness a mere intellectual discipline, springing instead from what seems to have been for him a creative obligation to identify with the sufferings of other people.

The sceptic is entitled to yawn at this point and demand to know how so saintly an apostle of moral rectitude managed to sign so many letters and articles traducing his real beliefs – and the simplest answer has to be: with difficulty. Valentin Berlinsky of the Borodin Quartet has said of Shostakovich that, while basically mild, 'he hated injustice, malice, pettiness – and when somebody of quality, somebody he valued, was humiliated, he became very angry'. How pained he was by having to conspire in his own betrayal can be measured both in the isolated bouts of fury in his late music and in the occasional revealing anecdote. Mstislav Rostropovich, for example, records that, at a press conference at the Edinburgh Festival in 1962, a reporter asked Shostakovich if he agreed with the Party criticism voiced in 1948. 'Yes, yes, yes, I agree,' replied the composer, eagerly. 'And not only do I agree, but I'm *grateful* to the Party because the Party taught me.' Turning to Rostropovich immediately after this, he muttered 'That son of a bitch! How could he dare ask that question? Doesn't he understand that I can't answer it?'

Seemingly an instinctive repetition of his defensive *yurodivy* exaggerations of 1948, Shostakovich's 'eager' answer to the Edinburgh reporter will naturally appear to those used to being able to say what they think as, at the very least,

---

[1] Maxim Shostakovich emphatically denies it.

distasteful. Unusual conditions, however, call forth unusual ethics. Nadezhda Mandelstam clarifies this in connection with a Stalin-praising article attributed to the biologist Alexei Bakh but widely thought to have been written by an official and shown to Bakh solely for the purpose of obtaining his signature.

> What, objectively speaking, could Academician Bakh have done? Could he have revised the text a little, so that his name would not appear under an obviously official document? I doubt it. Or could he have thrown out the journalist who came to collect his signature? Can one expect people to behave like this, knowing what the consequences will be? I do not think so, and I do not know how to answer these questions. The distinguishing feature of terror is that everybody is completely paralysed and doesn't dare resist in any way.

Pressures like these can be applied to public figures in the USSR at any time and it is salutory to note that, during the very period in 1973 in which Chingiz Aitmatov and Royal Brown were marvelling at Shostakovich's inner strength, he was forced to forswear his liberalism by signing a denunciation of the country's leading dissident, Andrei Sakharov.

Complicated by personal rivalry and professional jealousy, the reality behind the games of *Ketman* continually going on in Russian public life has often been vague even to those members of the Soviet intelligentsia taking part in them. In *Testimony*, for example, Volkov plausibly presents Shostakovich as disdainful of Sakharov's right to preach to the Soviet people: 'Some major geniuses and future famous humanists are behaving extremely flippantly, to put it mildly. First they invent a powerful weapon and hand it over to the tyrants and then they write snide brochures.[1] But one doesn't balance out the other. There aren't any brochures that could balance the hydrogen bomb.' However critical he may have been of Sakharov, it is inconceivable that Shostakovich would have put his name to the 1973 denunciation without coercion. (In fact, every composer and musician in the USSR seems to have been rounded up to sign it.) Yet the resentment was there – and this despite the restraints he must have known bound Sakharov every bit as tightly as those confining his own capacity for expression.

Shostakovich's edgy relationship with Sakharov and Solzhenitsyn derived partly from the moral superiority the younger men enjoyed through their willingness to flout the state and suffer the consequences – a martyrdom which, in his sixties, the composer was no longer prepared to risk. (Solzhenitsyn knew, when he invited him to sign a letter against the Soviet invasion of Czechoslovakia in 1968, that 'the shackled genius Shostakovich would thrash about like a wounded thing, clasp himself with tightly folded arms so that his fingers could not hold a pen'.) But just as important to maintaining a suspicious

---

[1] The 'brochure' referred to was Sakharov's polemic calling for an end to the nuclear arms race, for which he was later awarded the Nobel Peace Prize.

distance between members of the liberal intellectual community in Russia is the difficulty of evaluating the motives of others in what is necessarily a society of masks, behind not a few of which lurk KGB informers. Not that Shostakovich could have imagined Sakharov or Solzhenitsyn were such; yet segregation in itself breeds incomprehension and he seems sometimes to have taken the line of least resistance, thinking ill of others rather than risk betrayal by getting close enough to them to discover the truth. The critic Boris Asafiev, for example, sniped at in several passages of *Testimony* for apparently turning on the composer in 1948, was, according to his pupil Andrei Olkhovsky, no more the author of the unfortunate statements ascribed to him than Shostakovich was. He, too, was coerced. And, of course, the cycle of mistrust perpetuates itself. Yevtushenko, with whom Shostakovich later planned a symphony called *Torments of Conscience*, once asked him bluntly why he signed such stupid articles. 'Look,' replied the composer, wearily, 'words are not my genre. I never lie in music. That's enough.'

From this, it may seem inevitable that most Western experts were initially unable to accept *Testimony*'s suggestion that Shostakovich was far from the docile conformist pedalled by Soviet propaganda. Yet they should have known from experience that, under Soviet conditions, the most orthodox mask could conceal the face of a secret dissident. Perhaps the best-known case of this was the novelist and journalist Ilya Ehrenburg, who kept the world guessing for nearly fifty years – but there have been dozens like him. Prior to his public break with the Soviet system, Andrei Sakharov was three times made a Hero of Socialist Labour, his role of state honours matching those of Shostakovich medal for medal. Nor has membership of the Soviet Communist Party ever guaranteed anyone's true beliefs. Party members Anatoly Kuznetsov (author of the outstanding novel *Babi Yar*) and Kyrill Kondrashin (Shostakovich's favourite conductor after Mravinsky) were both perfect counterfeits of conformism before – to the astonishment of all but the most knowledgeable of Sovietologists – they defected to the West.

All in all, it ought to have been no surprise that Shostakovich should turn out to be different from his Soviet-manufactured public persona: specifically, far brighter than the platitudinous middlebrow his Communist masters fashioned in their own image. What is extraordinary is that the truth was not realised earlier. It should have been obvious from his literary tastes and acquaintances alone that he could not possibly have been as earnestly dim as he has often been painted. And, from there, it ought to have been a short step to realising that he had been, all along, quietly in control of musical effects formerly assumed to have been merely the interesting symptoms of a neurotic subjectivity.

As with all tragedy, the poignance of *Hamlet* consists in the fact that the hero cannot avoid being destroyed by the situation in which he is enmeshed. However, while Hamlet enjoys the consolation of being recognised by his fellow players as the most intelligent figure on the stage, Shostakovich has been travestied by all but a few of his interpreters. Moreover, without admitting the possibility that, even in the unlikeliest moments, his music may be telling us something quite different from what we have led ourselves to expect, the presence of his princely intelligence remains effectively unrecognised.

Leaving aside the issue of Shostakovich's unsuspected cleverness and the existence of the code language in which it partly expresses itself, how is it that Western academics have been able to study Shostakovich's music for so long while remaining deaf to its emotional content? There have, after all, been many advance warnings that it was not entirely as advertised in *Pravda* – for example, in Nikolai Nabokov's *Old Friends and New Music*, published in 1951, and in Andrei Olkhovsky's *Music Under the Soviets*, which came out four years later. Granted, these books appeared at a time when the first wave of Soviet 'camp literature' was being ritually dismissed by Western liberal critics as Cold War propaganda; still, one might have expected the ring of truth in Nabokov and Olkhovsky to have alerted the attention of at least some of the trained ears in the universities of Europe and America. Olkhovsky, in particular, did not beat about the bush in portraying Shostakovich as a tragic figure struggling to maintain integrity in a repressive environment: 'The sources of the composer's musical thoughts are not the abundance of his spiritual forces, but rather their impairment. In what other contemporary composer is the intensity of musical pulsation accompanied by such strong sensations of fading light and gathering dusk?' This was a good question – yet even the few in the West who shared Olkhovsky's impression failed to draw the logical conclusion that such music was the stuff of a disaffected independent conscience, rather than the errors of an unusually witless 'Honest Communist' or the depressive self-indulgences of a Hamlet figure. Ignoring the increasingly obvious signals to the contrary, most Western critics continued to waste their energy on justifying Shostakovich's music in the terms fed to them by Soviet disinformation agencies, while those few who could not stomach this prevaricated, apparently incapable of verifying their suspicions through research.

Ultimately, Western confusion over the emotional tone of Shostakovich's music is traceable to two main causes: firstly, left-liberal self-deception concerning the realities of Communism; and secondly, the tendency of twentieth-century music to emphasize form over content.

From the thirties (when to most progressive intellectuals it seemed that the only choice was between the enlightened collectivism of Russia and the reactionary collectivism of Germany), Western left-liberal opinion on the Soviet 'socialist experiment' has been fatally distorted by a well-meaning refusal to dwell on the Revolution's 'negative side-effects'. Before the Second World War, much use was made, both inside and outside Russia, of a well-known maxim concerning the unfeasibility of making an omelette without cracking eggs. Certain isolated figures of the time (notably George Orwell and Arthur Koestler) made themselves highly unpopular with their fellow men and women of conscience by pointing out that the eggs being smashed to make

Stalin's omelette were people and that one murder sanctioned in the name of the future was, in theory, a licence for millions of supplementary murders. How far theory had become fact continued to be a topic of hot dispute until quite recently when, under Gorbachev's *perestroika*, it was admitted in the Soviet press that, during his twenty-five years at the helm of the Soviet state, Stalin had done for around fifty million Soviet citizens. During the forties, however, the broader debate over Communism was clouded by understandable emotion over the heroic sacrifices Russia had made in the war against Hitler. In effect, as Solzhenitsyn has sourly observed, the West forgave Stalin his thirties purges 'in gratitude for Stalingrad'. This gratitude kept left-liberal opinion in thrall to the USSR for decades afterwards and Western left-wing idealisation of Soviet Communism, having in many cases survived the invasions of Hungary and Czechoslovakia, thrives even today.[1]

The secret of this persistent myth is no mystery. Russia and her satellites march under a 'progressive' banner and forward-thinking intellectuals are prepared to make endless allowances for anyone claiming to be walking their way. 'The land of Socialism,' notes Solzhenitsyn, 'can be forgiven for atrocities immeasurably greater than those of Hitler, for its victims are offered up on a resplendent altar.' Forgiveness, however, is a passive thing. Had it not been for the active self-deception and occasional downright mendacity of its many influential Western apologists, the Soviet Union would never have managed to appear so spotless for a state so long and deep in its own blood. *Testimony*'s bitter swipes at the 'great humanists' George Bernard Shaw and Romain Rolland voice an outrage over the betrayal of Russian liberals by Western ones which can be found in many other dissident memoirs of recent years. (Nadezhda Mandelstam, for example, castigates Louis Aragon, while Solzhenitsyn vents his contempt on Sartre.)

As fellow travellers, some of Shostakovich's Western misrepresentatives have been so by design, reinforcing his image as a Communist in the interests of bolstering the parent ideology. Mostly, though, they have been stock left-liberal intellectuals, their critical antennae dulled by 'gratitude for Stalingrad' and awe of the USSR's 'progressive' mystique. Beyond this caucus of opinion-makers, the corps of musicians and their public have remained more or less oblivious to the issues at stake in Shostakovich's art. Indeed, in the absence of a clear outcome to the *Testimony* affair, a new breed of aesthete has begun to suggest through the classical review columns of the Western press that the political truth of Shostakovich's music is irrelevant and that it can and should be appreciated as 'pure' music. The limp inanity of this contention should be clear to anyone who has read this far. Yet still more damaging to the chances of a reassessment of the composer is the half-baked idealism that sees any sustained criticism of Soviet Communism (such as is embodied in his music) as

---

[1] Though not, presumably, after the Gorbachev-inspired de-Stalinisation of Eastern Europe, in progress as this book goes to print.

Cold-War-mongering. Without dislodging this misplaced faith in the decency of the Leninist system, little can be done to demonstrate the value of Shostakovich's achievement as an artist. (More seriously, nothing at all can be done towards planning the mixed-market, democratically devolved replacement for old-style centralised Socialism of which the world now stands in desperate need.)

All discussion of issues related to Communism must begin from the fact that this political system has so far, world-wide, been responsible for the deaths of around seventy-five million of its own citizens. Agreement even on this is, however, insufficient to ensure that speculation on the life and work of someone like Shostakovich will run along appropriate lines. In his introduction to Sandor Kopacsi's '*In the Name of the Working Class*', George Jonas writes: 'It is next to fraudulent to hold any opinions about the nature of the Soviet system without knowing certain facts. This knowledge can be acquired through first-hand experience or – rather less painfully – by reading a dozen or so seminal books.' Among the books Jonas lists is one which no recent writer on Shostakovich can be forgiven for not having read. This is Solzhenitsyn's *The Gulag Archipelago*, a work whose appearance was hailed by the essayist Lydia Chukovskaya as the most important event in post-war Russian history after Stalin's death. 'To live now and not know this work,' wrote an English reviewer with justice, 'is to be a kind of historical fool missing a crucial part of the consciousness of the age.' Suffice it to say that, for most listeners outside the Communist bloc, listening to Shostakovich's music without knowing *The Gulag Archipelago* is equivalent to listening to spoken Russian without a translation. Similarly crucial to an appreciation of Shostakovich's general intellectual environment are Nadezhda Mandelstam's memoirs *Hope Against Hope* and *Hope Abandoned*, while Anatoli Rybakov's novel *Children of the Arbat* is a considerable help towards understanding the composer's crucial period between 1931 and 1936. Many other books provide vital insights into the world which shaped Shostakovich's mind and work: Panteleimon Romanov's novel *Three Pairs of Silk Stockings*, for example, paints a vivid picture of life in Russia during 'proletarianization'; Eugenia Ginzburg's *Into the Whirlwind* provides an invaluable feminine slant on the matters surveyed by Solzhenitsyn in *The Gulag Archipelago*; Vasily Grossman's *Life and Fate* shows how far Stalin and even Lenin were blamed for state terrorism in ordinary conversation during the war; and Anna Akhmatova's poems (in particular *Requiem*) communicate the emotional core of Russian twentieth-century experience with a force directly comparable to Shostakovich's music itself.

Relying on Soviet articles spuriously attributed to the composer and books (like those by Martynov, Rabinovich, and the Sollertinskys) which skate across his career without a single mention of Stalin, most Western writers on Shostakovich have been working in a vacuum filled, in the main, by their own vaguely pro-Soviet wishful thinking. Behind the academic tiffs over the finale of the Fifth Symphony lies an immensely banal ignorance of the forces that made the music what it is. It is, for example, extraordinary how many of the contributors to Christopher Norris's 1982 symposium *Shostakovich: The Man and His Music* take the theory of Socialist Realism seriously. Described by Andrei Olkhovsky as 'a disaster', by Galina Vishnevskaya as 'insane gibberish' and by Yuri Yelagin as 'the most tragic event in the history of Russian culture', Socialist Realism was a bad joke even to its creators – yet here we find 'experts' tying themselves in knots in an attempt to reconcile contradictions in it which were always entirely arbitrary. While one can only assume that they enjoy this sort of thing, the fact remains that modern Soviet intellectuals would find their arguments as divorced from reality as those of biblical fundamentalists are to Darwinian biologists.

As the aesthetic of bureaucracy, Socialist Realism ruined Russian culture by replacing the vitality of the individual voice with a clanking choir of yea-saying robots. To the twenties' richness of form and poverty of content, it added poverty of form while subtracting freedom of expression. More subtly than that, it was a flexible device allowing those in control to justify the contradictory demands made of Soviet artists without any change in terminology. In general, this meant that the significance of words like 'Realism' and 'Formalism' could be adjusted at will to suit alterations in the political climate. In particular, it allowed the authorities to attack an artist for 'petty bourgeois philistinism' – yet, when he 'strayed' into (say) Modernism, to order him to develop those parts of his work which most closely approximated to the conventions of 'bourgeois' art. Having been abundantly present in both of the major musical purges at which Shostakovich received public reprimands, this devious institutionalised hypocrisy renders Western squabbles over whether or not he benefited from the Party's advice worthless in that it is impossible to say, in stable language, what that advice was.

That the 'advice' delivered to Shostakovich in 1936 and 1948 was nonsensical did not matter. All that was important was that the occasions frightened him sufficiently to stop him writing too much like himself, since the mere *sound* of an individual voice in a collectivistic environment is fundamentally subversive. Objectively speaking, 1936 drained the variety out of his music, but increased its concentration. Those who place a premium on formal clarity will see this as an advance; those who value spontaneity and adventure may find it regrettable. It is a matter of opinion. Less of a matter of opinion is that the experience scarred the composer for life and deprived the world of an ambitious sequence of what would probably have been first-rate operas. In other respects, it had no effect on him at all and he simply continued writing in the tragic-satiric style and from the anti-Communist standpoint he had arrived at with *Lady Macbeth*. As for 1948, it was a dangerous and depressing farce which left no mark on his music other than some creases due to being stored in a drawer for several years.

The Soviet version of 1936 is, of course, quite different, contending that, not only had it speeded Shostakovich's passage from youth to maturity, but that the Party's timely intervention had saved him from an artistic fate worse than death. What exactly that fate was supposed to be is hard to discern. Dmitri Rabinovich's summary of the issue, for example, is a characteristic Soviet blend of platitudes and portentous obscurities: 'Had Shostakovich been left to his own devices, despite his great talent, the danger of finding himself in a trap from which there was no escape would have threatened him; it threatened a number of talented musicians of the Modernist school and they were trapped. To his good fortune, Shostakovich's Soviet environment and the strength of public opinion helped him overcome the infantile disorders of Modernism.' Meaningless though such writing is, it decisively influenced Western understanding of Shostakovich for many years. Critics capable of swallowing the ludicrous idea of a psychopathic philistine like Stalin making deep pronouncements on language and logic found no difficulty in falling for such nonsense – especially when it was rounded off by edifying invocations to the folk wisdom of the Soviet people.[1] Indeed, even relatively knowledgeable commentators like Alexander Werth took the black comedy of the 1948 conference seriously, seeing it as a necessary disciplining of Russia's over-sophisticated and self-indulgent composing fraternity at a time when foreign escalation of the Cold War demanded a renewal of national accord. (How humiliating Shostakovich and Prokofiev could have drawn the nation together is hard to envisage. As for the Cold War, no one was prosecuting that more assiduously than Stalin.)

The fact is that, far from caring for Russian music, the Soviet Communist Party has, since 1917, done a very conscientious job of all but destroying it. Nor, save in the West, has this ever been much of a secret. The ruination of Russian culture and degeneration of artistic teaching under Marxism has been sworn to by almost every defector during the last thirty years and is analysed in detail from the musical angle by Olkhovsky, Schwarz, Ashkenazy, and Vishnevskaya. In truth, the decent music written in the Soviet Union – by Shostakovich, Prokofiev, Myaskovsky, Khachaturian, and a few others – has been written in spite of the country's political system rather than because of it. Had political logic been ruthlessly pursued, all trace of creative individuality in these composers would, over the years, have been gradually ground away. 'The fundamental theme of their work,' writes Olkhovsky, summarising the achievements of the 'Big Four', 'is the formation of personality under the conditions of its enslavement.' Common sense, if nothing else, could have told us this fifty years ago.

It is to be hoped that future writers on Soviet music will not allow their judgements to be clouded by an obsolete idealisation of what, in terms of

---

[1] To the ordinary Russian, Shostakovich was – and remains – a composer of popular songs and clamorous occasional pieces. (Older citizens might vaguely recall that he also wrote the *Leningrad* symphony.) Of his main output, as seen from abroad – the orchestral works, operas, and chamber music – most Soviet citizens know nothing. In fact, so thoroughly was the composer erased from public life during the fifties, that it is a common belief even among Soviet intellectuals that he was discovered in the West and only later became famous in Russia as a result of foreign interest.

mortalities alone, is the most catastrophic social system ever to have inflicted itself on the human race.

The persistent misinterpretation of Shostakovich's music is arguably the most grotesque cultural scandal of our time – not because it has caused his music to be devalued (he has long been deemed one of the century's half-dozen great composers), but because it allowed it to become highly rated for entirely the wrong reasons. The ordinary music-lover may find this concept obscure. Why should it matter whether we admire a work for the 'wrong' reasons? Surely there is only good and bad music? If the piece is good in itself, the things we see in it should be up to our individual imaginations. What the great requiem composers – Mozart, Berlioz, Verdi, Fauré – really thought about religion is irrelevant. All that counts is that we respond to the force of their inspiration.

However true this might be, its inherent flaw can be shown by a simple question: What would you think of someone's 'admiration' for a requiem if they had mistaken it for a comedy? (Or an heroic epic, or a party political broadcast?) The fact is that, with a few honourable exceptions, Western criticism on Shostakovich so far has amounted to a great deal of talk about the vicar's fine speaking-voice without the slightest understanding of his sermon.

Shostakovich's mistaken identity may have been chiefly a product of misplaced Western left-liberal awe of the Soviet Union, but there has also been another, more subtly pervasive factor involved: the increasing emphasis on form in modern music, with its attendant decline in emphasis on meaning.

Meaning in music [muses Volkov's Shostakovich in *Testimony*], that must sound very strange for most people. Particularly in the West. It's here in Russia that the question is usually posed: What was the composer trying to say, after all, with this musical work? What was he trying to make clear? The questions are naive, of course, but despite their naiveté and crudity, they definitely merit being asked. And I would add to them, for instance: Can music attack evil? Can it make man stop and think? Can it cry out and thereby draw man's attention to various vile acts to which he has grown accustomed? to the things he passes without any interest?

If it is true that Russians worry more about the meaning of music than Westerners, it may be because, as 'Asiatics' – and despite the atheistic religion of Communism imposed on them during the last seventy years – they still inhabit the pre-scientific 'soul culture' which holds the inner being of a thing as more real and permanent than its outward form. Of course, the West was itself largely living in this same soul-culture until approximately the outbreak of the First World War and, in those days, music was still assumed to have meaning in much the way that literature and painting did. On this view, far from being a merely technical development, abstraction in the modern arts has been a creative response to the spiritual vacuum left by the passing of the soul-culture. Losing their sense of the inner being of things, artists began to turn to an exploration of their outward forms, so that, by the mid-century, the inner dimensions of painting or music were either denied as flatly as they were in contemporary philosophy or allowed only token existence as expressions of fleeting emotion.

This trend towards externalism had a particularly marked effect on music in that, uniquely among the arts, it has two modes of existence: as score and as manufactured sound. Essentially a glorified aide-mémoire to sound-events, the musical score has endless formal interests of its own and at certain times in history these have exercised a greater fascination on composers than the contents of their auditory imaginations. Without touching further on an enormous subject, it is true to say that, after Schoenberg, the musical score came increasingly to be seen as a productive system in its own right, independent of the auditory imagination. Some composers became interested in music as meaningless sound, others as meaningless shape. For a while, the way a piece of music looked on paper became more important than what it sounded like (which was purely contingent and often completely random). The recent neo-Romantic reaction to this art-of-the-extreme-surface has been, in effect, an attempt to reinvest music with the sense of depth it possessed before the First World War. However, since the soul is no longer real to our culture, that depth has largely eluded an approach which sees Late Romanticism as a technical style rather than as an expression of being. Whereas the music of the nineteenth century contained thoughts (not just feelings) and dramas (not just psychodramas), the neo-Romantics embrace little more than the general emotional associations of traditional tonality. What result are expressionistic splurges of colour and feeling composed, with comic self-importance, in the shadow of Mahler's 'farewell' final period. (Mahler was saying 'farewell' to the soul-culture; contemporary neo-Romantics are saying farewell to having anything serious to say farewell to.)

Reinforcing this historical effect is what might be called the aesthetic bias of music. Musicians are naturally taught to make a 'beautiful' sound and, left to their own devices, that is usually *all* they'll make. In an age like ours, confined to the surface of things, 'beauty' inevitably comes to be thought of primarily as beauty of appearance rather than beauty of character or mind (or 'soul'). Thus, contemporary performing values stress smoothness, homogeneity, and glamour at the expense of all other qualities – despite the fact that these other qualities compose seventy-five percent of art, which is great, when it is great, not because it is beautiful but because it is true. Composers like Mussorgsky, Mahler, Berg, Britten, and Shostakovich – for whom the articulacy of sound is so critical as to teeter perpetually on the verge of speech – can be utterly obliterated by performers and critics whose interest is in beauty rather than truth, form rather than being, the score rather than the mind behind it.

Too many in the world of classical music believe they are getting to the heart of a given piece of music if they 'breathe with it' or 'draw out its expression' in a hammy mime of soulfulness. Nothing could be further from the truth – which resides not in musical notes, but in life, the source of all creative energy. Imagine *King Lear* played by the glamorous doll-like creatures of *Dynasty* and you have a not too exaggerated picture of many Western performances of Shostakovich. That beauty of sound matters less in Shostakovich than in any other more or less traditionally tonal composer should be clear to anyone who takes more than a minute to think about it. What is less obvious in this age of meaningless beautification is that all music withers if smothered in rouge and sequins. (Most Western performances of the elegant and melodically supercharged Prokofiev are hideously cosmeticized, too.)

Music's inherent susceptibility to the vacuously gorgeous has been further encouraged in our time by its score-fixated sense of separation from its fellow arts. Whereas figures like Ferruccio Busoni, Adolf Busch, and Artur Schnabel carried on nineteenth-century traditions of grounding music in life by relating it to poetry, painting, drama, and philosophy, modern instructors generally impart immaculate technique supported by a 'manner' of performance which is really no more than a physical impersonation of the middlebrow idea of what artistic profundity ought to *look* like. (If it were within their power to supply their students with high foreheads, wild hair, and eyes that gazed into eternity, they would doubtless do so at no extra charge.) It may be true that most performers are, after all, of average character – which is to say pleasantly bland – but character is there to be developed and art, as Shostakovich insists, should be an agent for that development rather than an entertaining confirmation of shallow passivity. Discussing the work of Heinrich Neuhaus, director of the Moscow Conservatoire in the early thirties, Yuri Yelagin describes how Emil Gilels, then one of the usual limitless supply of technically dazzling Russian pianists, became one of his students: 'On numerous occasions, instead of discussing the different methods of playing, Neuhaus read to his pupil his favourite poets, especially Pasternak. Or else he took him on a tour of the Moscow picture galleries. The results of this extraordinary approach were striking. The brilliant but superficial and cold performances by Gilels underwent a change and began to show a serious master and erudite artist.' There may be few nascent Gilelses in the world, but all of us are capable of travelling further into the interior if we look hard enough for the signposts or are shown them by those who have gone on ahead.

Quite apart from the pernicious mystique of Soviet Communism, then, Shostakovich's meaning has been obscured by a musical environment in which meaning itself is treated on the one hand as an anachronism, and on the other as a sort of magic ointment one can rub into one's performances by gesticulating in the approved manner. For long regarded by the score-worshipping post-Schoenbergian establishment as technically conservative and thus uninstructive, Shostakovich in fact offers a vital clue to contemporary composers as to how to escape their present imprisonment in an over-intellectualized and emotionally bogus aestheticism. Located as close to real life as he could get it, his music is intensely observant both of human characteristics – speech-rhythms, mannerisms, expressions – and of the tragi-comic drama of what might be called the moral theatre of existence. Calling himself a worker (proletarian) primarily to distance himself from the untrustworthiness of many of the *intelligenty* he knew, Shostakovich meant also that he saw himself as an ordinary human being whose job happened to be that of composing music. No snob, he could write one day for his fellow intellectuals and the next for the crowds in the street – and while the language of these extremes may have been different, there was always a continuity between them which kept him in touch with the demotic energy without which art relapses into self-absorption. Slap in the middle of this very wide spectrum of expression, the Twelfth Symphony, with its unpretentious language and satirical hidden depths, might still prove to be a key text for young composers in our century's last decade. Be that as it may, if they could rid themselves of their inbred horror of commonness and listen more to the sounds of life instead of playing with shapes on score-paper, they might yet cease to be captives of style and find their way back to the broad audience so impatiently awaiting them.

Interviewed about Shostakovich in 1976 by Pierre Vidal, the conductor Kyrill Kondrashin referred to him with respect and affection as 'the moral conscience of music in Russia'.

Conscience depends on memory. So relentlessly have Lenin's heirs striven to wipe clean the national memory – first by shooting millions of Russians through the brain-stem, later by denying that such things ever happened – that almost all the creative energy of the country's artists and intellectuals since 1917 has gone into the genre of the memoir. Plays, novels, poems – the majority of these, too, are memoirs in disguise. Shostakovich's music is no different. Remembrance is his theme, and if he tells the same story over and over again, it is because for him, as for nearly every other modern Russian, there is no other story to tell. On one occasion berating Solzhenitsyn for his refusal to let the regime off the hook and concentrate instead on its achievements, Alexander Tvardovsky thumped his *Novy Mir* editor's desk in exasperation: 'You refuse to forget anything. *You have much too good a memory*.' Notwithstanding their mutual suspicion, Solzhenitsyn and Shostakovich were co-workers in a massive effort to keep memory alive in Russia through the mid-twentieth century. Obsessed by the monstrous genocidal injustice of their country's political system, they return time and again in their works to the scene of the crime to paint its horror from a different angle or to bring fresh wreaths for those tens of millions of graves.

If Solzhenitsyn is the greater memoirist, Shostakovich was the finer artist. Unburdened by theories of history or a vision of Christian redemption, he looked reality in the eye and recorded what he saw with wry understatement and enormous tragic force. His music – not of a neurotic victim, but of an uncomfortably acute observer – is by turns ironic and appalled (and always dryer than it seems). Blessed with phenomenal inner energy, he worked steadily round his subject, summarising it in a language which, by his death, he had refined to a high degree of aphoristic concentration. Half-jester, half-Jeremiah, he evolved a distinctive 'tragic-satiric' style by crossing elements taken from nineteenth-century Russian literature with the work of Mahler, Mussorgsky, and Stravinsky. In so doing, he created a unique artistic dual personality which, in old age, became stamped on his face by the stroke that confined his smile to one side of his mouth, leaving the other curved down in an almost boyish expression of hurt resentment.

From the point of view of form, Shostakovich's greatness resides in his maintenance of an accessible style during a time in which the perceived mainstream of classical music turned away from the mass audience in pursuit of its own linguistic destiny. To say that this was not solely a matter of his own choosing – that had he done anything else in Stalin's Russia, he would not have survived – is to ignore the fact that, inseparable as it was from his personality, his musical language is unlikely to have developed along radically different lines had he lived anywhere else. More importantly, it is impossible to divorce Shostakovich's style from his outlook as a realist – which is to say that he was *in control* of his means of expression and not, as earlier critics have argued, in uneasy thrall to it. Just as George Orwell saw the necessity of plain speaking in an age of delusive rhetoric and thought-crippling clichés, so Shostakovich (and writers like Zamyatin, Bulgakov, Platonov, and Zoshchenko) recognised in the prefabricated overstatement of Soviet discourse a device intended to condition the minds of its audience to impotent obedience. One of Orwell's most valuable achievements as a critic was to show that the more habituated we become to inflated language, the more likely we are to be infected by a masochistic worship of energy and power. Filled with ready-made phrases such as 'stormy applause rising to an ovation' and 'caught up in the elemental force of events', the language of Soviet reportage during the Stalin era was a classic example of conditioning by rhetoric. ('Elemental force' is very congenial to power-seekers and the open-mouthed admiration of it in their audiences is always encouraged; 'storm' metaphors, too, are ubiquitous in both Bolshevik and Nazi political literature.) In his music – and, if we accept its essential authenticity, in *Testimony* – Shostakovich is at pains not only to remember what really happened, but to do so in realistic language. To have retreated into a musical equivalent of linguistic philosophy may not have been an option to him, but, thinking as he did, he would in any case have considered this no more of a *moral* option than that of adopting the surrogate nineteenth-century nationalism of the Socialist Realist 'Red Romantic' style. By raising the musically downbeat to the level of high art, Shostakovich availed himself of an undeceivable street-corner irony far more articulate in its historical context than the analytic complications of the Schoenberg–Webern tradition.

From the point of view of content it is arguable that, more than that of any other modern composer, Shostakovich's music *is* the twentieth century. Living, in every aspect other than the purely technical, on the frontline of modernity, he witnessed its effects on the emotional, intellectual, and moral life of a great culture during a crucial fifty years. Many would accept the history of the USSR as, in a heightened and localised way, the story of our time. The fact that Shostakovich expressed this so successfully through music automatically submits him for consideration as the century's leading composer. Whether he will, in fact, be thought so remains to be seen.

'If the twentieth century has any lesson for mankind, it is we who will teach the West, not the West us. Excessive ease and prosperity have weakened their will and their reason.' Solzhenitsyn's verdict has understandably not been a popular one on this side of the Iron Curtain and conceivably the message of Shostakovich's music, as re-interpreted here, will for some time remain equally unwelcome. Certainly the sort of limp aestheticism which regards the 'political' aspect of the composer's art as a regrettable hindrance to its subjective enjoyment will find plenty to deplore, not least in the present study. That Shostakovich is more concerned with 'spiritual' values and communicates on a more 'universal' plane than many a composer customarily thought to be his superior in such things will not easily be conceded – if at all. At the very least, we can look forward to some productive argument.

As for *Testimony*, in the absence of a minute exegesis by Solomon Volkov, a final judgement on it will have to be indefinitely postponed. For now, only provisional opinions are in order – and, for what it's worth, the opinion of the present writer, based partly on instinct and partly on the book's many curious conjunctions of information (such as those surrounding *Portrait Gallery* and the 1932 *Hamlet*), is that it is substantially authentic both in tone and content. Indeed, as a guide to the music, it is next to invaluable – not so much on precise points of interpretation, which will have to remain in dispute, as in illuminating the state of mind behind it. (In particular, *Testimony* is, both directly and indirectly, a profoundly convincing commentary on the structure of thought operative in the late period.) Why Volkov falsified his text has to remain conjectural. Obviously 'Shostakovich's memoirs' were far more of a commercial prospect than just another biography – even one containing swathes of verbatim quotes collected by a writer who had known the composer personally. The decision to abandon the one for the other may have been made by Volkov once in America and aware of the cost of living; there again, his use of signed pages argues a considerable degree of forethought. But whatever the truth of its provenance, *Testimony* remains the one indispensable source on Shostakovich. Even considered as a volume of 'dramatised' criticism, its sophistication puts it streets ahead of its competitors.

Dying in the depths of the Brezhnev freeze in 1975, Shostakovich never had the satisfaction of knowing that his message had been received by the world at large. Raised in a harsher age, he had grown used to opposing tyranny from behind a mask and thus had to forgo the grim satisfaction of younger men like Solzhenitsyn, Rostropovich, and Vladimir Bukovsky, who confronted Soviet Communism so openly that they had to be thrown out of the country. 'We,' writes Bukovsky, speaking for his fellow dissidents in his own 'testimony' *To Build a Castle*, 'had conducted a desperate war against this regime of utter scum. We were a handful of unarmed men facing a mighty State in possession of the most monstrous machinery of oppression in the entire world. And we had won.' All Shostakovich could do by comparison was confide some relatively oblique anecdotes to Solomon Volkov, eschewing so much as a moderately detailed account of his personal experiences during the Terror on the grounds that a sensitive reader would not require one and a fool not understand it. Even his music carries in it a fatalistic sense that one can tell nobody anything that they don't already know – that standing on a soapbox is self-defeating, distorting what ought to be an intimate communication.

Fated to follow an individualistic métier in a militantly collectivistic environment, Shostakovich arrived at a sharper awareness of the moral undertow to 'political' issues than most living in a democracy can begin to appreciate. 'For him,' insists Volkov, 'always the rights of the individual, the happiness of the individual, were more important than some abstract happiness of everybody.' Idealists – particularly young idealists – may find it hard to identify with the composer in this. As probably the central issue of our time, it is, however, worth pondering at length – and particularly in the company of his music, which is without doubt among the greatest art of this cautionary century.

Note

Stormy Applause, violinist Rostislav Dubinsky's eye-opening account of thirty years of internecine political struggle in the Borodin Quartet, appeared too recently for its merciless mockery of Soviet culture and racy vignettes of Shostakovich to be incorporated into the present text. Suffice it to say that Dubinsky's memoir confirms Volkov's in considerable detail and that his portrait of the composer accords perfectly with that on offer in *Testimony*. Of particular significance, in view of remarks made in the closing section of this study, is a passage describing how on one occasion the Borodins played Shostakovich's Fourth String Quartet in two entirely different ways: first, truthfully, emphasizing 'everything that Socialist Realism conceals'; and second, lyingly, with all 'anti-Soviet insinuations' removed – faster and lighter, disguising the music's dour message with spurious gracefulness and false smiles. Dubinsky's book effectively settles the argument about *Testimony*: Solomon Volkov may have to some extent misrepresented his material, but its essential truth is now altogether beyond doubt.

STALINISM AND

NINETEEN EIGHTY-FOUR

IT IS, perhaps, useful for Westerners unfamiliar with the Soviet background to know that a book which many of them will have read, George Orwell's *Nineteen Eighty-Four*, gives what many insiders consider to be a remarkably accurate satirical picture of Stalin's Russia around the time the novel itself was written (1946-8).

Three years older than Shostakovich, Orwell shared several characteristics with him: discipline, honesty, physical aloofness, a populist taste in literature, a preference for plain language, and a political outlook predicated on decency. Driven by a strong sense of obligation, both men identified with the worst-off in society and worked hard for the cultural departments of their countries' national broadcasting systems during the war. Just as Shostakovich, under stress, tended to retreat in his work to memories of his happy childhood, so Orwell returned often in his writing to an idyllic vision of pre-1914 rural England – the 'Golden Country' of *Nineteen Eighty-Four* (revisited at length in *Coming Up for Air*). Likewise, both men suffered towards the ends of their lives from illnesses which some critics see as having accentuated the pessimism of their later works. (The intensity of the torture scenes in *Nineteen Eighty-Four* and the 'waves of pain' in Shostakovich's Thirteenth Quartet have alike been ascribed to the unpleasant medical tests each went through shortly before writing these passages.)

While Orwell, unlike Shostakovich, could write what he liked, he chose to disguise the message of his two masterpieces, the tragi-satiric anti-Communist allegories *Animal Farm* and *Nineteen Eighty-Four*, by setting them in fictional worlds, much as Soviet satirists like Zamyatin, Bulgakov, and Platonov did under duress.[1] Banned for forty years in the USSR as counter-revolutionary propaganda, these books have recently been published there as part of Mikhail Gorbachev's drive to discredit Stalinism. Long famous by repute throughout the Communist bloc, they would have been known of by Shostakovich, though he is unlikely to have read them.

---

[1] See Gleb Struve in Coppard and Crick, pp. 260–1.

Many features of Orwell's imaginary superstate, Oceania, are ironic translations from Stalinist reality: the puritanical Komsomol (Young Communists) appear as the Anti-Sex League; the young informers of the Pioneers turn up as the Spies; Soviet Five-Year Plans shrink into Oceanian Three-Year Plans; and state-regulated vodka metamorphoses into Victory Gin. Soviet jargon, though sometimes parodied – bourgeois individualism becomes 'ownlife' – is more often taken over unaltered. Thus, like Stalin's USSR, Oceania has its 'renegades and backsliders' who are arrested at night, questioned by relays of interrogators, 'unmasked' and 'unpersoned' for 'counter-revolutionary activities' and then either sent to the 'salt-mines' or 'vaporised' (liquidated). To avoid such a fate, Orwell's hero Winston Smith adopts an 'expression of quiet optimism' so as not to be accused of 'facecrime' (a genuine Stalinist misdemeanour defined by the critic Ronald Hingley as 'the inability to simulate an adequate degree of righteous indignation').[1] As in Russia, the 'comrades' of Oceania are regaled with news bulletins consisting almost entirely of lists of industrial production figures, most of which are triumphantly announced as 'overfulfilled' and none of which are believed. As in Russia there are constant power-cuts and shortages, all essentials being obtained through the underground 'free market'. The only thing in Oceania unknown under Stalinism is Orwell's two-way telescreen; the only aspect of Stalinism left out of Oceania is compulsory collectivism (instead of living in a communal apartment, Winston Smith has his own flat).

Winston's job is that of 'rectification' in the newspaper section of the Ministry of Truth (known as Minitrue, in accordance with the Soviet penchant for modern-brutal abbreviations, like 'Orgburo' and 'Diamat'). In this building – whose 'enormous pyramidal structure' symbolises the organisation of the Communist state – books and periodicals are rewritten and photographs altered to reflect the 'correct' (that is, the latest) view of past events. Sometimes taken by Western readers to be a flight of surrealist fantasy, this is a barely inflated parody of what actually happened under Stalinism. Soviet defector Arkady Shevchenko has written of his student days that 'facts and concepts were always being "corrected" in textbooks and lectures. As policy shifted at Stalin's whim, men and nations who had been in favour became pariahs overnight; established dogma turned into heresy. It could be disastrous to miss a lecture where the revised truth of the day was proclaimed for us to copy down.' Stalin's most outrageous 'correction' of the past, the Soviet-Nazi pact of 1939, is satirised in *Nineteen Eighty-Four* as the alliance of Oceania with its arch-enemy Eurasia against its former ally Eastasia ('Oceania was at war with Eastasia: Oceania had always been at war with Eastasia.'). Orwell's observation that in Oceania the same updating of reality applied to poetry as political writing is similarly based on Stalinist fact.

Big Brother, the all-seeing leader who murders his rivals, decrees 'a new,

---

[1] *Nightingale Fever*, p. 208.

happy life' and, from ubiquitous posters and hoardings, broods over a populace conditioned by terror to love him, is, of course, Stalin 'the Omniscient, the Omnipresent' himself. ('Big Brother' is what the East European satellite nations began calling Russia just after the war.) Just as in Soviet mythology the quasi-supernatural Lenin 'lives', so in Oceania 'Big Brother cannot die'. Equally perpetual is Oceania's devil-figure, Emmanuel Goldstein, counter-revolutionary author of 'the book', against whom the state wages an endless struggle: 'Always there were fresh dupes waiting to be seduced by him. A day never passed when spies and saboteurs acting under his directions were not unmasked by the Thought Police. He was the commander of a vast shadowy army, an underground network of conspirators dedicated to the overthrow of the State.' This is the way Trotsky was portrayed to the Soviet people during the thirties, a political myth which allowed Stalin's NKVD to repress millions for the imaginary crime of 'Trotskyism' just as Big Brother's Thought Police repress the alleged followers of Goldstein. (Goldstein's book is a probable allusion to Trotsky's *The Revolution Betrayed*.)

On the subject of Oceania's purges, Orwell is particularly literal, shifting Big Brother's Terror from the thirties to the sixties but otherwise reproducing the pattern of events in Stalin's Russia with great precision. Last of Big Brother's rivals to survive are the prominent Party members Jones, Aaranson, and Rutherford:

As so often happened, they had vanished for a year or more, so that one did not know whether they were alive or dead, and then had suddenly been brought forth to incriminate themselves in the usual way. They had confessed to intelligence with the enemy (at that date, too, the enemy was Eurasia), embezzlement of public funds, the murder of various trusted Party members, intrigues against the leadership of Big Brother which had started long before the Revolution happened, and acts of sabotage causing the deaths of hundreds of thousands of people. After confessing to these things they had been pardoned, reinstated in the Party, and given posts which were in fact sinecures but which sounded important. All three had written long, abject articles in *The Times*, analysing the reasons for their defection and promising to make amends . . . A little later all three were re-arrested. It appeared that they had engaged in fresh conspiracies from the very moment of their release. At their second trial they confessed to all their old crimes over again, with a whole string of new ones.

Jones, Aaranson, and Rutherford probably stand for Kamenev, Zinoviev, and Radek, to whom the events described by Orwell most closely apply. They confessed to spying for Japan, murdering Kirov, trying to murder Stalin, wanting to have murdered Lenin, and general 'Trotskyite sabotage' – crimes for which they apologised at length, accompanied by fulsome expressions of admiration for Stalin, in *Pravda*. Rubashov's similar confession in Arthur

Koestler's novel of 1940, *Darkness at Noon*, is a genteel affair compared to the ordeal inflicted on Winston Smith, but there is good reason to suppose Orwell's crueller picture was closer to the truth. In *Let History Judge*, for example, Roy Medvedev quotes the deposition of Mikhail Yakubovich in 1967 concerning his alleged participation in the All-Union Bureau of Mensheviks. The trial of this non-existent counter-revolutionary organisation took place in 1931, six years after the last Mensheviks had been liquidated. Yakubovich, a Bolshevik, was understandably reluctant to confess to membership of this imaginary party and, though tortured on 'the conveyor' (that is, driven continuously between interrogation cells by blows), he refused to comply with his captors' demands until the State Prosecutor himself, Nikolai Krylenko, paid him a visit. Summoning Yakubovich before him in the Butyrki Prison, Krylenko told him: 'I have no doubt that you personally are not guilty of anything. We are both performing our duty to the Party – I have considered and consider you a Communist. I will be the prosecutor at the trial, and you will confirm the testimony given during the investigation. This is our duty to the Party, yours and mine . . . Have we agreed?' Yakubovich recalls: 'I mumbled something indistinctly, but to the effect that I promised to do my duty. I think there were tears in my eyes. Krylenko made a gesture of approval. I left.'[1]

Confused, like Winston Smith, by beatings and sleep-deprivation, the NKVD's victims rarely had any will left to argue with their interrogators' nonsensical assertions. In fact, many were so bamboozled by propaganda and Stalin-worship that they confessed instantly to whatever crimes they were accused of, preferring *on principle* the Party's version of their past to their own. The eager confession of Orwell's burlesque character Parsons ('Of course I'm guilty! You don't think the Party would arrest an innocent man, do you?') is only partly a joke. Eugenia Ginzburg heard similar sentiments expressed by imprisoned Party members while she herself was in the Butyrki between 1937 and 1939.

Readers behind the Iron Curtain often express amazement at Orwell's minute familiarity with their way of life: the scarcity of telephone directories; the unavailability of any books published more than twenty years previously; the material privileges enjoyed by the Soviet *nomenklatura* (Oceania's Inner Party); the use of swearing as an antidote to officialese; the routine corruption of the labour-camp system; the employment of criminals to supervise political prisoners; and so on. Some of this trickled through to the West via the newspaper columns of foreign correspondents and Orwell evidently kept his eye out for such data. For example, he incorporated the raising of the maximum Soviet hard-labour sentence to twenty-five years when Tass announced it in 1947 while he was writing *Nineteen Eighty-Four* on Jura. Similarly, O'Brien's claim that the Party was above the laws of nature is likely to have been based on newspaper reports of Trofim Lysenko's speech to the Congress of the Soviet

---

[1] Medvedev, p. 130.

Academy of Agricultural Sciences in August 1948. Otherwise, he depended on talking to visitors to and defectors from the Soviet bloc, and on the books and pamphlets by such people that he amassed in his personal library. Much of the verisimilitude of the novel is owed to writings of this kind, including the famous formula '2+2=5', derived from an 'acceleration slogan' of 1929 (indicating that the targets of the First Five-Year Plan were achievable a year early) which he found in Eugene Lyons's *Assignment in Utopia*.

How far the theoretical apparatus of *Nineteen Eighty-Four* – Newspeak, Doublethink, and so on – was taken from accounts of Socialist Realism is difficult to say, since much of the thought behind the technical side of Orwell's book derived from his own critical essays on language and politics. There is, though, a discrete step between imagining a mode of discourse in which ready-made phrases block free thought (Communist examples of which he collected avidly) and a language in which a word or phrase means the exact opposite of what it seems to mean. Paradoxical concepts like 'democratic centralism' (meaning totalitarianism) may have given him a lead, as may the convolutions of Socialist Realist theory, but essentially Newspeak appears to have been an inspired deduction – the closest *Nineteen Eighty-Four* approaches to science fiction. (Not that this has prevented the Poles from recognising in it a satirical projection of their own brand of officialese and taking it into their language as *nowomowa*. Nor, indeed, are Orwell's theoretical constructs by any means regarded as fanciful by Soviet intellectuals. A Russian acquaintance of Orwell's *Tribune* colleague Tosco Fyvel told him in 1982: 'With his Newspeak and Doublethink, Orwell wrote for us! No Westerner could understand him as intimately as we in the Soviet Union felt he understood our lives.')

Further instances of Orwell's logic leading him to endow Oceania with features in advance of its Stalinist model include 'reality control' (a concept paralleled thirty years later by the doctrine of Soviet 'information space') and O'Brien's insistence that Winston is insane (twelve years before Soviet courts started sending dissidents to psychiatric wards). Even Orwell's 'exaggerations' have more often than not turned out to be justified. The Two Minutes Hate, for example, is anticipated by a piece in *Pionerskaya Pravda* for 17 December 1932 announcing that the paper's main educational mission to Soviet youth was 'the cultivation of hatred'. More extraordinary still, recent research shows that in 1921 the Kiev secret police were executing captives with rats, much as occurs in *Nineteen Eighty-Four*'s ghastly Room 101.[1]

With this level of incisiveness, Orwell's masterpiece was bound to make a major impact in Europe where, in the words of its publisher Fredric Warburg, it was 'the most powerful anti-Soviet tract that you could find – and treated as such'. Robert Tucker, now Professor of Politics at Princeton, was on the staff of the American Embassy in Moscow after the war and read *Nineteen Eighty-Four* soon after it appeared. In his opinion the novel, far from being a fantasy about

---

[1] Leggett, p. 198.

the future, was then happening in reality outside the embassy compound.[1] Oceania 'actually existed' in Russia in 1949.

For some years, *Nineteen Eighty-Four* was little more than a legend behind the Iron Curtain. Referring to the novel in *The Captive Mind* in 1953, Czeslaw Milosz observed that 'because it is both difficult to obtain and dangerous to possess, it is known only to certain members of the Inner Party. Orwell fascinates them through his insight into details they know well . . . [They] are amazed that a writer who never lived in Russia should have so keen a perception into its life.' Fifteen years on, *Nineteen Eighty-Four* was sufficiently familiar to the Russian intelligentsia for Eugenia Ginzburg to make casual allusions to it in her memoirs. The Polish philosopher Leszek Kolakowski has since praised its analytic brilliance while, in their recent history of the Soviet Union *Utopia in Power*, Mikhail Heller and Aleksandr Nekrich single out Orwell as 'perhaps the only Western writer who profoundly understood the essence of the Soviet world'.

---

[1] Steinhoff, p. 95.

AKHMATOVA, SHOSTAKOVICH, AND THE 'SEVENTH'

THERE IS no doubt that Shostakovich greatly admired Akhmatova as an artist. A portrait of her hung in his Moscow apartment and, in *Testimony* (p. 274), he acknowledges his regard for her work, making special mention of *Requiem* and the 'incomparable' late verse of her last decade, 1955–66. Equally certain is that Akhmatova was fascinated by Shostakovich. Much affected by his Fifth Symphony, which she first heard during the late thirties, she thought sufficiently highly of him to have inscribed the 1958 Soviet selection of her verse *To Dmitri Dmitryevich Shostakovich, in whose epoch I lived on earth*. Indeed, so intense was her interest in his art that it occasionally claimed precedence over enquiries from devotees about her own. The scholar and translator Peter Norman recalls that, while visiting Akhmatova at Komarovo in 1964, his conversation with her was halted when the poet Anatoli Naiman arrived with a tape of new pieces by Shostakovich[1] which she insisted on hearing immediately. As for the composer himself, he records that she regularly attended his premières and (somewhat to his embarrassment) wrote poems about them.[2] One of these, dedicated to 'D. D. Sh.' and dated 1958, is translated by Richard McKane in his extensive selection of Akhmatova's verse:[3]

MUSIC

It creates miracles.
In its eyes limits are defined.
It alone talks with me
when others are afraid to come near,

---

[1] These were the Ninth and Tenth Quartets, premièred in Moscow by the Beethoven Quartet on 20 November 1964 and brought to Komarovo by Galina Shostakovich's husband Yevgeny Chukovsky. According to Anatoli Naiman, Akhmatova and her circle listened to the quartets 'repeatedly, day after day'.

[2] *Testimony*, p. 273.

[3] *Anna Akhmatova: Selected Poems*, reprinted here by permission of Bloodaxe Books © 1989.

> when the last friend has turned his eyes away.
> It was with me in my grave
> and sang like the first storm,
> or as though all the flowers had burst into speech.

While their respect for each other as artists was deep, Shostakovich and Akhmatova were very dissimilar people and *Testimony*'s reminiscences of her are wry with faint amusement over her famously cultivated mystique. Remembered by all who knew her as the most dignified person they ever met, she moved through the flustered shallows of modernity with the anachronistic grace of a Renaissance galleon. Shostakovich's iconoclastic streak, however, prevented him from viewing Akhmatova's majestic demeanour without irony and, while he prized the serene translucence of her language, he was unable to share her Christian acceptance of suffering. Intellectually, he had more in common with her sister in verse Marina Tsvetayeva who, like him, had Polish blood, identified with the Jew as a fellow outsider, and was restlessly preoccupied with death.

Banned in the USSR between 1922 and 1956, Tsvetayeva's work came to his attention only in his sixties, whereupon he marked his belated acquaintance with it by writing the *Six Romances*, Opus 143, of 1973. The last and longest of these, *To Anna Akhmatova*, is based on a poem saluting a uniquely stately and incorruptible spirit in words whose turbulence paradoxically draws from Shostakovich a setting of stark gravity. His reverence for Akhmatova, elsewhere tempered by his innate scepticism, is here unequivocal. If, as a satirist, he was essentially as foreign to her as their mutual friend Mikhail Zoshchenko (whose supremacy in the domain of prose she conceded with awe), as a tragedian he was very close to her and *To Anna Akhmatova* remains one of his most solemn and imposing musical monuments. (His only explicit memorial to her, it quotes the first movement of the Second Violin Concerto, suggesting that something of her is likewise to be found in that unsung creation of 1967. More Akhmatovian meditations may figure in the similarly neglected Second Cello Concerto, written soon after her death in 1966.)

For her part, Akhmatova shared the misgivings of several of Shostakovich's literary friends concerning the quality of some of the texts he chose to set. (Biased to the vernacular, he was intrigued by the poignant and ironic aspects of artlessness; in *Testimony*, he records with a patient shrug her fastidious disapproval of the 'weak words'[1] of *From Jewish Folk Poetry*.) Despite this, her poet's hypersensitive ear made Akhmatova highly susceptible to music and she seems to have heard in Shostakovich's work a clear enough continuity with her favourite composers (Bach, Mozart, Beethoven, and Chopin) for any reservations about his general outlook to be of little account to her. Taking a more

---

[1] According to Anatoli Naiman, Akhmatova's actual pejorative was 'kitsch' and her anger on the subject unassuageable.

mysterious – if not religious – view of inspiration than he could, she perhaps saw deeper into him than he himself did.

On the subject of inspiration, Akhmatova's sense of a sublime, causative 'music' immanent in the lines of her verse – a sense very much shared by Osip Mandelstam[1] – is nowhere more apparent than in her incantatory *Poem Without a Hero,* commenced in 1940 and thereafter endlessly revisited by her for the purpose of fine tuning. Approving the poet Mikhail Zenkevich's description of the poem as a 'Tragic Symphony' and herself twice exploring its potential as a ballet scenario, she clearly found the boundaries between her text and the media of abstract sound and movement pregnantly vague. Dense with shadowy allusions, *Poem Without a Hero* is of special interest to Shostakovich students for its characteristically manifold reference to 'my Seventh' (II, ix), usually held simultaneously to concern Shostakovich's *Leningrad* Symphony, Beethoven's Seventh (her favourite),[2] and her own ill-fated 'Seventh Book' of poems. The cause of Akhmatova's particular attachment to Shostakovich's Seventh is unknown, though the likeliest explanation is that her sentiment was based on a feeling of identity with the symphony's fate. According to the latest Soviet scholarship,[3] she bore the manuscript of its first movement on her lap when evacuated by plane from Leningrad on 29 September 1941 – implying that Shostakovich, who left the city three days later, had insured himself against bad luck and enemy anti-aircraft guns by entrusting a copy to her. Since he cannot have had time to duplicate the orchestral score, this would seem to have been the piano reduction he played to a small audience in his apartment on September 17[4] – although a rejected draft of the Epilogue of *Poem Without a Hero* (here translated by Richard McKane) suggests an intriguing alternative:

> All of you would have been able to admire me,
> when I saved myself from evil pursuit,
> in the belly of the flying fish
> and flew over lake Ladoga and the forest
> as though possessed by the devil
> to Brocken like a witch in the night.
> And the Seventh, as it called itself,
> was after me, its secret sparkling,
> rushing to a feast that had never been heard of.
> The famed Leningrad
> in the guise of a notebook with notes in it
> returned into the native ether.

---

[1] See Nadezhda Mandelstam, *Hope Against Hope*, pp. 70–71.

[2] Gleb Struve and Boris Filippov, *Anna Akhmatova: Collected Works*, Inter-Language Literary Asociates (1968), II, p. 387.

[3] Notes to *Poem Without a Hero*, Knizhnaya Palata edition (Moscow), 1989.

[4] This being the day on which both he and Akhmatova addressed Leningrad by radio, it seems likely that she was among his guests that evening.

Did the 'notebook with notes in it' contain Shostakovich's jottings towards his first movement, or was it a complete version in short-score? Inasmuch as he is known to have done most of his composing in his head, the second possibility seems likelier.

Akhmatova's mission to rescue the symphony from the flames understandably resonated in her mind as a metaphor for the salvation, by individual conscience, of Russian culture. More than a mere symbol, though, the *Leningrad* assumed for her the significance of a major creative landmark in itself. Anatoli Naiman, a close friend of Akhmatova during the early sixties,[1] reveals that the musical subtext of *Poem Without a Hero* 'begins' with Stravinsky's *Petrushka* and 'ends' with Shostakovich's Seventh Symphony. Behind this, he explains, lies her vision of the first quarter of the century as being, artistically speaking, 'under the sign of Stravinsky' and of its middle years as 'under the sign of Shostakovich'.[2] While Western literary audiences may find this classification strange, it should be said that Akhmatova seems to have felt music to be a form of supraverbal speech and that her taste in it was, consequently, fairly sophisticated. Her group of pupils and admirers regularly circulated records, mostly of baroque music – Bach, Vivaldi, and Purcell (*Dido and Aeneas* being a special enthusiasm) – while she herself stretched as far as early Schoenberg and even *Wozzeck*.[3]

Much of what Akhmatova said or wrote possessed a double meaning. *Poem Without a Hero*, for example, is a masque in which the good and evil of two eras in a single city (the pre-revolutionary Petersburg of 1913 and the Soviet Leningrad of 1941) confront each other in a hall of mirrors. Conceivably, her idea of musico-astrological 'signs' in connection with Stravinsky and Shostakovich is similarly ambiguous. Taking for granted her love for their music, there is room for speculation that she saw these composers as archetypes representing not only the propitious but also the unfortunate sides of their respective periods. Just as, for instance, Stravinsky's individualism and ironic sense of style epitomise the best of the St Petersburg of Akhmatova's *Poem*, so the city's dark side stands reflected in his shortcomings: the capricious modishness noted by Schoenberg; the superficiality regretted by Nijinsky ('Stravinsky is a good composer, but he does not know life – his compositions have no purpose'). In the same way, while the tragic stoicism and unflinching honesty of Shostakovich accord with what was positive about Leningrad in 1941, his sceptical materialism can be said to represent – at least to someone of Akhmatova's spirituality – its inauspicious obverse. Whether, had she lived to

---

[1] As a distinguished poet, Naiman has collaborated with Shostakovich's foremost pupil Boris Tishchenko, himself the composer of a setting (1966) of Akhmatova's *Requiem* (see *Testimony*, p. 274).

[2] Personal communication with the present writer.

[3] It is tempting to wonder whether Shostakovich, who loved Berg, had any influence over Akhmatova in this.

hear it, she would have shared her fellow believer Solzhenitsyn's disapproval of Shostakovich's pessimistic Fourteenth Symphony is impossible to say; aesthetically a pantheist, she was broadminded enough to admire the expressive virtuosity of any amount of art whose philosophy she deplored. More to the point is that she would have seen Shostakovich's despair as implicit in his godless outlook – and that her favourite work of Stravinsky's was the *Symphony of Psalms*.

Yet another link to the 'Seventh' nexus in *Poem Without a Hero* may be Akhmatova's *Seventh Northern Elegy* (1958–64). Incomplete and only recently published in the USSR, it was of great personal significance to her and forms something of a poetic analogue to the predominantly still and quiet music of Shostakovich's late period. Richard McKane's translation, reproduced here with his permission, is the first English version of this important poem to appear in a book.

From the SEVENTH NORTHERN ELEGY

And I have been silent, silent for thirty years.
For countless nights
silence surrounds me like arctic ice.

It comes to blow out my candle.
The dead are silent too – but that is understandable,
and less terrifying . . .

My silence is heard everywhere,
it fills the hall at my trial
and it could outshout the very roar
of rumours, and like a miracle
leave its imprint on everything.
My God, it takes part in everything!
Who could cast me in such a role?
O Lord, let me, even for just a moment,
become a little bit more like everyone else.

Didn't I drink hemlock?
Why then did I not die
right then as I ought to have done?

My own dream does not light on those persons
nor do I give them my blessing,
no, not to those who seek out my books,
who stole them, who even had them bound,
who carry them as though they are secret chains,

who remember their every syllable by heart,
but I do give it to those persons who dared to write
my silence on a banner for all to see,
who lived with it and believed it,
who measured the black abyss . . .

My silence is in music and song
and in a chilling love,
in partings, in books,
      in what is more unknown
than anything in this world.

Even I am frightened by it sometimes
when it squeezes me with its full weight,
breathing and moving in on me.
There's no defence, there's nothing faster.
Who knows how it turned to stone;
and how its flames
burnt the heart? Whatever happens
everyone is so cosy with it, so used to it.
You are all happy to share it with me.
And yet it is always my own.

It almost wolfed my soul.
It deforms my fate.
But one day I shall break the silence,
in order to call death to the pillory.

APPENDIX 3:
CHRONOLOGY

YEAR	SHOSTAKOVICH: LIFE AND WORKS	CONTEMPORARY SOVIET MUSIC	CONTEMPORARY SOVIET CULTURE	CONTEMPORARY SOVIET LIFE
1915	8–9. First piano lessons.			
1916	9–10. Joins Gliasser's class. *The Soldier (Ode to Liberty)* for pf (not written down).			
1917	10–11. Bored by Gliasser's pedantic approach, studies with Rozanova at her house on the Fontanka. *Funeral March for the Victims of the Revolution* for pf (not written down). Gives first recital at Stoyunina's grammar school.		FEBRUARY: Bogdanov founds Proletkult with main base in Moscow. NOVEMBER: Lunacharsky made Commissar for Enlightenment. Mandelstam publishes poem supporting Kerensky and calling Lenin 'October's upstart'. Press censorship introduced.	FEBRUARY: workers' protests lead to creation of Provisional Government under Kerensky in Petrograd. OCTOBER 21–25: Bolshevik coup. DECEMBER 7: formation of the Cheka. WINTER: unrestrained anarchy in the cities – many killed.
1918	11–12. Playing for family friends. Fedin (hearing him at Grekov's): 'The bony boy is transformed at the piano into a bold musician with a man's strength and arresting rhythmic drive.' *The Gipsies* (opera) and *Rusalochka* (ballet), both destroyed in 1926.	MYASKOVSKY: Symphonies Nos. 4 and 5	MAY: Mayakovsky demands abolition of libraries, theatres, and galleries. JULY 16: Lenin suppresses Gorky's journal *New Life* for criticising the Bolsheviks. All non-Party papers and periodicals banned. DECEMBER 11: birth of Solzhenitsyn. ⸻ BLOK: *The Twelve* (poem)	JANUARY: Lenin orders summary shooting of 'bourgeois recalcitrants'. APRIL: Civil War breaks out. JUNE: first concentration camps. JULY: general collapse of industry. AUGUST 31: attempt on Lenin's life provokes Red Terror; Cheka sets out 'to exterminate the bourgeoisie'.

1919	12–13. Accepted full-time at Conservatoire (pf under Nikolayev). SUMMER: privately coached by Petrov in composition. AUTUMN: accepted into Steinberg's composition class. WINTER: Scherzo for orchestra in F sharp minor, Op. 1 (ded.: Steinberg).		MARCH: 'war against superstition'. Churches sacked and closed. NOVEMBER: programme of 'social prophylaxis' brings mass arrests of intelligentsia in Petrograd. —— EHRENBURG: *Julio Jurenito* (novel)	War Communism brings food and fuel shortages. Cities depopulate. SPRING: Tambov Rebellion begins. SUMMER: peasant revolts all over Russia. Genocidal suppression of Don Cossack uprising. AUTUMN: Red Army victorious on all fronts. Liquidation of the Cadets.
1920	13–14. SPRING: 8 Preludes, Op. 2. (1st ded.: Kustodiev, 2nd–5th ded.: sister Maria, 6th–8th ded.: Natasha Kuba, first girlfriend). Glazunov awards S. grant from Borodin Fund for student composers. MAY 8: portrait painted by Boris Kustodiev.	ROSLAVETS: Quartet No. 3 MYASKOVSKY: Piano Sonata No. 3	Meyerhold Theatre opens in Moscow. NOVEMBER 7: Yevreinov's *Storming of the Winter Palace* (spectacle). DECEMBER: Lenin bans Proletkult. —— ZAMYATIN: *We* (novel, unpublished) MAYAKOVSKY: *150 Million* (poem) AKHMATOVA: *Anno Domini MCMXI* (poems) ESENIN: *Mass for the Dead* (poem)	JANUARY: Entente blockade lifted. APRIL 23: Lenin's 50th birthday marks beginning of his cult. APRIL–OCTOBER: war with Poland. NOVEMBER: Civil War ends. Peasant War continues. Ten million have died since 1918.

1921

14–15. Suffers malnutrition. Glazunov requests extra rations for S. from Lunacharsky.
2 *Krylov Fables* for mezzo and orchestra, Op. 4. Orchestrates Rimsky-Korsakov's *I Waited for Thee in a Grotto*.
WINTER: begins Op. 3.

SHCHERBACHOV: *Inventions* (suite)
MYASKOVSKY: *Verses by Blok*

Zamyatin and Malevich complain of restrictions. Gorky goes abroad. Voronsky deputed to humour Fellow Travellers. Serapion Brothers form.
AUGUST 7: Blok dies, disillusioned with the Revolution.
AUGUST: Akhmatova's husband, poet Nikolai Gumilov, shot for alleged involvement in Kronstadt Uprising.

JANUARY: bread ration reduced. Riots and strikes. Mass arrests follow.
FEBRUARY: martial law in Petrograd.
MARCH: Kronstadt Uprising and Tambov Rebellion put down by Tukhachevsky. Peasant War ends. Left Opposition liquidated. Lenin decrees New Economic Policy (NEP).
SUMMER–WINTER: terrible famine kills five million.

1922

15–16. SPRING: finishes *Theme and Variations* in B flat. Op. 3 (ded.: N. Sokolov, polyphony teacher); *3 Fantastic Dances* for pf, Op. 5.
FEBRUARY: death of S.'s father.
MARCH: Suite in F sharp for 2 pfs, Op. 6, composed in his father's memory.
S.'s mother gets job as a cashier; sister Maria obtains pianist's diploma and finds employment at College of Choreography, thereby enabling S. to go on studying.

ROSLAVETS: Symphony

PILNYAK: *St Petersburg* (novel)
General suppression of the church. 8,000 priests, monks and nuns die. Chagall leaves Russia.
FEBRUARY: Orgburo resolution against 'bourgeois ideology' in literature.
MAY: further purge of intellectuals. Tsvetayeva leaves Russia, denouncing Bolshevik barbarism.
AUGUST: new censorship body, Glavlit, bans Zamyatin's *We*.
AUTUMN: deportation of 'reactionary intelligentsia'.

Harvest good. NEP brings recovery in the countryside. Kulaks, repressed in 1918, reappear as consequence of surplus incentive-schemes. Markets and entrepreneurial economy return to cities. Life regains its colour.
FEBRUARY 6: Cheka renamed the GPU.
MARCH: attending his final Congress, Lenin observes that the Party has enough political and economic power – 'what is lacking is culture'.

1923	16–17. SPRING: completes pf course and sketches symphony. Unable to continue owing to malnutrition and tuberculosis. SUMMER: recovers in Crimean sanatorium. Meets Tanya Glivenko, his fiancée till her marriage in 1929. AUTUMN: obliged to find a job, S. becomes accompanist in Bright Reel cinema, Petrograd. Piano Trio No. 1 in C minor, Op. 8 (ded.: Tanya). WINTER: begins Opp. 7 and 9.	MYASKOVSKY: Symphonies Nos 6 and 7 KASTALSKY: *Agricultural Symphony* SHEBALIN: Quartet No. 1	PASTERNAK: *My Sister Life* (poems) V. IVANOV: *Armoured Train 14–69* (story) PILNYAK: *The Naked Year* (novel) MANDELSTAM: *Tristia* (poems) Vakhtangov's *The Dybbuk* (theatre production) Formation of proletarian literary group October (forerunner of RAPP). Centrist Pereval group founded. ACM set up in Leningrad and RAPM formed in Moscow to oppose it.	APRIL 2: Stalin elected General Secretary of the Central Committee. MAY 26: Lenin suffers first stroke. JUNE: show-trial of the SRs. DECEMBER 16: Lenin's second stroke. DECEMBER 30: foundation of the USSR. The 'scissors crisis': cost of living in cities rises as that of the country falls. Wild fluctuation in prices. Chaos in industry produces surge in unemployment. MARCH 3: Lenin's third stroke ends his participation in government. JULY: adoption of Constitution of the USSR. AUGUST: wave of strikes and unrest among workers.
1924	17–18. SPRING: finishes 3 Pieces for vc and pf, Op. 9 (lost). S.'s mother ill with malaria. He plays in various cinemas to support his family. Unable to compose.	MYASKOVSKY: Piano Sonata No. 4 SHAPORIN: Piano Sonata No. 1 MOSOLOV: Piano Sonatas Nos. 1 a:1d 2	FURMANOV: *Chapayev* (novel) A. TOLSTOY: *Aelita* (novel) PASTERNAK: *Themes and Variations* (poems) Students strike for right of assembly and removal of indoctrination from university curricula. Many arrested in Leningrad.	JANUARY 21: death of Lenin. Stalin insists on embalming his body and building the Red Square mausoleum. Petrograd renamed Leningrad. Leadership

OCTOBER: finishes Scherzo for pf and orchestra in E flat, Op. 7. Begins symphony again.

NOVEMBER: S.'s mother attacked by robber outside family apartment.

DECEMBER: stops work on symphony to write Prelude for string octet, Op. 11a, in memory of his friend, the young poet Volodya Kurchavov.

1925

18–19. FEBRUARY: stops cinema work. Opp. 5, 10 and 11a accepted for publication.

MARCH 20: gives concert at Moscow Conservatoire (Opp. 1, 6 and 8).

JULY 1: finishes Symphony No. 1 in F minor, Op. 10. Graduates from Leningrad Conservatoire.

JULY: Scherzo for string octet, Op. 11b.

MYASKOVSKY: Symphony No. 8

MOSOLOV: Piano Sonatas Nos. 4 and 5; *Twilight* (symphonic poem)

SHAPORIN: *Paulina Goebel* (opera)

SHEBALIN: Symphony No. 1

EISENSTEIN: *Strike* (film)

FEDIN: *Cities and Years* (novel)

LEONOV: *The Badgers* (novel)

SERAFIMOVICH: *The Iron Flood* (novel)

ERDMAN: *The Warrant* (play)

BULGAKOV: *The White Guard* (unpublished novel)

MAYAKOVSKY: *Vladimir Ilyich Lenin* (poem)

FEBRUARY: CP meeting on 'the problem of the intelligentsia'. Bukharin calls for 'standardised intellectuals, as though from a factory'.

JULY: proletarian 'zealots' demand suppression of Fellow Travellers.

NOVEMBER 28: 'people's poet' Esenin hangs himself.

———

EISENSTEIN: *Battleship Potemkin* (film)

KULESHOV: *Death-Ray* (film)

GLADKOV: *Cement* (novel)

BULGAKOV: *Heart of a Dog* (story, published 1987)

passes to a triumvirate of Zinoviev, Kamenev and Stalin.

MARCH: currency reform stabilises economy. 'Lenin enrolment' swells Party by two-thirds – step from élite corps to mass organisation capable of running the country.

SUMMER: recovery. Confidence grows.

DECEMBER: Stalin's first reference to 'socialism in one country'.

Permissiveness rules: free sex, divorce and abortion, overruling of parental authority, educational experimentalism, etc.

APRIL: Bukharin exhorts peasants to 'enrich' themselves.

MAY: 'Menshevik students' arrested.

SEPTEMBER: Zinoviev attacks 'moral degeneracy' of NEP.

OCTOBER: Stalin's crony Voroshilov replaces Frunze as Minister of War.

WINTER: Zinoviev (Leningrad – for workers' world

			SHOLOKHOV: *Tales from the Don* ZAMYATIN: *The Flea* (play)	revolution) versus Stalin (Moscow – for peasants and socialism in one country).
1926	19–20. APRIL: recommended for higher degree course. MAY 12: première of Symphony No. 1 in Leningrad. Great success. MAY 26: plays pf reduction of 1st Symphony for Myaskovsky in Moscow. SUMMER: during creative crisis, destroys juvenilia, incl. Fantasy for 2 pfs; *In the Forest* for pf; *The Gipsies* (opera); *Rusalochka* (ballet); *Revolutionary Symphony*. AUTUMN: Piano Sonata No. 1, Op. 12.	SHCHERBACHOV: Symphony No. 2 (*Blok*) GNESIN: *1905–1917* ('symphonic monument') MOSOLOV: *Nocturnes*; Quartet No. 1; *Steel* (ballet); *Blok Poems* DESHEVOV: *The Rails* KREIN: *Lenin Ode* SHAPORIN: *Zamyatin Songs*	Zamyatin's *We* published in Prague. Zabolotsky founds Dadaist Oberiu group in Leningrad. OCTOBER 2: Mayakovsky demands legal reprisals against Bulgakov's play *The Days of the Turbins*. PUDOVKIN: *Mother* (film) BABEL: *Red Cavalry* (stories) KATAYEV: *The Embezzlers* (novel) FADEYEV: *The Rout* (novel) MAYAKOVSKY: *To Esenin* (poem) TSVETAYEVA: *Rat-Catcher* (poem)	Height of NEP. Stalin inches quietly towards total power. JULY: Zinoviev expelled from Politburo. Kirov becomes Leningrad boss. Death of Dzerzhinsky, head of GPU. (Replaced by Menzhinsky.) OCTOBER: new legal code attacks 'bourgeois family'. OCTOBER 23: Trotsky and Kamenev expelled from Politburo.
1927	20–21. JANUARY 9: plays 1st Piano Sonata in Moscow. JANUARY 28–30: competes in First International Chopin Competition (Warsaw). Lev Oborin wins. FEBRUARY: to Berlin. Meets Bruno Walter. Tours Poland. Returns to Leningrad and meets Prokofiev.	MYASKOVSKY: Symphonies Nos. 9 and 10 POPOV: Chamber Symphony ZHIVOTOV: Suite for Orchestra MOSOLOV: Piano Concerto No. 1 GLIER: *The Red Poppy* (ballet) KNIPPER: Symphony No. 1 KABALEVSKY: *3 Poems of Blok*	Bulgakov's *The Days of the Turbins* and Olesha's novella *Envy* the literary sensations of the year. Berg's *Wozzeck* staged in Leningrad. EISENSTEIN: *October* (film) PUDOVKIN: *The End of St Petersburg* (film)	Stalin creates 'war scare' to cover his campaign against his enemies. SUMMER: United Opposition (Trotsky, Zinoviev, Kamenev) criticise Stalin in the Central Committee. AUTUMN: protesting low prices, peasants hoard their grain.

APRIL: meets Sollertinsky.
Aphorisms for pf, Op. 13.
JUNE: Symphony No. 2 in B,
Op. 14 (*To October*).
Becomes musical director of
TRAM. Begins *The Nose*.
AUGUST: meets Nina Varzar.
NOVEMBER 5: première of
Symphony No. 2 in
Leningrad.
NOVEMBER 22: Walter
conducts 1st Symphony in
Berlin.

1928 21–22. SPRING: stays in
Moscow with Meyerhold as
head of his music
department. Writes Act II of
The Nose. Returns to
Leningrad.
MAY: finishes *The Nose*,
Op. 15.
JULY: completes postgraduate
course.
AUTUMN: *Tahiti Trot*, Op. 16;
2 Scarlatti Pieces, Op. 17;
first three *Japanese Romances*
(see 1932).
NOVEMBER 2: Stokowski gives
US première of 1st
Symphony in New York.
NOVEMBER 25: suite from *The
Nose* performed in Moscow.

MOSOLOV: *The Iron Foundry*
ZHIVOTOV: *Fragments for Nonet*
SHAPORIN: *The Flea* (suite)
KABALEVSKY: Piano Concerto
No. 1
KNIPER: Symphony No. 2
POLOVINKIN: *Last Sonata*
ROSLAVETS: *October* (cantata)

SUMMER: Central Committee
resolution against creative
'backsliding'. Eisenstein and
Pudovkin call for 'ideological
dictatorship' in the cinema.
The cultural revolution
begins. Gorky returns to
Russia.
DECEMBER: Central Com-
mittee decrees Communist
hegemony in art. RAPP
ascendant in literature.
———
PUDOVKIN: *Storm Over Asia*
(film)
ERDMAN: *The Suicide* (play)
ILF AND PETROV: *The Twelve
Chairs* (novel)

SHUB: *The Fall of the
Romanovs* (film)
DOVZHENKO: *Zvenigora* (film)
LEONOV: *The Thief* (novel)
PASTERNAK: *The Year 1905*
(poem)
BABEL: *Odessa Stories*; *Sunset*
(play)

SEPTEMBER: climax of political
feud. Demonstrations in
Moscow.
NOVEMBER 12: Trotsky and
Zinoviev expelled from the
Party.
DECEMBER: Zinoviev and
Kamenev banished to
Kaluga. Stalin reigns
supreme. End of legal
opposition; unification of
Party and state.

JANUARY: Trotsky internally
exiled to Alma-Ata. Stalin
visits Siberia and orders
'extraordinary measures' for
seizing grain.
MAY–JULY: Shakhty case
(first show-trial since 1922)
of 53 'wreckers' from the
Donbass. Press whips up
hate campaign against the
accused.
JULY: Comintern condemns
Social Democrats as 'social
fascists'.
OCTOBER 1: official beginning
of 1st Five-Year Plan.
NOVEMBER: food shortages
again. Bread-cards in
Leningrad.

1929

22–23. FEBRUARY: *New Babylon*, Op. 18 and *The Bedbug*, Op. 19. The latter causes a furious scandal.

MARCH: Cinema orchestras refuse to play *New Babylon*. Score shelved till Marius Constant performs it in Paris in 1975.

MARCH: 2 Pieces for Dressel's 'Columbus', Op. 23.

MAY: announces engagement to Nina.

JUNE: attends First All-Russian Musical Conference in Leningrad.

JUNE 16: concert performance of *The Nose* provokes savage controversy.

JULY: Symphony No. 3 in E flat, Op. 20 (*First of May*).

AUGUST: *The Shot*, Op. 24 (lost).

SEPTEMBER: begins *The Golden Age*.

MYASKOVSKY: 3 Pieces, Op. 32
SHEBALIN: Symphony No. 2

JANUARY: Voronsky arrested.

MAY: Bulgakov's plays banned. Propagation of religion becomes crime against state. Christians hounded.

SUMMER: leading historians arrested.

AUTUMN: orchestrated campaign of vilification against Zamyatin and Pilnyak. They are forbidden publication and their works are banned.

DECEMBER: proletarian groups awarded supreme power over Soviet culture. Mayakovsky joins RAPP. Commissariat for Enlightenment abolished.

EISENSTEIN: *The General Line* (film)

DOVZHENKO: *Arsenal* (film)
ROMANOV: *Comrade Kishyakov* (novel)

PILNYAK: *Mahogany* (novel, banned)

'Superindustrialisation' heralds Russia's new Iron Age. Collectivism is the watchword in every sphere of Soviet life. 'Shock-workers' appear.

JANUARY: Trotsky exiled from USSR.

APRIL: Stalin announces Shakhtyites ('bourgeois wreckers') at work in all branches of industry – they must be 'rooted out'. Party purged.

NOVEMBER: Stalin defeats right wing. Bukharin expelled from Politburo.

DECEMBER 21: extraordinary national 'celebrations' of Stalin's 50th birthday. Foundation of the 'cult of personality'.

DECEMBER 27: Stalin announces 'total collectivisation' and 'liquidation of the kulaks as a class'.

| 1930 | 23–24. JANUARY: controversial premières of *The Nose* and Symphony No. 3 in Leningrad.
FEBRUARY: finishes *The Golden Age*, Op. 22.
MARCH: declines commission from Bolshoi Theatre to write opera *Battleship Potemkin*.
APRIL: *Soil*, Op. 25 (lost).
JULY: holiday on Black Sea coast. Begins *The Bolt*.
SEPTEMBER: begins *Alone*.
OCTOBER: begins work on libretto for *Lady Macbeth*. *The Golden Age* premièred in Leningrad (failure). | KNIPPER: *The North Wind* (opera)
DESHEVOV: *Ice and Steel* (opera)
MYASKOVSKY: Quartets Nos. 1–3
KABALEVSKY: *Poem of Struggle* | Height of cultural revolution. Stalin writes in *Pravda*, demanding end to non-Bolshevik literature. Proletarians take over universities and conservatoires. Serapion Brothers, Pereval, Oberiu, and ACM repressed. All pre-1917 culture outlawed.
MARCH: Mayakovsky's *The Bathhouse* a failure. He is howled down during a recital at the House of Komosol.
APRIL 14: Mayakovsky shoots himself.
NOVEMBER: Gorky's *If the Enemy Does Not Surrender, He Must Be Destroyed*. Kharkov Congress on Proletarian Art calls for an end to 'individualism'. | JANUARY–FEBRUARY: six million peasants expropriated. They slaughter their livestock in protest and a drastic meat shortage ensues.
MARCH 2: Stalin's *Dizzy with Success* temporarily halts collectivisation.
MAY: end to trips abroad for Soviet citizens. Russia's borders sealed.
SEPTEMBER: closed trial of 'Famine Organizers' (agronomists accused of wrecking meat industry). All shot.
NOVEMBER–DECEMBER: show-trial of the 'Industrial Party' (group accused of wrecking factories and plotting to overthrow Stalin). All shot. |
| 1931 | 24–25. JANUARY: finishes *The Bolt*, Op. 27 and film score *Alone*, Op. 26.
APRIL: *Rule, Britannia!*, Op. 28. *The Bolt* premièred in Leningrad (failure).
SUMMER: filmscore *Golden Mountains*, Op. 30 and revue *Allegedly Murdered*, Op. 31. | SHEBALIN: *Lenin Symphony*
SHCHERBACHOV: Symphony No. 3 | Under proletarian rule, Soviet art is battered into compliance. Babel adopts 'genre of silence'. Pilnyak and Olesha conform. Nonconformist Mandelstam thrown out of Leningrad. Zamyatin writes to Stalin asking permission to emigrate; | Treason, wrecking, espionage 'discovered' everywhere. Persecution of technical intelligentsia superseded by hounding of 'gold-hoarders'. Torture now institutionalised.
JANUARY: major Party purge begins. |

S. pulls out of theatre contracts (including TRAM) and goes on holiday to the Black Sea.

OCTOBER: *Alone* released. Becomes international hit, largely due to S.'s score.

NOVEMBER: finishes Act I of *Lady Macbeth*, 4th *Japanese Romance*.

DECEMBER 5: interviewed by *New York Times* in Leningrad.

1932 25–26. FEBRUARY: begins symphony *From Karl Marx to Our Own Days*.

MARCH: finishes Act II of *Lady Macbeth*.

APRIL: finishes *6 Japanese Romances*, Op. 21. Joins new Composers' Union. Abandons *Karl Marx*.

MAY 13: marries Nina Varzar.

MAY 19: première of *Hamlet*, Op. 32, at Vakhtangov Theatre, Moscow, causes wild scandal.

JUNE: film score *Counterplan*, Op. 33. Score a popular success.

MYASKOVSKY: Symphonies Nos. 11 and 12 (*Collective Farm*)

MOSOLOV: Piano Concerto No. 2

DZERZHINSKY: Piano Concerto No. 1

ZHIVOTOV: *West* (choruses)

KABALEVSKY: Symphony No. 1

Gorky intercedes; permission granted. Zamyatin goes to Paris. Bulgakov's similar request denied.

———

AFINOGENOV: *Fear* (play)

SHAGINYAN: *Hydrocentral* (novel)

LEONOV: *Sot* (novel)

ILF AND PETROV: *The Golden Calf* (novel)

OLESHA: *A List of Assets* (play)

Gorky advises Stalin to dissolve the proletarian artistic organisations. Stalin orders private performance of Bulgakov's *Days of the Turbins*. Gorky leads 'brigade' of writers on propaganda trip to White Sea Canal.

APRIL 23: Central Committee resolution on restructuring of creative groups. Preferential treatment offered to 'co-operative' artists. Proletarian organisations banned.

MAY: launch of five-year-plan

MARCH: show-trial of 'All-Union Bureau of Mensheviks' (non-existent subversive party supposedly engaged in sabotaging the planning sector).

AUGUST: bread-queues in every city. G. B. Shaw, on flying visit, remarks 'there is no hunger in Russia'.

SEPTEMBER: beginning of ill-fated White Sea Canal project.

OCTOBER: Stalin usurps control of Party ideology and history.

Last year of the 1st Five-Year Plan. Exhaustion and disillusion set in (mood of rebellion similar to that of early 1921).

FEBRUARY: Stalin introduces wage-differentials, condemning equal pay as 'egalitarianism'.

SUMMER: only Party protest is from the 'Ryutin Platform'. Failing to move Politburo to have protesters shot, Stalin intensifies purge.

AUGUST: death penalty introduced for damaging state property.

AUGUST: Act III of Lady Macbeth.
DECEMBER: finishes Lady Macbeth of Mtsensk District, Op. 29. Begins 24 Preludes.

DOVZHENKO: A Simple Case (film)
SHOLOKHOV: Virgin Soil Upturned (Pt 1) (novel)
KATAYEV: Time, Forward! (novel)
LEONOV: Skutarevsky (novel)

for the elimination of religion.
—
SEPTEMBER: Pavlik Morozov declared a hero for denouncing his father.
DECEMBER: introduction of internal passports allows only townsfolk to travel (peasants bound to farms).

1933

26–27. MARCH: finishes 24 Preludes for pf, Op. 34. Begins Tale of a Priest and His Servant Balda (see 1934) and Piano Concerto No. 1.
APRIL: The Age of Gold criticised in Moscow press for frivolity.
JULY: finishes Piano Concerto No. 1 in C minor, Op. 35.
AUTUMN: preparations for staging of Lady Macbeth.
NOVEMBER: elected deputy to Leningrad's Oktyabrsky District soviet.

MYASKOVSKY: Symphonies Nos. 13 and 14
PROKOFIEV: Symphonic Song; Lieutenant Kije
KNIPPER: Symphony No. 3 (To the Far Eastern Red Army)
SHAPORIN: Symphony
KABALEVSKY: Symphony No. 2
KHRENNIKOV: Piano Concerto No. 1

Nobel Prize for Literature awarded to émigré novelist Ivan Bunin. Pasternak, appalled at events in the USSR, stops writing.
AUGUST: Mandelstam's Journey to Armenia denounced by Pravda.
NOVEMBER: Mandelstam privately circulates his Poem About Stalin, which describes him as 'murderer and peasant-slayer'.

Severe winter. Stalin continues to export grain to raise foreign currency. Famine in the Ukraine kills seven million. Eight million more die during collectivisation.
JANUARY: end of purge (one million victims since 1931). Beginning of 2nd Five-Year Plan.
MARCH: show-trial of Metro-Vickers 'spies'.
APRIL: White Sea Canal finished (at cost of a hundred thousand lives).

1934

27–28. WINTER: incidental music for The Human Comedy, Op. 37.
JANUARY: Lady Macbeth premièred in Leningrad and

MYASKOVSKY: Symphony No. 15
POPOV: Symphony No. 1
DZERZHINSKY: Piano Concerto No. 2

AFINOGENOV: The Lie (play)
PUDOVKIN: Deserter (film)

MAY 14: Mandelstam arrested. Pasternak and Akhmatova protest. He receives three years' internal exile.

JANUARY: 17th Party Congress ('Congress of Victors'). Stalin declares all targets fulfilled and Socialism achieved. His cult now

Moscow. Biggest success since Symphony No. 1.
FEBRUARY: Suite No. 1 for Dance Band.
SUMMER: film score *Love and Hate*, Op. 38.
AUGUST–SEPTEMBER: S. argues with Nina; temporarily they separate. Cello Sonata in D minor, Op. 40.
NOVEMBER: finishes *Tale of a Priest and His Servant Balda*, Op. 36.
DECEMBER: film scores *Maxim's Youth*, Op. 41 No. 1 and *Girlfriends*, Op. 41 No. 2.
DECEMBER 25: première of Cello Sonata in Leningrad.

1935
28–29, JANUARY: *The Limpid Stream*, Op. 39.
FEBRUARY 4–6: angry debate on Soviet symphonism in Composers' Union.
APRIL 3: S. defends *Lady Macbeth* against charges of Formalism in *Izvestia*.
APRIL 26: 5 Fragments, Op. 42.
JUNE: *The Limpid Stream* premièred in Leningrad. Success.
SEPTEMBER: concert tour of Turkey. Begins Symphony

SHEBALIN: Symphony No. 3; Quartet No. 2
KNIPPER: Symphony No. 4 (*Poem of the Fighting Komsomol*)
KABALEVSKY: Symphony No. 3
IPPOLITOV-IVANOV: Symphony No. 2
KOVAL: *Pushkiniana*

PROKOFIEV: Violin Concerto No. 2
A.KHACHATURIAN: Symphony No. 1
SHCHERBACHOV: Symphony No. 4 (*Izhorsk*)
SHEBALIN: Symphony No. 4 (*Heroes of Perekop*)
ZHIVTOV: *Kirov Elegy*
KHRENNIKOV: Symphony No. 1
KOVAL: *Tale of the Partisan*
KABALEVSKY: Piano Concerto No. 2

AUGUST: 1st Congress of Writers' Union. Mandelstam, Akhmatova, Bulgakov, Platonov and Zabolotsky are excluded. Gorky announces Socialist Realism as the new Soviet aesthetic. Critic Viktor Shklovsky denounces Dostoyevsky as a posthumous traitor to the Revolution.

VERTOV: *Three Songs of Lenin* (film)
POGODIN: *Aristocrats* (play)
SHOLOKHOV: *And Quiet Flows The Don* (novel)
OSTROVSKY: *How the Steel Was Tempered* (novel)

Stalin decrees that 'life has become more joyful'. Optimism in art now compulsory. Akhmatova's husband and son arrested. CP sponsors campaign against 'Meyerholdism'.
JULY: first gymnastic display in Red Square, following Nazi model.
DECEMBER: Stalin declares Mayakovsky 'the best, the most talented'. The poet's cult begins.

gargantuan. Radek eulogises him as 'great chief of toilers . . . wisest of the wise'. Zinoviev, Kamenev, and Bukharin are made to confess that Stalin always right. Sensing unease in the Party, Stalin prepares to move against it.
JULY: GPU renamed NKVD under Yagoda.
DECEMBER 1: Stalin engineers murder of rival Kirov in Leningrad. Forty thousand Leningraders deported to Siberia for conspiracy to assassinate. The Great Terror begins.

FEBRUARY: beginning of new purge of the Party. Mass-arrests, shootings and deportations. Gorky, arguing that Terror is counter-productive, falls out of favour with Stalin.
Attempting to leave the country, he finds his visa withdrawn.
MAY 1: huge intensification of the Stalin-cult. Massive floral pictures of him carried in Red Square. New slogans portray him as 'good and

No. 4.
NOVEMBER: *The Limpid Stream* premiered in Moscow.
DECEMBER: new production of *Lady Macbeth* opens in Moscow.

1936
29–30. JANUARY 28: *Pravda* attacks *Lady Macbeth*.
FEBRUARY 6: *Pravda* attacks *The Limpid Stream*.
FEBRUARY 10/13/15: 'stormy debates' in Composers' Union around the *Pravda* controversy. S. condemned as a Formalist.
MAY 20: finishes Symphony No. 4 in C minor, Op. 43.
MAY 30: daughter Galya born.
OCTOBER–NOVEMBER: incidental music for Afinogenov's *Salute to Spain*, Op. 44 (play banned soon after opening in Moscow).
DECEMBER: film of *Tale of a Priest* stopped in production. Symphony No. 4 withdrawn from rehearsal.

DZERZHINSKY: *The Quiet Don* (opera)
KNIPPER: Symphony No. 5

PROKOFIEV: *Romeo and Juliet*; *Peter and the Wolf*
MYASKOVSKY: Symphony No. 16 (*The Aviators*)
A.KHACHATURIAN: Piano Concerto
SHEBALIN: *Overture on Mari Themes*
KNIPPER: Symphony No. 6 (*Red Cavalry*)

DOVZHENKO: *Aerograd* (film)
S./G. VASILIEV: *Chapayev* (film)
SEREBRYAKOVA: *Marx's Youth* (novel)
MANDELSTAM: *First Voronezh Notebook* (unpublished)

Criticism of Shostakovich triggers a general wave of attacks on culture. Gide, visiting USSR, condemns intellectual slavery under Stalinism.
JANUARY: *Pravda* damns 'unscientific' historians, so endorsing the trend towards falsification of the past.
FEBRUARY: Bulgakov's *Molière*, first banned in 1930, taken off after 7 nights at the Moscow Arts Theatre.
Pravda criticizes 'cacophony' in architecture.
MARCH: *Pravda* castigates artistic 'daubers' and theatrical 'glitter'.
JUNE: Gorky dies (or is murdered).
AUGUST: *Pravda* declares Serebryakova and Pilnyak enemies of the people.

KATAYEV: *Lonely White Sail* (novel)

kind', 'Beloved Leader'.
AUGUST 30: shockworker A. Stakhanov overfulfills his norm by fifteen times (a publicity stunt). Birth of the 'Stakhanovite' movement.

The Terror continues. With millions disappearing, demoralisation sets in and society begins to atomise.
JUNE 27: anti-abortion law and new family and marriage codes.
SUMMER: massive wave of arrests.
AUGUST 19–24: show-trial of the so-called 'United Centre' (Zinoviev, Kamenev and 14 'accomplices') for murder of Kirov and planned murder of Stalin. Mass-hysteria surrounds the proceedings; papers are full of letters demanding death-penalty for 'these Gestapo agents'. All shot.
SEPTEMBER: Yagoda arrested for being 'four years late' in uncovering the 'Trotskyite-Zinovievite bloc'. He is replaced by Yezhov.

1937	30–31. WINTER: film score *Maxim's Return*, Op. 45. JANUARY: *4 Pushkin Romances*, Op. 46 and film score *Volochayevsk Days*, Op. 48. SPRING: Leningrad Conservatoire invites S. to give tutorials in composition and orchestration. APRIL–JULY: Symphony No. 5 in D minor, Op. 47. AUTUMN: drafts operetta *The Twelve Chairs* (scrapped 1938). NOVEMBER 21: Symphony No. 5 premièred in Leningrad. Great success.	PROKOVIEV: *Cantata for the 20th Anniversary of the Revolution*. MYASKOVSKY: Symphonies Nos. 17 and 18, Quartet No. 4. A.KHACHATURIAN: *Song of Stalin* (cantata). DZERZHINSKY: *Virgin Soil Upturned* (opera). CHISHKO: *Battleship Potemkin* (opera).	Cultural purge continues. Dovzhenko and Eisenstein reprimanded. Meyerhold vilified. 100 films stopped in production. Half the latest plays taken off and 20 theatres closed. JANUARY: at the end of his tether, Mandelstam writes conformist *Ode to Stalin*. His gesture ignored. FEBRUARY: Eugenia Ginzburg arrested. ROMM: *Lenin in October* (film) BULGAKOV: *Black Snow* (novel, unpublished till 1965) MANDELSTAM: *Second and Third Voronezh Notebooks* (unpublished)	Apex of the Terror. Five million deported, half a million shot. Stalin calls for 'intensified struggle' against the 'enemies of the People'. *Pravda* accuses Yagoda of having run the labour camps 'like health-resorts'. JANUARY 23–30: second Moscow show-trial (of Pyatakov, Radek and their 'accomplices'), 13 shot. APRIL: end of 2nd Five-Year Plan. JUNE: arrest of Tukhachevsky and 80,000 senior military. Many are executed without trial.
1938	31–32. JANUARY 29: Symphony No. 5 premièred in Moscow. MARCH: Toscanini gives US première of 5th Symphony in New York. APRIL: begins choral 'Lenin' symphony (never finished). MAY 10: son Maxim born. MAY–JULY: Quartet No. 1 in C, Op. 49.	PROKOFIEV: Cello Concerto No. 1; *Alexander Nevsky*. MYASKOVSKY: Violin Concerto. SHAPORIN: *The Field of Kolikovo* (cantata). KABALEVSKY: *Colas Breugnon* (opera). KNIPPER: Symphony No. 7 (*Miliary*); *Marya* (opera). ZHELOBINSKY: *Mother* (opera). SHEBALIN: Quartet No. 3.	Cultural purge continues. Pilnyak shot as Japanese spy, Mandelstam, Olesha and Zabolotsky imprisoned. Kirshon 'disappears'. Bulgakov finishes *The Master and Margarita* (unpublished till 1966). JANUARY: Meyerhold Theatre closed. MARCH: second arrest of	Wholesale massacre of officials in every walk of life (and increasingly of security forces too). At least two million shot. MARCH: show-trial of so-called 'Right-Trotskyite Centre' (Rykov, Bukharin, Yagoda and others). 18 shot. SEPTEMBER: Stalin's *History of the Communist Party of the*

	Shostakovich's life	Music	Arts	Historical events
	AUTUMN: Suite No. 2 for Dance Band and film scores *Friends*, Op. 52, *The Man With a Gun*, Op. 53, and *The Vyborg Side*, Op. 50.	PROKOVIEV: *Semyon Kotko* (opera); *Hail to Stalin* (cantata) MYASKOVSKY: Symphony No. 19; Quartet No. 5; *Salutation Overture* KHRENNIKOV: *Into the Storm* (opera) A.KHACHATURIAN: *Happiness* (ballet)	Akhmatova's son Lev Gumilov (see 1935). DECEMBER: Mandelstam dies in transit camp near Vladivostok. ——— EISENSTEIN: *Alexander Nevsky* (film) GERASIMOV: *Komsomolsk* (film) DONSKOI: *Childhood of Gorky* (film)	*Soviet Union: Short Course.* DECEMBER: Yezhov replaced by Beria. The Terror abates.
1939	32–33. FEBRUARY: film score *The Great Citizen (Part 2)*, Op. 55. MARCH: film score *The Silly Little Mouse*, Op. 56 (lost). APRIL: begins Symphony No. 6. MAY 23: confirmed as professor at Leningrad Conservatoire. OCTOBER: finishes Symphony No. 6 in B minor, Op. 54. NOVEMBER 5: Symphony No. 6 premièred in Leningrad. Begins re-orchestration of *Boris Godunov*. DECEMBER: elected to Leningrad city soviet.		Cultural purge eases. Tretyakov shot. Kornilov 'disappears'. Akhmatova begins *Requiem*. MAY: Babel arrested. JUNE: Meyerhold arrested, tortured. Tsvetayeva returns to Russia. SEPTEMBER: Tsvetayeva's husband and daughter arrested. DECEMBER: Meyerhold dies in prison. ——— DOVZHENKO: *Shchors* (film) GERASIMOV: *Uchitel* (film) ROMM: *Lenin in 1918* (film) DONSKOI: *My Apprenticeships* (film)	Mass-arrests cease. Around seven million arrested since 1936. The Terror blamed on the Trotskyites. JANUARY: Yezhov arrested and charged with trying to kill Stalin. MAY: Molotov replaces Litvinov. AUGUST: Russia and Nazi Germany sign non-aggression pact. SEPTEMBER: joint Nazi–Soviet invasion of Poland. NOVEMBER: Russia invades Finland. DECEMBER: Russia expelled from the League of Nations.

| 1940 | 33–34. Continues work on *Boris Godunov*, Op. 58, No. 1, finishing score in June.
MAY 20: Order of the Red Banner of Labour (for film work).
JULY–SEPTEMBER: Piano Quintet in G minor, Op. 57. AUTUMN: incidental music for *King Lear*, Op. 58, No. 2, 3 Pieces for vn, and film score *The Adventures of Korzinkina*, Op. 59. Opera *Katyusha Maslova* begun and abandoned.
NOVEMBER 23: Piano Quintet premièred in Moscow. Great success. | MYASKOVSKY: Symphonies Nos. 20 and 21; Quartet No. 6
PROKOVIEV: Piano Sonata No. 6
A.KHACHATURIAN: Violin Concerto
KABALEVSKY: *The Comedians* (suite)
SHEBALIN: Violin Concerto; Quartet No. 4
DZERZHINSKY: *The Storm* (opera)
SVIRIDOV: Symphony No. 1 | Bulgakov dies. Pasternak translates *Hamlet and Sonnet 66*.
MARCH: Akhmatova completes *Requiem* (published in Russia in 1987).
———
SHOLOKHOV: *The Don Flows Home to the Sea* (novel)
ZOSHCHENKO: *The Poker* (story)
YUTKEVICH: *Yakov Sverdlov* (film)
KULESHOV: *Siberians* (film)
DONSKOI: *My Universities* (film) | FEBRUARY: Nazi–Soviet trade agreement. Russia supplies Germany with food and raw materials.
MARCH 12: Finland's small reservist force surrenders, having inflicted half a million casualties on ill-led Red Army three times its size.
APRIL: NKVD massacre 15,000 Polish POWs in Katyn forest.
AUGUST: Russia annexes Lithuania, Latvia and Estonia.
AUGUST 20: Trotsky assassinated by Soviet agent in Mexico. |
| 1941 | 34–35. MARCH: *King Lear* premièred in Leningrad. Two performances of re-orchestrated *Vienna Blood*.
APRIL: tours, playing Piano Quintet and 1st Piano Concerto.
MAY: Piano Quintet wins Stalin Prize, First Grade. 6th Symphony harshly attacked at meeting of Composers' Union in Leningrad. | PROKOVIEV: *The Year 1941* (suite); *Betrothal in a Monastery* (opera); Quartet No. 2
MYASKOVSKY: Symphonies Nos. 22 and 23; Quartet No. 7
KABALEVSKY: *Parade of Youth* (cantata)
DZERZHINSKY: *Blood of the People* (opera) | AUGUST: Tsvetaeva hangs herself.
SEPTEMBER: Akhmatova's radio speech to the women of Leningrad.
OCTOBER: Akhmatova and Lydia Chukovskaya evacuated to Tashkent, there joining Nadezhda Mandelstam.
NOVEMBER: Vera Inber notes in her diary that people of Leningrad reduced to eating their pets. | Stalin ignores warnings that Hitler about to attack USSR.
JUNE 22: Germany invades Russia.
JUNE 28: fall of Minsk.
JULY 3: Stalin appeals to Russian people to defend the Motherland.
JULY 19: fall of Smolensk.
AUGUST: development of the 'Kiev pocket'.
SEPTEMBER 19: fall of Kiev. |

JULY 12–14: *Vow of the People's Commissar*, 27 arrangements for front-line ensembles (Beethoven, Bizet, Dargomyzhsky, etc.).
JULY 15: *The Fearless Regiments Are on the Move* (song).
LATE JULY: begins 7th Symphony.
SEPTEMBER 17: S. broadcasts to citizens of Leningrad.
OCTOBER 2: S. and family flown out to Moscow.
OCTOBER 15–22: in transit by train to Kuibyshev.
DECEMBER 27: finishes Symphony No. 7 in C, Op. 60 (*To the City of Leningrad*).
DECEMBER 28: begins *The Gamblers* (opera).

FADEYEV: *Last of the Udege* (novel)
BORODIN: *Dmitri Donskoi* (novel)
A. TOLSTOI: *Ivan the Terrible Part I* (play)
PUDOVKIN: *General Suvarov* (film)
GERASIMOV/KALATOZOV: *The Invincible* (film)

SEPTEMBER–OCTOBER: German drive on Moscow. Battle of Vyazma – Soviet armies defeated. Leningrad besieged. German advance slows down.
DECEMBER: German patrols in sight of Moscow. Russians defend as the city is evacuated. German advance halts in −40°F temperatures.
DECEMBER 5–6: Russians attack in front of Moscow, driving Germans back. Red Army losses for 1941: three million (half of them prisoners).

1942

35–36. MARCH 5: 7th Symphony premiered in Kuibyshev.
MARCH 29: 7th Symphony premiered in Moscow.
MAY: begins *English Poets*.
SUMMER: visits Sollertinsky in Novosibirsk.
AUGUST 9: Leningrad premiere of 7th Symphony.

PROKOFIEV: Piano Sonata No. 7
A.KHACHATURIAN: *Gayane* (ballet)
MYASKOVSKY: Quartet No. 8
SHEBALIN: Quartet No. 5 (*Slavonic*)
KABALEVSKY: *The Mighty Homeland*; *The People's Avengers* (cantatas)

INBER: *The Pulkovo Meridian* (poem)
EHRENBURG: *The Fall of Paris* (novel)
LEONOV: *Invasion* (play)
S/G. VASILIEV: *Defence of Tsaritsin* (film)
DONSKOI: *How the Steel was Tempered* (film)

JANUARY–FEBRUARY: NKVD renamed NKGB under Beria. Russian counter-offensive pushes German line back everywhere except around Leningrad.
MARCH–MAY: Russians halt. Stalemate.
APRIL: end of 3rd Five-Year Plan.

AUGUST: *Native Leningrad*, Op. 63, and *Solemn March* for military band.
OCTOBER: Honoured Artist of the RSFSR.
OCTOBER 25: finishes *6 Romances on Verses by English Poets*, Op. 62.
DECEMBER: abandons *The Gamblers*. Falls ill with gastric typhoid.

1943
36–37. JANUARY 11: still ill, begins 2nd Piano Sonata.
MARCH 18: finishes Piano Sonata No. 2 in B minor, Op. 61, in a sanatorium near Moscow.
APRIL: moves to Moscow with Nina. Children remain in Kuibyshev.
MAY: *8 British and American Folksongs*.
JULY 1: begins 8th Symphony.
AUGUST: *Song of the Red Army* (with Khachaturian for National Anthem competition).
SEPTEMBER 9: finishes Symphony No. 8 in C minor, Op. 65.
NOVEMBER 4: Moscow première of 8th Symphony.

KARAYEV: *Quartet No. 1*
KOVAL: *Emelyan Pugachev* (opera); *National Holy War* (oratorio)
VAYNBERG: Symphony No. 1
KHRENNIKOV: Symphony No. 2

PROKOFIEV: *War and Peace* (Pt 1); *Ballad of an Unknown Boy* (cantata)
MYASKOVSKY: Symphony No. 24; Quartet No. 9
SHEBALIN: Quartet No. 6
ZHIVOTOV: *Happiness* (song-cycle)
KNIPPER: Symphony No. 8; Violin Concerto
KARAYEV: Symphony No. 1
GLIER: Coloratura Concerto
A.KHACHATURIAN: Symphony No. 2

ZOSHCHENKO: *Before Sunrise* (autobiography)
A.TOLSTOY: *The Way Through Hell* (novel); *Ivan the Terrible Pt II* (play)
YUTKEVICH: *The Good Soldier Schweik* (film)

MAY–JUNE: Germans begin new attack. Russians defeated at Kharkov. Fall of Sevastopol.
JUNE–JULY: German summer offensive. Fall of Voronezh.
JULY–AUGUST: Germans break through and advance on Stalingrad.
AUGUST–DECEMBER: Battle of Stalingrad. German army enclosed.

JANUARY 12–18: partial lifting of siege of Leningrad. 630,000 of the city's occupants have starved to death since the end of 1941.
FEBRUARY 2: Germans surrender at Stalingrad. Start of Russian winter offensive.
FEBRUARY–MARCH: attack and counter-attack. Manstein checks the Russian advance.
MARCH–JUNE: lull during the thaw.
JULY–AUGUST: world's largest tank-battle at Kursk. Germans defeated.
JULY–NOVEMBER: Russian offensive recaptures Kiev and Smolensk.
NOVEMBER: Teheran conference.

1944	37–38. FEBRUARY 15: hearing of death of Sollertinsky, begins 2nd Piano Trio. APRIL: the children join S. and Nina in Moscow. JUNE: film score *Zoya*, Op. 64. AUGUST 13: finishes Piano Trio No. 2 in E minor, Op. 67. SEPTEMBER: Quartet No. 2 in A, Op. 68 NOVEMBER 14: Moscow première of 2nd Piano Trio and 2nd Quartet. DECEMBER 6: *Children's Notebook* for pf, Op. 69, and *Russian River* (spectacle), Op. 66.	PROKOFIEV: Symphony No. 5; Violin Sonata No. 2; Piano Sonata No. 8; *Cinderella* (ballet) SHAPORIN: *Battle for the Russian Land* (cantata) POPOV: Symphony No. 2 (*Fatherland*) MYASKOVSKY: Piano Sonatas Nos. 5 and 6 ZHIVOTOV: *Songs of Leningrad* A.KHACHATURIAN: *Masquerade* (suite)	MAY: Akhmatova gives recital in Moscow. Standing ovation greets her appearance. Stalin demands to know who 'organised' the applause. ——— SIMONOV: *The Last Summer* (novel) EISENSTEIN: *Ivan the Terrible Pt 1* (film) DONSKOI: *Rainbow* (film)	JANUARY 27: final liberation of Leningrad. FEBRUARY–JUNE: continuous fighting. JUNE–JULY: Russian summer offensive breaks through at Smolensk. JULY 3: recapture of Minsk. JULY–AUGUST: Red Army drives into Poland. AUGUST–SEPTEMBER: Warsaw uprising. Under Stalin's orders, Russians hold off, allowing Germans to crush the insurgents. SEPTEMBER–DECEMBER: Russians drive into Eastern Europe. Armed national resistance against them begins.
1945	38–39. JULY–AUGUST: Symphony No. 9 in E flat, Op. 70. NOVEMBER 3: 9th Symphony premiered in Leningrad. DECEMBER: film score *Simple Folk*, Op. 71, and incidental music for *Victorious Spring*, Op. 72.	MYASKOVSKY: Quartets Nos. 10 and 11; Cello Concerto; Sinfonietta No. 2 PROKOFIEV: *Ode to the End of War* DZERZHINSKY: Piano Concerto No. 3 KABALEVSKY: Quartet No. 2 SVIRIDOV: Piano Trio MOSOLOV: Cello Concerto	TVARDOVSKY: *Vasily Tyorkin* (poem) FADEYEV: *The Young Guard* (novel, first version) ZOSHCHENKO: *Adventures of a Monkey* (story) FEDIN: *Early Joys* (novel)	JANUARY–FEBRUARY: Russians enter Germany. FEBRUARY: Yalta conference. APRIL–MAY: final attack on Berlin. MAY 2: fall of Berlin. MAY 8: Germans surrender. JULY–AUGUST: Potsdam conference. SEPTEMBER 3: end of Second World War.

1946	39–40. JANUARY 26 – AUGUST 2: Quartet No. 3 in F, Op. 73. SEPTEMBER 4: *Simple Folk* banned as 'unSoviet and anti-People'. SEPTEMBER 25: Order of Lenin. DECEMBER 16: 3rd Quartet premièred in Moscow.	PROKOFIEV: *Ivan the Terrible*; Violin Sonata No. 1 MYASKOVSKY: Symphony No. 25 A. KHACHATURIAN: Cello Concerto SHEBALIN: *Moscow* (cantata) GLIER: Cello Concerto VAYNBERG: Symphony No. 2 KARAYEV: Symphony No. 2; Quartet No. 2 KOVAL: *Defenders of Sevastopol* (opera) KNIPPER: Symphony No. 10	Pasternak begins *Doctor Zhivago*. JUNE: Pasternak and Akhmatova give recital in Moscow. Ovations. AUGUST: Zhdanov attacks Akhmatova and Zoshchenko for 'reactionary individualism'. They are expelled from the Writers' Union. SEPTEMBER: Zhdanov attacks Pudovkin and Eisenstein. ——— EISENSTEIN: *Ivan the Terrible Pt 2* (film, not released till 1958)	NKGB renamed MGB under Beria. MARCH: Churchill's 'Iron Curtain' speech at Fulton, Missouri. Cold War begins. Uprisings in Gulag. AUTUMN: beginning of campaign against 'kowtowing to the West'. DECEMBER: Russia builds its first nuclear reactor.
1947	40–41. FEBRUARY: elected chairman of Leningrad Composers' Union. MAY: attends Prague Festival. SUMMER: elected Leningrad deputy to Supreme Soviet of RSFSR; *Poem of the Motherland* (cantata), Op. 74; film score *Pirogov*, Op. 76. AUTUMN: begins *The Young Guard*; 3 Pieces for Orchestra (ms. only). OCTOBER: begins 1st Violin Concerto.	PROKOFIEV: Symphony No. 6; *War and Peace* (Pt 2); *Thirty Years* ('festive poem') MYASKOVSKY: Quartet No. 12; Violin Sonata; *The Kremlin at Night* (cantata) A. KHACHATURIAN: Symphony No. 3 KABALEVSKY: *The Taras Family* (opera) POPOV: Symphony No. 3 SHEBALIN: Piano Trio	Spate of publications claiming all inventions credited to Westerners actually made by obscure Russians. MARCH: Pasternak, Gladkov, and Olga Berggolts publically criticised. JUNE: Zhdanov begins witch-hunt of non-Lysenko biologists. ——— EHRENBURG: *The Storm* (novel) YUTKEVICH: *Light Over Russia* (film, banned)	The post-war freeze intensifies. Beginning of the Zhdanovshchina. WINTER – SPRING: severe famine in the Ukraine and southern USSR. SEPTEMBER: founding of Cominform. NOVEMBER – DECEMBER: drive against foreigners and those 'associated' with them.

| 1948 | 41–42. JANUARY: Zhdanov chairs the First Congress of the Composers' Union in Moscow. FEBRUARY 10: Resolution 'On the Opera *The Great Friendship* by V. Muradeli': Shostakovich, Prokofiev, Myaskovsky, Popov, Khachaturian, and Shebalin condemned as 'Formalists'. S. demoted in Composers' Union. MARCH: finishes Violin Concerto No. 1 in A minor, Op. 77; cantata *Portrait Gallery*; film score *The Young Guard*, Op. 75. SUMMER: film score *Michurin*, Op. 78; *From Jewish Folk Poetry*, Op. 79. AUTUMN: film score *Meeting on the Elbe*, Op. 80. S. sacked from his teaching posts. OCTOBER: People's Artist of the RSFSR. | PROKOFIEV: *The Story of a Real Man* (opera) MYASKOVSKY: Symphony No. 26 SHCHERBACHOV: Symphony No. 5 (*Russian*) K. KHACHATURIAN: *Blossom and Prosper, Youth* (cantata) SHEBALIN: Quartet No. 7 KNIPPER: *On Lake Baikal* (opera) KABALEVSKY: Violin Concerto | Gladkov arrested, Mikhoëls murdered. SEPTEMBER: Anti-Fascist League dissolved. Jewish newspapers closed. Yiddish writers arrested. FEDIN: *No Ordinary Summer* (novel) AZHAYEV: *Far From Moscow* (novel) | Mass-arrests for 'spying', 'revealing state secrets', 'kowtowing to the West', 'praising American technology' and so forth. Re-arrests of those given ten-year sentences in 1937–8 (the 'repeaters'). Arrests also of children of those in the Gulag. AUGUST: Lysenko enforces 'Michurinism' over genetics at Soviet Congress of Agricultural Sciences. AUGUST 31: Death of Zhdanov. OCTOBER: 'The Great Stalinist Plan for Remaking Nature' – 15-year scheme to change climate in Central Asia by planting new forests. (Abandoned in 1953.) |
| 1949 | 42–43. FEBRUARY: Khrennikov leads attacks on 'Formalist' critics and musicologists (especially those friendly to S.). | PROKOFIEV: *The Stone Flower* (ballet); Cello Sonata VAYNBERG: Symphony No. 3 TAKTAKISHVILI: Symphony No. 1 | Akhmatova's son Lev Gumilov arrested for the third time and sent to the camps. Pasternak's mistress Olga Ivinskaya deported to | Anti-Semitism becomes official in the USSR: the campaign against 'rootless cosmopolitanism'. JANUARY: *Komsomolskaya* |

MARCH: to New York with Soviet Committee for the Defence of Peace. Plays scherzo from 5th Symphony at Madison Square Garden. SUMMER: *Song of the Forests* (oratorio), Op. 81; film score *The Fall of Berlin*, Op. 82; Quartet No. 4 in D, Op. 83.

MYASKOVSKY: Symphony No. 27; Viola Sonata; Piano Sonatas Nos. 7–9; Quartet No. 13
KNIPPER: *Source of Life* (opera)
GLIER: *The Bronze Horseman* (ballet)
KABALEVSKY: Cello Concerto No. 1
POPOV: Symphony No. 4

Siberia.
JANUARY: *Pravda* attacks 'anti-patriotic' (Jewish) theatre critics.
FEBRUARY: Ehrenburg banned from publication (as a Jew).

Pravda claims the aeroplane a Russian invention.
SPRING: show-trial and sensational 'confession' of Cardinal Mindszenty in Hungary. (He had been tortured.)
SEPTEMBER: first Soviet A-bomb tested.
WINTER: the 'Leningrad Affair'. Beria and Malenkov liquidate Zhdanov's clique in the Party. Hundreds shot.

1950

43–44. SPRING: to Warsaw for 2nd World Peace Congress.
JULY: Bach bicentenary in Leipzig.
AUGUST: *2 Lermontov Songs*, Op. 84; film score *Belinsky*, Op. 85. Starts giving recitals to earn money.
OCTOBER 10: begins 24 Preludes and Fugues.

PROKOFIEV: *On Guard for Peace* (oratorio)
MOSOLOV: *Kubanskaya*
SVIRIDOV: *Land of My Fathers*

Akhmatova writes the conformist cycle *Glory To Peace*, praising Stalin, in hope of getting her son released from the Gulag. She fails.
SUMMER: repression of 'perfidious Zionism' in Soviet biology.

Camp revolts provoke mass-executions in the Gulag. Many political show-trials in Eastern Europe.

1951

44–45. FEBRUARY 25: finishes 24 Preludes and Fugues for pf, Op. 87.
SPRING: tours Baltic states, giving recitals.
SUMMER: *4 Dolmatovsky Songs*, Op. 86; *10 Poems on*

PROKOFIEV: *The Volga Meets the Don* ('festive poem')
SHEBALIN: *Sinfonietta on Russian Themes*
SHCHEDRIN: *Collective Farm Holiday*

EHRENBURG: *The Ninth Wave* (novel)
FADEYEV: *The Young Guard* (novel, second version)

More show-trials in Eastern Europe. Revolts in the Gulag continue.

Year		Other composers	Events
	Revolutionary Texts for chorus, Op. 88; film score *The Unforgettable Year 1919*, Op. 89. OCTOBER 10: *10 Poems* premièred in Moscow.		Execution of members of the Jewish Anti-Fascist Committee (arrested in 1948). Stalin, now paranoid, is increasingly obsessed with imaginary conspiracies. OCTOBER: the 19th Party Congress. Stalin reorganises the Party in preparation for a major purge.
1952	45–46. SPRING: *The Sun Shines Over Our Motherland* (cantata), Op. 90; *4 Pushkin Monologues*, Op. 91. Tours Transcaucasus, giving recitals. APRIL: to E. Germany for Beethoven Festival. SEPTEMBER 7 – NOVEMBER 1: Quartet No. 5 in B flat, Op. 92. NOVEMBER: *7 Dances of the Dolls*. DECEMBER: attends Vienna Peace Congress. DECEMBER 23/28: Tatiana Nikolayeva premières 24 Preludes and Fugues (1950–51) in Leningrad.	PROKOFIEV: Symphony-Concerto ('Sinfonia concertante'); Symphony No. 7 A. KHACHATURIAN: *Battle for Stalingrad* (suite) GLIER: *Taras Bulba* (ballet) KNIPPER: Cello Concerto KABALEVSKY: Piano Concerto No. 3 KARAYEV: *Seven Beauties* (ballet) VOLKONSKY: *Dead Souls*; *The Vision of the World* (cantatas)	Climax of 'Lysenkoist' attack on legitimate science: denial of Theory of Relativity ('reactionary Einsteinism'). APRIL: literary scene so dead that *Pravda* calls for new Soviet Gogols and Saltykov-Shchedrins to revive social satire so as to illuminate shortcomings of Soviet society. Few writers take the bait. Those who do are attacked for 'anti-patriotic slander' and arrested.
1953	46–47. JUNE 4: première of film *Belinsky* (1950). JULY–OCTOBER 25: Symphony No. 10 in E minor, Op. 93. NOVEMBER 13: 5th Quartet premièred in Moscow. DECEMBER 3: 4th Quartet	SHAPORIN: *The Decembrists* (opera) A. KHACHATURIAN: *The Widow of Valencia* (suite) VOLKONSKY: Concerto for Orchestra TAKTAKISHVILI: Symphony No. 2	Pasternak finishes *Dr Zhivago*. NOVEMBER: *Pravda* advocates a 'broad-minded' view on Socialist Realism. Beginning of the first 'thaw'. DECEMBER: Pomerantsev's *On Sincerity in Literature* published in *Novy Mir*, JANUARY: 'Vigilance' campaign. The 'Doctors' Plot' (intended beginning of new era of mass terror). MARCH 5: Stalin dies. Succeeded by a triumvirate of Malenkov, Beria and Molotov. Power-struggle

premièred in Moscow.
DECEMBER: Concertino for 2 pfs, Op. 94.
DECEMBER 17: 10th Symphony premièred in Leningrad. Initial response mixed. Discussions convened to 'determine' whether it is failure or success.

1954 47–48. JANUARY 20: Concertino premièred in Moscow.
MARCH: 29–30: angry debates about 10th Symphony in Composers' Union.
APRIL: Incidental music for Kozintsev's *Hamlet*.
SUMMER: film score *Seven Rivers*, Op. 95.
AUTUMN: *Festival Overture* Op. 96 (for 37th anniversary of October).
OCTOBER: People's Artist of the USSR.
DECEMBER 5: death of Nina.

A.KHACHATURIAN: *Spartacus* (ballet)
SHCHEDRIN: Piano Concerto No. 1
KNIPPER: Symphony No. 14
VOLKONSKY: *Capriccio*
KABALEVSKY: Symphony No. 4

(seminal essay deploring Socialist Realist 'prettifying' of reality.)

LEONOV: *The Russian Forest* (novel)
YEVTUSHENKO: *Winter Station* (poem)

———

Short Philosophic Dictionary condemns 'the reactionary pseudo-science of cybernetics'.
MARCH: Ehrenburg's novel *The Thaw* is published.
DECEMBER: Tvardovsky sacked from *Novy Mir* for publishing Pomerantsev (see 1953). First 'thaw' ends.

S. VASILIEV: *The Heroes of Shipka* (film)

---

begins.
APRIL: 'Doctors' Plot' described as a 'provocation' and discredited.
JUNE: anti-Stalinist demonstrations in Czechoslovakia. Unrest in Hungary. Uprising in East Berlin put down by Soviet tanks (500 killed).
JULY: Khrushchev replaces Beria.
AUGUST: first Soviet H-bomb tested.
DECEMBER: Beria executed.

———

Removal and execution of top Soviet security figures. Secret service (MGB/MVD) reformed as KGB.
APRIL: major Gulag revolt in Central Asia – the 'Forty Days of Kengir'. Rebellion crushed by tanks.

	Shostakovich	Compositions	Literature/Arts	Politics
1955	48–49, JANUARY 15: première of *From Jewish Folk Poetry* (1948) in Moscow. SPRING: film score *The Gadfly*, Op. 97; *5 Dolmatovsky Romances (Songs of our Days)*, Op. 98. SUMMER: S. looks after his mother at Komarovo, composing little. OCTOBER 29: première of 1st Violin Concerto (1947–8) in Leningrad (soloist: David Oistrakh). NOVEMBER 9: S.'s mother dies. DECEMBER: begins *The First Echelon*.	KABALEVSKY: *Nikita Vershinin* (opera) K. KHACHATURIAN: Symphony No. 1 VOLKONSKY: Piano Quintet SVIRIDOV: *Burns Songs* DENISOV: Symphony	Mayakovsky's *The Bedbug* is produced for the first time since 1929; a great success. ___ YUTKEVICH: *Othello* (film)	'Virgin lands' scheme to open up Kazakhstan, Siberia, and the Urals. Campaign for 'closer ties with real life': everyone (except senior politicians) to do some menial work. FEBRUARY: Malenkov is manoeuvred into resignation and replaced by Bulganin. MAY: formation of the Warsaw Pact.
1956	49–50, JANUARY: receives diploma of St Cecilia in Rome; finishes film score *The First Echelon*, Op. 99. SUMMER: *6 Spanish Songs*, Op. 100. *Simple Folk* (1945) released. Marries Margarita Kainova. AUGUST: Quartet No. 6 in G, Op. 101. SEPTEMBER 25: Order of Lenin.	SHEBALIN: *The Taming of the Shrew* (opera) SHCHEDRIN: *The Little Humpbacked Horse* (ballet) GILER: Violin Concerto VOLKONSKY: *Musica Stricta* SVIRIDOV: *To the Memory of Esenin* KABALEVSKY: *Romeo and Juliet* ESHPAY: Violin Concerto No. 1 VAYNBERG: Cello Concerto	Second 'thaw'. Large wave of rehabilitated intellectuals returns from Siberia (including Akhmatova's son). MAY: Fadeyev shoots himself. ___ DUDINTSEV: *Not By Bread Alone* (novel) KHIKMET: *Did Ivan Ivanovich Ever Exist?* (play) NILIN: *Probationary Period* (novella)	The 'Year of Protest'. Widespread unrest in the Soviet bloc. FEBRUARY: Khrushchev 'unmasks' Stalin in his 'Secret Speech' to the 20th Party Congress. JUNE 28–29: Poznan strike in Poland put down by Soviet tanks. JUNE 30: Central Committee issues resolution on

	Shostakovich's life	Music	Literature	History
	AUTUMN: begins revising *Lady Macbeth* (as *Katerina Ismailova*).		YASHIN: *Levers* (novella) *Literary Moscow I & II* (anthologies) YEVTUSHENKO: *Zima Junction* (poem) KOZINTSEV: *Don Quixote* (film) CHUKRAI: *The Fortyfirst* (film)	'overcoming the personality cult' (of J.V. Stalin). OCTOBER–NOVEMBER: Hungarian Uprising crushed by Red Army. 25,000 die. End of liberalisation.
1957	50–51. SPRING: guest at Prague Spring Festival. Piano Concerto No. 2 in F, Op. 102. MARCH 28 – APRIL 5: attends 2nd Congress of Composers' Union. SUMMER: Symphony No. 11 in G minor, Op. 103 (*The Year 1905*) for the 40th anniversary of October. SEPTEMBER: S. made a Secretary of Union of Soviet Composers. OCTOBER 30: 11th Symphony premiered in Moscow. Greatest popular success since 7th Symphony. NOVEMBER: *2 Russian Folk Songs* (*Cultivation*), Op. 104.	KARAYEV: *Path of Thunder* (ballet) VOLKONSKY: *Music for 12 Instruments* VAYNBERG: Symphony No. 4 KHRENNIKOV: *The Mother* (opera) DENISOV: Quartet No. 1 GUBAYDULINA: Piano Quintet TISHCHENKO: Quartet No. 1; Piano Sonata No. 1 SCHNITTKE: Violin Concerto No. 1	Clamp-down. Khrushchev reprimands Dudintsev. Yevtushenko criticised. November: *Doctor Zhivago* published in Italy and Germany. ——— NIKOLAYEVA: *A Running Battle* (novel) KALATAZOV: *The Cranes are Flying* (film)	First high-rise housing complexes (e.g. Cheryomushki). Beginning of campaign against 'parasites' (nominally 'anti-social elements'; in practice, nonconformist writers and artists). JULY: Khrushchev liquidates 'anti-Party opposition' (Malenkov, Kaganovich, Molotov), gaining supreme power. OCTOBER 3: riots in Warsaw. OCTOBER 4: *Sputnik*, first satellite. OCTOBER 26: Khrushchev eliminates his chief supporter in July, Marshal Zhukov, for 'Bonapartism'.
1958	51–52. SPRING: operetta *Moscow, Cheryomushki*, Op. 105.	TISHCHENKO: Violin Concerto No. 1	Nationwide drive against religion.	Milovan Djilas's *The New Class* published in

303

APRIL 22: Lenin Prize for 11th Symphony.
MAY 28: CP Resolution to correct 'errors' of 1948 decree.
JUNE: Honorary Doctorate, Oxford.
SUMMER: re-orchestrates *Khovanshchina* for film, Op. 106. Begins to feel pain in right hand.
DECEMBER: meets Irina Supinskaya.

SHCHEDRIN: Symphony No. 1
VOLKONSKY: Quartet No. 2; *Serenade for an Insect*
KABALEVSKY: *Song of Morning, Spring and Peace* (cantata)
GUBAYDULINA: Symphony
SCHNITTKE: *Nagasaki* (oratorio)

OCTOBER: Pasternak awarded Nobel Prize for *Doctor Zhivago*. Forced to renounce it, he is thrown out of the Writers' Union.
NOVEMBER: Official campaign of harassment against Pasternak.
DECEMBER: Sakharov appeals to Khrushchev to stop H-bomb tests.

GERASIMOV: *The Quiet Don* (film)

Yugoslavia. Unrest in universities leads to trial of Union of Patriots of Russia (protesting Moscow students).
MARCH 27: Khrushchev ousts Bulganin, becoming chairman of Council of Ministers.

1959

52–53. JANUARY 24: première of *Moscow, Cheryomushki* in Moscow.
MARCH: visits USA and Mexico.
MAY 23: *Khovanshchina* premièred.
SUMMER: Cello Concerto No. 1 in E flat, Op. 107.
OCTOBER 4: 1st Cello Concerto premièred in Leningrad (soloist: Mstislav Rostropovich).
OCTOBER: visits USA.
NOVEMBER 4: re-orchestration of *Boris Godunov* (1939–40) premièred in Leningrad.
DECEMBER: buys dacha in Zhukovka outside Moscow.

SVIRIDOV: *Pathetic Oratorio*
SHEBALIN: *The Sun Over the Steppe* (opera)
KABALEVSKY: *The Leninists* (choruses)
KARAYEV: *Our Party* (cantata)
VAYNBERG: Violin Concerto
GUBAYDULINA: Piano Concerto
TISHCHENKO: Quartet No. 2
ESHPAY: Symphony No. 1
KHRENNIKOV: Violin Concerto

Beginning of poetry readings in Mayakovsky Square, Moscow.
MAY: Khrushchev's address to the Third Congress of Writers' Union.

SHOLOKHOV: *Virgin Soil Upturned Pt 2* (novel)
SIMONOV: *The Living and the Dead* (novel)
CHUKRAI: *Ballad of a Soldier* (film)
BONDARCHUK: *Destiny of a Man* (film)

Dissident protest grows in all walks of life. Start of seven-year plan to regenerate Soviet agriculture.
September: Khrushchev visits USA. Beginning of détente.

1960

53–54. JANUARY: hospitalised for treatment to right hand.
FEBRUARY–MARCH: Quartet No. 7 in F sharp minor, Op. 108.
APRIL 9: re-elected First Secretary of RSFSR Composers' Union.
MARCH–JUNE: 5 Satires (Pictures of the Past), Op. 109.
MAY 15: 7th Quartet premièred in Leningrad.
JULY 12–14: Quartet No. 8 in C minor, Op. 110, in Dresden.
AUGUST: film score Five Days, Five Nights, Op. 111, in E. Germany.
SEPTEMBER: Novorossiisk Chimes.
SEPTEMBER 14: accepted as candidate member of the Communist Party. Ban on 8th Symphony rescinded.
OCTOBER 2: 8th Quartet premièred in Leningrad. Great success.
NOVEMBER: leaves Margarita Kainova.

SHEBALIN: Quartet No. 8
TISHCHENKO: Piano Sonata No. 2
VOLKONSKY: Viola Sonata; Mirror Suite
KABALEVSKY: Spring (symphonic poem)
SCHNITTKE: Piano Concerto

MAY 30: Pasternak dies at Peredelkino.
—
KATAYEV: Winter Wind (novel)
TVARDOVSKY: Beyond the Far Distance (poem)
SINYAVSKY ('Abraham Tertz'): The Trial Begins (novel)
GROSSMAN: Life and Fate (novel, unpublished)

Authorities start confining dissidents in psychiatric hospitals.
JANUARY 20: successful ballistic missile test in the Pacific.
APRIL: beginning of break between Russia and China.
MAY 1: V-2 spy-plane shot down over Sverdlovsk.
MAY 17: Khrushchev disrupts summit conference over V-2 incident.

Year		Music	Literature	Politics
1961	54–55. FEBRUARY 22: *Pictures of the Past* premièred in Moscow (soloist: Galina Vishnevskaya). SPRING: Leningrad University invite S. to give postgraduate classes in composition. SUMMER: Symphony No. 12 in D minor, Op. 112 (*The Year 1917*). AUGUST: grandson Dmitri born. OCTOBER 1: 12th Symphony premièred at 22nd Congress of Soviet CP. OCTOBER: becomes full member of Communist Party. To Liszt–Bartók Festival in Budapest. DECEMBER 30: 4th Symphony (1935–6) premièred in Moscow.	SHCHEDRIN: *Not Love Alone* (opera) DENISOV: *Siberian Soil* (oratorio) GUBAYDULINA: *Intermezzo* TISHCHENKO: Symphony No. 1 SCHNITTKE: *Poem About Cosmos* VAYNBERG: Flute Concerto VOLKONSKY: *Les Plaintes de Chtchaza*	Third thaw begins. OCTOBER: Bukovsky and Kuznetsov arrested. YEVTUSHENKO: *Babi Yar* (poem) PAUSTOVSKY (ed.): *Tarusa Pages* (anthology) KOCHETOV: *The Secretary of the Oblast Committee* (novel) AKSYONOV: *A Ticket to the Stars* (story) SINYAVSKY: ('Abraham Tertz'): *The Icicle* (stories) SEREBRYAKOVA: *The Theft of Fire* (novel) KATAYEV: *The Catacombs* (novel)	APRIL 12: cosmonaut Yuri Gagarin in *Vostok* first man in space. JUNE: Berlin crisis begins. AUGUST: building of Berlin Wall. SEPTEMBER: Grigorenko warns of new 'cult of personality' surrounding Khrushchev. OCTOBER: 22nd Party Congress. Khrushchev's second anti-Stalin speech. Removal of Stalin's remains from the mausoleum in Red Square. High-water mark of pre-Gorbachev 'de-Stalinisation'. DECEMBER: Albania breaks off relations with USSR over de-Stalinisation.
1962	55–56. SPRING: orchestrates *Songs and Dances of Death* (Mussorgsky). MARCH 25 – APRIL 3: 2nd Congress of the Composers' Union. MAY: elected delegate to Supreme Soviet of USSR.	SHEBALIN: Symphony No. 5 KABALEVSKY: Requiem A. KHACHATURIAN: Concert Rhapsody for violin and orchestra VAYNBERG: Symphony No. 5 SHCHEDRIN: Piano Sonata VOLKONSKY: *Game for Three*;	Serebryakova attacks literary nonconformists. OCTOBER: *Pravda* prints Yevtushenko's *The Heirs of Stalin* (poem) NOVEMBER: *Novy Mir* publishes *One Day in the Life of Ivan Denisovich*.	JUNE 2: workers peacefully protesting price-rises in Novocherkassk are violently suppressed by the army. Around 80 killed. OCTOBER: Khrushchev announces a 'return to Leninist norms'.

Life	Works	Cultural	Political
JUNE 20–JULY 20: hospitalised. Begins 13th Symphony. AUGUST: arranges 2 *Davidenko Choruses*, Op. 124; finishes Symphony No. 13 in B flat minor, Op. 113. SEPTEMBER: to Edinburgh Festival. DECEMBER 18: 13th Symphony premièred in Moscow. Great controversy. DECEMBER: marries Irina Supinskaya. DECEMBER 26: première of *Katerina Ismailova* in Leningrad.	*Jam Session* ESHPAY: Symphony No. 2 TISHCHENKO: Piano Concerto	DECEMBER: Khrushchev enraged by exhibition of abstract art at the Manège. Demands new discipline among intelligentsia. End of third thaw. ——— SOLZHENITSYN: *One Day in the Life of Ivan Denisovich* (novella) BONDAREV: *Silence* (novel) STADNYUK: *People are Not Angels* (novel) SEREBRYAKOVA: *Life's Summits* (novel) TARKOVSKY: *Ivan's Childhood* (film) GERASIMOV: *Men and Beasts* (film)	OCTOBER 17: Sino-Soviet rift becomes official. OCTOBER–NOVEMBER: Cuban missile crisis.
1963 56–57. JANUARY 8: première of *Katerina Ismailova* in Moscow. SUMMER: re-orchestrates Schumann's Cello Concerto, Op. 125; orchestrates *From Jewish Folk Poetry* (1948); *Overture on Russian and Khirghiz Themes*, Op. 115; arranges Prelude and Fugue No. 15 and *Tarantella* (from *The Gadfly*) for 2 pfs. DECEMBER: begins *Hamlet*.	TISHCHENKO: Cello Concerto No. 1; *The Twelve* (ballet) A. KHACHATURIAN: Concert Rhapsody for cello and orchestra SVIRIDOV: *Petersburg Songs* SHEBALIN: Quartet No. 9 MOSOLOV: Quartet No. 2 VAYNBERG: Symphony No. 6 SHCHEDRIN: Concerto for Orchestra No. 1 (*Merry Ditties*)	MARCH 8: Khrushchev's speech on discipline in the arts. He dictates the line to writers, artists and directors. DECEMBER: Serebryakova attacks Ehrenburg with Khrushchev's approval. YEVTUSHENKO: *Precocious Autobiography* TVARDOVSKY: *Tyorkin in the Other World* (poem) SHEPITKO: *Heat* (film)	Failure of 'Virgin Lands' scheme. Severe food shortages. Khrushchev buys wheat from Canada. Unrest and strikes across the USSR. JULY 25: Limited Nuclear Test Ban Treaty.

1964

57–58. JANUARY: finishes film score *Hamlet*, Op. 116, at Repino.
FEBRUARY 15–23: festival of S.'s work in Gorky.
APRIL: to Tashkent for festival.
MAY: meets Sholokhov at Don Festival. Announces opera *The Quiet Don* (a smokescreen for his other work, finally abandoned in 1967).
MAY: Quartet No. 9 in E flat, Op. 117.
JULY: visits Armenia. Quartet No. 10 in A flat, Op. 118.
AUGUST–SEPTEMBER: *The Execution of Stepan Razin* (cantata), Op. 119.
NOVEMBER 20: première of 9th and 10th Quartets in Moscow.
DECEMBER 28: première of *Stepan Razin* in Moscow.

DENISOV: *Sun of the Incas* (cantata)
KABALEVSKY: Cello Concerto No. 2
A. KHACHATURIAN: Concert Rhapsody for piano and orchestra
SVIRIDOV: *Kursk Songs*
KHRENNIKOV: Cello Concerto
VAYNBERG: Symphonies Nos. 7 and 8

Brodsky tried for 'parasitism' in Leningrad. Sentenced to five years' internal exile. Relaxation while Brezhnev/Kosygin regime settles in: beginning of fourth thaw.

GORBATOV: *Years Off My Life* (memoir)
SINYAVSKY: ('Abraham Tertz'): *The Makepeace Experiment* (novel)
YUTKEVICH: *Lenin in Poland* (film)
KOZINTSEV: *Hamlet* (film)
BONDARCHUK: *War and Peace* (film)

MAY: KGB sets fire to library of Ukrainian National Academy of Sciences, destroying some national treasures.
OCTOBER 14: Khrushchev deposed. Brezhnev elected first secretary of the Central Committee.

1965

58–59. JANUARY: celebrates New Year with Britten in Zhukhovka.
JANUARY: hospitalised in neurological unit.
FEBRUARY: to Vienna for

TISHCHENKO: Symphony No. 2; Piano Sonata No. 3
POPOV: Symphony No. 5
KARAYEV: Symphony No. 3
GUBAYDULINA: Piano Sonata; *Etudes*

SEPTEMBER: KGB seize manuscript of Solzhenitsyn's *The First Circle*. Daniel and Sinyavsky arrested. Panic in the literary underground: *samizdat* and illegal emigré

Purge of Ukrainian nationalists.
MARCH: unrest in universities leads to new crack-down on dissidents.

	SHOSTAKOVICH	MUSIC	OTHER ARTS / EVENTS	HISTORY
	production of *Katerina Ismailova*. MARCH–APRIL: to Bulgaria for festival of Soviet music. APRIL 26: première of *5 Fragments*, Op. 42 (1935) in Leningrad. SUMMER: convalescence and holiday in Byelorussia. AUGUST: death of Vasili Shirinsky. AUTUMN: film score *A Year as Long as a Lifetime*, Op. 120; *5 Romances on Texts from Krokodil*, Op. 121; work on film of *Katerina Ismailova*. NOVEMBER 22: celebrates birthday of Britten, then visiting Russia. DECEMBER: to Budapest for production of *Katerina Ismailova*.	SCHNITTKE: *Dialogues* SHCHEDRIN: Symphony No. 2 MOSOLOV: Symphony No. 5 DENISOV: *Crescendo and Diminuendo* KABALEVSKY: *Homeland* (cantata); *Heroes of Gerlovka* (symphonic poem)	material hastily rehidden. OCTOBER: Sholokhov awarded Nobel Prize. ——— TARSIS: *Ward Seven* (study) CHUKOVSKAYA: *The Deserted House* (novel) TARKOVSKY: *Andrei Rublev* (film)	MAY: at Central Committee plenum on agriculture, Brezhnev acknowledges failure of agricultural seven-year plan. Reduction of compulsory farm quotas to encourage production. DECEMBER: pro-constitution demonstration in Pushkin Square.
1966	**59–60.** JANUARY: Quartet No. 11 in F minor, Op. 122, at Repino. FEBRUARY: *Preface to My Collected Works and Brief Reflections on This Preface*, Op. 123. MARCH 25: première of 11th Quartet in Moscow.	TISHCHENKO: Symphony No. 3; *Requiem* (after Akhmatova) SCHNITTKE: Violin Concerto No. 2; Quartet No. 2 ESHPAY: Symphony No. 3; Piano Sonata SHCHEDRIN: Piano Concerto No. 2 DENISOV: *Laments*	FEBRUARY: trial of writers Daniel and Sinyavsky. Sholokhov demands death sentence. They are sentenced to seven years' hard labour. End of fourth thaw. Beginning of Export Only literature and rapid growth of *samizdat* literature.	End of 'de-Stalinisation'. Moves to rehabilitate the dictator. Khrushchev 'unpersoned'. Wave of repressive political trials all over Russia. Censorship reinforced. MARCH–APRIL: 23rd Party Congress. Restoring

MARCH–APRIL: attends 23rd
Congress of CP as
Leningrad delegate.
APRIL: falls ill. Convalesces in
sanatorium in the Crimea.
Cello Concerto No. 2 in G,
Op. 126.
APRIL 24: première of 6
Japanese Romances, Op. 21
(1928–32) in Leningrad.
MAY 28: première of 5
Krokodil Romances in
Leningrad. Suffers heart-
attack after concert.
JUNE: Leningrad White
Nights Festival devoted to
S.'s music.
JUNE–AUGUST: hospitalised.
SEPTEMBER 25: 60th birthday.
Order of Lenin and Hero of
Socialist Labour. Premières
of 2nd Cello Concerto
(soloist: Mstislav
Rostropovich) and film of
Katerina Ismailova.
AUTUMN–WINTER: works
quietly on Blok cycle at
Zhukovka.

1967   60–61. Celebrates New Year
with Britten at Zhukovka.
SPRING: finishes 7 *Romances on
Poems of Alexander Blok*, Op.

KARAYEV: Violin Concerto
ESHPAY: Concerto for
orchestra
SVIRIDOV: *Time, Forward!*

MARCH: intellectuals protest
Soviet injustice and deplore
the trend towards
rehabilitation of Stalin.
MARCH 5: Akhmatova dies at
Komarovo.

KUZNETSOV: *Babi Yar* (novel)
SHALAMOV: *Kolyma Tales*
(stories, published in
samizdat)

Aleksandr Ginzburg arrested
for publishing 'seditious'
material.
MAY: Solzhenitsyn writes to

Politburo, Brezhnev makes
himself General Secretary.
SEPTEMBER: penal code
revised to facilitate action
against dissidents.

More political trials.
Beginning of Brezhevian
'stagnation'.

	VAYNBERG: Symphony No. 9; Trumpet Concerto SHCHEDRIN: Concerto for Orchestra No. 2 (*Chimes*) MOSOLOV: *Hail, Moscow* (cantata) VOLKONSKY: *Itinerant Concerto*	Fourth Congress of the Writers' Union, demanding an end to censorship. ——— E. GINZBURG: *Into the Whirlwind* (memoir, published in *samizdat*) FEDIN: *The Bonfire* (novel) SEREBRYAKOVA: *Tornado* (memoir) GERASIMOV: *The Journalist* (film)	

127; song *Spring, spring*, Op. 128.
MAY: Violin Concerto No. 2 in C sharp minor, Op. 129, at Repino.
AUGUST: holiday in Byelorussia. Car accident in Moscow: breaks leg. *Funeral-Triumphal Prelude*, Op. 130, and symphonic poem *October*, Op. 131, for 50th anniversary of the revolution.
SEPTEMBER 13: 2nd Violin Concerto premièred in Bolshevo (soloist: David Oistrakh).
AUTUMN: film score *Sofia Perovskaya*, Op. 132.
OCTOBER: Blok cycle premièred in Moscow.

1968 61–62. SPRING: orchestration of Fleishman's *Rothschild's Violin*.
MARCH 11: finishes Quartet No. 12 in D flat, Op. 133.
APRIL: steps down as First Secretary of RSFSR Composers' Union. *Rothschild's Violin* premièred in Leningrad.
JUNE 14: 12th Quartet premièred in Moscow.

GUBAYDULINA: *Night in Memphis* (cantata)
ESHPAY: *Lenin is With Us* (cantata)
SHCHEDRIN: *Carmen Suite*
DENISOV: *Autumn*
K. KHACHATURIAN: Symphony No. 2
VAYNBERG: Symphony No. 10

FEBRUARY: Aleksandr Ginzburg given seven years in the Gulag.
MARCH–APRIL: trial of Christian group in Leningrad.
APRIL: first issue of *Chronicle of Current Events*.
JUNE: Sakharov's *Progress, Coexistence and Intellectual Freedom* (*samizdat*)
———

JANUARY: Dubček succeeds Novotný in Czechoslovakia. Liberalisation — the 'Prague spring'.
MAY: Czech leaders visit Moscow.
JULY: 'Warsaw letter' ultimatum to Prague.
AUGUST 20: Soviet Pact forces invade Czechoslovakia.
AUGUST 25: dissident protests in Red Square against

AUGUST: Violin Sonata, Op. 134.
SUMMER: tour through Karelia with Irina.

SOLZHENITSYN: *The First Circle; Cancer Ward* (novels)
ABRAMOV: *Two Winters, Three Summers* (novel)

Soviet intervention in Czechoslovakia.
OCTOBER: trial of Red Square demonstrators.

1969 62–63. JANUARY 8: Violin Sonata premièred in Moscow (soloist: David Oistrakh).
JANUARY–FEBRUARY: hospitalised in neurological unit. Composes Symphony No. 14, Op. 135.
MARCH: re-orchestrates Tishchenko's Cello Concerto No. 1 (1963).
SUMMER: holidays in Armenia and Siberia.
SEPTEMBER 29: 14th Symphony premièred in Leningrad (soloists: Vishnevskaya, Mark Reshetin).

DENISOV: *D-S-C-H; Wind Quintet*
GUBAYDULINA: *Rubayat* (cantata)
TISHCHENKO: Cello Concerto No. 3
VOLKONSKY: *Les Mailles du temps*

Solzhenitsyn thrown out of the Writers' Union. Rostropovich gives him refuge.
———
SOLZHENITSYN: *The Lovegirl and the Innocent* (play)
MARCHENKO: *My Testimony* (memoir)
TRIFONOV: *The Exchange* (novel)
DONSKOI: *Chaliapin* (film)

Zorin and Alexeyev: the 'Leningrad Programme'. *Samizdat* analysis of *nomenklatura* as Soviet ruling class.
MARCH: Sino-Soviet border clashes on the Ussuri River.
MAY: formation of action group for defence of civil rights in USSR. General Grigorenko arrested and imprisoned in psychiatric ward.
JUNE: Crimean Tatars demonstrate in Moscow.
DECEMBER: Soviet negotiators are recalled from Peking.

1970 63–64. JANUARY–FEBRUARY: *Loyalty* (8 choruses), Op. 136, for Lenin's centenary.
APRIL–MAY: hospitalised (Ilizarov clinic in Kurgan).
JUNE–JULY: film score *King Lear*, Op. 137.

GUBAYDULINA: *Vivente, non vivente*
SHCHEDRIN: 24 Preludes and Fugues
VAYNBERG: Symphony No. 11
VOLKONSKY: *Replica*
POPOV: Symphony No. 6;

Tvardovsky sacked from editorship of *Novy Mir*. Solzhenitsyn invited to leave USSR; he refuses to go. Zhores Medvedev sent to mental hospital for criticising the Soviet regime.

Sakharov, Tverdokhlebov and Chalidze found Soviet Human Rights Committee.
MARCH 5: Sakharov writes to Soviet leadership, protesting lack of intellectual freedom.
JUNE: beginning of Jewish

	SUMMER: Moscow, for Tchaikovsky Competition. SEPTEMBER–OCTOBER: Ilizarov clinic again. Quartet No. 13 in B flat minor, Op. 138; *March of the Soviet Police*, Op. 139. DECEMBER 11: premiere of 13th Quartet in Moscow.	Organ Concerto DENISOV: *Peinture* TISHCHENKO: *Sinfonia Robusta*; Quartet No. 3; *Tsvetayeva Songs*	Solzhenitsyn protests, calling it 'spiritual murder'. OCTOBER: Solzhenitsyn awarded Nobel Prize. ___ N. MANDELSTAM: *Hope Against Hope* (memoir) GROSSMAN: *Forever Flowing* (novel) BONDARCHUK: *Waterloo* (film)	emigration movement. AUGUST: diplomatic relations with China re-opened. DECEMBER: trial of Jewish dissidents who tried to hijack plane in Leningrad. Jailed for fifteen years. Polish price-riots in Gdansk. Gierek replaces Gomulka.
1971	64–65. SPRING: orchestrates *6 Romances on Verses by English Poets* (1942), Op. 140. JULY–AUGUST: Symphony No. 15 in A, Op. 141. SEPTEMBER: suffers second heart-attack during rehearsals of 15th Symphony. OCTOBER: Order of the October Revolution. WINTER: hospitalised.	DENISOV: Piano Trio GUBAYDULINA: Quartet No. 1; *Fairytale* K. KHACHATURIAN: *A Moment of History* (cantata) KHRENNIKOV: Piano Concerto No. 2	SOLZHENITSYN: *August 1914* (novel) MAKSIMOV: *Seven Days of Creation* (novel)	Nadir of Brezhnevian repression. Widespread crime, alcoholism and corruption. MARCH: 24th Party Congress. Italian and Rumanian delegates reject Brezhnev Doctrine of unlimited sovereignty. Indo-Soviet friendship treaty. SEPTEMBER: Khrushchev dies. Brezhnev meets Tito in Belgrade.
1972	65–66. JANUARY 8: 15th Symphony premiered in Moscow. MAY: visits E. Germany. SUMMER: to Aldeburgh to stay with Britten. Begins 14th Quartet. AUTUMN–WINTER:	SHCHEDRIN: *Lenin Lives* (cantata) KABALEVSKY: *Letter to the 30th Century* (oratorio) DENISOV: Cello Concerto SCHNITTKE: Symphony No. 1 ESHPAY: Violin Concerto No. 2	JANUARY: KGB crack-down. *Chronicle of Current Events* banned. JUNE: arrest of Petr Yakir. KOZINTSEV: *King Lear* (film) TARKOVSKY: *Solaris* (film)	New wave of censorship. Trials of 'liberals' in Czechoslovakia. MAY: army suppresses nationalist demonstration in Lithuania. MAY: Nixon visits Moscow. MAY 30: signing of SALT 1

	hospitalised with renal colic and lung cancer. Undergoes radiation therapy.	GUBAYDULINA: *Roses* (song-cycle) TISHCHENKO: Piano Sonata No. 4		treaty on limitation of strategic nuclear weapons.
1973	66–67. FEBRUARY: to Berlin for productions of *Katerina Ismailova* and *The Nose*. MARCH: further radiation therapy. APRIL 23: finishes Quartet No. 14 in F sharp, Op. 142, at Repino. MAY: to Copenhagen for production of *Katerina Ismailova*. JUNE: sails to New York. JULY: back to Moscow via England. AUGUST: *6 Romances on Poems by Marina Tsvetayeva*, Op. 143. OCTOBER 30: 14th Quartet premièred in Moscow. DECEMBER 27: *Tsvetayeva Songs* premièred in Moscow.	DENISOV: *La vie en rouge* TISHCHENKO: Piano Sonata No. 5 KHRENNIKOV: Symphony No. 3 KNIPPER: Symphony No. 20	Mandelstam's poetry published for the first time since the 1920s. AUGUST: trial of Yakir and Krasin. They 'repent' and plead guilty. AUGUST 23: Elizaveta Voronyanskaya murdered by KGB after confessing to possession of manuscript copy of Solzhenitsyn's *Gulag Archipelago*. SEPTEMBER: Solzhenitsyn's *Letter to the Soviet Leaders*. TRIFONOV: *Impatience* (novel) MARKOV: *Siberia* (novel)	No change on freedom of expression. JUNE 22: Soviet–American agreement on prevention of nuclear war.
1974	67–68. JANUARY: orchestrates *Tsvetayeva Songs*, Op. 143a. FEBRUARY–MAY 17: Quartet No. 15 in E flat minor, Op. 144, at Repino. JUNE–JULY: *Suite on Verses by Michelangelo*, Op. 145. AUTUMN: rehearsals of *The*	TISHCHENKO: Symphony No. 4 DENISOV: Piano Concerto SCHNITTKE: *Hymnus I–III* GUBAYDULINA: *Preludes*	JANUARY: Solzhenitsyn subjected to campaign of harassment following publication abroad of volume 1 of *The Gulag Archipelago*. FEBRUARY: Solzhenitsyn expelled from the USSR.	Bad harvest forces massive wheat imports from America. FEBRUARY: Volga Germans demonstrate in Moscow and Tallin for repatriation. DECEMBER: Brezhnev and Ford agree SALT timetable.

Chukovskaya and Voynovich thrown out of the Writers' Union.
———
N. MANDELSTAM: *Hope Abandoned* (memoir)

Another bad harvest. Soviet farming in state of collapse. More huge wheat imports from America.
AUGUST 1: Helsinki Accord on human rights.

DECEMBER: Sakharov awarded Nobel Peace Prize.

VOYNOVICH: *Ivan Chonkin* (novel)
SOLZHENITSYN: *The Oak and the Calf* (memoir)
VLADIMOV: *Faithful Ruslan* (novella)

TISHCHENKO: Piano Sonata No. 6
GUBAYDULINA: *Laudatio Pacis*
SCHNITTKE: *Praeludium in Memoriam D. Shostakovich*

Nose at new Moscow Chamber Opera Theatre.
OCTOBER 20: Sergei Shirinsky dies.
OCTOBER 25: 15th Quartet premièred in Leningrad.
DECEMBER 23: *Michelangelo Suite* premièred in Leningrad.

1975 68–69. JANUARY: orchestrates *Michelangelo Suite*, Op. 145a, and *Song of the Flea* (Beethoven); *4 Verses of Captain Lebyadkin*, Op. 146.
MARCH: hospitalised.
APRIL–MAY: convalescing.
JUNE–JULY 6: Viola Sonata, Op. 147, Repino and Moscow.
JULY–AUGUST: hospitalised.
AUGUST 9: dies in hospital.
AUGUST 14: buried in Novodevichy Cemetery, Moscow.
OCTOBER 1: première of Viola Sonata in Leningrad.

Some Recommended Recordings

Recordings by Russian or East European performers invariably emerge as the most convincing. Western performances of the symphonies, though usually better recorded, are by comparison vague, sluggish, and undercharacterised. The composer's favourite conductor Mravinsky has left classic performances of the Sixth (HMV, 1965*), Eighth (Philips, 1982), Tenth (Saga, 1954), and Eleventh (Melodiya, 1960). Kondrashin's versions of the Fourth (HMV, 1962), Ninth (HMV, 1965), Twelfth (HMV, 1972), and Thirteenth (HMV, 1967) are similarly in a class of their own. His complete cycle, currently available in five CD boxes (Le Chant du Monde, import), is preferable to Rozhdestvensky's recent, eccentrically ill-recorded, rival set on Olympia (although Rozhdestvensky's Fifth stands as the best version of the last ten years). Volume One of the Kondrashin cycle includes the Fourth (a première recording and, despite a flawed transfer here, still better than all subsequent attempts). Best buy in this series is Volume Four, featuring the Eleventh, Twelfth, and a probably unsurpassable Thirteenth. Like Kondrashin's Thirteenth, the best versions of the Fourteenth (Barshai, HMV, 1970) and Fifteenth (Maxim Shostakovich, HMV, 1972) are première recordings. Karel Ancerl's readings of the Fifth (Supraphon, 1965) and Seventh (Supraphon, 1959) remain arguably supreme for each. Since some of these versions are unavailable at present, buyers seeking fair substitutes in modern sound are advised to try Neeme Järvi's recordings for Chandos (1986-9).

For the cello concertos, Rostropovich's versions of the First (CBS, 1959) and Second (Deutsche Grammophon, 1976) are definitive; likewise Oistrakh in the First (HMV, 1956) and Second (HMV, 1967) violin concertos. Oistrakh's recordings are currently available on a single disc from Le Chant du Monde, a company which has reissued several classic Shostakovich recordings on CD. Of special interest in this range is a set of some of the composer's own recordings (including the Piano Quintet and *From Jewish Folk Poetry*) and a coupling of Oistrakh and Richter in the Violin Sonata with Druzhinin and Muntyan in the Viola Sonata (both uniquely authoritative première versions). In the absence of reissues of the Beethoven Quartet's cycle of the string quartets, the Borodins' second set (HMV, 1979-84) heads the list, though the Fitzwilliams (Decca, 1975-9) are by no means completely outclassed by their Russian colleagues and occasionally even surpass them (for example, in the Ninth). Richter and the Borodins offer the finest Piano Quintet (HMV, 1983); Turovsky and Edlina are best in the Cello Sonata (Chandos, 1982); Boris Berman is outstanding in the Second Piano Sonata (Ottavo, 1988); and so on.

---

* Dates refer to years of recording.

Source Notes

Prelude: Truth

1-2 'I never tried to flatter the authorities' – *Testimony*, p. 94. **2** 'A man has no significance in a totalitarian state' – Ibid., pp. 211–12. **2** 'Don't believe humanists, citizens' – Ibid., p. 205. **4** *Sunday Times* quote. – 17 May 1981. **5** 'I think that it is clear . . . what happens in the Fifth' – *Testimony*, p. 183. **5** 'Too shrewd to be hoodwinked' – *Gramophone*, February 1983, p. 892. **6** Maxim's 'devastating holes' – Schwarz, p. 645. **6** Barshai's 'ambiguities' – Interview with Michael Oliver, BBC Radio 3, 1983. **6** A memorial to the 'destruction of Russian culture' – Norman Lebrecht, *Sunday Times Magazine*, April 1984. **6** 'If music can be anti-Communist' – Vishnevskaya, p. 400. **6** Ashkenazy quotes – Parrott, pp. 55–6. **7** Two Shostakoviches – Lebrecht, op. cit. **8** 'Second great *yurodivy* composer' – *Testimony*, xxv. **9** The word *yurodivy* applied to S. in Russian music circles – Ibid., xxvii. **9** 'relinquished all responsibility for anything he said' – Ibid., xxvii. **10** Maxim on S.'s signing – Schwarz, p. 645; interview with Geoffrey Norris, *Daily Telegraph*, 27 September 1986. **10** Vishnevskaya records as 'common knowledge' – Vishnevskaya, p. 399. **11–12** Milosz quotes – Milosz, pp. 78–9. **12** The convict Petya Kishkin – *Gulag Archipelago*, III, pp. 119–23. **13** 'reacted in an agonizing, physical way' – Vishnevskaya, p. 225. **13** 'that shackled genius . . .' – Solzhenitsyn, *The Oak and the Calf*, pp. 221, 405.

Chapter One. Innocence 1906–1925

Epigraph: Akhmatova, tr. Amanda Haight. **16** 'A billowing sea of people' – D. and L. Sollertinsky, p. 9. **16** 'If I had been told . . . what a luminary was arriving' – *Testimony*, p. 7. **20** Families of Stravinsky and Prokofiev – Ibid., pp. 7–8. **20** Attitudes to 1905 – Ibid., xi–xii, p. 8. **24** 'what moves what' – Ibid., p. 9. **25** Incident on the Nevsky Prospekt – Ibid., p. 7. **28** Sacked for laughing – Leyda, p. 190. **29** 'the . . . closing of . . . a large book' – Blokker and Dearling, p. 44.

Chapter Two. Experience 1926–1931

Epigraph: Akhmatova, *Why is our century worse than any other?*, tr. D.M. Thomas. **32** A suitcase ready – Peter Maniura, *Shostakovich: a career*, BBC2, 1987. **35** Lenin on 'class war' – Leggett, pp. 54–5. **36** A programme of 'social extermination' – Ibid., pp. 56–7; Heller, pp. 44–5, 121, etc. **36** Thousands of bourgeois shot, etc. – Leggett, pp. 148–9, 197–8. **36** Criminals able to blackmail by posing as Chekists – Ibid., p. 118. **36** S. family origin a handicap – Seroff, *Shostakovich*, p. 121. **36** Sofia cursed Nadia for 'her' revolution. – Ibid., p. 91. **37** Sofia's letter to Nadia – Ibid., p. 131. **37** Malko on S.'s political exam – *A Certain Art*, p. 186. 37 Kronstadt a deep influence – *Testimony*, pp. 15n, 97. 38 'brass-throated horns' – *Conversation With a Tax-Collector About Poetry*, 1926. 38 Decline of the word *dusha* – Hingley, *The Russian Mind*, p. 64. 39 'bordering on sadism' – Hingley, *Russian Writers and Soviet Society*, p. 173. 39 Othello story – Gyseghem, p. 38. 39 'Fictions' like freedom – Mandelstam, *Hope Against Hope*, pp. 162–3. 39–40 'generation that roars with laughter' – Ehrenburg, *The Truce*, p. 69. 40 'Something in the air' – Mandelstam, *Hope Against Hope*, p. 163. 40 'As a youth, I was . . . harsh' – *Testimony*, pp. 22–3. 40 Debunking the poet Sologub – Ibid., pp. 11–14. 40 Cinema work gave him insomnia – Lukyanova, p. 33. 40 Akim Volynsky – *Testimony*, pp. 9–11. 41 'a petty and silly vanity' – Malko, pp. 174ff. 41 Bulgakov tags – *Testimony*, xvii. 42 RAPM instigated by the Central Committee – Olkhovsky, p. 148. 43 'Of course I am not a "proletarian" composer' – Schwarz, p. 54. 44 Theme of 5th Prelude – Brown, 'Interview with Shostakovich', p. 88. 45 Malko on S. and Sollertinsky. – op. cit., pp. 147, 187–9. 46 Hearing *Wozzeck* – *Testimony*, pp. 42–4. 46 Disowned Second and Third Symphonies – Schwarz, p. 646. 47 'Our family had Narodnik leanings' – *Testimony*, p. 7. 48 'Watch out, or they'll adopt you' – Mandelstam, *Hope Against Hope*, p. 151. 48 500 roubles – D. and L. Sollertinsky, p. 46. 49 S's opinion of RAPM – Malko, p. 204; Vishnevskaya, p. 205. 49 Sokolovsky, etc. – *Testimony*, p. 31. 49 'S. did not like [Bezymensky's words]' – Malko, p. 204. 50 'They're all off their heads' – Ehrenburg, *First Years of Revolution*, p. 9. 50 Official statements about Scriabin – Grigoryev and Platek, pp. 304–5. 50 Remarks about *Funeral March for Victims of the Revolution*, – *Testimony*, p. 7. 51 Decision to become a *yurodivy* – Ibid., xxvii. 51 *The Nose* 'a horror-story, not a joke' – Ibid., p. 208. 52 Nostalgia for his teenage reading habits – Ibid., pp. 206–8. 52 Oberiu and Zoshchenko *yurodivye* – Ibid., xxvi. 52 Pilnyak a *yurodivy* – Ehrenburg, *The Truce*, p. 24. 52 'A . . . cascade of musical witticisms' – Rabinovich, p. 27. 53 A 'musico-theatrical symphony' – Ibid., p. 232. 53 Dismisses Berg influences – *Testimony*, p. 43. 53 Unimpressed by *Love for Three Oranges* – Ibid., p. 208. 54 Denies Meyerhold influence – Ibid., p. 207. 54 Acknowledges erotic undercurrent in *The Nose* – Ibid., p. 18. 56 Romanov quote – *Comrade Kislyakov*, p. 116. 57 'to kill human sensibility' – Heller and Nekrich, p. 243; Heller, pp. 78–86. 59 'a mighty and big-striding animal' – Eastman, p. 63. 59 S. on Mayakovsky – Grigoryev and Platek, p. 182. 59 *The Bedbug* a front for satirising the government – Symons, p. 180. 59 S. on *The Bedbug* – *Testimony*, p. 247. 60 *New Babylon* given in Moscow cinema – Martynov, p. 32. 60 S. disappointed by ending of *Days of the Turbins* – D. and L. Sollertinsky, p. 50. 62 Abraham on Third Symphony – *Eight Soviet Composers*, p. 18. 62 Mussorgsky 'an entire academy' for S. – *Testimony*, p. 226. 62 'I always felt that the ethical basis of *Boris* was my own' – Ibid., p. 232. 64 Stalin on *The Shot* – Symons, p. 184. 65 Ilya Selvinsky quote – Eastman, p. 4. 65 'a red slave in the People's harem' – Heller, p. 252. 65 Vladimir Kirshon quote – Ibid., p. 248. 66 'a veritable pogrom' – Eastman, p. 109. 66 'Every writer . . . obliged . . . to spit at Pilnyak' – Lyons, p. 246. 67 Panteleimon Romanov's confession – Eastman, pp. 94–100. 67 Everyone wearing a mask – Mandelstam, *Hope Against Hope*, p. 328. 68 Faked workers' denunciations – *Testimony*, p. 111. 68 TRAM scores as insurance – Ibid., p. 112. 69 'the crucifixion of the intelligentsia' – Romanov, p. 58. 69 'Up with mediocrity' – *Literary Gazette*, 10 June 1929. 70 Two hundred hours a year as paid labourers – Schwarz, p. 102. 70 Moscow students graduate on two or three mass-songs – Abraham, *New Oxford History of Music*, X, p. 642. 70 Shebalin's complaint – Schwarz, p. 58. 70 Yuri Yelagin quote – *Taming of the Arts*, pp. 188–9. 70 Maximilian Steinberg quote – Schwarz, p. 102. 71 S. on campaign against light music – Grigoryev and Platek, p. 29. 71 Gorky's dilemma – Heller and Nekrich, pp. 272–6. 72 'People under dictatorships' – Lyons, p. 341. 72 Solzhenitsyn's applause story – *Gulag Archipelago*, I, pp. 69–70. 72 Heller's applause story. – *Cogs in the Soviet Wheel*, p. 238. 72 600,000 in the Gulag – Conquest, *The Great*

Terror, pp. 333ff. **73** 'Wrecking . . . never existed' – Medvedev, pp. 112. **73** 'A monstrous theatrical presentation' – Ibid., p. 179. **73** An extraordinary Punch-and-Judy farce – *Gulag Archipelago*, I, pp. 376–99. **4** 'Hour after hour as night engulfed the city' – Lyons, p. 372. **74** 'Epoch of great fear' – Heller, *Cogs in the Soviet Wheel*, p. 117. **75** Quote about Myaskovsky's Eleventh – Ikonnikov, p. 49. **75** S.'s withdrawal from theatre-contracts, etc. – Lukyanova, pp. 69–71. **76** Eastman on Pilnyak's humiliation – *Artists in Uniform*, p. 108. **77** Nadezhda Mandelstam and 'the young English gerund' – *Hope Abandoned*, p. 381. **77** Komsomol attack RAPP – Brown, *The Proletarian Episode in Russian Literature*, p. 185. **77** Osip Mandelstam quote – *First Moscow Notebook*, 1931.

Chapter Three. Uncertainty 1932–1934

Epigraph: Akhmatova, *Neither by cart nor boat*, tr. D.M. Thomas. **81** Shostakovich and the 1932 resolution – *Testimony*, pp. 85, 112; Vishnevskaya, pp. 204–5. **81** A composer of incidental music – Lukyanova, p. 69. **81–2** Yelagin on S. at the Vakhtangov, 1932 – Jelagin, p. 35. **84** First Piano Concerto not one of his best works – Grigoryev and Platek, p. 235. **84** 'Under the influence of American folk music' – Ibid., p. 318. **85** S.'s comic work just as deep and humane – Ibid., pp. 47, 53. **87** Yelagin on S. during *The Human Comedy* – Jelagin, pp. 92–3. **87–8** S. quotes on *Lady Macbeth* – *Testimony*, pp. 106–7. **88** Rostropovich quote – Rothstein, p. 50. **00** 'A quiet Russian family' – *Testimony*, p. 268. **89** 'a petty scoundrel' – S.'s introduction to the opera, published with the libretto, 1935. **89** 'how love could have been' – *Testimony*, p. 108. **90** S. admits eroticism dominates *Lady Macbeth* – Ibid., p. 18. **90** The 'abolition of love' – Ibid., pp. 108–9. **91** S. no sympathy with sadism – Ibid., pp. 123–5. **91** 'Irrelevant and distracting from the main idea' – Brown, 'Interview with Shostakovich', p. 89. **91** A 'tragic-satiric opera' – Ibid., p. 107. **93** 'I wanted to remind the audience' – Ibid., p. 110. **94** Olesha quote – Ehrenburg, *Eve of War*, p. 42. **95** Olkhovsky quote – *Music Under the Soviets*, p. 162. **96** Solomon Volkov on Cello Sonata – Sleeve-note, Chandos CHAN 8340.

Chapter Four. Terror 1935–1938

Epigraph: Akhmatova, *You are no longer among the living*, tr. Amanda Haight. **99** 'Nearly fifteen million peasants had died' – Conquest, *Harvest of Sorrow*, p. 306. **102** S. quotes on Socialist Realism – Grigoryev and Platek, p. 50; Schwarz, p. 76. **102** 'I have never been a Formalist' – *Izvestia*, 3 April 1935. **102** Vishnevskaya quote – *Galina*, p. 208. **105** 'a weak-willed, neurasthenic, and sacrificial concept' – Schwarz, p. 78. **105** *Pravda* quote – Seroff, *Dmitri Shostakovich*, pp. 214–15. **106** Tukhachevsky story – D. and L. Sollertinsky, p. 78; *Testimony*, pp. 98–9. **106** S. to Shebalin – D. and L. Sollertinsky, p. 79. **106** S. quotes – *Testimony*, pp. 118–19. **106** Volkov quote – *Testimony*, xxix. **107** Mandelstam quote – *Hope Against Hope*, p. 148. **109** 'Astronomical figures and projections on a planetary scale' – Basily, p. 263. **110** Hingley quote – *The Russian Mind*, p. 84. **111** *Pravda* quotes – Basily, pp. 208n, 210. **112** 'An existence like this' – Mandelstam, *Hope Against Hope*, p. 88. **112** 'An inner pain' – Mandelstam, *Hope Abandoned*, p. 7. **112** 'If you live in a state of constant terror' – Ibid., p. 251. **113** 'as if happy to be back' – Blokker and Dearling, p. 60. **115** 'Show–whipping', etc. – *Testimony*, pp. 98, 119. **117** 1936 a Proletkult plot – Vishnevskaya, pp. 207–10. **119** 'Better scared than spared' – Mandelstam, *Hope Abandoned*, p. 174. **120** 'a gargantuan effort of will' – Kay, p. 30. **120** Solzhenitsyn quote – *Gulag Archipelago*, I, p. 76. **120** Soviet Criminal Code – Ibid., I, pp. 60–7. **120** Mandelstam quotes – *Hope Against Hope*, pp. 86–7, 90.

121 Arrests by quota – Heller and Nekrich, p. 303; Heller, p. 73; Solzhenitsyn, op. cit., I, p. 71. 121 Absurd arrest charges – Conquest, *The Great Terror*, pp. 312–14; Mandelstam, *Hope Abandoned*, p. 222. 121 Ehrenburg stories – *Eve of War*, p. 193. 122 'The principles of terror' – Mandelstam, *Hope Against Hope*, pp. 316–17. 122 Slave labour one-fifth of Russia's work force – Heller and Nekrich, p. 320. 123 'The word "conscience"' – Mandelstam, *Hope Against Hope*, p. 67. 123 Essential to smile – Ibid., pp. 286, 304–5. 124 Volkov quote – Peter Maniura, *Shostakovich: a career*, BBC2, 1987. 124 'Of course they understood' – *Testimony*, p. 135. 124 Maxim quote – Schwarz, p. 646. 125 Yelagin quote – *Taming of the Arts*, pp. 166–8. 125 Von Meck reference – *As I Remember Them*, p. 422. 128 Vishnevskaya quote – *Galina*, p. 213. 131 'It was a terrible blow' – *Testimony*, p. 116. 134 'come back to life' – *Testimony*, p. 136. 138 'almost derisively uncomplicated' – Kay, p. 37.

Chapter Five. *Togetherness 1938–1946*

Epigraph: Akhmatova, *Requiem*, tr. D. M. Thomas. 139 Ginzburg quote – *Into the Whirlwind*, p. 109. 140 Meyerhold's speech – Jelagin, pp. 169–73. 142 A thousand per day in Moscow – Medvedev, p. 239. 143 S. quote – *Testimony*, p. 229. 144 Lukyanova quote – *Shostakovich*, p. 93. 144 S. on Sixth – *Testimony*, p. 119. 146–7 S. on *Boris* – *Testimony*, pp. 229–33. 147 'almost simultaneously' – Ibid., p. 224. 149 A political demonstration – Olkhovsky, p. 191. 150 'The withering away of illusions' – *Testimony*, p. 85. 150 Deprived of the will to compose – Ibid., p. 136. 151 'We could talk about it' – *Testimony*, p. 136. 152 Inber quote – *Leningrad Diary*, 22 September 1941. 155 'I have nothing against calling the Seventh the *Leningrad* Symphony. . . ' – *Testimony*, p. 156. 155–6 S. quotes – Ibid., pp. 154–5. 156 'a tremendous requiem' – Rabinovich, p. 8. 156 'Akhmatova wrote her *Requiem*' – *Testimony*, p. 136. 157 Blokker and Dearling quotes – *The Music of Dmitri Shostakovich*, pp. 82–93. 159 Mravinsky quote – *Testimony*, xxxiii–iv. 159 Rabinovich quote – *Dmitri Shostakovich*, p. 68. 160 'I'll go and see Maxim' – *Testimony*, p. xxxiv. 162 S. on the Psalms – Ibid., p. 184. 165 S. on *The Gamblers* – Ibid., pp. 222–3. 165 'I intended to use a full orchestra' – Brown, 'Interview with Shostakovich', p. 89. 166 Rabinovich quotes – *Dmitri Shostakovich*, p. 80. 168–70 S. on Eighth Symphony's meaning – *Testimony*, pp. 136, 155. 175 'A musical portrait of Stalin' – Ibid., p. 141. 176 'They wanted a fanfare' – *Testimony*, p. 140. 177–8 Mravinsky on the Ninth Symphony – D. and L. Sollertinsky, p. 122. 178 Stradling quote – Norris, pp. 200–1. 178 S. on the Ninth – *Testimony*, pp. 140–1. 178 S. on Wagner – *Testimony*, p. 128–34. 180 Two and a quarter million repatriated – Heller and Nekrich, p. 452. 182 Ehrenburg quote – *Post-War Years*, p. 11.

Chapter Six. *Isolation 1946–1953*

Epigraph: Akhmatova, *Everyone has gone and no-one has returned*, tr. Amanda Haight. 185 S. on Zoshchenko – *Testimony*, pp. 271–2. 187 Soviet anti-Semitism – Kochan, pp. 299ff. 187–8 S. on anti-Semitism – *Testimony*, pp. 156–7. 188 Humiliation of professors – Heller and Nekrich, pp. 491–2. 188–9 Mandelstam quote – *Hope Against Hope*, pp. 33–4. 189 Volkov quote – *Testimony*, xxxvii. 190 Planning of 1948 'Formalist' campaign – Vishnevskaya, p. 219. 190 Werth quote and further quotes from the 1948 Congress – *Musical Uproar in Moscow*, passim. 193 Orwell quote – *Writers and Leviathan* (March 1948). 193 Ivinskaya quote – *A Captive of Time*, pp. 130–1. 193 Lyubimov quote – Peter Maniura, *Shostakovich: a career*, BBC2, 1987. 194 Rostropovich quote –

Rothstein, p. 50. **198** 'Not one of these works could be performed' – *Testimony*, pp. 157–8. **198** 'People say it must have been an interesting trip' – Ibid., p. 198. **198–9** Nabokov quotes – *Old Friends and New Music*, pp. 204–5. **199** 'I thought, This is it' – *Testimony*, p. 148. **204** Hundreds crushed by MGB tanks at Stalin's funeral – Kopacsi, p. 82.

Chapter Seven. Assertion 1953–1975

Epigraph: Akhmatova, *Fifth Northern Elegy*, tr. D. M. Thomas. **210** Roseberry quote – *Dmitri Shostakovich*, p. 141. **210** Vishnevskaya on S.'s poverty – *Galina*, p. 222. **211** Schwarz on S.'s interview – *Music and Musical Life in Soviet Russia*, p. 284. **211** Vishnevskaya on S.'s attitude to his children – *Galina*, p. 223. **212** Maxim quote – Peter Maniura, *Shostakovich: a career*, BBC2, 1987. **215** S. on Eleventh Symphony – *Testimony*, p. 8. **216** Bukovsky quote – *To Build a Castle*, p. 88. **219** Vishnevskaya on S.'s reaction to the 1958 CC resolution – *Galina*, p. 243. **219–20** Pasternak's persecution – Ivinskaya, pp. 273–8. **222** Vishnevskaya on the Eighth Quartet – *Galina*, p. 229. **222** S. on the Eighth Quartet – *Testimony*, p. 156. **223** Schwarz on S.'s *Pravda* article of 13 June 1958 – *Music and Musical Life in Soviet Russia*, p. 312. **224** Volkov and Ashkenazy on S.'s enrolment in the Communist Party – *Testimony*, xxxix; Parrott, pp. 55–6. **224** Schwarz on S.'s *Pravda* article of 7 September 1960 – *Music and Musical Life in Soviet Russia*, p. 336. **224** Vishnevskaya on *Pictures of the Past* – *Galina*, pp. 267–71. **226** S. on the Twelfth – *Testimony*, p. 141. **229–30** Campaign against Thirteenth Symphony – Vishnevskaya, pp. 274–9; Scammell, p. 462; Johnson and Labedz, *passim*. **232** 'They'll talk about beauty . . .' – *Testimony*, p. 159. **238** S. on cynicism – *Testimony*, pp. 175–7. **238–9** S.'s activities as a 'signer' – Scammell, pp. 553, 576. **239** Malcolm MacDonald quote – Norris, p. 137. **240** S. on Fifteenth Symphony – *Trud*, 15 January 1972. **241** Maxim on Fifteenth Symphony – Schwarz, p. 646. **242** 'We are all marionettes' – Hulme, p. 36. **243** Mandelstam quote – *Hope Against Hope*, p. 287.

Postlude: Immortality

Epigraph: Akhmatova, *In 1940*, tr. D. M. Thomas. **247** Norris, Stradling quotes. – Norris, pp. 167, 202. **248** Werth quote – *Musical Uproar in Moscow*, xvi. **248** Fanning quote – *The Breath of the Symphonist*, p. 6. **249** Lukyanova's witness – *Shostakovich*, p. 100. **249** Dmitri Frederiks on S. – D. and L. Sollertinsky, p. 209. **249** Boris Tishchenko on S. – Ibid., p. 184. **249–50** Sollertinskys' impressions – Ibid., pp. 184–6. **250** Royal S. Brown on S. – 'Interview with Shostakovich', p. 87. **250** Vishnevskaya on S. – *Galina*, pp. 225–6. **250** Berlinsky quote – Interview with Michael Oliver, *Music Magazine*, BBC Radio 3, 1983. **250** Rostropovich anecdote – Rothstein, p. 50. **251** Mandelstam quote – *Hope Against Hope*, p. 231. **251** S. signs letter denouncing Sakharov – Scammell, p. 807. **251** Solzhenitsyn on Czechoslovakia protest – *The Oak and the Calf*, p. 271. **252** Olkhovsky on Asafiev – *Music Under the Soviets*, pp. 81–4. **252** Yevtushenko quote – Peter Maniura, *Shostakovich: a career*, BBC2, 1987. **253** Olkhovsky on S. – *Music Under the Soviets*, pp. 215–17. **254** 'around fifty million Soviet citizens' – *Nedelya* April 1988. **254** Solzhenitsyn quote – *The Oak and the Calf*, p. 389. **254** Mandelstam on Aragon – *Hope Abandoned*, p. 139. **254** Solzhenitsyn on Sartre – *The Oak and the Calf*, p. 119. **257** Rabinovich quote – *Dmitri Shostakovich*, p. 9. **257** Olkhovsky quote – *Music Under the Soviets*, p. 192. **258** S. on meaning in music – *Testimony*, p. 234. **260** Yelagin on Neuhaus – *Taming of the Arts*, pp. 199–200. **261** Kondrashin interview – *DSCH*, xiii (August 1989). **263** Solzhenitsyn quote – *The Oak and the Calf*, p. 119. **362–4** Bukovsky quote – *To Build a Castle*, p. 342. **264** Volkov quote – *Saturday Review*, BBC2, 1986.

SELECT BIBLIOGRAPHY

Abraham, Gerald. *Eight Soviet Composers*. Oxford University Press, 1943.
Akhmatova, Anna. *Requiem and Poem Without a Hero* (tr. D. M. Thomas). Elek, 1976.
— *Way of All the Earth* (tr. D.M. Thomas). Secker & Warburg, 1979.
— *Selected Poems* (tr. Richard McKane). Bloodaxe, 1989.
Bakst, James. *A History of Russian–Soviet Music*. Dodd, Mead, 1966.
Basily, N. de (Nikolai Bazilli). *Russia under Soviet Rule: twenty years of Bolshevik Experiment*. Allen & Unwin, 1938.
Beausobre, Julia de. *The Woman Who Could Not Die*. Gollancz, 1948.
Bennett, John Reginald. *Melodiya: a Soviet Russian discography*. Greenwood, 1981.
Bloch, Sidney and Peter Reddaway. *Russia's Political Hospitals: the abuse of psychiatry in the Soviet Union*. Gollancz. 1977.
Blokker, Roy and Robert Dearling. *The Music of Dmitri Shostakovich: the symphonies.* Tantivy Press, 1979.
Brown, Douglas. *Doomsday 1917: the destruction of Russia's ruling class*. Sidgwick & Jackson, 1975.
Brown, Edward J. *The Proletarian Episode in Russian Literature, 1928–32*. Columbia University Press, 1953.
Brown, Malcolm Hamrick (ed.). *Russian and Soviet Music: essays for Boris Schwarz*. UMI Research, 1984.
Brown, Royal S. 'Interview with Shostakovich.' *High Fidelity*, 23 (October 1973).
Bukovsky, Vladimir. *To Build a Castle: my life as a dissenter*. Viking, 1979.
Bulgakov, Mikhail. *The Heart of a Dog*. Collins Harvill, 1989.
Cheng, Nien. *Life and Death in Shanghai*. Grafton, 1986.
Conquest, Robert. *The Nation Killers: the Soviet deportation of nationalities*. Macmillan, 1960.
— *The Great Terror: Stalin's purge of the thirties*. Macmillan, 1968.
— *Kolyma: the Arctic death camps*. Macmillan, 1978.
— *Harvest of Sorrow: Soviet collectivization and the terror famine*. Hutchinson, 1986.
— *Stalin and the Kirov Murder*. Hutchinson, 1989.
Coppard, Audrey and Bernard Crick (eds). *Orwell Remembered*. Ariel, 1984.
Deutscher, Isaac, Tamara Deutscher, David King. *The Great Purges*. Blackwell, 1984.
Devlin, James. *Shostakovich*. Novello, 1983.
Dubinsky, Rostislav. *Stormy Applause: making music in a workers' state*. Hutchinson, 1989.
Eastman, Max. *Artists in Uniform: a study of literature and bureaucraticism*. Alfred A. Knopf, 1934.
Ehrenburg, Ilya. *People, Years – Life*. 5 vols. MacGibbon & Kee, 1962–6.
Fanning, David. *The Breath of the Symphonist: Shostakovich's Tenth*. Royal Musical Association, 1988.
Fay, Laurel E. 'Shostakovich vs Volkov: whose Testimony?' *The Russian Review* (October 1980), pp. 484–93.
Fitzpatrick, Sheila (ed.). *Cultural Revolution in Russia 1928–31*. Indiana University Press, 1978.

Fyvel, T. R. *George Orwell: a personal memoir*. Hutchinson, 1982.

Gehrkens, K. W. 'Is Shostakovich a satirist?' *Etude*, 63 (December 1945), p. 686.

Ginzburg, Eugenia. *Into the Whirlwind*. Collins, Harvill, 1967.

— *Within the Whirlwind*. Collins, 1981.

Gleason, Abbot, Peter Kenez, Richard Stites (eds). *Bolshevik Culture: experiment and order in the Russian Revolution*. Indiana University Press, 1985.

Gogol, Nikolai. *Diary of a Madman and Other Stories*. Penguin, 1972.

Golomstock, Igor. *Totalitarian Art*. Collins Harvill, 1990.

Grigoryev, L. and Y. Platek (eds). *Dmitri Shostakovich: about himself and his times*. Progress, 1981.

Grossman, Vasily. *Life and Fate*. Collins Harvill, 1985.

Günther, Hans (ed.). *The Culture of the Stalin Period*. Macmillan/SSEES, 1990.

Gunther, John. *Inside Russia Today*. Hamish Hamilton, 1958.

Gyseghem, André van. *Theatre in Soviet Russia*. Faber, 1943.

Hackel, Sergei. *The Poet and the Revolution: Aleksandr Blok's 'The Twelve'*. Clarendon Press, 1975.

Haight, Amanda. *Anna Akhmatova: a poetic pilgrimage*. Oxford University Press, 1976.

Haraszti, Miklós. *The Velvet Prison: artists under state socialism*. Penguin, 1989.

Heller, Mikhail. *Cogs in the Soviet Wheel: the formation of Soviet man*. Collins Harvill, 1988.

Heller, Mikhail and Aleksandr Nekrich. *Utopia in Power*. Hutchinson, 1985.

Hingley, Ronald. *The Russian Mind*. Bodley Head, 1977.

— *Russian Writers and Soviet Society, 1917–78*. Weidenfeld & Nicolson, 1979.

— *Nightingale Fever: Russian poets in revolution*. Weidenfeld & Nicolson, 1982.

Howe, Irving (ed.). *1984 Revisited: totalitarianism in our century*. Harper & Row, 1983.

Hulme, Derek C. *Dmitri Shostakovich: catalogue, bibliography, & discography*. Kyle & Glen, 1982.

Hunt, R. N. Carew. *A Guide to Communist Jargon*. Bles, 1957.

Ikonnikov, Alexei. *Myaskovsky: his life and work*. Philosophical Library, 1946.

Inber, Vera. *Leningrad Diary*. Hutchinson, 1971.

Ivinskaya, Olga. *A Captive of Time: my years with Pasternak*. Collins & Harvill, 1979.

Jelagin, Juri (Yury Yelagin). *Taming of the Arts*. Dutton, 1951.

Johnson, Priscilla and Leopold Labedz (eds). *Khrushchev and the Arts: the politics of Soviet culture, 1962–64*. MIT Press, 1965.

Kagarlitsky, Boris. *The Thinking Reed: intellectuals and the Soviet state from 1917 to the present*. Verso, 1988.

Karlinsky, Simon. *Marina Cvetaeva: the woman, her soul and her poetry*. Cambridge University Press, 1985.

— *The Sexual Labyrinth of Nikolai Gogol*. Harvard University Press, 1976.

Kay, Norman. *Dmitri Shostakovich*. Oxford University Press, 1971.

Kochan, Lionel (ed.). *The Jews in Soviet Russia since 1917*. Oxford University Press, 1972.

Kopacsi, Sandor. *'In the Name of the Working Class.'* Fontana, 1989.

Krebs, Stanley Dale. *Soviet Composers and the Development of Soviet Music*. Allen & Unwin, 1970.

Kuznetsov, Anatoli. *Babi Yar: a document in the form of a novel*. 2nd edition. Jonathan Cape, 1970.

Laqueur, Walter and George Lichtheim (eds). *The Soviet Cultural Scene: 1956–7*. Praeger, 1958.

Lee, Rose. 'D. Szostakovitch.' *New York Times*, 20 December 1931.

Leggett, George. *The Cheka: Lenin's secret police*. Clarendon, 1981.

Leskov, Nikolai. *Lady Macbeth of Mtsensk District*. (in: R. Jarrell, *Six Russian Short Novels*, Doubleday, 1963.)
Levin, Dan. *Stormy Petrel: the life and work of Maxim Gorky*. Frederick Muller, 1965.
Leyda, Jay. *Kino: a history of the Russian and Soviet film*. Allen & Unwin, 1960.
Lukyanova, N. V. *Shostakovich*. Paganiniana Publications, 1984.
Lyons, Eugene. *Assignment in Utopia*. Harrap, 1938.
MacDonald, Ian. 'Shostakovich and Communism.' *Music and Musicians*, Vol. 36 No. 8 (April 1988), pp. 12–15.
— 'Shostakovich and Bulgakov.' *DSCH*, Vol. 18 (1991).
MacDonald, Malcolm. *Dmitri Shostakovich: a complete catalogue*. 2nd edition. Boosey & Hawkes, 1985.
Malko, Nikolai. *A Certain Art*. Morrow, 1966.
Mandelstam, Nadezhda. *Hope Against Hope*. Collins & Harvill, 1971.
— *Hope Abandoned*. Collins Harvill, 1974.
Martynov, Ivan. *Dmitri Shostakovich: the man and his work*. Philosophical Library, 1947.
Mayakovsky, Vladimir. *The Bedbug and Selected Poetry*. Weidenfeld & Nicolson, 1961.
— *The Bathhouse*. (in: A. R. MacAndrew, *20th Century Russian Drama*, Bantam, 1963.)
Meck, Galina von. *As I Remember Them*. Dobson, 1973.
Medvedev, Roy. *Let History Judge: the origins and consequences of Stalinism*. Macmillan, 1971.
Milosz, Czesław. *The Captive Mind*. Secker & Warburg, 1953.
Moldon, David. *Bibliography of Russian Composers*. White Lion, 1976.
Muggeridge, Malcolm. *Winter in Moscow*. Eyre & Spottiswode, 1934.
Nabokov, Nicolas. *Old Friends and New Music*. Little, Brown, 1951.
Nappelbaum, Moses (ed. Ilya Rudiak). *Our Age*. Ardis, 1984.
Norris, Christopher (ed.). *Shostakovich: the man and his music*. Lawrence & Wishart, 1982.
Olesha, Yury. *Envy*. Woolf, 1936.
Olkhovsky, Andrei. *Music under the Soviets: the agony of an art*. Praeger, 1955.
Ottaway, Hugh, *Shostakovich Symphonies*. BBC, 1978.
Parrott, Jasper with Vladimir Ashkenazy. *Beyond Frontiers*. Collins, 1984.
Pasternak, Boris. *An Essay in Autobiography*. Collins & Harvill, 1959.
Pownall, David. *Master Class*. Faber & Faber, 1983.
Rabinovich, David. *Dmitri Shostakovich, Composer*. Lawrence & Wishart, 1959.
Reck, Vera T. *Boris Pilnyak: a Soviet writer in conflict with the State*. McGill-Queen's, 1975.
Robinson, Harlow. *Sergei Prokofiev: a biography*. Hale, 1987.
Romanov, Panteleimon. *Three Pairs of Silk Stockings (Comrade Kislyakov): a novel of the life of the educated class under the Soviets*. Benn, 1931.
Roseberry, Eric. *Shostakovich*. Midas, 1982.
Rosenberg, William G. *Bolshevik Visions: the first phase of the cultural revolution in Soviet Russia*. Ardis, 1984.
Rothstein, Edward. 'A labour of love.' *Independent Magazine*, 12 November 1988, pp. 49–52.
Rudnitsky, Konstantin. *Russian and Soviet Theatre: tradition and the avant-garde*. Thames & Hudson, 1988.
Rybakov, Anatoli. *Children of the Arbat*. Hutchinson, 1988.
Salisbury, Harrison. 'A Visit with Dmitri Shostakovich.' *New York Times*, 8 August 1954.
— *The 900 Days: the siege of Leningrad*. Secker & Warburg, 1969.
Scammell, Michael. *Solzhenitsyn: a biography*. Hutchinson, 1984.

Schwarz, Boris. *Music and Musical Life in Soviet Russia, 1917–81*. 2nd edition. Indiana University Press, 1983.

Seroff, Viktor. *Sergei Prokofiev: a Soviet tragedy*. Funk & Wagnalls, 1968.

Seroff, Viktor with Nadezhda Galli-Shohat. *Dmitri Shostakovich: the life and background of a Soviet composer*. Alfred A. Knopf, 1943.

Shostakovich, Dmitri. *Collected Works*. 42 vols. State Publishers, Moscow, 1979–87.

Shostakovich, Dmitri (et al.). *Russian Symphony: thoughts about Tchaikovsky*. Philosophical Library, 1947.

Sollertinsky, Dmitri and Ludmilla. *Pages from the Life of Dmitri Shostakovich*. Hale, 1981.

Solzhenitsyn, Alexander. *The Gulag Archipelago*. 3 vols. Harvill, 1973–5.

— *The Oak and the Calf: sketches of literary life in the Soviet Union*. Collins Harvill, 1980.

Steinhoff, William. *The Road to 1984*. Weidenfeld & Nicolson, 1975.

Struve, Gleb. *Russian Literature under Lenin and Stalin, 1917–1953*. Routledge & Kegan Paul, 1972.

Swayze, Harold. *Political Control of Literature in the USSR, 1949–1959*. Harvard University Press, 1962.

Symons, James M. *Meyerhold's Theatre of the Grotesque: the post-revolutionary productions, 1920–1932*. Rivers Press, 1973.

Terras, Victor (ed.). *Handbook of Russian Literature*. Yale University, 1985.

Tumarkin, Nina. *Lenin Lives! The Lenin cult in Soviet Russia*. Harvard University Press, 1983.

Ulam, Adam B. *Stalin: the man and his era*. Allen Lane, 1973.

Vishnevskaya, Galina. *Galina: a Russian story*. Hodder & Stoughton, 1984.

Volkov, Solomon (ed.). *Testimony: the memoirs of Dmitri Shostakovich*. Harper & Row, 1979.

Werth, Alexander. *Musical Uproar in Moscow*. Turnstile, 1949.

— *Russia: the post-war years*. Hale, 1971.

Whitney, Thomas P. *Russia in my Life*. Harrap, 1962.

Xianling, Zhang. *Half of Man is Woman*. Viking, 1988.

Yelagin, Yuri. *see* Jelagin, Juri.

Zamyatin, Yevgeny. *We*. Cape, 1970.

INDEX OF COMPOSITIONS

Adventures of Korzinkina, The, 150, 293
Allegedly Murdered,, 75, 286
Alone, 75, 76, 286-7
Aphorisms, 46, 105, 284

Ballet Suites Nos.1-3, 100, 201
Ballet Suite No.4, 186n
Bedbug, The, 58-60, 285
Belinsky, 299-300
Big Lightning, 83, 83n
Bolt, The, 73-4, 86, 99, 103, 201, 286
Boris Godunov (Mussorgsky, re-
    orchestration), 135, 143, 146-7, 149,
    228, 292-3, 304

Cello Concerto (Schumann, re-
    orchestration), 307
Cello Concerto (Tishchenko, re-
    orchestration), 312
Cello Sonata, 96-7, 111, 137, 147, 148,
    173, 289, 316
Children's Notebook, 176, 296
Concertino, 211, 301
Counterplan, 83, 99, 196, 287

Eight British and American Folksongs, 295
Eighth Quartet, 147, 221-4, 226, 228,
    305
Eighth Symphony, 156, 156-7n, 167-
    72, 175, 177, 181, 187, 191, 199,
    203, 207, 213, 214, 218, 222, 224,
    231, 231n, 239, 295, 305, 316
Eleventh Quartet, 235, 236, 243n, 309
Eleventh Symphony, 20, 26, 44, 144,
    214-19, 222, 223, 225, 227, 232,
    233, 243, 243n, 303-4, 316
Execution of Stepan Razin, The, 232-233,
    236, 241, 308

Fall of Berlin, The, 201, 201n, 299
Fantasy for Two Pianos, 283
Fearless Regiments are on the Move, The,
    151-2, 294
Festival Overture, 211, 301
Fifth Quartet, 174, 202-3, 205, 206,
    212, 300
Fifth Symphony, 1, 5-6, 14, 15, 50,
    110, 120-34, 136, 137-8, 140, 141,
    144-6, 148, 149, 150, 155, 157,
    157n, 159, 162, 163, 169, 170, 172,
    173, 176, 179, 181, 183, 189, 199,
    200, 221, 222, 227, 255, 271, 291,
    299, 316
Fifteenth Quartet, 236, 237, 243n, 314
Fifteenth Symphony, 143n, 220, 232,
    240-4, 313, 316
First Cello Concerto, 219-22, 222, 232,
    239, 304, 316
First Echelon, The, 302
First Piano Concerto, 84-6, 288, 293
First Piano Sonata, 45, 46, 283
First Piano Trio, 26, 281
First Quartet, 135, 136-8, 147, 173,
    174, 181, 213, 291
First Suite for Dance Band, 87n, 289
First Symphony, 28-30, 38, 41-2, 43,
    44, 45, 48-51, 53, 62, 74, 87, 115,
    128n, 130, 131, 143, 148n, 223,
    242, 246, 282-4, 289
First Violin Concerto, 186-90, 194,
    198, 200, 200n, 207, 212, 220, 239,
    297-8, 302, 316
Five Days, Five Nights, 217n, 222, 305
Five Fragments for Small Orchestra,
    103, 289, 309
Four Monologues on Verses by Pushkin,
    300
Five Satires (Pictures Of The Past), 224,
    305-6
Five Songs on Texts from Krokodil, 234,
    309-10
*Five Songs on Verses by Dolmatovsky
    (Songs of Our Days)*, 201n, 302
Four Songs on Verses by Dolmatovsky,

201n, 299
Four Songs on Verses by Pushkin, 119,
    131-2, 132n, 291
Four Verses of Captain Lebyadkin, 236,
    315
Fourteenth Quartet, 236, 250, 313-14
Fourteenth Symphony, 115, 220, 231n
    232, 237, 238, 238n, 241, 242n,
    243n, 275, 312, 316
Fourth Quartet, 186, 187, 199-201,
    202, 206, 212, 231, 234, 264,
    299-301
Fourth Symphony, 103, 106-117, 118,
    128, 128n 129-31, 143-6, 147, 157,
    163, 165, 170, 172, 175, 178, 179,
    189, 207, 214, 224, 225, 228, 231,
    232, 240, 241, 242n, 246, 289-90,
    306, 316
Friends, 136, 292
From Jewish Folk Poetry, 186, 187, 197-
    8, 212, 233, 272, 272n, 298, 302,
    307, 316
From Karl Marx to Our Own Days, 75,
    78, 81, 136, 176, 287
Funeral March for the Victims of the
    Revolution, 25, 44-5, 50, 158, 163,
    225, 227, 242, 278
Funeral-Triumphal Prelude, 235n, 311

Gadfly, The, 212, 226n, 302, 307
Gamblers, The, 164-5, 166, 294-5
Gipsies, The, 26, 278, 283
Girlfriends, 99, 102, 289
Golden Age, The, 60, 64, 68, 69, 71, 74,
    85, 86, 87n, 99, 103, 130, 136n,
    201, 285-6
Golden Mountains, 118, 286
Great Citizen, The, 136, 149, 149n, 292

Hamlet (1932), 76, 81-2, 82n 150, 263,
    287
Hamlet (1954), 301
Hamlet (1964), 232-3, 236, 307-8
Human Comedy, The, 87, 201, 288

In the Forest, 283

Katerina Ismailova, 90, 165, 232, 233,
    233n, 303, 307-10, 314
Katyusha Maslova, 150n, 293
Khovanshchina (Mussorgsky, re-
    orchestration), 214, 228, 304

King Lear (1941), 112n, 150, 165, 293
King Lear (1970), 115, 237, 312

Lady Macbeth of Mtsensk, 74, 75, 76, 78
    81, 83, 84, 85, 87-93, 95, 100, 102,
    103, 104, 110, 112, 115, 117-18,
    118n, 127, 130, 134, 136, 136n,
    153, 178, 190, 201, 202-3, 222, 223,
    226, 226n, 232, 246, 256, 286-90,
    303
'Lenin Symphony', 135-6, 141, 144, 176,
    199, 291
Limpid Stream, The, 99-100, 102, 103,
    104, 135, 201, 289-90
Love and Hate, 289
Loyalty, 201n, 235, 312

Man with a Gun, The, 292
March of the Soviet Police, 235n, 313
Maxim's Return, 119, 291
Maxim's Youth, 99, 100, 289
Meeting on the Elbe, The, 196, 201, 201n,
    298
Michurin, 83n, 195-6, 201, 298
Moscow, Cheryomushki, 83n, 214, 303-4

Native Leningrad, 46, 165-6, 201n, 295
New Babylon, 58, 60, 76, 285
Ninth Quartet, 233-4, 243n, 271n, 304,
    316
Ninth Symphony, 143n, 158, 174, 176-
    80, 181, 183, 202, 208, 225, 241,
    296, 316
Nose, The, 38, 39, 51-5, 56, 58, 61, 67,
    68, 74, 75, 85, 90, 91, 99, 105, 284-
    6, 314-15
Novorossisk Chimes, 305

October (symphonic poem), 46, 225n,
    232, 235n, 311
Overture on Russian and Khirghiz Themes,
    307

Patriotic Song, 167n, 201n, 295
Piano Quintet, 97, 147-50, 162, 171,
    173, 174, 175, 181, 203, 236, 293,
    316
Pirogov, 186, 201, 297
Poem of the Motherland, 83n, 186, 189,
    196n, 297
Portrait Gallery (Rayok), 194-5, 194n,

198, 265, 298
Preface to my Collected Works, 194, 309
Prelude and Scherzo, 45, 95, 136n, 282
Preludes (Opus 2), 25, 25n, 44, 45, 217, 217n, 279

'*Quiet Don, The*', 308

Revolutionary Symphony, 44, 45, 283
Rothschild's Violin (Fleishman, orchestration), 153, 311
Rule Britannia!, 75, 286
Rusalochka, 26, 278, 283
Russian River, 176, 296

Salute to Spain!, 118, 290
Scherzo (Opus 1), 25, 279
Scherzo (Opus 7), 44, 281-2
Second Cello Concerto, 235, 236, 237, 239-40, 242n, 272, 310, 316
Second Piano Concerto, 215, 303
Second Piano Sonata, 166, 171, 295, 316
Second Piano Trio, 173-4, 173n 175, 176, 178n, 182, 182n, 189, 198, 200, 222, 296
Second Quartet, 173n, 174-6, 179, 181, 182, 190, 200n, 202, 203, 206, 296, 305
Second Suite for Dance Band, 135, 142, 292
Second Symphony, 18, 46-51, 55, 60, 62, 64, 131, 143n, 219, 225, 284
Second Violin Concerto, 231n, 237, 238-9, 272, 311, 316
Seven Dances of the Dolls, 201, 300
Seven Rivers, 301
Seven Romances on Verses by Alexander Blok, 235, 236, 237, 310-11
Seventh Quartet, 221, 300
Seventh Symphony, 50, 124, 143n, 152-64, 165, 167, 169, 170, 172, 173, 174, 183, 191, 203, 206, 214, 221, 244, 257n, 273-4, 294, 303, 316
Shot, The, 64, 285
Silly Little Mouse, The, 135, 143, 292
Simple Folk, 186, 296-7, 302
Six Japanese Romances, 284, 287, 310
Six Romances on Verses by English Poets, 165, 182, 231, 231n, 294-5, 313

Six Romances on Verses by Marina Tsvetayeva, 239, 274, 314
Six Spanish Songs, 302
Sixth Quartet, 212-14, 216, 217, 231, 243, 302
Sixth Symphony, 135, 137, 141, 142-6, 147, 149, 157, 157n, 170, 179, 189, 208, 292-3, 316
Sofia Perovskaya (film), 311
Sofia Perovskaya (opera), 88, 128
Soil, 68, 286
Soldier, The (Ode To Liberty), 278
Solemn March, 295
Song of the Forests, 199, 201, 201n, 299
Song of the Red Army, 295
Songs and Dances of Death (Mussorgsky, orchestration), 228, 306
Spring, Spring, 311
Suite for Two Pianos, 24, 25, 237, 280
Suite on Verses by Michelangelo, 236, 238, 243n, 314-15
Sun Shines Over Our Motherland, The, 201n, 300

Tahiti Trot, 71, 284
Tale of a Priest and his servant Balda, The, 118n, 288-90
Ten Poems on Revolutionary Texts, 44, 201, 216, 217, 299-300
Tenth Quartet, 233-4, 271n, 308
Tenth Symphony, 113, 161, 169, 175, 182, 189, 203, 204-8 212, 224, 247, 300-1, 316
Theme and Variations, 25, 280
Third Quartet, 180-3, 186, 190, 200, 203, 206, 212, 297
Third Symphony, 18, 46, 61-4, 68, 78, 129, 143n, 280
Thirteenth Quartet, 236, 265, 281
Thirteenth Symphony, 133, 228-33, 233n, 243n, 245, 297
Three Fantastic Dances, 46, 280
Three Pieces for Cello and Piano, 95, 281
Three Pieces for Orchestra, 186, 186n, 297
Three Pieces for Solo Violin, 150, 293
Twelfth Quartet, 232, 235, 236, 237, 243n, 248, 311
Twelfth Symphony, 50, 225-7, 226n, 228, 261, 306, 316

Twelve Chairs, The, 89n, 291

Twenty-four Preludes (Opus 34), 83-5, 86, 201n, 292

Twenty-four Preludes and Fugues (Opus 87), 166, 186, 201-2, 299-300, 307

Two Davidenko Choruses, 229n, 307

Two Krylov Fables, 280

Two Pieces for Dressel's *Columbus*, 285

Two Pieces for String Quartet, 136n

Two Russian Folksongs (Cultivation), 303

Two Scarlatti Pieces, 284

Two Songs on Verses by Lermontov, 299

Unforgettable Year 1919, The, 300

Victorious Spring, 176, 201n, 296

Vienna Blood (Strauss, re-orchestration), 141, 293

Viola Sonata, 235, 236, 237, 315, 316

Violin Sonata, 232, 235, 236, 237, 312, 316

Volochayevsk Days, 119, 136, 291

Vow of the People's Commissar, 151, 294

Vyborg Side, The, 292

Year as Long as a Lifetime, A, 235n, 309

Young Guard, The, 197, 201, 203, 222, 236, 297-8

Zoya, 84, 174, 296

Index of Characters

Abakumov, Viktor, 204
Abraham, Gerald, 4, 62
Abramov, Fyodor, 312
ACM, 41-43, 45, 49, 51, 60, 61, 66-68,
    74, 93, 281, 286
Afinogenov, Alexander, 74, 86n, 118,
    287-8, 290
Aitmatov, Chingiz, 250, 251
Akhmatova, Anna, 14, 26, 27, 28, 30-1,
    39-40, 65-6, 93, 94, 98, 99, 107,
    122, 130, 134, 137, 139; 152, 156,
    170, 184-6, 185n 189, 201, 208,
    211, 219, 234n, 255, 271-6, 279-80,
    288-9, 292-3, 296-9, 302, 310;
    Poem Without a Hero,, 27, 273-5;
    Requiem, 130, 170, 255; *Seventh
    Northern Elegy,* 275-6
Akimov, Nikolai, 76, 81-2
Aksyonov, Vasily, 306
Alexander II, 19n, 88
Alexandrov, Grigori, 195
Alliluyeva, Nadezhda, 99
Alliluyeva, Svetlana, 204
Ancerl, Karel, 316
Andersen, Hans, 22, 26
Apostolov, Pavel, 194
Aragon, Louis, 254
Ardov, Viktor, 234n
Arnshtam, Lev, 76
Asafiev, Boris, 39n, 42, 62, 63, 105,
    127, 252
Aseyev, Nikolai, 78, 83
Ashkenazy, Vladimir, 6, 120n, 224, 257
Atoumyan, Lev, 201
Authors' League, 66
Avdeyenko, Alexander, 111
Averbakh, Leopold, 67n, 77-8, 100
Azhayev, Vasily, 298

Babel, Isaac, 41, 44, 76, 94, 95, 117,
    118n, 121, 122, 134, 139, 139n, 149,
    283-4, 286, 292

Bach, J.S., 22, 85, 143, 147, 175, 201,
    272, 274
Bakh, Alexei, 251
Balakirev, Mily, 26
Balzac, Honoré de, 87
Barshai, Rudolf, 4, 6, 7, 246, 316
Bartok, Bela, 45
Basily, Nicholas de, 109
Beausobre, Julia de, 36n
Beckett, Samuel, 240
Beecham, Sir Thomas, 14
Beethoven, Ludwig van, 42, 69, 85,
    113-14, 151, 222, 235, 240, 272;
    Third Symphony, 33, 160; Sixth
    Symphony, 161; Seventh Symphony,
    273; Thirteenth Quartet, 202;
    Fourteenth Piano Sonata, 237;
    Thirty-second Piano Sonata, 166
Beethoven Quartet, 83, 147, 148n, 149,
    176, 182, 250, 271n, 316
Belyi, Viktor, 43, 191-2
Berg, Alban, 74, 259, 274n; *Wozzeck,*
    29, 46, 53, 274, 283
Berggolts, Olga, 297
Beria, Lavrenti, 139, 209, 219, 292,
    294, 299-301
Berkeley, Michael, 7
Berlinsky, Valentin, 181n, 250
Berlioz, Hector, 247, 258
Berman, Boris, 316
Bezymensky, Alexander, 49, 50, 64, 219
Bizet, Georges, 151
Blok, Alexander, 21, 27, 44, 278, 280
Blokker, Roy, 29, 113, 157
Bogdanov, Alexander, 42, 278
Bondarchuk, Sergei, 304, 308, 313
Bondarev, Yuri, 307
Borodin, Alexander, 88
Borodin Quartet, 6, 181n, 251, 264,
    316
Borodin, Sergei, 294
Brecht, Bertold, 49, 197

Brezhnev, Leonid, 234, 238, 240, 242, 263, 308-10, 313-14
Britten, Benjamin, 85, 137, 161, 163, 173, 236, 259, 308-10, 313
Brodsky, Josef, 234, 234n, 308
Brown, Royal, 250, 251
Bukharin, Nikolai, 43, 134-5, 134n, 136, 282, 285, 289, 291
Bukovsky, Vladimir, 216, 263-4, 306
Bulgakov, Mikhail, 41, 52, 60-1, 61n, 64, 93, 107n, 134, 262, 265, 282-3, 285, 287, 289-91, 293
Bulganin, Nikolai, 302, 304
Bunin, Ivan, 57, 228, 288
Busch, Adolf, 260
Busoni, Ferruccio, 260

Carroll, Lewis, 116, 242
Chagall, Marc, 280
Chalidze, Valery, 312
Chaplin, Charlie, 28, 29
Cheka, 36, 36n, 37, 44, 56, 278, 280
Chekhov, Mikhail, 16, 88n, 244
Cheng, Nien, 34
Cherny, Alexander, 224
Chishko, Oles, 291
Chopin, Frederic, 272
Chukovskaya, Lydia, 130, 255, 293, 309, 315
Chukovsky, Kornei, 238
Chukovsky, Yevgeny, 271n
Chukrai, Grigori, 303-4
Chulaki, Mikhail, 192
Churchill, Winston, 132, 297
Conquest, Robert, 99, 121, 122n
Constant, Marius, 285

Daniel, Yuli, 157n 234, 308, 309
Dargomyzhsky, Alexander, 151
Davidenko, Alexander, 43, 68, 82, 229n
Dearling, Robert, 157
Denisov, Edison, 11, 302-3, 306, 308-9, 311-4
Dery, Tibor, 216
Deshevov, Vladimir, 42, 68, 283, 286
Diaghilev, Serge, 27
Djilas, Milovan, 303
Dolmatovsky, Yevgeny, 201,201n
Donskoi, Mark, 292, 293, 294, 296, 312
Dostoyevsky, Fyodor, 26, 53n, 54, 87,

218, 289
Dovzhenko, Alexander, 65, 119, 195, 284-5, 288, 290-2
Dubcek, Alexander, 311
Dubinsky, Rostislav, 6, 7, 264
Dudintsev, Vladimir, 213, 216-7, 302-3
Dzerzhinsky, Feliks, 283
Dzerzhinsky, Ivan, 117, 117n, 127, 191, 191n, 204, 287-8, 290-1, 293, 296
Dzhabayev, Dzhambul, 135

Eastman, Max, 59, 66, 76
Edlina, Luba, 316
Ehrenburg, Ilya, 28, 39-40, 50, 52, 64, 94, 107n, 117, 121, 122, 151, 156-7n, 182, 209, 252, 279, 294, 297, 299, 301, 307
Eikhenbaum, Boris, 65, 185n
Eisenstein, Sergei, 28, 39, 65, 75, 89n, 119, 140, 178, 186, 282-5, 291-2, 296-7
Eisler, Hanns, 87n
Elias, Karl, 154
Engels, Friedrich, 114
Erdman, Nikolai, 58, 65, 282, 284
Esenin, Sergei, 28, 279, 282
Eshpay, Andrei, 302, 304, 306, 309, 310-11, 313

Fadeyev, Alexander, 101, 283, 294, 296, 299, 302
Fanning, David, 205n, 248
Fauré, Gabriel, 96, 240, 258
Fay, Laurel, 3-4, 8, 245
Fedin, Konstantin, 118n, 278, 282, 296, 298, 311
Fitzwilliam, Quartet, 316
Fleishman, Veniamin, 143, 151, 153
Ford, Gerald, 314
Frederiks, Dmitri, 249
Frunze, Mikhail, 66n, 282
Furmanov, Dmitri, 281
Fyvel, Tosco, 269

Gagarin, Yuri, 201n, 306
Galli-Shohat, J.A., 24-5
Galli-Shohat, Nadezhda, 19-22, 24, 36-7, 41
Gerasimov, Sergei, 101, 195, 292, 294, 304, 307, 311
Gide, André, 290

Gierek, Edward, 313
Gilels, Emil, 260
Ginzburg, Alexander, 310-11
Ginzburg, Eugenia, 139, 188n, 255, 268, 270, 291, 311
Gladkov, Fedor, 282, 297-8
Glass, Philip, 237
Glazunov, Alexander, 22, 25, 26, 28, 245, 279-80
Gliasser, Ignati, 278
Glier, Reinhold, 51, 283, 295, 297, 299, 300, 302
Glikman, Isaak, 194n
Glinka, Mikhail, 243-4
Glivenko, Tanya, 281
Gnesin, Mikhail, 283
Gogol, Nikolai, 2, 26, 51-4, 52-3n, 62, 87, 164-5
Gomulka, Wladislaw, 313
Gorbachev, Mikhail, 254, 254n, 265
Gorbatov, A.V., 308
Gorky, Maxim, 71, 73, 77, 93, 100, 239, 278, 280, 284, 286-7, 289-90
Govorov, Leonid, 154
GPU, 56, 58, 280, 283, 289
Grekov, Ivan, 27
Grigorenko, Petr, 238, 306, 312
Gromadsky, Vitaly, 230
Grossman, Vasily, 255, 305, 313
Grosz, George, 145
Gubaydulina, Sofia, 303-4, 306, 308, 311-15
Gumilov, Lev, 292, 298-9, 302
Gumilov, Nikolai, 280

Hay, Gyula, 216
Haydn, Joseph, 85
Heller, Mikhail, 57, 72, 123n, 270
Hingley, Ronald, 39, 109-10, 266
Hitler, Adolf, 110, 131, 131n, 141, 142, 150, 151, 155, 159, 162, 172, 175n, 178, 179, 254, 293

Ilf (Ilya) and Petrov (Yevgeny), 41, 59, 88n, 284, 287
Inber, Vera, 152, 153, 293-4
Ionin, Georgi, 52, 52n
Ippolitov-Ivanov, Mikhail, 289
Ivanov, Vsevolod, 118n, 281
Ivinskaya, Olga, 166n, 193, 193n, 298

Janacek, Leos, 237
Järvi, Neeme, 316
Jonas, Georg, 255

Kabalevsky, Dmitri, 42, 43, 49, 68, 74, 233, 283-4, 286-9, 291, 293-4, 296-302, 304-6, 308-9, 313
Kaganovich, Lazar, 303
Kalatozov, Mikhail, 294, 303
Kalinin, Mikhail, 111
Kamenev, Sergei, 13, 267, 283-4, 289-90
Kapitsa, Petr, 238
Kaplan, Fanny, 35
Karayev, Kara, 143, 295, 297, 300, 303-4, 308, 310
Karlinsky, Simon, 3, 4, 245
Karsavina, Tamara, 27
Kastalsky, Alexander, 42, 281
Katayev, Valentin, 41, 59, 65n, 66, 94, 118n, 283, 288, 290, 305-6
Kay, Norman, 120, 137-8
Keaton, Buster, 28
Kerensky, Alexander, 278
Khachaturian, Aram, 167n, 180, 190-4, 209, 211, 229, 257, 289-98, 300-1, 306-8, 311
Khachaturian, Karen, 298, 302, 313
Khenkin, Vladimir, 32
Khentova, Sofia, 118n, 150
Khikmet, Nazym, (Nazim Hikmet), 302
Khrennikov, Tikhon, 11n, 105, 167, 190-3, 191n, 192n, 197, 199, 204, 223, 233, 288-9, 292, 295, 298, 303-4, 308, 313-14
Khrushchev, Nikita, 108, 151n, 209, 212, 214, 216, 219, 220, 223, 227, 229-30, 234, 302-9, 313
Kim, Yuli, 238
Kirov, Sergei, 97, 98-9, 102, 140, 149n, 267, 283, 289-90
Kirsanov, Semyon, 61, 78
Kirshon, Vladimir, 65, 291
Kishkin, Petya, 12
Knipper, Lev, 75, 94-5, 105, 117n, 127, 283-4, 286, 288-91, 295, 297-301, 314
Kochetov, Vsevolod, 306
Koestler, Arthur, 253, 267-8
Kogan, Petr, 65
Kokoulin, Yasha, 21

Kokoulina, Lyubochka, 20, 22, 25
Kolakowski, Leszek, 270
Kollontai, Alexandra, 38, 185n
Komsomol, 43, 47, 49, 58, 60, 64, 68,
    74, 77-8, 221, 266
Kondrashin, Kyrill, 4, 7, 108, 108n,
    115, 229, 252, 261, 316
Kopacsi, Sandor, 255
Kornilov, Boris, 83, 139, 292
Kostrykin, Maxim, 20
Kosygin, Alexei, 308
Koval, Marian, 43, 192, 204, 289, 295,
    297
Kozintsev, Grigori, 58, 76, 150, 152,
    186, 232, 237, 301, 303, 308
Krasin, Viktor, 314
Krein, Alexander, 43, 283
Krylenko, Nikolai, 268
Krylov, Ivan, 22
Kuba, Natasha, 279
Kubatsky, Viktor, 96-7
Kuleshov, Lev, 282, 293
Kurchavov, Volodya, 282
Kustodiev, Boris, 279
Kuznetsov, Anatoli, 151, 252, 306, 310

Lambert, Constant, 247
Lamm, Pavel, 62
Lebrecht, Norman, 6
Lee, Rose, 32-3, 77, 92
Lenin, Vladimir, 2, 16-18, 21, 27n, 33,
    35-6, 42, 47, 55, 67n, 69, 71, 80,
    134-6, 136n, 144, 218, 225-7, 225n,
    235n, 238, 255, 261, 267, 278, 279-
    81; dissolves Constituent Assembly,
    19n; foments class war, 35-6;
    suppresses Kronstadt Uprising, 37n
Leonov, Leonid, 94, 110, 118n, 168,
    282, 284, 287-8, 294, 301
Lermontov, Mikhail, 141
Leskov, Nikolai, 75, 87, 90-2
Lischke, André, 194n
Liszt, Franz, 45, 226, 240
Litvinov, Maxim, 292
Lukacs, Georg, 216
Lukyanova, N.V., 144, 249
Lunacharsky, Anatoli, 43, 45, 67, 278,
    280
Lyons, Eugene, 32, 59, 66, 69, 72, 73,
    269
Lysenko, Trofim, 196, 196n, 268,

297-8
Lyubimov, Yuri, 193

MacDonald, Malcolm, 239
Mahler, Gustav, 14-15, 26, 46, 63, 85,
    112, 114, 116, 128, 138, 159, 161,
    164, 189, 207, 217, 242, 248, 249,
    259, 262; First Symphony, 129, 132,
    217n; Second Symphony, 145, 161;
    Third Symphony, 159; Fourth
    Symphony, 127, 181, 212, 241; Fifth
    Symphony, 114, 162, 241n; Sixth
    Symphony, 130; Seventh Symphony,
    162, 248; Ninth Symphony, 74, 173;
    Tenth Symphony, 144, 169; Des
    Knaben Wunderhorn, 150, 189, 197
Maksimov, Vladimir, 313
Malenkov, Georgi, 196n, 209, 219, 299,
    300, 302-3
Malevich, Kasimir, 280
Malko, Nikolai, 28, 37, 41, 45, 49, 71,
    136n, 148n
Mandelstam, Nadezhda, 17, 30, 47, 48,
    77, 99, 107, 111-2, 119, 120, 121,
    122, 123-4, 127, 139, 151, 188, 202,
    242, 243, 251, 254, 255, 293, 313,
    315
Mandelstam, Osip, 27, 30, 39, 65, 77,
    93, 94, 98-9, 107, 127, 134, 139,
    149, 187, 273, 278, 281, 286, 288-
    92, 314
Mao Tse-tung, 35, 67, 69, 73, 199n
Marchenko, Anatoly, 312
Markov, Georgi, 314
Martynov, Ivan, 39n, 83, 145, 255
Marx, Karl, 35, 114, 235n
Maryengov, Anatoli, 150n
Mayakovsky, Vladimir, 31, 38, 40, 57,
    61, 66, 68-9, 77, 78, 83, 135, 136,
    139, 141, 184, 278-9, 282-3, 285-6,
    289, 302; denounces Akhmatova,
    30; denounces Bulgakov, 60; The
    Bedbug, 58-60, 63, 77, 78
McKane, Richard, 271, 273, 275
Meck, Galina von, 92n, 122n, 125
Medtner, Nikolai, 25
Medvedev, Roy, 73, 268
Medvedev, Zhores, 312
Mendelssohn, Felix, 143n
Menzhinsky, Vyacheslav, 283
Messiaen, Olivier, 29

Meyerhold, Vsevolod, 27, 39, 46, 49, 54, 58-60, 64, 78, 125n, 134, 139-41, 149, 229, 245, 284, 291, 292; biomechanics, theory of, 39n, 49
MGB, 204-5, 297, 301
Michurin, Ivan, 196, 197n
Mikoëls, Solomon, 298
Mikoyan, Anastas, 121n
Milosz, Czeslaw, 11-12, 71, 133, 211, 270
Mindszenty, Joszef, 299
Molotov, Vyacheslav, 117, 209, 219, 292, 300, 303
Morozov, Pavlik, 89, 89n, 288
Mosolov, Alexander, 42, 45, 68, 281-4, 287, 296, 299, 307, 309, 311
Mozart, W.A., 143n, 258, 272
Mravinsky, Yevgeny, 9, 124, 126, 153, 159, 167, 171, 177, 204, 212, 252, 316
Muradeli, Vano, 190-2, 195, 298
Mussorgsky, Modest, 8, 26, 62-3, 69, 146-7, 149, 151, 214, 215, 228, 233, 259, 262; *Boris Godunov*, 5, 62-3, 126, 135, 143, 146-7
Myaskovsky, Nikolai, 42-3, 44, 45, 54, 74-5, 104, 105, 108, 108n, 146, 149, 190-3, 257, 278-83, 285-8, 290-9; Sixth Symphony, 44, 105; Eleventh Symphony, 45, 75; Twelfth Symphony, 75; Sixteenth Symphony, 108n; Cello Concerto, 180, 191; Violin Concerto, 137; Lyric Concertino, Op.32. No.3, 74n

Nabokov, Nikolai, 198-9, 253
Naiman, Anatoli, 234n, 271, 271n, 272n, 274, 274n
Narodniks, 36, 37, 47, 88, 144, 215, 217, 225
Nechayev, Sergei, 218
Nechipaylo, Viktor, 229-30
Nekrich, Aleksandr, 57, 270
Nestyev, Israel, 191n
Neuhaus, Heinrich, 260
Nicholas II, 217
Nielsen, Carl, 161, 174; Fourth Symphony, 182; Fifth Symphony, 161; Sixth Symphony, 172, 173, 243
Nijinsky, Vaslav, 27, 274
Nikolayev, Leonid (piano teacher), 22-3, 279
Nikolayev, Leonid (assassin) 97, 98
Nikolayeva, Galina, 303
Nikolayeva, Tatiana, 300
Nilin, Pavel, 302
Nixon, Richard, 313
NKVD, 98-9, 113, 120-2, 122n, 131n, 149, 166, 180, 267, 270, 289, 293-4
Norman, Peter, 271
Norris, Christopher, 5, 247, 256
Novotny, Antonin, 311

Oberiu, 52, 283, 286
Oborin, Lev, 153, 166, 283
Oistrakh, David, 6, 186, 212, 302, 311-12, 316
Olesha, Yuri, 39, 40, 41, 52, 59, 76, 82, 92, 94, 118n, 283, 286-7, 291; *A List of Assets*, 82n, 92, 126; *Envy*, 41, 52
Olkhovsky, Andrei, 95, 149, 192n, 229n, 249, 252, 253, 256, 257
Orwell, George, 32, 77, 113, 157n, 158, 193, 196n, 202, 253, 262, 265-70; *Nineteen Eighty-Four*, 32, 90, 113, 197n, 202, 265-70
Ostrovsky, Nikolai, 289
Ottaway, Hugh, 109, 159n, 178

Pasternak, Boris, 13, 48, 57, 93, 98-9, 107, 107n, 110, 118n, 121, 127, 134, 139, 140, 151, 165, 165-6n, 184, 186, 193, 193n, 219-21, 227, 260, 281, 284, 288, 293, 297-8, 300, 304-5; the 'Sixty-sixth', 1656n; *Dr Zhivago*, 219-20, 297, 303-4
Paustovsky, Konstantin, 228, 238, 306
Pavlov, Ivan, 39n, 123, 196n
Pavlova, Anna, 27
Penderecki, Krzysztof, 171
Perovskaya, Sofia, 88
Pertsov, Viktor, 219
Peter the Great, 26
Pilnyak, Boris, 41, 52, 66, 66n 68, 76, 76n, 86, 87, 104, 118n, 139, 157n, 193, 219, 280-1, 285-6, 290-1
Piscator, Erwin, 49
Platonov, Andrei, 94, 262, 265, 289
Pogodin, Nikolai, 289
Polovinkin, Leonid, 45, 284
Pomerantsev, Vladimir, 209, 300-1

Popov, Gavril, 42, 68, 283, 288, 296-8, 308, 312
Poulenc, Francis, 84
Pownall, David, 248
Preis, Alexander, 52, 52-3n, 88n, 90
Prokofiev, Lina, 188n
Prokofiev, Sergei, 20, 26, 45, 67, 95-6, 100, 104, 137, 142, 146, 149, 180, 188n, 190-4, 192n, 197, 198, 241, 247-8, 248n, 257, 260, 283, 289-98, 300; Fifth Symphony, 249n; Sixth Symphony, 180, 191, 197, 248n; First Piano Concerto, 84; Second Quartet, 248n; First Violin Sonata, 180, 248n; Sixth Piano Sonata, 148, 166; *Visions Fugitives*, 45; *Love for Three Oranges*, 53; *Pas d'acier*, 67-8; *Cantata for the 20th Anniversary of October*, 127
Prokoll, 43, 67, 229n
Proletkult, 42-4, 49, 58, 60, 64, 66-71, 73, 74-5, 74n, 78, 79, 81, 82, 82n, 84, 89, 95, 97, 100, 103, 117, 127, 136, 167, 177, 190, 191, 197, 205, 219, 229n
Pudovkin, Vsevolod, 28, 65, 186, 283-4, 288, 294, 297
Purcell, Henry, 274
Pushkin, Alexander, 22, 26, 118n, 131-2, 157n
Pyatakov, Yuri, 294

Rabinovich, Dmitri, 96, 105, 132n, 145, 156, 159, 164, 166, 178n, 191n, 255, 257
Rachmaninov, Sergei, 24, 25, 84, 250
Radek, Karl, 82, 110, 267, 289, 291
Raikh, Zinaida, 141
Rákosi, Matyas, 215
RAPM, 34, 41-3, 45, 49, 51, 60, 61, 64, 66-8, 71, 74-6, 79-80, 82, 114, 281
RAPP, 42, 43, 60, 61n, 64, 66-67, 67n, 74, 75, 77, 79, 118, 281, 284-5
Ravel, Maurice, 51
Reisner, Larissa, 88
Rellstab, Heinrich, 237
Repin, Ilya, 157n
Reshetin, Mark, 312
Rezac, Tomas, 247
Richter, Sviatoslav, 177, 261n, 316
Rimsky-Korsakov, Nikolai, 22, 25, 26,

280; *Tsar Saltan*, 22
Rolland, Romain, 254
Romanko, Zhenya, 88
Romanov, Panteleimon, 56, 67, 255, 285
Rome, Harold, 83
Romm, Mikhail, 291-2
Roseberry, Eric, 210
Roslavets, Nikolai, 42-4, 70, 70n, 279-80, 284
Rossini, Gioacchino, 116, 178; *Barber of Seville*, 233n; *William Tell*, 241-2
Rostropovich, Mstislav, 6, 7, 88, 125n, 194, 194n, 219, 229, 250, 263, 310, 312, 316
Rozanova, Alexandra, 278
Rozhdestvensky, Gennadi, 83n, 115, 316
Rybakov, Anatoli, 255
Rykov, Alexei, 291
Ryutin, Mikhail, 287

Sakharov, Andrei, 238, 251-2, 251n, 304, 311-12, 315
Salisbury, Harrison, 210-11
Saltykov-Shchedrin, Mikhail, 88n
Samosud, Samuel, 55, 105, 146-7, 153
Sartre, Jean Paul, 254
Satie, Erik, 46
Schnabel, Artur, 260
Schnittke, Alfred, 171, 303-6, 309, 313-15
Schoenberg, Arnold, 10, 29, 224, 259, 260, 262, 274
Schwarz, Boris, 6, 7, 10, 211, 223, 224, 241, 257
Scriabin, Alexander, 33, 45, 50, 53
Selvinsky, Ilya, 65
Serafimovich, Alexander, 282
Serebryakova, Galina, 118n, 235n, 290, 306-7, 311
Seroff, Viktor, 36-7, 192n
Shaginyan, Marietta, 94, 287
Shakespeare, William, 165, 221; *Hamlet*, 8, 81-2, 82n, 92, 126, 150, 254; *King Lear*, 8-9 112n, 150, 237, 240, 260; *Othello*, 39, 49, 53
Shalamov, Varlam, 310
Shaporin, Yuri, 281-4, 288-9, 291, 296, 300
Shaw, George Bernard, 254, 287

Shchedrin, Rodion, 233, 299, 301-2, 304, 306-7, 309, 311-13

Shcherbachov, Vladimir, 42, 68, 70, 70n, 280, 283, 286, 289, 298

Shebalin, Vissarion, 42-3, 68, 70, 74, 106, 108, 108n, 135-6, 149, 153, 166, 176, 191-2, 194, 197, 281-2, 285-6, 289-91, 293-5, 297-9, 302, 304-7

Shekhter, Boris, 43

Shepitko, Larissa, 307

Shevchenko, Arkady, 266

Shirinsky, Sergei, 315

Shirinsky, Vasili, 309

Shklovsky, Viktor, 289

Sholokhov, Mikhail, 94, 101, 283, 288-9, 293, 304, 308-9

Shostakovich, Dmitri B. (father), 18-20, 22, 24-5, 28, 44, 280

Shostakovich, Dmitri D., *passim; see also under Appendix 3; see also under Index of Compositions;* cynicism, 238; Hamlet theory, 5, 8, 126, 132, 145, 156, 164, 247-8, 249, 252-3; Kronstadt Uprising, thoughts on, 37, 47; *New York Times* interviews, 32-4, 77-8, 210-11; Proletkult, attitude to, 45, 49, 82, 84; 'puppet' motif, 24, 29-30, 53, 174, 242, 242n, 244; speeches and writings, Soviet, 3-6, 10-14, 247; *yurodivy*, 8-9, 12, 51-2, 103, 106-8, 147, 149, 160, 162, 235-6

Shostakovich, Dmitri M. (grandson), 306

Shostakovich, Galina, 108, 153, 167, 174, 176, 211, 214n, 218, 271n, 290, 296

Shostakovich, Irina (Supinskaya), 3, 9, 194, 194n, 232, 245, 304, 307, 312

Shostakovich, Margarita (Kainova), 212, 302, 305

Shostakovich, Maria, 18, 28, 41, 153, 164, 279-80

Shostakovich, Maxim, 4-7, 10, 16, 20, 32, 46, 124, 138, 153, 160, 167, 174, 194, 210, 211, 212, 214, 214n, 241, 245, 250n, 291, 296, 316

Shostakovich, Nina (Varzar), 58, 61, 81, 83, 95, 96, 105, 108, 138, 152, 153, 167, 211, 212, 221, 284-5, 287-8,

296, 301

Shostakovich, Sofia (Kokoulina), 18-20, 22-5, 28, 36-7, 56, 83, 93, 95, 153, 164, 167, 280-2

Shostakovich, Zoya, 18

Shub, Esfer, 284

Simonov, Konstantin, 296, 304

Sinyavsky, Andrei, 157n, 234, 305-6, 308-9

Smirnov, Sergei, 238

Smolich, Nikolai, 55

Socialist Revolutionaries, 18-19n, 20, 36

Sokolovsky, Mikhail, 49, 64

Sollertinsky, Dmitri and Ludmilla, 251, 249, 255

Sollertinsky, Ivan, 45-6, 48, 51, 68, 78, 90-1, 95, 103, 105, 152, 166, 172-3, 174, 284, 296

Sologub, Fyodor, 40

Soloviev-Sedoi, Vasili, 214

Solzhenitsyn, Alexander, 6, 12-13, 15, 17, 32, 72, 72n, 119-20, 133, 170, 172, 213, 229, 233, 238-9, 238n, 247, 251-2, 254, 255, 261, 263, 275, 278, 307-8, 311-15

Spasski, Sergei, 121

Stadnyuk, Ivan, 307

Stakhanov, Alexei, 290

Stalin, Joseph, 2, 18, 23, 27, 32, 34, 55-7, 60, 61n, 63, 64, 66-9, 66n, 71-3, 78-80, 86n, 89n, 90, 92-95, 97, 98-101, 103-4, 106-8, 110-11, 117-18, 120-3, 129-31, 131n, 135-7, 139-42, 146, 148-50, 150n, 151, 151n, 155, 157n, 161-3, 165-6n, 167, 167n, 168, 170, 172, 174, 174n, 175-82, 184-5, 187, 190, 192, 195-6, 196n, 197n, 198, 199n, 202-9, 210-13, 215, 217-23, 225n, 227, 228, 228n, 234, 235-6, 240, 242, 248, 253-7, 262-3, 265-7, 281-93, 296, 299, 300, 303, 306, 310

Steinberg, Maximilian, 22, 70, 279

Stiedry, Fritz, 108

Stokowski, Leopold, 41, 284

Stolyarov, Grigori, 153

Stradling, Robert, 178, 247

Strauss, Johann (II), 141

Strauss, Richard, 160, 222, 243

Stravinsky, Igor, 10-11, 20, 26, 29, 69,

198, 262, 274-5; *Apollon Musagètes*,
128; *Jeu de Cartes*, 116; *Oedipus Rex*,
162; *Petrushka*, 29-30, 174, 274;
Piano Concerto, 162; *Pulcinella*, 165;
Symphony of Psalms, 144, 162, 275
Stroeva, Vera, 214
Surikov, Vasili, 157n
Suslov, Mikhail, 224
Sviridov, Georgi, 143, 293, 296, 299,
302, 304, 307-8, 311

Taktakishvili, Otar, 298, 300
Tarkovsky, Andrei, 307, 309, 313
Tarsis, Valeri, 309
Tchaikovsky, Petr, 26, 29-30, 41, 53,
136n, 160, 163, 218, 226n; Fourth
Symphony, 84; Fifth Symphony,
160; Sixth Symphony, 133; *1812*,
156, 169; *Queen of Spades*, 87
Timoshenko, Semen, 150
Tippett, Michael, 29
Tishchenko, Boris, 11, 108n, 240, 245,
249, 274n, 303-9, 312-15
Tito, Josip, 313
Tkachev, Petr, 218
Tolstoy, Alexei, 50, 281, 294-5
Tolstoy, Leo, 16, 67n, 150n, 157n
Toscanini, Arturo, 154
TRAM, 49, 64, 68, 75, 284, 287
Trauberg, Leonid, 58, 76, 186
Tretyakov, Sergei, 139
Trifonov, Yuri, 312, 314
Trotsky, Leon, 46, 69, 267, 283-5
Tsekhanovsky, Mikhail, 118n
Tsvetayeva, Marina, 28, 184, 228,
233n, 272, 280, 283, 292-3
Tsyganov, Dmitri, 70, 83
Tucker, Robert, 269
Tukhachevsky, Mikhail, 13, 37n, 106,
121, 130-1, 131n, 149, 280, 291
Turovsky, Yuli, 316
Tvardovsky, Alexander, 209, 229, 261,
296, 301, 305, 307, 312
Tverdokhlebov, Andrei, 312

Vasiliev, Georgi, 290, 294
Vasiliev, Sergei, 290, 294, 301
Vasilyeva, Raya, 102
Vaughan, Williams, Ralph, 243
Vaynberg, Moisei (Moses Weinberg),
229, 295, 297-8, 302-4, 306-8,

311-12
Verdi, Giuseppe, 95, 258; *Don Carlos*,
230
Vertov, Dziga, 289
Vidal, Pierre, 261
Vishnevskaya, Galina, 6, 7, 10, 13, 102,
117, 128, 133n, 201, 210, 211-12,
214n, 219, 222, 224, 228, 229, 247,
249, 250, 256, 257, 305, 312
Vivaldi, Antonio, 274
Vladimov, Georgi, 315
Volkonsky, Andrei, 11, 300-5, 307,
311-12
Volkov, Solomon, 1-10, 12, 16, 17, 47,
51-2, 96, 106-9, 124, 143, 155-6,
156n, 160, 185n, 1945, 215, 225,
238, 244, 245, 249, 251, 258, 263,
264; plagiarism of, 3-5, 155-6;
Testimony, authenticity of, 3-4, 6-7,
8, 10, 245-7, 263; *Testimony*,
approved by Shostakovich family, 7,
9, 10
Volynsky, Akim, 40
Voronyanskaya, Elizaveta, 314
Voronsky, Alexander, 60, 280, 285
Voroshilov, Kliment, 66n, 282
Voynovich, Vladimir, 315

Wagner, Richard, 33, 95, 161, 178, 179,
243
Walter, Bruno, 41, 283-4
Warburg, Fredric, 269
Weber, Carl Maria von, 85
Webern, Anton, 262
Weill, Kurt, 87n, 197
Werth, Alexander, 190, 247-8, 257
Whitney, Thomas, 199n

Yagoda, Genrikh, 289-91
Yakir, Petr, 238, 313-14
Yakubovich, Mikhail, 268
Yanovitsky, Vyacheslav, 20, 21, 36
Yarustovsky, Boris, 204
Yashin, Alexander, 303
Yelagin, Yuri, 70, 81-2, 87, 125, 140,
142, 256, 260
Yevreinov, Nikolai, 279
Yevtushenko, Yevgeny, 228-31, 252,
301, 303, 306-7
Yezhov, Nikolai, 121-2, 121n, 139, 290,
292

Yudina, Maria, 107
Yutkevich, Sergei, 293, 295, 297, 302, 308

Zabolotsky, Nikolai, 118n, 228, 283, 289, 308
Zakharov, Vladimir, 191-2
Zamyatin, Yevgeny, 41, 52, 52n, 55, 66-7, 87, 104, 157n, 219, 262, 265, 279-80, 283, 286-7
Zenkevich, Mikhail, 273
Zhang, Xianling, 34-5
Zhdanov, Andrei, 99, 183, 184-6, 185n, 188, 189-96, 197, 211, 218, 220, 223, 248, 297-9
Zhelobinsky, Valery, 291
Zhitomirsky, Daniel, 61
Zhivotov, Alexei, 68, 283-4, 287, 289, 295-6
Zhukov, Georgi, 174, 174n, 303
Zinoviev, Alexander, 17
Zinoviev, Grigori, 13, 99, 267, 282-4, 289, 290
Zoshchenko, Mikhail, 41, 44, 52, 87, 93, 106, 185-6, 189, 201, 211, 235n, 245, 262, 272, 293, 295-7